AMERICAN FOREIGN RELATIONS 1972

A DOCUMENTARY RECORD

COUNCIL ON FOREIGN RELATIONS BOOKS

Founded in 1921, the Council on Foreign Relations, Inc. is a non-profit and non-partisan organization of individuals devoted to the promotion of a better and wider understanding of international affairs through the free interchange of ideas. The membership of the Council, which numbers about 1,600, is made up of men and women throughout the United States elected by the Board of Directors on the basis of an estimate of their special interest, experience and involvement in international affairs and their standing in their own communities. The Council does not take any position on questions of foreign policy, and no person is authorized to speak for the Council on such matters. The Council has no affiliation with and receives no funding from any part of the United States government.

The Council conducts a meetings program to provide its members an opportunity to talk with invited guests who have special experience, expertise or involvement in international affairs, and conducts a studies program of research directed to political, economic and strategic problems related to United States foreign policy. Since 1922 the Council has published the quarterly journal, *Foreign Affairs*. From time to time the Council also publishes books and monographs which in the judgment of the Committee on Studies of the Council's Board of Directors are responsible treatments of significant international topics worthy of presentation to the public. The individual authors of articles in *Foreign Affairs* and of Council books and monographs are solely responsible for all statements of fact and expressions of opinion contained in them.

AMERICAN FOREIGN RELATIONS 1972
A DOCUMENTARY RECORD

Continuing the Series
DOCUMENTS ON AMERICAN FOREIGN RELATIONS

Edited by RICHARD P. STEBBINS and ELAINE P. ADAM

A Council on Foreign Relations Book
Published by
New York University Press ● New York ● 1976

PREFACE

This volume presents a documentary record of the foreign relations of the United States in 1972, a year made memorable by presidential visits to China and the Soviet Union, the conclusion of pioneer agreements limiting the U.S.-Soviet strategic arms race, and President Nixon's re-election in the midst of complicated maneuvers looking toward a settlement of the Vietnam war. Continuing the *Documents on American Foreign Relations* series initiated by the World Peace Foundation in 1939 and carried forward since 1952 by the Council on Foreign Relations, the present publication also offers background information and critical commentary of the sort provided since 1931 through the annual volumes of the parallel Council on Foreign Relations series, *The United States in World Affairs*.

As with earlier volumes in the documentary series, the present collection is made up of documents that are already in the public domain and whose permanent significance has been thought to warrant their republication in coherent sequence and in verified and annotated form. While questions directly involving the United States have naturally been treated in greatest detail, an effort has been made to indicate the essentials of the American position on all foreign policy matters of current concern. Documents have been selected solely on the basis of their historical relevance, and the inclusion of a given document signifies neither approval nor disapproval of its contents. Editorial treatment of the individual documents has been limited mainly to the correction of obvious textual errors, the insertion within square brackets of needed supplementary details, and the elucidation of any remaining obscurities through explanatory footnotes. For the broad historical context the reader is referred to the editorial commentaries that preface each group of documents and, in this volume, are set off by square brackets.

Although the editing of the present volume was substantially completed in April 1975, some supplementary information of later appearance has been added as a convenience to the reader. Publications referred to by abbreviated titles in the footnotes are fully identified in the Appendix, which lists the sources found most useful in the preparation of the volume. The editors take this opportunity of noting their indebtedness to Grace Darling Griffin, Publications Manager, and Robert E. Valkenier, Editor, of the Council on Foreign Relations; to Donald Wasson, Librarian Emeritus, Janet Rigney, Librarian, and others of the Council's admirable Library staff; and to Despina Papazoglou and other friends at NYU Press. They are likewise indebted to several national and international agencies which have provided documentary material, and to *The New York Times* for permission to reprint texts or excerpts from documents appearing in its pages. The editors themselves are responsible for the choice and presentation of the documents and for the form and content of the editorial matter.

R.P.S.
E.P.A.

January 1, 1976

CONTENTS

I.
WORLD AFFAIRS
THROUGH
AMERICAN EYES

[Americans have seldom been brought as close to the inner workings of foreign policy as was true in the final year of President Nixon's first administration. Elaborate television coverage of the President's visits to China and the Soviet Union offered uniquely vivid glimpses of some of the principal actors in world affairs and of the setting of some of the most significant acts of foreign policy. A series of extraordinary, "on-the-record" news conferences by Dr. Henry A. Kissinger, the President's Assistant for National Security Affairs, provided a sense of almost personal participation both in the dealings with China and the U.S.S.R. and in the secret Paris negotiations aimed at a peace agreement on Vietnam. Such novel insights gave a new dimension to the conventional exposés of foreign policy that flowed in increasing volume from the White House, the Department of State, and other governmental quarters. Perennial questions about the relationship between the President and Congress in the conduct of foreign policy were meanwhile illuminated from fresh angles as Congress struggled to confine executive discretion in this area within acceptable limits. Concurrently, the presidential election campaign gave rise to trenchant criticism as well as reasoned reaffirmation of foreign policy fundamentals as seen by the Nixon administration. Discourse in each of these modes contributed to the nation's overall perception of its role in the world and its relationship to the innumerable problems involved in the coexistence of national societies in the 1970s.]

A. America and the World.

["This Administration attaches fundamental importance to the articulation as well as the execution of foreign policy," wrote President Nixon in transmitting to Congress the fourth of his annual surveys of the nation's foreign affairs, concerned essentially with

1

the events of the year 1972. "Public understanding is, of course, essential in a democracy. It is all the more urgent in a fast changing world, which requires continuing, though redefined, American leadership. One of my basic goals is to build a new consensus of support in the Congress and among the American people for a responsible foreign policy for the 1970's."[1]

The series of annual "State of the World" reports made public by the President since 1970 under the general title of *U.S. Foreign Policy for the 1970's*[2] represented a major though by no means the only instrument of this novel educational effort. Numerous additional details were offered each year in the parallel reports made public by the Secretaries of State[3] and Defense;[4] while the President himself, in his communications to Congress on the State of the Union each January, continued at times to touch on foreign policy questions that might be further elaborated in later analyses of the State of the World.

The State of the Union address which President Nixon delivered to the Congress on January 20, 1972 (Document 1) offered a particularly illuminating appraisal of the status of the national foreign policy as seen within a context of overall national trends. Together with the condensation of the State of the World document that was made public in a presidential broadcast of February 9, 1972 (Document 2), it affords valuable insights into the national situation on the eve of the epoch-making ventures in personal diplomacy that were to take the President to mainland China in February and to the Soviet Union in May.]

(1) The State of the Union: Address by President Richard M. Nixon to a Joint Session of the Congress, January 20, 1972.[5]

(Excerpts)

The PRESIDENT. Mr. Speaker, Mr. President, my colleagues in the Congress, our distinguished guests and my fellow Americans:

Twenty-five years ago I sat here as a freshman Congressman—along

[1] Nixon Report, 1973, p. v.
[2] See Appendix under "Nixon Reports."
[3] See Appendix under "Rogers Reports."
[4] See Appendix under "Laird Posture Statement, FY 1973." For discussion of U.S. defense policy see also Nixon Report, 1972, pp. 154-70; same, 1973, pp. 178-93; Rogers Report, 1972, pp. 75-80.
[5] House Document 92-201; text from *Congressional Record* (Daily Edition), Jan. 20, 1972, pp. H 145-8.

with Speaker [Carl] ALBERT—and listened for the first time to the President address the State of the Union.[6]

I shall never forget that moment. The Senate, the diplomatic corps, the Supreme Court, the Cabinet entered the Chamber, and then the President of the United States. As all of you are aware, I had some differences with President Truman; he had some with me. But I remember that on that day, the day he addressed that joint session of the newly elected Republican 80th Congress, he spoke not as a partisan but as President of all the people—calling upon the Congress to put aside partisan considerations in the national interest.

The Greek-Turkish aid program, the Marshall plan, the great foreign policy initiatives which have been responsible for avoiding a world war for over 25 years were approved by the 80th Congress, by a bipartisan majority of which I was proud to be a part.

1972 is now before us. It holds precious time in which to accomplish good for the Nation. We must not waste it. I know the political pressures in this session of the Congress will be great. There are more candidates for the Presidency in this Chamber today than there probably have been at any one time in the whole history of the Republic. And there is an honest difference of opinion, not only between the parties but within each party on some foreign policy issues and on some domestic policy issues.

However, there are great national problems that are so vital that they transcend partisanship. So let us have our debates. Let us have our honest differences. But let us join in keeping the national interest first. Let us join in making sure that legislation the Nation needs does not become hostage to the political interests of any party or any person.

There is ample precedent, in this election year, for me to present you with a huge list of new proposals, knowing full well that there would not be any possibility of your passing them if you worked night and day.

I shall not do that.

I have presented to the leaders of the Congress today a message of 15,000 words[7] discussing in some detail where the Nation stands and setting forth specific legislative items on which I ask the Congress to act. Much of this is legislation which I proposed in 1969 and in 1970, and also in the first session of this 92d Congress, and on which I feel it is essential that action be completed this year.

I am not presenting proposals which have attractive labels but no hope of passage. I am presenting only vital programs which are within

---

[6] Message by President Harry S. Truman, Jan. 5, 1947; excerpts in *Documents, 1947*, pp. 1-2.
[7] House Document 92-201; text in *Congressional Record* (Daily Edition), Jan. 20, 1972, pp. H 148-60; excerpts in *Bulletin*, Feb. 7, 1972, pp. 144-51.

the capacity of this Congress to enact, within the capacity of the budget to finance, and which I believe should be above partisanship—programs which deal with urgent priorities for the Nation, which should and must be the subject of bipartisan action by this Congress in the interests of the country in 1972.

When I took the oath of office on the steps of this building just 3 years ago today, the Nation was ending one of the most tortured decades in its history.

The 1960's were a time of great progress in many areas. But as we all know, they were also times of great agony—the agonies of war, of inflation, of rapidly rising crime, of deteriorating cities—of hopes raised and disappointed, and of anger and frustration that led finally to violence, and to the worst civil disorder in a century.

I recall these troubles not to point any fingers of blame. The Nation was so torn in those final years of the sixties that many in both parties questioned whether America could be governed at all.

The Nation has made significant progress in these first years of the seventies.

Our cities are no longer engulfed by civil disorders.

Our colleges and universities have again become places of learning instead of battlegrounds.

A beginning has been made on preserving and protecting our environment.

The rate of increase in crime has been slowed—and here in the District of Columbia, the one city where the Federal Government has direct jurisdiction, serious crime in 1971 was actually reduced by 13 percent from the year before.

Most important, because of the beginnings that have been made, we can say today that this year, 1972, can be the year in which America may make the greatest progress in 25 years toward achieving our goal of being at peace with all the nations of the world.

As our involvement in the war in Vietnam comes to an end, we must now go on to build a generation of peace.

To achieve that goal, we must first face realistically the need to maintain our defenses.

In the past 3 years, we have reduced the burden of arms. For the first time in 20 years, spending on defense has been brought below spending on human resources.

As we look to the future, we find encouraging progress in our negotiations with the Soviet Union on limitation of strategic arms. And looking further into the future, we hope there can eventually be agreement on the mutual reduction of arms. But until there is such a mutual agreement we must maintain the strength necessary to deter war.

And that is why, because of rising research and development costs, because of increases in military and civilian pay, because of the need to proceed with new weapons systems, my budget for the coming fiscal year will provide for an increase in defense spending.[8]

Strong military defenses are not the enemy of peace. They are the guardians of peace.

There could be no more misguided set of priorities than one which would tempt others by weakening America, and thereby endanger the peace of the world.

In our foreign policies, we have entered a new era. The world has changed greatly in the 11 years since President John F. Kennedy said, in his inaugural address, "We shall pay any price, bear any burden, meet any hardship, support any friend, oppose any foe, to assure the survival and the success of liberty."[9]

Our policy has been carefully and deliberately adjusted to meet the new realities of the new world we live in.

We make today only those commitments we are able and prepared to meet.

Our commitment to freedom remains strong and unshakable. But others must bear their share of the burden of defending freedom around the world.

And so this, then, is our policy:

We will maintain a nuclear deterrent adequate to meet any threat to the security of the United States or of our allies.

We will help other nations develop the capability of defending themselves.

We will faithfully honor all of our treaty commitments.

We will act to defend our interests whenever and wherever they are threatened any place in the world.

But where our interests or our treaty commitments are not involved our role will be limited.

We will not intervene militarily.

But we will use our influence to prevent war. If war comes we will use our influence to stop it.

And once it is over we will do our share in helping to bind up the wounds of those who have participated in it.

As you know, I will soon be visiting the People's Republic of China and the Soviet Union. I go there with no illusions. We have great differences with both powers. We will continue to have great differences. But peace depends on the ability of great powers to live together on the same planet despite their differences. We would not be

---

[8] The budget for fiscal year 1973, presented Jan. 24, 1972, estimated defense outlays at $76.5 billion and new budget authority at $83.4 billion, an increase of $6.3 billion over the preceding year. Military personnel on active duty was scheduled to decrease from 2,391,000 to 2,358,000. For details see Laird Posture Statement, FY 1973.

[9] *Documents, 1961*, p. 13.

true to our obligation to generations yet unborn if we failed to seize this moment to do everything in our power to insure that we will be able to talk about these differences rather than to fight about them in the future.

As we look back over this century let us in the highest spirit of bipartisanship recognize that we can be proud of our Nation's record in foreign affairs.

America has given more generously of itself toward maintaining freedom, preserving peace and alleviating human suffering around the globe than any nation has ever done in the history of man.

We have fought wars in this century, but our power has never been used to break the peace, only to keep it; never been used to destroy freedom, only to defend it. We now have within our reach the goal of ensuring that the next generation can be the first generation in this century to be spared the scourges of war.

Turning to our problems at home, we are making progress toward our goal of a new prosperity without war.

Industrial production, consumer spending, retail sales and personal income all have been rising. Total employment and real income are the highest in history. New homebuilding starts this past year reached the highest level ever. Business and consumer confidence have both been rising. Interest rates are down, and the rate of inflation is down. We can look with confidence to 1972 as the year when the back of inflation will be broken.

Now, this is a good record, but it is not good enough—not when we still have an unemployment rate of 6 percent.

It is not enough to point out that this was the rate of the early, peacetime years of the 1960's, or that, if the more than 2 million men released from the Armed Forces and defense-related industries were still on their wartime jobs, unemployment would be far lower.

Our goal in this country is full employment in peacetime—and we intend to meet that goal—and we can.

The Congress has helped to meet that goal by passing our job-creating tax program last month.[10]

The historic monetary agreements we have reached with the major European nations, Canada and Japan[11] will help meet it, by providing new markets for American products—new jobs for American workers.

Our budget will help meet it, by being expansionary without being inflationary—a job-producing budget that will help take up the gap as the economy expands to full employment.

Our program to raise farm income will help meet it, by helping to

---

[10] Public Law 92-210 (Economic Stabilization Act), Dec. 22, 1971. For Nixon signature statement see *Public Papers, 1971*, pp. 1202-4.
[11] *A.F.R., 1971*, no. 150.

revitalize rural America—by giving to American farmers their fair share of America's increasing productivity.

We also will help meet our goal of full employment in peacetime with a set of major initiatives to stimulate more imaginative use of America's great capacity for technological advance, and to direct it toward improving the quality of life for every American.

In reaching the moon, we demonstrated what miracles American technology is capable of achieving. Now the time has come to move more deliberately toward making full use of that technology here on earth, in harnessing the wonders of science to the service of man.

I shall soon send to the Congress a special message[12] proposing a new program of Federal partnership in technological research and development—with Federal incentives to increase private research, and federally supported research on projects designed to improve our everyday lives in ways that will range from improving mass transit to developing new systems of emergency health care that could save thousands of lives annually.

Historically, our superior technology and high productivity have made it possible for America's workers to be the most highly paid in the world by far, and yet for our goods still to compete in world markets.

Now we face a new situation. As other nations are moving rapidly forward in technology, the answer to the new competition is not to build a wall around America, but rather to remain competitive by improving our own technology still further, and by increasing productivity in American industry.

Our new monetary and trade agreements will make it possible for American goods to compete fairly in the world's markets—but they still must compete. The new technology program will put to use the skills of many highly trained Americans—skills that might otherwise be wasted. It will also meet the growing technological challenge from abroad, and it will thus help to create new industries as well as creating more jobs for America's workers in producing for the world's markets.

This second session of the 92d Congress already has before it more than 90 major administration proposals which still await action.

I have discussed these in the extensive written message that I have presented to the Congress today.[13]

They include among others our programs to improve life for the aging; to combat crime and drug abuse; to improve health services and to ensure that no one will be denied needed health care because of inability to pay; to protect workers' pension rights; to promote equal

---

12 Message on science and technology, Mar. 16, 1972, in *Public Papers, 1972*, pp. 416-25.
13 Cf. note 7 above.

opportunity for members of minorities and others who have been left behind; to expand consumer protection; to improve the environment; to revitalize rural America; to help the cities; to launch new initiatives in education; to improve transportation, and to put an end to costly labor tieups in transportation.

The west coast dock strike is a case in point. This Nation cannot and will not tolerate that kind of irresponsible labor tieup in the future.

The messages also include basic reforms which are essential if our structure of government is to be adequate to the needs in the decades ahead.

They include reform of our wasteful and outmoded welfare system— and substitution of a new system that provides work requirements and work incentives for those who can help themselves, income support for those who cannot help themselves, and fairness for the working poor.

They include a $17.6 billion program of Federal revenue sharing with the States and localities—as an investment in their renewal, and an investment also of faith in the American people.

They also include a sweeping reorganization of the executive branch of the Federal Government, so that it will be more efficient, more responsive, and able to meet the challenges of the decades ahead.

One year ago, standing in this place, I laid before the opening session of this Congress six great goals.[14]

One of these was welfare reform. That proposal has been before the Congress now for nearly two and a half years.

My proposals on revenue sharing, government reorganization, health care, and the environment have now been before the Congress for nearly a year. Many of the other major proposals that I have referred to have been here that long or longer.[15]

Now, 1971, we can say, was a year of consideration of these measures. Now let us join in making 1972 a year of action on them—action by the Congress, for the Nation and for the people of America.[16]

*   *   *

As we look ahead over the coming decades, vast new growth and

---

[14] State of the Union Message, Jan. 22, 1971, in *Public Papers, 1971*, pp. 51-8.

[15] Cf. special message resubmitting legislative proposals, Jan. 26, 1971, in same, pp. 61-73.

[16] A modified version of the revenue-sharing bill was enacted by Congress and signed Oct. 20, 1972 as Public Law 92-512 (State and Local Fiscal Assistance Act of 1972). Welfare reform proposals were approved by the House but died in the Senate; the President's plan for governmental reorganization failed to reach the floor of either house.

In the omitted passage of his State of the Union address, the President promised to make recommendations concerning the financing of public primary and secondary education from sources other than local property taxes.

changes are not only certainties, they will be the dominant realities of this world and particularly of our life in America.

Surveying the certainty of rapid change, we can be like a fallen rider caught in the stirrups—or we can sit high in the saddle, the masters of change, directing it on a course that we choose.

The secret of mastering change in today's world is to reach back to old and proven principles, and to adapt them, with imagination and intelligence, to the new realities of a new age.

And that is what we have done in the proposals that I have laid before the Congress. They are rooted in basic principles that are as enduring as human nature, as robust as the American experience; and they are responsive to new conditions. Thus they represent a spirit of change that is truly renewal.

As we look back at these old principles, we find them as timely as they are timeless.

We believe in independence, and self-reliance, and the creative value of the competitive spirit.

We believe in full and equal opportunity for all Americans, and in the protection of individual rights and liberties.

We believe in the family as the keystone of the community, and in the community as the keystone of the Nation.

We believe in compassion for those in need.

We believe in a system of law, justice, and order as the basis of a genuinely free society.

We believe that a person should get what he works for—and that those who can should work for what they get.

We believe in the capacity of people to make their own decisions, in their own lives and their own communities—and we believe in their right to make those decisions.

In applying these principles, we have done so with a full understanding that what we seek in the seventies, what our quest is, is not merely for more, but for better—for a better quality of life for all Americans.

Thus, for example, we are giving a new measure of attention to cleaning up our air and water, making our surroundings more attractive. We are providing broader support for the arts, and helping stimulate a deeper appreciation of what they can contribute to the Nation's activities and to our individual lives.

But nothing really matters more to the quality of our lives than the way we treat one another—than our capacity to live respectfully together as a unified society, with a full and generous regard for the rights of others and also for the feelings of others.

As we recover from the turmoil and violence of recent years, as we learn once again to speak with one another instead of shouting at one another, we are regaining that capacity.

As is customary here, on this occasion, I have been talking about programs. Programs are important. But even more important than programs is what we are as a nation—what we mean as a nation, to ourselves and to the world.

In New York Harbor stands one of the most famous statues in the world—the Statue of Liberty, the gift in 1886 of the people of France to the people of the United States. This statue is more than a landmark; it is a symbol—a symbol of what America has meant to the world.

It reminds us that what America has meant is not its wealth and not its power, but its spirit and purpose—a land that enshrines liberty and opportunity, and that it has held out a hand of welcome to millions in search of a better and a fuller and above all, a freer life.

The world's hopes poured into America, along with its people—and those hopes, those dreams, that have been brought here from every corner of the world, have become a part of the hope that we now hold out to the world.

Four years from now, America will celebrate the 200th anniversary of its founding as a nation.

And there are those who say that the old Spirit of '76 is dead—that we no longer have the strength of character, the idealism, and the faith in our founding purposes, that that spirit represents.

But those who say this do now[17] know America.

We have been undergoing self-doubts and self-criticism. But these are only the other side of our growing sensitivity to the persistence of want in the midst of plenty, and our impatience with the slowness with which age-old ills are being overcome.

If we were indifferent to the shortcomings of our society, or complacent about our institutions, or blind to the lingering inequities—then we would have lost our way.

But the fact that we have those concerns is evidence that our ideals deep down are still strong. Indeed, they remind us that what is really best about America is its compassion. They remind us that in the final analysis America is great, not because it is strong, not because it is rich, but because this is a good country.

Let us reject the narrow visions of those who would tell us that we are evil because we are not yet perfect; that we are corrupt because we are not yet pure; that all the sweat and toil and sacrifice that have gone into the building of America were for naught because the building is not yet done.

Let us see that the path we are traveling is wide, with room in it for all of us, and that its direction is toward a better nation in a more peaceful world.

Never has it mattered more that we go forward together.

17 The word "now" appears as "not" in the definitive text as published in *Public Papers, 1972*, p. 40.

Look at this Chamber. The leadership of America is here today—the Supreme Court, the Cabinet, the Senate, the House of Representatives.

Together we hold the future of the nation, and the conscience of the nation, in our hands.

Because this year is an election year, it will be a time of great pressure.

If we yield to that pressure, and fail to deal seriously with the historic challenges that we face, then we will have failed the trust of millions of Americans, and shaken the confidence they have a right to place in us, in their government.

Never has a Congress had a greater opportunity to leave a legacy of profound and constructive reform for the nation than this Congress.

If we succeed in these tasks, there will be credit enough for all—not only for doing what is right, but doing it in the right way, by rising above partisan interest to serve the national interest.

If we fail, more than any one of us, America will be the loser.

That is why my call upon the Congress today is for a high statesmanship—so that in the years to come Americans will look back and say that because it withstood the intense pressures of a political year, and achieved such great good for the American people, and for the future of this Nation—this was truly a great Congress.

(2) "United States Foreign Policy for the 1970's—The Emerging Structure of Peace": Radio Address by President Nixon on Transmitting His Third Annual Foreign Affairs Report to the Congress, February 9, 1972. [18]

(Complete Text)

Good morning. Today I have submitted to the Congress my third annual report on United States foreign policy.[19] I want to share my thoughts with you now on some of the highlights of that report.

For the first time in a generation, the most powerful nation in the world and the most populous nation in the world, the United States and the People's Republic of China, have begun a process of communication.

For the first time in a generation, we have taken a series of steps that could mean a new relationship with the Soviet Union.

For the first time in a generation, our alliances with the nations of Europe, Japan, and other nations have been reshaped to reflect their new capacity to assume a greater responsibility for their own defense.

For the first time in a generation, we have laid a new basis for fair

[18]*Presidential Documents*, Feb. 14, 1972, pp. 232-4. For further discussion cf. Rogers Report, 1972, pp. i-xviii.
[19] Nixon Report, 1972 (for full citation see Appendix).

competition in world trade that will mean more jobs for American workers.

These are great changes. They have brought the world closer to a stable peace. They did not happen by accident. These breakthroughs toward peace took place in the past year for good reason.

Three years ago we stopped reacting on the basis of yesterday's habits and started acting to deal with the realities of today and the opportunites of tomorrow.

Where has this new attitude taken us?

In our relations with the Soviet Union, these were the elements of the breakthrough that took place over the past 12 months.

We broke the deadlock in the arms limitation negotiation and agreed on a framework for progress in the SALT talks.[20]

We agreed on a treaty barring weapons of mass destruction from the ocean floor,[21] and on another treaty to remove the threat of germ warfare.[22]

We agreed on a more reliable "hot line" between Washington and Moscow, and found new ways to consult each other in emergencies which will reduce the risk of accidental nuclear war.[23]

And in a step of the greatest importance, we reached an agreement on Berlin.[24] If there was one city where World War III could have broken out in the past 20 years, it was Berlin. This new agreement reduces the danger of the superpowers in direct confrontation.

There are other areas where we have had, and continue to have, serious differences with the Soviet Union. On balance, however, I have concluded that Soviet willingness to take positive steps toward peace in the past year makes a meeting at the highest level timely, particularly in arms limitation and economic cooperation.

And that is why, for the first time, a President of the United States will visit Moscow. I will go to that meeting in May[25] with no naive illusions, but with some reasonable expectations.

Our relations with the Soviet Union were helped by the fact that our two nations have had long-established communications. Because we deeply understood what our real differences were, we could move to negotiate them.

When it came to dealing with the People's Republic of China, 25 years of hostility stood in the way. Accordingly, I began what is now 3 years of the most painstaking and necessarily discreet preparation for an opening to the world's most populous nation.

20 *A.F.R., 1971*, no. 21.
21 Same, no. 13.
22 Same, no. 19.
23 Same, nos. 26-28.
24 Same, no. 39.
25 Cf. Documents 9-12.

In 2 weeks, I shall begin my journey for peace to Peking. The agreement to meet, and the mutual trust needed to make the arrangements for the first American state visit to the People's Republic of China[26] is a breakthrough of great importance.

We do not expect instant solutions to deep-seated differences. But the visit is a beginning. Now, in the relations between our countries, the old exchange of denunciations can be replaced with a constructive exchange of views.

Just as we have established a creative relationship with our adversaries, we have developed a more balanced alliance with our friends.

Not so long ago, our alliances were addressed exclusively to the containment of the Soviet Union and the People's Republic of China. But now there has to be more to our alliance. It is fairly simple to unite about what you are against. It is a lot more complicated to hold together an alliance on the basis of what you are for.

We do not shy away from this complexity because now, in this time of breakthroughs, there has never been a greater need for a sense of common purpose among the non-Communist nations. There is no requirement that we all march in lockstep; but there is a need to move forward in the same direction.

And that is why we encourage initiative and self-reliance on the part of our allies. That is why our alliance is becoming what we need in the real world of the seventies—a dynamic coalition of self-assured and independent nations.

Our former dependents have become our competitors. That is good for them, and it is also good for us.

But as the roles change, the rules change. The old international monetary and trading system had become unfair to the American workers and to American business. Facing vigorous, healthy competitors, the United States could no longer be expected to compete with one hand tied behind its back.

Nothing would have happened unless we made it happen. Last August, we took action to stimulate a worldwide settlement of the problem.[27] Within a few months, a general realignment of currencies took place,[28] the first step toward complete reform.

We succeeded in moving the non-Communist world away from the constant state of monetary crisis of the past decade, and we removed a danger to the unity of the free world.

Let me turn now to Vietnam. This has been America's longest and most difficult war. It began long before I became President. And I have been doing everything I can honorably do to end it.

---

[26] Cf. Documents 53-56.
[27] *A.F.R., 1971*, nos. 142-145.
[28] Same, no. 150.

I have brought almost one-half million men home from Vietnam. As high as 300 a week were being killed in action when I took office. This week there were two. We have reduced air sorties, budget costs, and draft calls. And we have made the most generous peace offer in the history of warfare.[29]

I have no complaint over the fact that during this period, when I have been ending a war I did not begin, I have been subjected to vigorous criticism. I do not question the patriotism or the sincerity of those who disagree with my policies to bring peace, but as I said in 1968 when I was a candidate for President, we have only one President at a time, and only the President can negotiate an end to the war.

There should always be free debate and criticism, so that our policy will represent the best thinking of our Nation, but a candidate for President has a higher responsibility than the ordinary critic. A candidate should make any criticism he believes would contribute to bringing an honorable peace. But I would hope that anyone seeking the Presidency would examine his statements carefully to be sure that nothing he says might give the enemy an incentive to prolong the war until after the election.

Trust in the United States among the 45 nations with which we have treaty commitments is essential if peace and freedom are to be preserved in the world. Let us end our involvement in the war in Vietnam in a way which will not destroy that trust.

Looking ahead on the world scene, how can we move ahead to make the most of the breakthroughs of the past year? We must advance the delicate process of creating a more constructive relationship between ourselves and the People's Republic of China.

We must bring the arms race under control, and by so doing, lay the basis for other major steps toward peace that can be taken together by the United States and the Soviet Union. And equally important, we must continue to strengthen the partnership with our friends. We must work with friends and adversaries to build an international structure of peace which everyone will work to preserve because each nation will realize its stake in its preservation.

We must continue the process of reforming the world's financial and trading systems so that workers and consumers can benefit in America and in every country that has a competitive spirit.

Those are by no means the only items on our international agenda. We want to see the cease-fire in the Middle East, which we initiated,[30] moved toward a more secure and permanent peace. We want to work out with our friends in Latin America, Africa, and non-Communist Asia new ways of helping them help themselves. We want to shore up the eroding confidence in the United Nations.

---

[29] Cf. Documents 43-44.
[30] *Documents, 1970*, pp. 131-5.

There is much unfinished business. But there is a new awareness of reality growing in the world. Movement and progress can be felt today where there was stagnation and frustration before.

By facing the realities of the world today—as this breakthrough year has shown we are capable of doing—we can make peace a reality in the generation ahead.

Thank you and good morning.

B. Congress and Foreign Policy.

[While President Nixon ventured into uncharted realms of personal diplomacy, important elements within the U.S. Congress persisted in their efforts to reassert the position of the legislature as a coequal partner in the conduct of foreign affairs. Increasing disagreement with particular aspects of administration foreign policy, particularly in Southeast Asia, reinforced the broader constitutional and political considerations that were felt by influential members of Congress to call for new restrictions on executive freedom of action in foreign affairs. On neither the regional nor the constitutional level, however, was dissent sufficiently focused or intense to have much impact on administration actions during 1972. Détente with Peking and Moscow had few enemies in Congress, and there was little serious resistance to Senate approval of the Treaty on the Limitation of Anti-Ballistic Missile Systems. Even the accompanying Interim Agreement on limitation of strategic offensive arms was endorsed by overwhelming majorities, once the intent of Congress had been clarified by an amendment to the resolution of approval.[31] Attempts to force a conclusion to the war in Indochina, primarily through the (Senator Edward W.) Brooke Amendment stipulating that all U.S. forces be withdrawn within four months, were repeatedly approved by the Senate, but failed to gain the approval of the House at a time when American forces were withdrawing anyway and serious peace negotiations were taking place in Paris.[32] The resolution of Senator Mike Mansfield, who for years had been calling for a substantial reduction of U.S. forces in Europe,[33] was not at issue during 1972; and, although Congress trimmed the administration's requests for new weapons and other defense items, it refrained from challenging the essentials of defense policy. Even its failure to enact coherent foreign aid legislation for the fiscal years 1972 and 1973 was partially offset by the adoption

[31] Documents 13-14; for congressional action, cf. Documents 15-16.
[32] Cf. Chapter V at notes 61-64.
[33] Cf. *A.F.R., 1971*, nos. 33-34 and 41.

of continuing resolutions permitting foreign aid spending to go forward at previously established rates.[34]]

1. The "War Powers" Bill.

[Attempts at a broader redefinition of presidential and congressional responsibilities in the general area of foreign affairs remained almost equally inconclusive. The most significant development in this field was the approval by the Senate, after nearly two years of preliminary effort, of a "war powers" bill, sponsored by Republican Senator Jacob K. Javits of New York and Democratic Senator William B. Spong, Jr., of Virginia, which sought to impose a 30-day limit on any emergency use of the Armed Forces by the President in the absence of a declaration of war or specific authorization by the Congress.[35] Described by the Senate Foreign Relations Committee as an important contribution toward restoring "the confidence of the American people in the processes of their government, particularly as they relate to the vital and overriding questions of war and peace,"[36] the bill was viewed by Secretary of State William P. Rogers as both "unconstitutional and unwise" because, in addition to limiting authority that had been left unlimited by the Constitution, it would in his opinion increase the risks of undesired hostilities and cast doubt on the reliability of the United States as an ally.[37] Although the bill was nevertheless adopted by a 68 to 16 vote of the Senate on April 13, 1972 (Document 3), the House of Representatives shied away from such far-reaching action and contented itself with the readoption on August 14, 1972 of the (Representative Clement J.) Zablocki Resolution, previously approved in 1970 and 1971, which merely called on the President to seek "appropriate consultation" with the Congress and to submit a written report in the event of any significant military action undertaken without prior congressional authorization.[38] In consequence of these differences, no war powers legislation was enacted in 1972, and it was not until the fall of 1973 that House and Senate were able to agree on the war powers resolution (with a 60-day limit on

---

[34] Cf. Chapter X at notes 59-62.
[35] S. 2956, 92d Congress (Document 3); for background cf. *A.F.R., 1971*, nos. 6-8.
[36] Senate Report 92-606, Feb. 9, 1972, p. 23; details in Senate Foreign Relations Committee History, pp. 116-20.
[37] Letter to Senator Gordon Allott, Mar. 24, 1972, in *Bulletin*, Apr. 17, 1972, pp. 580-82; for a fuller statement see *A.F.R., 1971*, no. 8.
[38] S. 2956, 92d Congress, as approved by a 344-13 vote of the House of Representatives on Aug. 14, 1972; previously approved Aug. 2, 1971 as House Joint Resolution 1, 92d Congress (*A.F.R., 1971*, no. 6b).

discretionary use of the Armed Forces) which was enacted over President Nixon's veto on November 7, 1973.[39]

(3) The "War Powers Act," Passed by the Senate April 13, 1972 But Not Accepted by the House of Representatives.[40]

(Complete Text)
S. 2956

An act to make rules governing the use of the Armed Forces of the United States in the absence of a declaration of war by the Congress

Be it enacted by the Senate and House of Representatives of the United States of America in Congress assembled,

SHORT TITLE

SECTION 1. This Act may be cited as the "War Powers Act".

PURPOSE AND POLICY

SEC. 2. It is the purpose of this Act to fulfill the intent of the framers of the Constitution of the United States and insure that the collective judgment of both the Congress and the President will apply to the introduction of the Armed Forces of the United States in hostilities, or in situations where imminent involvement in hostilities is clearly indicated by the circumstances, and to the continued use of such forces in hostilities or in such situations after they have been introduced in hostilities or in such situations.

Under article I, section 8, of the Constitution, it is specifically provided that the Congress shall have the power to make all laws necessary and proper for carrying into execution, not only its own powers but also all other powers vested by this Constitution in the Government of the United States, or in any department or officer thereof. At the same time, this Act is not intended to encroach upon the recognized powers of the President, as Commander in Chief and Chief Executive, to conduct hostilities authorized by the Congress, to respond to attacks or the imminent threat of attacks upon the United States, including its

[39] House Joint Resolution 542, 93d Congress, enacted as Public Law 93-148, effective Nov. 7, 1973. President Nixon's veto message of Oct. 24, 1973 appears in *Presidential Documents*, Oct. 29, 1973, pp. 1285-7.
[40] S. 2956, 92d Congress, as approved by a 68-16 vote of the Senate on Apr. 13, 1972; text from *Congressional Record* (Daily Edition), April 13, 1972, pp. S 6101-2. For action by the House of Representatives, cf. above at note 38.

territories and possessions, to repel attacks or forestall the imminent threat of attacks against the Armed Forces of the United States, and, under proper circumstances, to rescue endangered citizens and nationals of the United States located in foreign countries.

EMERGENCY USE OF THE ARMED FORCES

SEC. 3. In the absence of a declaration of war by the Congress, the Armed Forces of the United States may be introduced in hostilities, or in situations where imminent involvement in hostilities is clearly indicated by the circumstances, only—

(1) to repel an armed attack upon the United States, its territories and possessions; to take necessary and appropriate retaliatory actions in the event of such an attack; and to forestall the direct and imminent threat of such an attack;

(2) to repel an armed attack against the Armed Forces of the United States located outside of the United States, its territories and possessions, and to forestall the direct and imminent threat of such an attack;

(3) to protect while evacuating citizens and nationals of the United States, as rapidly as possible, from (A) any situation on the high seas involving a direct and imminent threat to the lives of such citizens and nationals, or (B) any country in which such citizens and nationals are present with the express or tacit consent of the government of such country and are being subjected to a direct and imminent threat to their lives, either sponsored by such government or beyond the power of such government to control; but the President shall make every effort to terminate such a threat without using the Armed Forces of the United States, and shall, where possible, obtain the consent of the government of such country before using the Armed Forces of the United States to protect citizens and nationals of the United States being evacuated from such country; or

(4) pursuant to specific statutory authorization, but authority to introduce the Armed Forces of the United States in hostilities or in any such situation shall not be inferred (A) from any provision of law hereafter enacted, including any provision contained in any appropriation Act, unless such provision specifically authorizes the introduction of [the Armed Forces of the United States in hostilities or in such situation and specifically exempts the introduction of] such Armed Forces from compliance with the provisions of this Act, or (B) from any treaty hereafter ratified unless such treaty is implemented by legislation specifically authorizing the introduction of the Armed Forces of the United States in hostilities or in such situation and specifically exempting the introduction of such Armed Forces from compliance with the provisions of this Act. Specific statutory authorization is required for the assignment of members of the Armed Forces of the United

States to command, coordinate, participate in the movement of, or accompany the regular or irregular military forces of any foreign country or government when such Armed Forces are engaged, or there exists an imminent threat that such forces will become engaged, in hostilities. No treaty in force at the time of the enactment of this Act shall be construed as specific statutory authorization for, or a specific exemption permitting, the introduction of the Armed Forces of the United States in hostilities or in any such situation, within the meaning of this clause (4); and no provision of law in force at the time of the enactment of this Act shall be so construed unless such provision specifically authorizes the introduction of such Armed Forces in hostilities or in any such situation.

REPORTS

SEC. 4. The introduction of the Armed Forces of the United States in hostilities, or in any situation where imminent involvement in hostilities is clearly indicated by the circumstances, under any of the conditions described in section 3 of this Act shall be reported promptly in writing by the President to the Speaker of the House of Representatives and the President of the Senate, together with a full account of the circumstances under which such Armed Forces were introduced in such hostilities or in such situation, the estimated scope of such hostilities or situation, and the consistency of the introduction of such forces in such hostilities or situation with the provisions of section 3 of this Act. Whenever Armed Forces of the United States are engaged in hostilities or in any such situation outside of the United States, its territories and possessions, the President shall, so long as such Armed Forces continue to be engaged in such hostilities or in such situation, report to the Congress periodically on the status of such hostilities or situation as well as the scope and expected duration of such hostilities or situation, but in no event shall he report to the Congress less often than every six months.

THIRTY-DAY AUTHORIZATION PERIOD

SEC. 5. The use of the Armed Forces of the United States in hostilities, or in any situation where imminent involvement in hostilities is clearly indicated by the circumstances, under any of the conditions described in section 3 of this Act shall not be sustained beyond thirty days from the date of the introduction of such Armed Forces in hostilities or in any such situation unless (1) the President determines and certifies to the Congress in writing that unavoidable military necessity respecting the safety of Armed Forces of the United States engaged pursuant to section 3(1) or 3(2) of this Act requires the continued use of such Armed Forces in the course of bringing about a prompt disengagement from such hostilities; or (2) Congress is physically unable to meet as a result of an armed attack upon the United States; or (3) the continued use of such Armed Forces in such hostilities or in such situation has been authorized in specific legislation enacted for that purpose by the Congress and pursuant to the provisions thereof.

TERMINATION WITHIN 30-DAY PERIOD

SEC. 6. The use of the Armed Forces of the United States in hostilities, or in any situation where imminent involvement in hostilities is clearly indicated by the circumstances, under any of the conditions described in section 3 of this Act may be terminated prior to the thirty-day period specified in section 5 of this Act by an Act or joint resolution of Congress, except in a case where the President has determined and certified to the Congress in writing that unavoidable military necessity respecting the safety of Armed Forces of the United States engaged pursuant to section 3(1) or 3(2) of this Act requires the continued use of such Armed Forces in the course of bringing about a prompt disengagement from such hostilities.

CONGRESSIONAL PRIORITY PROVISIONS

SEC. 7. (a) Any bill or joint resolution authorizing a continuation of the use of the Armed Forces of the United States in hostilities, or in any situation where imminent involvement in hostilities is clearly indicated by the circumstances under any of the conditions described in section 3 of this Act, or any bill or joint resolution terminating the use of Armed Forces of the United States in hostilities, as provided in section 6 of this Act, shall, if sponsored or cosponsored by one-third of the Members of the House of Congress in which it is introduced, be considered reported to the floor of such House no later than one day following its introduction unless the Members of such House otherwise determine by yeas and nays. Any such bill or joint resolution, after having been passed by the House of Congress in which it originated, shall be considered reported to the floor of the other House of Congress within one day after it has been passed by the House in which it originated and sent to the other House, unless the Members of the other House shall otherwise determine by yeas and nays.

(b) Any bill or joint resolution reported to the floor pursuant to subsection (a) or when placed directly on the calendar shall immediately become the pending business of the House in which such bill or joint resolution is reported or placed directly on the calendar, and shall be voted upon within three days after it has been reported or placed directly on the calendar, as the case may be, unless such House shall otherwise determine by yeas and nays.

SEPARABILITY CLAUSE

SEC. 8. If any provision of this Act or the application thereof to any person or circumstance is held invalid, the remainder of the Act and the application of such provision to any other person or circumstance shall not be affected thereby.

EFFECTIVE DATE AND APPLICABILITY

SEC. 9. This Act shall take effect on the date of its enactment but shall not apply to hostilities in which the Armed Forces of the United States are involved on the effective date of this Act. Nothing in section 3 (4) of this Act shall be construed to require any further specific statutory authorization to permit members of the Armed Forces of the United States to participate jointly with members of the armed forces of one or more foreign countries in the headquarters operations of high-level military commands which were established prior to the date of enactment of this Act and pursuant to the United Nations Charter or any treaty ratified by the United States prior to such date.

2. The Problem of Executive Agreements.

[In still another manifestation of uneasiness about the extent of executive power in foreign affairs, both houses of Congress displayed discomfort during 1971 concerning the administration's frequent practice of concluding international agreements in a form that did not require subsequent congressional review. Formal treaties, under the Constitution, require the advice and consent of the Senate before they can be ratified and enter into force; but a much larger number of international arrangements involving the United States in recent decades had taken the form of so-called executive agreements, which, by definition, had been exempt from congressional scrutiny. As of January 1, 1972, the United States was a party to 947 treaties and no fewer than 4,359 executive agreements; between the beginning of President Nixon's term on January 20, 1969 and May 1, 1972, it concluded a total of 71 treaties and 608 executive agreements.[41]

[41] John R. Stevenson, State Department Legal Adviser, "Constitutional Aspects of the Executive Agreement Procedure" (*Bulletin*, June 19, 1972, pp. 840-51), p. 840.

Congressional uneasiness about the lack of legislative oversight in this area had been stimulated by the conclusion of a controversial defense arrangement with Spain in 1970[42] and was brought to a head by the conclusion in December 1971 of two further executive agreements that likewise involved the use of military facilities abroad. One of these was an exchange of notes with Portugal on December 9, 1971 that extended the validity of an existing agreement permitting peacetime stationing of U.S. forces at Lajes Field in the Azores;[43] the other was an exchange of notes with Bahrain on December 23, 1971 that provided for continued use of support facilities in that country by the U.S. Navy's Middle East Force.[44]

The conclusion of these agreements, both of which were concluded without prior consultation with the Congress, added impetus to a move already initiated by Republican Senator Clifford P. Case of New Jersey with a view to insisting that any international agreement, other than a treaty, to which the United States was a party should be transmitted to Congress within 60 days of its entry into force, subject to special security safeguards in the case of secret agreements. Legislation embodying this requirement, which in no way challenged the President's right to conclude executive agreements but merely called for their subsequent communication to the Congress, had been introduced by Senator Case on February 4, 1971. Adopted by an 81 to 0 vote of the Senate on February 16, 1972, the Case bill was subsequently endorsed by a voice vote of the House on August 14, 1972 and signed into law by the President on August 22, 1972.[45]

Independently of the reporting requirement, it was felt by Senator Case and other members of the Foreign Relations Committee that the 1971 agreements with Portugal and Bahrain were sufficiently important to justify their submission to the Senate as treaties. A resolution stating this view was introduced by Senator Case and approved, in amended form, by a Senate vote of 50 to 6 on March 3, 1972.[46] Since the administration chose merely to "note" this expression but gave no sign of any intention to comply, the Foreign Relations Committee subsequently attached an amendment by Senator Case to the pending foreign aid bill stipulating that

---

[42] *Documents, 1970*, pp. 107-14.
[43] TIAS 7254 (22 UST 2106); cf. *A.F.R., 1971*, no. 47, and Document 21, below.
[44] TIAS 7263 (22 UST 2184); for details cf. *Bulletin*, Feb. 28, 1972, p. 282.
[45] Public Law 92-403, Aug. 22, 1972; details in Senate Foreign Relations Committee History, pp. 109-11. For White House comment, see *Bulletin*, Oct. 23, 1972, pp. 480-81.
[46] Senate Resolution 214, 92d Congress, in *Congressional Record* (Daily Edition), Mar. 3, 1972, p. S 3290; details in Senate Report 92-1182, Sept. 19, 1972, p. 24, and Senate Foreign Relations Committee History, pp. 111-14.

no funds to implement the two agreements could be provided until they were submitted to the Senate in treaty form. A motion to delete this provision was rejected by a 41 to 36 vote of the Senate on June 19, 1972, but reference to the Bahrain agreement was subsequently deleted by another Senate vote of 50 to 30,[47] and the stipulation regarding the Portuguese agreement eventually perished amid the general debacle of the fiscal year 1973 foreign aid legislation.[48] Also stillborn was a proposal by Senator Case to require Senate approval of any agreement involving the stationing of U.S. combat forces abroad, as well as a proposal by Democratic Senator Sam J. Ervin, Jr., of North Carolina to delay the entry into force of executive agreements for a period of 60 days during which Congress might disapprove them.[49]

In an exception to the usual procedure with regard to executive agreements, the administration did submit for congressional approval the Interim Agreement on the limitation of strategic offensive weapons which President Nixon signed in Moscow on May 26, 1972 (Document 14). As explained in the next chapter, this procedure was legally obligatory because of the special subject matter of the agreement and did not reflect any change in the administration position on the constitutional issues involved.]

3. Governmental Organization for Foreign Affairs.

[Two measures bearing on the organization of the government for the conduct of foreign policy were approved by Congress at its 1972 session. By the Foreign Relations Act of 1972,[50] it established a twelve-member Commission on the Organization of the Government for the Conduct of Foreign Policy, to be composed of presidential and congressional nominees from government and private life, to study and make recommendations in this area by the middle of 1974. (The deadline was later extended to mid-1975.)[51]

By the International Economic Policy Act of 1972,[52] Congress

---

[47] Same, pp. 59-60.
[48] Details in same, pp. 57-64, and Senate Report 92-1182, pp. 23-7. On the foreign aid legislation cf. Chapter X at notes 59-62.
[49] For details, cf. Senate Report 92-1182, pp. 27-9, and Stevenson, *loc. cit.* (n. 41), pp. 849-50.
[50] Title VI, Public Law 92-352, July 13, 1972.
[51] Public Law 93-126, Oct. 18, 1973. The names of the four presidential appointees (Robert D. Murphy, David M. Abshire, William J. Casey, and Anne L. Armstrong) were made public Mar. 9, 1973 (*Presidential Documents*, Mar. 12, 1973, p. 245). For further discussion on foreign affairs management cf. Nixon Report, 1972, pp. 208-12, and Rogers Report, 1972, pp. 229-55.
[52] Title II, Public Law 92-412, Aug. 29, 1972.

gave formal status to the Council on International Economic Policy established by the President in 1971;[53] charged that body with making "recommendations to the President for domestic and foreign programs which will promote a more consistent international economic policy on the part of the United States and private industry"; and called for the submission of an annual report on the international economic position of the United States within 60 days after the beginning of each new session of Congress.[54]]

C. The Presidential Nominations.

[Recollection of the presidential campaign of 1972 is inevitably dominated by the memory of the Watergate scandals that ultimately led to the resignation of President Nixon under threat of impeachment on August 9, 1974. At the time, however, few Americans attached such far-reaching importance to the arrest inside the Democratic National Committee headquarters on June 17, 1972 of five individuals, equipped with special cameras and electronic listening devices, who turned out to be connected in various ways with the Central Intelligence Agency, the Republican National Committee, the Committee for the Re-election of the President, and members of the White House staff. Political espionage, corruption, and "dirty tricks" did not develop into really major issues during the 1972 campaign and entered the foreground of public consciousness only after President Nixon's reelection on November 7, 1972 and his inauguration for a second four-year term on January 20, 1973.

To Republican perception, the main objective of the 1972 campaign was to ensure for President Nixon the mandate he would need to bring to completion the domestic and foreign enterprises initiated over the past three and one-half years, among them the withdrawal of American military forces from Vietnam, the normal-

---

[53] *A.F.R., 1971*, no. 5.

[54] Under the terms of the Act, the original members of the Commission were the President; the Secretaries of State, Treasury, Defense, Agriculture, Commerce, and Labor; the Director of the Office of Management and Budget; the Chairman of the Council of Economic Advisers; and the Special Representative for Trade Negotiations. (Membership was later modified by Public Law 93-121 of Oct. 4, 1973.) Peter M. Flanigan, who succeeded Peter G. Peterson as Executive Director of the Council in Jan. 1972, was confirmed in that position on Dec. 1, 1972 when Secretary of the Treasury George P. Shultz was designated as an Assistant to the President and Chairman of the Council (*Public Papers, 1972*, Appendix E, pp. 4-6). The first of the annual reports required by the Act was transmitted Mar. 22, 1973 and is listed in note 172 to Chapter II.

ization of relations with mainland China, and the promotion of détente with the Soviet Union and its allies. For Democrats, the primary task was to select a candidate and devise a platform with some chance of overcoming the inherent advantage enjoyed by the incumbent administration. A further problem initially confronting both major parties was the threat of an effective populist-style campaign by Governor George Wallace of Alabama, whose prospects of entering the race as a third-party candidate were cut short only by his serious wounding in an assassination attempt on May 15, 1972.

Among the leading Democratic candidates—Senator Hubert H. Humphrey of Minnesota, Senator Edmund S. Muskie of Maine, and Senator George McGovern of South Dakota—all were on record as favoring a prompt withdrawal from Indochina and a settlement of the war on terms substantially more lenient than the administration had been prepared to contemplate. Senator McGovern, in a departure from the mainstream of Democratic sentiment, had also outlined a series of left-wing positions involving, among other things, a sharp curtailment of overseas commitments and military expenditures,[55] elimination of tax discrimination in favor of the wealthy, and increased investment in human resources through expanded social security, education, and job-creation programs. Above all, the South Dakota Senator insisted upon the need for a reaffirmation of the underlying ideals that had inspired the American nation at its birth, but, in his view, had been largely lost to sight in recent years. Nominated on the first ballot at the Democratic National Convention in Miami Beach, Florida, on July 12, 1972, Senator McGovern defined his position next day in an acceptance speech (Document 4) that was equally characteristic in its insistence on an end to the war and its invocation of neglected elements in the national tradition. But the McGovern candidacy had seriously divisive effects within the Senator's own party, and the sense of disarray was subsequently heightened by a switch in vice-presidential candidates when Senator Thomas F. Eagleton of Missouri was superseded by Sargent Shriver, former Ambassador to Paris.

Dissension in the Democratic camp could only strengthen the outlook for reelection of President Nixon, who won the expected first ballot nomination at the Republican National Convention, also held in Miami Beach, on August 22, 1972.[56] Vice-President Spiro T. Agnew, the President's choice as running mate, was likewise endorsed by the convention on the following day. An interim

---

55 Cf. note 61 below.
56 One vote out of 1,348 was cast for an antiwar candidate, Representative Paul N. McCloskey of California.

report on the achievements and hopes of his administration in the field of foreign policy was among the salient features of President Nixon's acceptance speech delivered on August 23, 1972 (Document 5).]

(4) The Democratic Challenge: Address by Senator George McGovern Accepting the Democratic Presidential Nomination, Miami Beach, July 13, 1972.[57]

(Excerpts)

*   *   *

In Scripture and in the music of our children we are told: "To everything there is a season, and a time to every purpose under heaven."

And for America, the time has come at last.

This is the time for truth, not falsehood.

In a democratic nation, no one likes to say that his inspiration came from secret arrangements behind closed doors. But in a sense that is how my candidacy began. I am here as your candidate tonight in large part because during four administrations of both parties, a terrible war has been charted behind closed doors.

I want those doors opened, and I want that war closed. And I make these pledges above all others—the doors of government will be open, and that brutal war will be closed.

Truth is a habit of integrity, not a strategy of politics. And if we nurture the habit of candor in this campaign, we will continue to be candid once we are in the White House. Let us say to Americans, as Woodrow Wilson said in his first campaign: "Let me inside [the government] and I will tell you everything that is going on in there."

And this is a time not for death, but for life.

In 1968, Americans voted to bring our sons home from Vietnam in peace—and since then, 20,000 have come home in coffins.

I have no secret plan for peace. I have a public plan.

As one whose heart has ached for 10 years over the agony of Vietnam, I will halt the senseless bombing of Indochina on Inauguration Day.

There will be no more Asian children running ablaze from bombed-out schools.

There will be no more talk of bombing the dikes or the cities of the North.

Within 90 days of my inauguration, every American soldier and every

57 Prepared text as printed in *New York Times*, July 14, 1972.

American prisoner will be out of the jungle and out of their cells and back home in America where they belong.

And then let us resolve that never again will we shed the precious young blood of this nation to perpetuate an unrepresentative client abroad.

Let us choose life, not death, this is the time.

This is also the time to turn away from excessive preoccupation overseas to rebuilding our own nation.

America must be restored to her proper role in the world. But we can do that only through the recovery of confidence in ourselves. The greatest contribution America can make to our fellow mortals is to heal our own great but deeply troubled land. We must respond to that ancient command: "Physician, heal thyself."

It is necessary in an age of nuclear power and hostile ideology that we be militarily strong. America must never become a second-rate nation. As one who has tasted the bitter fruits of our weakness before Pearl Harbor, 1941, I give you my sacred pledge that if I become President of the United States, America will keep its defenses alert and fully sufficient to meet any danger. We will do that not only for ourselves, but for those who deserve and need the shield of our strength—our old allies in Europe, and elsewhere, including the people of Israel, who will always have our help to hold their promised land.

Yet we know that for 30 years we have been so absorbed with fear and danger from abroad that we have permitted our own house to fall into disarray. We must now show that peace and prosperity can exist side by side—indeed, each now depends on the other.

National strength includes the credibility of our system in the eyes of our own people as well as the credibility of our deterrent in the eyes of others abroad.

National security includes schools for our children as well as silos for our missiles, the health of our families as much as the size of our bombs, the safety of our streets and the condition of our cities and not just the engines of war.

And if we some day choke on the pollution of our own air, there will be little consolation in leaving behind a dying continent ringed with steel.

Let us protect ourselves abroad and perfect ourselves at home.

This is the time.

*   *   *

We are not content with things as they are. We reject the view of those who say: "America—love it or leave it." We reply: "Let us change it so we can love it the more."

And this is the time. It is the time for this land to become again a witness to the world for what is noble and just in human affairs. It is the time to live more with faith and less with fear—with an abiding confidence that can sweep away the strongest barriers between us and teach us that we truly are brothers and sisters.

So join with me in this campaign, lend me your strength and your support, give me your voice—and together, we will call America home to the founding ideals that nourished us in the beginning.

From secrecy and deception in high places, come home, America.

From a conflict in Indochina which maims our ideals as well as our soldiers, come home, America.

From military spending so wasteful that it weakens our nation, come home, America.

From the entrenchment of special privilege and tax favoritism, come home, America.

From the waste of idle hands to the joy of useful labor, come home, America.

From the prejudice of race and sex, come home, America.

From the loneliness of the aging poor and the despair of the neglected sick, come home, America.

Come home to the affirmation that we have a dream.

Come home to the conviction that we can move our country forward.

Come home to the belief that we can seek a newer world.

For:

> *This land is your land,*
> *This land is my land,*
> *From California to the New York Island,*
> *From the Redwood Forest*
> *To the Gulfstream waters,*
> *This land was made for you and me.*

May God grant us the wisdom to cherish this good land to meet the great challenge that beckons us home.

(5) The Republican Response: Address by President Nixon Accepting the Republican Presidential Nomination, Miami Beach, August 23, 1972.[58]

(Excerpt)

*   *   *

Now, I turn to an issue of overriding importance not only to this

[58] *Presidential Documents*, Aug. 28, 1972, pp. 1267-70.

election, but for generations to come—the progress we have made in building a new structure of peace in the world.

Peace is too important for partisanship. There have been five Presidents in my political lifetime—Franklin D. Roosevelt, Harry Truman, Dwight Eisenhower, John F. Kennedy, and Lyndon Johnson.

They had differences on some issues, but they were united in their belief that where the security of America or the peace of the world is involved we are not Republicans, we are not Democrats. We are Americans, first, last, and always.

These five Presidents were united in their total opposition to isolation for America and in their belief that the interests of the United States and the interests of world peace require that America be strong enough and intelligent enough to assume the responsibilities of leadership in the world.

They were united in the conviction that the United States should have a defense second to none in the world.

They were all men who hated war and were dedicated to peace.

But not one of these five men and no President in our history believed that America should ask an enemy for peace on terms that would betray our allies and destroy respect for the United States all over the world.

As your President, I pledge that I shall always uphold that proud bipartisan tradition. Standing in this Convention Hall 4 years ago, I pledged to seek an honorable end to the war in Vietnam.[59] We have made great progress toward that end. We have brought over half a million men home and more will be coming home. We have ended America's ground combat role. No draftees are being sent to Vietnam. We have reduced our casualties by 98 percent. We have gone the extra mile, in fact, we have gone tens of thousands of miles trying to seek a negotiated settlement of the war. We have offered a cease-fire, a total withdrawal of all American forces, an exchange of all prisoners of war, internationally supervised free elections with the Communists participating in the elections and in the supervision.[60]

There are three things, however, that we have not and that we will not offer.

We will never abandon our prisoners of war.

Second, we will not join our enemies in imposing a Communist government on our allies—the 17 million people of South Vietnam.

And we will never stain the honor of the United States of America.

Now I realize that many, particularly in this political year, wonder why we insist on an honorable peace in Vietnam. From a political

[59] Acceptance speech, Republican National Convention, Aug. 8, 1968; text in *New York Times*, Aug. 9, 1968.
[60] Cf. Document 44.

standpoint they suggest that since I was not in office when over a half million American men were sent there, that I should end the war by agreeing to impose a Communist government on the people of South Vietnam and just blame the whole catastrophe on my predecessors.

This might be good politics, but it would be disastrous to the cause of peace in the world. If, at this time, we betray our allies, it will discourage our friends abroad and it will encourage our enemies to engage in aggression.

In areas like the Mideast, which are danger areas, small nations who rely on the friendship and support of the United States would be in deadly jeopardy.

To our friends and allies in Europe, Asia, the Mideast, and Latin America, I say the United States will continue its great bipartisan tradition—to stand by our friends and never to desert them.

Now in discussing Vietnam, I have noted that in this election year there has been a great deal of talk about providing amnesty for those few hundred Americans who chose to desert their country rather than to serve it in Vietnam. I think it is time that we put the emphasis where it belongs. The real heroes are two and one-half million young Americans who chose to serve their country rather than desert it. I say to you tonight, in these times when there is so much of a tendency to run down those who have served America in the past and who serve it today, let us give those who serve in our Armed Forces and those who have served in Vietnam the honor and the respect that they deserve and that they have earned.

Finally, in this connection, let one thing be clearly understood in this election campaign: The American people will not tolerate any attempt by our enemies to interfere in the cherished right of the American voter to make his own decision with regard to what is best for America, without outside intervention.

Now it is understandable that Vietnam has been a major concern in foreign policy. But we have not allowed the war in Vietnam to paralyze our capacity to initiate historic new policies to construct a lasting and just peace in the world.

When the history of this period is written, I believe it will be recorded that our most significant contributions to peace resulted from our trips to Peking and to Moscow.

The dialogue that we have begun with the People's Republic of China has reduced the danger of war and has increased the chance for peaceful cooperation between two great peoples.

Within the space of 4 years in our relations with the Soviet Union we have moved from confrontation to negotiation, and then to cooperation in the interest of peace.

We have taken the first step in limiting the nuclear arms race.

We have laid the foundation for further limitations on nuclear weapons and eventually of reducing the armaments in the nuclear area. We can thereby not only reduce the enormous cost of arms for both our countries, but we can increase the chances for peace.

More than on any other single issue, I ask you, my fellow Americans, to give us the chance to continue these great initiatives that can contribute so much to the future peace in the world.

It can truly be said that as a result of our initiatives, the danger of war is less today than it was; the chances for peace are greater.

But a note of warning needs to be sounded. We cannot be complacent. Our opponents have proposed massive cuts in our defense budget[61] which would have the inevitable effect of making the United States the second strongest nation in the world.

For the United States unilaterally to reduce its strength with the naive hope that other nations would do likewise would increase the danger of war in the world.

It would completely remove any incentive of other nations to agree to a mutual limitation or reduction of arms.

The promising initiatives we have undertaken to limit arms would be destroyed.

The security of the United States and all the nations in the world who depend upon our friendship and support would be threatened.

Let's look at the record on defense expenditures. We have cut spending in our Administration. It now takes the lowest percentage of our national product in 20 years. We should not spend more on defense than we need. But we must never spend less than we need.

What we must understand is, spending what we need on defense will cost us money. Spending less than we need could cost us our lives or our freedom.

So tonight, my fellow Americans, I say, let us take risks for peace, but let us never risk the security of the United States of America.

It is for that reason that I pledge that we will continue to seek peace and the mutual reduction of arms. The United States, during this period, however, will always have a defense second to none.

There are those who believe that we can entrust the security of America to the good will of our adversaries.

[61] In an "alternative defense budget" originally put forward in Jan. 1972 and subsequently elaborated, Senator McGovern proposed a reduction of defense spending to an annual level of approximately $55 billion over the next three years through the elimination of "waste . . . excess . . . fat and . . . overkill capability"; reduction of military manpower from about 2.5 million to 1.75 million; a reduction of U.S. ground forces in Western Europe from 4-1/3 divisions to 2 divisions, or from 310,000 to 130,000 men; a reduction in the number of aircraft carrier task forces; disbandment of nine tactical air wings; and elimination of antiballistic missile defenses. For details, cf. *New York Times*, Jan. 20, 1972; *U.S. News & World Report*, Aug. 7, 1972, p. 20; *Christian Science Monitor*, Sept. 15, 1972.

Those who hold this view do not know the real world. We can negotiate limitation of arms and we have done so. We can make agreements to reduce the danger of war, and we have done so.

But one unchangeable rule of international diplomacy that I have learned over many, many years is that, in negotiations between great powers, you can only get something if you have something to give in return.

That is why I say tonight: Let us always be sure that when the President of the United States goes to the conference table, he never has to negotiate from weakness.

There is no such thing as a retreat to peace.

My fellow Americans, we stand today on the threshold of one of the most exciting and challenging eras in the history of relations between nations.

We have the opportunity in our time to be the peacemakers of the world, because the world trusts and respects us, and because the world knows that we shall only use our power to defend freedom, never to destroy it; to keep the peace, never to break it.

A strong America is not the enemy of peace; it is the guardian of peace.

The initiatives that we have begun can result in reducing the danger of arms, as well as the danger of war which hangs over the world today.

Even more important, it means that the enormous creative energies of the Russian people and the Chinese people and the American people and all the great peoples of the world can be turned away from production [for] war and turned toward production for peace.

In America it means that we can undertake programs for progress at home that will be just as exciting as the great initiatives we have undertaken in building a new structure of peace abroad.

My fellow Americans, the peace dividend that we hear so much about has too often been described solely in monetary terms—how much money we could take out of the arms budget and apply to our domestic needs. By far the biggest dividend, however, is that achieving our goal of a lasting peace in the world would reflect the deepest hopes and ideals of all of the American people.

Speaking on behalf of the American people, I was proud to be able to say in my television address to the Russian people in May:[62] "We covet no one else's territory. We seek no dominion over any other nation. We seek peace not only for ourselves, but for all the people of the world."

This dedication to idealism runs through America's history.

During the tragic War Between the States, Abraham Lincoln was asked whether God was on his side. He replied, "My concern is not whether God is on our side, but whether we are on God's side."

May that always be our prayer for America.

[62] Document 9.

We hold the future of peace in the world and our own future in our hands. Let us reject therefore the policies of those who whine and whimper about our frustrations and call on us to turn inward.

Let us not turn away from greatness.

The chance America now has to lead the way to a lasting peace in the world may never come again.

With faith in God and faith in ourselves and faith in our country, let us have the vision and the courage to seize the moment and meet the challenge before it slips away.

*   *   *

D. Foreign Policy in the Campaign.

[The foreign policy views put forward by Senator McGovern and President Nixon in their respective acceptance statements were too far apart to lend themselves to subsequent debate. While the President continued to emphasize defense and foreign policy in his postconvention statements,[63] Senator McGovern had little new to say on these subjects until early October, when he released a comprehensive written statement on foreign policy (Document 6) and, five days later, broadcast a highly critical appraisal of the administration's policies in Vietnam (Document 48). President Nixon, whose hopes for a Vietnam settlement in advance of the November 7 election were doomed to last-minute disappointment,[64] confined himself in the closing days of the campaign to a series of short broadcasts rebutting the McGovern views on defense and foreign policy (Document 7), underlining his own determination to hold out for satisfactory peace terms,[65] and again reviewing the international achievements of his administration (Document 8).

That the Nixon record afforded greater reassurance to the public than the untried expedients of the McGovern formula seemed evident from the overwhelming nature of President Nixon's electoral victory on November 7, in which he carried every state but Massachusetts (and the District of Columbia), acquiring 521 of the 538 electoral votes and winning 60.7 percent of the popular vote to McGovern's 37.5 percent. The Democrats nevertheless retained their control of Congress, winning two additional Senate seats (for a total of 57) and retaining a 243 to 192 lead in the House of Representatives.

Interpreting his victory as an unequivocal expression of national

---

[63] American Legion address, Chicago, Aug. 24, 1972, in *Public Papers, 1972*, pp. 795-803; San Francisco address, Sept. 27, 1972, in same, pp. 925-32.
[64] Cf. Chapter V at notes 79-80.
[65] Broadcast statement, Nov. 2, 1972, in *Public Papers, 1972*, pp. 1084-9.

confidence, the President gave few immediate indications of his plans for the second term. In a newspaper interview granted two days before the election and published on November 9, he intimated that "while the next four years will not be as spectacular as the year 1972, where we had the opening to Peking, the first summit with the Russians, and the August 15 [1971] international monetary moves, ... the next four years will build on those and will really accomplish more, because those were basically the first steps which opened the way for much bigger steps in the future."[66]

Late in November it was announced that Secretary of State Rogers would continue to serve under the new administration, with Kenneth Rush succeeding John N. Irwin II as Deputy Secretary of State, William J. Porter succeeding U. Alexis Johnson as Under Secretary for Political Affairs, and William J. Casey moving into the new post of Under Secretary for Economic Affairs.[67] At the Defense Department, Melvin R. Laird was to be succeeded by Elliot L. Richardson;[68] at the Treasury, Secretary George P. Shultz would be gaining new authority over economic policy as an Assistant to the President and chairman of the new Council on International Economic Policy.[69] At the beginning of December, the White House further revealed that Dr. Kissinger would continue during the new term to exercise his responsibilities as an Assistant to the President.[70]]

(6) "The New Internationalism": Foreign Policy Statement Issued by Senator McGovern, October 5, 1972.[71]

(Complete Text)

Next week on television I will address the American people on the subject of Vietnam.[72] In that speech I will demonstrate a public plan— as distinct from Mr. Nixon's secret plan—to achieve peace in Indochina. In that same speech I will set forth my own vision of what American society can be once the tragedy of Vietnam is behind us.

---

[66] Interview with Garnett D. Horner, *Washington Star-News*, Nov. 9, 1972, in *Bulletin*, Dec. 4, 1972, p. 653.
[67] *Public Papers, 1972*, Appendix E, pp. 3-4. Irwin was subsequently named Ambassador to France, while Johnson became head of the U.S. delegation to the Strategic Arms Limitation Talks (SALT).
[68] *Public Papers, 1972*, Appendix E, pp. 1-2.
[69] Same, Appendix E, pp. 4-6; cf. above at note 54.
[70] Same, Appendix E, p. 6.
[71] Text from *New York Times*, Oct. 6, 1972 (subtitles omitted). A portion of the statement was delivered in an address before the City Club of Cleveland, Ohio.
[72] Document 48.

But before then, I want to share my more general views of America's role in the world of the 1970's. And I want to contrast my own approach with the record of the Nixon years, so that in this critical area the American people can understand clearly what the choices are.

Mr. Nixon stated his current vision of the world this past January.[73] He declared that:

> The only time in the history of the world that we have had any extended period[s] of peace is when there has been balance of power. It is when one nation becomes infinitely more powerful in relation to its potential competitor that the danger of war arises. So I believe in a world in which the United States is powerful. I think it will be a safer world and a better world if we have a strong, healthy United States, Europe, Soviet Union, China, Japan, each balancing the other, not playing one against the other, an even balance.[74]

But I begin today by asking whether that is all we want. And I ask, too, whether it is relevant and realistic in today's world—or does it simply resurrect an old world, of kings and princes and empires, that we will never see again.

That five-power, balance of power thesis attempts to force onto the contemporary world a naive pre-nuclear view dating back to the 19th century and before.

Today, in the military sense, we have but two superpowers—capable of destroying ourselves and most of humanity many times over.

That will likely be the case for some time. Europe is not one entity yet, and at best, it will be a long time before it functions as one nation. Japan, though clearly a dominant economic and political power, may not seek entry into the military balance at all—and will probably profit from that decision. And we have discovered a China that seems as determined to avoid direct military entanglements outside her borders as she is to assume her proper role as a great society in world diplomacy and commerce.

It is a naive delusion as well to believe that there is some arbitrary number of actors who will determine whether the world has war or peace. There may have been periods of relative peace under a balance of power. But Mr. Nixon forgets that no balance among the giants can eradicate the causes of war among the rest of mankind. Nor can it dispel the demand of some 140 countries to have a say in the issues which determine their survival.

[73] "An Interview with the President: 'The Jury Is Out'," *Time*, Jan. 3, 1972, pp. 14-15.
[74] Same, p. 15.

And finally, that balance of power neglects other ominous threats to our safety. On May 9, 1969, the then-Secretary General of the United Nations, U Thant, issued this warning:[75]

> ... the members of the United Nations have perhaps 10 years left in which to subordinate their ancient quarrels and launch a global partnership to curb the arms race, to improve the human environment, to defuse the population explosion, and to supply the required momentum to world development efforts.
>
> If such a global partnership is not forged within the next decade, then I very much fear that the problems I have mentioned will have reached such staggering proportions that they will be beyond our [capacity to] control.

We have lost precious time since 1969, and there are precious few years left. Our preoccupation with a military balance leaves untouched the deadly imbalances among population, resources and wealth—and they, too, endanger our lives.

So we face a much different world from the one we knew as we grew up, or as we served in World War II, or even as we watched our country slip into a disastrous Asian war.

Less than 12 years ago John F. Kennedy was inaugurated, and on that bright January day everything seemed possible. If our sturdy American spirit did not give reason enough for that faith, we had as well a new figure and a new voice to personify the optimism and boldness of a new generation.

In January, 1961, no one could predict the Bay of Pigs ... the Cuban Missile Crisis, the tragic murders of John and Robert Kennedy and Martin Luther King ... the Dominican Intervention ... the alienation of many in our own society—least of all, the endless minefield in which we would find ourselves in Vietnam.

Yet, in the years that were to follow, we as a people would be buffeted by one shock and disillusionment after another until finally, in Vietnam, we would lose our innocence—and much of our confidence.

And today we are moving toward a mature knowledge that while we are deeply involved and have vast influence in the world, forces beyond our control will have the most to do with shaping the political arrangements of the future. We can see the error of assuming, since World War II, that our actions would be decisive in either "winning" or "losing" China ... in causing or preventing revolution of the Right or Left in much of Latin America and the rest of the developing world ... or in determining the outcome of a distant civil war in Southeast Asia.

[75] Statement at a conference on "The Second United Nations Development Decade," *UN Monthly Chronicle*, July 1969, p. ii.

But at the same time we must be aware that as the richest and most powerful nation in the earth's history, what we do both here and elsewhere will be more important than what anyone else does in moving this planet closer to either its final destruction or a more peaceful and happy future.

Possessed now with a sense of tragedy and of our own limitations, we as a people may finally be ready to play a more responsible and constructive role in the world than we ever have before.

More than 25 years ago, Adlai Stevenson, in his Godkin Lectures at Harvard, offered us these lines—and good advice—from Keats's "Hyperion."

For to bear all naked truths,
And to envisage circumstances [sic], all calm,
That is the top of sovereignty . . .

What shall our role be?

I know of no responsible person who would knowingly call for a return to isolationism.

Modern communications, and the existence of intercontinental weapons systems, have made that a practical impossibility.

Yet, in many ways, the foreign policies of the present Administration are isolating us.

¶ We are isolated from our allies and trading partners in Europe and Asia, and even from Canada, because of sixgun economic diplomacy and failure to consult.

¶ We are isolated from the developing nations by a policy which tells them that "what's good for Pepsi-Cola and the First National City Bank is more than good enough for you";

¶ We are isolated from reality by the insistence that tough talk and big Pentagon budgets are somehow synonymous with national manhood.

¶ And most of all, we are isolated from our own ideals as we back a corrupt dictatorship in Saigon, by raining fire and death on helpless people all over Indochina.

I suggest that we must reject this unconscious isolationism in favor of a New Internationalism based not only upon our vital interests, but also upon the kind of nation we can and should be.

Where are our vital interests?

By one measure, they certainly lie in the world's North Temperate Zone.

North America, Europe, the Soviet Union and Japan do produce some 80 per cent of the world's goods. This is where the power—in the sense of wealth, technology, developed human skills, and the capacity to wage modern war—most largely resides.

And this is where both we and the Soviet Union, as the two super-powers, will for the foreseeable future continue to have the highest interest in averting any attempt by the other to threaten or subvert our respective systems of security.

The North Temperate Zone, is in short, where a final World War III would be fought—and where its potential causes must most carefully be guarded against.

But our vital interests go further.

The Arab-Israeli confrontation in the Middle East, with its potential for even more dangerous United States-Soviet confrontation, is an immediate threat to general peace. And we have a firm and deep obligation to the security and integrity of the State of Israel.

Communist China has little power in terms of conventional measure-ment (by 1975 Japanese per capita G.N.P. will be 12 times that of China's) but she possesses nuclear weapons and a desire to reassert her ancient prestige.

The Indian Subcontinent and Indonesia especially compel our atten-tion in Asia, as do several states in Africa and in our own hemisphere.

What of the hundreds of other sovereign nations existing in the 1970's—including those to the south lying within the purview of the Monroe Doctrine?

All, in one way or another, have some importance to us.

But must we be committed to their armed defense?

Under what conceivable circumstances should we ever become involved in supporting their present governments in the face of domestic turmoil?

These are questions we had better ask ourselves today, rather than later.

I believe that America's New Internationalism in the 1970's must follow several clear guidelines.

First, it must be supported by a strong national defense, but one free of waste, as I have previously outlined;[76] forces fully adequate to defend our own land and to fill vital defense commitments.

Second, it must look toward prudent relaxation of tension with potential adversary powers, such as the Soviet Union and China.

Third, it must look to reestablishment of healthy economic and political relationships with our principal allies and trading partners in Europe, Japan, Canada and Latin America.

Fourth, it must avoid the kind of reflexive interventionism that has foolishly involved us in the internal political affairs of other countries.

Fifth, it must envision a world community with the capacity to re-solve disputes among nations, and to end the war between man and his own environment.

Sixth, it must reassert America's role as a beacon—and friend—to

[76] Cf. note 61 above.

those millions in the human family desperately striving to achieve the elemental human dignity which all men seek.

The kind of interventionism I would favor as President would be agricultural and technical assistance ... the building of roads and schools ... the training of skilled personnel, in concert with other nations and through multilateral institutions.

Finally, at the bottom of it all, must lie a just and prosperous domestic society, where all our people—and the people's representatives—are involved in decision-making.

As my old friend Senator [Hubert H.] Humphrey has often said: America's most important foreign policy act in the 1960's was the passage of the Civil Rights Act of 1964.[77]

I agree.

How then, should we proceed[?]

My first act of American foreign policy on Inauguration Day must be—will be an immediate and total end to our involvement in the Indochina War.

As Richard Nixon said in 1968: "Those who have had a chance for four years and could not produce peace, should not be given another chance."[78]

We have had enough of secret plans to end the war. We need a public plan for peace.

As we look beyond Vietnam, the prevention of nuclear war remains the first charge on America's commitments.

During the 1960's, we built a great arsenal to protect the United States and our allies against a nuclear threat from any quarter. And we must continue to maintain the power we need.

But we also know that too much power is self-defeating.

We have seen the deadly spiral of the arms race, and drawn no comfort from it.

We have seen that if we build weapons we do not need, we only provoke the Soviet Union to follow suit.

The agreements with the Soviet Union to slow the arms race[79] are a significant achievement. Yet they have shortcomings, for they are now used as an excuse not to halt but to escalate the race in nuclear arms.[80]

We must not push the upward [sic], and lose the chances for a lasting peace that are before us now.

Let us have the defense we need. But let us not permit the insatiable appetite of our military to replace our good sense, and undermine the prospects [for] reduction in the balance of nuclear terror.

President Nixon's trip to Moscow this May[81] was historic. It was the

---

[77] Public Law 88-352, July 2, 1964.
[78] *New York Times*, Oct. 10, 1968.
[79] Documents 13-14.
[80] Cf. Chapter II at notes 115-117.
[81] Documents 9-12.

culmination of many years of effort that began when President
Kennedy signed the Limited-Test Ban Treaty.[82] This effort continued
under three Presidents, both Democratic and Republican.

We must now build upon this effort. That is why it makes no sense
for the President to return from Moscow with an arms reduction agreement and then call on the Congress to add another $4-billion to
military spending.

¶ We must work to bring the arms race under control;

¶ We must seek areas of agreement with the Soviet Union consistent
with the needs and interests of our friends and Allies. We should press
for justice for Soviet Jews rather than abandon them for a trade agreement.[83] Surely we have learned the lesson at great cost that a free
people cannot sit by and merely witness the oppression of a religious
minority by a totalitarian society.

¶ We should, of course, encourage expanded trade between our two
countries.

¶ And we must spare no effort to build the structure of a lasting
peace.

In limiting the arms race we do not begin with excessive trust in the
Russians, for we retain more than enough for deterrence.

In reducing our excess we do not rely on Moscow's good intentions,
we will remain strong enough to meet any test.

We need only act in our sure defense by seeking areas of genuine
mutual interest and by tailoring our armed forces to the reality of the
world around us.

If the Soviet Union responds with the cooperation dictated by her
own interest as much as ours, then we can build toward a future that is
not based on outdated stereotypes of military confrontation and power
politics. Instead we can build toward a world of diversity in which we
are secure, a world in which there are new ways of thinking and be-
having, and a world where there are real prospects for enduring peace.

I also welcome the progress that the President has made in relations
with China[84]—a course I have advocated for 20 years.

We must build on this progress, by encouraging China's full participation in the community of nations, to take part in providing for Asian
security, instead of threatening it.

As President, I will begin by recognizing the government in Peking.

The future of Asia will depend in part upon China. But it will also
depend upon Japan, the third most powerful economic nation in the
world, a nation of vigor and purpose, and a long-standing friend of the
United States.

---

[82] *Documents, 1963*, pp. 130-32.
[83] Cf. Chapter II at note 182.
[84] Cf. Documents 53-60.

In recent years our relations with Japan have been in steady, but needless decline.

President Nixon announced his trip to China[85] without consulting Japan, betraying the trust that nation had placed in our Asian partnership. He imposed the New Economic Policy[86] without consulting Japan, and then blamed Japan for problems that were largely of his own making. And after these shocks, President Nixon took a year to convene a summit meeting with the Prime Minister of Japan.[87]

This was a diplomacy of insult, and it must not continue. For as we seek new accommodations with our adversaries, we must never neglect old and treasured friends.

We must treat Japan as an equal, consult with her in trust. As President, I would begin the painstaking renewal of our cooperative relationship with this key nation in Asia.

There will be tough negotiations and vigorous competition on important matters of trade and economics, where both our nations have interests to protect. We will expect fair treatment by Japan on matters of trade and investment, and greater understanding of our domestic economic problems. But Japan also expects fair treatment from us, not the patronizing attitude that the President has shown, or the sixgun diplomacy of John [B.] Connally.[88]

At the same time, we must recognize that Japan has a chance to become the first great power without a massive military arsenal. We must not crush that hopeful experiment. I will ensure that remaining U.S. forces in Japan serve the original purpose designed for them—to help provide for the defense of Japan, and not to become involved in military ventures in Southeast Asia;

I will place the support of the United States behind membership for Japan in the United Nations Security Council;

And I will begin laying the groundwork with Japan in East Asia that will improve the chances that security in that troubled part of the world will be based on economic cooperation and effort, and never again on the kind of war we have been uselessly and destructively fighting in Indochina.

In Western Europe, there has been great progress toward a relaxation of tensions, and toward resolution of problems left over from World War II.

Much of the credit belongs to Chancellor [Willy] Brandt of West Germany, despite occasional opposition from the Nixon Administration. There is a treaty on Berlin,[89] and there are West German

---

[85] *A.F.R., 1971*, no. 91.
[86] Same, no. 142.
[87] But cf. Documents 62-63.
[88] Secretary of the Treasury, Feb. 11, 1971-June 12, 1972.
[89] Cf. Document 25.

treaties with Poland and the Soviet Union.[90] And we will soon see a Conference on Security and Cooperation.[91]

Our Western European neighbors are fulfilling our mutual hopes and expectations of the past quarter-century.

But in Western Europe's success, there are grave implications for the United States. There will be vigorous economic competition across the Atlantic—and we should welcome it.

The Atlantic Partnership no longer needs single-handed American leadership nor do our partners want it. Nor should we.

But again there are diplomatic failures and challenges to American statesmanship.

President Nixon does not consult adequately with our allies on critical allies [sic: questions ?] of detente, raising fears in Western Europe that we will reach agreements with the Soviet Union at their expense. He talks of cooperation, yet he permitted his Secretary of the Treasury, John Connally, to badger and bully the countries with whom we most need to maintain a cooperative spirit. He talks of the future, but does not understand the importance of good economic relations in preserving and strengthening Atlantic ties.

We must restore good economic and political relations across the Atlantic. And we must restore Europe's faith in our commitment to the success of the European Community.

At the same time I believe in a thorough review of the military aspects of European security.

We no longer need to maintain 319,000 American troops in Europe to deter aggression, 27 years after the Second World War. But the way we reduce our forces—and share burdens more equally—is critical to the future of the Alliance and to European security.

The key to force reductions on the side of the Warsaw Pact does not lie in the number of American troops stationed in the West, rather it lies in the cohesion, cooperation, and common purpose of the Western Alliance.

If we make some force reductions, yet strengthen these attitudes and practices, then there is nothing the Soviet Union can do to weaken us or our allies, or to reduce our security.

We retain a special concern about the Middle East. All Americans have been heartened by the reduction of Soviet involvement in Egypt.[92] But we recognize that this does not end the threat to Israel.

We must remain committed to Israel's future, to her right to live at peace with her neighbors behind secure and recognized borders.

We must continue to supply those arms that will permit Israel to guarantee its own security. In my Administration, we will do this be-

[90] Cf. Chapter III at notes 30-31.
[91] Cf. Documents 23 and 31.
[92] Cf. Chapter IV at note 48.

cause of our deep and abiding concern for Israel, not adopt one policy for election year, and another for the years that follow.

We must continue to retain sufficient American power in the area to ensure that there is no doubt of our commitment to Israel's security.

We must intensify our efforts to end the international terrorism that most recently appalled the world at Munich,[93] and that is a threat to us all.

And we must show a deep regard for the economic and human needs of the Palestine refugees.

Today, we have long since met the demands of a world dominated by military concerns. But we are rapidly losing the world in which economic power and relations will have their day.

The international economic system is near collapse—and for a year President Nixon did almost nothing.

Our Alliances with Europe and Japan are in disarray over economic issues—and President Nixon does nothing.

The problems of two and one-half billion poor people in the world are insistent and demanding—and President Nixon does nothing.

Under President Nixon, we are becoming a second-rate nation in the terms that will really count in the 1970's.

It is more than a year since the New Economic Policy began. Yet, only now has the Administration begun an effort to restructure the international economic system, while the United States balance of trade continues in the worst deficit in 100 years, and the United States dollar has been devalued as a result of the Nixon inflation at home. We have still not recovered our sense of responsibility for this economic system, upon which our prosperity, and that of other nations, depends.

We must repair our damaged friendships abroad; we must begin sorting out the difficult problems that must be solved in order to create a new international economic system. We must begin the urgent task of monetary reform not through confrontation, but by restoring and building on the international cooperation and commercial partnership that we had until this Administration. We must work out new rules of international conduct in trade and commerce. And we must begin building an awareness and understanding of international economic policy into the councils of government at all levels.

Last week, I made several concrete proposals to begin this effort:

¶ New rules governing changes in exchange rates.

¶ Cooperative arrangements to cushion large disruptive flows of short-term capital.

¶ More special drawing rights—and more of them for developing countries.

¶ Steps to resolve fairly the problem of the dollar "overhang."

---

93 Cf. Document 36.

We must help businesses that are uncompetitive to shift to new products.

And we must guarantee every working man and woman a good job at good pay in industries that can compete in world markets.

American will is being tested. President Nixon has decided that our will is weak—that we cannot pass the test—that we can survive economically only by having inflated military budgets and by blaming others for our difficulties. But I say this: Give Americans a chance, and we will prove that we can have the strongest economy in the world, and a prosperity in which everyone will share.

In virtually every statement, every act, of this administration, nearly two and a half billion human beings in the world have been left out.

These are the people who have too little power to figure in a new balance of power based on the military giants; they are the people who are too meek to command the attention given to generals and weapons manufacturers producing excess weapons we do not need; they are the people whose crime was to be born poor.

Ten years ago, I was President Kennedy's first Director of Food for Peace.

He declared then: "If we do not help the many who are poor, we cannot hope to save the few who are rich."[94]

Today, this statement is more true than ever.

Today, the ability of people from the rich countries to trade, travel, and invest in the developing countries depends upon our helping them to meet their critical problems of development.

Our future success in preserving the environment will require the help of developing countries. And even the international system of trade and monetary relations is beginning to depend on developing-country cooperation. They deserve and demand a voice, and they desperately need our help.

We have seen little to inspire our confidence in these past four years. Mr. Nixon pledged to untie aid, and then reneged; he talked of the need for development, then slashed the budget and put his lobbying efforts in Congress behind the supply of arms instead of technical assistance to developing countries. He extended the 10 per cent surcharge on imports to poor-country products as well as rich.[95] He has used the power of his office to bully and intimidate Latin-American nations. He has defied the conscience of mankind by giving up United States opposition to racism in Southern Africa.

He threatened to intervene in the war between India and Pakistan,[96] against our interests, against what was right and against the conscience

---

[94] Paraphrased from Inaugural Address, Jan. 20, 1961, in *Documents, 1961*, pp. 13-14.
[95] But cf. *A.F.R., 1971*, no. 151.
[96] Cf. same, p. 239.

of the civilized world. He then waited five months before recognizing the infant, struggling nation of Bangladesh[97] that has suffered so much for so long. And he still has not restored aid to India—aid for schools and roads and health care—that he cut off when the war began. Indeed, the mistaken anti-India pro-Pakistan stand of the Nixon Administration while Pakistan was murdering its poor people by the hundreds of thousands was not only morally wrong, it has cost us the goodwill of India— the world's largest democratic nation.

These have been callous displays toward the poor of the world, for fully two-thirds of mankind. As a great nation, America cannot turn its back on their suffering. And we cannot stand aside as development— this great human adventure—goes on.

We cannot continue to abdicate our moral and political responsibility to so many people, and ultimately to the United States itself.

The New Internationalism will chart another course.

We will make a full commitment of the United States to the multilateral institutions that are helping with development, not with military weapons that make war and suffering more likely, but with the economic and technological tools that help men to improve their own lives.

We will put our relations with individual developing countries on a firm footing, not relegate them to an insignificant place in a balance of power.

We will show that we can live up to our commitments to our neighbors in Latin America, not demand that they quietly accept our domination.

We will show that we are concerned for all of Africa, and abandon this Administration's support for the racist regimes of Southern Africa. We will show our concern for the racist expulsion of Asians from Uganda.

We will renew our commitment to the efforts of the United Nations for peace and for development. And we will show that we, too, can respond to the demands that membership in the human family places upon us. The United Nations peace-keeping capacity must be strengthened and utilized. It is an essential framework for international cooperation.

The making of decisions of defense and foreign policy is an awesome task, too great for any one man—or any one branch of government. And here, too, we cry out for reform.

Long ago, we recognized that the powers of the Presidency could isolate the man and his decisions from the American people.

So we protected the nation—and the Presidency itself—from the "man on horseback," by adopting methods for the close scrutiny of foreign and defense policy.

97 Cf. Documents 40-41.

Under President Nixon, these methods have decayed and Congress itself has been thwarted in its efforts to discharge its Constitutional responsibilities.

The executive agreement has often replaced the treaty subject to Senate approval.[98]

Wars are fought in secret, in Laos and Cambodia, and paid for by secret funds in defiance of the will of Congress.

Under President Nixon, however, the Secretary of State has become a minor functionary, and was not even permitted to take part in the most critical negotiations the President had in Peking.

No American President should be permitted to escape the Constitutional restraints on Executive power.

Under my Administration, the Congress will be fully informed, it will be fully consulted, and it will have restored to it the full powers set down for it in the Constitution of the United States.

And I will not permit the basic trends of American foreign and defense policy to be set in the inner sanctum of the White House, by men who are hidden from public view and removed from public responsibility.

There will be a Secretary of State of great capability and unquestioned stature.

No foreign policy can be effective if it is backed by weakness at home. President Nixon wants us to believe that talking of America's problems denies its greatness.

But I believe that our greatness lies in part in our ability to look at ourselves, to recognize what we have to do, and then to do something about it.

If we have four more years of the same at home, the wisdom of our foreign policy may not matter very much.

We will be condemned to be a second-rate nation at home.

We must and we can have a strong economy, with a good job at good pay for everyone who wants to work ... an end to crippling inflation and an end to the Nixon recession.

We must have real tax reform ... a reduction of crime ... improved health care ... and genuine quality education for all our children.

We must resume building a society in which government helps to bring people together, not drives them apart; where it helps to increase opportunity, not limit it; and where it taps the deep roots of the American spirit, not stifles them in indifference to the need for America to grow and change.

I believe that we can have that America, again—a first-rate nation at home and abroad, where American greatness and commitment to international cooperation will again become a thing of wonder in the world.

[98] Cf. above at note 41.

As a nation, we must bring to an end our time of tragedy:

¶When Americans have lost faith in what their Government tells them;

¶When a bitter and needless war has divided our people, and threatened our spirit and confidence as a nation.

Few other countries have faced what we have in these past few years.

But I believe that we are now prepared to use what we have learned from our past, from success and from failure, to meet our responsibilities both at home and in the world—to the lasting benefit of the American people and all mankind.

In the final analysis, our foreign policy is no more than who and what we are. It is a reflection of our attitudes towards ourselves, towards our country, and towards the rest of mankind. We cannot separate what we do abroad from what we do at home.

How we live in the neighborhoods and communities of America will determine how we live with our international neighbors, and in the broader world community.

Today, we can aspire to a maturity in our actions abroad, and maturity as a great nation—a great people—at home.

This is a challenge appropriate to our ideals, and to all that we have dared and won in the nearly two hundred years of our independence. As Abraham Lincoln once said, in a dark hour for America:

We shall nobly save or meanly lose the last, best hope on [sic] earth.

I have faith that we shall nobly save that "last best hope on earth."

(7) "Defense Policy": Radio Address by President Nixon, October 29, 1972. [99]

(Complete Text)

Good afternoon.

I want to talk to you this afternoon about national defense. Defense policy is the most important single issue in this election. It represents a choice which must be made not on the basis of name-calling or appeals to emotion, but on the basis of thoughtful analysis of the alternatives. That is the purpose of my talk this afternoon.

When a President thinks of his responsibilities to the American people, he must think first of all about the need to keep this country

---

[99] *Presidential Documents*, Nov. 6, 1972, pp. 1600-1602. Time for the broadcast was purchased by the Committee for the Re-election of the President.

strong, about the need to maintain a national defense second to none in the world.

A President also has an obligation to spend no more of the Nation's limited resources on defense than is absolutely required, because he knows there are other urgent human needs to be met.

Today, no nation on earth is more powerful than the United States. Not only are our nuclear deterrent forces fully sufficient for their role in keeping the peace, our conventional forces also are modern, strong, prepared, and credible to any adversary.

During the past 4 years, however, because of the progress we have made in bringing the Vietnam war to an honorable conclusion and in reducing tensions among the great powers, we have also been able to reduce substantially the size of our military establishment.

We have reduced our total military manpower by nearly one-third from the 1968 level. We have closed large numbers of unneeded military bases and installations. Under the Nixon Doctrine, we have successfully persuaded our allies to take up a greater share of the free world defense burden than they have in the past.

Before we took office, less than a third of every dollar the Federal Government spent was devoted to human resources, while close to half of every budget dollar was spent for defense. Today those proportions are reversed, with the military down to a third and human resources getting nearly a half.

Most important, all of this has been achieved without jeopardizing our security and without betraying our allies.

But now in this campaign our opponents have proposed massive new cuts in military spending[100]—cuts which would drastically slash away not just the fat, but the very muscle of our defense.

These are the specific proposals they have made: America's strategic bomber force would be cut by 60 percent, our tactical air wings by 30 percent, development of the new B–1 bomber would be cancelled.

The number of Navy warships would be cut almost in half. Our aircraft carrier fleet would be cut from 16 to 6. They would cut the Marine Corps by almost one-third. The 7th Fleet in the Far East and the 6th Fleet in the Mediterranean would be sharply reduced and weakened.

Missile modernization programs like the Minuteman III and the Poseidon would be halted.

The result would be to leave America with the second strongest Army, the second strongest Navy, the second strongest Air Force in the world.

Now some might ask, what is wrong with being second? Isn't it jingoistic and nationalistic for the United States always to have to be Number One?

[100] Cf. note 61.

The answer to that question is that the day the United States becomes the second strongest nation in the world, peace and freedom will be in deadly jeopardy everywhere in the world.

We do not seek power for its own sake. What we seek is the assurance that our survival and that of other free nations will never be threatened by some other nation whose intentions are less peaceful than ours, and whose military forces are more powerful than those of the United States.

History has taught us again and again that war is caused not by the strength of one nation alone, but by the weakness of one nation in relation to another.

Last spring in Moscow I signed an agreement for the limitation of offensive and defensive nuclear weapons on the part of the United States and the Soviet Union.[101] We would never have reached that agreement if the United States had unilaterally given up the ABM as some had recommended, or if we had begun stripping away our offensive missile forces.

If we were to take such action now, we would destroy any chance for further arms limitations in the second round of strategic nuclear arms limitation talks which are to begin with the Soviet Union next month.[102] If we unilaterally reduced the forces now supporting our NATO allies in Western Europe, as has also been proposed by our opponents, we would throw away the prospect of mutual and balanced reductions of Soviet forces in Eastern Europe.[103]

Strength and resolution command respect. They are an incentive for negotiation leading to peace. But weakness and naive sentimentality breed contempt. They are an open invitation to pressure tactics and aggression leading to war.

That is why I say let us never send the President of the United States to the conference table as the head of the second strongest nation in the world.

It may be argued that as long as we have our nuclear weapons we have nothing to worry about. Because the United States relied heavily on a deterrent policy of massive nuclear retaliation during the 1950's, this theory says, we can safely gut our conventional forces today and go back to the policy of massive nuclear retaliation in the 1970's.

The flaw in that argument is that during the Eisenhower years the United States held a 15 to 1 or even a 20 to 1 ratio of nuclear superiority over the Soviet Union. Massive retaliation was credible then, in the 1950's, and it was credible during the Cuban missile crisis of 1962, when our nuclear advantage was about 8 to 1. No enemy would dare to test such overwhelming odds.

[101] Documents 13-14.
[102] Cf. Document 17.
[103] Cf. Document 30.

However, when I came into office in January 1969, I found that this massive nuclear superiority no longer existed. For 6 years the Soviet Union had moved forward with a massive buildup of their nuclear forces, while the United States was standing still. As a result, today the United States and the Soviet Union are equal in nuclear capability.

It has, therefore, become totally unrealistic to believe that we could any longer deter aggression against a small nation, particularly one whose survival did not directly affect our own survival, if our only option were a nuclear retaliation which would lead to nuclear suicide for the United States.

The mutual destruction would be too great, and both sides would know it. No potential aggressor would respect America's security commitments to our friends and allies under those conditions.

The Middle East is an example. In the fall of 1970, when Syrian tanks poured into Jordan, what might have become a grave world crisis was quietly defused by the movement of the United States 6th Fleet into the eastern Mediterranean.[104] The possibility of a war which could have threatened the existence of Israel and dragged in the great powers was averted.

American naval superiority kept the peace in that situation, where nuclear threats would have been powerless to do so. That is why, for the sake of Israel and other small nations we are committed to defend, as well as for our own sake, we must never give up our superiority on the sea and in the air in the name of false economy.

The time has come to stand up and answer those of our own countrymen who complain that American power is an evil force in the world, those who say that our foreign policy is selfish and bad.

We can be proud of the fact that in four wars in this century the United States has fought only to defend freedom, never to destroy it; only to keep the peace, never to break it.

The men and women who have fought in those wars deserve the highest respect this Nation can pay them, as do those who serve in our peace forces today, and those who will serve in years to come as we end the draft next summer and move to a volunteer armed force.[105] They are the real heroes of our time.

Rather than talking about amnesty for a few hundred who chose to

---

[104] Cf. *The United States in World Affairs, 1970*, pp. 109-11.

[105] Recalling his 1968 campaign pledge to work toward ending the military draft and establishing an all-volunteer armed force, President Nixon reported on Aug. 28, 1972 that the enactment of pending legislation by the Congress would eliminate any need for peacetime conscription into the armed forces after July 1973 (*Public Papers, 1972*, pp. 825-6).

desert America, let us honor the millions who chose to serve America in Vietnam. As this long and difficult war draws to an end, it is time to draw the line on this issue once and for all. There will be no amnesty for draft dodgers and deserters after the war.

Millions of Americans chose to serve their country in Vietnam. Many gave their lives for their choice. The few hundred who refused to serve, or who deserted their country, must pay a penalty for their choice.

A few days before I left for Peking last February, I had as a guest at the White House the brilliant French thinker and statesman Andre [sic] Malraux. Let me share with you a comment which he made to me that night.

"The United States," he said, "is the only nation ever to become the most powerful in the world without seeking to."

Think for a moment of how true this statement is and what it means. This country did not push its way to the position of world leadership which we have occupied for a generation. That position came to us unsought, but we have borne it nobly and well, guided not by ambition or greed or ideology, but only by the high ideals of human liberty and lasting peace.

Uniquely among the great powers of the world in our own time or in any previous time, the United States is trusted with power by all the peoples of the earth. No nation which refrains from aggression against its neighbors has anything to fear from America, and all nations know that is true.

For the United States to abdicate its leadership role in the world, or to attempt to meet its responsibilities through good intentions alone, without the backing of a strong defense, would be one of the greatest tragedies of history.

Let us never go down that road. That is the road which led an unprepared America into two world wars earlier in this century.

Let us remain instead on the high road of peace through strength, the road mapped out by five successive Presidents in our time, Democrats and Republicans alike—by Franklin D. Roosevelt, Harry Truman, Dwight Eisenhower, John Kennedy, Lyndon Johnson.

As long as I am your President, I shall keep America on that road. I shall keep this country strong militarily, strong economically, and strong in the moral values and the trust in God which is our ultimate defense.

Only in this way can we make certain that the 1970's will not be the twilight of America's greatness, but the dawn of a new age; not a time of tension and turmoil, but the beginning of a full generation of peace for us and for all mankind.

Thank you and good afternoon.

(8) "Foreign Policy": Radio Address by President Nixon, November 4, 1972.[106]

(Complete Text)

Good afternoon.

Through the long years of America's involvement in Vietnam, our people's yearning for peace has largely been focused on winning an end to that difficult war. As a result, there has often been a tendency to lose sight of the larger prospects for peace in the rest of the world. As peace in Vietnam comes closer,[107] we can look to the larger world and the long-term future with hope and satisfaction.

Four years ago I promised that we would move from an era of confrontation to an era of negotiation.[108] I also said that we would maintain our own strength and work to restore that of our alliances, because the way to make real progress toward peace is to negotiate from strength and not from weakness. Because we have done so, the world today is more peaceful by far than it was 4 years ago. The prospects for a full generation of peace are brighter than at any time since the end of World War II.

In the past 4 years, we have concluded more and more significant agreements with the Soviets than in all the previous years since World War II. We have ended nearly a quarter century of mutual isolation between the United States and the People's Republic of China. All over the world, the tide toward negotiation is moving. North and South Korea are negotiating with one another. East and West Germany are negotiating with one another. A cease-fire has been in effect for more than 2 years in the Middle East. The leaders of India and Pakistan are talking with one another. The nations of Europe, of NATO, and of the Warsaw Pact, are preparing to meet next year in a European Security Conference, and preparations are underway for negotiations on mutual and balanced reduction of armed forces in Central Europe.[109]

All this is evidence of solid progress toward a world in which we can talk about our differences rather than fight about them.

1972 has been a year of more achievement for peace than any year since the end of World War II. This progress did not just happen by itself.

In my Inaugural Address nearly 4 years ago, I said that the greatest honor history can bestow is the title of peacemaker, but I also pointed out that peace does not come through wishing for it, that there is no

---

[106] *Presidential Documents*, Nov. 13, 1972, pp. 1639-41. Time for the broadcast was purchased by the Committee for the Re-election of the President.
[107] Cf. Documents 50-52.
[108] Same as note 59.
[109] Cf. Documents 30-32.

substitute for days and even years of patient and prolonged diplomacy.[110]

For the past 4 years this Nation has engaged in patient and prolonged diplomacy, in every corner of the world, and we have also maintained the strength that has made our diplomacy credible and peace possible. As a result, we are well on the way toward erecting what I have often referred to as a structure of peace, a structure that rests on the hard concrete of common interests and mutual agreements, and not on the shifting sands of naive sentimentality.

That term, "a structure of peace," speaks an important truth about the nature of peace in today's world. Peace cannot be wished into being. It has to be carefully and painstakingly built in many ways and on many fronts, through networks of alliances, through respect for commitments, through patient negotiations, through balancing military forces and expanding economic interdependence, through reaching one agreement that opens the way to others, through developing patterns of international behavior that will be accepted by other powers. Most important of all, the structure of peace has to be built in such a way that all those who might be tempted to destroy it will instead have a stake in preserving it.

In the past 4 years, my efforts to build that structure of peace have taken me to 22 countries, including four world capitals never visited by an American President before, Peking, Moscow, Warsaw, and Bucharest. Everywhere I have traveled I have seen evidence that the times are on the side of peace, if America maintains its strength and continues on course. For example, ever since World War II, the world's people and its statesmen have dreamed of putting the nuclear genie back in the bottle, of controlling the dreaded nuclear arms race, but always that race remained unchecked until this year.

In Moscow last May, we and the Soviet Union reached the first agreement ever for limiting strategic nuclear arms. We signed that agreement last month in Washington.[111] This was an historic beginning. It moved back the frontiers of fear. It helped check the dangerous spiral of nuclear weapons. It opened the way to further negotiations on further limitations on nuclear arsenals which will soon begin.[112]

As we pursue these negotiations, however, let us remember that no country will pay a price for something that another country will give up for nothing. If we had scrapped the ABM missile system, as many advocated, we would never have achieved the first arms agreement with the Soviets. If we unilaterally slashed our defenses now as our oppo-

---

[110] *Documents, 1968-69*, pp. 39 and 42.
[111] The treaty and interim agreement signed in Moscow May 26, 1972 (Documents 13-14) entered into force Oct. 3, 1972. Cf. Chapter II at note 125.
[112] Cf. Document 17.

nents in this election advocate, the Soviets would have no incentive to negotiate further arms limitations.

Or take another example. After 10 years of recurring international monetary crises, we took bold actions a year ago[113] to strengthen the dollar and to bring about a reformed international monetary system that would be fair to the United States and fair to the world. The result of these actions has been a solid and substantial beginning on just such a system, and the stage is now set for an international effort to achieve some of the most important monetary and trade reforms in history.[114] As we complete these reforms in the years ahead, we can usher in a new age of world prosperity, a prosperity made even greater by the rapid expansion of peaceful trade that is now taking place, not only with our traditional trading partners, but also with nations that have been our adversaries.

I cite these simply as examples of the broad, unfinished agenda of peace that now lies before us, the agenda of new starts made, of negotiations begun, of new relationships established, which now we must build on with the same initiative and imagination that achieved the initial breakthroughs. As we move forward on this agenda, we can see vast areas of peaceful cooperation to be explored.

We agreed in Peking to pursue cultural, journalistic, educational, and other exchanges, so that the world's most prosperous nation and its most populous nation can get to know one another again.[115]

We agreed in Moscow to cooperate in protecting the environment, explore in space, fight disease.[116] This means the day is fast approaching when a Russian cosmonaut and an American astronaut will shake hands in space, when a Russian chemist and an American biologist will work side by side to find a cure for cancer, and each time our nations join hands in the works of peace, we advance the day when nations will no longer raise their hands in warfare.

Throughout the world today America is respected. This is partly because we have entered a new era of initiative in American foreign policy, and the world's leaders and its people have seen the results. But it is also because the world has come to know America. It knows we are a nation of peaceful intentions, of honorable purposes, true to our commitments. We are respected because for a third of a century under six Presidents we have met the responsibilities of a great and free nation. We have not retreated from the world. We have not betrayed our allies. We have not fallen into the foolish illusion that we could somehow build a wall around America, here to enjoy our comforts, oblivious to the cries or the threats of others. We have maintained our strength.

113 *A.F.R., 1971*, no. 142.
114 Cf. Documents 94-96.
115 Cf. Document 54.
116 Cf. Document 10.

There are those today who condemn as a relic of a cold war mentality the idea that peace requires strength. There are those who ridicule military expenditures as wasteful and immoral. Our opponents in this campaign have even described the great bipartisan tradition of negotiating from strength as one of the most damaging and costly clichés in the American vocabulary. If the day ever comes when the President of the United States has to negotiate from weakness, that will be a dangerous day, not only for America, but for the whole world.

Those who scoff at balance of power diplomacy should recognize that the only alternative to a balance of power is an imbalance of power, and history shows that nothing so drastically escalates the danger of war as such an imbalance. It is precisely the fact that the elements of balance now exist that gives us a rare opportunity to create a system of stability that can maintain the peace, not just for a decade, but for a generation and more.

The years ahead will not be easy. The choices will not be simple. They will require an extra measure of care in distinguishing between rhetoric and reality, between the easy temptation and the hard necessity. We will be told that all the things we want to do at home could be painlessly financed if we slashed our military spending. We will be told that we can have peace merely by asking for it, that if we simply demonstrate good will and good faith, our adversaries will do likewise, and that we need do no more. This is dangerous nonsense.

A heavy responsibility lies on the shoulders of those who hold or seek power in today's world, a responsibility not to court the public favor by fostering illusions that peace can be either achieved or kept without maintaining our strength and meeting our responsibilities.

As we approach the end of the war in Vietnam, the great question is whether the end of that war will be only an interlude between wars or the beginning of a generation of peace for the world.

Five months ago, I delivered the first television address to the Soviet people ever made by an American President.[117] I tried to tell them something about America, about the people of America, about our hopes, our desire for peace and progress, not only for ourselves, but for all the people of the world. In that talk, I repeated an old story told in Russia about a traveler who was walking to another village, who stopped and asked a woodsman how long it would take him to get there. The woodsman replied he did not know. The traveler was angry, because he was sure the woodsman lived in the village and knew how far it was. But then as soon as he had gone a few steps further down the road, the woodsman called out to him to stop. "It will take you 15 minutes," the woodsman said. "Why didn't you tell me that in the first place?" the traveler demanded. And the woodsman answered, "Because then I didn't know the length of your stride."

[117] Document 9.

In these past 4 years, we and the other nations of the world have had a chance to measure the length of our strides. At last we are traveling in the same direction toward a world of peace, toward an era of negotiation, and of expanding cooperation. In the next 4 years, the President of the United States, whoever he is, will negotiate with the leaders of many nations on a broad range of issues vital to America, vital to the world. As we cast our ballots next Tuesday [November 7], the world will see whether we have changed the length of our stride.

If you approve the beginnings we have made, then your vote on Election Day to support those policies will be a message to the leaders of all other nations that the American people are not going to retreat, are not going to surrender. It will strengthen the President's hand immensely as we continue to move from confrontation to negotiation to cooperation all around the world as we build toward a generation of peace.

Thank you and good afternoon.

II.
ARMS CONTROL AND
U.S.-SOVIET RELATIONS

[The year 1972 marked a clearly historic turning point in the relationship between the two leading world powers and in the struggle to reduce the danger of a military clash between them. President Nixon's nine-day visit to the Soviet Union on May 22-30, 1972 consolidated a process of détente that had been under way for several years and established a basis for further development of mutually beneficial relations in various directions. Among the numerous agreements concluded during the presidential visit, the Treaty on the Limitation of Anti-Ballistic Missile Systems and the accompanying Interim Agreement on Certain Measures with Respect to the Limitation of Strategic Offensive Weapons completed the first stage of the Strategic Arms Limitation Talks (SALT) initiated in 1969, imposing the first agreed limitations on the expansion of the two powers' strategic forces and opening up at least a theoretical possibility of subsequent reduction in their respective strategic armories. The entry into force of the two accords on October 3, 1972 was followed in November by the opening in Geneva of SALT II, the second phase of SALT talks. Other agreements concluded during or after the presidential visit facilitated the large-scale grain purchases effected by the Soviet Union during the summer of 1972 and appeared to create conditions for a general expansion of U.S.-Soviet trade over the next several years, although these expectations later proved to have been exaggerated in some important respects.]

A. President Nixon's Visit to the Soviet Union, May 22-30, 1972.

1. The Background.

[Many factors combined to bring about the conditions that enabled President Nixon to undertake an official visit to the Soviet

Union in May 1972, thus realizing an objective that had consistently eluded such predecessors as Dwight D. Eisenhower[1] and Lyndon B. Johnson.[2] By the early 1970s, the overall relationship between the U.S.S.R. and the principal Western powers had largely recovered from the effects of Moscow's repressive action in Czechoslovakia in 1968. A relaxation of tension in Europe had recently made possible the negotiation of an important four-power agreement on Berlin[3] and opened up a prospect for diplomatic talks both on security and cooperation in Europe and on mutual and balanced reduction of military forces in that continent. Disarmament negotiations on a multilateral basis had led to such significant achievements as the signature of a Seabed Arms Control Treaty[4] and the completion of a Convention on the Prohibition of Bacteriological (Biological) and Toxin Weapons.[5] Most important of all, perhaps, a "breakthrough" in the bilateral Strategic Arms Limitation Talks (SALT) between the United States and the U.S.S.R. had led in May 1971 to a new agreement on objectives and priorities[6] which had been followed in September 1971 by a pair of subsidiary agreements on measures to reduce the risk of outbreak of nuclear war between the two powers and to improve the direct communications link or "hot line" between them.[7] These developments had been particularly stressed by President Nixon in his announcement on October 12, 1971 that he planned to meet with the Soviet leaders in Moscow in the latter part of May 1972 for a review of "all major issues, with a view towards further improving [the two powers'] bilateral relations and enhancing the prospects of world peace."[8]

"In Moscow, we will have three central objectives," the President further noted in the "State of the World" report he released on February 9, 1972. "We want to complete work on those issues which have been carried to the point of final decision. We want to establish a political framework for dealing with the issues still in dispute. And we want to examine with the Soviet leaders the further development of the U.S.-Soviet relationship in the years ahead. . . .

[1] *The United States in World Affairs, 1960*, p. 30.
[2] Lyndon Baines Johnson, *The Vantage Point: Perspectives of the Presidency 1963-1969* (New York: Holt, Rinehart and Winston, 1971), pp. 487-90.
[3] *A.F.R., 1971*, no. 39; cf. Document 25, below.
[4] Cf. note 149 below.
[5] Cf. note 150 below.
[6] *A.F.R., 1971*, no. 21; cf. below at note 93.
[7] *A.F.R., 1971*, nos. 26-28.
[8] Same, no. 29.

"We do not, of course, expect the Soviet Union to give up its pursuit of its own interests. We do not expect to give up pursuing our own. We do expect, and are prepared ourselves to demonstrate, self-restraint in the pursuit of those interests. We do expect a recognition of the fact that the general improvement in our relationship transcends in importance the kind of narrow advantages which can be sought only by imperiling the cooperation between our two countries. . . .

"The USSR has the choice: whether the current period of relaxation is to be merely another offensive tactic or truly an opportunity to develop an international system resting on the stability of relations between the superpowers. Its choice will be demonstrated in actions prior to and after our meetings. . . ."[9]

Soviet actions during the winter and spring of 1972 seemed generally attuned to the promotion of a continued U.S.-Soviet détente, despite the strain imposed on the relations of the two powers by the India-Pakistan crisis of December 1971[10] and the threat of a renewed deterioration in South Vietnam.[11] Bilateral American-Soviet relations continued to develop over a broad front. An agreement providing for a limited expansion in air services between the two countries was signed on March 17, 1972,[12] and an expanded Agreement on Exchanges and Cooperation in Scientific, Technical, Educational, Cultural and Other Fields, covering the two-year period 1972-73, was signed on April 11 retroactive to the beginning of the year.[13] Officials from various U.S. Government departments engaged their Soviet opposites in preliminary discussion of commercial shipping, lend-lease issues, possible grain sales, and other matters that might be taken up in the Moscow talks or subsequently.

In Vienna, the sixth round of Strategic Arms Limitation Talks (SALT) concluded on February 4 with a joint announcement of "progress . . . on a number of issues" and an expression of the two delegations' determination to continue their efforts at a further session that would begin in Helsinki on March 28.[14] Conceding that

[9] Nixon Report, 1972, pp. 24-5. For fuller discussion cf. same, pp. 16-25; Nixon Report, 1973, pp. 26-39; Rogers Report, 1972, pp. 308-14.
[10] A.F.R., 1971, nos. 30 and 56-64.
[11] Cf. Document 43.
[12] TIAS 7287 (23 UST 158); announcement in Bulletin, May 22, 1972, p. 740.
[13] TIAS 7343 (23 UST 790); announcement and text in Bulletin, May 15, 1972, pp. 707-13.
[14] Joint communiqué, Feb. 4, 1972, in Documents on Disarmament, 1972, pp. 18-19. (Materials reprinted in Documents on Disarmament are also frequently available in Bulletin and/or Presidential Documents and Public Papers.)

the two parties remained "very far apart on some fundamental issues," President Nixon suggested on March 24 that there was still a good chance that the differences would be narrowed sufficiently to permit an agreement to be reached in Moscow.[15]

These favorable prospects were once again called in question by the launching on March 30 of a new North Vietnamese offensive in South Vietnam and the subsequent resumption by the United States of air and naval strikes against military targets in North Vietnam, eliciting a sharp Soviet protest and claims of damage to Soviet shipping in the harbor of Haiphong. Plans for the presidential visit were nevertheless kept alive with the aid of a secret trip to Moscow by Dr. Kissinger on April 20-24,[16] and President Nixon appealed directly to the Soviet leaders in the speech of May 8 in which he announced the mining of North Vietnamese harbors by the United States.[17] "We ... are on the threshold of a new relationship that can serve not only the interests of our two countries but the cause of world peace," the President told the Soviet leaders. "We are prepared to continue to build up this relationship. The responsibility is yours if we fail to do so."

To the general relief, Moscow refrained from canceling the presidential visit and limited its reaction to Vietnam developments to a diplomatic protest that was considered mild under the circumstances. In what was construed as a signal of continued Soviet interest in détente, a leading Soviet "hard-liner," Ukrainian party boss P.Y. Shelest, was stripped of his Communist Party functions on the very day before the President's arrival in Moscow.[18]

"Everybody in this Government," Mr. Nixon remarked at a White House farewell on May 19, "has worked extremely hard on this trip over the past months—some for years: the SALT delegation, our State Department people, the people in the other departments I have mentioned, the White House Staff, Dr. Kissinger, of course, has made an enormous contribution with the trip he has made to the Soviet Union, in talking with Mr. [Leonid I.] Brezhnev and the other Soviet leaders. It is basically one where we are all going with one common purpose, and that is to attempt to establish a different relationship, one in which there will still be very significant differences—we must always remember this—and philosophy and approach and so forth, but one in which the two great powers, each

---

[15] News conference, Mar. 24, 1972, in *Documents on Disarmament, 1972*, p. 113; cf. below at note 94.
[16] White House announcement, Apr. 25, 1972, in *Presidential Documents*, May 1, 1972, p. 789; see also Document 46 and Kalb, *Kissinger*, pp. 291-6.
[17] Document 47.
[18] *The World This Year, 1973*, p. 117.

looking to its interest, decides that in certain areas we should work together rather than against each other."[19]]

2. The Visit.

[The main events of the presidential journey were reported by a host of newsmen and are well reflected in the official statements and communiqués that marked its course.[20] Leaving Washington on Saturday, May 20, the presidential party spent the weekend in Salzburg, Austria, where the President conferred with Chancellor Bruno Kreisky.[21] Monday, May 22 marked the arrival in Moscow and the commencement of a strenuous round of discussions with General Secretary Brezhnev and other Soviet leaders that was to continue into the following week, punctuated by numerous banquets and ceremonial observances and by the almost daily signature of bilateral agreements on topics of mutual interest. Among the highlights of the visit were the signature on May 26 of the Anti-Ballistic Missile (ABM) Treaty and the Interim Agreement; a presidential visit to Leningrad on May 27; Mr. Nixon's radio-television address to the Soviet people on Sunday, May 28 (Document 9); and the issuance on May 29 of an official communiqué (Document 10) and a statement enunciating "Basic Principles of Relations Between the United States of America and the Union of Soviet Socialist Republics" (Document 11). A visit to Kiev on May 29-30 preceded the departure of the presidential party for brief stopovers in Iran[22] and Poland[23] before the return to Washington on Thursday, June 1 (Document 12).]

(9) President Nixon's Radio-Television Address to the Soviet People, May 28, 1972.[24]

(Complete Text)

Dobryy vecher [Good Evening] .

I deeply appreciate this opportunity your Government has given me

---

[19] *Public Papers, 1972*, pp. 606-7.
[20] Full chronology and documentation appear in *Public Papers, 1972*, pp. 611-66, and *Bulletin*, June 26, 1972, pp. 863-927. For a detailed unofficial account, cf. Kalb, *Kissinger*, pp. 312-34.
[21] *Public Papers, 1972*, pp. 614-17.
[22] Same, pp. 643-52.
[23] Same, pp. 652-60; cf. Document 26.
[24] *Presidential Documents*, June 5, 1972, pp. 939-42.

to speak directly with the people of the Soviet Union, to bring you a message of friendship from all the people of the United States and to share with you some of my thoughts about the relations between our two countries and about the way to peace and progress in the world.

This is my fourth visit to the Soviet Union. On these visits I have gained a great respect for the peoples of the Soviet Union, for your strength, your generosity, your determination, for the diversity and richness of your cultural heritage, for your many achievements.

In the 3 years I have been in office, one of my principal aims has been to establish a better relationship between the United States and the Soviet Union. Our two countries have much in common. Most important of all, we have never fought one another in war. On the contrary, the memory of your soldiers and ours embracing at the Elbe, as allies, in 1945, remains strong in millions of hearts in both of our countries. It is my hope that that memory can serve as an inspiration for the renewal of Soviet-American cooperation in the 1970's.

As great powers, we shall sometimes be competitors, but we need never be enemies.

Thirteen years ago, when I visited your country as Vice-President, I addressed the people of the Soviet Union on radio and television,[25] as I am addressing you tonight. I said then, "Let us have peaceful competition, not only in producing the best factories, but in producing better lives for our people. Let us cooperate in our exploration of outer space. . . . Let our aim be not victory over other peoples, but the victory of all mankind over hunger, want, misery, and disease, wherever it exists in the world."

In our meetings this week, we have begun to bring some of those hopes to fruition. Shortly after we arrived here on Monday afternoon [May 22], a brief rain fell on Moscow, of a kind that I am told is called a mushroom rain, a warm rain, with sunshine breaking through, that makes the mushrooms grow and is therefore considered a good omen. The month of May is early for mushrooms, but as our talks progressed this week, what did grow was even better. A far-reaching set of agreements[26] that can lead to a better life for both of our peoples, to a better chance for peace in the world.

We have agreed on joint ventures in space. We have agreed on ways of working together to protect the environment, to advance health, to cooperate in science and technology. We have agreed on means of preventing incidents at sea. We have established a commission to expand trade between our two nations.

Most important, we have taken an historic first step in the limitation

[25] Radio-TV address, Aug. 1, 1959, in *Documents, 1959*, pp. 183-93; quoted passage on p. 191.
[26] For details, see Document 10.

of nuclear strategic arms. This arms control agreement[27] is not for the purpose of giving either side an advantage over the other. Both of our nations are strong, each respects the strength of the other, each will maintain the strength necessary to defend its independence.

But in an unchecked arms race between two great nations, there would be no winners, only losers. By setting this limitation together, the people of both of our nations, and of all nations, can be winners. If we continue in the spirit of serious purpose that has marked our discussions this week, these agreements can start us on a new road of cooperation for the benefit of our people, for the benefit of all peoples.

There is an old proverb that says, "Make peace with man and quarrel with your sins." The hardships and evils that beset all men and all nations, these and these alone are what we should make war upon.

As we look at the prospects for peace, we see that we have made significant progress at reducing the possible sources of direct conflict between us. But history tells us that great nations have often been dragged into war without intending it, by conflicts between smaller nations. As great powers, we can and should use our influence to prevent this from happening. Our goal should be to discourage aggression in other parts of the world and particularly among those smaller nations that look to us for leadership and example.

With great power goes great responsibility. When a man walks with a giant tread, he must be careful where he sets his feet. There can be true peace only when the weak are as safe as the strong. The wealthier and more powerful our own nations become, the more we have to lose from war and the threat of war, anywhere in the world.

Speaking for the United States, I can say this: We covet no one else's territory, we seek no dominion over any other people, we seek the right to live in peace, not only for ourselves, but for all the peoples of this earth. Our power will only be used to keep the peace, never to break it, only to defend freedom, never to destroy it. No nation that does not threaten its neighbors has anything to fear from the United States.

Soviet citizens have often asked me, "Does America truly want peace?"

I believe that our actions answer that question far better than any words could do. If we did not want peace, we would not have reduced the size of our armed forces by a million men, by almost one-third, during the past 3 years. If we did not want peace, we would not have worked so hard at reaching an agreement on the limitation of nuclear arms, at achieving a settlement of Berlin, at maintaining peace in the Middle East, at establishing better relations with the Soviet Union, with the People's Republic of China, with other nations of the world.

Mrs. Nixon and I feel very fortunate to have had the opportunity to

[27] Documents 13-14.

visit the Soviet Union, to get to know the people of the Soviet Union, friendly and hospitable, courageous and strong. Most Americans will never have a chance to visit the Soviet Union and most Soviet citizens will never have a chance to visit America. Most of you know our country only through what you read in your newspapers and what you hear and see on radio and television and motion pictures. This is only a part of the real America.

I would like to take this opportunity to try to convey to you something of what America is really like, not in terms of its scenic beauties, its great cities, its factories, its farms, or its highways, but in terms of its people.

In many ways, the people of our two countries are very much alike. Like the Soviet Union, ours is a large and diverse nation. Our people, like yours, are hard-working. Like you, we Americans have a strong spirit of competition, but we also have a great love of music and poetry, of sports, and of humor. Above all, we, like you, are an open, natural, and friendly people. We love our country. We love our children. And we want for you and for your children the same peace and abundance that we want for ourselves and for our children.

We Americans are idealists. We believe deeply in our system of government. We cherish our personal liberty. We would fight to defend it, if necessary, as we have done before. But we also believe deeply in the right of each nation to choose its own system. Therefore, however much we like our own system for ourselves, we have no desire to impose it on anyone else.

As we conclude this week of talks, there are certain fundamental premises of the American point of view which I believe deserve emphasis. In conducting these talks, it has not been our aim to divide up the world into spheres of influence, to establish a condominium, or in any way to conspire together against the interests of any other nation. Rather we have sought to construct a better framework of understanding between our two nations, to make progress in our bilateral relationships, to find ways of ensuring that future frictions between us would never embroil our two nations, and therefore, the world, in war.

While ours are both great and powerful nations, the world is no longer dominated by two superpowers. The world is a better and safer place because its power and resources are more widely distributed.

Beyond this, since World War II, more than 70 new nations have come into being. We cannot have true peace unless they, and all nations, can feel that they share it.

America seeks better relations, not only with the Soviet Union, but with all nations. The only sound basis for a peaceful and progressive international order is sovereign equality and mutual respect. We believe in the right of each nation to chart its own course, to choose its own system, to go its own way, without interference from other nations.

As we look to the longer term, peace depends also on continued progress in the developing nations. Together with other advanced industrial countries, the United States and the Soviet Union share a twofold responsibility in this regard.

On the one hand, to practice restraint in those activities, such as the supply of arms, that might endanger the peace of developing nations. And second, to assist them in their orderly economic and social development, without political interference.

Some of you may have heard an old story told in Russia of a traveler who was walking to another village. He knew the way, but not the distance. Finally he came upon a woodsman chopping wood by the side of the road and he asked the woodsman, "How long will it take to reach the village?"

The woodsman replied, "I don't know."

The traveler was angry, because he was sure the woodsman was from the village and therefore knew how far it was. And so he started off down the road again. After he had gone a few steps, the woodsman called out, "Stop. It will take you about 15 minutes."

The traveler turned and demanded, "Why didn't you tell me that in the first place?"

The woodsman replied, "Because then I didn't know the length of your stride."

In our talks this week with the leaders of the Soviet Union, both sides have had a chance to measure the length of our strides toward peace and security. I believe that those strides have been substantial and that now we have well begun the long journey which will lead us to a new age in the relations between our two countries. It is important to both of our peoples that we continue those strides.

As our two countries learn to work together, our people will be able to get to know one another better. Greater cooperation can also mean a great deal in our daily lives. As we learn to cooperate in space, in health and the environment, in science and technology, our cooperation can help sick people get well. It can help industries produce more consumer goods. It can help all of us enjoy cleaner air and water. It can increase our knowledge of the world around us.

As we expand our trade, each of our countries can buy more of the other's goods and market more of our own. As we gain experience with arms control, we can bring closer the day when further agreements can lessen the arms burden of our two nations and lessen the threat of war in the world.

Through all the pages of history, through all the centuries, the world's people have struggled to be free from fear, whether fear of the elements or fear of hunger or fear of their own rulers or fear of their neighbors in other countries. And yet, time and again, people have vanquished the source of one fear only to fall prey to another.

Let our goal now be a world free of fear. A world in which nation will no longer prey upon nation, in which human energies will be turned away from production for war and toward more production for peace, away from conquest and toward invention, development, creation. A world in which together we can establish that peace which is more than the absence of war, which enables man to pursue those higher goals that the spirit yearns for.

Yesterday, I laid a wreath at the cemetery which commemorates the brave people who died during the siege of Leningrad in World War II. At the cemetery, I saw the picture of a 12-year-old girl. She was a beautiful child. Her name was Tanya. The pages of her diary tell the terrible story of war. In the simple words of a child, she wrote of the deaths of the members of her family: Zhenya in December. Grannie in January. Leka then next. Then Uncle Vasya. Then Uncle Lyosha. Then Mama. And then the Savichevs. And then finally these words, the last words in her diary, "All are dead. Only Tanya is left."

As we work toward a more peaceful world, let us think of Tanya and of the other Tanyas and their brothers and sisters everywhere. Let us do all that we can to insure that no other children will have to endure what Tanya did and that your children and ours, all the children of the world can live their full lives together in friendship and in peace.

Spasibo y do svidaniye [Thank you and good-bye].

(10) Joint United States-Soviet Communiqué Issued at the Conclusion of the President's Visit, May 29, 1972.[28]

(Complete Text)

By mutual agreement between the United States of America and the Union of Soviet Socialist Republics, the President of the United States and Mrs. Richard Nixon paid an official visit to the Soviet Union from May 22 to May 30, 1972. The President was accompanied by Secretary of State William P. Rogers, Assistant to the President Dr. Henry A. Kissinger, and other American officials. During his stay in the USSR President Nixon visited, in addition to Moscow, the cities of Leningrad and Kiev.

President Nixon and L. I. Brezhnev, General Secretary of the Central Committee of the Communist Party of the Soviet Union, N. V. Podgorny, Chairman of the Presidium of the Supreme Soviet of the USSR, and A. N. Kosygin, Chairman of the Council of Ministers of the USSR conducted talks on fundamental problems of American-Soviet relations and the current international situation.

[28] *Presidential Documents*, June 5, 1972, pp. 945-51.

Also taking part in the conversations were:

On the American side: William P. Rogers, Secretary of State; Jacob D. Beam, American Ambassador to the USSR; Dr. Henry A. Kissinger, Assistant to the President for National Security Affairs; Peter M. Flanigan, Assistant to the President; and Martin J. Hillenbrand, Assistant Secretary of State for European Affairs.

On the Soviet side: A. A. Gromyko, Minister of Foreign Affairs of the USSR; N. S. Patolichev, Minister of Foreign Trade; V. V. Kuznetsov, Deputy Minister of Foreign Affairs of the USSR; A. F. Dobrynin, Soviet Ambassador to the USA; A. M. Aleksandrov, Assistant to the General Secretary of the Central Committee, CPSU [Communist Party of the Soviet Union]; G. M. Korniyenko, Member of the Collegium of the Ministry of Foreign Affairs of the USSR.

The discussions covered a wide range of questions of mutual interest and were frank and thorough. They defined more precisely those areas where there are prospects for developing greater cooperation between the two countries, as well as those areas where the positions of the two Sides are different.

I. BILATERAL RELATIONS

Guided by the desire to place US-Soviet relations on a more stable and constructive foundation, and mindful of their responsibilities for maintaining world peace and for facilitating the relaxation of international tension, the two Sides adopted a document entitled: "Basic Principles of Mutual Relations between the United States of America and the Union of Soviet Socialist Republics," signed on behalf of the US by President Nixon and on behalf of the USSR by General Secretary Brezhnev.[29]

Both Sides are convinced that the provisions of that document open new possibilities for the development of peaceful relations and mutually beneficial cooperation between the USA and the USSR.

Having considered various areas of bilateral US-Soviet relations, the two Sides agreed that an improvement of relations is possible and desirable. They expressed their firm intention to act in accordance with the provisions set forth in the above-mentioned document.

As a result of progress made in negotiations which preceded the summit meeting, and in the course of the meeting itself, a number of significant agreements were reached. This will intensify bilateral cooperation in areas of common concern as well as in areas relevant to the cause of peace and international cooperation.

[29] Document 11.

Limitation of Strategic Armaments

The two Sides gave primary attention to the problem of reducing the danger of nuclear war. They believe that curbing the competition in strategic arms will make a significant and tangible contribution to this cause.

The two Sides attach great importance to the Treaty on the Limitation of Anti-Ballistic Missile Systems[30] and the Interim Agreement on Certain Measures with Respect to the Limitation of Strategic Offensive Arms[31] concluded between them.

These agreements, which were concluded as a result of the negotiations in Moscow, constitute a major step towards curbing and ultimately ending the arms race.

They are a concrete expression of the intention of the two Sides to contribute to the relaxation of international tension and the strengthening of confidence between states, as well as to carry out the obligations assumed by them in the Treaty on the Non-Proliferation of Nuclear Weapons (Article VI).[32] Both Sides are convinced that the achievement of the above agreements is a practical step towards saving mankind from the threat of the outbreak of nuclear war. Accordingly, it corresponds to the vital interests of the American and Soviet peoples as well as to the vital interests of all other peoples.

The two Sides intend to continue active negotiations for the limitation of strategic offensive arms[33] and to conduct them in a spirit of goodwill, respect for each other's legitimate interests and observance of the principle of equal security.

Both Sides are also convinced that the agreement on Measures to Reduce the Risk of Outbreak of Nuclear War Between the USA and the USSR, signed in Washington on September 30, 1971,[34] serves the interests not only of the Soviet and American peoples, but of all mankind.

Commercial and Economic Relations

Both Sides agreed on measures designed to establish more favorable conditions for developing commercial and other economic ties between the USA and the USSR. The two Sides agree that realistic conditions

[30] Document 13.
[31] Document 14.
[32] Signed at Washington, London, and Moscow July 1, 1968 and entered into force Mar. 5, 1970 (TIAS 6839; 21 UST 490); text in *Documents, 1968-69*, pp. 62-8. Article VI reads: "Each of the Parties to the Treaty undertakes to pursue negotiations in good faith on effective measures relating to cessation of the nuclear arms race at an early date and to nuclear disarmament, and on a treaty on general and complete disarmament under strict and effective international control."
[33] Cf. Document 17.
[34] *A.F.R., 1971*, no. 27.

exist for increasing economic ties. These ties should develop on the basis of mutual benefit and in accordance with generally accepted international practice.

Believing that these aims would be served by conclusion of a trade agreement between the USA and the USSR, the two Sides decided to complete in the near future the work necessary to conclude such an agreement. They agreed on the desirability of credit arrangements to develop mutual trade and of early efforts to resolve other financial and economic issues. It was agreed that a lend-lease settlement will be negotiated concurrently with a trade agreement.[35]

In the interests of broadening and facilitating commercial ties between the two countries, and to work out specific arrangements, the two Sides decided to create a US–Soviet Joint Commercial Commission.[36] Its first meeting will be held in Moscow in the summer of 1972.[37]

Each Side will help promote the establishment of effective working arrangements between organizations and firms of both countries and encouraging the conclusion of long-term contracts.

Maritime Matters—Incidents at Sea

The Two Sides agreed to continue the negotiations aimed at reaching an agreement on maritime and related matters. They believe that such an agreement would mark a positive step in facilitating the expansion of commerce between the United States and the Soviet Union.[38]

An Agreement was concluded between the two Sides on measures to prevent incidents at sea and in air space over it between vessels and aircraft of the US and Soviet Navies.[39] By providing agreed procedures for ships and aircraft of the two navies operating in close proximity, this agreement will diminish the chances of dangerous accidents.

Cooperation in Science and Technology

It was recognized that the cooperation now underway in areas such as atomic energy research, space research, health and other fields benefits both nations and has contributed positively to their over-all relations. It was agreed that increased scientific and technical cooperation on the

---

35 Cf. Document 19.
36 Cf. joint communiqué of May 26, 1972 in *Public Papers, 1972*, pp. 623-4.
37 Cf. below at note 166.
38 Cf. below at notes 176-8.
39 Agreement Between the Government of the United States of America and the Government of the Union of Soviet Socialist Republics on the Prevention of Incidents on and Over the Sea, signed May 25, 1972 by Secretary of the Navy John W. Warner and Sergei G. Gorshkov, Commander-in-Chief of the Soviet Navy and Deputy Minister of Defense (TIAS 7379; 23 UST 1168); text in *Presidential Documents*, June 5, 1972, pp. 922-3.

basis of mutual benefit and shared effort for common goals is in the interest of both nations and would contribute to a further improvement in their bilateral relations. For these purposes the two Sides signed an agreement for cooperation in the fields of science and technology.[40] A US-Soviet Joint Commission on Scientific and Technical Cooperation will be created for identifying and establishing cooperative programs.[41]

Cooperation in Space

Having in mind the role played by the US and the USSR in the peaceful exploration of outer space, both Sides emphasized the importance of further bilateral cooperation in this sphere. In order to increase the safety of man's flights in outer space and the future prospects of joint scientific experiments, the two Sides agreed to make suitable arrangements to permit the docking of American and Soviet spacecraft and stations.[42] The first joint docking experiment of the two countries' piloted spacecraft, with visits by astronauts and cosmonauts to each other's spacecraft, is contemplated for 1975. The planning and implementation of this flight will be carried out by the US National Aeronautics and Space Administration and the USSR Academy of Sciences, according to principles and procedures developed through mutual consultations.

Cooperation in the Field of Health

The two Sides concluded an agreement on health cooperation[43] which marks a fruitful beginning of sharing knowledge about, and collaborative attacks on, the common enemies, disease and disability. The

[40] Agreement Between the Government of the United States of America and the Government of the Union of Soviet Socialist Republics on Cooperation in the Fields of Science and Technology, signed May 24, 1972 by Secretary of State Rogers and V.A. Kirillin, Chairman of the State Committee for Science and Technology (TIAS 7346; 23 UST 856); text in *Presidential Documents*, June 5, 1972, pp. 921-2.

[41] A framework for the Joint Commission was established by U.S. and Soviet officials in July 1972 and the Commission held its first meeting in Mar. 1973 (*Bulletin*, Aug. 21, 1972, pp. 214-16; same, May 7, 1973, pp. 584-5).

[42] Agreement Between the United States of America and the Union of Soviet Socialist Republics Concerning Cooperation in the Exploration and Use of Outer Space for Peaceful Purposes, signed May 24, 1972 by President Nixon and Chairman Kosygin (TIAS 7347; 23 UST 867); text in *Presidential Documents*, June 5, 1972, pp. 920-21.

[43] Agreement Between the Government of the United States of America and the Government of the Union of Soviet Socialist Republics on Cooperation in the Field of Medical Science and Public Health, signed May 23, 1972 by Secretary of State Rogers and Minister of Health Boris V. Petrovsky (TIAS 7344; 23 UST 836); text in *Presidential Documents*, June 5, 1972, pp. 919-20.

initial research efforts of the program will concentrate on health problems important to the whole world—cancer, heart diseases, and the environmental health sciences. This cooperation subsequently will be broadened to include other health problems of mutual interest. The two Sides pledged their full support for the health cooperation program and agreed to continue the active participation of the two governments in the work of international organizations in the health field.

Environmental Cooperation

The two Sides agreed to initiate a program of cooperation in the protection and enhancement of man's environment.[44] Through joint research and joint measures, the United States and the USSR hope to contribute to the preservation of a healthful environment in their countries and throughout the world. Under the new agreement on environmental cooperation there will be consultations in the near future in Moscow on specific cooperative projects.

Exchanges in the Fields of Science, Technology, Education, and Culture

Both Sides note the importance of the Agreement on Exchanges and Cooperation in Scientific, Technical, Educational, Cultural, and Other Fields in 1972–1973, signed in Moscow on April 11, 1972.[45] Continuation and expansion of bilateral exchanges in these fields will lead to better understanding and help improve the general state of relations between the two countries. Within the broad framework provided by this Agreement the two Sides have agreed to expand the areas of cooperation, as reflected in new agreements concerning space, health, the environment and science and technology.

The US side, noting the existence of an extensive program of English language instruction in the Soviet Union, indicated its intention to encourage Russian language programs in the United States.

II. INTERNATIONAL ISSUES

Europe

In the course of the discussions on the international situation, both

---

[44] Agreement on Cooperation in the Field of Environmental Protection Between the United States of America and the Union of Soviet Socialist Republics, signed May 23, 1972 by President Nixon and Chairman Podgorny (TIAS 7345; 23 UST 845); text in *Presidential Documents*, June 5, 1972, pp. 917-19. Detailed plans for the implementation of the agreement were agreed upon at the first meeting of the U.S.-Soviet Joint Committee on Cooperation in the Field of Environmental Protection, held in Moscow Sept. 18-21, 1972 (*Bulletin*, Oct. 16, 1972, pp. 451-5).

[45] Cf. above at note 13.

Sides took note of favorable developments in the relaxation of tensions in Europe.

Recognizing the importance to world peace of developments in Europe, where both World Wars originated, and mindful of the responsibilities and commitments which they share with other powers under appropriate agreements, the USA and the USSR intend to make further efforts to ensure a peaceful future for Europe, free of tensions, crises and conflicts.

They agree that the territorial integrity of all states in Europe should be respected.

Both Sides view the September 3, 1971 Quadripartite Agreement relating to the Western Sectors of Berlin[46] as a good example of fruitful cooperation between the states concerned, including the USA and the USSR. The two Sides believe that the implementation of that agreement in the near future, along with other steps, will further improve the European situation and contribute to the necessary trust among states.

Both Sides welcomed the treaty between the USSR and the Federal Republic of Germany signed on August 12, 1970.[47] They noted the significance of the provisions of this treaty as well as of other recent agreements in contributing to confidence and cooperation among the European states.

The USA and the USSR are prepared to make appropriate contributions to the positive trends on the European continent toward a genuine detente and the development of relations of peaceful cooperation among states in Europe on the basis of the principles of territorial integrity and inviolability of frontiers, non-interference in internal affairs, sovereign equality, independence and renunciation of the use or threat of force.

The US and the USSR are in accord that multilateral consultations looking toward a Conference on Security and Cooperation in Europe could begin after the signature of the Final Quadripartite Protocol of the Agreement of September 3, 1971.[48] The two governments agree that the conference should be carefully prepared in order that it may concretely consider specific problems of security and cooperation and thus contribute to the progressive reduction of the underlying causes of tension in Europe. This conference should be convened at a time to be agreed by the countries concerned, but without undue delay.[49]

Both Sides believe that the goal of ensuring stability and security in Europe would be served by a reciprocal reduction of armed forces and armaments, first of all in Central Europe. Any agreement on this question should not diminish the security of any of the Sides. Appropriate

[46] A.F.R., 1971, no. 38.
[47] Documents, 1970, pp. 105-6; cf. Chapter III at note 30.
[48] The protocol was signed June 3, 1972; cf. Document 25, below.
[49] Cf. Document 31.

agreement should be reached as soon as practicable between the states concerned on the procedures for negotiations on this subject in a special forum.[50]

The Middle East

The two Sides set out their positions on this question. They reaffirm their support for a peaceful settlement in the Middle East in accordance with Security Council Resolution 242.[51]

Noting the significance of constructive cooperation of the parties concerned with the Special Representative of the UN Secretary General, Ambassador [Gunnar V.] Jarring, the US and the USSR confirm their desire to contribute to his mission's success and also declare their readiness to play their part in bringing about a peaceful settlement in the Middle East. In the view of the US and the USSR, the achievement of such a settlement would open prospects for the normalization of the Middle East situation and would permit, in particular, consideration of further steps to bring about a military relaxation in that area.[52]

Indochina

Each side set forth its respective standpoint with regard to the continuing war in Vietnam and the situation in the area of Indochina as a whole.

The US side emphasized the need to bring an end to the military conflict as soon as possible and reaffirmed its commitment to the principle that the political future of South Vietnam should be left for the South Vietnamese people to decide for themselves, free from outside interference.

The US side explained its view that the quickest and most effective way to attain the above-mentioned objectives is through negotiations leading to the return of all Americans held captive in the region, the implementation of an internationally supervised Indochina-wide cease-fire and the subsequent withdrawal of all American forces stationed in South Vietnam within four months, leaving the political questions to be resolved by the Indochinese peoples themselves.

The United States reiterated its willingness to enter into serious negotiations with the North Vietnamese Side to settle the war in Indochina on a basis just to all.

The Soviet Side stressed its solidarity with the just struggle of the peoples of Vietnam, Laos and Cambodia for their freedom, independence and social progress. Firmly supporting the proposals of the

[50] Cf. Document 30.
[51] U.N. Security Council Resolution 242 (1967), Nov. 22, 1967, in *Documents, 1967*, pp. 169-70; cf. Chapter IV at note 41.
[52] Cf. Document 35.

DRV [Democratic Republic of Vietnam] and the Republic of South Vietnam,[53] which provide a realistic and constructive basis for settling the Vietnam problem, the Soviet Union stands for a cessation of bombings of the DRV, for a complete and unequivocal withdrawal of the troops of the USA and its allies from South Vietnam, so that the peoples of Indochina would have the possibility to determine for themselves their fate without any outside interference.

Disarmament Issues

The two Sides expressed their positions on arms limitation and disarmament issues.

The two Sides note that in recent years their joint and parallel actions have facilitated the working out and conclusion of treaties which curb the arms race or ban some of the most dangerous types of weapons. They note further that these treaties were welcomed by a large majority of the states in the world, which became parties to them.

Both sides regard the Convention on the Prohibition of the Development, Production and Stockpiling of Bacteriological (Biological) and Toxic [Toxin] Weapons and on their Destruction,[54] as an essential disarmament measure. Along with Great Britain, they are the depositories for the Convention which was recently opened for signature by all states. The USA and the USSR will continue their efforts to reach an international agreement regarding chemical weapons.

The USA and the USSR, proceeding from the need to take into account the security interests of both countries on the basis of the principle of equality, and without prejudice to the security interests of third countries, will actively participate in negotiations aimed at working out new measures designed to curb and end the arms race. The ultimate purpose is general and complete disarmament, including nuclear disarmament, under strict international control. A world disarmament conference could play a role in this process at an appropriate time.

Strengthening the United Nations

Both Sides will strive to strengthen the effectiveness of the United Nations on the basis of strict observance of the UN Charter. They regard the United Nations as an instrument for maintaining world peace and security, discouraging conflicts, and developing international cooperation. Accordingly, they will do their best to support United Nations efforts in the interests of international peace.

Both Sides emphasized that agreements and understandings reached

[53] Usually referred to as the "Provisional Revolutionary Government of the Republic of South Vietnam."
[54] Cf. note 150.

in the negotiations in Moscow, as well as the contents and nature of these negotiations, are not in any way directed against any other country. Both Sides proceed from the recognition of the role, the responsibility and the prerogatives of other interested states, existing international obligations and agreements, and the principles and purposes of the UN Charter.

Both Sides believe that positive results were accomplished in the course of the talks at the highest level. These results indicate that despite the differences between the USA and the USSR in social systems, ideologies, and policy principles, it is possible to develop mutually advantageous cooperation between the peoples of both countries, in the interests of strengthening peace and international security.

Both Sides expressed the desire to continue close contact on a number of issues that were under discussion. They agreed that regular consultations on questions of mutual interest, including meetings at the highest level, would be useful.

In expressing his appreciation for the hospitality accorded him in the Soviet Union, President Nixon invited General Secretary L. I. Brezhnev, Chairman N. V. Podgorny, and Chairman A. N. Kosygin to visit the United States at a mutually convenient time. This invitation was accepted.[55]

(11) "Basic Principles of Mutual Relations Between the United States of America and the Union of Soviet Socialist Republics," Signed in Moscow May 29, 1972.[56]

(Complete Text)

The United States of America and the Union of Soviet Socialist Republics,

Guided by their obligations under the Charter of the United Nations and by a desire to strengthen peaceful relations with each other and to place these relations on the firmest possible basis,

Aware of the need to make every effort to remove the threat of war and to create conditions which promote the reduction of tensions in the world and the strengthening of universal security and international cooperation,

Believing that the improvement of US-Soviet relations and their mutually advantageous development in such areas as economics, science and culture, will meet these objectives and contribute to better mutual

[55] General Secretary Brezhnev visited the United States on June 17-25, 1973; cf. *Presidential Documents*, June 25, 1973, pp. 787-827 and same, July 2, 1973, pp. 831-55.
[56] *Presidential Documents*, June 5, 1972, pp. 943-4.

understanding and business-like cooperation, without in any way prejudicing the interests of third countries,

Conscious that these objectives reflect the interests of the peoples of both countries,

Have agreed as follows:

First. They will proceed from the common determination that in the nuclear age there is no alternative to conducting their mutual relations on the basis of peaceful coexistence. Differences in ideology and in the social systems of the USA and the USSR are not obstacles to the bilateral development of normal relations based on the principles of sovereignty, equality, non-interference in internal affairs and mutual advantage.

Second. The USA and the USSR attach major importance to preventing the development of situations capable of causing a dangerous exacerbation of their relations. Therefore, they will do their utmost to avoid military confrontations and to prevent the outbreak of nuclear war. They will always exercise restraint in their mutual relations, and will be prepared to negotiate and settle differences by peaceful means. Discussions and negotiations on outstanding issues will be conducted in a spirit of reciprocity, mutual accommodation and mutual benefit.

Both sides recognize that efforts to obtain unilateral advantage at the expense of the other, directly or indirectly, are inconsistent with these objectives. The prerequisites for maintaining and strengthening peaceful relations between the USA and the USSR are the recognition of the security interests of the Parties based on the principle of equality and the renunciation of the use or threat of force.

Third. The USA and the USSR have a special responsibility, as do other countries which are permanent members of the United Nations Security Council, to do everything in their power so that conflicts or situations will not arise which would serve to increase international tensions. Accordingly, they will seek to promote conditions in which all countries will live in peace and security and will not be subject to outside interference in their internal affairs.

Fourth. The USA and the USSR intend to widen the juridical basis of their mutual relations and to exert the necessary efforts so that bilateral agreements which they have concluded and multilateral treaties and agreements to which they are jointly parties are faithfully implemented.

Fifth. The USA and the USSR reaffirm their readiness to continue the practice of exchanging views on problems of mutual interest and, when necessary, to conduct such exchanges at the highest level, including meetings between leaders of the two countries.

The two governments welcome and will facilitate an increase in productive contacts between representatives of the legislative bodies of the two countries.

Sixth. The Parties will continue their efforts to limit armaments on a bilateral as well as on a multilateral basis. They will continue to make special efforts to limit strategic armaments.[57] Whenever possible, they will conclude concrete agreements aimed at achieving these purposes.

The USA and the USSR regard as the ultimate objective of their efforts the achievement of general and complete disarmament and the establishment of an effective system of international security in accordance with the purposes and principles of the United Nations.

Seventh. The USA and the USSR regard commercial and economic ties as an important and necessary element in the strengthening of their bilateral relations and thus will actively promote the growth of such ties. They will facilitate cooperation between the relevant organizations and enterprises of the two countries and the conclusion of appropriate agreements and contracts, including long-term ones.[58]

The two countries will contribute to the improvement of maritime and air communications between them.[59]

Eighth. The two sides consider it timely and useful to develop mutual contacts and cooperation in the fields of science and technology. Where suitable, the USA and the USSR will conclude appropriate agreements dealing with concrete cooperation in these fields.[60]

Ninth. The two sides reaffirm their intention to deepen cultural ties with one another and to encourage fuller familiarization with each other's cultural values.[61] They will promote improved conditions for cultural exchanges and tourism.

Tenth. The USA and the USSR will seek to ensure that their ties and cooperation in all the above-mentioned fields and in any others in their mutual interest are built on a firm and long-term basis. To give a permanent character to these efforts, they will establish in all fields where this is feasible joint commissions or other joint bodies.

Eleventh. The USA and the USSR make no claim for themselves and would not recognize the claims of anyone else to any special rights or advantages in world affairs. They recognize the sovereign equality of all states.

The development of U.S.-Soviet relations is not directed against third countries and their interests.

[57] Cf. Document 17.
[58] Cf. Document 19.
[59] Cf. below at notes 176-178.
[60] Cf. above at notes 40-44.
[61] Cf. above at note 45.

Twelfth. The basic principles set forth in this document do not affect any obligations with respect to other countries earlier assumed by the USA and the USSR.

MOSCOW, MAY 29, 1972

FOR THE UNITED STATES OF AMERICA
RICHARD NIXON
    President of the United States of America

FOR THE UNION OF SOVIET SOCIALIST REPUBLICS
LEONID I. BREZHNEV
    General Secretary of the Central Committee, CPSU

3. Report to Congress.

[An event of such importance as President Nixon's visit to the U.S.S.R. left ample traces in the annals of the Nixon administration. Dr. Kissinger, emerging for the first time as the administration's principal spokesman on international affairs, provided an abundance of background and interpretation in a series of news briefings held while the presidential party was still on Soviet soil.[62] The President himself, arriving at Andrews Air Force Base on the evening of June 1, proceeded directly to Capitol Hill for an address to Congress which was also broadcast live on radio and television. The freshness and immediacy of this presentation (Document 12) entitle it to rank with the more analytical account included almost eleven months later in the President's 1973 report on the State of the World.[63]]

(12) Address by President Nixon to a Joint Session of the Congress, June 1, 1972.[64]

(Complete Text)

Mr. Speaker, Mr. President, Members of the Congress, our distinguished guests, my fellow Americans:

Your welcome in this great chamber tonight has a very special meaning to Mrs. Nixon and to me. We feel very fortunate to have traveled abroad so often representing the United States of America. But

---

[62] *Presidential Documents*, June 5, 1972, pp. 929-37 and 951-63.
[63] Nixon Report, 1973, pp. 32-8.
[64] *Presidential Documents*, June 5, 1972, pp. 975-81.

we both agree after each journey that the best part of any trip abroad is coming home to America again.

During the past 13 days we have flown more than 16,000 miles and we visited four countries. Everywhere we went—to Austria, the Soviet Union, Iran, Poland[65]—we could feel the quickening pace of change in old international relationships, and the people's genuine desire for friendship for the American people. Everywhere new hopes are rising for a world no longer shadowed by fear and want and war, and as Americans we can be proud that we now have an historic opportunity to play a great role in helping to achieve man's oldest dream—a world in which all nations can enjoy the blessings of peace.

On this journey we saw many memorable sights, but one picture will always remain indelible in our memory—the flag of the United States of America flying high in the spring breeze above Moscow's ancient Kremlin fortress.

To millions of Americans for the past quarter century the Kremlin has stood for implacable hostility toward all that we cherish, and to millions of Russians, the American flag has long been held up as a symbol of evil. No one would have believed, even a short time ago, that these two apparently irreconcilable symbols would be seen together as we saw them for those few days.

But this does not mean that we bring back from Moscow the promise of instant peace, but we do bring the beginning of a process that can lead to a lasting peace. And that is why I have taken the extraordinary action of requesting this special joint session of the Congress because we have before us an extraordinary opportunity.

I have not come here this evening to make new announcements in a dramatic setting. This summit has already made its news. It has barely begun, however, to make its mark on our world, and I ask you to join me tonight—while events are fresh, while the iron is hot—in starting to consider how we can help to make that mark what we want it to be.

The foundation has been laid for a new relationship between the two most powerful nations in the world. Now it is up to us—to all of us here in this Chamber, to all of us across America—to join with other nations in building a new house upon that foundation, one that can be a home for the hopes of mankind and a shelter against the storms of conflict.

As a preliminary, therefore, to requesting your concurrence in some of the agreements we reached and your approval of funds to carry out others, and also as a keynote for the unity in which this Government and this Nation must go forward from here, I am rendering this immediate report to the Congress on the results of the Moscow summit.

The pattern of U.S.-Soviet summit diplomacy in the cold war era is well known to all those in this Chamber. One meeting after another produced a brief euphoric mood—the spirit of Geneva, the spirit of

65 For documentation on the visits to Austria, Iran, and Poland, cf. notes 21-23.

Camp David, the spirit of Vienna, the spirit of Glassboro[66]—but without producing significant progress on the really difficult issues.

And so early in this Administration I stated[67] that the prospect of concrete results, not atmospherics, would be our criterion for meetings at the highest level. I also announced our intention to pursue negotiations with the Soviet Union across a broad front of related issues, with the purpose of creating a momentum of achievement in which progress in one area could contribute to progress in others.

This is the basis on which we prepared for and conducted last week's talks. This was a working summit. We sought to establish not a superficial spirit of Moscow, but a solid record of progress on solving the difficult issues which for so long have divided our two nations and also have divided the world. Reviewing the number and the scope of the agreements that emerged, I think we have accomplished that goal.

Recognizing the responsibility of the advanced industrial nations to set an example in combatting mankind's common enemies, the United States and the Soviet Union have agreed to cooperate in efforts to reduce pollution and enhance environmental quality.[68] We have agreed to work together in the field of medical science and public health, particularly in the conquest of cancer and heart disease.[69]

Recognizing that the quest for useful knowledge transcends differences between ideologies and social systems, we have agreed to expand United States-Soviet cooperation in many areas of science and technology.[70]

We have joined in plans for an exciting new adventure, a new adventure in the cooperative exploration of space, which will begin—subject to Congressional approval of funding—with a joint orbital mission of an Apollo vehicle and a Soviet spacecraft in 1975.[71]

By forming habits of cooperation and strengthening institutional ties in areas of peaceful enterprise, these four agreements, to which I have referred, will create on both sides a steadily growing vested interest in the maintenance of good relations between our two countries.

Expanded United States-Soviet trade will also yield advantages to both of our nations. When the two largest economies in the world start trading with each other on a much larger scale, living standards in both

[66] Four-power Heads of Government conference, Geneva, July 18-23, 1955 (*Documents, 1955*, pp. 171-232); Eisenhower-Khrushchev meeting, Camp David, Md., Sept. 28, 1959 (*Documents, 1959*, pp. 193-200); Kennedy-Khrushchev meeting, Vienna, June 3-4, 1961 (*Documents, 1961*, pp. 136-41); Johnson-Kosygin meeting, Glassboro, N.J., June 23 and 25, 1967 (*Documents, 1967*, pp. 52-9).

[67] News conference statement, Feb. 6, 1969, in *Public Papers, 1969*, p. 67.

[68] Cf. note 44.

[69] Cf. note 43.

[70] Cf. note 40.

[71] Cf. note 42.

nations will rise, and the stake which both have in peace will increase.

Progress in this area is proceeding on schedule. At the summit, we established a Joint Commercial Commission[72] which will complete the negotiations for a comprehensive trade agreement between the United States and the USSR.

And we expect the final terms of such an agreement to be settled, later this year.[73]

Two further accords which were reached last week have a much more direct bearing on the search for peace and security in the world.

One is the agreement between the American and Soviet navies aimed at significantly reducing the chances of dangerous incidents between our ships and aircraft at sea.[74]

And second, and most important, there is the treaty and the related executive agreement which will limit, for the first time, both offensive and defensive strategic nuclear weapons in the arsenals of the United States and the Soviet Union.[75]

Three-fifths of all the people alive in the world today have spent their whole lifetimes under the shadow of a nuclear war which could be touched off by the arms race among the great powers. Last Friday [May 26] in Moscow we witnessed the beginning of the end of that era which began in 1945. We took the first step toward a new era of mutually agreed restraint and arms limitation between the two principal nuclear powers.

With this step we have enhanced the security of both nations. We have begun to check the wasteful and dangerous spiral of nuclear arms which has dominated relations between our two countries for a generation. We have begun to reduce the level of fear by reducing the causes of fear, for our two peoples and for all peoples in the world.

The ABM Treaty will be submitted promptly for the Senate's advice and consent to ratification[76] and the interim agreement limiting certain offensive weapons will be submitted to both Houses for concurrence. Because we can undertake agreements as important as these only on a basis of full partnership between the executive and legislative branches of our Government.

I ask from this Congress and I ask from the Nation the fullest scrutiny of these accords. I am confident such examination will underscore the truth of what I told the Soviet people on television just a few nights ago—that this is an agreement in the interest of both nations.[77] From the standpoint of the United States, when we consider what the stra-

72 Cf. note 36 and see below at notes 166 and 186.
73 Document 19.
74 Cf. note 39.
75 Documents 13-14.
76 Cf. Document 15.
77 Document 9.

tegic balance would have looked like later in the Seventies, if there had been no arms limitation, it is clear that the agreements forestall a major spiraling of the arms race—one which would have worked to our disadvantage, since we have no current building programs for the categories of weapons which have been frozen, and since no new building program could have produced any new weapons in those categories during the period of the freeze.

My colleagues in the Congress, I have studied the strategic balance in great detail with my senior advisers for more than 3 years. I can assure you, the Members of the Congress, and the American people tonight that the present and planned strategic forces of the United States are without question sufficient for the maintenance of our security and the protection of our vital interests.

No power on earth is stronger than the United States of America today. And none will be stronger than the United States of America in the future.

This is the only national defense posture which can ever be acceptable to the United States. This is the posture I ask the Senate and the Congress to protect by approving the arms limitation agreements to which I have referred. This is the posture which, with the responsible cooperation of the Congress, I will take all necessary steps to maintain in our future defense programs.

In addition to the talks which led to the specific agreements I have listed, I also had full, very frank, and extensive discussions with General Secretary Brezhnev and his colleagues about several parts of the world where American and Soviet interests have come in conflict.

With regard to the reduction of tensions in Europe, we recorded our intention of proceeding later this year with multilateral consultations looking toward a conference on security and cooperation in all of Europe. We have also jointly agreed to move forward with negotiations on mutual and balanced force reductions in central Europe.[78]

The problem of ending the Vietnam war, which engages the hopes of all Americans, was one of the most extensively discussed subjects on our agenda. It would only jeopardize the search for peace if I were to review here all that was said on the subject. I will simply say this: Each side obviously has its own point of view and its own approach to this very difficult issue. But at the same time, both the United States and the Soviet Union share an overriding desire to achieve a more stable peace in the world. I emphasize to you once again that this Administration has no higher goal, a goal that I know all of you share, than bringing the Vietnam war to an early and honorable end. We are ending the war in Vietnam, but we shall end it in a way which will not betray our friends, risk the lives of the courageous Americans still serving in

Vietnam, break faith with those held prisoners by the enemy, or stain the honor of the United States of America.

Another area where we had very full, frank, and extensive discussions was the Middle East. I reiterated the American people's commitment to the survival of the state of Israel and to a settlement just to all the countries in the area. Both sides stated in the communiqué[79] their intention to support the Jarring peace mission and other appropriate efforts to achieve this objective.

The final achievement of the Moscow conference was the signing of a landmark declaration entitled "Basic Principles of Mutual Relations Between the United States and the USSR."[80] As these 12 basic principles are put into practice, they can provide a solid framework for the future development of better American-Soviet relations.

They begin with the recognition that two nuclear nations, each of which has the power to destroy humanity, have no alternative but to coexist peacefully because in a nuclear war there would be no winners, only losers.

The basic principles commit both sides to avoid direct military confrontation and to exercise constructive leadership and restraint with respect to smaller conflicts in other parts of the world which could drag the major powers into war.

They disavow any intention to create spheres of influence or to conspire against the interests of any other nation—a point I would underscore by saying once again tonight that America values its ties with all nations—from our oldest allies in Europe and Asia, as I emphasized by my visit to Iran, to our good friends in the third world, and to our new relationship with the People's Republic of China.

The improvement of relations depends not only, of course, on words, but far more on actions. The principles to which we agreed in Moscow are like a road map. Now that the map has been laid out, it is up to each country to follow it. The United States intends to adhere to these principles. The leaders of the Soviet Union have indicated a similar intention.

However, we must remember that Soviet ideology still proclaims hostility to some of America's most basic values. The Soviet leaders remain committed to that ideology. Like the nation they lead, they are and they will continue to be totally dedicated competitors of the United States of America.

As we shape our policies for the period ahead, therefore, we must maintain our defenses at an adequate level until there is mutual agreement to limit forces. The time-tested policies of vigilance and firmness which have brought us to this summit are the only ones that can safely

[79] Document 10 at note 52.
[80] Document 11.

carry us forward to further progress in reaching agreements to reduce the danger of war.

Our successes in the strategic arms talks and in the Berlin negotiations,[81] which opened the road to Moscow, came about because over the past 3 years we have consistently refused proposals for unilaterally abandoning the ABM, unilaterally pulling back our forces from Europe, and drastically cutting the defense budget. The Congress deserves the appreciation of the American people for having the courage to vote such proposals down and to maintain the strength America needs to protect its interests.

As we continue the strategic arms talks, seeking a permanent offensive weapons treaty, we must bear the lessons of the earlier talks well in mind.

By the same token, we must stand steadfastly with our NATO partners if negotiations leading to a new détente and a mutual reduction of forces in Europe are to be productive. Maintaining the strength, integrity, and steadfastness of our free world alliances is the foundation on which all of our other initiatives for peace and security in the world must rest. As we seek better relations with those who have been our adversaries, we will not let down our friends and allies around the world.

And in this period we must keep our economy vigorous and competitive if the opening for greater East-West trade is to mean anything at all, and if we do not wish to be shouldered aside in world markets by the growing potential of the economies of Japan, Western Europe, the Soviet Union, and the People's Republic of China. For America to continue its role of helping to build a more peaceful world, we must keep America number one economically in the world.

We must maintain our own momentum of domestic innovation, growth, and reform if the opportunities for joint action with the Soviets are to fulfill their promise. As we seek agreements to build peace abroad, we must keep America moving forward at home.

Most importantly, if the new age we seek is ever to become a reality, we must keep America strong in spirit—a nation proud of its greatness as a free society, confident of its mission in the world. Let us be committed to our way of life as wholeheartedly as the Communist leaders with whom we seek a new relationship are committed to their system. Let us always be proud to show in our words and actions what we know in our hearts—that we believe in America.

These are just some of the challenges of peace. They are in some ways even more difficult than the challenges of war. But we are equal to them. As we meet them, we will be able to go forward and explore the sweeping possibilities for peace which this season of summits has now opened up for the world.

81 Cf. *A.F.R., 1971*, no. 38.

For decades, America has been locked in hostile confrontation with the two great Communist powers, the Soviet Union and the People's Republic of China. We were engaged with the one at many points and almost totally isolated from the other, but our relationships with both had reached a deadly impasse. All three countries were victims of the kind of bondage about which George Washington long ago warned in these words: "The nation which indulges toward another [an] habitual hatred is a slave to its own animosity."[82]

But now in the brief space of 4 months, these journeys to Peking[83] and to Moscow have begun to free us from perpetual confrontation. We have moved toward better understanding, mutual respect, and point-by-point settlement of differences with both the major Communist powers.

This one series of meetings has not rendered an imperfect world suddenly perfect. There still are deep philosophical differences; there still are parts of the world in which age-old hatreds persist. The threat of war has not been eliminated—it has been reduced. We are making progress toward a world in which leaders of nations will settle their differences by negotiation, not by force, and in which they learn to live with their differences so that their sons will not have to die for those differences.

It was particularly fitting that this trip, aimed at building such a world, should have concluded in Poland.[84]

No country in the world has suffered more from war than Poland has—and no country has more to gain from peace. The faces of the people who gave us such a heartwarming welcome in Warsaw yesterday, and again this morning and this afternoon, told an eloquent story of suffering in the past and of hope for peace in the future. One could see it in their faces. It made me more determined than ever that America must do all in its power to help that hope come true for all people.

As we continue that effort, our unity of purpose and action will be all-important.

For the summits of 1972 have not belonged just to one person or one party or to one branch of our Government alone. Rather they are part of a great national journey for peace. Every American can claim a share in the credit for the success of that journey so far, and every American has a major stake in its success for the future.

An unparalleled opportunity has been placed in America's hands. Never has there been a time when hope was more justified or when complacency was more dangerous. We have made a good beginning.

---

[82] The original quotation from Washington's Farewell Address reads: "The Nation which indulges toward another an habitual hatred or an habitual fondness is in some degree a slave. It is a slave to its animosity or to its affection. . . ."

[83] Documents 53-56.

[84] Cf. Document 21.

And because we have begun, history now lays upon us a special obligation to see it through. We can seize this moment or we can lose it; we can make good this opportunity to build a new structure of peace in the world, or let it slip away. Together, therefore, let us seize the moment so that our children and the world's children live free of the fears and free of the hatreds that have been the lot of mankind through the centuries.

Then the historians of some future age will write of the year 1972, not that this was the year America went up to the summit and then down to the depths of the valley again—but that this was the year when America helped to lead the world up out of the lowlands of constant war, and onto the high plateau of lasting peace.

B. The ABM Treaty, the Interim Agreement, and the Beginning of SALT II.

1. The Background.

[The Treaty and Interim Agreement signed by President Nixon and General Secretary Brezhnev in Moscow on May 26, 1972 completed a diplomatic process that reached back into the mid-1960s. Perturbed by signs that the U.S.S.R. had embarked on a long-term buildup of its offensive missile strength and was also commencing the deployment of an anti-ballistic missile (ABM) defense system, the United States had begun at that time to urge that the two powers negotiate an agreement whereby they would mutually refrain from extending the arms race into this new area. In the absence of Soviet agreement to the holding of exploratory talks on a limitation of strategic arms, the United States had determined in 1967 to deploy its own "light" ABM system, known as "Sentinel"; and the Nixon administration in 1969 had adopted a modified ABM program under the name of "Safeguard" that was intended to provide for local defense of selected intercontinental ballistic missile (ICBM) sites plus an area defense for the protection of U.S. bomber bases and command and control authorities. Of the twelve ABM sites that were intended to make up the full Safeguard program, the construction of a site at Grand Forks, North Dakota, was about 80 percent complete by the beginning of 1972, and a second site at Malmstrom Air Force Base, Montana, was scheduled for completion in early 1976.[85]

[85] *Documents, 1967*, pp. 74-81; same, *1968-69*, pp. 83-7; Laird Posture Statement, FY 1973, p. 76. For more detailed discussion of arms control matters, cf. Nixon Report, 1972, pp. 171-81; same, 1973, pp. 194-208; Rogers Report, 1972, pp. 81-90.

Although bilateral Strategic Arms Limitation Talks (SALT) between U.S. and Soviet representatives had eventually been initiated in late 1969, they had not as yet resulted in any agreement to curb the deployment of either defensive or offensive strategic armaments. Continuing the long-term expansion of its offensive armory of ICBM's and submarine-launched ballistic missiles (SLBMs), the U.S.S.R. had also introduced a variety of technical improvements which, President Nixon had repeatedly warned, raised serious doubt about its long-range intentions. "The Soviet Union," the President wrote in his "State of the World" report for 1972, "is continuing to create strategic capabilities beyond a level which by any reasonable standard already seems sufficient. It is therefore inevitable that we ask whether the Soviet Union seeks the numbers and types of forces needed to attack and destroy vital elements of our own strategic forces."[86]

The United States had not, thus far, attempted to match the growing Soviet missile armory on a numerical basis. Its own strategic offensive forces, which included "1,000 MINUTEMAN missiles, 54 TITAN missiles, 455 B-52 aircraft (26 squadrons), 72 FB-111 aircraft (four squadrons), and 656 POLARIS and POSEIDON missiles carried in 41 nuclear submarines,"[87] still seemed sufficient for any eventuality and, moreover, were being continuously strengthened through the replacement of older Minuteman and Polaris missiles with the more advanced Minuteman III and Poseidon missiles equipped with multiple independently targetable reentry vehicles (MIRVs). Yet Washington displayed increasing concern about the steady growth of the Soviet offensive missile armory, which continued to increase at an average rate of over 200 land-based and 100 sea-based missiles a year[88] and, by the end of 1971, had already reached a total of 1,520 ICBMs (to the United States' 1,054) and 500 SLBMs (to the United States' 656). "We are approaching a crucial point in our strategic arms programs," President Nixon warned early in 1972. "If the Soviet Union continues to expand strategic forces, compensating U.S. programs will be mandatory ... under no circumstances will I permit the further erosion of the strategic balance with the USSR."[89]

Although the United States still planned no important addition to its own strategic offensive forces, it continued (in the words of Secretary of Defense Melvin R. Laird) "to move forward with planned improvements to all elements of our deterrent in light of the continuing momentum of the Soviet threat." In addition, Wash-

[86] Nixon Report, 1972, p. 159.
[87] Laird Posture Statement, FY 1973, p. 67.
[88] Kissinger statement, June 15, 1972, in *Documents on Disarmament, 1972*, p. 301.
[89] Nixon Report, 1972, p. 160.

ington was already looking ahead to a new generation of offensive weapon systems that might be needed by the late 1970s or early 1980s. The budget of the Department of Defense for the fiscal year 1973 provided for vigorous development of two such systems, at a combined cost slightly under $1.4 billion. One of these was a new Undersea Long-Range Missile System (ULMS), later dubbed "Trident," with a wider cruising range and a larger missile capacity than the existing Polaris submarines, which was scheduled for initial deployment in 1978. The other was the supersonic B-1 intercontinental manned bomber, already in process of development as an eventual replacement for the aging B-52 bomber fleet.[90]

In the meantime, the United States continued to emphasize its preference for limiting the arms race through "a combination of mutual restraint and an agreement in SALT."[91] Thus far in the SALT talks, however, the U.S.S.R. had shown only a rather tepid interest in agreements that would curb the growth of its strategic offensive weapon systems. After failing in an initial attempt to persuade the United States to cut back the American forward-based aircraft and carrier forces, by early 1971 the Soviet negotiators had taken the position "that only the ABM's should be limited, and that offensive systems should be left aside." The United States, however, saw serious flaws in a plan that would "limit our option of developing the ABM system without at the same time checking the growth of the Soviet offensive threat." In the American view, as Dr. Kissinger later explained, "the still incipient ABM systems on both sides were far from the most dynamic or dangerous factors in the strategic equation. It was the Soviet offensive programs . . . which we felt constituted the most urgent issue."[92]

Exchanges between President Nixon and the Soviet leaders during the spring of 1971 had resulted in a compromise on this particular issue. As announced May 20, 1971, the two governments agreed "to concentrate this year [1971] on working out an agreement for the limitation of the deployment of anti-ballistic missile systems (ABMs)," but also to agree concurrently on "certain measures with respect to the limitation of offensive strategic weapons." In other words, according to President Nixon's later interpretation, "we would concentrate the negotiations on a permanent treaty limiting ABM systems, while working out an Interim Agreement freezing only certain strategic offensive systems and leaving aside other systems for consideration in a further agreement."[93]

Still to be determined, under this arrangement, were the level of

[90] Laird Posture Statement, FY 1973, pp. 67-71.
[91] Nixon Report, 1972, 160.
[92] Same as note 88.
[93] A.F.R., 1971, no. 21; Nixon Report, 1973, p. 199.

ABM defense to be allowed the two sides, and the choice of offensive weapons to be included in the interim freeze. Discussion of these vital matters occupied the SALT negotiators for another year, continuing right up to the time of the Moscow summit in May 1972. By early 1972, the two governments were broadly agreed that (1) each party would be limited to two ABM sites, one for its national capital and one for the protection of an ICBM launcher site; (2) the interim freeze would include both sides' ICBMs; but (3) it would *not* include bombers and so-called forward-based systems, in which the United States held an advantage. The crucial question was whether or not the freeze would also extend to submarine-launched ballistic missiles, a point to which the U.S. Joint Chiefs of Staff attached essential importance. Once again, Dr. Kissinger later reported, the President "used his direct channel to the Soviet leaders, this time to urge the inclusion of missile-launching submarines in the offensive agreement. After a long period of hesitation, the Soviet leaders agreed in principle at the end of April [1972]. Final details were worked out in Moscow between the President and the Soviet leaders" even while the last technicalities were being smoothed away by the two SALT delegations in Helsinki.[94]]

2. The Texts.

[The provisions of the ABM Treaty, the Interim Agreement and Protocol, and the various agreed and unagreed interpretations put forward in the course of negotiation were exhaustively analyzed in an official report of the Secretary of State and were also explained at length by Dr. Kissinger, Secretary Rogers, and Ambassador Gerard C. Smith (Director of the U.S. Arms Control and Disarmament Agency and leader of the SALT negotiating team) in appearances before congressional committee members.[95] Material drawn from their statements is essential to the comprehension of these extraordinarily intricate agreements.]

---

[94] Kissinger statement, June 15, 1972, in *Documents on Disarmament, 1972*, p. 303; on the concluding negotiations, see also Kissinger-Smith news conference, May 26, 1972, in same, pp. 207-17, and Kalb, *Kissinger*, pp. 319-29.

[95] The Secretary of State's report of June 10, 1972 (S. Ex. L, 92d Cong., 2d sess.) appears in *Documents on Disarmament, 1972*, pp. 267-86; statements by Kissinger, Rogers, and Smith appear in same, pp. 295-309, 311-18, 422-9, 488-97, and 518-28. (Much of this material is also available in *Presidential Documents* and *Bulletin.*) Annexed to the report of the Secretary of State are various "Agreed Interpretations, Common Understandings, and Unilateral Statements" which, though not formally a part of the Treaty or Interim Agreement, are also appended to the official U.S. texts as cited in notes 96 and 104.

a. The ABM Treaty.

[The essential feature of the Treaty on the Limitation of Anti-Ballistic Missile Systems (Document 13) was a permanent restriction (barring amendment of the treaty or withdrawal by one of the parties) on the deployment of ABM systems by either party. Not only did each party renounce the establishment of a nationwide ABM defense; it also agreed to limit itself to two ABM sites, situated at least 1,300 kilometers apart, one centered on its national capital and the other on a single ICBM launcher site (for the United States, the ICBM base at Grand Forks, North Dakota). Compliance with the treaty's provisions was to be observed by "national technical means of verification" (i.e., reconnaissance satellites), and each party undertook not to interfere with the other's verification efforts so long as these were conducted in a legal manner. The parties also agreed to establish a Standing Consultative Commission to monitor compliance with the treaty and, when appropriate, consider further measures aimed at limiting strategic arms.]

(13) Treaty Between the United States of America and the Union of Soviet Socialist Republics on the Limitation of Anti-Ballistic Missile Systems, Signed in Moscow May 26, 1972. [96]

(Complete Text)

The United States of America and the Union of Soviet Socialist Republics, hereinafter referred to as the Parties,

Proceeding from the premise that nuclear war would have devastating consequences for all mankind,

Considering that effective measures to limit anti-ballistic missile systems would be a substantial factor in curbing the race in strategic offensive arms and would lead to a decrease in the risk of outbreak of war involving nuclear weapons,

Proceeding from the premise that the limitation of anti-ballistic missile systems, as well as certain agreed measures with respect to the limitation of strategic offensive arms,[97] would contribute to the creation of more favorable conditions for further negotiations on limiting strategic arms,

Mindful of their obligations under Article VI of the Treaty on the Non-Proliferation of Nuclear Weapons,[98]

Declaring their intention to achieve at the earliest possible date the

---

[96] TIAS 7503 (23 UST 3435); entered into force Oct. 3, 1972.
[97] Cf. Document 14.
[98] Cf. note 32, above.

cessation of the nuclear arms race and to take effective measures toward reductions in strategic arms, nuclear disarmament, and general and complete disarmament,

Desiring to contribute to the relaxation of international tension and the strengthening of trust between States,

Have agreed as follows:

ARTICLE I

1. Each Party undertakes to limit anti-ballistic missile (ABM) systems and to adopt other measures in accordance with the provisions of this Treaty.

2. Each Party undertakes not to deploy ABM systems for a defense of the territory of its country and not to provide a base for such a defense, and not to deploy ABM systems for defense of an individual region except as provided for in Article III of this Treaty.

ARTICLE II

1. For the purposes of this Treaty an ABM system is a system to counter strategic ballistic missiles or their elements in flight trajectory, currently consisting of:

(a) ABM interceptor missiles, which are interceptor missiles constructed and deployed for an ABM role, or of a type tested in an ABM mode;

(b) ABM launchers, which are launchers constructed and deployed for launching ABM interceptor missiles; and

(c) ABM radars, which are radars constructed and deployed for an ABM role, or a type tested in an ABM mode.

2. The ABM system components listed in paragraph 1 of this Article include those which are:

(a) operational;
(b) under construction;
(c) undergoing testing;
(d) undergoing overhaul, repair or conversion; or
(e) mothballed.

ARTICLE III

Each Party undertakes not to deploy ABM systems or their components except that:

(a) within one ABM system deployment area having a radius of one hundred and fifty kilometers and centered on the Party's national capital, a Party may deploy: (1) no more than one hundred ABM launchers and no more than one hundred ABM interceptor missiles at launch sites, and (2) ABM radars within no more than six ABM radar complexes, the area of each complex being circular and having a diameter of no more than three kilometers; and

(b) within one ABM system deployment area having a radius of one hundred and fifty kilometers and containing ICBM silo launchers, a Party may deploy: (1) no more than one hundred ABM launchers and no more than one hundred ABM interceptor missiles at launch sites, (2) two large phased-array ABM radars comparable in potential to corresponding ABM radars operational or under construction on the date of signature of the Treaty in an ABM system deployment area containing ICBM silo launchers, and (3) no more than eighteen ABM radars each having a potential less than the potential of the smaller of the above-mentioned two large phased-array ABM radars.[99]

ARTICLE IV

The limitations provided for in Article III shall not apply to ABM systems or their components used for development or testing, and located within current or additionally agreed test ranges. Each Party may have no more than a total of fifteen ABM launchers at test ranges.

ARTICLE V

1. Each Party undertakes not to develop, test, or deploy ABM systems or components which are sea-based, air-based, space-based, or mobile land-based.

2. Each Party undertakes not to develop, test, or deploy ABM launchers for launching more than one ABM interceptor missile at a time from each launcher, nor to modify deployed launchers to provide them with such a capability, nor to develop, test, or deploy automatic or semi-automatic or other similar systems for rapid reload of ABM launchers.

ARTICLE VI

To enhance assurance of the effectiveness of the limitations on ABM

---

[99] The series of agreed statements initialed by the heads of the delegations on May 26, 1972 includes the following additional stipulation: "The Parties understand that the center of the ABM system deployment area centered on the national capital and the center of the ABM system deployment area containing ICBM silo launchers for each party shall be separated by no less than thirteen hundred kilometers" (23 UST 3456). In this connection, the United States gave notice that its ABM system deployment area for defense of ICBM silo launchers would be centered in the Grand Forks (North Dakota) ICBM silo launcher deployment area (same, p. 3457).

systems and their components provided by this Treaty, each Party undertakes:

(a) not to give missiles, launchers, or radars, other than ABM interceptor missiles, ABM launchers, or ABM radars, capabilities to counter strategic ballistic missiles or their elements in flight trajectory, and not to test them in an ABM mode; and

(b) not to deploy in the future radars for early warning of strategic ballistic missile attack except at locations along the periphery of its national territory and oriented outward.

ARTICLE VII

Subject to the provisions of this Treaty, modernization and replacement of ABM systems or their components may be carried out.

ARTICLE VIII

ABM systems or their components in excess of the numbers or outside the areas specified in this Treaty, as well as ABM systems or their components prohibited by this Treaty, shall be destroyed or dismantled under agreed procedures within the shortest possible agreed period of time.

ARTICLE IX

To assure the viability and effectiveness of this Treaty, each Party undertakes not to transfer to other States, and not to deploy outside its national territory, ABM systems or their components limited by this Treaty.

ARTICLE X

Each Party undertakes not to assume any international obligations which would conflict with this Treaty.

ARTICLE XI

The Parties undertake to continue active negotiations for limitations on strategic offensive arms.

ARTICLE XII

1. For the purpose of providing assurance of compliance with the provisions of this Treaty, each Party shall use national technical means

of verification at its disposal in a manner consistent with generally recognized principles of international law.

2. Each Party undertakes not to interfere with the national technical means of verification of the other Party operating in accordance with paragraph 1 of this Article.

3. Each Party undertakes not to use deliberate concealment measures which impede verification by national technical means of compliance with the provisions of this Treaty. This obligation shall not require changes in current construction, assembly, conversion, or overhaul practices.

ARTICLE XIII

1. To promote the objectives and implementation of the provisions of this Treaty, the Parties shall establish promptly a Standing Consultative Commission, within the framework of which they will:

(a) consider questions concerning compliance with the obligations assumed and related situations which may be considered ambiguous;

(b) provide on a voluntary basis such information as either Party considers necessary to assure confidence in compliance with the obligations assumed;

(c) consider questions involving unintended interference with national technical means of verification;

(d) consider possible changes in the strategic situation which have a bearing on the provisions of this Treaty;

(e) agree upon procedures and dates for destruction or dismantling of ABM systems or their components in cases provided for by the provisions of this Treaty;

(f) consider, as appropriate, possible proposals for further increasing the viability of this Treaty, including proposals for amendments in accordance with the provisions of this Treaty;

(g) consider, as appropriate, proposals for further measures aimed at limiting strategic arms.

2. The Parties through consultation shall establish, and may amend as appropriate, Regulations for the Standing Consultative Commission governing procedures, composition and other relevant matters.[100]

ARTICLE XIV

1. Each Party may propose amendments to this Treaty. Agreed amendments shall enter into force in accordance with the procedures governing the entry into force of this Treaty.

2. Five years after entry into force of this Treaty, and at five-year

[100] Cf. Document 17b and note 148.

intervals thereafter, the Parties shall together conduct a review of this Treaty.

ARTICLE XV

1. This Treaty shall be of unlimited duration.
2. Each Party shall, in exercising its national sovereignty, have the right to withdraw from this Treaty if it decides that extraordinary events related to the subject matter of this Treaty have jeopardized its supreme interests. It shall give notice of its decision to the other Party six months prior to withdrawal from the Treaty. Such notice shall include a statement of the extraordinary events the notifying Party regards as having jeopardized its supreme interests.

ARTICLE XVI

1. This Treaty shall be subject to ratification in accordance with the constitutional procedures of each Party. The Treaty shall enter into force on the day of the exchange of instruments of ratification.[101]
2. This Treaty shall be registered pursuant to Article 102 of the Charter of the United Nations.

Done at Moscow on May 26, 1972, in two copies, each in the English and Russian languages, both texts being equally authentic.

FOR THE UNITED STATES
OF AMERICA:

FOR THE UNION OF SOVIET
SOCIALIST REPUBLICS:

(*Signed*) Richard Nixon

(*Signed*) L. I. Brezhnev

President of the United States
of America

General Secretary of the
Central Committee of the CPSU
[Communist Party of the
Soviet Union]

b. The Interim Agreement

[Having accepted a permanent limitation on their ABM defenses, the two parties by the provisions of the Interim Agreement on Certain Measures with Respect to the Limitation of Strategic Offensive Arms (Document 14) undertook the further obligation to limit the growth of their strategic offensive weaponry in certain

---

[101] The treaty entered into force Oct. 3, 1972; cf. below at note 125.

respects during the next five years while continuing the search for more complete measures limiting strategic offensive arms. The essential function of the Interim Agreement, as Dr. Kissinger pointed out, was to "freeze the numbers of strategic offensive missiles on both sides at approximately the levels currently operational and under construction." Although the U.S.S.R. would thus retain an assured numerical advantage in both land-based and submarine-launched missiles, it would be prevented from further widening the gap; and in accepting a "freeze" on heavy ICBM launchers, it agreed to limit those weapons that were considered most threatening to the American strategic forces. At the same time, Dr. Kissinger emphasized, the United States was left free to pursue its own "current and planned strategic offensive programs." Specifically, the agreement would not interfere with the ongoing conversion of U.S. missiles from single to multiple warheads (MIRVs); nor would it stand in the way of new weapon systems like the B-1 strategic bomber or the proposed Trident submarine system, which were planned for deployment after the expiration date of the five-year Interim Agreement.[102]

The "freeze" on the two powers' offensive strategic missiles actually consisted of three separate but interrelated elements, corresponding to the first three articles of the Interim Agreement:

(1) By Article I, the parties undertook not to start construction of additional fixed land-based ICBM launchers after July 1, 1972. The effect of this article, as interpreted by U.S. authorities, was to limit the number of land-based ICBM launchers available to the two parties during the lifetime of the agreement (excluding those for testing and training purposes) to the numbers that were operational or under construction on May 26, 1972—viz., 1,054 for the United States and 1,618 for the U.S.S.R.

(2) By Article II, the parties undertook not to convert land-based launchers for light ICBMs, or ICBMs of older types, into land-based launchers for heavy ICBMs such as the U.S. Titan or the Soviet SS-7, SS-8, or SS-9.

(3) By Article III, the parties undertook to place numerical limits on their respective submarine-launched ballistic missile (SLBM) launchers and modern ballistic missile submarines. In principle, these items would be limited to the numbers operational or under construction on the date of signature—amounting, in SLBMs, to 656 for the United States and 740 for the U.S.S.R. These limitations, however, were not absolute because the parties would also be permitted to increase their SLBM strength within certain limits—provided, however, that any such expansion was compensated by the retirement of equal numbers of older ICBM launchers or of

---

[102] White House briefing, June 15, 1972, in *Documents on Disarmament, 1972*, p. 304.

ballistic missile launchers on older submarines. The upper limits of this permitted expansion were set forth in a Protocol to the Interim Agreement which stated that the United States would be entitled to a maximum of 710 SLBMs and 44 modern ballistic missile submarines, while the U.S.S.R. would be permitted a maximum of 950 SLBMs and 62 modern ballistic missile submarines.

This complicated arrangement subsequently gave rise to a good deal of confusion, in part because not all of the President's and Dr. Kissinger's exchanges with the Soviet Government were included in the official record provided to the Congress. Responding to later rumors of possible "secret deals" at the Moscow summit, Dr. Kissinger (by this time Secretary of State) offered two important clarifications at a news conference on June 24, 1974:

(1) Although the United States insisted for reasons of "symmetry" on reserving the right to retire its 54 land-based Titan ICBMs and increase its SLBM force by an equivalent number of missile launchers (from 656 to 710), it had never intended to exercise this option, and the President had so informed the Soviets on the last day of the summit conference.

(2) Any possibility that the U.S.S.R. might try to evade its numerical limit of 950 SLBMs by deploying modern SLBM launchers on its obsolescent G-class diesel-powered submarines had been eliminated through the signature of an agreed "interpretive statement" by Dr. Kissinger and Soviet Ambassador Anatoly F. Dobrynin in June 1972.[103]

As with the ABM Treaty, verification of compliance with the Interim Agreement was to be effected by "national technical means" without interference by the other party. The agreement would enter into force concurrently with the ABM Treaty, and would remain in force for five years unless replaced earlier by a permanent agreement.]

(14) Interim Agreement Between the United States of America and the Union of Soviet Socialist Republics on Certain Measures with Respect to the Limitation of Strategic Offensive Arms, Signed in Moscow May 26, 1972.[104]

(Complete Text)

The United States of America and the Union of Soviet Socialist Republics, hereinafter referred to as the Parties,

---

[103] Kissinger news conference, June 24, 1974, in *Bulletin*, July 22, 1974, pp. 133-45. For further discussion, cf. Kissinger news conference, June 26, 1974. in same, July 29, 1974, pp. 198-201; also Leslie H. Gelb, "Washington Dateline: The Story of a Flap," *Foreign Policy*, no. 16, Fall 1974, pp. 165-81.
[104] TIAS 7504 (23 UST 3462); entered into force Oct. 3, 1972.

Convinced that the Treaty on the Limitation of Anti-Ballistic Missile Systems[105] and this Interim Agreement on Certain Measures with Respect to the Limitation of Strategic Offensive Arms will contribute to the creation of more favorable conditions for active negotiations on limiting strategic arms as well as to the relaxation of international tension and the strengthening of trust between States,

Taking into account the relationship between strategic offensive and defensive arms,

Mindful of their obligations under Article VI of the Treaty on the Non-Proliferation of Nuclear Weapons,[106]

Have agreed as follows:

ARTICLE I

The Parties undertake not to start construction of additional fixed land-based intercontinental ballistic missile (ICBM) launchers after July 1, 1972.

ARTICLE II

The Parties undertake not to convert land-based launchers for light ICBMs, or for ICBMs of older types deployed prior to 1964, into land-based launchers for heavy ICBMs of types deployed after that time.

ARTICLE III

The Parties undertake to limit submarine-launched ballistic missile (SLBM) launchers and modern ballistic missile submarines to the numbers operational and under construction on the date of signature of this Interim Agreement, and in addition to launchers and submarines constructed under procedures established by the Parties as replacements for an equal number of ICBM launchers of older types deployed prior to 1964 or for launchers on older submarines.

ARTICLE IV

Subject to the provisions of this Interim Agreement, modernization and replacement of strategic offensive ballistic missiles and launchers covered by this Interim Agreement may be undertaken.[107]

[105] Document 13.
[106] Cf. note 32.
[107] The series of agreed statements initialed by the heads of the delegations on May 26, 1972 includes the following additional stipulation: "The Parties understand that in the process of modernization and replacement the dimensions of land-based ICBM silo launchers will not be significantly increased" (23 UST 3478).

ARTICLE V

1. For the purpose of providing assurance of compliance with the provisions of this Interim Agreement, each Party shall use national technical means of verification at its disposal in a manner consistent with generally recognized principles of international law.

2. Each Party undertakes not to interfere with the national technical means of verification of the other Party operating in accordance with paragraph 1 of this Article.

3. Each Party undertakes not to use deliberate concealment measures which impede verification by national technical means of compliance with the provisions of this Interim Agreement. This obligation shall not require changes in current construction, assembly, conversion, or overhaul practices.

ARTICLE VI

To promote the objectives and implementation of the provisions of this Interim Agreement, the Parties shall use the Standing Consultative Commission established under Article XIII of the Treaty on the Limitation of Anti-Ballistic Missile Systems[108] in accordance with the provisions of that Article.

ARTICLE VII

The Parties undertake to continue active negotiations for limitations on strategic offensive arms.[109] The obligations provided for in this Interim Agreement shall not prejudice the scope or terms of the limitations on strategic offensive arms which may be worked out in the course of further negotiations.

ARTICLE VIII

1. This Interim Agreement shall enter into force upon exchange of written notices of acceptance by each Party, which exchange shall take place simultaneously with the exchange of instruments of ratification of the Treaty on the Limitation of Anti-Ballistic Missile Systems.[110]

2. This Interim Agreement shall remain in force for a period of five years unless replaced earlier by an agreement on more complete measures limiting strategic offensive arms. It is the objective of the Parties to conduct active follow-on negotiations with the aim of concluding such an agreement as soon as possible.

[108] Cf. Document 13 at note 100.
[109] Cf. Document 17.
[110] The Interim Agreement entered into force Oct. 3, 1972; cf. below at note 125.

3. Each Party shall, in exercising its national sovereignty, have the right to withdraw from this Interim Agreement if it decides that extraordinary events related to the subject matter of this Interim Agreement have jeopardized its supreme interests. It shall give notice of its decision to the other Party six months prior to withdrawal from this Interim Agreement. Such notice shall include a statement of the extraordinary events the notifying Party regards as having jeopardized its supreme interests.

Done at Moscow on May 26, 1972, in two copies, each in the English and Russian languages, both texts being equally authentic.

FOR THE UNITED STATES   FOR THE UNION OF SOVIET
OF AMERICA: SOCIALIST REPUBLICS:

(*Signed*) Richard Nixon   (*Signed*) L. I. Brezhnev

President of the United States   General Secretary of the
of America   Central Committee of the CPSU

PROTOCOL

TO THE INTERIM AGREEMENT BETWEEN
THE UNITED STATES OF AMERICA AND THE UNION OF SOVIET
SOCIALIST REPUBLICS ON CERTAIN MEASURES WITH RESPECT
TO THE LIMITATION OF STRATEGIC OFFENSIVE ARMS

The United States of America and the Union of Soviet Socialist Republics, hereinafter referred to as the Parties,
Having agreed on certain limitations relating to submarine-launched ballistic missile launchers and modern ballistic missile submarines, and to replacement procedures, in the Interim Agreement,
Have agreed as follows:
The Parties understand that, under Article III of the Interim Agreement, for the period during which that Agreement remains in force:
The US may have no more than 710 ballistic missile launchers on submarines (SLBMs) and no more than 44 modern ballistic missile submarines. The Soviet Union may have no more than 950 ballistic missile launchers on submarines and no more than 62 modern ballistic missile submarines.
Additional ballistic missile launchers on submarines up to the above-mentioned levels, in the U.S.—over 656 ballistic missile launchers on nuclear-powered submarines, and in the U.S.S.R.—over 740 ballistic missile launchers on nuclear-powered submarines, operational and

under construction, may become operational as replacements for equal numbers of ballistic missile launchers of older types deployed prior to 1964 or of ballistic missile launchers on older submarines.

The deployment of modern SLBMs on any submarine, regardless of type, will be counted against the total level of SLBMs permitted for the U.S. and the U.S.S.R.

This Protocol shall be considered an integral part of the Interim Agreement.

Done at Moscow this 26th day of May, 1972.

FOR THE UNITED STATES
OF AMERICA

FOR THE UNION OF SOVIET
SOCIALIST REPUBLICS

(*Signed*) Richard Nixon

(*Signed*) L. I. Brezhnev

President of the United States
of America

General Secretary of the
Central Committee of the CPSU

3. Approval and Entry Into Force.

[Immediately on his return to Washington, the President gave notice that he would submit the ABM Treaty for Senate approval and, in addition, intended to submit the Interim Agreement to both houses of Congress "for concurrence." "Agreements as important as these," Mr. Nixon said, could be undertaken "only on a basis of full partnership between the executive and legislative branches of the Government."[111] In parallel communications addressed on June 13 to the Senate and to the Speaker of the House of Representatives, the President asked for Senate support of both the Treaty and the Interim Agreement (Document 15), while recommending that the House support the Interim Agreement.[112] As noted in the preceding chapter, the administration did not consider that Congress had any regular right of review over executive agreements, as distinguished from treaties.[113] Apart from the special importance of the U.S.-Soviet Interim Agreement, however, the administration was undoubtedly aware that the 1961 Arms Control and Disarmament Act prohibited any action that would obligate the United States to disarm or limit its military strength "except pursuant to the treaty making power of the President or unless authorized by further affirmative legislation of the Congress. . . ."[114]

[111] Document 12 at note 76.
[112] *Documents on Disarmament, 1972*, pp. 288-9.
[113] Cf. note 41 to Chapter I.
[114] Sec. 33, Public Law 87-297, Sept. 26, 1961.

The presidential communications to the two houses were also noteworthy for their insistence on the need to continue the development of U.S. military power within the limits laid down by the Moscow accords. Although these agreements represented "an important first step in checking the arms race," the President said, they were "only a first step" and did not "close off all avenues of strategic competition." Continuation of "a sound strategic modernization program," Mr. Nixon asserted, was as essential as ever, "to maintain our security and to ensure that more permanent and comprehensive arms limitation agreements can be reached."

Such intimations were disconcerting to those who had seen the Moscow agreements as the beginning of a definite downturn in the arms race. Not all of the President's own advisers appeared to think the moment well chosen for an invigoration of the U.S. arms program. The Joint Chiefs of Staff, however, made clear that their support of the Moscow arrangements was contingent on precise assurances that there would be no "degradation" of the national security posture;[115] while Secretary of Defense Laird particularly stressed the need to persevere with the strategic programs already included in the defense budget for Fiscal Year 1973. Singled out for special emphasis were the Trident undersea long-range missile system (ULMS) and the B-1 manned bomber, both of which were scheduled to come to fruition shortly after the Interim Agreement expired in 1977.[116]

The question of approval of the Moscow agreements thus became enmeshed with that of the administration's ongoing military programs. Both the Moscow agreements and the military programs were indispensable, President Nixon continued to insist. Not only were the proposed military programs essential to U.S. security, he reiterated; the Russians clearly intended to press ahead in those armament categories that were not limited by the Moscow agreements, and he himself would never permit the United States to become the "second most powerful nation." Without the military programs, Mr. Nixon added, the chances for success in the next phase of SALT would be severely limited, since the U.S.S.R. would then have no incentive to agree on cutting back its own programs.[117]

Although the Senate Foreign Relations Committee voiced reser-

---

[115] Statement of Adm. Thomas H. Moorer to the Senate Armed Services Committee, June 20, 1972, in *Documents on Disarmament, 1972*, pp. 375-6.

[116] Statements to Senate Armed Services Committee, June 6, 1972, in same, pp. 262-3; cf. above at note 90.

[117] Congressional briefing, June 15, 1972, in *Documents on Disarmament, 1972*, pp. 293-5; news conference, June 22, 1972, in same, 406-8; news conference, June 29, 1972, in same, pp. 437-8; similarly American Legion speech, Chicago, Aug. 24, 1972, in *Public Papers, 1972*, pp. 799-800.

vations about this "bargaining-chip" approach,[118] consideration of the ABM Treaty was not directly affected. Unanimously approved by the Foreign Relations Committee on July 21, the treaty was endorsed by an 88 to 2 vote of the full Senate on August 3, 1972.[119]

Approval of the Interim Agreement and the accompanying Protocol gave rise to a more complex debate, not only because both houses of Congress were involved but also because the limitation of strategic offensive weapons was a more controversial subject than the limitation of ABM systems. Some interested Americans, among them a majority of the members of the Senate Foreign Relations Committee, inclined to think the United States already had enough strategic offensive weapons and that the moment was poorly chosen for proceeding "full steam ahead" with new weapon systems, as the administration was proposing.[120] But there were others in the Senate and elsewhere who felt less optimism about the current and prospective military balance, were disturbed by the disparities in the numerical limits under the Interim Agreement, and feared the United States might be sliding into a position of permanent strategic inferiority.

The strongest exponent of this viewpoint was Democratic Senator Henry M. Jackson of Washington, who scouted the favorable Foreign Relations Committee estimate of the Interim Agreement and joined with 23 (later 43) colleagues of both parties in submitting an amendment to the resolution of acceptance that aimed at discouraging any letup in U.S. strategic preparedness. Insisting on the vital importance of the "survivability" of U.S. strategic deterrent forces, the Jackson amendment in effect urged the President to try to negotiate a treaty in which the United States would *not* be limited to levels of intercontinental strategic forces inferior to those provided for the Soviet Union. Meanwhile, the amendment called for maintenance of "a vigorous research and development and modernization program as required by a prudent strategic posture."[121] With the support of the administration, which had not requested the amendment but found no serious fault with it, the Jackson amendment was accepted by a 56 to 35 vote of the Senate on September 14 and was included (with other, less noteworthy amendments) in the resolution of approval that was adopted by a

---

[118] S. Rept. 92-979, July 21, 1972, in *Documents on Disarmament, 1972*, pp. 506-14.

[119] Negative votes were cast by Senators James B. Allen (Democrat, Alabama) and James L. Buckley (Conservative-Republican, New York). For details see S. Ex. Rept. 92-28, July 21, 1972, in *Documents on Disarmament, 1972*, pp. 497-505; also Senate Foreign Relations Committee History, pp. 29-31.

[120] Same as note 118.

[121] *Documents on Disarmament, 1972*, pp. 546-7 and 652-3.

Senate vote of 88 to 2 on September 14[122] and a House vote of 307 to 4 on September 25, 1972.[123]

Soviet ratification procedures were completed shortly afterward with the approval of the two accords by the Supreme Soviet and the ratification of the ABM Treaty by Head of State Nikolai V. Podgorny on September 29, 1972. On September 30, in turn, President Nixon ratified the ABM Treaty on behalf of the United States and signed the Joint Congressional Resolution authorizing approval of the Interim Agreement and Protocol (Document 16).[124] The two accords entered into force simultaneously on October 3, 1972 as ratifications of the ABM Treaty were exchanged in Washington and President Nixon notified the Soviet Head of State of U.S. acceptance of the Interim Agreement and Protocol.[125]

Funds to implement the administration's recommendations with respect to the Trident submarine system and the B-1 bomber were duly included in the defense legislation enacted by Congress for the fiscal year 1973, although administration proposals were disregarded in one respect with the elimination of funds to construct an ABM site around Washington, D.C. This, however, was not a point to which the administration attached great importance. Less than two years later, the whole idea of having two ABM sites was abandoned with the signature on July 3, 1974, during President Nixon's second and last visit to Moscow, of a protocol to the ABM Treaty in which the two powers agreed to limit themselves to a single ABM site each, the U.S. site at Grand Forks and the Soviet site at Moscow.[126]]

(15) Transmission of the ABM Treaty and the Interim Agreement on Strategic Offensive Arms to the Congress: Message from President Nixon to the Senate, June 13, 1972. [127]

(Complete Text)

To the Senate of the United States:
 I transmit herewith the Treaty on the Limitation of Anti-Ballistic

---

[122] Negative votes were cast by Senators James B. Allen (Democrat, Alabama) and Ernest F. Hollings (Democrat, South Carolina). For details, see *Documents on Disarmament, 1972,* pp. 654-6 and 681-3; also Senate Foreign Relations Committee History, pp. 31-4.

[123] The House had previously approved on Aug. 18, 1972 a resolution of approval without any policy statement (cf. *Documents on Disarmament, 1972,* pp. 555-61 and 577).

[124] Signature statement in *Documents on Disarmament, 1972,* pp. 683-4.

[125] Same, 684-7; letter to Podgorny in *Presidential Documents,* Oct. 9, 1972, p. 1484.

[126] Cf. below at note 202.

[127] *Presidential Documents,* June 19, 1972, p. 1026.

Missile Systems and the Interim Agreement on Certain Measures with respect to the Limitation of Strategic Offensive Arms signed in Moscow on May 26, 1972.[128] Copies of these agreements are also being forwarded to the Speaker of the House of Representatives.[129] I ask the Senate's advice and consent to ratification of the Treaty, and an expression of support from both Houses of the Congress for the Interim Agreement on Strategic Offensive Arms.

These agreements, the product of a major effort of this administration, are a significant step into a new era of mutually agreed restraint and arms limitation between the two principal nuclear powers.

The provisions of the agreements are explained in detail in the Report of the Secretary of State, which I attach.[130] Their main effect is this: The ABM Treaty limits the deployment of anti-ballistic missile systems to two designated areas, and at a low level. The Interim Agreement limits the overall level of strategic offensive missile forces. Together the two agreements provide for a more stable strategic balance in the next several years than would be possible if strategic arms competition continued unchecked. This benefits not only the United States and the Soviet Union, but all the nations of the world.

The agreements are an important first step in checking the arms race, but only a first step; they do not close off all avenues of strategic competition. Just as the maintenance of a strong strategic posture was an essential element in the success of these negotiations, it is now equally essential that we carry forward a sound strategic modernization program to maintain our security and to ensure that more permanent and comprehensive arms limitation agreements can be reached.

The defense capabilities of the United States are second to none in the world today. I am determined that they shall remain so. The terms of the ABM Treaty and Interim Agreement will permit the United States to take the steps we deem necessary to maintain a strategic posture which protects our vital interests and guarantees our continued security.

Besides enhancing our national security, these agreements open the opportunity for a new and more constructive U.S.-Soviet relationship, characterized by negotiated settlement of differences, rather than by the hostility and confrontation of decades past.

These accords offer tangible evidence that mankind need not live forever in the dark shadow of nuclear war. They provide renewed hope that men and nations working together can succeed in building a lasting peace.

Because these agreements effectively serve one of this Nation's most cherished purposes—a more secure and peaceful world in which America's security is fully protected—I strongly recommend that the Senate

[128] Documents 13-14.
[129] *Documents on Disarmament, 1972*, pp. 288-9.
[130] Cf. note 95, above.

support them, and that its deliberations be conducted without delay.[131]

RICHARD NIXON

The White House
June 13, 1972

(16) Congressional Resolution Approving the Interim Agreement: Public Law 92-448, Approved September 30, 1972.[132]

(Complete Text)

JOINT RESOLUTION

Approval and authorization for the President of the United States to accept an Interim Agreement Between the United States of America and the Union of Soviet Socialist Republics on Certain Measures With Respect to the Limitation of Strategic Offensive Arms.

Resolved by the Senate and House of Representatives of the United States of America in Congress assembled, That the Congress hereby endorses those portions of the Declaration of Basic Principles of Mutual Relations Between the United States of America and the Union of Soviet Socialist Republics signed by President Nixon and General Secretary Brezhnev at Moscow on May 29, 1972,[133] which relate to the dangers of military confrontation and which read as follows:

"The United States of America and the Union of Soviet Socialist Republics attach major importance to preventing the development of situations capable of causing a dangerous exacerbation of their relations . . ." and "will do their utmost to avoid military confrontations and to prevent the outbreak of nuclear war" and "will always exercise restraint in their mutual relations," and "on outstanding issues will conduct" their discussions and negotiations "in a spirit of reciprocity, mutual accommodation and mutual benefit," and

"Both sides recognize that efforts to obtain unilateral advantage at the expense of the other, directly or indirectly, are inconsistent with these objectives," and

"The prerequisites for maintaining and strengthening peaceful relations between the United States of American and the Union of Soviet

---

[131]Cf. above at notes 119 and 122..
[132] H.J. Res. 92-448 (86 Stat. 746), approved by the Senate on Sept. 14 and by the House on Sept. 25, 1972 (cf. above at notes 122 and 123).
[133] Document 11.

Socialist Republics are the recognition of the security interests of the parties based on the principle of equality and the renunciation of the use or threat of force."

SEC. 2. The President is hereby authorized to approve on behalf of the United States the interim agreement between the United States of America and the Union of Soviet Socialist Republics on certain measures with respect to the limitation of strategic offensive arms, and the protocol related thereto, signed at Moscow on May 26, 1972, by Richard Nixon, President of the United States of America and Leonid I. Brezhnev, General Secretary of the Central Committee of the Communist Party of the Soviet Union.[134]

SEC. 3. The Government and the people of the United States ardently desire a stable international strategic balance that maintains peace and deters aggression. The Congress supports the stated policy of the United States that, were a more complete strategic offensive arms agreement not achieved within the five years of the interim agreement, and were the survivability of the strategic deterrent forces of the United States to be threatened as a result of such failure, this could jeopardize the supreme national interests of the United States; the Congress recognizes the difficulty of maintaining a stable strategic balance in a period of rapidly developing technology; the Congress recognizes the principle of United States-Soviet Union equality reflected in the antiballistic missile treaty,[135] and urges and requests the President to seek a future treaty that, inter alia, would not limit the United States to levels of intercontinental strategic forces inferior to the limits provided for the Soviet Union; and the Congress considers that the success of these agreements and the attainment of more permanent and comprehensive agreements are dependent upon the maintenance under present world conditions of a vigorous research and development and modernization program as required by a prudent strategic posture.

SEC. 4. The Congress hereby commends the President for having successfully concluded agreements with the Soviet Union limiting the production and deployment of antiballistic missiles and certain strategic offensive armaments, and it supports the announced intention of the President to seek further limits on the production and deployment of strategic armaments at future Strategic Arms Limitation Talks. At the same time, the Senate [sic] takes cognizance of the fact that agreements to limit the further escalation of the arms race are only preliminary steps, however important, toward the attainment of world stability and national security. The Congress therefore urges the President to seek at the earliest practicable moment Strategic Arms Reduction Talks (SART) with the Soviet Union, the People's Republic of

[134] Document 14.
[135] Document 13.

China, and other countries, and simultaneously to work toward reductions in conventional armaments, in order to bring about agreements for mutual decreases in the production and development of weapons of mass destruction so as to eliminate the threat of large-scale devastation and the ever-mounting costs of arms production and weapons modernization, thereby freeing world resources for constructive, peaceful use.

SEC. 5. Pursuant to paragraph six of the Declaration of Principles of Nixon and Brezhnev on May 29, 1972, which states that the United States and the Union of Soviet Socialist Republics: "will continue to make special efforts to limit strategic armaments. Whenever possible, they will conclude concrete agreements aimed at achieving these purposes"; Congress considers that the success of the interim agreement and the attainment of more permanent and comprehensive agreements are dependent upon the preservation of longstanding United States policy that neither the Soviet Union nor the United States should seek unilateral advantage by developing a first-strike potential.

Approved September 30, 1972.

4. The Beginning of SALT II.

[In concluding the ABM Treaty and Interim Agreement, the United States and the U.S.S.R. reaffirmed their general commitment to continue negotiations aimed at curbing the nuclear arms race, and specifically promised to seek agreement on "more complete measures limiting strategic offensive arms."[136] A continuation of the SALT talks was considered by both governments to provide the most suitable framework for this effort, and a joint approach to Switzerland elicited that country's agreement during the summer to the holding of the second phase of the talks in Geneva, thus obviating the administrative problems encountered in the previous rotation between Helsinki and Vienna.[137] On October 19 it was announced that the talks would resume in Geneva on November 21, 1972.[138]

"We have much unfinished business in the realm of strategic offensive weapons," Ambassador Smith remarked on his arrival in Geneva. "In SALT Two we will endeavor to bring strategic offensive weapons under permanent limitation. In addition, we will

[136] Document 14, Article VII.
[137] Arms Control and Disarmament Agency Press Release, Aug. 15, 1972, in *Bulletin*, Sept. 11, 1972, p. 284.
[138] White House announcement, Oct. 19, 1972, in *Presidential Documents*, Oct. 23, 1972, p. 1534.

seek to reduce the levels of strategic arms. All of this will take time. This year, in the session now about to take place, we expect to begin the serious exploratory work which should serve as a foundation for success in SALT Two.

"It is our hope that we may arrive at a permanent agreement on offensive systems—which would be the companion piece of the ABM Treaty—well before the five-year life expectancy of the interim agreement.

"I hope," Ambassador Smith added, "that we will promptly arrive at a charter establishing the Standing Consultative Commission as provided for in the ABM Treaty."[139]

The establishment of a Standing Consultative Commission, intended as a permament organ to help promote the objectives and implementation of existing U.S.-Soviet bilateral agreements, was in fact the most tangible achievement of the initial round of SALT II discussions. In a month of talks that concluded with the issuance of a formal communiqué on December 21, 1972 (Document 17a), the two delegations reached general understanding on the range of questions to be taken up in 1973 and signed a Memorandum of Understanding establishing the Standing Consultative Commission and defining its terms of reference (Document 17b). (For later developments, see pp. 127-130.)]

(17) SALT II, Round One: Joint United States-Soviet Communiqué and Memorandum of Understanding, Geneva, December 21, 1972.

(a) Communiqué.[140]

(Complete Text)

The US-USSR negotiations on limiting strategic arms continued from November 21, 1972, to December 21, 1972, in Geneva.

The US Delegation was headed by the Director of the US Arms Control and Disarmament Agency, Gerard Smith. Members of the Delegation Philip J. Farley, Paul Nitze, Harold Brown, and Royal Allison participated in the negotiations.

The USSR Delegation was headed by Deputy Minister of Foreign Affairs of the USSR, V. S. Semenov. Members of the Delegation K. A. Trusov, P. S. Pleshakov, A. N. Shchukin, and O. A. Grinevsky participated in the negotiations.

The Delegations were accompanied by advisors and experts.

---

[139] Statement of Nov. 17, 1972, in *Documents on Disarmament, 1972*, p. 811. On the Standing Consultative Commission, see Document 13, Article XIII.
[140] *Bulletin*, Jan. 15, 1973, p. 60.

In accordance with the agreement reached in May, 1972 to continue active US-Soviet negotiations on the limitation of strategic offensive arms,[141] the Delegations engaged in further consideration of the issues relating to achieving an agreement on more complete measures limiting strategic offensive arms.

During the course of these preliminary discussions a wide range of questions relating to this subject was considered. The discussion was useful for both sides in preparing for further negotiations next year. An understanding was reached on the general range of questions which will be the subject of further US-Soviet discussions.

During the negotiations, a Memorandum of Understanding[142] establishing a Standing Consultative Commission pursuant to Article XIII of the Treaty between the US and the USSR on the Limitation of Anti-Ballistic Missile Systems[143] was agreed and signed.

The two sides express their appreciation to the Government of Switzerland for creating favorable conditions for holding the negotiations and for the hospitality which was extended to them.

Agreement was reached that negotiations between the US Delegation and the USSR Delegation will be resumed on February 27, 1973, in Geneva.[144]

December 21, 1972
GENEVA

(b) Memorandum of Understanding Between the Government of the United States of America and the Government of the Union of Soviet Socialist Republics Regarding the Establishment of a Standing Consultative Commission. [145]

(Complete Text)

I.

The Government of the United States of America and the Government of the Union of Soviet Socialist Republics hereby establish a Standing Consultative Commission.

---

[141] Document 14, Article VII.
[142] Document 17b.
[143] Document 13.
[144] SALT discussions were resumed in Geneva on Mar. 12, 1973, with U. Alexis Johnson replacing Ambassador Smith as head of the U.S. delegation.
[145] TIAS 7545 (24 UST 238); entered into force Dec. 21, 1972.

II.

The Standing Consultative Commission shall promote the objectives and implementation of the provisions of the Treaty between the USA and the USSR on the Limitation of Anti-Ballistic Missile Systems of May 26, 1972, the Interim Agreement between the USA and the USSR on Certain Measures with Respect to the Limitation of Strategic Offensive Arms of May 26, 1972,[146] and the Agreement on Measures to Reduce the Risk of Outbreak of Nuclear War between the USA and the USSR of September 30, 1971,[147] and shall exercise its competence in accordance with the provisions of Article XIII of said Treaty, Article VI of said Interim Agreement, and Article 7 of said Agreement on Measures.

III.

Each Government shall be represented on the Standing Consultative Commission by a Commissioner and a Deputy Commissioner, assisted by such staff as it deems necessary.

IV.

The Standing Consultative Commission shall hold periodic sessions on dates mutually agreed by the Commissioners but no less than two times per year. Sessions shall also be convened as soon as possible, following reasonable notice, at the request of either Commissioner.

V.

The Standing Consultative Commission shall establish and approve Regulations governing procedures and other relevant matters and may amend them as it deems appropriate.[148]

VI.

The Standing Consultative Commission will meet in Geneva. It may also meet at such other places as may be agreed.

Done in Geneva, on December 21, 1972, in two copies, each in the

[146] Documents 13-14.
[147] *A.F.R., 1971*, no. 27.
[148] Regulations governing procedures and other relevant matters of the Commission were embodied in a protocol signed at Geneva on May 30, 1973 by U.S. Commissioner Johnson and Soviet Commissioner Ustinov (TIAS 7637; 24 UST 1124).

English and Russian languages, both texts being equally authentic.

<table>
<tr><td>For the Government
of the
United States of America</td><td>For the Government
of the
Union of the Soviet Socialist Republics</td></tr>
<tr><td>(*Signed*) Gerard C. Smith</td><td>(*Signed*) V. S. Semenov</td></tr>
</table>

C. Multilateral Disarmament Efforts.

[The signature and entry into force of the ABM Treaty and Interim Agreement were widely hailed as the most significant disarmament development of 1972 if not of the entire postwar period. As such, they tended to overshadow the multilateral disarmament efforts that continued to inch forward under the auspices of the United Nations and the 25-nation, U.N.-sponsored Conference of the Committee on Disarmament (CCD). At least one of these efforts, however, achieved definitive success in 1972 with the entry into force on May 18 of the Seabed Arms Control Treaty concluded the previous year.[149] The Convention on the Prohibition of Bacteriological (Biological) Weapons, completed in 1971, was also opened for signature on April 10, 1972 and promptly signed by over 74 nations, although ratification and entry into force were delayed until March 26, 1975.[150] Additional projects, notably the attempt

---

[149] Treaty on the Prohibition of the Emplacement of Nuclear Weapons and Other Weapons of Mass Destruction on the Seabed and the Ocean Floor and in the Subsoil Thereof, done at Washington, London, and Moscow Feb. 11, 1971 (TIAS 7337; 23 UST 701); text in *Documents, 1970*, pp. 69-73; related documents in *A.F.R., 1971*, nos. 13-14. Approved by an 83-0 vote of the U.S. Senate on Feb. 15, 1972, the treaty entered into force with the deposit of ratifications by the U.S., the U.K., and the U.S.S.R. on May 18, 1972. For details, cf. *Documents on Disarmament, 1972*, pp. 8-18 and 44-7.

[150] Convention on the Prohibition of the Development, Production, and Stockpiling of Bacteriological (Biological) and Toxin Weapons and on Their Destruction, opened for signature in Washington, London, and Moscow on Apr. 10, 1972; text in *A.F.R., 1971*, no. 19; related documentation in same, nos. 17-18. Transmitted to the Senate by President Nixon on Aug. 10, 1972, the convention was approved by a 90-0 vote of that body on Dec. 16, 1974, ratified by President Ford on Jan. 22, 1975, and entered into force with the deposit of ratifications by the U.S.S.R., U.K., and U.S. on Mar. 26, 1975. (For details, see especially *Documents on Disarmament, 1972*, pp. 138-9, 380-86, and 553-5.) Completed at the same time was U.S. adherence to the 1925 Geneva Protocol for the Prohibition of the Use in War of Asphyxiating, Poisonous, or Other Gases, and of Bacteriological Methods of Warfare, done at Geneva June 17, 1925. Approved (with a reservation) by a 90-0 vote of the Senate on Dec. 16, 1974, the convention was ratified by President Ford on Jan. 22, 1975 and entered into force for the U.S. with the deposit of its instrument of ratification on Apr. 10, 1975. The Geneva Protocal bears TIAS no. 8061; the Bacteriological Weapons Convention bears TIAS no. 8062.

to achieve a comparable ban on chemical weapons and a total prohibition of nuclear weapon tests, failed to advance significantly at two further sessions of the CCD on February 29-April 27 and June 20-September 7, 1972.[151] Though disappointed at the inconclusive outcome of these discussions, disarmament advocates derived encouragement from the successful negotiation in the framework of the Nuclear Nonproliferation Treaty[152] of a "safeguards agreement" between the International Atomic Energy Agency (I.A.E.A.) and the European Atomic Energy Community and five of its member states.[153] In a different context, the year brought definite progress toward the opening of preliminary talks on mutual and balanced force reduction (M.B.F.R.) in Europe.[154]

Disarmament discussions at the 27th (1972) Regular Session of the U.N. General Assembly focused largely on two proposals originated by the Soviet Union but found unacceptable by the United States on both political and practical grounds. One was a year-old plan for the convening of a world disarmament conference; the other, a proposed declaration by U.N. member states renouncing the use or threat of force in international relations and permanently prohibiting the use of nuclear weapons. Asserting that a world disarmament conference under existing circumstances might do more harm than good, the United States registered a solitary abstention when the Assembly voted 105 to 0 to set up a 35-member committee to study the project and report to its next session.[155] The second Soviet proposal, which was felt by the American delegation to fly "in the face of reality and law," was also adopted by an Assembly vote of 73 to 4, although the abstentions in this instance numbered 46 and included numerous allied and friendly powers as well as the United States.[156]

Similar considerations governed the U.S. stand on other disarmament proposals in the General Assembly. The American delegation abstained, for various reasons, on a resolution deploring the use of napalm and other incendiary weapons in armed conflict;[157] on another resolution that attempted to set standards for achievement

---

151 Report to the General Assembly and the Disarmament Committee, Sept. 7, 1972 (U.N. document CCD/329), in *Documents on Disarmament, 1972*, pp. 626-51; *12th Annual Report of the United States Arms Control and Disarmament Agency, Jan. 31, 1973*, in same, pp. 881-8.
152 Cf. note 32, above.
153 *Documents on Disarmament, 1972*, p. 891.
154 Chapter III.
155 Resolution 2930 (XXVII), Nov. 29, 1972, in *Documents on Disarmament, 1972*, pp. 835-6; for the U.S. position see same, pp. 615-18, 709-10, and 885-6.
156 Resolution 2936 (XXVII), Nov. 29, 1972, in same, pp. 848-9; U.S. position in same, pp. 830-31.
157 Resolution 2932 (XXVII) A, Nov. 29, 1972, in same, pp. 837-9; adopted by a vote of 99-0-5.

in SALT II;[158] on two resolutions calling for a comprehensive nuclear test ban but failing to provide for satisfactory verification procedures;[159] and on one that sought to further the status of the Indian Ocean as a U.N.-proclaimed "zone of peace."[160] On the other hand, the United States voted in favor of resolutions that urged a cessation of nuclear testing in the atmosphere,[161] called for great power support of the Treaty for the Prohibition of Nuclear Weapons in Latin America (Treaty of Tlatelolco),[162] and advocated priority efforts to negotiate a ban on chemical weapons.[163]]

D. Promoting Bilateral Relations.

[Limitation of strategic armaments was but one of the bilateral issues discussed at the Moscow summit in May 1972. In addition to concluding agreements for cooperation in various scientific and technical fields, the leaders of the American and Soviet governments in Moscow laid emphasis on their determination to promote a broader development of commercial and economic ties through such means as the conclusion of a trade agreement and lend-lease settlement, creation of a Joint Commercial Commission, and completion of an agreement on maritime and related matters.[164]

Considerable preliminary work in these areas had been accomplished in the year that preceded the summit meeting. As early as May 1971, the United States had agreed to let American firms participate in the construction of a large Soviet truck manufactory on the Kama River, and in the fall of that year the U.S.S.R. had purchased $150 million worth of American corn and other feed grains. Secretary of Commerce Maurice H. Stans had been received with "marked cordiality" when he visited the U.S.S.R. in November 1971 to initiate discussions looking toward a general normalization of economic relations. Secretary of Agriculture Earl L. Butz had also proceeded to the U.S.S.R. in April 1972 in the hope of arranging for increased shipments of U.S. feed grains in the wake of

---

[158] Resolution 2932 (XXVII) B, Nov. 29, 1972, in same, pp. 839-40; adopted by a vote of 87-0-27; U.S. position in same, p. 797.

[159] Resolution 2934 (XXVII) B and C, in same, pp. 844-6; adopted respectively by votes of 89-4-23 and 80-4-29; U.S. position in same, pp. 799-800.

[160] Resolution 2992 (XXVII), Dec. 15, 1972, in same, pp. 861-2; adopted by a vote of 95-0-33; U.S. position in same, pp. 851-2.

[161] Resolution 2934 (XXVII) A, Nov. 29, 1972, in same, pp. 842-3; adopted by a vote of 105-4-9; U.S. position in same, p. 799.

[162] Resolution 2935 (XXVII), Nov. 29, 1972, in same, pp. 847-8; adopted by a vote of 101-0-17. Cf. A.F.R., 1971, pp. 456-9.

[163] Resolution 2933 (XXVII), Nov. 29, 1972, in same, pp. 840-41; adopted by a vote of 113-0-2.

[164] Cf. Document 10 at notes 35-38.

a mediocre Soviet harvest. Soviet ministers with comparable responsibilities had also visited the United States; negotiations had been commenced on a maritime agreement to facilitate orderly transport of goods between the two countries; and preliminary talks had been held about the need to settle the perennial issue of Moscow's World War II lend-lease debt, a step the United States deemed indispensable to any extension of trade credits and most-favored-nation tariff treatment.[165]

The pace was quickened in the months that followed the 1972 summit meeting. A three-year agreement on U.S. grain sales to the U.S.S.R. was signed July 8, 1972. Later in that month, Secretary of Commerce Peter G. Peterson was in Moscow to attend the initial meeting of the Joint U.S.-U.S.S.R. Commercial Commission, which lasted from July 20 to August 1 and vigorously addressed itself to the complexities of credits, lend-lease, licenses, patents, copyrights, taxes, and maritime affairs.[166] In September, Dr. Kissinger was again in Moscow for follow-up discussions reflecting, as he said, the President's idea of "a global approach that would tie together the issues of lend-lease, most-favored-nation, a trade agreement, a maritime agreement, into one overall negotiation in which we would set ourselves an objective of where we wanted to be and then work towards it."[167]

Although the grain agreement (Document 18) was concluded with a rapidity that testified to the eagerness of both parties, the negotiation of the trade and maritime agreements was fraught with considerable difficulty. Aside from the widely divergent views of the two governments about the proper terms for a settlement of Moscow's lend-lease indebtedness—in effect, the key to the entire arrangement—an unexpected threat to agreement arose from the critical American reaction to Soviet measures restricting the emigration of Soviet Jews. Although total Jewish emigration from the U.S.S.R. in 1972 was to attain a figure of some 31,000, approximately double the 1971 rate, such progress was offset in the eyes of interested Americans by the imposition in August 1972 of a special education tax whereby some prospective emigrants were called upon to pay sums as high as $25,000 before being granted permission to leave.

Advising against any overt pressure on the Soviet Government in this sensitive matter, the U.S. administration intimated that "quiet

[165] These developments are summarized in Rogers Report, 1971, pp. 33-5; Nixon Report, 1972, p. 23; same, 1973, pp. 31-4.
[166] Peterson news conference, Moscow, Aug. 1, 1972, in *Bulletin*, Sept. 11, 1972, pp. 285-92.
[167] Kissinger news conference, Sept. 16, 1972, in *Presidential Documents*, Sept. 18, 1972, p. 1380; cf. also Kalb, *Kissinger*, pp. 346-8.

diplomacy" would be the best means of getting such restrictions removed. A majority of the U.S. Senate, however, favored a more vigorous approach, and 72 Senators—again headed by Senator Jackson of Washington—joined on October 4, 1972 in introducing an amendment to a pending East-West trade bill that would have the effect of barring the extension of credits, credit guarantees, or most-favored-nation treatment to the U.S.S.R. as long as it persisted in such unacceptable practices.[168] Although the Senators' action did not prevent the conclusion by the two governments of agreements purporting to establish Moscow's eligibility for credits and most-favored-nation treatment (Document 19), such treatment would in fact be unavailable and even credits would remain precarious until such time as Congress might be satisfied on the emigration issue.]

1. The Grain Agreement of July 8, 1972.

[Officially hailed as "the largest long-term trade purchase agreement ever made between two countries," the three-year agreement providing for Soviet purchase on credit of $750 million worth of U.S.-grown grains could be described without exaggeration as "a very important, concrete forward step in the commercial relations between the United States and the Soviet Union."[169] Signed in Washington on July 8, 1972 by Secretary of Commerce Peterson, Secretary of Agriculture Butz, and M.R. Kuzmin, Soviet First Deputy Minister of Foreign Trade, the agreement (summarized in Document 18) obligated the U.S.S.R. not merely to purchase at least $750 million worth of U.S.-grown grain over the three-year period August 1, 1972-July 31, 1975, but to purchase at least $200 million worth of this amount during the first twelve months. Purchases and sales were to be negotiated directly with U.S. private commercial exporters, but governmental credits up to a maximum of $500 million at any one time were to be made available through the Commodity Credit Corporation (C.C.C.) at its current going interest rates. Shipping arrangements were left in abeyance pending conclusion of the separate negotiations for a bilateral maritime agreement.

Largely because the U.S.S.R. was facing a disastrous harvest and consequently was anxious to purchase as much grain as possible, the economic impact of the agreement on the United States was unexpectedly sharp. "As a result of adverse weather conditions in the

---

[168] *New York Times*, Oct. 5, 1972.
[169] Statement by Ronald L. Ziegler, presidential Press Secretary, July 8, 1972, in *Presidential Documents*, July 17, 1972, pp. 1142-3. For the background of the agreement, cf. the statement by Dr. Kissinger in same, pp. 1143-4.

U.S.S.R. in 1972," wrote Secretary Rogers early in 1973, "total Soviet purchases of U.S. grain, for cash as well as credit, have already exceeded the $750 million projected for the entire three years. U.S. firms have sold the Soviet Union more than 18 million tons of wheat, corn, and soybeans, with a total value of $1.2 billion. The sales of grain to the Soviet Union have had, of course, beneficial effects on our balance of payments and have reduced the expense to the American taxpayer of storing surplus agricultural products."[170]

But these advantages, in the eyes of millions of Americans, were more than offset by the negative effects of a transaction that was soon being blamed for many of the economic ills besetting the average householder. Critics of the Government alleged that the details of the deal had been incompetently if not dishonestly handled, that the prices paid had been inordinately low, that exporting firms had profited at the expense of farmers and taxpayers, and that the Soviet purchases were directly responsible for a 30 percent increase in world wheat prices and similar increases in the prices of meat and other foodstuffs. In a preliminary response to some of these criticisms, President Nixon ridiculed the notion that "we got snookered by the Russians" and insisted that while "they got something they needed ... it was also good for us."[171] Not open to dispute is the fact that the Soviet demand for agricultural products contributed to a dramatic increase in U.S.-Soviet trade in 1972, a year when U.S. exports to the U.S.S.R. more than tripled, from $162 million in 1971 to $547 million, and U.S. imports from the Soviets increased from $57 million to $96 million. The resultant $451 million surplus in overall trade with the U.S.S.R. in 1972 was actually the largest surplus in U.S. trade with any single country during that year.[172]]

(18) Summary of Agreement with Respect to Purchases of Grain by the Soviet Union in the United States, Signed in Washington July 8, 1972.[173]

(Excerpt)

1. The President announced on July 8 the successful negotiation of a

---

[170] Rogers Report, 1972, pp. 313-14.

[171] News conference, Oct. 5, 1972, in *Public Papers, 1972*, pp. 955-6.

[172] *International Economic Report of the President, Together with the Annual Report of the Council on International Economic Policy, Transmitted to the Congress March 1973* (Washington: G.P.O., 1973), p. 51.

[173] White House Press Release (San Clemente), June 8, 1972; text from *Bulletin*, July 31, 1972, pp. 144-5. Two statistical tables accompanying the original release are not reprinted.

three-year grain agreement between the United States and the Soviet Union[174] totaling $750 million of U.S.-grown grains (wheat, corn, barley, sorghum, rye, oats—at the Soviet Union's option) for the period from August 1, 1972, through July 31, 1975. As part of the agreement, the United States will make available credit through the Commodity Credit Corporation (CCC) for repayment in three years from the dates of deliveries, with the total amount of credit outstanding not to exceed $500 million.[175] Under the agreement the Soviet Union will purchase for deliveries during the first year, August 1, 1972, through July 31, 1973, at least $200 million of U.S.-grown grains.

2. The purchases and sales will be as negotiated between the Soviet Union and the U.S. private commercial exporters. The credits on deliveries made through March 31, 1973, will carry CCC's present going interest rates (which are 6-1/8 percent per annum on letters of credit issued by U.S. banks and 7-1/8 percent on letters of credit issued by foreign banks). Under the CCC program, the principal is payable in ·three equal annual installments following the delivery and accrued interest is paid with each installment.

3. The Soviet Union purchased $150 million of feed grains (mainly corn) from U.S. grain traders in the fall of 1971. This was a cash transaction. In 1963 U.S. exporters sold the Soviet Union about $140 million of wheat. Thus, this is the largest Soviet grain purchase in history.

4. This sale to the Soviet Union will put that country in a second position among purchasers of U.S. grain. Average annual grain purchases of these six grains over the last three years are:

Japan	$437 million
Netherlands	135 "
Canada	126 "
United Kingdom	102 "
Italy	86 "
West Germany	75 "
Belgium-Luxembourg	48 "
Venezuela	46 "
Republic of Korea	36 "
Republic of China	27 "

5. The average purchase rate of $250 million annually would increase U.S. exports of the six grains by almost 17 percent annually over the average of the three previous years, 1969–71.

6. Agricultural experts estimate that about 3,000 to 5,000 additional

---

[174] TIAS 7423 (23 UST 1447); entered into force July 8, 1972.
[175] Article 1 of the agreement established the total amount of credit to be made available at $750 million, subject to possible increase by the U.S.

jobs are created for $100 million of grain exports. Since at least $750 million is involved, it could be estimated that a range of 22,500 to 37,500 man-years of work for U.S. workers is involved in this deal.

2. The Maritime Agreement of October 14, 1972.

[The U.S.-Soviet Agreement Regarding Certain Maritime Matters, signed in Washington October 14, 1972[176] by Secretary of Commerce Peterson and Soviet Merchant Marine Minister Timofey B. Guzhenko, was developed in the course of negotiations that had begun in the latter part of 1971 and continued in a series of meetings in Washington and Moscow throughout most of 1972. Essentially technical in character, the agreement had two main purposes: (1) "to open the channels of maritime commerce between the two nations by opening major U.S. and Soviet commercial ports to calls by specified kinds of U.S.-flag and Soviet-flag vessels"; and (2) "to afford to U.S.-flag vessels and Soviet-flag vessels the opportunity to participate equally and substantially in the carriage of all cargoes moving by sea between the two nations."[177] By the terms of the agreement, 40 ports in each nation were opened to access by the other's vessels, normally on four days' advance notice. Each country's vessels were further assured of the opportunity to carry at least one-third of the waterborne trade between the two countries, this requirement being made retroactive to July 1, 1972 in the case of grain shipments. Special freight rates, reflecting current market conditions and backed by U.S. subsidies in the case of agricultural cargo, were established for the benefit of U.S. carriers in view of their higher operating costs.[178] As an executive agreement, the accord did not require congressional approval but entered into force November 22, 1972 for the period ending December 31, 1975.]

3. Agreements on Trade and Lend-Lease, October 18, 1972.

[Negotiations for a comprehensive settlement of U.S.-Soviet commercial and financial issues were successfully completed at the second meeting of the Joint U.S.-U.S.S.R. Commercial Commission, held in Washington in mid-October, and the completed agreements were promptly signed in the U.S. capital on October 18, 1972. Described in some detail in a White House "Fact Sheet" (Document 19), this diplomatic package comprised a trade agreement, a lend-

---

[176] TIAS 7513 (23 UST 3573); partial text in *Bulletin*, Dec. 4, 1972, pp. 664-70.
[177] White House Press Release, Oct. 14, 1972, in same, p. 661.
[178] Same, pp. 663-4; also *New York Times*, Oct. 15, 1972.

lease settlement, and certain subsidiary arrangements relating to the extension of commercial credits.

The Agreement Regarding Trade,[179] concluded for a period of three years, established various guidelines aimed at promoting an expanded trade flow, notably an assurance that each country would accord most-favored-nation treatment to the other's products and that each could establish official commercial representation in the other's capital. In concluding the agreements, the parties voiced an expectation "that total bilateral trade in comparison with the period 1969-1971 will at least triple over the three-year period," to an aggregate amount envisioned by the United States as not less than $1.5 billion.

The Agreement Regarding Settlement of Lend Lease, Reciprocal Aid and Claims,[180] intended as a final settlement of Moscow's indebtedness for a total of $11.1 billion in wartime lend-lease aid, established the net sum due the United States at $722 million and laid down a schedule for repayment in installments ending July 1, 2001.

In addition, the two parties agreed to provide each other with normal credit facilities, which, in the case of the United States, would be furnished through the Export-Import Bank on a nondiscriminatory basis. A formal determination permitting the extension of Eximbank credits and guarantees was signed by President Nixon on October 18, 1972.[181]

Although the lend-lease agreement and the financial arrangements entered into force immediately, the terms of the trade agreement provided that it would not enter into force until the two parties exchanged formal notices of acceptance; nor could this occur until Congress enacted legislation assuring most-favored-nation treatment of Soviet products in accordance with the provisions of the agreement itself. While the White House planned to submit proposals to this end to Congress early in 1973, it was already known that many senators would be disinclined to grant such treatment (or to approve the granting of Eximbank credits) so long as the U.S.S.R. continued to interfere with emigration by its Jewish citizens.[182] This situation inevitably gave rise to some uncertainty about the real significance of the trade agreement and the prospects of its entering into force within the foreseeable future. Even the lend-lease settlement, moreover, appeared unlikely to be fully carried out in the absence of a grant of most-favored-nation treatment. Although in signing the agreement the U.S.S.R. had undertaken to

179 Cf. note 188 below.
180 Cf. note 189.
181 Cf. note 187.
182 Cf. above at note 168.

pay a total of $48 million on specified dates between 1972 and 1975, no payments toward the balance of $674 million were called for by the terms of the agreement until such time as the U.S.S.R. received official notice that most-favored-nation treatment was in effect. (For later developments, see pp. 127-130.)]

(19) Agreements and Arrangements on Trade and Other Matters: White House Fact Sheet, Released October 18, 1972. [183]

(Excerpts)

The successful negotiation was completed today of a comprehensive series of agreements and arrangements between the United States and the Soviet Union covering trade matters, reciprocal trade credits, expanded business facilities, and the settlement of outstanding lend-lease obligations. These agreements reflect the Basic Principles of Relations Between the United States of America and the Union of Soviet Socialist Republics signed by the President and General Secretary Brezhnev at last May's summit meeting. [184] The seventh principle provided: "The USA and the USSR regard commercial and economic ties as an important and necessary element in the strengthening of their bilateral relations and thus will actively promote the growth of such ties. They will facilitate cooperation between the relevant organizations and enterprises of the two countries and the conclusion of appropriate agreements and contracts, including long-term ones." At the summit meeting, the Joint U.S.-U.S.S.R. Commercial Commission was established, [185] chaired by U.S. Secretary of Commerce Peter G. Peterson for the American side and Minister of Foreign Trade N. S. Patolichev for the Soviet side. The full Commission met in Moscow in July of this year [186] and again in Washington for the past week. Specific work groups of the Commission have been in specific negotiations for the past few weeks.

The President signed today the determination making the Soviet Union eligible for credits from the Export-Import Bank of the United States. [187] Secretary Peterson and Soviet Minister Patolichev signed the

183 White House Press Release, Oct. 18, 1972; text from *Bulletin*, Nov. 20, 1972, pp. 592-5. For additional comment, cf. Rogers-Peterson news conference, Oct. 18, 1972, in same, pp. 581-92.
184 Document 11.
185 Cf. Document 10 at note 36.
186 Cf. above at note 166.
187 Presidential Determination No. 72-18100 (37 Federal Register 22573); text in *Bulletin*, Nov. 20, 1972, p. 604.

trade agreement.[188] Secretary William P. Rogers and Minister Patolichev signed the lend-lease agreement.[189]

Trade Agreement. Consistent with the U.S. objective of creating a comprehensive and clear framework within which private American firms can participate in U.S.-Soviet trade, the trade agreement spells out guidelines in specified critical areas to facilitate the flow of trade. The agreement provides for reciprocal granting of trading access equal to that granted for most of our trading partners in the free world; for protection against disruption of domestic markets; for the placement of substantial orders by the Soviet Union for U.S. machinery, plant and equipment, agricultural products, industrial products, and consumer goods; for the availability of U.S. business facilities in the Soviet Union equivalent to those granted representatives of other nations; for the establishment of a U.S. commercial office in Moscow and a Soviet trade representation in Washington; and for the encouragement of third-country-supervised arbitration in the settlement of commercial disputes. The agreement provides an exception for each side relating to national security interests. U.S. export controls are not negotiable and were not therefore discussed. However, such regulations have been and will continue to be under review.

Level of Trade. The trade agreement contemplates that total trade during its three-year period will at least triple over the 1969–71 period to an aggregate amount of at least $1.5 billion. The Soviet Government states that it expects substantial orders to be placed in the United States for "machinery, plant and equipment, agricultural products, industrial products and consumer goods." For example, the Soviet Government has indicated a desire to purchase several million dollars' worth of U.S. equipment to manufacture tableware. Also, U.S. firms have applied for export licenses for equipment valued at well over $1 billion in anticipation of bidding successfully on contracts associated with the huge Kama River truck plant construction projects. It is estimated that U.S. companies could capture between 250 and 500 million dollars' worth of the equipment contracts for this project. Substantial grain purchases are expected to continue during the period of the agreement. Machinery and equipment exports to the Soviet Union are expected to grow substantially. Currently, electrical and nonelectrical machinery accounts for only $60 million (or 37 percent of our total exports to the Soviet Union in 1971), even though total U.S. machinery

---

[188] Agreement Between the Government of the United States of America and the Government of the Union of Soviet Socialist Republics Regarding Trade, signed in Washington Oct. 18, 1972 but not in force as of early 1975; text and annexes in *Bulletin*, Nov. 20, 1972, pp. 595-603.

[189] Agreement Between the Government of the United States of America and the Government of the Union of Soviet Socialist Republics Regarding Settlement of Lend Lease, Reciprocal Aid and Claims (TIAS 7478; 23 UST 2910); text in *Bulletin*, Nov. 20, 1972, pp. 603-4.

exports to all countries in 1971 were $11.6 billion. Several large-scale joint projects are currently under discussion or negotiation. These include industrial installations for the production of polystyrene, metal fasteners, fertilizers, metal mining, and natural gas extraction and transmission. The U.S. balance of trade with the Soviet Union has traditionally run heavily in favor of the United States—generally by a ratio of 3 to 1. This trend can be expected to continue over the period of the trade agreement resulting in a favorable trade balance in the probable range of at least a few hundred million dollars a year. Furthermore, U.S. exports to the Soviet Union traditionally have been much more job intensive than Soviet exports to the United States, largely raw materials which are much less job intensive.

Most-Favored-Nation Provisions. The agreement provides that each country will reduce its tariffs with respect to the products of the other to the level generally applicable to like products of most other countries. This will require action by the U.S. Congress. The President currently plans to submit such legislation early in next year's session.[190] It is anticipated the trade agreement will not enter into force, and its three-year period will not begin to run, until such legislation is enacted. Between 1935 and 1951 such tariff treatment was also accorded to the Soviet Union, but it was withdrawn by statute in 1951 during the Korean war.[191] Yugoslavia was not affected by the 1951 statute. A subsequent amendment made possible the granting of this tariff treatment to Poland in 1960.[192] The granting of tariff treatment, at a level generally applicable to like products of most other countries, to the Soviet Union is fully consistent with U.S. membership in GATT [General Agreement on Tariffs and Trade].

Market Disruption Provision. Through state trading monopolies, the Soviet Union controls both the importation and exportation of all goods. In the Soviet economy, costs and prices do not necessarily play the same role as they do in a market economy. Accordingly, the Soviets have agreed to a procedure under which, after consultations, they will not ship products to the United States which the U.S. Government has advised will "cause, threaten or contribute to disruption of its domestic market." In the event the Soviets request limitation of U.S. exports, the U.S. Government is obliged to make such information available to the U.S. business community.

Reciprocal Trade Credits. Each government agreed to make available to the other, on a reciprocal basis, trade credit arrangements which are usual and customary in the financing of exports. The President has therefore determined that the Export-Import Bank of the United States

---

190 Cf. below at note 207.
191 Public Law 82-50, June 16, 1951; cf. *The United States in World Affairs, 1951*, pp. 227-8.
192 Cf. same, *1960*, p. 107.

may engage in transactions with the Soviet Union. The Soviets have given assurances that the facilities of the Foreign Trade Bank of the Soviet Union and the credit facilities of more than 40 Soviet foreign trade organizations will be available to American importers.

The Soviets have executed an operating agreement with Eximbank which provides that with respect to all matters—amount of credit, interest rate, repayment provisions—they will be treated in the same manner as any other country. Eximbank policies concerning private participation in credit facilitation will apply, and all credits in excess of $10 million will be subject to the usual review by the National Advisory Council.

Expanded Business and Commercial Facilities–Commercial Office. The trade agreement provides that the United States may establish a governmentally sponsored commercial office in Moscow to be operated through the U.S. Embassy there. The Soviets will be permitted to establish a trade representation in Washington. The U.S. commercial office in Moscow will provide the U.S. business community with up-to-date information on Soviet markets, facilitate introductions of U.S. businessmen to the appropriate Soviet ministries, provide such facilities as bilingual stenographers and communications, and provide critical expertise in advising U.S. businessmen in making their sales and purchases. Because members of the Soviet trade representation will have diplomatic immunity, they will not be permitted to negotiate or execute any transactions.

Business Facilities in Moscow. Like all foreign firms, U.S. business firms may not establish a permanent office in Moscow with the power to hire local personnel and the right to receive office space, facilities, and housing without accreditation by the Soviet Government. Until very recently, only two U.S. firms, both engaged in the travel and tourism industry, were accredited. Since negotiations were commenced, two industrial firms have been accredited, and the Soviets have agreed that they will continue to accredit U.S. firms on a basis no less favorable than that accorded firms of any third country. Any problems arising out of these accreditation procedures will be resolved through the Joint Commercial Commission. The Soviets have given written assurances that U.S. accredited companies will be authorized to employ Soviet personnel, acquire needed telephones, telex equipment, and other such communications facilities promptly, import promptly needed equipment such as typewriters, calculators, dictation and copying equipment, and automobiles and personal items such as furniture and appliances, have access to suitable housing, and receive prompt processing of visa requests.[193]

[193] A protocol relating to expansion and improvement of commercial facilities in Washington and Moscow, signed in Washington June 22, 1973 (TIAS 7657; *Presidential Documents*, June 25, 1973, pp. 821-2), provided among other things for the simultaneous opening of a Soviet trade representation in Washington and a U.S. commercial office in Moscow not later than Oct. 31, 1973.

Large Trade Center Complex. The Soviets also have said they will construct a large office-hotel-apartment trade center in Moscow. It is contemplated that the trade center will contain a substantial number of company offices, first-class hotel rooms and apartments, and related support activities. The center will be the first of its kind in the Soviet Union and is expected to be in full operation in the next few years. The Soviets will invite U.S. companies to make proposals and cooperate in the financing and construction of the trade center. The Soviet Government is also planning to construct a trade and economic exposition center and has offered to lease a pavilion to the United States for display of American products. The United States will assist the Soviets in establishing in New York a Soviet office for the purpose of purchasing American equipment for use in the Kama River truck plant.[194]

Arbitration. For the last 40 years the Soviets have had a policy of encouraging arbitration under the auspices of the Foreign Trade Arbitration Commission in Moscow, which is composed of 15 Soviet nationals. Arbitration in a third country was agreed to by the Soviet foreign trade organizations only if the Western firm demanded and was able to negotiate a third-country provision in the purchase or sale contract. By contrast, the rules of the American Arbitration Association provide that where a party to an arbitration proceeding is not an American, he has a right to have the controlling arbitrator be from a third country. The trade agreement encourages settlement of commercial disputes by arbitration under the Arbitration Rules of the Economic Commission for Europe, a United Nations agency, in a country other than the Soviet Union and the United States with arbitrators appointed by an authority in a country other than the Soviet Union and the United States. Parties to contracts, however, are free to decide on any other means of arbitration "which they mutually prefer and agree best suits their particular needs." In addition, U.S. firms are guaranteed the right to use the processes of Soviet courts and comparable Soviet organizations are assured similar access to U.S. courts.

Lend-Lease Settlement

Background. Outstanding Soviet lend-lease obligations have been a deterrent to U.S.-Soviet commercial relations since World War II. Negotiations which were conducted immediately after the war, in 1951, and in 1960 all ended in failure. The lend-lease statute[195] gives the President full power to settle the obligation within very broad limits. The

---

[194] A separate agreement on the establishment of a temporary purchasing commission was effected by exchange of letters signed at Washington Oct. 18, 1972 (TIAS 7772; partial text in *Bulletin*, Nov. 20, 1972, pp. 602-3).
[195] Lend-Lease Act of Mar. 11, 1941 (Public Law 77-11); text in *Documents, 1940-41*, pp. 712-15.

agreement under which lend-lease aid was extended to the Soviets[196] followed other similar agreements in providing only the most general language concerning how contributions to the war effort by each side were to be settled. Consequently, the actual 1945 settlement with the British,[197] the principal beneficiaries of lend-lease aid, provided the guidelines for the settlement with the Soviet Union, which received about half as much aid as the British but more than five times as much as any other country.[198] The principal issues were the amount of the total settlement, whether and how much interest should be charged, the length of time for repayment, a grace period, and a right to postpone annual installments under certain conditions. Negotiations were complicated by the length of time which had elapsed since World War II, the difference between current interest rates and those prevailing at the end of World War II, and the fact that Soviet products have been subject to higher tariff levels during the intervening period than have been the products of the British.

The Soviet Settlement. Outstanding Soviet lend-lease obligations will be settled by the payment by the Soviets to the United States of an amount at least $722 million payable over the period ending July 1, 2001. Twelve million dollars is being paid today; $24 million will be paid July 1, 1973, and $12 million on July 1, 1975. The balance will be paid in equal annual installments ($24,071,429 for each of 28 installments, assuming the first such annual payment is on July 1, 1974[199]) ending on July 1, 2001. The exact total amount will depend upon when and how many of the four allowable annual deferments are taken by the Soviets. If the Soviets were to take their four postponements early in the period, interest on deferments could amount to as much as $37 million, making the total amount payable between now and 2001 equal to $759 million. Such deferments, if taken, will nonetheless be repaid by July 1, 2001, and will bear interest at the rate of 3 percent per annum. The British pay 2 percent interest on any deferments and are permitted to add a year beyond 2001 for each deferment. The median interest rate for total interest-bearing public debt between 1946 and

[196] Signed at Washington June 11, 1942; cf. *Documents, 1941-42*, p. 238.
[197] Signed Washington Mar. 27, 1946 (TIAS 1509); cf. *Documents, 1945-46*, pp. 132-9.
[198] A detailed comparison of the British and Soviet lend-lease settlements, included in the source document but not reprinted here, shows total aid extended to the U.K. as $21.5 billion and total aid to the U.S.S.R. at $11.1 billion. The total amounts to be repaid are listed as $895 million for the U.K. and $921 million (including previous payments of $199 million) for the U.S.S.R.
[199] If such MFN [most-favored-nation treatment] is granted between June 1 and December 1, the first lend-lease payment is due not more than 30 days thereafter. If MFN is granted from December 2 through May 31 of the following year, then the first lend-lease payment is due on July 1 of that year. The earlier [sic: earliest?] payment date of such annual installments is July 1, 1974. [Footnote in original.]

1972 is 2.867 percent (which is coincidently the interest rate for the year 1959). The settlement also includes remaining amounts due on the "pipeline account" for lend-lease goods delivered (approximately $45 million due) to the Soviets immediately after World War II and for which they have been paying since 1954.

*   *   *

Copyrights and Tax Treaties. Significant progress was made on both the copyright and tax treaty issues, and work is continuing on both scores in special work groups in each of these subjects. It is expected that additional major progress on these issues will be made prior to the next Commission meeting.

Joint U.S.-U.S.S.R. Commercial Commission. Commercial relations between the two countries will continue to be monitored by the Joint Commercial Commission. The U.S. delegation on the Commission is chaired by Peter G. Peterson, Secretary of Commerce, and is composed of James T. Lynn, Under Secretary of Commerce, as Vice Chairman; Jack F. Bennett, Deputy Under Secretary of Treasury, Willis Armstrong, Assistant Secretary of State, and Andrew E. Gibson, Assistant Secretary of Commerce, as members; James L. Mitchell as General Counsel; and Steven Lazarus as Executive Secretary.

E. Summary of 1973-75 Developments.

[The significance of the various U.S.-Soviet agreements concluded during 1972 cannot be adequately assessed without some reference to the developments of the two following years, particularly in the areas of strategic arms limitation and trade and economic relations.

The quest for a "SALT II" agreement on the limitation and eventual reduction of strategic armaments occupied the American and Soviet leaders at three further meetings during 1973-74: a visit by General Secretary Brezhnev to the United States on June 17-25, 1973; a second visit by President Nixon to the U.S.S.R. on June 27-July 3, 1974; and a meeting between President Ford and General Secretary Brezhnev at Vladivostok on November 23-24, 1974.

The intention of the two governments to continue active negotiation with a view to a permanent agreement on strategic arms limitation and eventual reduction was reaffirmed by President Nixon and General Secretary Brezhnev in an agreement on "Basic Principles of Negotiations on the Further Limitation of Strategic Offensive Arms" which was signed in Washington on June 21, 1973.[200] In this document, the two sides pledged "serious efforts"

[200]TIAS 7653 (24 UST 1472); text in *Presidential Documents*, June 25, 1973, p. 812.

to work out the provisions of a permanent agreement during the next two years, with the objective of signing it in 1974.

No permanent agreement, however, had been made ready for signature when President Nixon revisited the U.S.S.R. the following year. In a joint communiqué made public in Moscow on July 3, 1974,[201] the two sides nevertheless recorded their joint determination that a new agreement on the limitation of strategic arms should be completed before the current Interim Agreement expired in 1977 and "should cover the period until 1985 and deal with both quantitative and qualitative limitations." Also signed during the President's second Moscow visit were (1) a protocol limiting each side (subject to ratification) to a single deployment area for ABM systems, instead of the two areas permitted by the 1972 ABM Treaty;[202] (2) two protocols on procedures governing replacement, dismantling or destruction for strategic offensive arms and for ABM systems and components; (3) a Treaty on the Limitation of Underground Nuclear Weapon Tests (or "Threshold Test Ban Treaty"), providing (again subject to ratification) for the complete cessation starting March 31, 1976 of nuclear weapon tests with a yield exceeding 150 kilotons and for "confining other underground tests to a minimum";[203] and (4) a joint statement advocating effective measures against "the dangers of the use of environmental modification techniques for military purposes."[204]

The subsequent meeting of President Ford and General Secretary Brezhnev at Vladivostok broke new ground in the form of a preliminary agreement on the establishment of numerical limits for each side's strategic delivery vehicles. In a joint statement issued on November 24, 1974,[205] the two leaders reaffirmed the intention to conclude a new agreement to last through 1985; asserted that favorable prospects existed for completing work on this agreement in 1975; and announced that they had already agreed on certain key provisions of the new accord. Specifically, it was later disclosed, each side was to be permitted a total of not more than 2,400 strategic delivery vehicles, of which not more than 1,320 could be

[201] Same, July 8, 1974, pp. 755-6.
[202] Protocol to the Treaty Between the United States of America and the Union of Soviet Socialist Republics on the Limitation of Anti-Ballistic Missile Systems, done at Moscow July 3, 1974; text in *Presidential Documents*, July 8, 1974, pp. 750-51 (cf. above at note 126). The Protocol was transmitted to the Senate Sept. 19, 1974 (S. Ex. I, 93-2; *Presidential Documents*, Sept. 23, 1974, pp. 1170-71) and was approved by that body on Nov. 10, 1975.
[203] Treaty Between the United States of American and the Union of Soviet Socialist Republics on the Limitation of Underground Nuclear Weapon Tests, and Protocol, done at Moscow July 3, 1974; text in *Presidential Documents*, July 8, 1974, pp. 751-3.
[204] Communiqué, *loc. cit.*, p. 756; text of joint statement in same, p. 753.
[205] *Presidential Documents*, Dec. 2, 1974, p. 1489.

equipped with multiple warheads (MIRVs).[206] Negotiations to work out the new agreement were scheduled to resume in Geneva in January 1975, and it was hoped that the agreement would be ready for signature when General Secretary Brezhnev paid a contemplated visit to the United States later in that year.

The sequel to the trade and lend-lease agreements concluded in 1972 (Document 19) was far less positive, primarily because of the Soviet Government's unwillingness to adjust its emigration policies to meet specifications laid down by the U.S. Congress. As already noted, the entry into force of the trade agreement—and continued Soviet payments under the lend-lease agreement—required the enactment of legislation assuring most-favored-nation (M.F.N.) tariff treatment of Soviet products entering the American market. Although provision for such treatment was included in the draft Trade Reform Act sent to Congress by President Nixon on April 10, 1973,[207] most legislators remained unwilling to sanction M.F.N. in the absence of free emigration for Soviet Jews. Under amendments introduced by Senator Jackson and by Democratic Representative Charles A. Vanik of Ohio, the U.S.S.R. and most other Eastern European countries would be denied M.F.N. treatment and would also be ineligible for governmental export credits unless their nationals were permitted to emigrate freely.

In a compromise arrangement negotiated by Secretary of State Kissinger and embodied in an exchange of letters with Senator Jackson on October 18, 1974, Mr. Jackson agreed to relax the restrictions in the pending legislation on the understanding that restrictions on Soviet emigration would also be eased and that such emigration would increase promptly to a rate of at least 60,000 per year. Although this understanding was vigorously repudiated in Soviet quarters, it formed the basis of the legislation approved by Congress late in 1974 and formally known as the Trade Act of 1974.[208] Section 402 of the law prohibited M.F.N. treatment or credits, after an eighteen-month grace period, for any nonmarket economy (Communist) country that denied its citizens the right or opportunity to emigrate or impeded the exercise of this right. Section 613 imposed additional restraints on the expansion of U.S.-Soviet trade by limiting U.S. Government credits (other than agricultural credits) to the U.S.S.R. to a total of $300,000,000.

This legislation was signed by President Ford on January 3, 1975. One week later, on January 10, 1975, the Soviet Government gave formal notice that it would be unable to accept a trading relation-

---

[206] Ford news conference, Dec. 2, 1974, in same, Dec. 9, 1974, p. 1514.
[207] Same, Apr. 16, 1973, p. 350.
[208] Public Law 93-618, Jan. 3, 1975; background in Keesing's, pp. 26850-51 and 26993-4.

ship based on legislation which it viewed as contravening both the terms of the 1972 agreement and the principle of noninterference in domestic affairs. "The Soviet Government," Secretary Kissinger revealed on January 14, 1975, "states that it does not intend to accept a trade status that is discriminatory and subject to political conditions and, accordingly, that it will not put into force the 1972 Trade Agreement. . . ." "Under these conditions," Secretary Kissinger continued, "we have concluded that the 1972 Trade Agreement cannot be brought into force at this time and that the President will therefore not take the steps required for this purpose. . . . The administration regrets this turn of events. It has regarded and continues to regard an orderly and mutually beneficial trade relationship with the Soviet Union as an important element in the overall improvement of relations. It will, of course, continue to pursue all available avenues for such an improvement, including efforts to obtain legislation that will permit normal trading relationships."[209]]

[209]*Bulletin*, Feb. 3, 1975, pp. 139-40.

III.
ATLANTIC ALLIANCE
AND DÉTENTE IN EUROPE

[A continuing reduction in East-West tensions helped set the course of European affairs in 1972 as President Nixon's visit to the U.S.S.R., the completion of a four-power agreement on Berlin, and the conclusion of a basic treaty between East and West Germany cleared the way for preliminary steps toward the holding of a Conference on Security and Cooperation in Europe (C.S.C.E.) and of talks on Mutual and Balanced Force Reduction (M.B.F.R.) between members of the North Atlantic Treaty Organization (NATO) and the Warsaw Pact. Accompanying and, to some extent, promoting this trend was a further development of relations between the United States and the Communist-governed countries of Eastern Europe, exemplified in particular by President Nixon's visit to Poland on his way home from the U.S.S.R. and by Secretary of State Rogers' later visit to Romania, Hungary, and Yugoslavia. The sense of harmony so evident in many East-West contacts was in some ways less apparent in the relations among the Western nations themselves, particularly in their attempts to deal with certain long-standing economic and political problems that had become a source of congenital friction between the United States and some of its Western associates.[1]]

A. Problems of the Western Family.

[Relations between the United States and other Western nations were not a top-priority concern of U.S. foreign policy in 1972, except to the extent that they impinged on more immediate strategic, political, or economic questions. Most of the internal problems of the Western family, American leaders seemed to feel, could be

---

[1] For more detailed discussion, cf. Nixon Report, 1972, pp. 38-51; same, 1973, pp. 76-93: Rogers Report, 1972, pp. 281-320.

temporarily set aside while the United States concentrated its diplomatic efforts on the consolidation of the U.S.-Soviet détente, the opening of a dialogue with the People's Republic of China, and the negotiation of a peace settlement in Vietnam. Decisive progress in these enterprises, in Washington's view, would make it possible to look toward 1973 as a "Year of Europe" specifically reserved for the consideration of Western problems.]

1. The United States and the European Communities.

[This broad disinterest in specifically Western affairs did not, however, extend to the developments that centered in the six-nation European Economic Community (E.E.C.), which, with its sister communities for coal and steel and for atomic energy, formed the economic core of industrialized Western Europe. Already wielding gigantic influence in international trade and monetary matters, the E.E.C. was on the verge of a formidable accretion of new strength with the expected accession to membership of Denmark, Ireland, Norway, and the United Kingdom. Under a treaty and related arrangements concluded in Brussels on January 22, 1972, all four of those countries were due to become members of the three communities on January 1, 1973.

Although Norwegian voters subsequently rejected accession to the communities in a referendum held September 24-25, 1972, the prospect of British, Irish, and Danish membership more than sufficed to heighten the existing tension between the United States and the E.E.C. on a variety of trade and monetary issues. As will be noted in a later chapter, many of these issues were due for basic reexamination as part of the complex of understandings that had made up the so-called Smithsonian Agreement on exchange rate adjustments of December 18, 1971.[2] An address by Nathaniel Samuels, Deputy Under Secretary of State for Economic Affairs, surveys these problems as they presented themselves early in the new year 1972.]

---

[2] *A.F.R., 1971*, no. 150; for further discussion, cf. Chapter X at note 3.

(20) "Europe and Its Atlantic Partner—the U.S.A.": Address by Nathaniel Samuels, Deputy Under Secretary of State for Economic Affairs, Before the Friedrich Ebert Stiftung (Foundation), Leverkusen, Germany, April 14, 1972.[3]

(Complete Text)

I am honored by the *Friedrich Ebert Stiftung* for their cordial invitation to attend this forum and for the opportunity to speculate among so distinguished an assemblage of speakers and audience on the relationship between a uniting Europe and its Atlantic partner, the United States of America.

The patterns of cooperation and of conflict between these two great partners are as numerous as they are complex. The underlying harmony which characterizes our relationship is sometimes profound and purposeful, while at other times it contains dissonance and confusion. In short, we are vibrant and living societies, and our relationship is not the repetitive strain of a wornout composition.

The music of the moment, while it retains its essential and indissoluble harmony, is not without its dissonance. Since none of us, I believe, wishes dissonance to dominate our relationship, it behooves us perhaps to alter some notes, to rearrange some chords, and to revise some themes so as to reassure the peoples of both sides of the Atlantic of a rhythm that accords with their innermost aspirations.

If I stress harmony rather than dissonance, it is because I believe that it is necessary to reaffirm at this point in time the continuing unity of our purposes rather than to stress and pursue the divergences in our short-term aims.

There has been taking place in recent years—let us be frank—a gradual shift in perceptions in the United States about Europe and in Europe about the United States. Some 20 years ago, when the European Community was beginning to take shape, many Americans asked themselves whether the massive support we gave to this great undertaking would help to create a powerful collaboration in world affairs or a powerful third force of uncertain direction. There were those who assumed that the former would be the case and were unstinting in their support for the concept and for the substance of an integrated and, ultimately, a united Europe. In response to those, on the other hand, who foresaw the emergence of a powerful and independent force in world affairs, the point was often made that such an eventuality was not to be feared by the United States—that the moral health of a nation, like that of an individual, is enhanced and enriched not by dominance but by the

---

[3] Department of State Press Release 87, Apr. 13, 1972; text from *Bulletin*, May 1, 1972, pp. 632-6.

necessity to resolve differences and to seek common policies on the basis of partnership.

Today, after two decades of experience in the processes of European unification, the reality has emerged of a powerful European entity in world affairs arising out of a fragmented pattern of national sovereignties, an entity which recognizes the fundamental nature of its ties with the United States but which seeks its own unique identity and is determined to be in a position to influence the course of events in accordance with its own perceptions and interests.

The materialization of our vision, however, and the success of our efforts has thrust upon Americans and Europeans alike the need to adjust our interrelationships to conform to the world of the 1970's, already so different from that of the 1950's, as the bipolar world of the 1950's gives way to the emergence of multiple power centers in the final quarter of this century.

For Americans, the unfolding of this historical drama, insofar as our relationship with Europe is concerned, has not been without its problems. We are conscious of the fact that we have applied enormous moral effort and material resources to the reconstruction of Europe, that in so doing we helped to create competitors as well as collaborators, that we exported capital in great volume and transferred technology in profusion in order to create economic wealth and to enhance political stability for others and ourselves together.

If we assess the economic consequences in the United States of this unprecedented effort we find that, on the one hand, our industrial exports to the European Community have risen sharply, our agricultural exports, despite being held down by trade barriers, have grown in the aggregate—although principally in nonprotected products—and our investments abroad have soared. The European Community, Europe as a whole, and the United States have all visibly been beneficiaries, as has been the developing world generally.

On the other hand, for some 20 years now we have gone into deficit in our balance of payments as public and private capital has poured out to Europe and other parts of the world, as worldwide trade and production patterns have been altered by this process, and as defense burdens have been sustained. High-technology industries have been creating their own competitors abroad, low-technology industries find it increasingly difficult to compete against lower wage levels in other countries, agriculture is prevented from hurdling protectionist barriers for certain of its important export products, and the areas of preferential treatment of trade, with adverse consequences for our interests, have spread from the Mediterranean to Africa and now back again to the non-Community European countries.[4]

---

[4] Association agreements between the E.E.C. and certain Mediterranean and

In the area of monetary affairs, if we look back over our experience of the past years prior to the recent realignment,[5] we often experienced only a grudging willingness on the part of some surplus countries to adjust their exchange rates, their internal fiscal and monetary policies, and their trade practices and policies to meet the needs of better international equilibrium.

RECONCILING DIVERGENT ATTITUDES

To an observer from outside Europe, a distinct if subtle change has occurred in recent years, wherein a weak and tentative Europe—resurgent yet afraid, prosperous without believing in its good fortune, resolute but not confident—has, almost imperceptibly, begun to feel its own strength and to pursue its own aims with only limited attention to the consequences for others.

I know that many of you will regard this as an inaccurate and unfair observation of some European policies and attitudes. Surely, if you look at the Atlantic partnership with European eyes, your rejection of this observation would be understandable. In your eyes, the policy of generally open industrial trade and investment has been highly beneficial to American exports and investments. If agricultural policy in the European Community has been prejudicial to certain United States farm exports, this has been necessary, in your view, in endeavoring to achieve certain internal European social and economic aims that can be attained only over a span of years. If trade preferences in favor of certain European and African countries have been extended and expanded, it is because the European Community believes it has accepted a responsibility for economic development and political stability in the Mediterranean and African world in which both Atlantic partners have a common interest. In European eyes, a similar policy is necessary with respect to that part of Europe which will not join the Community, not only for Europe's sake but for the fundamental and long-term interests of the United States. In the monetary sphere, Europe looks upon its enormous accumulation of American dollars as tangible evidence that it has acted as a silent partner passively accepting certain United States internal and external policies of which it not infrequently has disapproved.

If I have spent a considerable amount of time today in describing some of these changing perceptions within the Atlantic partnership, it is

African countries were supplemented during 1972 by agreements between the E.E.C. and member states of the European Free Trade Association (EFTA), signed in Brussels on July 22, 1972, providing for the establishment of free trade in manufactured goods throughout the E.E.C.-EFTA region over a five-year period beginning Jan. 1, 1973.

[5] Cf. above at note 2.

because I wish to point to a few intellectual and attitudinal modifications which, in my opinion, could once again bring into sharper focus our essential unity of purpose and of action while filtering out disturbing tendencies toward divisiveness and divergence.

—First, in the area of trade relationships, we must reconcile the principle of universalism and nondiscrimination with the growing practice of regionalism.

—Second, while preserving the political imperatives of agricultural policy that prevail in all our countries, we must not prevent rationalism from penetrating these policies on both sides of the Atlantic.

—Third, in monetary affairs, there is a wide intellectual gap that needs to be bridged between our convictions on the obligations of surplus as well as deficit countries with respect to balance of payments problems.

—Fourth, regarding the developing world, we must emerge from the conceptual morass in which we are all floundering on the principles applicable to countries which are in widely different stages of economic and political development.

—Fifth, we need to deepen our bilateral relationships while at the same time integrating them into the essential and increasingly necessary multilateral framework of our contemporary world. With respect to trade, including agriculture, we cannot assume that broadening a single market within a defined geographic area and extending a network of trading privileges to selected countries outside these geographic limits will automatically be in the general international interest. The expectation that underlay the Common Market was not only that the elimination of trade barriers among the Six would stimulate and enhance their own trade and economic growth but that the dynamic effects of this process would be beneficial to other countries not members of this customs union. As we all know, this expectation has become in most respects a reality, and the belief prevails that when the Six become Ten an even broader single market will continue to have stimulative economic effects on member countries and on nonmembers as well.

REGIONALISM AND UNIVERSALISM

Clearly, none of us can be certain as to the extent to which the European single market contributed to general trade and economic growth in the past decade and to what extent other factors played a role. We trust that the expansion of the European Community to include the United Kingdom, Denmark, Norway, and Ireland will contribute further to the economic well-being of Europe and of the world at large, but it behooves Europe in so doing to adhere to the vision of a universal and nondiscriminatory world rather than to seek to consolidate its gains behind walls of protectionism in agriculture and preferentialism with nonmember countries in Europe and beyond. As yet we see few, if any, signs of movement toward modification of certain policies adverse to the interests of nonmember countries. We appreciate the fact that the European Community cannot be oblivious to the problems created for the rest of Europe by her enlargement, but we expect that a genuine Atlantic partnership requires the Community and non-Community Europe to order their relationship between themselves in a way that will not impose unacceptable costs on the United States and other nonmember countries. We understand the solicitude of the European Community for its Mediterranean neighbors and former African colonies, but in the system of so-called reverse preferences[6] we detect the vestiges of colonial thinking and we look forward to an unraveling of this type of trading relationship.

The pursuance of preferentialism will inevitably bring a counter-reaction. There will be, and there already is, a tendency for some people in other countries to consider whether the formation of trading blocs would be in their interest, either to offset the one Europe has built or to preserve markets for themselves in parts of the world not covered by European preferences. Those developing countries that find themselves at a disadvantage as a result of European preferences are seized with this same problem from their point of view and wonder whether they, too, must become tied to certain industrialized markets.

However, one cannot extrapolate the unique conditions of Europe to the rest of the world. The geographic propinquity, historical and cultural ties, political evolution, and economic interrelationships which have made a European Community possible are not to be duplicated elsewhere. Regional cooperation has its logic, its practicality, and its value, but surely we can reconcile these benefits with a universal order and avoid the fragmentation of a world community that needs cooperation more than division.

INTERNATIONAL MONETARY ADJUSTMENT PROCESSES

In the monetary sphere, I have alluded to the obligations of deficit and surplus countries alike to accept adjustment processes as a normal part of international life. We operate within a monetary system in which generally there still prevails the outmoded view that deficit countries are obliged to alter their policies in order to achieve better balance whereas no such moral imperative is imposed upon surplus countries to adjust their surpluses. Both have problems of weighing internal versus external aims; and both, deficit and surplus countries alike, have obligations to make the international system work.

---

[6] Preferential access granted a former metropolitan country to the markets of a former colonial area.

There is great need on both sides of the Atlantic to accept as conviction the practical wisdom and the moral obligation of surplus as well as deficit countries to pursue internal and external policies that will tend to achieve equilibrium in our affairs. Much has been accomplished in this respect in recent years, and our European partners have shown an understanding, a consideration, and a patience that is well understood at home.

ASSISTING THE LESS DEVELOPED WORLD

Turning to the developing world, we are coming to recognize that certain countries within the developing world need to be differentiated from each other with respect to the levels and nature of their economic development. We do not all live in the same period in terms of economic development. When I spoke earlier of universalism and nondiscrimination, I was referring primarily to the more developed world in a broad sense, embracing the industrialized countries and a number of countries which hover between industrialized and nonindustrialized societies. However, we have not deviated from the principle of most-favored-nation in trade by virtue of moving toward the concept of generalized trade preferences for less developed countries, and it may be that in the future the world will find it useful to devise more sophisticated categories of differentiation for groups of less developed countries to accommodate different levels of economic development. The two great Atlantic partners have a common task and a common interest in sorting out our thinking with respect to assisting the less developed world.

Let me close by saying a word about a possible mechanism for deepening the Atlantic bilateral relationship; that is, between the United States and the European Community. The need to consider a mechanism grows out of the richness and the breadth and complexity of our partnership. American and European attitudes on scores of problems and issues are the powerful and often dominating elements of international life. There are, of course, innumerable interchanges between us on all manner of issues, and in the past 2 years we have constituted very informal consultative groups between the United States and the European Commission to consider certain problems of common concern. Interchanges have also occurred of a strictly informal, almost personal, nature outside the consultative group with the permanent representatives of the member states in Brussels. If the Community should, in the future, wish to propose a broader and more systematic mechanism or other means of conducting our business of common interest, we shall be ready to give consideration to their proposals.

Let us not lose sight of the fact, however, that if we should seek to strengthen our bilateral relationship, it is because this can enrich the multilateral processes of international life. If an appropriate bilateral mechanism will help insure that the policies of one partner take into account the interests of the other, this will help also to insure that we both take into account the interests of other countries and other continents.

If I do not speak today about our respective relationship with Japan, with Canada, with Latin America, with Australia and New Zealand, with the subcontinent of India and Pakistan, with the Communist world in Europe and in Asia, as well as our relationship with individual countries in all parts of the globe, it is because I am confining my remarks to the Atlantic relationship. But it is certain that the bilateral relationship between the European and American partners must not derogate in any way from the desired and essential bilateral relationship we enjoy with other countries and regions or from the multilateral relationships and institutions in which we are both deeply involved.

The United States and Europe, including both Community and non-Community Europe, are of a size and a grandeur that assign to each an enormous role and pervading influence in world affairs. The very origins of my country, our common Atlantic history, our cultural heritage, the agonies and the triumphs we have shared in all facets of human endeavor, and the structure of our economic interdependence all coalesce into a political, economic, and security relationship today that is as natural as it is necessary. Our destiny is cooperation not confrontation, competition but not conflict.

2. Problems With Portugal and Greece.

[A further source of friction between the United States and some allies was the close relationship maintained by Washington with certain governments which, though clearly undemocratic in character, were regarded as essential factors in American and allied security. In Europe, the governments of Greece, Portugal, and Spain were generally considered to fall within this category, and U.S. relations with Greece and Portugal—both of them allied with the United States through the North Atlantic Treaty—remained a subject of particularly lively debate in 1972.]

a. Portugal.

[Relations between the United States and the Portuguese Government of Prime Minister Marcello Caetano, which had been widely and vehemently criticized because of its opposition to popular movements at home and in the Portuguese African territories, had appeared to reach a new stage of intimacy with the disclosure on December 9, 1971 of a number of bilateral U.S.-Portuguese agreements that provided, among other things, for substantial U.S. economic assistance to Portugal as an apparent *quid pro quo* for continued U.S. use of an air base in the Portuguese Azores.[7] The rationale of these arrangements was explained by U. Alexis Johnson, Deputy Under Secretary of State for Political Affairs, in a statement presented before the Senate Foreign Relations Committee on February 1, 1972 in connection with that body's inquiry into the executive agreements procedure.[8]]

(21) Recent Agreements With Portugal: Statement by U. Alexis Johnson, Deputy Under Secretary of State for Political Affairs, Before the Senate Committee on Foreign Relations, February 1, 1972.[9]

(Excerpt)

*   *   *

AGREEMENT WITH PORTUGAL

With this general background in mind, let me now turn to the specific agreements involving the Azores[10] and Bahrain.[11] The texts of these agreements have been provided to the committee. The first agreement between the United States and Portugal continues United States rights to station forces at Lajes Airbase on Terceira Island in the Azores. Although the use by the United States of facilities in the Azores goes back to World War II, our present defense relationship with Portugal is based on the North Atlantic Treaty and the Defense Agreement between Portugal and the United States of September 6, 1951,[12] concluded pursuant to article 3 of the NATO Treaty.[13] This 1951 agreement, through various unilateral and bilateral extensions since that date, continues to govern the use of Lajes Airbase by United States

---

[7] *A.F.R., 1971*, no. 47.
[8] Cf. Chapter I at notes 43-48. (The Caetano regime was displaced Apr. 25, 1974 by a military junta which promised a return to democratic government. Elections to a constituent assembly were held Apr. 25, 1975.)
[9] *Bulletin*, Feb. 28, 1972, pp. 280-82.
[10] TIAS 7254 (22 UST 2106); cf. *A.F.R., 1971*, no. 47.
[11] TIAS 7263 (22 UST 2184); cf. Chapter I at note 44.
[12] TIAS 3087 (5 UST 2263).
[13] Signed at Washington Apr. 4, 1949 and entered into force Aug. 24, 1949 (TIAS 1964); text in *Documents 1949*, p. 613.

forces. This long history is set forth fully in a separate memorandum which I am submitting for the record.[14]

Simultaneously with the exchange of notes, the United States gave to the Government of Portugal:

—A letter of intent concerning various forms of economic assistance to Portugal;[15]

—A letter of explanation concerning possible Export-Import Bank financing of Portuguese projects;[16]   and

—A letter concerning support by the Government of Portugal of the United States Military Assistance Advisory Group in Lisbon.

The Department believes it was appropriate to conclude this agreement as an executive agreement for the following reasons:

1. The agreement contains no new defense commitment to Portugal— in fact, the grant to the United States of base rights in the Azores involves no defense or security commitments by the United States at all. We are not required to station troops at Lajes. We could, without violating this agreement, bring them all home tomorrow. We have obtained from Portugal a commitment to make facilities available to us for a specified period of time. That is a commitment by Portugal, not a commitment by the United States. To cast the agreement in the form of a treaty and submit it to the Senate for advice and consent might carry the misleading implication that the agreement does involve a new United States security commitment. Of course, our defense commitment to Portugal is contained in the North Atlantic Treaty, which did receive the advice and consent of the Senate. The agreement on the Azores neither adds to nor subtracts from our commitment to Portugal under the North Atlantic Treaty.

2. Agreements implementing treaties traditionally have been concluded by executive agreement. The 1951 Defense Agreement and the 1971 exchange of notes have been entered into pursuant to article 3 of the North Atlantic Treaty. In the context of the North Atlantic Treaty, the arrangement for stationing forces in the Azores is not unique or even unusual. The United States has concluded executive agreements for the stationing of forces with Belgium, Canada, Denmark, Germany, Greece, Iceland, the Netherlands, Turkey, and the United Kingdom.

3. In addition, it seems to me clear that as Commander in Chief of our Armed Forces, the President has constitutional power to conclude agreements providing for facilities for our military personnel abroad.

[14] Text in U.S. Senate, Committee on Foreign Relations, *Hearings on S. Res. 214 Relative to the Submission of Any Portuguese Base Agreement As a Treaty, 92d Cong., 2d. sess.* (Washington: G.P.O., 1972), pp. 16-17.
[15] *Bulletin*, Jan. 3, 1972, pp. 8-9.
[16] Same, p. 9.

4. Congress alone has the right to authorize and appropriate funds. Consequently, our commitments to Portugal for assistance are made specifically within the limitations of applicable United States legislation and appropriations.

Before turning to the agreement with Bahrain, I want to make a few additional observations about the Azores agreement. The military facilities in the Azores are important to the national security of the United States. The Azores have become increasingly important in recent years for antisubmarine surveillance in view of the buildup in submarine activity in the mid-Atlantic. Because of the strategic location of the Azores, the facility there is uniquely suited for this function, which could not be performed so efficiently from any other location. The airbase in the Azores is also valuable for aircraft refueling and staging over that part of the Atlantic, not only because of the location but also the good weather conditions prevailing in that area.

ASSISTANCE TO PORTUGAL

Now, a certain amount of confusion has arisen concerning our assistance obligation because of distorted accounts in the press of the nature of the agreement. The only direct assistance which we are furnishing to Portugal in connection with this agreement consists of (1) the loan of an oceanographic vessel, the U.S.N.S. *Kellar*, (2) $1 million for use in the Portuguese educational reform program in metropolitan Portugal, and (3) $5 million, measured in terms of initial acquisition cost and not current value, in non-military excess equipment. The rest of the agreement on assistance concerns credits which are mutually beneficial to both countries. The P.L. 480[17] program permits Portugal to purchase surplus U.S. agricultural commodities on favorable credit terms, but these are sales, not gifts, of these commodities. The letters which accompanied the exchange of notes state that Portugal may purchase surplus commodities up to $15 million per year for the next 2 years. The offer of Export-Import Bank financing, which it was agreed would be subject to the normal Eximbank criteria and procedures in actually making specific loans on specific projects, will likewise benefit U.S. suppliers to the extent Portugal avails itself of these credits.

The figure $400 million, which has been used in connection with the Eximbank financing, represents the approximate value of development projects in metropolitan Portugal which the Government of Portugal has indicated it plans to put into effect in the coming years. To the extent the Portuguese may choose to buy American goods or services

---

[17] Agricultural Trade Development and Assistance Act of 1954 (Public Law 83-480, July 10, 1954).

for use in these projects, we will receive and give expeditious handling to loan applications to the Eximbank they may care to submit. There is thus no commitment to extend any specific amount of credit.

As you know, the law which established the Export-Import Bank stated that the primary concern of that institution would be the promotion of the export of American products. Any future loan under the agreement to the Portuguese Government would be consistent with that purpose and in our own economic interest.

Some critics of 'the agreement have suggested that it provides assistance to Portugal which will help that country in its efforts to combat the insurgency in its various African territories. Newspaper accounts have inaccurately stated that the conflicts in Africa have put a strain on Portugal's foreign exchange reserves and that the new U.S. assistance to Portugal will relieve this strain.

In fact, Portugal's military efforts in the past seem to have been dictated by the military strategy it has chosen for Portuguese Africa rather than because of any budgetary considerations. Portuguese defense expenditures have risen only slightly in recent years and thus have declined in proportion to the total budget. Defense expenditures dropped from 45 percent of the total budget in 1968 to 33 percent in 1971. Portugal's balance of payments, likewise, has shown no sign of strain, continuing to register a surplus year after year. As a result, Portugal's gold and foreign exchange reserves have risen to an alltime high of almost $1.8 billion—equal to about 14 months' imports. By this standard no other country in the world is so well off. In the light of these facts it is clear that our grant assistance to Portugal is of little financial significance. Its significance is that it will permit us to initiate programs of cooperation in such fields as education and oceanography which otherwise would probably not have come into being. Thus, none of the assistance under this agreement has any relationship to the Portuguese territories in Africa, where our arms embargo continues fully in effect.

*   *   *

b. Greece.

[Five years after the 1967 coup against the parliamentary regime in Greece, the United States continued to be widely criticized for its political and military support of the government headed by Brigadier General (retired) George Papadopoulos. The following address by Secretary of State Rogers at the Fiftieth Anniversary Dinner of the Order of AHEPA (American Hellenic Educational and Progressive Association) is typical of a continuing effort by U.S. foreign policy spokesmen to explain and justify a relationship that was admittedly maintained primarily for military reasons.]

(22) United States Relations With Greece: Address by Secretary of State William P. Rogers Before the Fiftieth Anniversary Dinner of the Order of AHEPA, Atlanta, August 24, 1972.[18]

(Excerpts)

I am very pleased to join you in celebrating the golden anniversary of "The Order of Ahepa." In those fifty years AHEPA has established a remarkable record of achievement in philanthropy, in education, in civic action and—perhaps most important—in giving new and fresh life to those vibrant elements of your ancestors' culture which so enrich the lives of all Americans.

*   *   *

One of the main pillars of our collective security system is the North Atlantic Treaty Organization. For a generation, the durability, solidarity and determination of NATO have been the foundation of peace in Europe. NATO is the umbrella under which our friends in Europe have built prosperous societies while protecting and preserving the right of their citizens to live free of foreign domination.

NATO has also provided a base from which we have been able to move from confrontation to negotiation. And today the countries of Europe, with our participation, are currently engaged in unprecedented negotiating activity.

— Together with the United Kingdom, France, and the Soviet Union, we have achieved an agreement giving the two million brave people of West Berlin increased access to East Berlin and the German Democratic Republic.[19]

— West and East Germany have just begun formal negotiations on a treaty to improve relations between them.[20]

— We expect preliminary talks to begin this year looking toward a conference in 1973 on security and cooperation in Europe which will involve European nations as well as the United States and Canada.[21]

— We also look forward to early multilateral east-west talks on the mutual and balanced reduction of military forces in central Europe,[22] which, except for the Soviet-Chinese border, is the site of the largest concentration of ground forces in the world.

— Finally, in addition to the agreements we have completed with the

---

[18] Department of State Press Release 204, Aug. 24, 1972. For further comment on relations with Greece, see Document 33.
[19] Cf. Document 25.
[20] Cf. below at note 101.
[21] Cf. below at note 102.
[22] Cf. Document 30.

Soviet Union, involving arms limitation, science, the environment, health, cultural exchanges, space cooperation, and the prevention of incidents at sea between our navies,[23] we are seeking to reach a comprehensive trade agreement.[24] Even without one, our grain sales during the next year should make the Soviet Union our second largest agricultural market in the world—second only to Japan.

Nearly all Americans recognize the important role that NATO has played in contributing to these developments and to peace in Europe since World War II. But in the current climate of detente, the argument can be heard that because the alliance was built decades ago it is no longer relevant. Nothing could be further from the truth. As President Nixon said in his foreign policy report to the Congress earlier this year: "Today, the military balance underpins the overall stability that has brought these new opportunities about."[25]

One of our relationships within the Alliance has been a special target of critics. I refer of course to our partnership with Greece in NATO and our policy towards Greece.

What about that policy? As all of you know so well, there are strong bonds of friendship and confidence between the people of the United States and the people of Greece. They go back to the earliest days of our own Republic and the earliest days of the Greek struggle for independence. President James Monroe in his message to the Congress of December 22, 1822, observed that "Greece fills the mind with the most exalted sentiments.... Superior skill and refinement in the arts, gallantry in action, disinterested patriotism and devotion in favor of public liberty...." Relations between Greece and the United States remain of great importance and should be a subject for reflection and understanding by all Americans.

Greece and the United States were allies in World War II. Subsequently we joined together in defeating the communist attempt to wrest Greece from the community of free nations. We fought together under the flag of the United Nations in Korea. For more than twenty years we have been partners in the North Atlantic Alliance. That alliance has given Greece a guarantee of its sovereignty and integrity not subject to the whim of others. And, of course, Greece's role has provided the alliance with a vital link in the security of Europe and the West.

The United States has ideological links, too, with the people of

[23] Cf. Document 10.
[24] Cf. Document 19.
[25] The passage in Nixon Report, 1972, p. 42, reads as follows: "Today, the military balance underpins the overall stability on the Continent which makes detente feasible in the 1970's. East-West diplomacy in Europe is more active today than at any time since the Second World War; new hopes and new complexities are emerging. This is hardly the time for the West to abandon the very cohesion and stability that have brought these new opportunities about."

Greece. The heritage of classical Greece teaches us that authoritarian governments can be inflicted upon nations all too easily, but a democracy cannot be imposed. By its very nature a democracy grows out of the will of a people. Our Founding Fathers, too, built our own country with that knowledge.

We believe that a democratic system offers the best hope for achieving the spiritual and material aspirations of people everywhere. But the choice, except as it applies to our own country, is not ours to make. It would be the ultimate arrogance of power to think that we can, or should, impose our will on others—to threaten or coerce others even in the name of conscience. The kind of government other countries have must in the final analysis be what their people want or will permit.

Because of our long and close relationship with the people of Greece we would of course like to see their constitution speedily implemented and their parliamentary system reinstituted.[26] Some critics of our policy toward Greece have urged us to denounce the government of an allied country because it has failed to implement its constitution in a manner and at a pace they think desirable. Others would use the alliance as a means of pressure. As good friends and allies we can urge other governments to take certain steps. I do not believe that we should threaten retaliation or use coercive methods to insist that another government conduct its internal affairs in a manner to coincide with our views. Such a policy violates the concept of sovereignty and independence, and, in my opinion, would not be effective or in our best interests.

Alliances are made by governments, but in a more fundamental sense the most important aspect of alliances are people. Governments are transitory but the people are not. Many American governments and Greek governments have passed from the scene, and our people and the Greek people remain allies. Whatever the government of the United States and whatever the government of Greece, I hope Americans will continue to be bound to the people of Greece in friendship and common purpose.

Over the past 20 years the pressures on NATO have increased in the south, and today the weight of challenge falls heavily on the allies of the southern flank, particularly on Greece and Turkey. Soviet activity, military and political, in the Mediterranean has sharply increased in recent years. We and our allies must continue to give serious attention

---

[26] A new constitution declaring Greece a "crowned democracy" was approved by referendum and declared in force in 1968, but provisions relating to civil rights, political parties, and the election of a parliament remained inoperative pending further governmental action. (The military junta was replaced by a civilian regime on July 24, 1974 and parliamentary elections were held Nov. 17, 1974.)

to maintaining and strengthening our defense in this area which is so important to the peace of the world.

Within that framework we have obtained the agreement of our Greek allies to provide a homeport in Greece to one element of the Sixth Fleet. Early in September a squadron of six destroyers will take up anchorages in Greece and some 770 dependents of the crews will move into Athens. Homeporting in Greece will have advantages for the United States, for Greece, and for NATO. It will help improve the morale of our navy personnel by eliminating long periods of separation from their families. It will also make it easier for the Sixth Fleet to maintain the high state of readiness essential to its role as one of the key NATO defense forces on the southern flank of the alliance.

We have also undertaken over the past two decades to help Greece play an effective and necessary role in the deterrence which the alliance represents. We intend to continue providing that assistance because we believe it to be in the best interest of the Greek people, of the NATO alliance, and of the United States.

Let me leave you with this thought. In the search for an exit from the dangerous confrontations of the past decades, the desire for detente must not lead to a retreat from our responsibilities abroad. In a retreat to isolationism there are no safe havens to be found along the way. The threat to peace and security in the world has been reduced, but it would be foolhardy to think that it has quickly and completely evaporated. Our alliances must therefore remain strong.

In seeking improved relations with our former adversaries we must maintain warm and reassuring relations with our old and close friends in the world. That is the heart of our policy toward Europe and the heart of our policy toward Greece. It is my earnest hope that you support that policy.

*   *   *

B. Toward European Détente.

[The favorable development of East-West relations in Europe during 1971 had made it virtually certain that 1972 would bring further progress toward the opening of a dialogue on matters of concern to the NATO powers, the Warsaw Pact countries, and Europe's neutral and nonaligned states. Of special importance had been the signature on September 3, 1971 of a four-power agreement on Berlin[27] which not only promised an improvement of conditions in and around that divided city but also removed the chief obstacle to Western acquiescence in the Soviet plan for a

---

[27] *A.F.R., 1971*, no. 39.

Conference on Security and Cooperation in Europe (C.S.C.E.). In addition, the Berlin agreement strengthened Western hopes of inducing the U.S.S.R. and its allies to join in a discussion of Mutual and Balanced Force Reduction (M.B.F.R.) in Central Europe.[28]

Improving prospects for a limitation of military forces in Europe by mutual agreement resulted in a temporary relaxation of the pressure within the U.S. Congress for a substantial withdrawal of American forces from Europe as contemplated by the Mansfield resolution and amendment which had been defeated in 1971.[29] For similar reasons, a skeptical American administration had become increasingly resigned to the prospect of a European Security Conference, a project whose background and implications were examined in depth by Martin J. Hillenbrand, Assistant Secretary of State for European Affairs, in a statement delivered April 25, 1972 before the Subcommittee on Europe of the House Foreign Affairs Committee (Document 23).

Further important developments occurred in the weeks that followed the Hillenbrand statement. On May 23, 1972, President Gustav Heinemann of the Federal Republic of Germany completed ratification of the bilateral treaties normalizing West Germany's relations with the U.S.S.R.[30] and Poland,[31] both originally signed in 1970. This action, promptly reciprocated by the respective Communist governments, cleared the way for the entry into force of both treaties on June 3, 1972 and for the simultaneous entry into force of the 1971 Berlin agreement, which was formally brought into effect with the signature of a final protocol by the Foreign Ministers of the four powers in the former German capital (Document 25).

The settlement of these long-standing problems exerted a favorable influence on the American-Soviet summit meeting held in Moscow during the last week of May. According to the joint communiqué released May 29 (Document 10), the U.S. and Soviet governments took occasion of the Moscow meetings to affirm their readiness to make appropriate contributions to détente and peaceful cooperation in Europe; agreed that multilateral consultations looking toward a European Security Conference could begin after signature of the Berlin protocol; and expressed belief that stability and security in Europe would be promoted by "a reciprocal reduction of armed forces and armaments, first of all in Central Europe."

This sequence of developments was also hailed by the North

28 Same, no. 42.
29 Same, nos. 33-34 and 41.
30 Signed in Moscow Aug. 12, 1970; text in *Documents, 1970*, pp. 105-6.
31 Signed in Warsaw Dec. 12, 1970.

Atlantic Council, which met in Ministerial Session in Bonn on May 30-31, 1972 and, after years of hesitation, gave formal consent to the commencement of multilateral conversations looking toward the convening of a European Security Conference. In addition, ministers of those NATO countries identified with the M.B.F.R. proposal—in effect, all allied countries save France—proposed that multilateral explorations in this area be undertaken either before or in parallel with those on European Security (Document 24).]

(23) United States Interest in the Proposed Conference on Security and Cooperation in Europe (C.S.C.E.): Statement by Martin J. Hillenbrand, Assistant Secretary of State for European Affairs, Before the Subcommittee on Europe of the House Committee on Foreign Affairs, April 25, 1972.[32]

(Complete Text)

I am grateful for a chance to discuss before the subcommittee the United States interest in the proposed Conference on Security and Cooperation in Europe (CSCE). I shall begin by filling in a bit of the history of various Warsaw Pact proposals for such a conference which date back to 1954. Against that background, I would then like to say how we look at such a conference.

The first formal proposal to convene a conference to settle European political and security problems was made by the Soviet Union in 1954, and variations on the theme have been advanced several times since then. The proposals until 1969 seemed to amount to little more than a procedural gesture to divert attention from the absence of any substantive Soviet moves on a constructive postwar settlement in the European area. Western governments, while never rejecting these proposals, nonetheless have always insisted that a conference must be adequately prepared to give it a reasonable chance of success, must involve United States and Canadian participation at the outset, and should result in effective measures for improving security and cooperation rather than in new declarations of good intentions. In the past, close Western evaluation of these proposals failed to convince the allies that serious negotiations rather than propaganda points were the object of the proposals. In the present instance, we hope that a substantive focus can be developed and maintained for a conference on the very real problems facing Europe.

The Soviet Union first suggested a pan-European conference on future security arrangements as part of a broad initiative on European

[32] *Bulletin*, May 15, 1972, pp. 703-6.

settlement in 1954. In an effort patently designed to forestall West German rearmament, Foreign Minister [Vyacheslav M.] Molotov proposed a general European collective security treaty open to all European states in which a reunified, confederated Germany would play a part. The legitimacy of American interests in Europe would have been denied under this arrangement, with the United States having observer status in the organization to be set up by the treaty. The Western powers unanimously rejected this proposal.[33]

At the Geneva summit conference in mid-1955, the Soviets reintroduced the idea of a European security conference, this time including U.S. participation.[34] But with the rearmament of West Germany, Soviet interest in the conference waned.

Polish Foreign Minister [Adam] Rapacki revived the idea in 1964 before the United Nations General Assembly.[35] Rapacki assumed American participation in such a conference, which he saw as furthering the emergence of a new security system in Europe, one element of which would be nuclear arms limitations. The Warsaw Pact in January 1965 endorsed Rapacki's European security conference proposal without, however, mentioning the matter of U.S. participation. The Communists held out hope for "settlement of the German problem," while demanding acceptance of existing borders and "liquidation of the remnants of World War II."[36]

Secretary General Brezhnev's 1966 address to the 23d Congress of the Communist Party of the Soviet Union mentioned a conference again,[37] and the Warsaw Pact powers in July 1966 advanced the notion formally in the Bucharest Declaration.[38] While the specifics of a proposed conference were vague, Soviet aims in 1966 seem to have been to exploit any perceived frictions within the alliance and to reduce American influence in west Europe. At that time, Secretary General Brezhnev said that the United States "seeks some pretext to continue keeping its troops and war bases in Europe, twenty years after the end of the war and thereby exert direct influence on the economy and policies of the Western European countries." Continuing the same theme, the Bucharest Declaration proposing the conference argued that "there can be no doubt that the aims of the U.S. policy in Europe have nothing in common with the vital interests of the European peoples and the tasks of European security."

By mid-1968 no concrete agenda for a European security conference

---

[33] Documents, 1954, pp. 250-53.
[34] Documents, 1955, pp. 202-3.
[35] UN Monthly Chronicle, Jan. 1965, pp. 73-4.
[36] Cf. Warsaw Pact communiqué, Jan. 20, 1965, in Documents on Disarmament, 1965, pp. 5-9.
[37] Report to the 23d Congress, Mar. 29, 1966, in Current Digest of the Soviet Press, Apr. 13, 1966, p. 13.
[38] Declaration on Strengthening Peace and Security in Europe, July 6, 1966, in

had been proposed, nor had the desired European security system been defined.

The conference idea was revived yet again in March 1969, perhaps with the immediate purpose of resuming the East-West dialogue that had been interrupted by the invasion of Czechoslovakia. In the so-called Budapest Appeal,[39] Warsaw Pact Foreign Ministers listed three "basic prerequisites" of European security: the inviolability of the existing boundaries in Europe, including "the Oder-Neisse border and the border between the GDR [German Democratic Republic] and the German Federal Republic"; "recognition of the existence of the GDR and Federal Republic"; and renunciation by Bonn of possession of nuclear weapons in any form. Fulfillment of these conditions would then permit all-European cooperation in "great projects" on economic and environmental matters. The statement was generally conciliatory in tone and omitted the anti-German polemics that had marked earlier Warsaw Pact pronouncements on this subject.

The NATO Foreign Ministers responded, in effect, in their April 1969 communique by offering to explore with the Soviet Union and other eastern European states which "concrete issues" best lent themselves to fruitful negotiation and an early resolution. Additionally, the ministers pointed out that the United States and Canada, as well as the European states, should take part in any negotiations.[40]

In this way, there began a kind of dialogue of communiques between NATO and the Warsaw Pact on the timing and content of the conference.

In May 1969, I should add, the Finnish Government offered Helsinki as a possible conference site.

The recent Soviet and eastern European calls for a conference at an early date were met with growing interest in most west European countries, and since their December 1969 meeting,[41] the NATO Foreign Ministers have devoted a considerable portion of each of their semi-annual meetings to refining the alliance position on the holding of a conference. In Rome in May 1970, the ministers noted East-West negotiations had already been launched and asserted that as progress was made in these negotiations, in particular on Germany and Berlin, they would be prepared to enter into multilateral contacts with all interested governments to explore when it might be possible to enter into such a conference or series of conferences.[42]

The Warsaw Pact ministerial meeting in Budapest in June 1970 de-

Documents on Disarmament, 1966, pp. 407-20.
[39] March 17, 1969; text in same, *1969*, pp. 106-9.
[40] *Documents, 1968-69*, p. 155.
[41] Communiqué and Declaration, Dec. 5, 1969, in *Documents, 1968-69*, pp. 166-73.
[42] *Documents, 1970*, pp. 84-8.

clared that the United States and Canada, as well as the two Germanys and all European states, should participate equally in a conference.[43]

In the December 1970 and subsequent communiques, the NATO ministers made progressively more explicit what they meant by progress in ongoing talks and eventually linked the opening of multilateral East-West talks exclusively to satisfactory conclusion of the Berlin negotiations.[44]

Now the first two stages of the Berlin negotiations have been brought to a successful conclusion. However, the Soviet Union has not been prepared to sign the protocol until the Federal Republic of Germany ratifies the Moscow treaty earlier negotiated between the F.R.G. and U.S.S.R. In our view ratification of that bilateral treaty is an internal political question in West Germany, and it would be inappropriate for me to comment on this issue.

For our part we have indicated our willingness to sign the Final Quadripartite Protocol on Berlin, as have the British and the French, thus bringing the entire Berlin agreement into effect.[45] Once this is done by the Four Powers, the way will be clear for multilateral exploratory talks late this year.

No agenda for a conference has been agreed on. However, the dialogue of communiques has established four major topics which a conference might treat:

—Security issues, principles governing relations between states, including renunciation of force, and certain military aspects of security;
—Freer movement of people, ideas, and information, and cultural relations;
—Economic, scientific, technical, and environmental cooperation; and
—Permanent machinery.

Security Issues. The Warsaw Pact states made public in October 1969 a draft declaration in which CSCE participants would renounce the threat or the use of force and declare that they "recognize and unconditionally respect the territorial integrity of all European states within their existing borders."[46] For the Warsaw Pact, this topic is perhaps the core of the conference and would constitute the security element of the agenda.

NATO ministers, in their December 1969 and subsequent communi-

---

[43] *Documents on Disarmament, 1970*, pp. 245-8; cf. *The United States in World Affairs, 1970*, p. 44.
[44] NATO Council communiqués, Brussels, Dec. 3-4, 1970 (*Documents, 1970*, pp. 92-9); Lisbon, June 3-4, 1971 (*A.F.R., 1971*, no. 37); Brussels, Dec. 9-10, 1971 (same, no. 42).
[45] Cf. Document 25.
[46] Text (Prague, Oct. 31, 1969) in *Documents on Disarmament, 1969*, pp. 526-8.

ques, proposed broadening the discussion to encompass the generally accepted principles which would govern relations between states. These principles would apply to relations between all states, irrespective of their social and political systems.

In their December 1971 communique,[47] the NATO ministers suggested the study of certain military aspects of security with a view to their possible inclusion on an agenda.

Freer Movement of People, Ideas, and Information, and Cultural Relations. Real progress in this area would be a sign that Europe is ready to dismantle the barriers of fear and suspicion and move toward an era of peace. However, the Warsaw Pact states apparently prefer to limit the discussion to cultural relations in the traditional sense.

Cooperation. All parties could benefit from increased economic, scientific, and technological cooperation and from more active East-West cooperation in environmental problems shared by all modern societies.

Permanent Machinery. The Warsaw Pact states have proposed creation of a "standing body of all interested states participating at the conference which could continue after the termination of the conference in the joint work on the basis of an (agreement) concerning further steps in this respect." The allies have this question under study.

I should add that the Warsaw Pact's Prague communique, issued last January,[48] called for "creation of a system of commitments"—not precisely defined—that would preclude the use or threat of force and would guarantee all countries against acts of aggression. It then listed and elaborated upon seven basic principles of European security, adding that the conference, by taking these principles as a basis for relations between states, would "adopt a decision of great historical scope . . . capable of turning Europe into a truly peaceful continent." The seven principles are:

1. Inviolability of frontiers.
2. Nonuse of force.
3. Peaceful coexistence.
4. Good neighborly relations and cooperation in the interests of peace.
5. Mutually advantageous relations among the states.
6. Disarmament.
7. Support for the United Nations.

Whether this amounts to a new agenda proposal for the conference, in the strict sense, remains to be seen.

---

[47] *A.F.R., 1971*, no. 42.
[48] Text (Jan. 26, 1972) in *Documents on Disarmament, 1972*, pp. 1-8.

For our part, we believe the conference can constitute a modest step forward within a broader and long-range process of negotiation intended to lead toward more stable East-West relations—even though representatives of some 30 states of diverse interests and regimes cannot directly address the central problems of European security.

President Nixon in his February 1972 foreign policy report to Congress said that "The mere atmosphere of detente ... is insufficient. ..." However, the President said, "If such a conference is carefully prepared and will address substantive issues, the United States favors it."[49]

Secretary Rogers, in his speech of December 1, 1971, to the Overseas Writers,[50] outlined the basic approach we have taken toward the conference in somewhat more detail.

In the first place, he said, the conference must attempt to mitigate the underlying causes of tension, and not merely its superficial manifestations. It should deal with any security issues on the agenda in a concrete way.

In the second place, he pointed out, the discussions could address the basic principles that should govern relations among states by affirming the independence and equality of sovereign states whether their political or social systems are different or similar. The conference should thus encourage the reconciliation of European states, not confirm their division.

In the third place, a conference should give major emphasis to issues of cooperation on which East-West progress is attainable. However, the Secretary stressed, while a conference might contribute to enhanced security, experience has shown that detailed negotiations of complex and fundamental security issues, such as mutual and balanced force reductions, are more likely to be handled in less general and less highly visible fora.

Finally, he emphasized, the conference should go beyond the traditional pattern of cultural exchanges between East and West and take instead specific steps to encourage the freer movement of people, ideas, and information.

In summary, the Secretary stated that we view such a conference in dynamic rather than static terms. We would be firmly opposed to any attempt to use the conference to perpetuate the division of Europe. Instead, we see such a conference as one small step on the long road to a new situation in which the causes of tension are fewer, contacts are greater, and Europe could again be thought of as one continent rather than two parts.

This still remains our basic approach toward the conference. We have no illusions that the conference will solve the problems of a divided

[49] Nixon Report, 1972, pp. 49 and 48.
[50] *Bulletin*, Dec. 20, 1971, pp. 693-702.

Europe. Nor do we think that even modest improvements will come easily at a conference of over 30 sovereign states, each of which has somewhat different goals and different perceptions of what the conference should try to accomplish. But we do believe that if all concerned are willing to engage in careful preparations and to attempt to come to grips with some of the real problems, modest improvements might come about and the stage might be set for further progress.

(24) Ministerial Session of the North Atlantic Council, Bonn, May 30-31, 1972: Final Communiqué.[51]

(Complete Text)

1. The North Atlantic Council met in Ministerial Session in Bonn on 30th and 31st May, 1972.

2. Ministers reaffirmed that the purpose of the Alliance is to preserve the freedom and security of all its members. Defence and the relaxation of tension are inseparably linked. The solidarity of the Alliance is indispensable in this respect. Allied Governments seek an improvement in their relations with the countries of Eastern Europe and aim at a just and durable peace which would overcome the division of Germany and foster security in Europe.

3. Ministers noted progress in relations between Western and Eastern countries, increasing contacts between the leaders of these countries, and the conclusion of important agreements and arrangements. They welcomed these developments flowing from major initiatives undertaken by their governments, which had full and timely consultations on these subjects. Such consultations will continue.

4. Ministers welcomed the signing by the United States and the USSR of the Treaty on the Limitation of Anti-Ballistic Missile Systems and the interim agreement on Certain Measures with Respect to the Limitation of Strategic Offensive Arms.[52] They believe these two agreements limiting the strategic arms of the United States and the USSR will contribute to strategic stability, significantly strengthen international confidence, and reduce the danger of nuclear war. Ministers also welcomed the commitment by the United States and the USSR actively to continue negotiations on limiting strategic arms. They expressed the hope that these two agreements will be the beginning of a new and promising era of negotiations in the arms control field.

5. Ministers noted with satisfaction that the Treaty of 12th August, 1970, between the Federal Republic of Germany and the Soviet Union and the Treaty of 7th December, 1970, between the Federal Republic

---

[51] *Bulletin*, July 3, 1972, pp. 21-2.
[52] Documents 13-14.

of Germany and the Polish People's Republic are to enter into force in the near future.[53] They reaffirmed their opinion that these treaties are important, both as contributions towards the relaxation of tension in Europe and as elements of the modus vivendi which the Federal Republic of Germany wishes to establish with its Eastern neighbours. Ministers welcomed the Declaration of 17th May, 1972, in which the Federal Republic of Germany confirmed its policy to this end and reaffirmed its loyalty to the Atlantic Alliance as the basis of its security and freedom.[54] They noted that it remains the policy of the Federal Republic of Germany to work for circumstances of peace in Europe in which the German people, in free self-determination, can recover their unity; and that the existing treaties and agreements to which the Federal Republic of Germany is a party and the rights and responsibilities of the Four Powers relating to Berlin and Germany as a whole remain unaffected.

6. Ministers also welcomed the progress made since their last meeting in the talks between the Federal Republic of Germany and the GDR [German Democratic Republic]. They regard the conclusion of the agreements and arrangements between the competent German Authorities, which supplement the Quadripartite Agreement on Berlin of 3rd September, 1971,[55] as well as the signature of a Treaty on Questions of Traffic between the Federal Republic of Germany and the GDR,[56] as important steps in the effort to improve the situation in Germany. They thus feel encouraged in the hope that, in further negotiations between the Federal Republic of Germany and the GDR, agreement might be reached on more comprehensive arrangements which would take into account the special situation in Germany.[57]

7. Ministers noted with satisfaction that the Governments of France, the United Kingdom, the United States and the Soviet Union have arranged to sign the Final Protocol to the Quadripartite Agreement.[58] The entry into force of the entire Berlin Agreement being thus assured, the Ministers hope that a new era can begin for Berlin, free of the tension that has marked its history for the past quarter century.

8. In the light of these favourable developments, Ministers agreed to enter into multilateral conversations concerned with preparations for a Conference on Security and Co-operation in Europe [CSCE]. They accepted with gratitude the proposal of the Finnish Government to act as host for such talks in Helsinki at the level of Heads of Mission under

[53] Cf. above at notes 30-31.
[54] Joint resolution of the two houses of the West German Parliament, adopted May 17, 1972; English text in Keesing's, p. 25352.
[55] *Documents, 1971*, no. 39. The supplementary arrangements between "competent German Authorities" are listed in Document 25b, para. 2, below.
[56] Signed in East Berlin May 26, 1972; entered into force Oct. 17, 1972.
[57] Cf. below at note 101.
[58] Cf. Document 25.

the conditions set out in its aide-memoire of 24th November, 1970. Accordingly, they decided to work out with other interested governments the necessary arrangements for beginning the multilateral preparatory talks.[59]

9. Ministers stated that the aim of Allied Governments at the multilateral preparatory talks would be to ensure that their proposals were fully considered at a Conference and to establish that enough common ground existed among the participants to warrant reasonable expectations that a Conference would produce satisfactory results.

10. Prepared in this way, a Conference on Security and Co-operation in Europe should constitute an important factor in the process of reducing tension. It should help to eliminate obstacles to closer relations and co-operation among the participants while maintaining the security of all. Allied governments look forward to a serious examination of the real problems at issue and to a Conference which would yield practical results.

11. Ministers considered that, in the interest of security, the examination at a CSCE of appropriate measures, including certain military measures, aimed at strengthening confidence and increasing stability would contribute to the process of reducing the dangers of military confrontation.

12. Ministers noted the Report of the Council in Permanent Session concerning a Conference on Security and Co-operation in Europe. The Report examined the issues which might be included on the Agenda of a Conference as set forth in paragraph 13 of the Brussels Communiqué of 10th December, 1971,[60] as well as the procedural questions relating to the convening of a Conference. Ministers directed the Council in Permanent Session to develop further its substantive and procedural studies in preparation for a Conference.

13. Ministers representing countries which participate in NATO's Integrated Defence Programme recalled the offers to discuss mutual and balanced force reductions which they had made at Reykjavik in 1968, at Rome in 1970, and subsequently reaffirmed.[61]

14. These Ministers continue to aim at negotiations on mutual and balanced force reductions and related measures. They believe that these negotiations should be conducted on a multilateral basis and be preceded by suitable explorations. They regretted that the Soviet Government has failed to respond to the Allied offer of October 1971, to enter into exploratory talks.[62] They therefore now propose that multi-

[59] Cf. Document 31.
[60] *A.F.R., 1971*, no. 42.
[61] *Documents, 1968-69*, pp. 133-4; same, *1970*, pp. 89-90; *A.F.R., 1971*, nos. 37, 40, and 42. References to the participants in NATO's Integrated Defense Program technically encompass all allied countries except France and Iceland, which does not maintain military forces.
[62] *A.F.R., 1971*, no. 40.

lateral explorations on mutual and balanced force reductions be under-taken as soon as practicable, either before or in parallel with multilateral preparatory talks on a Conference on Security and Cooperation in Europe.

15. These Ministers noted the studies conducted since their last meeting on political, military and technical aspects of mutual and balanced force reductions. They instructed the Permanent Represent-atives to continue this work in preparation for eventual negotiations.

16. These Ministers stated that the present military balance of forces in Europe does not allow a unilateral relaxation of the defence efforts of the Allies. Unilateral force reductions would detract from the Alli-ance's efforts to achieve greater stability and détente and would jeop-ardise the prospects for mutual and balanced force reductions.

17. Ministers took note of a Report by the Council in Permanent Session on the situation in the Mediterranean. They expressed their concern regarding the factors of instability in the area which could endanger the security of the members of the Alliance. They instructed the Council in Permanent Session to follow closely the evolution of the situation and to report to them at their next meeting.

18. The next Ministerial Session of the North Atlantic Council will be held in Brussels in December 1972.[63]

19. Ministers requested the Foreign Minister of the Grand Duchy of Luxembourg [Gaston Thorn] to transmit this Communiqué on their behalf through diplomatic channels to all other interested parties, including neutral and non-aligned governments.

(25) Quadripartite Agreement on Berlin, Signed in Berlin September 3, 1971 and Entered Into Force June 3, 1972.

(a) Statement by Secretary of State Rogers on the Signing of the Final Quadripartite Protocol, Berlin, June 3, 1972.[64]

(Complete Text)

The signing of the final protocol to the Berlin agreement[65] is an act with profound meaning for the people of Berlin and Germany. It is an act with equally profound meaning for the people of Europe and for the cause of peace in the world. For over 25 years Berlin has been a major focus of tensions between East and West, tensions which at times

---

[63] Cf. Document 32.
[64] Department of State Press Release 132, June 5, 1972; text from *Bulletin*, July 3, 1972, p. 15. For the background and text of the Berlin agreement, see *A.F.R., 1971*, nos. 38-39.
[65] Document 25b.

threatened the stability of Europe and the world. The agreement we have just signed could serve to put those tensions to rest.

For the people of Berlin the agreement offers an improvement in daily life. Once only the stark effects of division could be seen in Berlin. Now the start of a healing process is in sight. Once virtually no visits to East Berlin and the German Democratic Republic were feasible. Now over a million Berliners have made such visits in only a few weeks, many of them seeing relatives and friends from whom they have been separated for years. For those who live here, Berlin is no longer an isolated island.

For the people of Europe, this agreement is a step in reducing barriers to contact—barriers which have too long divided this continent and this city. The success of these negotiations will spur further efforts on behalf of a Europe at peace and at one with itself. Berlin, for a quarter of a century a symbol of Europe's division, could become a symbol of hope for Europe's future.

For all who value peace, this agreement demonstrates that the most stubborn issues can yield to realistic and patient negotiation and that when the cause of peace is advanced there are no losers, only winners.

The four governments who today signed this protocol can take satisfaction in the work they have done. The German authorities, in concluding their indispensable supplementary agreements,[66] have also contributed fundamentally to the outcome. They now envisage additional negotiations, negotiations which we earnestly hope will further improve the relationship between them and will further remove obstacles to freer movement of peoples.[67]

I cannot let this occasion pass without paying tribute to the courageous people of Berlin. It is their spirit and their fortitude that have made it possible for us to be here today. This agreement is in a real sense their achievement. Those who sign it and those who are charged to carry it out undertake solemn responsibilities to Berliners.

This protocol commits each government to insure that the agreement is faithfully carried out. That, of course, is the heart of the matter; for it is in the implementation of the words of the agreement that true progress will come. The United States will fulfill its responsibilities under the agreement. And we will maintain our commitment to assure the security and viability of Berlin.

The people of America—who have a deep bond with the people of Berlin—share the hope that this day will be viewed in history as one which marked a better life for millions of Berliners and Germans. We hope it will be looked upon as a day when decisive progress was made in reconciliation among the peoples of all of Europe. We hope that

---

66 Cf. Document 25b, para. 2.
67 Cf. below at note 101.

today will be viewed as one of the most important days in the history of the last half of the 20th century.

Whether June 3, 1972, will hold that place in history depends on the determined effort of governments in both East and West. On behalf of President Nixon and the American people, I pledge the United States Government to that effort.

(b) Final Quadripartite Protocol, Signed at Berlin June 3, 1972.[68]

(Complete Text)

The Governments of the United States of America, the French Republic, the Union of Soviet Socialist Republics and the United Kingdom of Great Britain and Northern Ireland,

Having in mind Part III of the Quadripartite Agreement of September 3, 1971,[69] and taking note with satisfaction of the fact that the agreements and arrangements mentioned below have been concluded,

Have agreed on the following:

1. The four Governments, by virtue of this Protocol, bring into force the Quadripartite Agreement, which, like this Protocol, does not affect quadripartite agreements or decisions previously concluded or reached.

2. The four Governments proceed on the basis that the agreements and arrangements concluded between the competent German authorities:

"Agreement between the Government of the Federal Republic of Germany and the Government of the German Democratic Republic on the Transit Traffic of Civilian Persons and Goods between the Federal Republic of Germany and Berlin (West)" ("Abkommen zwischen der Regierung der Bundesrepublik Deutschland und der Regierung der Deutschen Demokratischen Republik ueber den Transitverkehr von zivilen Personen und Guetern zwischen der Bundesrepublik Deutschland und Berlin (West)") dated December 17, 1971;

"Arrangement between the Senat and the Government of the German Democratic Republic on Facilitations and Improvements in Travel and Visitor Traffic" ("Vereinbarung zwischen dem Senat und der Regierung der Deutschen Demokratischen Republik ueber Erleichterungen und Verbesserungen des Reise- und Besucherverkehrs") dated December 20, 1971;

[68] TIAS 7551 (24 UST 348). English texts of the agreements and arrangements listed in para. 2 appear in 24 UST 376-92.
[69] A.F.R. 1971, no. 39.

"Arrangement between the Senat and the Government of the German Democratic Republic on the Resolution of the Problem of Enclaves by Exchange of Territory" ("Vereinbarung zwischen dem Senat und der Regierung der Deutschen Demokratischen Republik ueber die Regelung der Frage von Enklaven durch Gebietsaustausch") dated December 20, 1971;

Points 6 and 7 of the "Protocol on Negotiations between a Delegation of the Federal Ministry for Post and Telecommunications of the Federal Republic of Germany and a Delegation of the Ministry for Post and Telecommunications of the German Democratic Republic" ("Protokoll ueber Verhandlungen zwischen einer Delegation des Bundesministeriums fuer das Post- und Fernmeldewesen der Bundesrepublik Deutschland und einer Delegation des Ministeriums fuer Post- und Fernmeldewesen der Deutschen Demokratischen Republik") dated September 30, 1971;

shall enter into force simultaneously with the Quadripartite Agreement.

3. The Quadripartite Agreement and the consequent agreements and arrangements of the competent German authorities referred to in this Protocol settle important issues examined in the course of the negotiations and shall remain in force together.

4. In the event of a difficulty in the application of the Quadripartite Agreement or any of the above-mentioned agreements or arrangements which any of the four Governments considers serious, or in the event of non-implementation of any part thereof, that Government will have the right to draw the attention of the other three Governments to the provisions of the Quadripartite Agreement and this Protocol and to conduct the requisite quadripartite consultations in order to ensure the observance of the commitments undertaken and to bring the situation into conformity with the Quadripartite Agreement and this Protocol.

5. This Protocol enters into force on the date of signature.

DONE at the building formerly occupied by the Allied Control Council in the American Sector of Berlin this third day of June, 1972, in four originals, each in the English, French and Russian languages, all texts being equally authentic.

For the Government of the United States of America:

(*Signed*) William P. Rogers

For the Government of the French Republic:

(*Signed*) Maurice Schumann

For the Government of the Union of Soviet
Socialist Republics:

(*Signed*) A. Gromyko

For the Government of the United Kingdom
of Great Britain and Northern Ireland:

(*Signed*) Alec Douglas-Home

C. The United States and Eastern Europe.

[The development of peaceful interchange between the United
States and the countries of Eastern Europe was seen in Washington
as an objective worth pursuing for its own sake, irrespective of the
immediate status of détente. "The improvement in our relations
with the Soviet Union during 1972 has created a better atmosphere
for our relations with the countries of Eastern Europe," wrote President Nixon in his annual foreign policy message early in 1973.
"But we do not regard our relations with any East European countries as a function of our relations with Moscow. We reject the idea
of special rights or advantages for outside powers in the region. We
welcomed and responded to opportunities to develop our relations
with the East European countries long before the Moscow Summit.
And we shall continue to seek ways to expand our economic, scientific, technological, and cultural contacts with them. Mutual benefit
and reciprocity are governing principles."[70]
Already known as the first American chief executive to visit
Romania (in 1969) and Yugoslavia (in 1970), President Nixon set
still another precedent by stopping over in Poland on May 31-June
1, 1972 on his return from the Moscow summit. Highlights of the
Polish visit, as recorded in the official communiqué (Document 26),
included a decision to create a joint Polish-American Trade Commission; agreement to expand cooperation in the economic, scientific, technological, and cultural fields; and the signature of a
consular convention by Secretary of State Rogers and Polish
Foreign Minister Stefan Olszowski.

[70] Nixon Report, 1973, p. 91.

Having accompanied the President on his visits to the U.S.S.R., Iran, and Poland, the Secretary of State proceeded in July 1972 to visit the capitals of Romania, Hungary, and Yugoslavia as well (Document 27). The first American Secretary of State to visit Romania and Hungary, Secretary Rogers signed consular conventions with both countries which were subsequently transmitted to the Senate, together with the earlier U.S.-Polish consular convention, on September 19, 1972 (Document 28). All three conventions were unanimously approved by the Senate on March 27, 1973 and entered into force July 6, 1973.]

(26) President Nixon's Visit to Poland, May 31-June 1, 1972: Joint United States-Polish Communiqué Issued at the Conclusion of the Visit, June 1, 1972. [71]

(Complete Text)

I.

At the invitation of the President of the Council of State of the Polish People's Republic, Mr. Henryk Jablonski, and the Chairman of the Council of Ministers, Mr. Piotr Jaroszewicz—the President of the United States, Mr. Richard Nixon, and Mrs. Nixon paid an official visit to Poland on May 31 and June 1.

On the first day of the visit, the First Secretary of the Central Committee of the Polish United Workers' Party [PUWP], Edward Gierek, conducted talks with President Nixon.

On June 1, President Nixon called on the President of the Council of State Henryk Jablonski and had talks with him.

On the second day of the visit talks were held between First Secretary of the Central Committee of the Polish United Workers' Party Edward Gierek, Chairman of the Council of Ministers Piotr Jaroszewicz, and President Nixon.

The following participated in these talks:

on the American side:

SECRETARY OF STATE WILLIAM P. ROGERS
AMBASSADOR OF THE UNITED STATES WALTER J. STOESSEL, JR.
ASSISTANT TO THE PRESIDENT FOR NATIONAL SECURITY AFFAIRS DR. HENRY KISSINGER
ASSISTANT SECRETARY OF STATE FOR EUROPEAN AFFAIRS MARTIN J. HILLENBRAND

[71] *Presidential Documents*, June 5, 1972, pp. 973-5.

on the Polish side:

VICE PREMIER AND CHAIRMAN OF THE PLANNING COMMISSION MIECZYSLAW JAGIELSKI
FOREIGN MINISTER STEFAN OLSZOWSKI
SECRETARY OF THE CENTRAL COMMITTEE OF THE PUWP FRANCISZEK SZLACHCIC
SECRETARY OF THE CENTRAL COMMITTEE OF THE PUWP JAN SZYDLAK
AMBASSADOR OF POLAND WITOLD TRAMPCZYNSKI
MINISTER OF SCIENCE, HIGHER EDUCATION AND TECHNOLOGY JAN KACZMAREK
MINISTER OF FOREIGN TRADE TADEUSZ OLECHOWSKI
DEPUTY CHAIRMAN OF THE PLANNING COMMISSION HENRYK KISIEL
VICE MINISTER OF FOREIGN AFFAIRS ROMUALD SPASOWSKI
GOVERNMENT SPOKESMAN UNDERSECRETARY OF STATE WLODZIMIERZ JANIUREK

Talks were also held between Secretary of State William P. Rogers and Minister of Foreign Affairs Stefan Olszowski.

During the talks, the two sides had a useful exchange of views on international questions of particular interest to them and discussed the most important subjects in the field of bilateral relations.

The talks were frank, businesslike and constructive. They were conducted in an atmosphere marked by a desire to better understand each other's position, and to expand and deepen mutual relations.

President and Mrs. Nixon expressed their warm appreciation for the hospitality they enjoyed in Poland. The President of the United States invited the First Secretary of the Central Committee of the Polish United Workers' Party, Mr. Edward Gierek, the President of the Council of State, Mr. Henryk Jablonski, and the Prime Minister, Mr. Piotr Jaroszewicz, to visit the United States at a time convenient to both sides. The invitation was accepted with pleasure.[72]

II.

1. Both sides agreed that the development of peaceful cooperation among states must be based on the principles of territorial integrity and inviolability of frontiers, non-interference in internal affairs, sovereign equality, independence and renunciation of the use or threat of use of force.

2. Both sides presented their views on the situation in Europe. They affirmed that the broadening of relations between all states interested in European security is of outstanding importance for world peace.

[72] First Secretary Gierek and other Polish leaders paid an official visit to the U.S. on Oct. 8-13, 1974 (*Presidential Documents*, Oct. 21, 1974, pp. 1280-82).

Both sides welcomed the expansion of cooperation in Europe in all fields and expressed their belief that true security is indivisible and can be attained only if Europe is considered as a whole. The relations between the United States and Poland, based on sovereign equality and mutual respect, contribute to peace and stability in Europe and to the favorable development of the overall international situation.

3. Both sides welcomed the treaty between Poland and the Federal Republic of Germany signed on December 7, 1970,[73] including its border provisions. They noted the significance of the provisions of this treaty as well as of other recent agreements in contributing to confidence and cooperation among the European states.

4. Both sides agreed that a reciprocal reduction of armed forces and armaments, first of all in Central Europe, would contribute to the goal of ensuring security and stability in Europe. Any agreement reached on this matter should not diminish the security of any of the sides. The two sides agreed that the states concerned should reach appropriate agreement as soon as practicable on procedures for negotiations on this question in a special forum. Reduction of armed forces and armaments in Central Europe would be an important step toward attaining the objective of general and complete disarmament.

5. Both sides expressed the belief that a European Conference on Security and Cooperation may constitute an important step forward in the extensive and long-range process of the normalization of relations and detente in Europe. They agreed that the Conference should be carefully prepared, and that multilateral consultations in that regard should begin without undue delay. The two sides declared their readiness to cooperate to achieve this aim.

6. Both sides presented their known positions on the war in Vietnam and the situation in Indochina. Essential views of the two sides in this question remained divergent.

III.

1. Both sides noted with satisfaction the increasing commercial and other economic ties between the two countries and concluded that there are considerable possibilities for their further expansion. With this in mind the two sides discussed issues related to commercial exchange and financial and credit matters.

The Polish side indicated an interest in increased purchases of capital goods, licenses and technology in the United States.

The U.S. side undertook to consider in a constructive manner further steps leading to increased bilateral trade and economic cooperation.

2. The two sides will exchange information leading to expanded

---

73 Cf. above at note 31.

trade relations. In the interest of broadening and facilitating trade relations between the two countries and working out concrete steps towards that end the two sides decided to create a joint Polish-American Trade Commission.

3. The two sides will encourage and support contacts and cooperation between economic organizations and enterprises of both countries.

4. The two sides expressed their satisfaction with the expanding program of scientific and technical cooperation and appraised positively its mutually advantageous results. Last year's exchange of visits at the cabinet level,[74] which gave attention to the development of scientific and technical cooperation, confirmed the desirability of continuing cooperation in this field.

The two sides expressed their interest in the conclusion of an intergovernmental agreement on comprehensive cooperation in science, technology and culture.[75] Appropriate institutional arrangements will be established to promote work in these fields.

5. The two sides agreed that the increase of mutual economic and personal contacts, including tourism, justifies further development of transportation links between Poland and the United States by sea as well as by air. The two sides expect to sign in the near future an air transport agreement[76] and to establish mutual and regular air connections.

6. The two sides expressed their interest in commemorating the five hundredth anniversary of the birth of Nicholas Copernicus and discussed ways of celebrating it.[77]

7. Both sides welcomed the signing of the Consular Convention by Secretary of State William P. Rogers and Minister of Foreign Affairs Stefan Olszowski[78] and the conclusion of an agreement on the simultaneous establishment on December 1, 1972 of new Consulates—in New York and Krakow, respectively. Both parties welcome these steps as concrete evidence of expanding relations between the two states.

8. The two sides emphasized the positive influence exerted on their mutual relations by the traditions of history, sentiment and friendship between the Polish and American peoples. A prominent part is played

---

[74] In a first exchange of cabinet-level visits with Poland during 1971, U.S. Secretary of Transportation John A. Volpe and Secretary of Commerce Maurice Stans visited Warsaw and Polish Science Minister Jan Kaczmarek visited Washington (Nixon Report, 1972, p. 51).

[75] An Agreement on Cooperation in Science and Technology was signed in Washington and Warsaw Oct. 31, 1972 and entered into force immediately. Text in TIAS 7565 (24 UST 465); comment in *Bulletin*, Nov. 27, 1972, p. 642.

[76] An Air Transport Agreement was signed in Warsaw July 19, 1972. Text in TIAS 7535 (23 UST 4269); comment in *Bulletin*, Aug. 21, 1972, p. 218.

[77] Cf. *Bulletin*, July 31, 1972, pp. 137-8.

[78] Cf. Document 28a.

in this respect by many United States citizens of Polish extraction who maintain an interest in the country of their ancestors. The two sides recognize that this interest and contacts resulting from it constitute a valuable contribution to the development of bilateral relations.

Signed in Warsaw, June 1, 1972.

(27) Secretary of State Rogers' Visit to Romania, Hungary, and Yugoslavia, July 1972.

(a) Toast at Luncheon Hosted by President Nicolae Ceauşescu, Bucharest, July 6, 1972.[79]

(Complete Text)

Mr. President, Madame Ceauşescu, ladies and gentlemen: We have just completed a morning of very successful talks. They confirm that the relations between our two countries are good and that they will continue to grow.

Three years ago these relations were limited. But the visit of President Nixon to Romania in August 1969[80] and your visit to the United States in October 1970[81] have begun a new and significant era.

In our talks yesterday and today we have demonstrated that this new era of cooperation will bring benefits to our peoples and closer relationships between our governments:

—We have signed the first consular convention between Romania and the United States since 1881. This convention[82] will contribute to the growth of normal travel and commercial contacts between our two countries.

—The United States has taken steps which will cut by more than half the time required for entry of Romanian ships and crews into United States ports, the first such measure we have taken with respect to countries in this part of Europe. We hope that this advance will lead to increased commerce and that American ships will soon be visiting Romanian ports as well.

—We have decided to make Export-Import Bank facilities available to Romania for the purchase of American equipment, materials, and technology.

[79] Department of State Press Release 167, July 7, 1972; text in *Bulletin*, Aug. 7, 1972, pp. 168-9.
[80] Aug. 2-3; *Public Papers, 1969*, pp. 604-12.
[81] Oct. 26; same, *1970*, pp. 942-3 and 946-8.
[82] Cf. Document 28b.

—We have removed travel restraints on Romanian diplomats in the United States which were remnants of a previous period of mutual restrictions.

These advances build upon other progress in the relationship between our countries:

—Our cultural exchange and relations are extensive and rapidly growing. The opening of a Romanian library in New York last December and of an American library in Bucharest in January will help to increase understanding between our peoples.

—Our cooperation in science and technology is equally advanced. In the last three years, more than 40 Romanian scientists have visited the United States. And just last week seven new areas of cooperation were approved, including work on controlling exhaust pollution from automobile engines, a matter of major concern in the United States. We look forward to a substantial increase both in areas of scientific cooperation and in numbers of projects.[83]

Mr. President, these specific advances in our bilateral relations are impressive. But they are not the whole story.

Our bilateral trade has more than tripled in the past three years. To increase it still further, we have urged and will continue to urge our Congress to approve legislation which will make it possible for Romanian exports to enter the United States on a most-favored-nation basis.

Our political relations have also prospered. Most importantly, Romania and the United States share a community of interest in Europe and in the world at large.

Last night Foreign Minister [Corneliu] Manescu spoke of transforming Europe into "A zone of peace, cooperation, and good neighborhood between sovereign countries enjoying equal rights." We, too, support this objective. Indeed, we would like to see the day when Europe is no longer divided. This will not be easy to achieve, but the Berlin agreement proves that marked progress is possible.

The conference next year on security and cooperation in Europe—if it takes concrete steps to increase contacts among Europeans—can also aid the process toward European reconciliation.

The United States and the Socialist Republic of Romania pursue world policies directed to similar objectives: to the peaceful resolution of disputes, to support for the United Nations, to the promotion of good relations with all countries. We also share a basic conviction that

---

[83] An expanded Agreement on Exchanges and Cooperation in Educational, Cultural, Scientific, Technical, and Other Fields in 1973-74 was signed in Washington Dec. 15, 1972; announcement and text in *Bulletin*, Jan. 29, 1973, pp. 119-23.

all countries, whatever their size or their location and whether they are in the same or in different social systems, are equally sovereign and equally independent and have an equal right to run their own affairs free of outside interference. My visit here underlines the devotion of the United States to that basic principle of relations among states.

Mr. President, President Nixon has asked me to bring this message to you and to the Romanian people: that the United States places a high value on its relations with your country and that it will do all it can to make those relations prosper in years to come.

I ask you now to join me in a toast: to President Ceausescu; to the growth in ties between the United States and the Socialist Republic of Romania; to the friendship between the American and the Romanian people.

(b) Remarks on Signing the United States-Hungarian Consular Convention, Budapest, July 7, 1972.[84]

(Complete Text)

In the quest for peace the United States believes that understanding among peoples is fundamental. Thus we favor a more open world, open to trade, to greater contacts among people, and to a greater flow of ideas. Both the agreements signed today, in modest but important ways, contribute to this goal.

The consular convention that Foreign Minister [Janos] Peter and I have signed[85] is a response, and an encouragement, to greater contact between Hungary and the United States. As American tourism to Hungary rises and as more Hungarians visit the United States, consular requirements are about to increase. We therefore have a mutual interest in developing a better basis for dealing with them.

I am happy to be present at the signing of the agreement on scientific and technical exchanges between the Institute of Cultural Relations and the National Science Foundation. This framework agreement will enable scientists in each country to share their knowledge and experience and to make the personal contacts which are so important to scientific progress.

Speaking for the United States Government, I welcome both these agreements not only for their own sake but because they indicate the mutual desire and ability of our two countries to seek improvement in our bilateral relations in a serious and realistic way.

---

84 Department of State Press Release 168, July 7, 1972; text from *Bulletin*, Aug. 7, 1972, p. 169.
85 Cf. Document 28c.

(c) Visit to Yugoslavia, July 7-9, 1972: Joint United States-Yugoslav Press Release, July 9, 1972.[86]

(Complete Text)

At the invitation of the Federal Secretary for Foreign Affairs of the Socialist Federal Republic of Yugoslavia [SFRY], Mirko Tepavac, the Secretary of State of the United States of America, William P. Rogers, accompanied by Mrs. Rogers, paid an official visit to Yugoslavia from July 7-9, 1972.

The President of the Socialist Federal Republic of Yugoslavia, Josip Broz Tito, received the Secretary of State at Brioni on July 9, 1972. Mr. Rogers was also received by the President of the Federal Executive Council, Dzemal Bijedic.

In the course of the visit talks were conducted on the international situation and on bilateral cooperation between the two countries.

The two Secretaries noted with satisfaction that relations between Yugoslavia and the United States have been traditionally good and mutually beneficial and are developing exceptionally well at the present time. They underlined the importance of the meetings of President Tito and President Nixon and of their joint statement of October 30, 1971,[87] which provides a long-term basis for cooperation between the two countries. They expressed satisfaction that on the basis of this document a further development of the close mutual relations between Yugoslavia and the United States has been registered in all fields.

The talks covered current international issues and developments, including recent visits made by the leaders of both countries, European cooperation and security, and the situations in the Middle East and Southeast Asia. The activities of non-aligned and developing countries were also discussed.

In the course of the exchange of views on international issues the two sides stated their respective positions in a candid and friendly manner. They agreed that solutions should be found for the problems which are burdening the present-day world on the basis of respect for independence, sovereignty, equality, and non-interference among all States, whether they are in the same or in different social, economic or political systems.

Emphasizing that the development of bilateral relations has been favorable in all fields, the Secretaries agreed further to develop and promote mutually beneficial cooperation between Yugoslavia and the United States. Special attention will be devoted to economic relations, which have recently received new incentives. Both countries also ex-

[86] Department of State Press Release 170, July 10, 1972; text from *Bulletin*, Aug. 7, 1972, pp. 169-70.
[87] Text in *Public Papers, 1971*, pp. 1070-72.

pressed their intention to continue to develop and enrich scientific, technical and cultural forms of cooperation. They considered that an important contribution to the development of bilateral relations is provided by United States citizens of Yugoslav descent.

The two Secretaries affirmed the importance of regular contacts and exchanges of views between representatives of the two countries in various fields, noting that they have been mutually useful and that they should be continued in the future, in the interest of the further development of relations and cooperation between the SFRY and USA, as well as of peace in the world.

(28) Consular Conventions with Poland, Romania, and Hungary: Messages from President Nixon to the Senate, September 19, 1972.

(a) Consular Convention Between the United States and the Polish People's Republic, Signed at Warsaw May 31, 1972.[88]

(Complete Text)

To the Senate of the United States:

I am pleased to transmit for the Senate's advice and consent to ratification the Consular Convention between the Government of the United States of America and the Government of the Polish People's Republic, with Protocols, signed at Warsaw on May 31, 1972,[89] on the occasion of my recent visit there. The Convention was accompanied by two related exchanges of notes, which are transmitted for the information of the Senate.[90]

The signing of this treaty is a significant step in the gradual process of improving and broadening the relationship between the United States and Poland. Consular relations between the two countries have not previously been subject to formal agreement. This Convention will establish firm obligations on such important matters as free communication between a citizen and his consul, notification to consular offices of the arrest and detention of their citizens, and permission for visits by consuls to citizens who are under detention.

The people of the United States and Poland enjoy a long tradition of friendship. I welcome the opportunity through this Consular Convention to strengthen the ties between our two nations. I urge the

---

[88] *Presidential Documents*, Sept. 25, 1972, p. 1410.
[89] S. Ex. U, 92d Cong., 2d sess.; entered into force as TIAS 7642 (24 UST 1231).
[90] 24 UST 1306-15.

Senate to give the Convention its prompt and favorable consideration.[91]

RICHARD NIXON

The White House
    September 19, 1972

(b) Consular Convention Between the United States and the Socialist Republic of Romania, Signed at Bucharest July 5, 1972.[92]

(Complete Text)

To the Senate of the United States:

I transmit herewith, for Senate advice and consent to ratification, the Consular Convention between the United States of America and the Socialist Republic of Romania, signed at Bucharest on July 5, 1972.[93]

The Convention was signed by Secretary of State William P. Rogers, who was paying an official visit to Romania,[94] and by Foreign Minister Corneliu Manescu. It is evidence of the continued improvement and expansion of United States-Romanian relations.

This new Convention, replacing one concluded in 1881,[95] will make possible improved consular services in both countries. It will ensure unhindered communication between a citizen and his consul and prompt visit by consuls to citizens who are detained. Under the Convention, American citizens in Romania will have a fuller degree of consular assistance and protection than ever before.

I hope that the Senate will act favorably on the Consular Convention with Romania at an early date.[96]

RICHARD NIXON

The White House
    September 19, 1972

---

[91] The Senate gave its advice and consent to ratification by a 90-0 vote on Mar. 27, 1973 and the convention entered into force July 6, 1973.

[92] *Presidential Documents*, Sept. 25, 1972, p. 1410.

[93] S. Ex. V, 92d Cong., 2d sess; entered into force as TIAS 7643 (24 UST 1317).

[94] Cf. Document 27a.

[95] Department of State *Treaty Series*, no. 297; 23 Stat. 711.

[96] The Senate gave its advice and consent to ratification by a 92-0 vote on Mar. 27, 1973 and the convention entered into force July 6, 1973.

(c) Consular Convention Between the United States and the Hungarian People's Republic, Signed at Budapest July 7, 1972.[97]

(Complete Text)

To the Senate of the United States:

I am transmitting for the Senate's advice and consent to ratification the Consular Convention between the United States of America and the Hungarian People's Republic, signed at Budapest on July 7, 1972.[98]

Secretary of State William P. Rogers signed the Convention for the United States during his official visit to Hungary.[99] It is the first bilateral treaty concluded between the Governments of the United States and Hungary since World War II and reflects the increasingly warm contacts developing between Americans and Hungarians as well as between their Governments.

The Consular Convention, like others recently negotiated with Poland and Romania, will make possible improved consular services, including guaranteed communication between a citizen and his consul and prompt notification in case of detention.

I believe that this Convention will provide a cornerstone for the development and maintenance of friendly relations with Hungary, and I recommend that the Senate advise and consent to its ratification.[100]

RICHARD NIXON

The White House
September 19, 1972

D. Further Steps Toward Détente.

[The entry into force of the German-Soviet and German-Polish treaties and of the four-power Berlin agreement (Document 25) gave added impetus to the processes of normalization and détente in Central Europe. Having successfully adjusted its relationships with the U.S.S.R. and Poland, the Federal Republic of Germany now addressed itself to the even more difficult task of establishing a modus vivendi with the rival German Democratic Republic. In negotiations opened in East Berlin on August 16, 1972, representatives of the two German governments were able to agree on the terms of

[97] *Presidential Documents*, Sept. 25, 1972, pp. 1410-11.
[98] S. Ex. W, 92d Cong., 2d sess.; entered into force as TIAS 7641 (24 UST 1141).
[99] Cf. Document 27b.
[100] The Senate gave its advice and consent to ratification by a 92-0 vote on Mar. 27, 1973 and the convention entered into force July 6, 1973.

a "Treaty on the Bases of Relations Between the Federal Republic of Germany and the German Democratic Republic," drawn up with the avowed objective of creating the "preconditions for cooperation" between the two German states for the benefit of their peoples.[101] Without renouncing their differing views on the question of German reunification, the two governments agreed among other things to develop normal good neighborly relations; to respect each other's frontiers, territorial integrity, independence, and sovereignty; to exchange permanent representative missions; and to make separate but coordinated applications for admission to the United Nations. Initialed in Bonn on November 8, 1972, the treaty was signed in East Berlin on December 21, 1972 and entered into force, following ratification, at midnight on June 20-21, 1973. Pursuant to their separate applications, both German governments were subsequently admitted to membership in the United Nations on September 18, 1973.

In view of the announced intention of the two German states to apply for U.N. membership, the four powers holding responsibilities in Germany issued a special statement on November 9, 1972 in which they expressed their intention to support the proposed applications and noted that such membership would in no way affect their own rights and responsibilities or the relevant quadripartite agreements, decisions, and practices (Document 29).

The corollary of this important step toward normalization of political relationships in Central Europe was a further improvement in the prospects for holding a Conference on Security and Cooperation in Europe (C.S.C.E.) and for the scheduling of talks on Mutual and Balanced Force Reductions (M.B.F.R.). When Dr. Kissinger visited Moscow in September 1972, the Soviet Government formally proposed that multilateral preparatory talks be held on both projects and that those on the Security Conference begin in Helsinki on November 22, 1972, in accordance with an invitation previously issued by the Finnish Government.[102] The United States, while apparently in agreement with this procedure, insisted that discussions of C.S.C.E. and M.B.F.R. should "take place in some related time frame"[103] and accordingly delayed its formal assent pending consultation with its allies about a new initiative on M.B.F.R.

As a sequel to these consultations, formal invitations to begin exploratory talks on force reduction in Central Europe on January

101 English text in Keesing's, pp. 25621-2.
102 12th Annual Report of the United States Arms Control and Disarmament Agency, Jan. 31, 1973, in Documents on Disarmament, 1972, p. 880. On the Kissinger visit to Moscow, cf. Chapter II at note 167.
103 Kissinger news conference, Sept. 16, 1972, in Bulletin, Oct. 9, 1972, p. 394.

31, 1973 were extended on November 15, 1972 by the seven NATO countries with troops or territory in that area (Belgium, Canada, Federal Republic of Germany, Luxembourg, Netherlands, United Kingdom, and United States) to four of the Warsaw Pact governments (Czechoslovakia, Hungary, Poland, and the U.S.S.R.). A separate invitation to the German Democratic Republic was extended by the Federal Republic of Germany. Five NATO "flank" countries (Denmark, Greece, Italy, Norway, and Turkey) also indicated their interest in being present on a rotating basis (Document 30).

Immediately following this initiative, the United States officially accepted the Finnish invitation to take part in multilateral consultations on a European Security Conference, to be held in Helsinki at ambassadorial level beginning November 22, 1972 (Document 31). It was understood in Washington that these preliminary consultations would focus on the drafting of an agenda for the proposed conference, the definition of the issues to be discussed, and the organization of the conference. Representatives of 34 governments, including the United States, Canada, and all European states except Albania, Andorra, and Monaco, took part in the first phase of the preliminary consultations, which began as scheduled on November 22, 1972 and continued until June 8, 1973. Thereafter, the 35-nation Conference on Security and Cooperation in Europe (including Monaco) was formally opened in the Finnish capital on July 3, 1973, and working sessions of the conference began in Geneva later in that year.

Preliminary consultations on M.B.F.R. were also commenced on schedule, although no reply to the NATO countries' invitation had been received up to the time of the North Atlantic Council's regular ministerial session held in Brussels on December 7-8, 1972. In a message read to the NATO Council by Secretary of State Rogers, President Nixon took note of the important negotiations in prospect and also renewed his promise "that given a similar approach by our Allies, we will maintain and improve our forces in Europe and will not reduce them unless there is reciprocal action from our adversaries" (Document 32a). Expressing satisfaction over the progress in East-West relations, all of the allied governments affirmed their intention to participate constructively in the Helsinki talks. Those that were involved in M.B.F.R.—in effect, all but France—expressed the further hope that exploratory conversations on that subject could still begin on January 31, 1973 and that formal negotiations could commence in the autumn of that year (Document 32b). Presumably the Communist governments had already signaled their willingness to abide by such a timetable; at all events, preparatory talks on M.B.F.R. did begin in Vienna on January 31, 1973, and a formal Conference on the Mutual Reduction of Forces and Armaments and Associated Measures in Central Europe opened in the Austrian capital on October 30, 1973.]

(29) Proposed German Membership in the United Nations: Quadripartite Declaration Issued November 9, 1972. [104]

(Complete Text)

DECLARATION OF THE GOVERNMENTS OF THE UNITED STATES OF AMERICA, THE FRENCH REPUBLIC, THE UNION OF SOVIET SOCIALIST REPUBLICS, AND THE UNITED KINGDOM OF GREAT BRITAIN AND NORTHERN IRELAND

The Governments of the United States of America, the French Republic, the Union of Soviet Socialist Republics, and the United Kingdom of Great Britain and Northern Ireland, having been represented by their Ambassadors, who held a series of meetings in the building formerly occupied by the Allied Control Council, are in agreement that they will support the applications for membership in the United Nations when submitted by the Federal Republic of Germany and the German Democratic Republic, and affirm in this connection that this membership shall in no way affect the rights and responsibilities of the Four Powers and the corresponding related Quadripartite agreements, decisions, and practices.

(30) Proposal for Exploratory Talks on Mutual and Balanced Force Reduction (M.B.F.R.): Statement Issued by the North Atlantic Treaty Organization, Brussels, November 16, 1972. [105]

(Complete Text)

Recognizing the importance of the question of mutual and balanced force reductions in Central Europe, governments of allied countries which issued the Declaration of Reykjavik[106] agreed to propose that

[104] *Bulletin*, Nov. 27, 1972, p. 623. Negotiated in Berlin by Ambassadors of the Four Powers, the declaration was issued in London, Moscow, Paris, and Washington following the initialing on Nov. 8, 1972 of the treaty referred to in note 101 above.

[105] *Bulletin*, Dec. 11, 1972, pp. 680-81. The statement was read to news correspondents in Washington by Charles W. Bray, III, Director of the State Department's Office of Press Relations. For further details, cf. above at note 103.

[106] *Documents, 1968-69*, pp. 133-4.

exploratory talks on this matter should be held beginning on 31 January 1973 in a place still to be agreed through diplomatic channels. The Governments of Belgium, Canada, the Federal Republic of Germany, Luxembourg, the Netherlands, the United Kingdom and the United States are communicating this proposal to the Governments of Czechoslovakia, Poland, Hungary and the USSR. The Government of the Federal Republic of Germany is communicating this proposal to the Government of the German Democratic Republic also.

The Governments of Denmark, Greece, Italy, Norway and Turkey will confirm their intention to be represented at the exploratory talks.

(31) Multilateral Consultations Regarding a Conference on Security and Cooperation in Europe (C.S.C.E.): Note from the American Embassy at Helsinki to the Finnish Ministry of Foreign Affairs, Delivered November 16, 1972.[107]

(Complete Text)

The Embassy of the United States of America presents its compliments to the Finnish Ministry of Foreign Affairs and, with reference to the Ministry's note of November 9, 1972, transmitting a memorandum and an annex, has the honor to accept the invitation of the Finnish Government to attend multilateral consultations in Helsinki, beginning on November 22, on the question of a conference on security and cooperation in Europe. The Government of the United States of America wishes to make clear in this connection that the acceptance of the invitation and participation does not affect the legal position that it has hitherto adopted on questions arising out of the special situation in Germany.

In accordance with the existing understanding, the United States will be represented for the duration of these multilateral consultations by the Chief of its Mission accredited in Helsinki.[108]

---

[107] *Bulletin*, Dec. 4, 1972, p. 660.
[108] Ambassador Val Peterson.

(32) Ministerial Session of the North Atlantic Council, Brussels, December 7-8, 1972.

  (a) Message from President Nixon to the Council, Read by Secretary of State Rogers December 7, 1972. [109]

(Complete Text)

As we approach 1973 we stand on the threshold of negotiations that could bring us closer to the lasting peace that is the goal of the North Atlantic Alliance:

—explorations have begun for a Conference on Security and Cooperation in Europe;
—explorations will begin soon regarding Mutual and Balanced Force Reductions;
—bilateral talks between individual Allies and members of the Warsaw Pact on issues of security and peace continue.

These prospects for peace, however, must rest on a foundation of continued military preparedness. Competing demands vie for the limited budgetary resources available to each Ally. Our peoples are increasingly sensitive to the just domestic needs of democratic and modern society, at the very time when the costs of modern and improved defense forces are increasing.

It will test the strength and vitality of this Alliance to maintain and improve our common defenses in these times. But this task must be accomplished.

For our part, the United States renews its pledge that given a similar approach by our Allies, we will maintain and improve our forces in Europe and will not reduce them unless there is reciprocal action from our adversaries.

We look to you—all of you—to continue the remarkable effort you have made in assuming a greater share of the burdens of common defense.

In our own way, each Ally must insure that its people understand the fundamental reasons that link a militarily strong NATO to successful negotiations. For without the understanding and the support of our peoples, this Alliance cannot survive. With this in mind, I am confident that the statesmen and the free peoples of the North Atlantic Alliance will continue to support an undiminished defense effort by each member.

RICHARD NIXON

[109] Department of State Press Release 307, Dec. 13, 1972; text from *Bulletin*, Jan. 1, 1973, p. 1.

(b) Final Communiqué, December 8, 1972.[110]

(Complete Text)

The North Atlantic Council met in Ministerial Session in Brussels on 7th and 8th December, 1972. Foreign and Defence Ministers were present.

2. In reviewing events since their May meeting,[111] Ministers noted with satisfaction the new progress in East-West relations. They observed that this progress flowed in large measure from initiatives taken by Allied Governments. They took the view that further significant improvements could be achieved during the coming year and indicated their readiness to press on with their efforts. They declared their resolve to bring about closer and more harmonious relationships, collectively and individually, among all peoples. They attached particular importance to freer movement of people, ideas and information.

3. Ministers were convinced that the objectives so far reached would not have been realized without the strength and cohesion of the Alliance. They expressed their determination, particularly in view of the continued strengthening of the Warsaw Pact military forces, to maintain the defensive capability of the Alliance. A healthy and strong Alliance is an indispensable condition for promoting stability and for achieving the aim of a just and lasting peace in Europe.

4. Ministers discussed the important developments concerning Germany which have taken place since their May meeting. They welcomed the initialling of the treaty on the basis of relations between the Federal Republic of Germany and the German Democratic Republic[112] on 8th November, 1972 and the statement of the Minister of Foreign Affairs of the Federal Republic of Germany that it is envisaged that this Treaty will be signed on 21st December, 1972 and thereafter will be submitted to the legislative bodies of the Federal Republic of Germany for approval. They took note of the statement of the Federal Foreign Minister that after the ratification of this treaty and after the domestic pre-conditions have been fulfilled the two German states will submit their applications for membership of the United Nations to be considered simultaneously by the competent organs of the world organization. Ministers took note of the declaration of the Four Powers of 9th November, 1972.[113] In this declaration the Four Powers recorded their agreement that they will support the applications for membership in the United Nations when submitted by the Federal Republic of Germany and the German Democratic Republic, and affirm in this

---

[110] *Bulletin*, Jan. 1, 1973, pp. 1-4.
[111] Document 24.
[112] Cf. above at note 101, where the treaty is correctly named.
[113] Document 29.

connection that this membership shall in no way affect the rights and responsibilities of the Four Powers and the corresponding, related quadripartite agreements, decisions, and practices. As regards the relations between France, the United Kingdom, the United States and the Federal Republic of Germany, Ministers noted that this declaration does not affect in any way the Convention on relations between the Three Powers and the Federal Republic of Germany and related Conventions and documents of 26th May, 1952 in the version of 23rd October, 1954.[114]

5. On the basis of these developments, individual member governments might wish to enter into negotiations with the German Democratic Republic with a view to establishing bilateral relations. In this connection Ministers reaffirmed the solidarity of the Alliance partners in questions concerning Germany, maintained since entry of the Federal Republic of Germany into the Alliance. The member states of the Atlantic Alliance expressed their continuing support for the policy of the Federal Republic of Germany to work towards a state of peace in Europe in which the German people regains its unity through free self-determination. Accordingly, they will continue to take fully into account the special situation in Germany, which is characterized by the fact that the German people today lives in two states, that a freely agreed contractual peace settlement for Germany is still outstanding and that until such a settlement is achieved, the above-mentioned rights and responsibilities of the Four Powers relating to Berlin and Germany as a whole will continue.

6. Ministers affirmed that their Governments would work constructively to establish necessary agreements in the multilateral preparatory talks, which have just started in Helsinki.[115] They recalled that the aim of their Governments at these talks would be to ensure that their proposals were fully considered at a Conference and to establish that enough common ground existed among the participants to warrant reasonable expectations that a Conference would produce satisfactory results. They considered that there should be agreement at these talks on the arrangements and guidelines necessary to enable such a Conference to produce constructive and specific results. They noted that such results could be achieved only through the process of detailed and serious negotiation, without artificial time limits.

7. Ministers confirmed that it is the goal of their Governments to increase the security of all Europe through negotiations concerning such questions as principles guiding relations between the participants and through appropriate measures, including military ones, aimed at strengthening confidence and increasing stability so as to contribute to the process of reducing the dangers of military confrontation; to im-

---

[114] *Documents, 1954*, pp. 136-42.
[115] Cf. Document 31.

prove co-operation in all fields; to bring about closer, more open and freer relationships between all people in Europe; to stimulate a wider flow of information and of ideas.

8. The Ministers representing countries which participate in NATO's integrated defence programme[116] noted with approval that the Governments of Belgium, Canada, the Federal Republic of Germany, Luxembourg, the Netherlands, United Kingdom, United States, Denmark, Greece, Italy, Norway and Turkey have proposed that the Governments of Czechoslovakia, the German Democratic Republic, Hungary, Poland and the Soviet Union join them in exploratory talks beginning on 31st January, 1973 on the question of Mutual and Balanced Force Reductions in Central Europe.[117] These Ministers recalled that this proposal accorded with past Allied initiatives and noted some indication of Eastern readiness to begin such talks at the time proposed. Ministers hoped that these talks would make it possible to commence negotiations on this subject in the Autumn of 1973. They noted that such a programme implied that talks on both Mutual and Balanced Force Reductions and on a Conference on Security and Co-operation in Europe would be going on in the same general period of time.

9. While considering it inappropriate to establish formal and specific links, these Ministers reaffirmed their view that progress in each set of the different negotiations would have a favourable effect on the others. None of them should be isolated from the general nature of the relations prevailing between the states concerned.

10. These Ministers took note of a report on guidelines for the conduct of the exploratory talks on Mutual and Balanced Force Reductions by the Allied countries involved, as well as of the work carried out in preparation for eventual negotiations. The Council in Permanent Session will continue consultations on all questions of objectives, policy and strategy pursued by Allied countries in these talks.

11. Recalling the Declaration of the Council in Rome in May 1970,[118] these Ministers confirmed their position that Mutual and Balanced Force Reductions in Central Europe should not operate to the military disadvantage of any side and should enhance stability and security in Europe as a whole. Their position is based on the conviction that the security of the Alliance is indivisible and that reductions in Central Europe should not diminish security in other areas.

12. Ministers expressed the hope that the SALT TWO negotiations between the United States and the Union of Soviet Socialist Republics[119] would achieve success. They considered that there should be renewed efforts in all fields of disarmament and arms control.

---

[116] Cf. note 61 to Document 24.
[117] Document 30.
[118] *Documents, 1970*, pp. 89-90.
[119] Cf. Document 17.

13. Ministers agreed that on all these questions the close and regular consultations which they have held so far and which have proved their value would continue.

14. Ministers took note of a new report on the situation in the Mediterranean prepared on their instructions by the Council in Permanent Session. Continuing instability in this region, which could endanger the security of the member countries, remains a cause for concern. Ministers instructed the Council in Permanent Session to continue keeping a close watch on developments and to report to them at their next meeting.

15. Ministers noted the progress achieved by the CCMS [Committee on the Challenges of Modern Society] especially in such areas as combatting oil pollution of the seas, disaster assistance, safety of motor vehicles, health care, waste water treatment, urban transportation, and also the recent signing of a memorandum of understanding by six member nations on low-pollution automobile engine development.

16. Ministers took note of the Report by the Conference of National Armaments Directors and of the views expressed on this paper by the Defence Ministers. Like the Defence Ministers, they welcomed the efforts being made to reduce duplication and waste of resources in the development and production of armaments. They instructed the Council in Permanent Session to make the necessary arrangements regarding the action to be taken on it and invited Armaments Directors to make suggestions for more effective co-operation.

17. Ministers of the countries participating in NATO's integrated defence programme met as the Defence Planning Committee and reviewed the military situation in the NATO area. They noted with concern that despite the political developments described above, the Soviet Union and her Allies seem determined to maintain and indeed increase their military capability which in both scale and nature appears to be greatly in excess of that required for purely defensive purposes; and that they continue to devote immense resources to the improvement and modernization of their land, air and naval forces confronting NATO. These Ministers stressed that NATO's requirements for defence are related directly to the reality of the military capabilities possessed by the Warsaw Pact.

18. These Ministers again gave attention to the growing Soviet maritime capability and in particular to the increase of Soviet naval activities in the Atlantic and Mediterranean which has taken place in recent years. They also considered the political and military implications of these activities and the measures being taken to counter them.

19. These Ministers emphasized the close relationship between the collective defence policy of NATO on the one hand and actual or potential developments in the international field on the other. They agreed that any unilateral reduction of effort on the part of the Alli-

ance would reduce the credibility of realistic deterrence and erode the stable balance of forces without which no satisfactory security arrangements can be negotiated. It was agreed that negotiations, in order to be successful, must proceed from a position of effective partnership and strength.

20. Accordingly these Ministers again endorsed the principle that the overall military capability of NATO should not be reduced except as part of a pattern of mutual force reductions balanced in scope and timing. In this context, they welcomed the reaffirmation by the United States that, given a similar approach by other countries of the Alliance, the United States would maintain and improve its forces in Europe and not reduce them unless there is reciprocal action by the other side.[120]

21. In the light of the considerations outlined earlier, these Ministers took note of the force commitment undertaken by each member nation for the year 1973, and adopted a five-year NATO Force Plan for the years 1973-1977. In doing so they emphasized the need to enhance the quality and effectiveness of national force contributions within the context of the total force concept, particularly through the implementation of the improvements recommended in the special report on Alliance Defence Problems for the 1970s.[121] They reviewed progress reported to date, and identified those areas in which such improvements are still most urgently required. In this connection they acknowledged the need to allocate more resources for the modernization and re-equipment of NATO forces.

22. These Ministers received from the Chairman of the Eurogroup an account of the Group's continuing work in order to reinforce the collective contribution of its members to Alliance defence.[122] They welcomed progress made, particularly towards fuller co-operation in equipment procurement.

23. These Ministers, recognizing the success of the NATO Common Infrastructure Programme in providing physical facilities fundamental to the Alliance's deterrent and defensive effectiveness, agreed to the continuation of the Infrastructure Programme during 1975-1979 as an essential element of the NATO defence effort.

24. Finally these Ministers noted with approval that the NATO Air Defence Ground Environment project (NADGE) would be virtually completed by the end of this year thus providing NATO, for the first time, with a fully integrated semi-automatic air defence system stretching from North Norway to the Eastern boundaries of Turkey.

25. The Defence Ministers comprising the Nuclear Defence Affairs Committee (Belgium, Canada, Denmark, Federal Republic of Germany,

---

[120] Cf. Document 32a.

[121] *Documents, 1970*, pp. 99-103.

[122] Cf. Eurogroup communiqué, Dec. 5, 1972, with annexes, in *NATO Review*, Nov.-Dec. 1972, pp. 26-7.

Greece, Italy, the Netherlands, Norway, Portugal, Turkey, the United Kingdom and the United States) also met to review the work of the Nuclear Planning Group during the past year and its plans for future activity.

26. The next meeting of the Defence Planning Committee at Ministerial level will take place in Brussels on 7th June, 1973.

27. The next Ministerial Session of the North Atlantic Council will be held in Copenhagen on 14th and 15th June, 1973.[123]

---

[123] Cf. communiqué, June 15, 1973, in Bulletin, July 16, 1973, pp. 89-90.

IV.
AMERICAN POLICY IN ASIA:
THE MIDDLE EAST
AND SOUTHERN ASIA

[A continuing deterioration of the Arab-Israeli relationship and a partial stabilization in the India-Pakistan subcontinent were the dominant trends of 1972 in the Middle East-South Asian region. The murder by Arab terrorists of eleven Israeli athletes at the Olympic Games in Munich bore witness to the implacable character of the Israeli-Arab conflict, five years after the defeat of the Arab armies and the occupation by Israel of vast tracts of Arab territory in the June War of 1967. The United States, concerned as always to preserve a "military balance" and encourage progress toward permanent peace between Arabs and Israelis, also found itself devoting increased attention to other Middle Eastern trends, among them the changing role of the Central Treaty Organization (CENTO) and the growing economic and strategic importance of the Persian (Arabian) Gulf region. In Southern Asia, meanwhile, American policy began to recover from the discomfitures it had experienced during the December 1971 war between India and Pakistan, the prelude to the emergence of the newly independent state of Bangladesh.]

A. A Regional Perspective.

[Joseph J. Sisco, the Assistant Secretary of State for Near Eastern and South Asian Affairs, emerges as the principal spokesman of the American Government on all the problems of this extensive region during the early 1970s. The following survey, delivered before the House Foreign Affairs Committee in March 1972, provides an introduction to many of these problems and suggests the underlying affinity among the separate geographic areas that compose the region.]

185

(33) Assistance to Near Eastern and South Asian Nations: Statement by Joseph J. Sisco, Assistant Secretary of State for Near Eastern and South Asian Affairs, Before the House Committee on Foreign Affairs, March 20, 1972. [1]

(Complete Text)

In a statement I made to this committee almost a year ago, I said that the Near East and South Asian region was one "where the search for peace must be relentless. The goal is an elusive one, the obstacles to be overcome to reach it formidable. And yet there is no alternative to persevering, for to pause is to court the risk of recourse to force."

The events of the past year have demonstrated just how elusive the goal of peace is. But we continue to persevere, ever mindful of the dangers of failure.

There would be no more satisfying experience than being able to come before you to report that our sustained efforts to help bring about the peaceful resolution of regional disputes was completely successful. Unfortunately, that is not possible. War, despite our energetic attempts to avert it, did break out in South Asia.[2] In the Middle East a peace settlement remains a hope rather than a reality although, on the plus side, the cease-fire, arranged on our initiative over a year and a half ago,[3] persists.

THE MIDDLE EAST

Let me review briefly where we stand in some of the more important areas.

In describing the situation in the Middle East, we must be mindful of the dangers. Only recently President Nixon noted that "The greatest threat to peace and stability in the Middle East remains the Arab-Israeli conflict."[4] While remaining fully alert to the dangers, we cannot lose sight of the element of hope. Our policies have incorporated both factors.

Within the past few weeks, military activities by Israel inside Lebanon, sparked by attacks on Israel by Arab irregular forces, provided ample evidence of the dangers that must be reckoned with so long as the dispute between Israel and its Arab neighbors remains unresolved—

---

[1] *Bulletin*, Apr. 24, 1972, pp. 605-8. For more detailed discussion of the Middle East, cf. Nixon Report, 1972, pp. 133-40; same, 1973, pp. 132-42; Rogers Report, 1972, pp. 375-88. For references on South Asia, see note 121 below.
[2] *A.F.R., 1971*, nos. 56-63.
[3] Cf. below at note 42.
[4] Nixon Report, 1972, p. 135.

so long as ways are not found to reconcile Israel's search for security with the Arab search for recovery of territory occupied in 1967 and for a just settlement for the Palestinian refugees.

But what has given the Arab-Israeli dispute its most dangerous dimension has been the deepened direct involvement of the Soviet Union. It has continued to furnish large amounts of modern weapons to certain of the Arab countries. And in Egypt it has established a substantial physical presence, with large numbers of Soviet personnel in operational as well as advisory capacities.

Since the U.S.S.R. has been unreceptive to U.S. suggestions for the exercise of restraint in the supply of military weapons to this volatile area, we have taken steps to maintain the arms balance.

The arms balance may not be a guarantee of peace. It is not a substitute for negotiations or an end in itself. But it is a deterrent to war, to a war which has the potential for escalation.

So long as peace remains an aspiration rather than a reality, the United States has an interest in assisting those countries which accept peace as the objective to be attained. We are providing assistance to both Israel and certain Arab states. They must be able to defend themselves against forces which represent threats to their own stability and survival and ultimately to an Arab-Israeli peace settlement.

One has only to recall that a year and a half ago Jordan was the scene of a battle for survival.[5] Civil war and invasion occurred simultaneously. This episode was instructive. It demonstrated that people with a will to survive can do so, but they need the wherewithal to do so. Today Jordan's security situation is much improved. But the traumatic events of September 1970 are a powerful reminder that it cannot afford to relax its vigilance or preparedness.

In addition to assuring that our friends in the area have the means for their legitimate self-defense, we have an interest in helping them remain economically strong and viable. In the case of Israel, recognizing the heavy defense burdens it bears and the additional strain on its resources resulting from the increased immigration of Soviet Jews, we have this year included in our fiscal year [19]73 budget presentation a request for $50 million in supporting assistance.

The Middle East is not without its hopeful signs. The cease-fire along the Suez Canal has held. Fragile though it has been, its existence has made it possible to save lives on both sides. Its continuation is in the interests of both sides, but it is not enough. A meaningful, viable, active diplomatic track is needed.

Ambassador [Gunnar] Jarring [U.N. Special Representative] has resumed his consultations with the parties under the mandate given him by Security Council Resolution 242 to promote agreement between the

5 *The United States in World Affairs, 1970*, pp. 109-13.

parties on the terms of a just and lasting peace.[6] He has our full support, and we continue to hope he will be able to give fresh impetus to a dialogue. Complementary to this effort, the United States remains available to the parties to pursue further the matter of an interim Suez Canal agreement.

GREECE AND TURKEY

Greece and Turkey—these two countries, NATO members, form NATO's southeastern flank and occupy strategic positions in the eastern Mediterranean. As NATO members, both countries have responsibilities to contribute to the military strength of the alliance. Both have demonstrated loyal support to the alliance.

Burdensome as their military expenditures have been, Greece and Turkey have felt it necessary to make them. The United States provided substantial assistance to them so that the military burdens would not weigh excessively on their economies. Greece's progress was rapid enough to permit the termination of U.S. economic assistance several years ago, and in more recent years we have been able increasingly to replace grant military assistance with credit. In Turkey, devaluation of the currency and a brisk demand for Turkish workers in western Europe have measurably strengthened Turkey's economic position. As a consequence, we now believe it possible that Turkey will be able over a period of time to make a gradual transition from military grant assistance to credits.

The friendship we have had with these two countries has been a durable one; it has stood the test of time. Changes of administration in this country and of governments in Greece[7] and Turkey have not altered that. Friendship has rested on a base of mutual respect, shared concerns, and common interests. We have not had a complete identity of views with either country; it would be unreasonable to expect it.

But friendship has bred close cooperation, and in no area has it been closer than in security matters. Cooperation over the years has been of mutual benefit.

Today the military forces of both countries need further modernization so that their contributions to NATO's overall strength will be more effective. Neither country has reached the point where it can achieve modernization without U.S. assistance. I believe it important that the Congress provide us with the funds essential to enable us to furnish that assistance.

In the highly dynamic world we live in, new problems are constantly arising. To the extent that they impinge on our relations with other

[6] Cf. below at note 41.
[7] For further comment on U.S.-Greek relations, see Document 22.

countries, it is of **great and** obvious advantage if our relations with others are firmly rooted in friendship.

No problem in recent years has exceeded in its concern to the American people the growth of drug abuse. President Nixon has made it a foreign policy priority.

Turkey has been one of the world's most important suppliers of opium. For the Turkish farmer, this has for years been a prime source of income, since the poppy has had many uses other than as a base for opium and heroin. But as the Turkish Government became more keenly aware of the human ravages caused by opium and heroin, it acted decisively and boldly. It banned the planting of the opium poppy after the harvest in June of last year.[8]

This was not an easy decision for the Turkish Government; it was a product of statesmanship and courage, and one that well merits the applause of the United States and the world community. We intend to provide $35.7 million in grant assistance over the next 3–4 years to offset legitimate foreign exchange losses and to help the Turkish Government to deal with problems they will confront in establishing alternative economic activities in the area affected by the poppy ban.

INTERCOMMUNAL PROBLEMS ON CYPRUS

The failure of the two communities—Greek and Turkish—to reconcile their differences has produced violent shock waves in the past which carried far beyond the shores of the idyllic island of Cyprus. In 1968 a negotiating process was established through international diplomacy to try to promote peaceful reconciliation of views. Three years of intercommunal talks failed to produce agreement, and in 1971 the specter of a collapse in negotiations emerged. International diplomacy was set in motion to head off a dangerous impasse, and early this year there appeared the hope that negotiations would resume under a new formula prepared by the Secretary General of the United Nations [Kurt Waldheim].[9]

More recently, new difficulties have arisen—this time the result of differences between the Governments of Greece and Cyprus. This has made it impossible to launch the new effort at negotiations suggested by the U.N. Secretary General.

We hope that these differences will be resolved by the governments concerned and that progress toward a satisfactory solution of the intercommunal problem on Cyprus will be made.

---

[8] Cf. Chapter IX at note 29.
[9] Cf. *UN Monthly Chronicle*, Apr. 1972, p. 45.

THE PERSIAN GULF REGION

Nineteen seventy-one was a year of transition for many countries of the Persian Gulf region. The British protective mantle was withdrawn, and three new political entities emerged—Bahrain, Qatar, and the United Arab Emirates. The United States promptly recognized them.

These three small countries now confront the challenge of beginning to consolidate their newly acquired independence. The area in which they are located is of major strategic and economic interest to us. It is a major source of oil for Europe and Japan. American companies have sizable participation in the oil industry in the peninsula. And we are interested in orderly political and social evolution in the area. We believe that these states are capable of meeting the challenges of independence and that cooperation among themselves as well as with their larger neighbors will best insure that.

Our own direct and formal relations with these states begin with what we regard as a fund of good will on both sides. This augurs well for our future, and for our part, we hope to enlarge the area of our cooperation with these states. Friendship and cooperation have been the hallmarks of our policy in this area in the past. We intend that they should remain so in the future.[10]

PRIORITY TASK IN SOUTH ASIA

In his foreign policy report to the Congress, President Nixon has said:[11]

The 700 million people of the subcontinent deserve a better future than the tragedy of 1971 seemed to portend. It is for them to fashion their own vision of such a future. The world has an interest in the regional peace and stability which are the preconditions for their achieving it.

Constructing the foundation on which that better future may be built is the priority task which lies ahead.

The problems that must be dealt with are immense in scope and pressing in their urgency.

Pakistan recognizes that it must undertake major political and economic adjustments flowing from the effects of the war. An outline for political and constitutional reconstruction has been recently announced. Recognizing that these are matters of Pakistan's internal affairs, we nevertheless welcome any developments that increase

---

[10] For more detailed discussion, see Document 39.
[11] Nixon Report, 1972, p. 152.

Pakistan's stability and strengthen its capacity to meet the problems which have arisen from the recent crisis.

Bangladesh faces the formidable task of relieving the massive human suffering caused by the events of the past year at the same time as it begins to rebuild a shattered economy and to create a viable political structure. We have indicated to the authorities in Dacca that we are prepared to assist in a major multilateral relief effort under U.N. auspices.[12]

Our relations with India were subjected to serious strain as a result of developments in South Asia in 1971. India has indicated a desire to renew better relations with the United States, and on our part we reciprocate this desire and are ready for a dialogue with India on subjects of mutual concern. The pattern of our future relations will be shaped by the outcome of our discussions with India. We hope for fruitful results.

Thus the year ahead will be one of readjustment and reconstruction in which we seek to develop mutually beneficial relations between ourselves and the countries of South Asia. In addition, the President has indicated his intentions of seeking a more constructive approach to great-power relations in South Asia in his discussions in Moscow.[13]

B. The Northern Tier.

[The Central Treaty Organization (CENTO), successor to the American-supported Baghdad Pact originally linking Britain, Turkey, Iran, Iraq, and Pakistan, continued active during the early 1970s despite the early withdrawal if Iraq and a more recent growth of doubts about the relevance of this regional defense alliance in a period of East-West détente and of improving relations between the Soviet Union and the countries on its southern flank. Although the military defeat of Pakistan by India in December 1971 was widely seen as still another blow to the alliance, Pakistan was represented as usual when the CENTO Council of Ministers held its Nineteenth Session in London on June 1-2, 1972. A statement by Assistant Secretary of State Sisco, who headed the U.S. observer delegation while awaiting the arrival of Secretary Rogers from Warsaw, provides a general survey of CENTO's current concerns (Document 34a). Many of these were further reviewed in the official communiqué issued at the conclusion of the meeting (Document 34b).]

---

[12] Cf. Documents 40-42.
[13] On the President's visit to the Soviet Union, cf. Document 10.

(34) Nineteenth Session of the Council of Ministers of the Central Treaty Organization (CENTO), London, June 1-2, 1972.

(a) Statement by Assistant Secretary of State Sisco, Acting Head of the United States Observer Delegation, June 1, 1972.[14]

(Complete Text)

Secretary Rogers regrets that he is unable to be here today, but as you know, he is accompanying President Nixon on the first visit an American President has ever made to Poland.[15] The Secretary has asked me to speak on his behalf at this opening session. And he is looking forward to meeting with you at the Council's session tomorrow.[16]

I should like to express our welcome to Secretary General [Nassir] Assar.[17] We were pleased to have seen him in Washington earlier this year and want to extend to him our best wishes for what I am confident will be a successful stewardship in his new position.

Since the Council of Ministers last met a year ago,[18] we have seen momentous events of interest and concern to all of us. It has been a year of profound change in world affairs—of change to which the United States, in the interests of peace, has sought to make its contribution.

President Nixon's unprecedented visits to China and the Soviet Union[19] have established the beginnings of a new dialogue with one and have set what we expect to be a more cooperative framework for our existing relationship with the other.

We trust that our efforts with the two leading Communist countries will be beneficial to the cause of peace and to all the world's peoples. And we are confident that the initial agreements to limit strategic arms,[20] and the more comprehensive agreement on which the United States and the Soviet Union must now concentrate, will help to increase the stability of the global environment in which we all live.

The past 12 months have also been a time of change in the area of most immediate concern to CENTO. Here constructive achievement has been mixed with tragedy, the preservation of peace with the descent into war.

From today's perspective, the year in South Asia was dominated by tragic events.[21] Looking to the future, what is needed is a durable

---

[14] *Bulletin,* July 3, 1972, pp. 23-5.
[15] Cf. Document 26.
[16] Cf. Document 34b.
[17] Of Iran; assumed office Feb. 1, 1972 for a three-year term ending Jan. 1, 1975.
[18] *A.F.R., 1971,* no. 50.
[19] Documents 53-56 and 9-12, respectively.
[20] Documents 13-14.
[21] Cf. below at note 121.

peace settlement, an era in which the energies and talents of the people of South Asia can be devoted in peace to constructive endeavors.

As President Nixon said earlier this year:[22]

> The 700 million people of the subcontinent deserve a better future than the tragedy of 1971 seemed to portend. It is for them to fashion their own vision of such a future. The world has an interest in the regional peace and stability which are the preconditions for their achieving it.

In keeping with the President's remarks on the need for a better future, we are pleased to note that the emissary-level talks between Pakistan and India have been successfully completed. We sincerely hope that the forthcoming summit meeting between the leaders of these two nations will be held in an atmosphere of mutual understanding and respect and will pave the way toward reconciliation and peaceful accommodation in the subcontinent.[23]

In the Middle East, the cease-fire along the Suez Canal[24] now nears its second anniversary. None of us has had any illusions about the difficulties which would have to be resolved if the parties to the conflict were to move from cease-fire to a permanent peace settlement based on the U.N. Security Council resolution of 1967.[25] Those difficulties are real and formidable. There have been too many lost opportunities in the tragic history of the Middle East. However, to dwell on them would distract us from the search for opportunities for peacemaking, which remains an overriding imperative. Diplomatic opportunities are available. Progress will depend on whether the countries of the Middle East exert the will, the vision, and the spirit of accommodation to grasp those opportunities. Others can help but cannot do this for them.

So long as the cease-fire continues in the Middle East, as in South Asia, it preserves the opportunity for diplomacy to concentrate on the search for peaceful reconciliation. Surely, the time has come for genuine negotiations looking toward the peaceful resolution of the disputes in both areas.

In our view, it is the antagonists in these disputes who must bear the primary responsibility for the construction of durable peace arrangements; for the solidity of arrangements to prevent future conflicts must depend in the final analysis on the will for peace among the parties to past conflicts.[26]

22 Nixon Report, 1972, p. 152.
23 For the Simla meeting between President Zulfikar Ali Bhutto of Pakistan and Prime Minister Indira Gandhi of India, cf. p. 229 below.
24 Cf. below at note 42.
25 Cf. below at note 41.
26 For further discussion, cf. Document 35.

Let me express at this point, on behalf of my government, our profound shock at the senseless attack at Israel's international airport Tuesday [May 30].[27] All of us who have sought a peaceful settlement in the Middle East are aware that deep passions and hostilities are involved. But this is no justification for violence. It is particularly outrageous, and particularly tragic, when innocent people are indiscriminately made the victims. This tragedy was brought home with special impact to Americans because so many of our own citizens were killed and wounded. The horror of the attack underscores the urgency of the need for greater effectiveness, by governments and by the international community, in measures to deal with such threats to travelers, in the Middle East and elsewhere as well.

In the Persian Gulf, a third area of direct concern to CENTO, the developments of the past year on the whole have been encouraging.

At the end of 1971 the British Government terminated its special treaty arrangements in the gulf. First Bahrain, then Qatar, and later the United Arab Emirates emerged as independent states. The consolidation and strengthening of independence is one of their more important tasks. Progress is being made, and we welcome the continued interest of the British Government in assisting these small states.[28]

We believe that the security of these small states and other countries in the gulf area can best be maintained through regional cooperation.

Yesterday in Tehran President Nixon and His Imperial Majesty the Shah of Iran agreed in their joint communique[29] "that the security and stability of the Persian Gulf is of vital importance to the littoral states. Both were of the view that the littoral states bore the primary responsibility for the security of the Persian Gulf. His Imperial Majesty reaffirmed Iran's determination to bear its share of this responsibility." We welcome this determination.

In this connection, President Nixon yesterday confirmed that the United States would, as in the past, continue to cooperate with Iran in strengthening its defense.[30]

Similarly, as a result of recent meetings which President Nixon held with then-Prime Minister [Nihat] Erim, the friendship and cooperation between our two countries, and in particular support for Turkey's security, have been strengthened.[31]

At the same time, the United States has entered direct diplomatic relations with new states of the gulf. Our policy is to assist them where possible in the development of their societies, their economies, and their new political institutions.

[27] Cf. below at note 51.
[28] See further Document 39.
[29] *Public Papers, 1972*, p. 651.
[30] Same, p. 652.
[31] Prime Minister Erim visited President Nixon Mar. 21-22, 1972; documentation in *Public Papers, 1972*, pp. 450-51 and 457-61.

At times of change in the world it is natural that nations should examine carefully many of their existing obligations and interests. My country, like many others, has been involved in such examinations. This is a good time, therefore, to state the United States position on CENTO, which we have supported since its inception and with which we have cooperated for 14 years:[32]

—We believe that CENTO continues to contribute measurably to stability and security in the area of its concern.

—We believe that it is a useful forum for consultation on problems affecting that area and, indeed, on broader problems.

—We believe that it contributes to respect, understanding, and cooperation among its members.

—And we believe that, in its practical recognition that security does not depend on military means alone, it plays a valuable role in promoting the economic and social well-being of the peoples in the area.

For these reasons, the United States continues to support CENTO and will continue to participate in its cooperative regional endeavors. We are sympathetic with the desire of the CENTO regional countries for further regional development and are ready to give serious consideration to new initiatives in the economic field within CENTO which are truly regional in scope.

(b) Final Communiqué, June 2, 1972.[33]

(Complete Text)

LONDON, June 2, 1972—The Council of Ministers of the Central Treaty Organization (CENTO) held their 19th Session at Lancaster House on June 1 and 2, 1972.

2. The leaders of the national delegations from the five CENTO countries were:

1. H.E. Mr. Abbas Ali Khalatbary,
   Minister for Foreign Affairs   Iran
2. H.E. Mr. Abdul Hafeez Pirzada,
   Minister for Education, Culture and Provincial
   Co-ordination   Pakistan
3. H.E. Mr. Halûk Bayülken,
   Minister for Foreign Affairs   Turkey

---

[32] Cf. Baghdad Pact Council declaration and communiqué, July 28-29, 1958, in *Documents, 1958*, pp. 376-8.
[33] *Bulletin*, July 3, 1972, pp. 25-6.

4. The Rt. Hon. Sir Alec Douglas-Home, KT, M.P.,
   Secretary of State for Foreign and Commonwealth   United
   Affairs   Kingdom
5. The Hon. William P. Rogers,
   Secretary of State   United States

   3. H.E. Mr. Nassir Assar, Secretary General of the Central Treaty
Organization, opened the Session.
   4. Following an address by the Rt. Hon. Mr. Edward Heath, Prime
Minister of the United Kingdom, in which he conveyed a message of
welcome from Her Majesty the Queen, opening statements were made
by the leaders of the delegations and the Secretary General of CENTO,
in which they expressed their appreciation of the Queen's gracious
message and the warm hospitality of the host country.
   5. As the leader of the delegation of the host country, the Rt. Hon.
Sir Alec Douglas-Home, Secretary of State for Foreign and Commonwealth Affairs of the United Kingdom, presided at the Session.
   6. In a wide-ranging exchange of views marked by traditional cor-
diality and understanding, the Council of Ministers reviewed the international developments since they met a year ago,[34] with special
reference to Iran, Pakistan and Turkey and the neighbouring areas.
   7. Regretting the recent clash of arms between Pakistan and India,
the Ministers expressed the hope that the two countries would in the
near future be able to arrive at an honourable and equitable settlement
of their outstanding disputes, so essential for ensuring lasting peace in
the sub-continent. They reaffirmed their support for the Security Council Resolution No. 307 of 21 December, 1971.[35] The Ministers also
wished success to the forthcoming meeting between the President of
Pakistan and the Prime Minister of India.[36]
   8. Expressing their concern at the continuing tense situation in the
Middle East, the Ministers reiterated their hopes for an early resolution
of the Middle East dispute and for the continuation of efforts aimed at
attaining a just and enduring peace in the area, in accordance with the
principles of international law, the Charter of the United Nations, and
the U.N. Security Council Resolution No. 242 of 22 November,
1967.[37]
   9. The Ministers also discussed other problems of peace and security
in the area, including subversive activities. They expressed the hope that
efforts would continue to be made to find solutions to these problems
in order to contribute to stability and progress for the nations of the
area.

[34] *A.F.R., 1971*, no. 50.
[35] Calling for strict observance of the cease-fire and early withdrawal of military
forces; *A.F.R., 1971*, no. 63.
[36] Cf. discussion preceding Document 40.
[37] Cf. below at note 41.

10. Concluding the review, the Ministers reaffirmed their faith in the importance of the Organization for its partners, especially for peace and progress in the Region.

11. In approving the Report of the Military Committee, the Ministers took note of the continuing collaboration among the CENTO countries.

12. Reaffirming their agreement that the programme of economic collaboration constitutes an important element of CENTO partnership, the Ministers noted with satisfaction the accelerated rate of economic expansion in the Regional countries as well as the increasing economic cooperation among them.

13. In reviewing the Report of the Economic Committee, the Ministers noted with pleasure the completion of the rail-link between Iran and Turkey.[38] They also noted with satisfaction that the communications projects had stimulated economic cooperation among the nations of the CENTO Region.

14. The Ministers directed the Economic Committee to give timely and sympathetic attention to projects submitted for consideration by the regional governments. They also endorsed recommendations for the expansion of the scope of the Multilateral Technical Cooperation Fund to provide greater intra-regional training.

15. The Ministers expressed their appreciation of the Annual Report of the Secretary General, who was attending the Ministerial Council for the first time,[39] and wished him every success.

16. The Council accepted the invitation of the Government of Iran to hold the next session in early May, 1973, in Tehran.[40]

C. The Arab-Israeli Conflict.

[The year 1972 stands near the end of the six-year period of "no war, no peace" that intervened between the third and fourth explosions of Israeli-Arab hostilities, often referred to as the June War of 1967 and the Yom Kippur War of October 1973. Although the imminent recurrence of a state of open warfare could not positively be foreseen in 1972, the possibility was sufficiently obvious to affect the thinking of all the interested parties as they picked their way amid the still-uncleared debris of the preceding conflict. While American diplomacy labored to preserve the Israeli-Egyptian ceasefire instituted in 1970 and to promote a settlement consistent with

[38] The rail link between Iran and Turkey was opened Sept. 27, 1971; cf. *A.F.R., 1971*, no. 55, note 62. For documentation on the meeting of the CENTO Economic Committee (Mar. 14-16, 1972), see *Bulletin*, Apr. 10, 1972, pp. 558-60.
[39] Cf. note 17 above.
[40] The 20th session was held in Tehran June 10-11, 1973; text of communiqué in *Bulletin*, July 16, 1973, pp. 83-5.

the basic United Nations resolution of 1967, its efforts were increasingly complicated by such factors as the continuing arms race in the region, proliferating terrorist attacks on Israeli interests, vigorous Israeli reprisal actions, and a waning of international support for Israel's position.]

1. Elements of the Conflict.

[Three principal strands made up the complex pattern of Israeli-Arab affairs as seen from Washington in 1972:

(1) *The search for a peace settlement* within the terms of U.N. Security Council Resolution 242 of November 22. 1967,[41] which called among other things for "(i) Withdrawal of Israeli armed forces from territories occupied in the recent conflict," and "(ii) Termination of all claims or states of belligerency and respect for and acknowledgement of the sovereignty, territorial integrity and political independence of every State in the area and their right to live in peace within secure and recognized boundaries free from threats or acts of force."

While Ambassador Gunnar V. Jarring of Sweden attempted to promote agreement among the 1967 belligerents in his capacity as Representative of the U.N. Secretary-General, the United States had undertaken a parallel effort that focused on Israel and the United Arab Republic (Egypt) and led in the summer of 1970 to the establishment of a cease-fire between the forces of those two countries along the Suez Canal.[42] In a continuation of this "step-by-step" approach, the United States had also been working since early 1971 to promote an interim agreement between Egypt and Israel that would permit the actual reopening of the canal, which had been closed since 1967, and a partial withdrawal of Israeli forces in the Sinai Peninsula.[43]

Although this effort had been undertaken in accordance with the express wish of the two parties, the latter had failed thus far to agree on a suitable format for the proposed negotiations. An American proposal looking toward so-called "proximity talks"—i.e., "indirect talks between representatives of the two sides brought together at the same location"—was eventually accepted by Israel in February 1972; Egypt, however, did not agree to this procedure and "expressed reservations about any negotiations in the absence of prior Israeli commitment to total withdrawal from Sinai in an

[41] *Documents, 1967*, pp. 169-70.
[42] Same, *1970*, pp. 131-5.
[43] *A.F.R., 1971*, nos. 50-52.

overall settlement."[44] Israel, on its side, had remained wholly averse to giving such a commitment, particularly at a time when its adversaries refused to honor its demand for direct negotiations.

(2) *The regional arms race* fueled by Soviet arms shipments to Egypt, Syria, and other Arab states, and the accompanying *danger of a Soviet-American confrontation* growing out of Moscow's identification with the Arabs and the United States' identification with Israel. President Nixon, in the "State of the World" report made public early in 1972, expressed particular concern about "the Soviet Union's effort to use the Arab-Israeli conflict to perpetuate and expand its own military position in Egypt" through such means as the introduction into that country of SA-6 mobile surface-to-air missiles, the FOXBAT and other advanced MIG aircraft, and TU-16 bombers equipped with long-range air-to-surface missiles—much of this equipment, he added, being "operated and defended exclusively by Soviets." In this situation, the President pointed out, it was the policy of the United States to ensure that a "military balance" was maintained, notwithstanding its realization that military equilibrium would not in itself assure peace.[45] Details of U.S. military shipments to Israel, as Secretary Rogers explained, were withheld from public announcement as a matter of policy;[46] nevertheless, the Secretary of State later reported, "Throughout 1972 we provided Israel and certain Arab states with the arms necessary for them to assure their self-defense."[47]

American apprehensions regarding the Soviet role in the Middle East were eased to some extent by developments during and subsequent to the Moscow summit meeting in May 1972. Although both sides took the opportunity of the Moscow conversations to reaffirm their opposing points of view, they also joined in stressing their commitment to a political solution (Document 10) and, more generally, acknowledged the importance of "preventing the development of situations capable of causing a dangerous exacerbation of their relations" (Document 11). The danger of Soviet military involvement in the Middle East appeared to have been further reduced by Egypt's subsequent request, disclosed by President Anwar es-Sadat on July 18, 1972, for withdrawal of the thousands of Soviet military experts and advisers stationed in that country in connection with its defense buildup. In spite of this important step—prompted, according to Sadat's later statements, by Moscow's persistent refusal to provide offensive weapons for a new campaign

---

[44] Nixon Report, 1973, p. 137.
[45] Nixon Report, 1972, pp. 138-9.
[46] Television interview, Feb. 6, 1972, in *Bulletin*, Feb. 28, 1972, pp. 272-3.
[47] Rogers Report, 1972, p. 377.

against Israel—the United States continued to show concern at the extent of the Soviet immersion in Middle East military affairs. "A significant Soviet presence and substantial Soviet military aid continue in the area," President Nixon was to note in his "State of the World" report for 1973. "The Soviet Union signed a friendship treaty with Iraq in April 1972. New shipments of Soviet military equipment have now been concentrated in Syria, Iraq, and the People's Democratic Republic of Yemen. The significant factor is whether the Soviet presence is paralleled by a Soviet interest in promoting peaceful solutions. The major powers have a continuing obligation to refrain from steps which will raise again the danger of their direct engagement in military conflict."[48]

(3) *The growth of irregular and terrorist operations* by Palestinian guerrilla groups, involving not only a continuance of the familiar frontier raids but also an increasing number of acts of violence affecting air travelers and other innocent persons in various parts of the world. Since the suppression of the guerrilla movements in Jordan by that country's government in 1970-71, the center of *fedayeen* activity had shifted to southern Lebanon and adjacent portions of Syria, where a persistent commando presence and sporadic raiding activities were answered by repeated instances of heavy air action and massive ground incursions by Israeli military forces. In February and again in June, 1972, large-scale Israeli raids into Lebanon evoked sharp reproof on the part of the U.N. Security Council, with the United States voting with the majority in the first instance[49] but abstaining in the second case on the ground that the resolution as drafted gave insufficient weight to the provocation suffered by Israel.[50]

Much more shocking to international opinion were the terrorist actions carried out in the name of Palestinian nationalism by such groups as the Beirut-based Popular Front for the Liberation of Palestine (P.F.L.P.) and the so-called Black September organization, whose name commemorated the suppression of the guerrillas in Jordan in September 1970. The killing of Jordanian Prime Minister Wasfi al-Tal by Black September terrorists in Cairo on November 28, 1971 proved to be only the first of a series of incidents of which the following are among the more notorious:[51]

—The hijacking by Arab terrorists of uncertain affiliation on Feb-

[48] Nixon Report, 1973, pp. 138-9.
[49] U.N. Security Council Resolution 313 (1972), Feb. 28, 1972, adopted unanimously.
[50] Resolution 316 (1972), June 26, 1972, adopted by a vote of 13-0-2 (Panama, U.S.); for the U.S. position, see *Bulletin*, July 24, 1972, pp. 126-8.
[51] Details in Keesing's, pp. 25365-7, 25409, and 25502.

ruary 22, 1972 of a West German airliner en route from Delhi to Athens which was diverted to Aden and ultimately released, with those on board, on payment of a ransom of $5,000,000.

—The seizure by Black September terrorists on May 8, 1972 of a Belgian airliner en route from Vienna to Israel's Lod (Lydda) International Airport, where 100 persons were held hostage until the hijackers were ultimately overpowered by Israeli security forces.

—The killing of some 26 persons and the wounding of at least 77 at Lod International Airport on May 30, 1972 when three Japanese terrorists affiliated with the P.F.L.P. attacked arriving passengers with hand grenades and automatic weapons. Some 17 of the dead were Roman Catholic religious pilgrims from Puerto Rico.

—Extensive sabotage on August 4, 1972, presumably by Black September terrorists, of the Trieste terminal of a transalpine pipeline leading to Ingolstadt (West Germany) and Vienna.

Such, in its major elements, was the status of the Arab-Israeli conflict in mid-August of 1972, when Assistant Secretary Sisco outlined the views of the United States in an address before the national convention of the Jewish War Veterans of the U.S.A. at Houston, Texas.]

(35) "The Step-by-Step Approach to Peace in the Middle East": Address by Assistant Secretary of State Sisco Before the National Convention of the Jewish War Veterans of the U.S.A., Houston, Texas, August 19, 1972.[52]

(Complete Text)

Mr. Plofsky [Ralph Plofsky, a past national commander, Jewish War Veterans], distinguished guests, and friends: First let me say thank you for your very generous introduction. I cannot help but recall the story of the man who fell off the 20th story of a building. After he passed the 10th floor, a friend stuck his head out of the window and shouted, "Joe, so far you are all right." There are times that in this job, which has been very challenging, I have felt a little bit like the fellow who fell off the 20th floor. But nevertheless it has been a labor of love, a labor of deep commitment to a political settlement which would result in a durable peace in the area.

There are three aspects of the Middle Eastern problem that help explain the continuing danger in the area.

There is the Arab-Israeli dispute, where the fundamental chasm is still deep, where mistrust between the parties remains.

52 *Bulletin*, Sept. 25, 1972, pp. 350-53.

There are the differences within the Arab world itself, the intra-Arab disputes that, in addition to the differences over the Arab-Israeli dispute, contribute to the present instability in the area. The objective of Arab unity still remains elusive.

And as if this were not enough, the fact that the Middle East is an area of potential conflict between the major powers helps to explain why it is high on the agenda of world trouble spots.

In my judgment, there is no satisfactory answer to the situation other than a stable and durable peace between the two sides—a peace agreement that will replace the 20 years of de facto cease-fire, a peace agreement in which each side undertakes obligations to the other, not a scotch-tape armistice arrangement, not undefined lines, but a peace agreement based on the fundamental philosophy of live-and-let-live.

As we look at the situation today, there are several positive elements.

The first is the cease-fire that has existed in the area well over two years.[53] There are many things that can be said about the cease-fire, but I would single out one in particular: The people on both sides have experienced a period of over two years of reduced violence. This period, I hope, in time will help create a new atmosphere in the Middle East, a new atmosphere which has begun to emerge—not only an atmosphere of live-and-let-live but an atmosphere where there can be deep and meaningful coexistence; where people can move freely; and where each side can have confidence that agreements entered into will be kept because they will be agreements serving the interests of both.

The second positive element is that the balance in the area has been and will be maintained. I am convinced that for American diplomacy in the area to be effective it has to be based on the maintenance of the balance within the region, as it has been these past years, and the maintenance of the global balance. It must also continue to be bulwarked by a strong American presence in the Mediterranean. Diplomacy must have teeth to be credible in the area.

A third element in the present situation has been the development of greater realism in the Arab world. I say this with some caution. Certainly the elements of violence in the Middle East are there. Certainly the people and the forces who see the military option as the answer still remain. But the forces of moderation are slowly getting the upper hand. The people in the area have an opportunity over the next three or four or five years to strengthen those voices of moderation; to move toward a peace shaped principally by the people and the countries of the area.

I am mindful of the fact that my words here tonight will be heard and scrutinized both in Cairo and in Tel Aviv. I hope you will bear this in mind. I have probably spoken to President Sadat for a longer period of time than any other official American since he has assumed the Presidency of his country. I want to say to this Jewish audience: I believe

---

[53] Cf. above at note 42.

he wants a peaceful solution. I believe he has unleashed certain expectations in his country which the people of his country want satisfied. I believe he wants to satisfy those expectations, both in terms of peace and the welfare of his people. I believe that a part of the greater realism in the Arab world, regardless of the strident rhetoric we hear daily, is the appreciation that going to war would not solve anything. It would not solve anything for the people or the countries in the area, nor would it get at the key issues of a binding contractual peace agreement or resolving the territorial issues that divide the two sides.

What's our objective? It is a stable peace in the area. We have in the Security Council resolution of November 1967[54] the framework of a binding peace agreement. But this Security Council resolution, important as it is, is no more than a bareboned framework. A basic assumption of that resolution was that there would be negotiations between the two sides in order to arrive at an agreement. Such negotiations would seek to resolve the key questions of withdrawal, of territory, of borders, of the opening of the Suez Canal, the question of the right of each state in the area to exist, and the problem of refugees. It is, as I say, a bareboned outline. It can have no lasting meaning in terms of implementation unless the details are filled out and agreed to by both sides and unless the resolution, in fact, in detail, and in reality, leads to a binding peace agreement arrived at by the two sides, not imposed from the outside. We have influence that we can bring to bear on the situation, but no major power has the capacity to impose a solution.

Where do matters stand? At the May summit in Moscow, the Middle East was not a primary item, though it was discussed thoroughly and in detail. The communique[55] endorsed a political solution based on the November 1967 resolution. We all know the 1967 resolution is interpreted differently in Israel and in the Arab world. The Egyptians have always insisted the resolution means total Israeli withdrawal to the lines that existed before the June war of 1967. Israel has never agreed with this interpretation. The resolution does call for withdrawal of Israeli forces from territories occupied during the June war. But it also calls for secure and recognized boundaries. The Security Council resolution neither endorses nor precludes the 1967 lines as the final lines. The assumption was that the final lines would have to be agreed between the two sides. I helped negotiate that resolution; and I am therefore fully familiar with its legislative history. The phrase "secure and recognized boundaries" is in the resolution, and it was adopted by a unanimous vote of the U.N. Security Council with each side applying its own interpretation in the explanations of vote. The Security Council did not endorse any specific lines as the final lines. This was and is a matter for the parties themselves to decide in the context of real negotiations,

---

54 Cf. above at note 41.
55 Document 10.

whether under the aegis of Ambassador Jarring or under other auspices.

In addition to the endorsement of a political solution in the summit communique, an important set of principles[56] was adopted: that each side should avoid confrontations over various trouble spots, that each ought to resort to peaceful means, that each should try to resist the temptation to derive unilateral benefit from one given trouble spot or another. There were no new departures. The communique tells the story: Neither major power wanted or wants to see the present situation break out again into hostilities between the two sides. Both sides remain committed to a political settlement based on the November 1967 Security Council resolution.

Since then there have been significant developments in Egypt. I am not in a position to say much about these developments. The events speak for themselves. This is an internal matter for the Egyptian people to decide. Moreover, not all of the facts are in; and before any firm judgments and conclusions can be drawn, we will want to be clear on what the situation is. That there has been a substantial reduction of the Soviet presence in Egypt has been confirmed. What it will mean in the future, what it will mean in terms of the "no war, no peace" situation in the area, what it will mean in terms of the possibilities of future negotiations, is difficult to predict at this point. At present the position on the substance of a settlement between the two sides remains unchanged.

There are diplomatic opportunities available. Ambassador Jarring has just concluded two weeks in New York. The United States has supported both the November 1967 resolution and Ambassador Jarring's mission. If Ambassador Jarring can break the impasse, it would be fine with us. But we have doubts on this score for one simple reason: Egypt says there must be total Israeli withdrawal to the lines which existed before the June war; Israel is equally insistent that there must be substantial change in the lines. Because this difference is fundamental at this stage and not bridgeable in the near future, we continue to feel the more practical approach is the step-by-step approach.

You will recall that a year ago both President Sadat and Prime Minister [Golda] Meir [of Israel] indicated a willingness to explore the possibilities of a so-called interim Suez Canal agreement. We, the United States, over the past year have tried to get these talks started, and we have not been successful. In October 1971 Egypt was favorable, Israel was not. Last February Israel took an affirmative decision to enter into so-called proximity talks under the aegis of the United States. The present Israeli position, in simple terms, is that it is willing to enter into these talks without conditions. The present Egyptian position is that before Egypt is willing to enter into such proximity talks it wants a prior commitment on the part of Israel to the memorandum submitted

[56] Document 11.

by Ambassador Jarring in February of 1971,[57] which would amount to a prior commitment to withdraw to the line with Egypt that existed before the June war of 1967.

In the last few weeks the Prime Minister of Israel has stressed once again and reaffirmed the desire of Israel to enter into these talks. We noted in particular that in her most recent speech she placed a certain amount of stress on the fact that Israel conceives of any interim Suez Canal agreement as temporary. A few days later Defense Minister [Moshe] Dayan placed similar emphasis on the desirability of such an interim agreement, indicating also some willingness to consider, in his words, "a line in the Sinai, temporary or permanent." The Israeli emphasis on the temporary nature of any interim Suez Canal agreement seems, in my judgment, to reflect a recognition on the part of Israel that one of the difficulties which Egypt has with the notion of an interim agreement is that it not become a new indefinite de facto status quo. Egypt is understandably concerned that any interim agreement not become a final agreement with Israel remaining in occupation of territory.

I can recall, since this has already been in the public domain, having visited Israel a year ago in May and having had long discussions with the Prime Minister. We discussed this particular point of Arab concern—that an interim agreement not be the final agreement. I was authorized at that time by the Government of Israel to communicate the following to President Sadat: First, that Israel would be willing to withdraw in the context of any interim agreement to whatever line is agreed to and that that line would not be the final line. And secondly, I was also authorized to communicate to President Sadat that Israel would be willing to withdraw in the context of an overall peace agreement to such other line that might be agreed to in the context of those negotiations.[58] This is not news, because the Foreign Minister of Israel [Abba Eban] indicated what I just said in these terms in his speech before the General Assembly a year ago.[59] But these two points, in addition to the emphasis on the temporary nature of any interim Suez Canal agreement, are intended, I believe, to try to reassure Egypt that an interim agreement, in fact, would open the resources of the Suez Canal to Egypt, since Israel has never questioned the sovereignty of Egypt over the Suez Canal; a step that would mean an extended cease-fire, would mean that the combatants in the area would be separated, would offer new opportunities for further efforts to achieve overall settlement. In short, it would be an agreement in the mutual interest of both sides because it

---

[57] A.F.R., 1971, no. 48b, para. 8.
[58] Cf. same, no. 50, and Bulletin, May 31, 1971, pp. 697-702.
[59] For a summary of Eban's speech to the General Assembly, Sept. 28, 1972, see UN Monthly Chronicle, Oct. 1972, pp. 100-101.

would be a practical and realistic test of peace on the ground. It would give a practical meaning to signed pieces of paper.

Let me leave you with one concluding thought. The "no war, no peace" situation in the area gives continuing opportunity to our adversary for penetration in the area, regardless of the recent developments that have occurred in Egypt. There is no satisfactory alternative to the unstable "no war, no peace" situation other than a stable peace agreement. The key is negotiations. Unfortunately, the concept of negotiations does not have the same meaning in the Arab world as it does in the Western world. Negotiations are the key because the day is long gone when the Middle East can claim to be unique in this regard. There have been three wars in the last two decades in the Middle East. If North Korea can talk to South Korea and the East Germans can talk to the West Germans, if the Indians can talk to the Pakistanis in the aftermath of a war, just a few months after a war, if we can talk to Peking when there has been no dialogue for 20 years, if we can talk to the Viet Cong every day in Paris—then the force of the argument that the Middle East must remain a unique exception in this regard is weak and unrealistic. I do not mean that such negotiations need start face-to-face at the outset. But there is need for a negotiating process to begin; proximity talks on an interim Suez Canal agreement are still the most feasible approach. So I hope as we look ahead that opportunities in time will develop. I believe the minimal conditions exist in the area for such opportunities to evolve in time. We remain available to play a role in promoting an interim Suez Canal agreement. I hope I can get together again with this audience, a year, two, three years from now, and find in existence not only a cease-fire but a peace meeting the legitimate concerns of both sides. I am convinced this is a do-able proposition.

2. The Munich Tragedy and Its Aftermath.

[The most sensational anti-Israeli action of the early 1970s was the killing of eleven Israeli athletes on September 5, 1972, by Black September terrorists who penetrated the Israeli living quarters at the Olympic Village in Munich, killing two of their victims and seizing the other nine to emphasize their demand for the release by Israel of two hundred Arab guerrillas detained in that country. The remaining Israeli captives, together with a German policeman and five of the eight terrorists, were killed in the course of a gun battle that erupted the same evening at the Fürstenfeldbruck military airfield, where the group had been conveyed pursuant to their demand for transportation to an Arab country. (The three remaining terrorists were later released by Bavarian authorities following the hijacking on October 29, 1972, by two other Arab terrorists, possibly affiliated with Black September, of a German airliner en route from Beirut to Ankara that was ultimately surrendered in Tripoli.)[60]

The statements of Secretary of State Rogers and President Nixon with regard to the Munich tragedy (Document 36) were typical of the horrified reaction of non-Arab world opinion, although King Hussein of Jordan was virtually the only Arab leader to condemn the terrorists.[61] In Israel, public demands for retaliatory action were followed on September 8, 1972 by the mounting of intensive air strikes against seven guerrilla bases in Syria and three in Lebanon, resulting in numerous civilian as well as guerrilla casualties.

The U.N. Security Council, meeting in emergency session at Syria's request on September 10, 1972, was prevented by differences among the permanent members from taking any clear-cut position on these events. A U.S. proposal stressing the obligation of states to combat terrorism (Document 37a) found little favor with the pro-Arab group and was ultimately not pressed to a vote, while a resolution submitted by Guinea, Somalia, and Yugoslavia that condemned Israeli actions but failed to deal with the terrorist issue was vetoed by the United States after amendments calling for an end to terrorist activities had been vetoed by China and the U.S.S.R. (Document 37b). In commenting on this second American veto in the history of the Security Council—the first had been cast on the Rhodesian issue on March 17, 1970[62]—U.S. Permanent Representative George Bush did not fail to stress the continued U.S. commitment to work for an end of terrorism as well as a just and lasting peace in the Middle East (Document 37c).]

(36) United States Government Reactions, September 5-6, 1972.

(a) Statements by Secretary of State Rogers, September 5, 1972.[63]

(Complete Texts)

I have asked the Israeli Ambassador [Yitzhak Rabin] to convey to the Israeli Government and people our profound sorrow and sense of horror at the callous, outrageous attack this morning on the Israeli athletes in their quarters in Olympic Village in Munich.

[60] Keesing's, pp. 25493-4 and 25579-80.
[61] Same, pp. 25495-6.
[62] *Documents, 1970*, pp. 246-7.
[63] Department of State Press Releases 209 and 211, Sept. 5, 1972; texts from *Bulletin*, Oct. 2, 1972, p. 364.

We extend our deepest condolences to the families of those Israelis who have lost their lives in this incident. With all nations and peoples around the world, we fervently hope that no further innocent lives will be sacrificed. This assault on the Israeli Olympic team is offensive to men and women of good will everywhere for whom the Olympic games are a symbol of man's striving for reconciliation and peace.

*   *   *

There are no words which can fully express our reaction to today's tragedy at the Olympic games. I know I speak for all Americans in extending the deepest sympathies of the United States to the families of those, Israelis and Germans alike, who have died because of this appalling, senseless deed.

(b) Remarks by President Nixon to Reporters, San Francisco, September 5, 1972.[64]

(Complete Text)

THE PRESIDENT. Gentlemen, I had the opportunity this morning before I left San Clemente to call Prime Minister Meir on the phone. I reached her just before we left. I talked with her about 7 or 8 minutes.

I expressed sympathy on behalf of all of the American people for the victims of this murderous action that occurred in the Olympic village in Munich. I also told her that she could expect total cooperation from the Government of the United States in any way that would be helpful in obtaining the release of the hostages.

In addition to that, I raised with her the problem of what we could do in the future in this respect. I asked her whether or not Israeli intelligence had any information with regard to the possibility of this happening. They did not have any information.

Incidentally, Israeli intelligence, we have found, is one of the best in the world. She said that, perhaps, the reason was that while the Olympic Games were being held there in Munich, there just weren't any expectations that this kind of a group would be able to get in and engage in the kind of activities that they have engaged in. However, we are dealing here with international outlaws of the worst sort who will stoop to anything in order to accomplish their goals, and who are totally unpredictable.

Under the circumstances, I said to the Prime Minister, that I thought that, looking to the future, we had to anticipate that Israeli citizens traveling abroad would be subjected to such activities in the future. Naturally, we cannot do anything with regard to what happens in other countries—that is their responsibility primarily, except to indicate our interest from the diplomatic standpoint. But I said in the United States

[64] *Presidential Documents*, Sept. 11, 1972, p. 1348.

that we would try to do everything we could with regard to groups of Israeli citizens traveling in the United States to see that where there is any information at all with regard to a possible attempt of this sort, that adequate security measures are taken.

Finally, as you know, the games, as I understand, are being postponed until the hostages are released and the people who are guilty are apprehended, or those charged with the guilt. There is very little that words can say to indicate the concern we have for the families of the victims. But to have this happen in an international event that has an unblemished record—this being the 20th Olympiad going back over 80 years—an unblemished record of no incidents of this sort, this is indeed a great tragedy and I know the whole world shares the views that I have expressed to Mrs. Meir.

Q. Are you satisfied about the security of American athletes, particularly American Jewish athletes at the Olympic Games?

THE PRESIDENT. I am never satisfied with security when you see incidents like this, but I believe that we have adequate security measures and, as I have indicated, or at least implied by my remarks here, since we are dealing with international outlaws who are unpredictable, we have to take extra security measures, extra security measures to protect those who might be the targets of this kind of activity in the future. That might include Americans of Israeli background, American citizens. It is more likely to be directed, however, against Israeli citizens, because what they want to do is get leverage with the Israeli Government with regard to people that are held by the Israeli Government. However, we are not taking any chances. We will do everything we can to protect our own citizens, whatever their background.

(c) Letter From President Nixon to Prime Minister Golda Meir of Israel, September 6, 1972. [65]

(Complete Text)

Dear Madame Prime Minister:

The heart of America goes out to you, to the bereaved families and to the Israeli people in the tragedy that has struck your Olympic athletes. This tragic and senseless act is a perversion of all the hopes and aspirations of mankind which the Olympic games symbolize. In a larger sense, it is a tragedy for all the peoples and nations of the world. We mourn with you the deaths of your innocent and brave athletes, and we share with you the determination that the spirit of brotherhood and peace they represented shall in the end persevere.

Sincerely,

RICHARD NIXON

[65] Presidential Documents, Sept. 11, 1972, p. 1348.

(37) Discussion in the United Nations Security Council, September 10, 1972.

(a) The Point of View of the United States: Statement by Ambassador George H. Bush, United States Representative to the United Nations.[66]

(Complete Text)

The Council is meeting today on a complaint by the Syrian Government.[67] The Middle East has again been the scene of violence, as it has so often in the past. The Council is again seized of a problem with which it has repeatedly failed in the past to come to grips in an equitable way.

We should all recall that until a few days ago the world had again dared to hope because a climate of reasonableness and realism seemed to be developing in the area. There were grounds to hope that new opportunities for progress toward peace in the Middle East were opening up before us. Then came "Munich"—the senseless act of terrorism there which cast a pall over these hopes. Yet we are now meeting on a complaint by Syria—a complaint that stands out for its unreality. It makes no reference to the tragic events at Munich. It gives no salve to the wounded conscience of an agonized world.

There is an obvious connection between the actions of which the Syrian Government now complains and the tragic events which took place in Munich this past Tuesday [September 5]. Did the Syrian Government join in complaint or expressions of outrage when terrorists invaded the Olympic Village, in violation not only of law but of the spirit of Olympic brotherhood, and murdered innocent athletes? Did we hear even a word of condemnation from the Government of Syria for this despicable act? No, quite the contrary. The Syrian Government continues to harbor and to give aid and encouragement to terrorist organizations which openly champion such acts.

And the Syrian Government is not alone in its encouragement of terrorism. Certain other governments in the area—whether by word and deed or by silent acquiescence and failure to disassociate themselves from the acts of a minority that preaches and practices lawlessness and violence—cannot be absolved of responsibility for the cycle of violence and counterviolence we have again witnessed this past week.

Mr. President,[68] the ultimate root of the problem is, of course, the

[66] USUN Press Release 91, Sept. 10, 1972; text in *Bulletin*, Oct. 2, 1972, pp. 365-7.
[67] U.N. documents S/10781 (A/8785), Sept. 8, 1972 and S/10782, Sept. 9, 1972; text in U.N. Security Council, *Official Records: 27th Year, Supplement for July, Aug. and Sept., 1972*, pp. 97-8.
[68] Huang Hua (China).

absence of peace in the Middle East. My government has labored long and hard in this cause; in the effort to achieve a just and durable peace the United States has been and will continue to be second to none.

We shall continue to work toward the goal of peace, but the absence of peace cannot be exploited as a pretext for violence on any side. Those who preach violence and employ it as a matter of policy always suffer its consequences, for violence always begets violence. The crimes that were carried out at Lod[69] and at Munich cannot but breed tragedy for their perpetrators and for those who befriend them. States which harbor and give succor to terrorists cannot then claim sanctuary for themselves. The greatest tragedy of all is that when violence is employed, innocent people on all sides are almost inevitably made to suffer. Slain Olympic athletes in Munich—or heartbroken mothers searching for dead under rubble in Rafid [Lebanon]—these are some of the immediate victims of terror. But indeed the whole civilized world is the real victim of terror. Mr. President, we deplore the loss of lives on both sides.

Today the United States is engaged in a major effort, along with other members of the international community, to make our airways, our sports fields, and our other gathering places safe from terrorism and violence. A beginning has been made, in various international conventions dealing with aircraft hijacking and related problems, to establish a strong framework of law in these matters among the nations of our interdependent world. Secretary Rogers has urged rapid and meaningful action in the subcommittee of ICAO [International Civil Aviation Organization] now meeting in Washington. He has urged rapid action in ratifying existing conventions by governments that have not yet done so.[70] But recent events make clear that the problem is much broader and more pernicious in nature. My government urges that the issue of terrorism in all its aspects receive the highest priority when the General Assembly convenes later this month.[71] The commendable initiative of the Secretary General in placing this question on the Assembly's agenda insures that the world can no longer close its eyes to this pressing matter.

Mr. President, the United States will continue to work for a just and lasting peace in the Middle East. But one-sided resolutions of the type which this Council has so frequently adopted in recent times[72] do not contribute to the goal of peace; indeed, they create an atmosphere in no way conducive to peace by encouraging perpetrators and supporters of acts of terrorism to believe they can escape the world's censure.

---

[69] Cf. above at note 51.
[70] Text of Rogers statement, Sept. 6, 1972, in *Bulletin*, Oct. 2, 1972, pp. 360-61; for details, see Chapter IX at note 74.
[71] Cf. Document 87.
[72] Cf. above at note 50.

Let us not put our heads in the sand and perpetuate the notion of "unreality" that is often assigned to the United Nations.

Munich was so horrible, so vicious, so brutal, so detrimental to order in the world and to peace in the Middle East that we simply must not act here as if it did not exist.

We believe each member of the Council, indeed of the entire international community, should make it unmistakably clear that acts of terror and violence practiced against innocent people as a matter of policy are unacceptable in a civilized world. Each of us has a responsibility to make clear that those who practice such acts, or aid and abet them in any way, are the ones deserving of censure and condemnation. Only then will we begin to eliminate this scourge from the earth and with it the acts of counterviolence to which history inevitably proves it gives rise.

Mr. President, in closing, I would like to read out the text of a resolution[73] which could be helpful to address itself to the thrust of our remarks here and which we would now like to introduce:

The Security Council,

Gravely concerned at the renewal of terrorist attacks on innocent persons,

Deploring the loss of innocent lives on both sides and the outbreak of renewed violence in the Middle East,

Convinced that acts of terrorism, and any encouragement and support for such acts, are totally unacceptable in a civilized society and are inimical to the maintenance of the cease-fire in the Middle East,

1. *Condemns* the senseless and unprovoked terrorist attack in Munich on September 5 by terrorists of the so-called Black September organization which resulted in the loss of life of numerous innocent victims;

2. *Calls upon* those States harbouring and supporting such terrorists and their activities to cease their encouragement and support of terrorists, and to take all necessary measures to bring about the immediate end of such senseless acts.

[73] U.N. document S/10785; not put to a vote.

(b) Draft Resolution Vetoed by the United States, with Amendments Previously Vetoed by China and the U.S.S.R. [74]

(Complete Texts)

Guinea, Somalia and Yugoslavia: draft resolution [75]

[Original: English]
[10 September 1972]

The Security Council,

Deeply concerned at the deteriorating situation in the Middle East,

Calls on the parties concerned to cease immediately all military operations and to exercise the greatest restraint in the interest of international peace and security.

Belgium, France, Italy and United Kingdom of Great Britain and Northern Ireland: amendments to document S/10784 [76]

[Original: English]
[10 September 1972]

1. Insert a second preambular paragraph as follows:

"*Deploring deeply* all acts of terrorism and violence and all breaches of the cease-fire in the Middle East,". [77]

2. In the operative paragraph:

(a) Replace "the parties" by "all parties"; [78]

(b) Delete "cease immediately all military operations" and substitute "take all measures for the immediate cessation and prevention of all military operations and terrorist activities". [79]

---

[74] U.N. Security Council, *Official Records: 27th Year, Supplement for July, Aug. and Sept., 1972*, pp. 98-9.

[75] U.N. document S/10784, rejected by a vote of 13 in favor, 1 against (U.S.), and 1 abstention (Panama).

[76] U.N. document S/10786.

[77] Rejected by a vote of 8 in favor (Argentina, Belgium, France, Italy, Japan, Panama, U.K., U.S.), 4 against (China, Guinea, Sudan, Yugoslavia), and 3 abstentions (India, Somalia, U.S.S.R.).

[78] Rejected by a vote of 9 in favor (Argentina, Belgium, France, India, Italy, Japan, Panama, U.K., U.S.) and 6 against (China, Guinea, Somalia, Sudan, U.S.S.R., Yugoslavia).

[79] Rejected by a vote of 8 in favor (Argentina, Belgium, France, Italy, Japan, Panama, U.K., U.S.) and 7 against (China, Guinea, India, Somalia, Sudan, U.S.S.R., Yugoslavia).

(c) Second Statement by Ambassador Bush.[80]

(Complete Text)

My delegation did not lightly decide to vote against the three-power resolution.[81] Our support of Resolution 242,[82] our abhorrence of violence, is a matter of record.

We, however, are deeply convinced that the Council would have done neither the parties nor itself any good by adopting a resolution which ignored realities, which spoke to one form of violence and not another, which looked to effect but not to cause.

We do not countenance violations of international law. We do not countenance terrorist acts. We seek and support a world in which athletes need not fear assassins and passengers on planes need not fear hijacking or assassination. We seek a just and lasting peace in the Middle East. And we will continue to work toward these ends.

It was said here today that we might be making a constructive move if we could contain the situation by calling for cessation of all military operations. But can anybody suggest that the situation today is unrelated to the Munich massacre? It is related. It is directly related. The fabric of violence in the Middle East is inextricably interwoven with the massacre in Munich.

Is it not a double standard to suggest that states must control their own forces, a point which we readily grant, but that these states need not control irregular forces in their territory, forces of murder, forces of terror?

We have been walking a very dangerous path by our silence on terrorism. We invite more terrorism by our silence on the disaster in Munich. Are we, indeed, inviting more Munichs?

We had hoped that all nations would deplore terrorism, deplore it by statement, deplore it by vote as well.

Mr. President, it is for these reasons that we cast a negative vote against the resolution.

3. Action by the United Nations General Assembly.

[Arab terrorism and Israeli retaliation continued to focus public attention during the 27th Regular Session of the U.N. General Assembly, held at U.N. Headquarters on September 19-December 19, 1972. In spite of widespread dismay that was kept alive by the

---

[80] USUN Press Release 92, Sept. 10, 1972; text from *Bulletin*, Oct. 2, 1972, pp. 367-8.
[81] Document 37b.
[82] Cf. above at note 41.

mailing of "letter bombs" and the hijacking of another German airliner,[83] the majority of the General Assembly proved unresponsive to the views set forth by Secretary of State Rogers[84] and unexpectedly favorable to the Arab position on all aspects of the Palestine question. This pro-Arab trend became particularly noticeable in the debate on a strongly worded statement of the Arab point of view which, with some moderating amendments, was adopted by the full Assembly despite the contrary counsels of Ambassador Bush (Document 38a). Approved by a vote of 86 to 7, with the United States and 30 others abstaining, the resolution (Document 38b) purported to reaffirm the principles of the 1967 Security Council resolution but went beyond it in some important respects, including a reference to "respect for the rights of the Palestinians" as an indispensable element in the establishment of a just and lasting peace. In explaining the reasons for the U.S. abstentions, Ambassador Bush again affirmed his government's determination to accord a high priority to encouraging meaningful negotiations between the parties (Document 38c).]

(38) Debate on the Middle East, December 1972.

(a) Views of the United States: Statement by Ambassador Bush in Plenary Session, December 5, 1972.[85]

(Complete Text)

Since the tragic war of 1967, a torrent of words on the Middle East has engulfed this and other U.N. chambers. Bitterness and invective have characterized many statements, and these have contributed little to finding the road to a durable peace.

For this reason the United States believed that unless there was a specific practical objective which clearly could have moved the area nearer to peace, it would have been wise to forgo yet another debate and resolution on the Middle East at this General Assembly. Others did not agree, and the debate is on. It is now for us—all of us—to do our best to see that what emerges from this debate contributes directly to an improvement in the atmosphere in the Middle East and to the prospects for peacemaking or, if this is not possible, to insure that opportunities for diplomacy in the months ahead are not seriously set back.

---

[83] Cf. above at note 60.
[84] Cf. Document 87.
[85] USUN Press Release 152, Dec. 5, 1972; text from *Bulletin*, Jan. 1, 1973, pp. 25-7.

Secretary Rogers outlined the views of my government during the general debate.[86] He cautioned that:

> ... the momentum toward a peace settlement must be regained. ...
> ... neither side has permanently closed the door to future diplomatic efforts. We believe that forces favoring a peaceful settlement still have the upper hand. Our task is to do everything possible to see that they are supported.

The basic framework for the long-sought peace has been in existence since 1967. So many pro forma and perfunctory references have been made to Security Council Resolution 242[87] in recent years that we tend to forget the landmark quality of that guideline to peace. It is a carefully balanced document, evolved with extraordinary care to address the concerns of the parties involved as well as to serve as a basis for reconciling interests and laying the foundation for a peaceful settlement which will endure. We would do well to bear always in mind that it is the essential agreed basis for United Nations peace efforts and that this body and all its members should be mindful of the need to preserve the negotiating asset that it represents.

The heart of this resolution is that a just and lasting peace in the Middle East should include the application of two—not one, but two—principles: withdrawal of Israeli armed forces from territories occupied in the 1967 conflict; and "termination of all claims or states of belligerency and respect for and acknowledgement of the sovereignty, territorial integrity and political independence of every State in the area and their right to live in peace within secure and recognized boundaries free from threats or acts of force."

Clearly, the inability of the countries in the area to move forward toward a settlement, despite determined efforts by a distinguished statesman, Ambassador Gunnar Jarring as the Secretary General's Special Representative, has resulted from varying interpretations of the principles contained in Resolution 242. The issues are complex and have deep historical and emotional roots. While my government regrets that more progress has not been made, we are also convinced that these difficulties are not insurmountable and that further efforts must be made to bring the benefits of a peaceful settlement to all the peoples of the Middle East. We know that each side is convinced of the justice of its cause, and we know that each side is concerned about its future security. We believe that a political settlement, based on mutual accommodation, could assure both.

Mr. President,[88] the U.S. Government and the American people have

---

86 Document 87.
87 Cf. above at note 41.
88 Stanislaw Trepczynski (Poland).

an important, substantial interest in maintaining peace in the Middle East, in preserving the cultural heritage and political independence of all its peoples, and in helping to create stable conditions in which they may freely pursue their own material and social development. We attach great importance to our relations with all the states and peoples of the area, relations which have deep and abiding roots. We are particularly pleased that in the last year cordial and fruitful relations have been reestablished between the United States and some Arab states.[89] We, on our part, are determined to conduct ourselves in a manner which will contribute to this trend of improving relations with old friends.

For this reason we supported, and continue to support, Security Council Resolution 242 and the mission of Ambassador Jarring. For this reason we welcomed, and continue to welcome, the establishment of a cease-fire in much of the area, which has reduced the loss of lives and resources and has given time for constructive reflection on the future of the area.

And what of that future? How is it to be assured in peace and harmony for the countries of the Middle East? We are still faced with the problem of the "how": how to get a reasonable process of discussion and accommodation underway so that the peoples of that area may enjoy the benefits of a more tranquil environment.

All of us are aware that progress on the great political issues of our time has come slowly and, in most cases, in small steps or stages. My government has long been convinced that the most hopeful and practical means of initiating a reasonable process of discussion and accommodation on the Middle East was through practical interim steps, such as those involved in the so-called interim Suez Canal agreement. The United States has publicly and privately indicated its willingness to play a role in helping the parties negotiate such an agreement if they so desire, and we remain available for this purpose.

Mr. President, the problems in the Middle East area are indeed complex and deeply rooted. But other problems around the world are also complex or the product of deep historical, cultural, or political divisions.

For our part, we are negotiating with the Soviet Union on the complex matter of nuclear arms and other matters.[90] We have taken the first steps toward reducing two decades of accumulated tensions between us and the People's Republic of China.[91] We are talking to North Viet-Nam about peace in Southeast Asia.[92]

In central Europe, the Federal Republic of Germany initiated a process that has led to the initialing of a basic treaty with the German

[89] Cf. below at notes 113 and 117.
[90] Cf. Document 17.
[91] Cf. Documents 53-60.
[92] Cf. Documents 50-52.

Democratic Republic[93] and to improved relations with the other neighbors to the east. The countries of North America and Europe are now engaged in a process of discussion of the issues that have divided Europe for almost three decades.[94]

Others have not been inactive in trying to bridge old animosities. Parties to the Cyprus dispute are participating in intercommunal talks. In south Asia, discussions are continuing among countries who only one year ago were engaged in active hostilities.[95] In Korea, representatives from both sides of the armistice line are engaged in exploring the prospects for greater peace and stability on their peninsula.[96]

It seems to us that all members of this organization have a strong interest in getting such processes started also on the problem of the Middle East. President Nixon recently indicated that a peaceful settlement in the Middle East will have a high priority for the United States.[97]

The guidelines for negotiations between the parties have already been established in Security Council Resolution 242. This Assembly must preserve the measure of agreement that already underlies this resolution. It cannot seek to redefine the essentials for peace in the Middle East. It cannot seek to impose courses of action on the countries directly concerned, either by making new demands or by favoring the proposals or positions of one side or the other. These approaches simply will not work and may in fact endanger the relative calm that has existed since 1970.

This Assembly must instead insure that its conclusions will reinforce the willingness of all parties in the months ahead to enter into a diplomatic process which alone can lead to the just and lasting settlement which is our common objective.

(b) "The Situation in the Middle East": General Assembly Resolution 2949 (XXVII), December 8, 1972.[98]

(Complete Text)

The General Assembly,

Having considered the item entitled "The situation in the Middle East",

---

[93] Cf. Chapter III at note 101.
[94] Cf. Documents 30-32.
[95] Cf. discussion preceding Document 40.
[96] Cf. note 85 to Chapter VI.
[97] Interview, Nov. 5, 1972, in *Washington Star-News*; excerpts in *Bulletin*, Dec. 4, 1972, p. 653.
[98] U.N. General Assembly, *Official Records: 27th Session, Supplement No. 30 (A/8730)*, pp. 6-7; adopted by a vote of 86-7-31 (U.S.).

Having received the report of the Secretary-General of 15 September 1972 on the activities of his Special Representative to the Middle East,[99]

Reaffirming that Security Council resolution 242 (1967) of 22 November 1967[100] must be implemented in all its parts,

Deeply perturbed that Security Council resolution 242 (1967) and General Assembly resolution 2799 (XXVI) of 13 December 1971[101] have not been implemented and, consequently, the envisaged just and lasting peace in the Middle East has not been achieved,

Reiterating its grave concern at the continuation of the Israeli occupation of Arab territories since 5 June 1967,

Reaffirming that the territory of a State shall not be the object of occupation or acquisition by another State resulting from the threat or use of force,

Affirming that changes in the physical character or demographic composition of occupied territories are contrary to the purposes and principles of the Charter of the United Nations, as well as to the provisions of the relevant applicable international conventions,

Convinced that the grave situation prevailing in the Middle East constitutes a serious threat to international peace and security,

Reaffirming the responsibility of the United Nations to restore peace and security in the Middle East in the immediate future,

1. *Reaffirms* its resolution 2799 (XXVI);

2. *Deplores* the non-compliance by Israel with General Assembly resolution 2799 (XXVI), which in particular called upon Israel to respond favourably to the peace initiative of the Special Representative of the Secretary-General to the Middle East;[102]

3. *Expresses its full support* for the efforts of the Secretary-General and his Special Representative;

4. *Declares once more* that the acquisition of territories by force is inadmissible and that, consequently, territories thus occupied must be restored;

5. *Reaffirms* that the establishment of a just and lasting peace in the Middle East should include the application of both the following principles:

(*a*) Withdrawal of Israeli armed forces from territories occupied in the recent conflict;

99 U.N. document S/10792; text in U.N. Security Council, *Official Records: Supplement for July, Aug. and Sept., 1972*, p. 102.
100 *Documents, 1967*, pp. 169-70; cf. above at note 41.
101 *A.F.R., 1971*, no. 54c; for the content, cf. operative para. 2 of Document 38b, below.
102 *A.F.R., 1971*, no. 48b, para. 9.

(b) Termination of all claims or states of belligerency and respect for and acknowledgement of the sovereignty, territorial integrity and political independence of every State in the area and its right to live in peace within secure and recognized boundaries free from threats or acts of force;

6. *Invites* Israel to declare publicly its adherence to the principle of non-annexation of territories through the use of force;

7. *Declares* that changes carried out by Israel in the occupied Arab territories in contravention of the Geneva Conventions of 12 August 1949[103] are null and void, and calls upon Israel to rescind forthwith all such measures and to desist from all policies and practices affecting the physical character or demographic composition of the occupied Arab territories;

8. *Calls upon* all States not to recognize any such changes and measures carried out by Israel in the occupied Arab territories and invites them to avoid actions, including actions in the field of aid, that could constitute recognition of that occupation;

9. *Recognizes* that respect for the rights of the Palestinians is an indispensable element in the establishment of a just and lasting peace in the Middle East;

10. *Requests* the Security Council, in consultation with the Secretary-General and his Special Representative, to take all appropriate steps with a view to the full and speedy implementation of Security Council resolution 242 (1967), taking into account all the relevant resolutions and documents of the United Nations in this connexion;

11. *Requests* the Secretary-General to report to the Security Council and the General Assembly on the progress made by him and his Special Representative in the implementation of Security Council resolution 242 (1967) and of the present resolution;

12. *Decides* to transmit the present resolution to the Security Council for its appropriate action and requests the Council to keep the General Assembly informed.

(c) Statement by Ambassador Bush in Plenary Session, December 8, 1972.[104]

(Complete Text)

We regret very much that the resolution which has just been voted[105] constitutes precisely the kind of resolution we had so much hoped could be avoided at this Assembly. This resolution cannot render con-

---

[103] TIAS 3362-5 (6 UST 3114, 3217, 3316, 3516).
[104] USUN Press Release 157, Dec. 8, 1972; text from *Bulletin*, Jan. 1, 1973, p. 27.
[105] Document 38b.

structive assistance to the processes of diplomacy. It cannot offer encouragement to the parties to reach a peaceful accommodation of their differences.

As we and others have noted many times before, Security Council Resolution 242[106] is a carefully balanced text whose provisions regarding the basic aspects of a settlement are integrally interrelated. Security Council Resolution 242 is designed to serve as the guideline for a peaceful settlement which meets the political, security, and economic interest of all the peoples in the area. It is the only agreed basis for such a settlement, and as I said four days ago, it is essential that we, and particularly the principal parties concerned, preserve the negotiating framework which Resolution 242 provides.

Several paragraphs of this resolution appear calculated to upset the careful balance of Security Council Resolution 242 between withdrawal from occupied territories and agreement between the parties on the terms of a just and lasting peace.

The United States was particularly concerned, as indicated in my intervention on a point of order earlier, over the language of operative paragraph 8 notwithstanding the efforts of a number of delegations to tone down the more objectionable features of the original language. I wish to record here and now that had we been permitted to vote on that paragraph separately, we would have voted "No." This paragraph is directly contrary to U.S. policy on the matter of assistance and cannot affect our attitude.

The Assembly cannot expect that by adopting such a resolution it can establish a new, agreed basis for peace in the Middle East.

Four days ago my government urged the members of this Assembly to insure that our debate contribute directly to an improvement in the atmosphere in the Middle East and to the prospects for peacemaking or, at a minimum, to insure that opportunities for diplomacy in the months ahead are not set back. As President Nixon said recently, the Middle East will have high priority.[107] Only this week Secretary Rogers reaffirmed in Brussels the U.S. intention to be active diplomatically to encourage meaningful negotiations between the parties.[108]

D. The Persian (Arabian) Gulf.

[Developments in the Gulf region during 1972 were more encouraging from an American viewpoint than were the vicissitudes of the Arab-Israeli conflict. The danger that a power vacuum might

106 Cf. above at note 41.
107 Cf. note 97 above.
108 Cf. Rogers news conference, Dec. 8, 1972, in *Bulletin*, Jan. 1, 1973, p. 9.

develop in the area in the wake of Britain's military withdrawal, completed late in 1971, had been at least temporarily staved off with the emergence of the independent states of Bahrain and Qatar in the summer of that year and the subsequent establishment of the new Union of Arab Emirates as successor to the former British-protected Trucial States. The problems of the region as seen from Washington were comprehensively surveyed by Assistant Secretary Sisco in a statement delivered on August 8, 1972 before the Subcommittee on the Near East of the House Committee on Foreign Affairs.]

(39) United States Policy Toward the Persian Gulf Region: Statement by Assistant Secretary of State Sisco Before the Subcommittee on the Near East of the House Committee on Foreign Affairs, August 8, 1972.[109]

(Complete Text)

Mr. Chairman:[110] I want to thank you and the members of the committee for providing the opportunity to come here to discuss the situation in the gulf and its adjacent region and to explain our policy toward this area. I have recently returned from Yemen, Bahrain, and Kuwait[111] impressed anew with the importance of the gulf region. I welcome the fact that this committee shares our interest in this matter.

Mr. Chairman, in our lifetimes we have seen many spectacular changes but few so striking as the transition of the gulf; from poverty to a number of areas of affluence, from traditional to more modern ways, from a position of international significance primarily as part of the British "lifeline" to India to a position of significant strategic and economic importance to many industrial countries. This change has been fueled, as the world increasingly is fueled, by oil. Growing concern about world energy requirements[112] focuses international attention on the gulf. Given recent political changes in the oil-rich gulf region, this has prompted some rather far-reaching speculation about the area's future and the impact of its future on our interests and energy needs. It is therefore timely for us to take a reasoned and realistic look at this region.

Mr. Chairman, the Persian Gulf contains areas of varying age and history. There are, on the one hand, monarchies like Iran and Saudi Arabia with long histories as independent nations with established in-

---

[109] *Bulletin*, Sept. 4, 1972, pp. 241-5.
[110] Lee H. Hamilton (Democrat, Indiana).
[111] Cf. note 117, below.
[112] Cf. Document 91.

fluence and interests in the area. On the other, there are states which have achieved full independence only recently. While greater attention of the outside world has been on the gulf in recent times, we must not forget that the nations of that region themselves have for long had interests in the gulf, which will continue. The present process of transition in the area was dramatized when the British made the decision to terminate their protective treaty relationships with the lower gulf states, an action completed by December 1971.

Iran and the Arabs who border the gulf have strong economic ties with, and unique importance to, the outside world. Consequently, the way in which outside nations view the gulf is significant. The relationships among the major world states will be reflected in their policies toward the gulf. As a strategic part of the world, the gulf is affected by the global strategic situation.

In addition to the tradition of Anglo-American cooperation throughout the world and the parallel nature of American and British interests in the Persian Gulf, the United States has had a long and fruitful tradition of cooperation with the two major regional powers, Iran and Saudi Arabia. We share with these two countries a strong mutual interest in the stability and orderly progress of the region, as do western European states and Japan. Along with the major regional powers and other interested states, we look forward to constructive relations with the newly independent smaller gulf states, and we are not unmindful of the commercial opportunities which exist there. We all share an interest in an orderly, expanding marketplace insulated insofar as possible from ideologically motivated disruptions.

PRINCIPLES GUIDING U.S. POLICY

As we have formulated our own policy toward the gulf, we have been guided by certain basic principles which derive from our policies round the world:

—Noninterference in the internal affairs of other nations.
—Encouragement of regional cooperation for peace and progress.
—Supporting friendly countries in their efforts to provide for their own security and development.
—The principles enunciated at the Moscow summit of avoiding confrontations in such areas of the world.
—Encouraging the international exchange of goods, services, and technology.

We have also recognized that the tensions arising from regional conflicts can spread to neighboring states and disrupt their stability and orderly development. The gulf area is not immune to the virus of the

Arab-Israeli conflict, whose peaceful and just resolution remains an overriding goal of our Middle East policy.

Holding to these principles, we have over the last few years carefully examined our posture toward the strategic gulf region—an area undergoing spectacular economic growth and social change, an area which has experienced a decade of historic political evolution, an area where American interests are of great significance.

The American interest in the gulf tends to be characterized in terms of oil. Undoubtedly, the United States has major strategic and economic interests in the oil of the gulf states. Its continued flow has been of vital importance to the economies of our NATO allies and of our friends east of Suez; assured sources of gulf petroleum are of growing importance to our own energy-hungry economy. American companies are heavily invested in the development of the oil resources of the region, and the returns on their investment have made substantial contributions to our international balance of payments.

But our interests in the region extend well beyond crude oil. From crude oil production the gulf states have derived spectacular and rapidly increasing wealth—wealth providing for growing economies, offering significant markets for American goods and services; wealth providing better lives for the peoples of the gulf through schemes of social and economic development, offering opportunities for American assistance in sharing technology and expert advice; wealth providing surplus capital for investment abroad and economic development throughout the world.

From these interests and our longstanding good relations with the peoples of the gulf derives an American interest in orderly political development there and regional cooperation to assure the tranquillity and progress of the area. Most governments of the gulf are friendly to the United States and welcome commercial and cultural contacts. Our policy toward the area is designed to support these governments in maintaining their independence and assuring peace, progress, and regional cooperation, without our interfering in the domestic affairs of these friendly countries.

EMPHASIS ON TECHNICAL ASSISTANCE

Mr. Chairman, United States policy toward the gulf recognizes that the states of the region want to provide for their own security and can. Our policy seeks to encourage Iran, Saudi Arabia, Kuwait, and the smaller states to cooperate wholeheartedly with one another to assure that the region remains secure. At the same time, we seek, in concert with other friendly non-gulf countries interested in the area, to assist these states where our help is needed and desired. The emphasis of our assistance will be in the provision of technology to those less advantaged. To those more advanced, credit through the Export-Import Bank and cooperation in the security field will be the main emphasis.

The states of the region, as a general rule, neither need nor desire American concessionary economic assistance and can pay their own way for the advice and technology which we provide. In the security field, we have for a number of years assisted in the modernization of the armed forces of Iran and Saudi Arabia to enable them to provide effectively for their own security and to foster the security of the region as a whole. The outsiders' role in this modernization process has not been exclusively American. The United Kingdom, France, and other countries have also participated. In the smaller states of the gulf, providing military advice and equipment has traditionally been a British undertaking. We stand ready to complement this British role in the areas where modest amounts of American equipment or training are desired and would make a real contribution to the self-defense and internal security of the states concerned. We would prefer, however, that the focus of American technical help in the smaller gulf states be on the improvement of the infrastructure of the civilian side of the governments and economies to strengthen the fabric of these rapidly developing societies.

U.S. FRIENDSHIP AND INTEREST

As the smaller states of the gulf have become fully independent, we have extended our diplomatic presence into the area. Specifically, in the past 12 months we have opened small missions in Bahrain, the United Arab Emirates, and Oman and have accredited our Ambassador in Kuwait[113] to these states and to Qatar. We believe that the resultant closer governmental contacts will contribute substantially to furthering our interests in commercial and technological exchange with these new states and in encouraging the trend toward cooperation among them.

United States friendship and interest has been further demonstrated over the last year by visits of top administration figures to the area—the President's visit to Iran;[114] the Vice President's visit to Iran, Saudi Arabia, and Kuwait;[115] and the Secretary of State's visits to Saudi Arabia,[116] and most recently, Kuwait, Bahrain, and the neighboring Yemen Arab Republic, which during his visit became the first Arab

[113] William A. Stoltzfus, Jr.
[114] May 30-31, 1972; documentation in *Public Papers, 1972*, pp. 643-52.
[115] Vice-President Agnew visited Kuwait, July 6-8, 1971; Saudi Arabia, July 8-10, 1971; and Iran, Oct. 13-16, 1971 (cf. *Bulletin*, Aug. 30, 1971, pp. 230-31; same, Nov. 29, 1971, p. 621).
[166] Secretary Rogers visited Saudi Arabia May 1-2, 1971 (cf. *Bulletin*, May 31, 1971, p. 694).

League member to resume broken diplomatic relations with the United States.[117]

As another manifestation of continuing American interest in the gulf and wider Indian Ocean region, we have maintained a small American naval contingent at Bahrain which has for a quarter century carried out the mission of visiting friendly ports in the region to symbolize American interest.[118] It is not our intention to expand this presence or to alter its role nor indeed to undertake an operational American military role in any state in the area. There is no need for the United States to assume responsibilities for security that the British exercised in the gulf in a different era. We do not seek to. We are making no new military commitments in the region but will support as we can the endeavors of the new states to consolidate their independence through economic and social progress and improvement of their means of self-defense and internal security.

There has been much said recently about the role of the Soviet Union in the Persian Gulf, a region in which there is historic Russian interest. The Soviet Union has developed close relations with Iraq at the head of the gulf, as well as in certain other Arab countries not bordering on this waterway. Soviet naval vessels have visited the area from time to time. The Soviet diplomatic and commercial presence is well established in Iran and in Kuwait. The Soviet Union has recognized the newly independent states in the lower gulf. The governments of these states are proud of their independence. They will make their own choices, perhaps in consultation with their neighbors, about the kind of contact which they desire with outside powers. In the gulf and beyond, in the Indian Ocean,[119] we seek no confrontation nor military competition with the Soviet Union. The only competition that we seek is a friendly and free one in the cultural, commercial, and technological fields.

PETROLEUM POLICIES

Mr. Chairman, I have noted the important United States strategic and commercial interest in the oil of the region and the expectation that this interest will increase. The maintenance of friendly relations with the governments of the area, of course, is important to assuring an environment in which economic cooperation in petroleum and other economic activities can flourish.

Today we are witnessing rather dramatic changes in the terms of the financial and concession arrangements between international oil com-

---

[117] Secretary Rogers visited the Yemen Arab Republic, Kuwait, and Bahrain on July 1-4, 1972. On the resumption of diplomatic relations with Yemen, broken by the latter in 1967, cf. *Bulletin*, Aug. 7, 1972, pp. 165-6.
[118] Cf. Chapter I at note 44.
[119] Cf. *A.F.R., 1971*, no. 65.

panies and the producer states. These changes reflect a strong and understandable impulse of economic nationalism. They are not restricted to the gulf region, and the oil policies of the gulf states will undoubtedly be influenced by trends in the international oil markets and concession relationships outside the area. States such as Iran, Saudi Arabia, and Kuwait, however, have consistently indicated by their approach to petroleum questions their recognition of a strong mutual economic interest with the major industrial nations. They have also recognized the useful role which international oil companies play in assuring the continuing and efficient flow from producer to consumer countries on financial terms acceptable to both. Difficult negotiations are currently underway on the question of "participation" as well as the recent moves by Libya and Iraq toward nationalization of certain Western oil operations in their countries. I do not wish to minimize either the economic significance or the complexity of these negotiations. It is my hope, however, that they can be conducted in a businesslike atmosphere toward conclusions which recognize the interdependence of the various national interests involved in the world petroleum picture.

PERIOD OF POLITICAL TRANSITION

Mr. Chairman, the lower gulf has emerged into a new era of full independence after a decade of historic political transition. This began when Kuwait became fully independent in 1961. The process was completed last year as the British protective relationships with the nine lower gulf sheikhdoms terminated and Bahrain and Qatar, along with the United Arab Emirates, took their places as fully independent members of the world community. At the same time, the Sultanate of Oman, which the United States has recognized since the 19th century as an independent state, emerged under new leadership from a period of isolation and began the process of modernization at home and normalization of contacts with other states in the Arab world and beyond.

This transition has required the resolution of longstanding conflicting territorial claims. The United States Government has never taken a position on the merits of these territorial claims but has consistently urged their resolution in a spirit of friendship and cooperation. The most notable achievement in solution of these problems was Iran's statesmanlike relinquishment of its claim to Bahrain.[120]

Iran, by virtue of its population, its economic and military strength, and its geographic position along the northern shore of the Persian Gulf, is destined to play a major role in providing for stability in the gulf and the continued flow of oil to consumer countries. Fortunately,

---

[120] Cf. *Documents, 1970*, pp. 147-8.

Iran has both the will and the capability to do so. At a press conference in July of this year in London, the Shah reiterated Iran's desire to live in peace and harmony with its neighbors on the other side of the Persian Gulf; he stated that Iran was prepared to offer assistance to the smaller gulf states should they wish it. Iran has given concrete evidence of its desire for cooperation by reaching median-line agreements with a number of its Arab neighbors, most notably Saudi Arabia.

Some territorial problems in the region remain, but on balance the solutions that have been found provide an excellent opportunity for the newly independent states to live in peace and cooperation with one another and their larger neighbors. The end of the British treaty relationship also involved an effort to achieve federation of the small gulf sheikhdoms. The United States and other friendly outside countries, as well as the larger gulf neighbors, supported this concept. At this stage, seven of the states, the so-called Trucial States, have formed a union, the United Arab Emirates. The remaining states, Bahrain and Qatar, have attained independence as separate entities but have expressed their continued dedication to the concept of federation.

Mr. Chairman, the political transition in the Persian Gulf inevitably has created uncertainties about the future there. Having just returned from the area, my conviction is reinforced that as they face the future, the governments of the region are determined to maintain their independence, assure the growing prosperity and welfare of their people, and give substance to their declared intention to cooperate with one another in the interest of security and stability in this important part of the world.

E. The Emergence of Bangladesh.

[For the Asian Subcontinent, 1972 was a year of readjustment and partial recovery from the shattering events of late 1971, when the outbreak of a major war between India and Pakistan assisted the 71 million Bengali inhabitants of Pakistan's eastern province in winning political independence in the new "People's Republic of Bangladesh."[121] The "tilt" toward Pakistan that characterized American policy in that crisis had seriously impaired U.S. relations with India and lessened American influence on developments in Pakistan and Bangladesh, whose people had been economically prostrated by the war and initially lacked firm political leadership as well.

[121] Cf. *A.F.R., 1971*, nos. 56-64. For more detailed discussion of South Asian affairs, cf. Nixon Report, 1972, pp. 141-52; same, 1973, pp. 143-52; Rogers Report, 1972, pp. 388-94.

The return to Bangladesh of Sheikh Mujibar Rahman, the princi-pal Bengali nationalist leader, at the beginning of 1972 initiated a process of recovery marked by the rapid withdrawal of Indian military forces; the conclusion on March 19, 1972 of a treaty of friendship and cooperation between Bangladesh and India; the establishment by Bangladesh of diplomatic relations with a majority of the world's governments; and the accession of the new state to membership in the Commonwealth of Nations. A proposal to admit Bangladesh to membership in the United Nations was, however, vetoed by China in the Security Council on August 25, 1972, and Bangladesh did not become a U.N. member until September 17, 1974.

Pakistan, under the civilian leadership of President Zulfikar Ali Bhutto, displayed a like resilience in beginning its recovery from the events of 1971, although its world position was considerably modified by its loss of East Pakistan, its withdrawal from the Commonwealth on January 30, 1972, and its subsequent determination to withdraw from the South-East Asia Treaty Organization (SEATO) as well. Relations between Pakistan and India also showed signs of improvement after President Bhutto and Indian Prime Minister Indira Gandhi met at Simla (India) on June 28-July 3, 1972 and agreed to a partial normalization based on a peaceful resolution of existing differences. Mutual military withdrawals from territories occupied in the recent conflict were completed later in 1972, although the status of the numerous prisoners and detainees being held in the two countries was not fully adjusted until 1974.

The ability of the United States to assist in getting these normalization processes under way was limited by the impairment of its own political relationships in the Subcontinent, which necessitated a fresh start in relations with all three countries. American policy, on the immediate issue of diplomatic recognition of Bangladesh remained undetermined for several weeks (Document 40) but was ultimately clarified in an announcement by Secretary of State Rogers on April 4, 1974 (Document 41). Meanwhile, the United States participated vigorously in an international relief effort which, in the words of an official announcement (Document 42), "helped avert starvation and widespread human suffering . . . among millions of men, women, and children in Bangladesh."]

(40) United States Policy Toward Bangladesh: Statement by Christopher Van Hollen, Deputy Assistant Secretary of State for Near Eastern and South Asian Affairs, Before the Senate Committee on Foreign Relations, March 6, 1972. [122]

(Complete Text)

Mr. Chairman:[123] It is a great pleasure for me to be here this morning before the Senate Foreign Relations Committee to discuss the question of Bangladesh, and with your permission, sir, I would like to read a brief introductory statement which sets forth the administration's views on this subject.

Insofar as the question of the recognition of Bangladesh is concerned, this matter is under active review but no decision has been taken.

President Nixon has made clear the context within which the issue of the recognition of Bangladesh is being considered. You will recall that in his February 10 press conference,[124] the President said that a decision on recognition should not be expected before his return from China. He noted, however, that "we have under study our whole relationship with the subcontinent" and that our relationship with "the 70 million people in Bangladesh" is, of course, part of that review. At the same time in a different context the President went on to say that "we are going to do everything that we can to develop a new relationship with the countries on the subcontinent that will be pro-Indian, pro-Bengalese, pro-Pakistan, but mostly pro-peace." That review is still in process, and no decision has been made.

These statements by the President make clear both our awareness of current political realities in South Asia and our concerns for peace and stability in that area. As a general proposition, however, many factors including political considerations determine decisions on recognition and its precise timing. The case of Bangladesh is set against the tragic background of the recent hostilities between India and Pakistan and of the political and military situation in the wake of the war which has yet to be fully clarified. Among other things, we are especially concerned about the continued presence of Indian troops in Bangladesh, and we also will wish to weigh the impact of our decisions on other countries both within and outside the region. In this context we are following developments in South Asia carefully in light of our interests, current problems, and humanitarian needs.

---

[122] *Bulletin*, Mar. 27, 1972, pp. 488-90.
[123] Senator Frank Church of Idaho presided in place of the Committee Chairman, Senator J. W. Fulbright of Arkansas.
[124] *Public Papers, 1972*, pp. 350-58; quoted passages on pp. 354 and 357. A further excerpt from this news conference appears below as Document 53.

The members of this committee are well aware that there has been historically a warm and close relationship between the American people and the people of East Bengal. The government and people of the United States have been in the forefront in contributing to development efforts in that area, and they have been deeply conscious of and sympathetic with the tremendous problems that have beset that area. This administration gave generously and promptly to the massive international effort that was launched to deal with the tragedy that befell East Bengal in the cyclone and tidal bore of 1970.[125] We played a strong leadership role in encouraging and supporting the U.N. relief work prior to the December hostilities, and our efforts contributed significantly to the prevention of famine, which threatened the area. Private Americans have long been active in that area in education, in public health, and in joint efforts in development.

All of us can be proud of that record. As the people and the Bangladesh authorities now again take up the tremendous tasks of rehabilitation and development, they can count on the support and help of the people and government of this country. As President Nixon pointed out in his foreign policy report to Congress for 1972:[126]

> Our relief effort in East Bengal will continue. The authorities face the grim challenge of creating a viable political structure and economy in one of the most impoverished—and now newly devastated—areas of the world. We have never been hostile to Bengali aspirations. Our aid program in the 1960's increasingly concentrated on development in East Bengal. We provided two-thirds of the world's emergency aid to the province in 1971. We would expect other nations to bear a proportionate share of that responsibility in the future, but as the United States strengthens new relationships in Asia, we have no intention of ignoring these 70 million people.

As tangible evidence of these remarks by the President, we have already announced a contribution of 175,000 tons of food grain, worth approximately $21 million, to the U.N. Secretary General's humanitarian relief appeal. We have also provided a total of $3.65 million to two American voluntary agencies long active in humanitarian work in East Bengal, CARE and Catholic Relief Services, to support the housing demonstration and construction projects that they have developed in coordination with the authorities of Bangladesh.

Additionally, we have provided $50,000 through the International Rescue Committee to the support of the Cholera Research Laboratory in Dacca and $300,000 for operating expenses of the U.N. mission in Dacca.

---

[125] Cf. *The United States in World Affairs, 1970*, p. 180.
[126] Nixon Report, 1972, p. 150.

As the U.N. effort develops, we are prepared to contribute our proportionate share of future assistance as requirements are clarified. In this common endeavor, we also believe it essential that other countries make substantial contributions on their own so that this will be a truly cooperative international effort in relief and rehabilitation.

It is in this broad political and humanitarian context that this government is closely considering its future relationship with Bangladesh, including the question of recognition, which is under active review.

(41) Extension of Diplomatic Recognition: Statement by Secretary of State Rogers, April 4, 1972.[127]

(Complete Text)

As you know, the question of recognition of Bangladesh has been under active review for some time. This review has now been completed, and I am pleased to announce this morning that the United States Government is extending recognition to Bangladesh Our principal officer in Dacca, Mr. Herbert D. Spivack, is now on his way back to Dacca following consultations here. He is carrying a message from the President to the Prime Minister, Sheikh Mujibur Rahman, informing him of our recognition and of our desire to establish diplomatic relations at the embassy level.

We look forward to good relations with this new country. The United States has had an official mission in Dacca since 1949, and many Americans, both in official and private capacities, have been associated over the years with the development efforts of the people of Bangladesh. President Nixon emphasized in his foreign policy report to Congress that as we strengthen new relationships in Asia this concern for the welfare of the people of Bangladesh will continue.[128]

As we now enter into an official relationship with the Government and people of Bangladesh, I want to express on behalf of all the American people our good wishes for the future. I also want to reaffirm our intention to develop friendly bilateral relations and be helpful as Bangladesh faces its immense task of relief and reconstruction.

[127] Department of State Press Release 79; text from *Bulletin*, Apr. 24, 1972, p. 597.
[128] Cf. above at note 126.

(42) Assistance to Bangladesh: Announcement by the Agency for International Development (AID), August 2, 1972. [129]

(Complete Text)

A massive humanitarian response by the United States has helped avert starvation and widespread human suffering in recent months among millions of men, women, and children in Bangladesh. So declared Maurice J. Williams, Deputy Administrator of the Agency for International Development, with the issuance on August 2 of a six-month report[130] detailing U.S. relief assistance to June 30, coinciding with the first half year of Bangladesh independence.[131]

The total U.S. contribution to help that emerging nation cope with the staggering social and economic problems growing out of last year's civil strife amounted to $267.5 million. That figure, Mr. Williams noted, represents about one-third of the combined contributions of all donor nations.

To counter the threat of famine, the United States has committed, since March alone, 700,000 tons of Food for Peace (P.L. 480)[132] foodgrains and edible oil, valued at $88.2 million, according to the report.

"But tonnage and dollar amounts hardly tell the whole story," Mr. Williams, who is also Coordinator of U.S. Relief Assistance to Bangladesh, pointed out. "What matters most is the people. They have suffered a tragedy of immense proportions. We are doing all in our power to help them."

In the six months covered by the report, U.S. relief contributions were shown to be in the form of: food and logistical support totaling $132 million; grants to U.S. voluntary agencies, $19.5 million; and economic assistance to the Government of Bangladesh, $115 million.

"Here, too," Mr. Williams declared, "it is essential to translate the report figures into human terms." He gave these illustrations:

—700,000 tons of Food for Peace wheat, rice, and vegetable oil will feed 4.4 million persons for a whole year.

—115,000 tons of fertilizer will increase Bangladesh's grain production by 690,000 tons, enough to feed another 4 million persons for a year.

—100,000 bales of cotton will clothe more than 16 million Bengalees

---

[129] AID Press Release 63, Aug. 2, 1972; text from *Bulletin*, Aug. 28, 1972, p. 231.

[130] Text in same, pp. 231-3.

[131] The independence of Bangladesh, originally proclaimed Mar. 26, 1971, was established *de facto* with the surrender of Pakistani armed forces to the Indian military command on Dec. 16, 1971.

[132] Cf. note 17 to Document 21.

234   THE MIDDLE EAST AND SOUTHERN ASIA

and provide employment for additional thousands in mills and factories now shut down.

—Repair to coastal embankments will give employment to 160,000 laborers this winter and provide protection from salt water damage to agricultural production while also protecting against cyclones following the present monsoons.

—U.S. voluntary agencies have focused on rehabilitation of individual families who have lost their homes. Nearly 2 million Bengalees who were without shelter have directly benefited from such assistance.

The U.S. aid report notes that "sustained international effort of rehabilitation assistance" will be required over the 1973 fiscal year and points out that the administration has requested a further $100 million "to permit the United States to do its proportionate share in this large scale humanitarian endeavor."[133]

---

[133] Cf. Nixon message on foreign assistance programs, Mar. 14, 1972, in *Public Papers, 1972*, p. 413.

V.
AMERICAN POLICY IN ASIA:
THE WAR
IN INDOCHINA

[Nineteen seventy-two was a climactic year in the protracted international military struggle over Indochina, in which the United States had become a direct participant with the commitment of the first American troops in support of the anti-Communist government of the Republic of Vietnam in 1961. The biggest Communist offensive of the war, unleashed by North Vietnamese and Vietcong forces on March 30, 1972 at a time when a withdrawal of American troops from South Vietnam was far advanced, precipitated a full-scale resumption of U.S. air operations against North Vietnam, accompanied for the first time by the mining of North Vietnam's ports and an attempt to sever all its overland communications. Secret peace negotiations between the United States and North Vietnam, in progress since 1969, continued during this period of heavy bombardment and reached a climax in the weeks preceding the United States' November election; but opposition by the Saigon government and disagreement over various technicalities delayed the actual signature of a peace agreement until January 27, 1973.[1]]

A. Disclosure of Secret Peace Negotiations.

[American policy with regard to the war in Indochina remained within the outlines sketched by President Nixon toward the end of his initial year in office. The guiding objective of the American Government, Mr. Nixon had explained on November 3, 1969, was "to end this war in a way that will bring us closer to . . . a just and lasting peace." If possible, this aim was to be realized through negotiation with the enemy; but should negotiation fail to work, it

[1] For more detailed discussion, cf. Nixon Report, 1972, pp. 110-32; same, 1973, pp. 42-74; Rogers Report, 1972, pp. 346-55; Kalb, *Kissinger*, pp. 284-311 and 336-418; Tad Szulc, "How Kissinger Did It: Behind the Vietnam Cease-fire Agreement," *Foreign Policy*, No. 15 (Summer 1974), pp. 21-69.

was anticipated that a policy of "Vietnamization," involving "the complete withdrawal of all U.S. ground combat forces, and their replacement by South Vietnamese forces on an orderly scheduled timetable," would "bring the war to an end regardless of what happens on the negotiating front."[2]

In major speeches during the earlier part of 1972, President Nixon described the progress of these efforts and defined the supplementary measures occasioned by the enemy's resistance to ending the war on American terms. In the first of these reports, a nationwide broadcast delivered January 25, 1972 (Document 43), the President claimed far-reaching success for the Vietnamization plan but conceded that there had been little progress toward a negotiated peace, despite extraordinary diplomatic efforts initiated even before his assumption of office. The main participants in the war— the United States, the southern Republic of Vietnam, the northern Democratic Republic of Vietnam (D.R.V.), and the insurgent Provisional Revolutionary Government of the Republic of South Vietnam (P.R.G.)—had been meeting openly in Paris since 1969 for the ostensible purpose of negotiating a peace settlement. Unknown to the public until the President's January 25 speech was the fact that secret exchanges had also been taking place in Paris since August 1969 between high-level representatives of the United States and North Vietnam. Dr. Kissinger, the President's Assistant for National Security Affairs, had handled these contacts on the American side, while North Vietnam had been represented by Le Duc Tho, a Special Adviser and influential member of the North Vietnamese Politburo, and/or Minister Xuan Thuy, head of the North Vietnamese delegation to the regular Paris talks.

Some information about the substance of these exchanges was included in the President's speech, and further details were offered in a January 26 news conference held by Dr. Kissinger; a polemical statement issued by the North Vietnamese delegation in Paris; and the "State of the World" report released by President Nixon on February 9, 1972.[3] This material made it clear that the obstacles to agreement, in the private as well as the semipublic talks, were essentially political in character and had less to do with the technicalities of a cease-fire or the release of prisoners held by the two sides than with the political future of South Vietnam. Ignoring the United States' repeated proposals that the military issues be settled on a priority basis and that political issues be held for separate resolution, the North Vietnamese and their P.R.G. allies had insisted not

[2] Documents, 1968-69, pp. 287, 282-3.
[3] Kissinger news conference in Presidential Documents, Jan. 31, 1972, pp. 126-33; North Vietnamese statement in Document 45; Nixon Report, 1972, pp. 113-19.

merely that the United States withdraw militarily from South Vietnam but also that it "stop supporting" the existing South Vietnamese leadership so that alternative political arrangements could be set up. Specifically, the P.R.G. had called repeatedly for the formation of a "provisional government of broad coalition" made up of three components: (1) persons already associated with the P.R.G.; (2) persons associated with the Saigon government but "really standing for peace, independence, neutrality and democracy"; and (3) persons unidentified with either camp and representing "various political and religious forces and tendencies standing for peace, independence, neutrality and democracy," including political exiles.[4] For President Nixon, such a program boiled down to the demand "that we overthrow the Government of South Vietnam" and "join our enemy to overthrow our ally." The North Vietnamese, the President wrote, "offer no political process except one that will ensure in advance that the Communists rule the South."[5]

While flatly refusing to abet a Communist takeover in this manner, the United States had nevertheless made various concessions in an attempt to meet at least a part of the Communist demands. Since the autumn of 1970, it had soft-pedaled its earlier demand for the withdrawal of North Vietnamese troops from South Vietnam, Laos, and Cambodia as the counterpart of an American (and allied) withdrawal from South Vietnam.[6] With the concurrence of South Vietnamese President Nguyen Van Thieu, it had also gone some way toward opening up the political processes of the Republic of Vietnam to Communist participation. In an eight-point proposal laid before the North Vietnamese on October 11, 1971, the United States and South Vietnam had offered an unprecedented arrangement that called for the resignation of President Thieu and Vice-President Tran Van Huong preliminary to the holding of a new presidential election, to be organized by an independent body and internationally supervised, within six months of the signature of a formal peace agreement.[7]

But North Vietnam's only reply to this proposal, President Nixon stated in his speech of January 25, 1972, had been "an increase in troop infiltration from North Vietnam and Communist military offensives in Laos and Cambodia." By the time the President spoke, there were strong indications that the enemy might be preparing to abandon his "talk and fight" strategy of the past three and one-half

[4] *Documents, 1970*, pp. 194-5; *A.F.R., 1971*, nos. 74a and 75.
[5] Document 43; Nixon Report, 1972, p. 119.
[6] Nixon broadcast, Oct. 7, 1970, in *Documents, 1970*, pp. 196-201; cf. *A.F.R., 1971*, p. 294.
[7] *A.F.R., 1971*, no. 76b; text made public Feb. 1, 1972.

years and mount a new offensive on the scale of the "Tet" attacks of 1968. In a gesture avowedly aimed in part at silencing his domestic critics, President Nixon nevertheless announced in the course of his January 25 speech that a slightly modified version of the American-South Vietnamese plan would be presented at the next regular session of the Paris peace talks, in the hope that public disclosure might gain it "the attention it deserves in Hanoi." Alternatively, Mr. Nixon added, "we remain willing to settle only the military issues and leave the political issues to the Vietnamese alone."

The new peace plan made public in the wake of the President's speech (Document 44) differed only in minor detail from the earlier version submitted October 11, 1971. The most conspicuous change was a slight speeding up of the timetable that would compress the withdrawal of U.S. and allied forces, the return of prisoners and detainees, and the holding of new presidential elections into a period of six months immediately following the conclusion of an agreement. As in the 1971 plan, there was reference to the principle "that all armed forces of the countries of Indochina must remain within their national frontiers," a formula that seemed to call for North Vietnamese withdrawal from Laos and Cambodia but failed to provide explicitly for a withdrawal from South Vietnam in view of Hanoi's longstanding contention that North and South Vietnam were parts of a single nation.

Although North Vietnam and the Vietcong-dominated P.R.G. did not explicitly reject the new American-South Vietnamese plan, they lost no time in complaining that it failed to provide a "serious answer" to their demands. The plan to hold new presidential elections in the South, the Vietcong protested, was merely a device for keeping intact the repressive apparatus of the Saigon regime.[8] Protesting the United States' alleged breach of confidence in making public these hitherto secret exchanges, the North Vietnamese delegation in Paris on January 31 released its own version of the secret talks (Document 45) together with some of the relevant documentary material. Again, Hanoi's delegation refrained from outright rejection of the plan; but its insistence on the reaffirmation of past positions left little hope of acceptance.

Hopes of a successful negotiation gained equally little support from a minor change in the Vietcong position disclosed at a session of the regular Paris talks on February 3, 1972. Instead of repeating its demand for the ouster of the entire Saigon regime, the P.R.G. delegation intimated on this occasion that the resignation of President Thieu, together with a reversal of his government's external

---

[8] North Vietnamese and P.R.G. statements, Jan. 26, 1972, in *New York Times*, Jan. 27, 1972.

and internal policies, would be sufficient in themselves to start a process of political settlement that would involve the formation of a "tripartite government of national concord" to organize elections and draw up a new constitution.[9] But even if President Thieu had been willing to resign in this manner, the idea of setting up a coalition government that would include Communist and neutral elements remained basically unacceptable to Saigon and, it appeared, to Washington as well.]

(43) "A Plan for Peace in Vietnam": Radio-Television Address by President Nixon, January 25, 1972.[10]

(Complete Text)

Good evening. I have asked for this television time tonight to make public a plan for peace that can end the war in Vietnam.

The offer that I shall now present, on behalf of the Government of the United States and the Government of South Vietnam, with the full knowledge and approval of President [Nguyen Van] Thieu, is both generous and far-reaching.

It is a plan to end the war now; it includes an offer to withdraw all American forces within 6 months of an agreement; its acceptance would mean the speedy return of all the prisoners of war to their homes.

Three years ago when I took office, there were 550,000 Americans in Vietnam; the number killed in action was running as high as 300 a week; there were no plans to bring any Americans home, and the only thing that had been settled in Paris was the shape of the conference table.

I immediately moved to fulfill a pledge I had made to the American people: to bring about a peace that could last, not only for the United States, but for the long-suffering people of Southeast Asia.

There were two honorable paths open to us.

The path of negotiation was, and is, the path we prefer. But it takes two to negotiate; there had to be another way in case the other side refused to negotiate.

That path we called Vietnamization. What it meant was training and equipping the South Vietnamese to defend themselves, and steadily withdrawing Americans, as they developed the capability to do so.

The path of Vietnamization has been successful. Two weeks ago, you will recall, I announced that by May 1, American forces in Vietnam

---

[9] Keesing's, p. 25319.
[10] Presidential Documents, Jan. 31, 1972, pp. 120-25.

would be down to 69,000.[11] That means almost one-half million Americans will have been brought home from Vietnam over the past 3 years. In terms of American lives, the losses of 300 a week have been reduced by over 95 percent—to less than 10 a week.

But the path of Vietnamization has been the long voyage home. It has strained the patience and tested the perseverance of the American people. What of the shortcut, the shortcut we prefer, the path of negotiation?

Progress here has been disappointing. The American people deserve an accounting of why it has been disappointing. Tonight I intend to give you that accounting, and in so doing, I am going to try to break the deadlock in the negotiations.

We have made a series of public proposals designed to bring an end to the conflict. But early in this administration, after 10 months of no progress in the public Paris talks, I became convinced that it was necessary to explore the possibility of negotiating in private channels, to see whether it would be possible to end the public deadlock.

After consultation with Secretary of State Rogers, our Ambassador in Saigon [Ellsworth Bunker] and our chief negotiator in Paris [Henry Cabot Lodge], and with the full knowledge and approval of President Thieu, I sent Dr. Kissinger to Paris as my personal representative on August 4, 1969, 30 months ago, to begin these secret peace negotiations.

Since that time, Dr. Kissinger has traveled to Paris 12 times on these secret missions. He has met seven times with Le Duc Tho, one of Hanoi's top political leaders, and Minister Xuan Thuy, head of the North Vietnamese delegation to the Paris talks, and he has met with Minister Xuan Thuy five times alone. I would like, incidentally, to take this opportunity to thank President [Georges] Pompidou of France for his personal assistance in helping to make the arrangements for these secret talks.

This is why I initiated these private negotiations: Privately, both sides can be more flexible in offering new approaches and also private discussions allow both sides to talk frankly, to take positions free from the pressure of public debate.

In seeking peace in Vietnam, with so many lives at stake, I felt we could not afford to let any opportunity go by—private or public—to negotiate a settlement. As I have stated on a number of occasions, I was prepared and I remain prepared to explore any avenue, public or private, to speed negotiations to end the war.

For 30 months, whenever Secretary Rogers, Dr. Kissinger, or I were asked about secret negotiations we would only say we were pursuing every possible channel in our search for peace. There was never a leak,

[11] Announcement of Jan. 13, 1972, in *Public Papers. 1972*, p. 30.

because we were determined not to jeopardize the secret negotiations. Until recently, this course showed signs of yielding some progress.

Now, however, it is my judgment that the purposes of peace will best be served by bringing out publicly the proposals we have been making in private.

Nothing is served by silence when the other side exploits our good faith to divide America and to avoid the conference table. Nothing is served by silence when it misleads some Americans into accusing their own government of failing to do what it has already done. Nothing is served by silence when it enables the other side to imply possible solutions publicly that it has already flatly rejected privately.

The time has come to lay the record of our secret negotiations on the table. Just as secret negotiations can sometimes break a public deadlock, public disclosure may help to break a secret deadlock.

Some Americans, who believed what the North Vietnamese led them to believe, have charged that the United States has not pursued negotiations intensively. As the record that I will now disclose will show, just the opposite is true.

Questions have been raised as to why we have not proposed a deadline for the withdrawal of all American forces in exchange for a cease-fire and the return of our prisoners of war; why we have not discussed the 7-point proposal made by the Vietcong last July in Paris;[12] why we have not submitted a new plan of our own to move the negotiations off dead center.

As the private record will show, we have taken all these steps and more and have been flatly rejected or ignored by the other side.

On May 31, 1971, 8 months ago, at one of the secret meetings in Paris, we offered specifically to agree to a deadline for the withdrawal of all American forces in exchange for the release of all prisoners of war and a cease-fire.

At the next private meeting, on June 26, the North Vietnamese rejected our offer. They privately proposed instead their own 9-point plan[13] which insisted that we overthrow the Government of South Vietnam.

Five days later, on July 1, the enemy publicly presented a different package of proposals—the 7-point Vietcong plan.[14]

That posed a dilemma: Which package should we respond to, the public plan or the secret plan?

On July 12, at another private meeting in Paris, Dr. Kissinger put that question to the North Vietnamese directly. They said we should deal with their 9-point secret plan, because it covered all of Indochina in-

[12] *A.F.R., 1971*, no. 74a; cf. above at note 4.
[13] *A.F.R., 1971*, no. 75; made public with Document 45, below.
[14] Same as note 12.

cluding Laos and Cambodia, while the Vietcong 7-point proposal was limited to Vietnam.

So that is what we did. But we went even beyond that, dealing with some of the points in the public plan that were not covered in the secret plan.

On August 16, at another private meeting, we went further. We offered the complete withdrawal of U.S. and allied forces within 9 months after an agreement on an overall settlement. On September 13, the North Vietnamese rejected that proposal. They continued to insist that we overthrow the South Vietnamese Government.[15]

Now, what has been the result of these private efforts? For months, the North Vietnamese have been berating us at the public sessions for not responding to their side's publicly presented 7-point plan.

The truth is that we did respond to the enemy's plan, in the manner they wanted us to respond—secretly. In full possession of our complete response, the North Vietnamese publicly denounced us for not having responded at all. They induced many Americans in the press and the Congress into echoing their propaganda—Americans who could not know they were being falsely used by the enemy to stir up divisiveness in this country.

I decided in October that we should make another attempt to break the deadlock. I consulted with President Thieu, who concurred fully in a new plan. On October 11, I sent a private communication to the North Vietnamese that contained new elements that could move negotiations forward. I urged a meeting on November 1 between Dr. Kissinger and Special Adviser Le Duc Tho, or some other appropriate official from Hanoi.[16]

On October 25, the North Vietnamese agreed to meet and suggested November 20 as the time for a meeting.[17] On November 17, just 3 days before the scheduled meeting, they said Le Duc Tho was ill.[18] We offered to meet as soon as he recovered, either with him, or immediately with any other authorized leader who could come from Hanoi[19]

Two months have passed since they called off that meeting. The only reply to our plan has been an increase in troop infiltration from North Vietnam and Communist military offensives in Laos and Cambodia. Our proposal for peace was answered by a step-up in the war on their part.

That is where matters stand today.

We are being asked publicly to respond to proposals that we answered, and in some respects accepted, months ago in private.

[15] Details in Nixon Report, 1972, p. 116 (quoted in *A.F.R., 1971*, pp. 302-3).
[16] *A.F.R., 1971*, no. 76; first made public with Document 45, below.
[17] *A.F.R., 1971*, no. 77a.
[18] Same, no. 77c.
[19] Same, no. 77d.

We are being asked publicly to set a terminal date for our withdrawals when we already offered one in private.

And the most comprehensive peace plan of this conflict lies ignored in a secret channel, while the enemy tries again for military victory.

That is why I have instructed Ambassador Porter[20] to present our plan publicly at this Thursday's session of the Paris peace talks, along with alternatives to make it even more flexible.[21]

We are publishing the full details of our plan tonight.[22] It will prove beyond doubt which side has made every effort to make these negotiations succeed. It will show unmistakably that Hanoi—not Washington or Saigon—has made the war go on.

Here is the essence of our peace plan; public disclosure may gain it the attention it deserves in Hanoi.

Within 6 months of an agreement:

—We shall withdraw all U.S. and allied forces from South Vietnam.

—We shall exchange all prisoners of war.

—There shall be a cease-fire throughout Indochina.

—There shall be a new presidential election in South Vietnam.

President Thieu will announce the elements of this election. These include international supervision; and an independent body to organize and run the election, representing all political forces in South Vietnam, including the National Liberation Front.

Furthermore, President Thieu has informed me that within the framework of the agreement outlined above, he makes the following offer: He and Vice President [Tran Van] Huong would be ready to resign one month before the new election. The Chairman of the Senate [Nguyen Van Huyen], as caretaker head of the government, would assume administrative responsibilities in South Vietnam, but the election would be the sole responsibility of the independent election body I have just described.

There are several other proposals in our new peace plan; for example, as we offered privately on July 26 of last year, we remain prepared to undertake a major reconstruction program throughout Indochina, including North Vietnam, to help all these peoples recover from the ravages of a generation of war.[23]

We will pursue any approach that will speed negotiations.

---

[20] William J. Porter, designated July 28, 1971 as head of the U.S. delegation to the Paris meetings on Vietnam.

[21] For Ambassador Porter's statement on Jan. 27, 1972, see *Bulletin*, Feb. 14, 1972, pp. 186-7.

[22] Document 44.

[23] In his "State of the World" report released Feb. 9, 1972, President Nixon stated: "We are prepared to undertake a massive 7½ billion dollar five-year reconstruction program in conjunction with an overall agreement, in which North Vietnam could share up to two and a half billion dollars" (Nixon Report, 1972, p. 119).

We are ready to negotiate the plan I have outlined tonight and conclude a comprehensive agreement on all military and political issues. Because some parts of this agreement could prove more difficult to negotiate than others, we would be willing to begin implementing certain military aspects while negotiations continue on the implementation of other issues, just as we suggested in our private proposal in October.

Or, as we proposed last May, we remain willing to settle only the military issues and leave the political issues to the Vietnamese alone. Under this approach, we would withdraw all U.S. and allied forces within 6 months in exchange for an Indochina cease-fire and the release of all prisoners.

The choice is up to the enemy.

This is a settlement offer which is fair to North Vietnam and fair to South Vietnam. It deserves the light of public scrutiny by these nations and by other nations throughout the world. And it deserves the united support of the American people.

We made the substance of this generous offer privately over 3 months ago. It has not been rejected, but it has been ignored. I reiterate that peace offer tonight. It can no longer be ignored.

The only thing this plan does not do is to join our enemy to overthrow our ally, which the United States of America will never do. If the enemy wants peace, it will have to recognize the important difference between settlement and surrender.

This has been a long and agonizing struggle. But it is difficult to see how anyone, regardless of his past position on the war, could now say that we have not gone the extra mile in offering a settlement that is fair, fair to everybody concerned.

By the steadiness of our withdrawal of troops, America has proved its resolution to end our involvement in the war; by our readiness to act in the spirit of conciliation, America has proved its desire to be involved in the building of a permanent peace throughout Indochina.

We are ready to negotiate peace immediately.

If the enemy rejects our offer to negotiate, we shall continue our program of ending American involvement in the war by withdrawing our remaining forces as the South Vietnamese develop the capability to defend themselves.

If the enemy's answer to our peace offer is to step up their military attacks, I shall fully meet my responsibility as Commander in Chief of our Armed Forces to protect our remaining troops.

We do not prefer this course of action.

We want to end the war not only for America but for all the people of Indochina. The plan I have proposed tonight can accomplish that goal.

Some of our citizens have become accustomed to thinking that whatever our Government says must be false, and whatever our enemies say must be true, as far as this war is concerned. Well, the record I have revealed tonight proves the contrary. We can now demonstrate publicly what we have long been demonstrating privately—that America has taken the initiative not only to end our participation in this war, but to end the war itself for all concerned.

This has been the longest, the most difficult war in American history.

Honest and patriotic Americans have disagreed as to whether we should have become involved ·at all 9 years ago; and there has been disagreement on the conduct of the war. The proposal I have made tonight is one on which we all can agree.

Let us unite now, unite in our search for peace—a peace that is fair to both sides—a peace that can last.

Thank you. And good night.

(44) *Joint Peace Proposal: Proposal of the Republic of Vietnam and the United States for a Negotiated Settlement of the Indochina Conflict, Made Public January 25, 1972.* [24]

(Complete Text)

1. There will be a total withdrawal from South Vietnam of all U.S. forces and other foreign forces allied with the government of South Vietnam within six months of an agreement.

2. The release of all military men and innocent civilians captured throughout Indochina will be carried out in parallel with the troop withdrawals mentioned in point 1. Both sides will present a complete list of military men and innocent civilians held throughout Indochina on the day the agreement is signed. The release will begin on the same day as the troop withdrawals and will be completed when they are completed.

3. The following principles will govern the political future of South Vietnam:

The political future of South Vietnam will be left for the South Vietnamese people to decide for themselves, free from outside interference.

There will be a free and democratic Presidential election in South Vietnam within six months of an agreement. This election will be organized and run by an independent body representing all political forces in South Vietnam which will assume its responsibilities on the date of the agreement. This body will, among other responsibilities,

---

[24] *Presidential Documents*, Jan. 31, 1972, pp. 125-6. The proposal was submitted in the 142d plenary session of the Paris peace talks on Jan. 27, 1972; cf. note 21 above.

determine the qualification of candidates. All political forces in South Vietnam can participate in the election and present candidates. There will be international supervision of this election.

One month before the Presidential election takes place, the incumbent President and Vice President of South Vietnam will resign. The Chairman of the Senate, as caretaker head of the government, will assume administrative responsibilities except for those pertaining to the election, which will remain with the independent election body.

The United States, for its part, declares that it:

—will support no candidate and will remain completely neutral in the election.

—will abide by the outcome of this election and any other political processes shaped by the South Vietnamese people themselves.

—is prepared to define its military and economic assistance relationship with any government that exists in South Vietnam.

Both sides agree that:

—South Vietnam, together with the other countries of Indochina, should adopt a foreign policy consistent with the military provisions of the 1954 Geneva Accords.[25]

—Reunification of Vietnam should be decided on the basis of discussions and agreements between North and South Vietnam without constraint and annexation from either party, and without foreign interference.

4. Both sides will respect the 1954 Geneva Agreements on Indochina and those of 1962 on Laos.[26] There will be no foreign intervention in the Indochinese countries and the Indochinese peoples will be left to settle their own affairs by themselves.

5. The problems existing among the Indochinese countries will be settled by the Indochinese parties on the basis of mutual respect for independence, sovereignty, territorial integrity and non-interference in each other's affairs. Among the problems that will be settled is the implementation of the principle that all armed forces of the countries of Indochina must remain within their national frontiers.

6. There will be a general cease-fire throughout Indochina, to begin when the agreement is signed. As part of the cease-fire, there will be no further infiltration of outside forces into any of the countries of Indochina.

7. There will be international supervision of the military aspects of this agreement including the cease-fire and its provisions, the release of prisoners of war and innocent civilians, the withdrawal of outside forces from Indochina, and the implementation of the principle that all armed

---

[25] *Documents, 1954*, pp. 283-310.
[26] Same, pp. 283-314; same, *1962*, pp. 284-94.

forces of the countries of Indochina must remain within their national frontiers.

8. There will be an international guarantee for the fundamental national rights of the Indochinese peoples, the status of all the countries in Indochina, and lasting peace in this region.

Both sides express their willingness to participate in an international conference for this and other appropriate purposes.

(45) North Vietnam's Version: Communiqué of the Delegation of the Democratic Republic of Vietnam to the Paris Peace Talks, January 31, 1972.[27]

(Complete Text)

In the peace negotiation on the Vietnam problem, the government of the DRVN [Democratic Republic of (North) Vietnam], with its constant goodwill, has always held that it was important to reach a peaceful settlement of the Vietnam problem on the basis of the guarantee for the Vietnamese people's fundamental national rights and that the form of negotiation, public sessions or private meetings, was not important. Starting from that point of view, the Government of the DRVN, with the full agreement of the Provisional Revolutionary Government of the Republic of South Vietnam [P.R.G. of the RSVN], has accepted to hold private meetings on the request of the U. S. party in order to peacefully settle the Vietnam problem.

The Government of the DRVN is of the view that the substance of the negotiations between the two parties should be made known to the public. However, as wished by the U.S. party, the Government of the DRVN agreed to the decision that the parties would refrain from publicizing the substance of the private meetings, yet President Nixon, in his Jan. 25, 1972, statement,[28] and Mr. H. Kissinger at his Jan. 26 press conference,[29] unilaterally divulged the substance of the private meetings between the U.S. and the DRVN; they even distorted the fact.

In so doing the Nixon Administration wants to make believe that it has goodwill and to shift onto the DRVN party the responsibility for the deadlock of the negotiations. The fact is just the contrary. The U.S. Government has broken its engagements and created serious obstacles to the negotiations. For its part, the DRVN party has always shown goodwill, which has been evidenced at the private meetings as well as at

---

[27]*New York Times*, Feb. 1, 1972. Printed here is the full text of the communiqué minus the annexes referred to at notes 35-39 below.

[28] Document 43.

[29] *Presidential Documents*, Jan. 31, 1972, pp. 126-33.

public sessions. However, the Nixon Administration has so far not answered to the two fundamental points mentioned in the proposals of the DRVN and the P.R.G. of the RSVN.

The just position of the DRVN is perfectly illustrated by the nine-point proposal presented to the U.S. party at the June 26, 1971, private meeting.[30] This proposal is fully conforming to the July 1, 1971, seven-point position of the P.R.G. of the RSVN on the peaceful settlement of the Vietnam problem.[31]

With regard to the problem of Laos and Cambodia, the Government of DRVN has already made known its invariable position, i.e.: The U.S. must respect the Geneva agreements of 1954 on Indochina and those of 1962 on Laos,[32] end its aggression and intervention in the Indochinese countries, and let the Indochinese peoples settle themselves their own affairs; the problems existing among the Indochinese countries will be settled by the Indochinese parties on the basis of mutual respect for independence, sovereignty and territorial integrity and noninterference in each other's internal affairs. This position is conforming to the spirit of the joint declaration of the Indochinese peoples' summit conference held in April, 1970.[33]

With regard to the cancellation of the private meeting on Nov. 20, 1971 between the DRVN and the U.S.:[34]

At some of the private meetings held until now, Mr. Le Duc Tho and Mr. Xuan Thuy met with Mr. H. Kissinger; at others, only Mr. Xuan Thuy conferred with Mr. Kissinger. On Oct. 11, 1971, Mr. H. Kissinger proposed a meeting to be held on Nov. 20, 1971, which was accepted by the DRVN party. On Nov. 17, 1971, the DRVN party informed the U.S. party that Mr. Le Duc Tho was taken ill and could not go to Paris, but Minister Xuan Thuy was prepared to meet with Mr. Kissinger on Nov. 20, 1971, as agreed upon. Yet, on Nov. 19, 1971, the U.S. party canceled this meeting. Thus, it was the U.S. party that canceled the Nov. 20, 1971, meeting, but it is now trying to distort the fact.

Of late world public opinion has condemned the U.S. [words missing] Paris conference on Vietnam and its repeated escalations of the air war against the DRVN.

In deciding now to unilaterally making public the substance of the private meetings between the DRVN and the U.S., the Nixon Administration has further laid bare its fallacy. This way of doing is aimed at deceiving public opinion in the U.S. and in the world, at serving Mr.

---

[30] *A.F.R., 1971*, no. 75; cf. above at note 4.
[31] *A.F.R., 1971*, no. 74a; cf. above at note 4.
[32] Cf. note 26 above.
[33] Apr. 25-26, 1970; cf. *The United States in World Affairs, 1970*, pp. 134 and 309.
[34] Cf. above at notes 17-19; for the original correspondence, see *A.F.R., 1971*, no. 77

Nixon's political objectives in this election year and at allowing him to pursue the "Vietnamization" of the war, and not "to serve in the best way the cause of peace," as he claims.

In the face of this situation, the Government of the DRVN is determined not to permit the U.S. party to mislead public opinion. In consequence, the delegation of the DRVN to the Paris conference deems it necessary to make public the following documents:

1. The full text of the nine points presented by the DRVN at the June 26, 1971, private meeting;[35] the full text of the July 1, 1971, seven points of the P.R.G. of the RSVN.[36]

2. The full text of the eight points handed by the U.S. to the DRVN on Oct. 11, 1971;[37] the full text of the eight published by the White House on Jan. 25, 1972[38] and presented at the Paris conference on Vietnam on Jan. 27, 1972.

3. The three messages of the U.S. party and the two messages of the DRVN party related to the cancellation of the private meeting scheduled for Nov. 20, 1971.[39]

Paris, Jan. 31, 1972

B. Communist Offensive and American Response.

[The publication of the new American-South Vietnamese peace proposal proved temporarily helpful in allaying domestic criticism of President Nixon's Vietnam policies, but did little to advance the prospect for a negotiated settlement or for the return of the estimated 1,500 American servicemen and 40 civilians reported captured or missing in territory held by North Vietnam and its allies. Likewise without visible effect on the situation in Vietnam were President Nixon's discussions with the Chinese leaders during his visit to the People's Republic of China on February 21-28, 1972 (Documents 53-56). Speculation to the effect that Peking might have undertaken to try to exercise a moderating influence on the North Vietnamese appeared to be refuted not only by the intransigence of the latter in the Paris peace talks but by their evident

---

[35] *A.F.R., 1971*, no. 75.
[36] Same, no. 74c.
[37] *A.F.R., 1971*, no. 76b. (The text published by the North Vietnamese was substantially identical to that made public by the Department of State on Feb. 1, 1972.)
[38] Document 44.
[39] *A.F.R., 1971*, no. 77.

distaste for the U.S.-Chinese *rapprochement* and their increasingly obvious preparations for a new, large-scale offensive. As these preparations became unmistakable, the meetings of the Paris peace negotiators became more infrequent, and on March 23, 1972 the United States announced the suspension of its participation in the formal Paris talks until the other side should again be ready for "serious discussion."[40] Exchanges looking toward a resumption of the private negotiations between American and North Vietnamese representatives also proved unproductive, although it was eventually decided to schedule a new meeting for April 24, 1972.

In the midst of these exchanges, the North Vietnamese army on March 30, 1972 launched a large-scale military offensive that began in areas immediately south of the Demilitarized Zone and later extended into more southerly provinces in the neighborhood of the Cambodian frontier, in the Central Highlands, and along the central coast. With American troops already reducing toward their May 1 target of 69,000, responsibility for meeting the offensive on the ground in this instance fell almost entirely upon the South Vietnamese. The United States, however, had retained the capability of renewing the air offensive, which had been discontinued by President Johnson in 1968 on the understanding that North Vietnam would not take military advantage of this action.[41] On April 6, 1972, the American Command in Saigon announced that Air Force tactical aircraft and Navy components were in fact engaged in "attacking military targets north of the demilitarized zone in order to help protect the lives of the diminishing U.S. forces in South Vietnam." B-52 bombers were also brought into action, and Hanoi and Haiphong were attacked on April 16 for the first time since 1968, occasioning civilian casualties as well as a Soviet protest claiming that four Soviet merchant ships had been damaged.

President Nixon's projected visit to the U.S.S.R. was less than a month away, and the United States, which strongly resented the Soviet arms shipments that had made Hanoi's offensive possible, was compelled to weigh each action in Vietnam in the light of its potential effect on the summit talks. Strong measures against the North Vietnamese might help impress the Kremlin with American resoluteness, but could also lead to outright cancellation of the meetings; the avoidance of such measures, on the other hand, might save the summit but convey a dangerously misleading impression of

---

[40] Porter statement, Mar. 23, 1972, in *Bulletin*, Apr. 10, 1972, pp. 537-8; for background, cf. Document 46 and Kissinger news conference, May 9, 1972, in *Presidential Documents*, May 15, 1972, pp. 842-5.
[41] Johnson address, Oct. 31, 1968, in *Documents, 1968-69*, pp. 243-8.

American weakness. Dr. Kissinger, on a presummit visit to Moscow on April 20-24, was apparently encouraged by the Soviet leaders to try to bring about a resumption of diplomatic negotiations;[42] and President Nixon announced in a broadcast on April 26 (Document 46) that the formal peace talks in Paris would in fact resume next day. Noting that the progressive withdrawal of U.S. military forces from South Vietnam had not been interrupted by the enemy offensive, the President warned nevertheless that "air and naval attacks on military installations in North Vietnam" would continue until the offensive was halted.

This admonition did not prevent a further intensification of the North Vietnamese and Vietcong offensive, which reached a climax in late April and early May with the Communist capture of Dong Ha and Quang Tri in the north and the seemingly imminent fall of Kontum in the center and An Loc in the south. New contacts in Paris revealed no change in the enemy's position, and President Nixon returned to the air waves on May 8, 1972 to announce decisions of the gravest import not only for North Vietnam but for the U.S.S.R. as well.

Hanoi's reckless actions and its refusal to negotiate, the President stated in his May 8 address (Document 47), had compelled the United States to take decisive action to deny it the weapons and supplies required to continue the aggression. Action was accordingly under way to implement a three-point program involving (1) the mining of all entrances to North Vietnamese ports; (2) the severance, so far as possible, of North Vietnam's rail and all other communications; and (3) continuance of air and naval strikes against military targets in North Vietnam. Appealing for the understanding of the Soviet leaders as well as the support of the American people,[43] the President also offered what amounted to a further relaxation of the American conditions for a peace settlement. Once all prisoners of war had been returned and an internationally supervised cease-fire was in effect throughout Indochina, he said, the United States would "proceed with a complete withdrawal of all American forces from Vietnam within 4 months." Nothing was said about political conditions or about a withdrawal of North Vietnamese forces from the South.]

---

[42] Cf. Document 47 and Kissinger news conference, May 9, 1972 (cited in note 40); also Kalb, *Kissinger*, pp. 291-5.
[43] Cf. Chapter II at note 17.

(46) "Report on Vietnam": Radio-Television Address by President Nixon, April 26, 1972. [44]

(Complete Text)

Good evening.

During the past 3 weeks you have been reading and hearing about the massive invasion of South Vietnam by the Communist armies of North Vietnam.

Tonight, I want to give you a firsthand report on the military situation in Vietnam, the decisions I have made with regard to the role of the United States in the conflict, and the efforts we are making to bring peace at the negotiating table.

Let me begin briefly by reviewing what the situation was when I took office and what we have done since then to end American involvement in the war and to bring peace to the long-suffering people of Southeast Asia.

On January 20, 1969, the American troop ceiling in Vietnam was 549,000. Our casualties were running as high as 300 a week. Thirty thousand young Americans were being drafted every month.

Today, 39 months later, through our program of Vietnamization— helping the South Vietnamese develop the capability of defending themselves—the number of Americans in Vietnam by Monday, May 1, will have been reduced to 69,000. [45] Our casualties—even during the present, all-out enemy offensive—have been reduced by 95 percent. And draft calls now average fewer than 5,000 men a month, and we expect to bring them to zero next year.

As I reported in my television address to the Nation on January 25, [46] we have offered the most generous peace terms in both public and private negotiating sessions. Our most recent proposal [47] provided for an immediate cease-fire; the exchange of all prisoners of war; the withdrawal of all of our forces within 6 months; and new elections in Vietnam, which would be internationally supervised, with all political elements including the Communists participating in and helping to run the elections. One month before such elections, President Thieu and Vice President Huong would resign.

Now, Hanoi's answer to this offer was a refusal even to discuss our proposals and, at the same time, a huge escalation of their military activities on the battlefield. Last October, the same month when we made this peace offer to Hanoi, our intelligence reports began to indicate that the enemy was building up for a major attack. And yet we

[44] *Presidential Documents*, May 1, 1972, pp. 790-94.
[45] Cf. note 11 to Document 43.
[46] Document 43.
[47] Document 44.

deliberately refrained from responding militarily. Instead we patiently continued with the Paris talks, because we wanted to give the enemy every chance to reach a negotiated settlement at the bargaining table rather than to seek a military victory on the battlefield—a victory they cannot be allowed to win.

Finally, 3 weeks ago, on Easter weekend,[48] they mounted their massive invasion of South Vietnam. Three North Vietnamese divisions swept across the demilitarized zone into South Vietnam—in violation of the treaties they had signed in 1954[49] and in violation of the understanding they had reached with President Johnson in 1968, when he stopped the bombing of North Vietnam in return for arrangements which included their pledge not to violate the DMZ.[50] Shortly after the invasion across the DMZ, another three North Vietnamese divisions invaded South Vietnam further south. As the offensive progressed, the enemy indiscriminately shelled civilian population centers in clear violation of the 1968 bombing halt understanding.

So the facts are clear. More than 120,000 North Vietnamese are now fighting in South Vietnam. There are no South Vietnamese troops anywhere in North Vietnam. Twelve of North Vietnam's 13 regular combat divisions have now left their own soil in order to carry aggressive war onto the territory of their neighbors. Whatever pretext there was of a civil war in South Vietnam has now been stripped away.

What we are witnessing here—what is being brutally inflicted upon the people of South Vietnam—is a clear case of naked and unprovoked aggression across an international border. There is only one word for it—invasion.

This attack has been resisted on the ground entirely by South Vietnamese forces, and in one area by South Korean forces. There are no United States ground troops involved. None will be involved. To support this defensive effort by the South Vietnamese, I have ordered attacks on enemy military targets in both North and South Vietnam by the air and naval forces of the United States.

I have here on my desk a report. I received it this morning from General Abrams.[51] He gives the following evaluation of the situation:

The South Vietnamese are fighting courageously and well in their self-defense. They are inflicting very heavy casualties on the invading force, which has not gained the easy victory some predicted for it 3 weeks ago.

Our air strikes have been essential in protecting our own remaining forces and in assisting the South Vietnamese in their efforts to protect

---

[48] Easter Sunday fell on Apr. 2, 1972.

[49] Agreement on the Cessation of Hostilities in Vietnam, July 20, 1954, in *Documents, 1954*, pp. 283-302.

[50] Same, *1968-69*, pp. 243-8.

[51] Gen. Creighton W. Abrams, Commander, U.S. Military Assistance Command in Vietnam.

their homes and their country from a Communist takeover.

General Abrams predicts in this report that there will be several more weeks of very hard fighting. Some battles will be lost, he says; others will be won by the South Vietnamese. But his conclusion is that if we continue to provide air and sea support, the enemy will fail in its desperate gamble to impose a Communist regime in South Vietnam, and the South Vietnamese will then have demonstrated their ability to defend themselves on the ground against future enemy attacks.

Based on this realistic assessment from General Abrams, and after consultation with President Thieu, Ambassador Bunker, Ambassador Porter, and my senior advisers in Washington, I have three decisions to announce tonight.

First, I have decided that Vietnamization has proved itself sufficiently that we can continue our program of withdrawing American forces without detriment to our overall goal of ensuring South Vietnam's survival as an independent country. Consequently, I am announcing tonight that over the next 2 months 20,000 more Americans will be brought home from Vietnam. This decision has the full approval of President Thieu and of General Abrams. It will bring our troop ceiling down to 49,000 by July 1—a reduction of half a million men since this Administration came into office.

Second, I have directed Ambassador Porter to return to the negotiating table in Paris tomorrow,[52] but with one very specific purpose in mind. We are not resuming the Paris talks simply in order to hear more empty propaganda and bombast from the North Vietnamese and Vietcong delegates, but to get on with the constructive business of making peace. We are resuming the Paris talks with the firm expectation that productive talks leading to rapid progress will follow through all available channels. As far as we are concerned, the first order of business will be to get the enemy to halt his invasion of South Vietnam and to return the American prisoners of war.

Finally, I have ordered that our air and naval attacks on military installations in North Vietnam be continued until the North Vietnamese stop their offensive in South Vietnam.

I have flatly rejected the proposal that we stop the bombing of North Vietnam as a condition for returning to the negotiating table. They sold that package to the United States once before, in 1968, and we are not going to buy it again in 1972.

Now, let's look at the record. By July 1 we will have withdrawn over 90 percent of our forces that were in Vietnam in 1969. Before the enemy's invasion began, we had cut our air sorties in half. We have offered exceedingly generous terms for peace. The only thing we have

---

[52] Cf. White House announcement, Apr. 25, 1972, in *Presidential Documents*, May 1, 1972, p. 790.

refused to do is to accede to the enemy's demand to overthrow the lawfully constituted Government of South Vietnam and to impose a Communist dictatorship in its place.

As you will recall, I have warned on a number of occasions over the past 3 years that if the enemy responded to our efforts to bring peace by stepping up the war, I would act to meet that attack, for these three very good reasons: first, to protect our remaining American forces; second, to permit continuation of our withdrawal program; and third, to prevent the imposition of a Communist regime on the people of South Vietnam against their will, with the inevitable bloodbath that would follow for hundreds of thousands who have dared to oppose Communist aggression.

The air and naval strikes of recent weeks have been carried out to achieve these objectives. They have been directed only against military targets which support the invasion of South Vietnam and they will not stop until the invasion stops.

The Communists have failed in their efforts to win over the people of South Vietnam politically. And General Abrams believes that they will fail in their efforts to conquer South Vietnam militarily. Their one remaining hope is to win in the Congress of the United States and among the people of the United States the victory they cannot win among the people of South Vietnam or on the battlefield in South Vietnam.

The great question then is how we, the American people, will respond to this final challenge.

Let us look at what the stakes are—not just for South Vietnam, but for the United States and for the cause of peace in the world. If one country, armed with the most modern weapons by major powers, can invade another nation and succeed in conquering it, other countries will be encouraged to do exactly the same thing—in the Mideast, in Europe, and in other international danger spots. If the Communists win militarily in Vietnam, the risk of war in other parts of the world would be enormously increased. But if, on the other hand, Communist aggression fails in Vietnam, it will be discouraged elsewhere and the chance for peace will be increased.

We are not trying to conquer North Vietnam or any other country in this world. We want no territory. We seek no bases. We have offered the most generous peace terms—peace with honor for both sides—with South Vietnam and North Vietnam each respecting the other's independence.

But we will not be defeated; and we will never surrender our friends to Communist aggression.

We have come a long way in this conflict. The South Vietnamese have made great progress; they are now bearing the brunt of the battle. We can now see the day when no more Americans will be involved there at all.

But as we come to the end of this long and difficult struggle, we must be steadfast. And we must not falter. For all that we have risked and all that we have gained over the years now hangs in the balance during the coming weeks and months. If we now let down our friends, we shall surely be letting down ourselves and our future as well. If we now persist, future generations will thank America for her courage and her vision in this time of testing.

That is why I say to you tonight, let us bring our men home from Vietnam; let us end the war in Vietnam. But let us end it in such a way that the younger brothers and the sons of the brave men who have fought in Vietnam will not have to fight again in some other Vietnam at some time in the future.

Any man who sits here in this office feels a profound sense of obligation to future generations. No man who sits here has the right to take any action which would abdicate America's great tradition of world leadership or weaken respect for the Office of President of the United States.

Earlier this year I traveled to Peking on an historic journey for peace.[53] Next month I shall travel to Moscow on what I hope will also be a journey for peace.[54] In the 18 countries I have visited as President I have found great respect for the Office of President of the United States. I have reason to expect, based on Dr. Kissinger's report, that I shall find that same respect for the office I hold when I visit Moscow.

I do not know who will be in this office in the years ahead. But I do know that future Presidents will travel to nations abroad as I have on journeys for peace. If the United States betrays the millions of people who have relied on us in Vietnam, the President of the United States, whoever he is, will not deserve nor receive the respect which is essential if the United States is to continue to play the great role we are destined to play of helping to build a new structure of peace in the world. It would amount to a renunciation of our morality, an abdication of our leadership among nations, and an invitation for the mighty to prey upon the weak all around the world. It would be to deny peace the chance peace deserves to have. This we shall never do.

My fellow Americans, let us therefore unite as a nation in a firm and wise policy of real peace—not the peace of surrender, but peace with honor—not just peace in our time, but peace for generations to come.

Thank you and good night.

[53] Cf. Documents 53-56.
[54] Cf. Documents 9-12.

(47) "The Situation in Southeast Asia": Radio-Television Address by President Nixon, May 8, 1972. [55]

(Complete Text)

Good evening. Five weeks ago, on Easter weekend, the Communist armies of North Vietnam launched a massive invasion of South Vietnam, an invasion that was made possible by tanks, artillery, and other advanced offensive weapons supplied to Hanoi by the Soviet Union and other Communist nations.

The South Vietnamese have fought bravely to repel this brutal assault. Casualties on both sides have been very high. Most tragically, there have been over 20,000 civilian casualties, including women and children, in the cities which the North Vietnamese have shelled in wanton disregard of human life.

As I announced in my report to the Nation 12 days ago,[56] the role of the United States in resisting this invasion has been limited to air and naval strikes on military targets in North and South Vietnam. As I also pointed out in that report, we have responded to North Vietnam's massive military offensive by undertaking wide-ranging new peace efforts aimed at ending the war through negotiation.

On April 20, I sent Dr. Kissinger to Moscow[57] for 4 days of meetings with General Secretary Brezhnev and other Soviet leaders. I instructed him to emphasize our desire for a rapid solution to the war and our willingness to look at all possible approaches. At that time, the Soviet leaders showed an interest in bringing the war to an end on a basis just to both sides. They urged resumption of negotiations in Paris, and they indicated they would use their constructive influence.

I authorized Dr. Kissinger to meet privately with the top North Vietnamese negotiator, Le Duc Tho, on Tuesday, May 2, in Paris. Ambassador Porter, as you know, resumed the public peace negotiations in Paris on April 27 and again on May 4. At those meetings, both public and private, all we heard from the enemy was bombastic rhetoric and a replaying of their demands for surrender. For example, at the May 2 secret meeting, I authorized Dr. Kissinger to talk about every conceivable avenue toward peace. The North Vietnamese flatly refused to consider any of these approaches. They refused to offer any new approach of their own. Instead, they simply read verbatim their previous public demands.

Here is what over 3 years of public and private negotiations with Hanoi has come down to: The United States, with the full concurrence

[55] *Presidential Documents*, May 15, 1972, pp. 838-42.
[56] Document 46.
[57] Cf. above at note 42.

of our South Vietnamese allies, has offered the maximum of what any President of the United States could offer.[58]

We have offered a deescalation of the fighting. We have offered a cease-fire with a deadline for withdrawal of all American forces. We have offered new elections which would be internationally supervised with the Communists participating both in the supervisory body and in the elections themselves.

President Thieu has offered to resign one month before the elections. We have offered an exchange of prisoners of war in a ratio of 10 North Vietnamese prisoners for every one American prisoner that they release. And North Vietnam has met each of these offers with insolence and insult. They have flatly and arrogantly refused to negotiate an end to the war and bring peace. Their answer to every peace offer we have made has been to escalate the war.

In the 2 weeks alone since I offered to resume negotiations Hanoi has launched three new military offensives in South Vietnam. In those 2 weeks the risk that a Communist government may be imposed on the 17 million people of South Vietnam has increased and the Communist offensive has now reached the point that it gravely threatens the lives of 60,000 American troops who are still in Vietnam.

There are only two issues left for us in this war. First, in the face of a massive invasion do we stand by, jeopardize the lives of 60,000 Americans, and leave the South Vietnamese to a long night of terror? This will not happen. We shall do whatever is required to safeguard American lives and American honor.

Second, in the face of complete intransigence at the conference table do we join with our enemy to install a Communist government in South Vietnam? This, too, will not happen. We will not cross the line from generosity to treachery.

We now have a clear, hard choice among three courses of action: immediate withdrawal of all American forces, continued attempts at negotiation, or decisive military action to end the war.

I know that many Americans favor the first course of action, immediate withdrawal. They believe the way to end the war is for the United States to get out and to remove the threat to our remaining forces by simply withdrawing them.

From a political standpoint, this would be a very easy choice for me to accept. After all, I did not send over one-half million Americans to Vietnam. I have brought 500,000 men home from Vietnam since I took office. But, abandoning our commitment in Vietnam here and now would mean turning 17 million South Vietnamese over to Communist tyranny and terror. It would mean leaving hundreds of American prisoners in Communist hands with no bargaining leverage to get them released.

[58] Cf. Document 44.

An American defeat in Vietnam would encourage this kind of aggression all over the world, aggression in which smaller nations armed by their major allies, could be tempted to attack neighboring nations at will in the Mid-East, in Europe, and other areas. World peace would be in grave jeopardy.

The second course of action is to keep on trying to negotiate a settlement. Now this is the course we have preferred from the beginning and we shall continue to pursue it. We want to negotiate, but we have made every reasonable offer and tried every possible path for ending this war at the conference table.

The problem is, as you all know. it takes two to negotiate and now, as throughout the past 4 years, the North Vietnamese arrogantly refuse to negotiate anything but an imposition, an ultimatum that the United States impose a Communist regime on 17 million people in South Vietnam who do not want a Communist government.

It is plain then that what appears to be a choice among three courses of action for the United States is really no choice at all. The killing in this tragic war must stop. By simply getting out, we would only worsen the bloodshed. By relying solely on negotiations, we would give an intransigent enemy the time he needs to press his aggression on the battlefield.

There is only one way to stop the killing. That is to keep the weapons of war out of the hands of the international outlaws of North Vietnam.

Throughout the war in Vietnam, the United States has exercised a degree of restraint unprecedented in the annals of war. That was our responsibility as a great nation, a nation which is interested—and we can be proud of this as Americans—as America has always been, in peace not conquest.

However, when the enemy abandons all restraint, throws its whole army into battle in the territory of its neighbor, refuses to negotiate, we simply face a new situation.

In these circumstances, with 60,000 Americans threatened, any President who failed to act decisively would have betrayed the trust of his country and betrayed the cause of world peace.

I therefore concluded that Hanoi must be denied the weapons and supplies it needs to continue the aggression. In full coordination with the Republic of Vietnam, I have ordered the following measures which are being implemented as I am speaking to you.

All entrances to North Vietnamese ports will be mined to prevent access to these ports and North Vietnamese naval operations from these ports. United States forces have been directed to take appropriate measures within the internal and claimed territorial waters of North Vietnam to interdict the delivery of any supplies. Rail and all other communications will be cut off to the maximum extent possible. Air and naval strikes against military targets in North Vietnam will continue.

These actions I have ordered will cease when the following conditions are met:

First, all American prisoners of war must be returned.

Second, there must be an internationally supervised cease-fire throughout Indochina.

Once prisoners of war are released, once the internationally supervised cease-fire has begun, we will stop all acts of force throughout Indochina, and at that time we will proceed with a complete withdrawal of all American forces from Vietnam within 4 months.

Now, these terms are generous terms. They are terms which would not require surrender and humiliation on the part of anybody. They would permit the United States to withdraw with honor. They would end the killing. They would bring our POW's home. They would allow negotiations on a political settlement between the Vietnamese themselves. They would permit all the nations which have suffered in this long war—Cambodia, Laos, North Vietnam, South Vietnam—to turn at last to the urgent works of healing and of peace. They deserve immediate acceptance by North Vietnam.

It is appropriate to conclude my remarks tonight with some comments directed individually to each of the major parties involved in the continuing tragedy of the Vietnam war.

First, to the leaders of Hanoi, your people have already suffered too much in your pursuit of conquest. Do not compound their agony with continued arrogance; choose instead the path of a peace that redeems your sacrifices, guarantees true independence for your country and ushers in an era of reconciliation.

To the people of South Vietnam, you shall continue to have our firm support in your resistance against aggression. It is your spirit that will determine the outcome of the battle. It is your will that will shape the future of your country.

To other nations, especially those which are allied with North Vietnam, the actions I have announced tonight are not directed against you. Their sole purpose is to protect the lives of 60,000 Americans who would be gravely endangered in the event that the Communist offensive continues to roll forward and to prevent the imposition of a Communist government by brutal aggression upon 17 million people.

I particularly direct my comments tonight to the Soviet Union. We respect the Soviet Union as a great power. We recognize the right of the Soviet Union to defend its interests when they are threatened. The Soviet Union in turn must recognize our right to defend our interests.

No Soviet soldiers are threatened in Vietnam. Sixty thousand Americans are threatened. We expect you to help your allies, and you cannot expect us to do other than to continue to help our allies, but let us, and let all great powers, help our allies only for the purpose of their defense, not for the purpose of launching invasions against their neighbors.

Otherwise the cause of peace, the cause in which we both have so great a stake, will be seriously jeopardized.

Our two nations have made significant progress in our negotiations in recent months. We are near major agreements on nuclear arms limitation, on trade, on a host of other issues.

Let us not slide back toward the dark shadows of a previous age. We do not ask you to sacrifice your principles, or your friends, but neither should you permit Hanoi's intransigence to blot out the prospects we together have so patiently prepared.

We, the United States and the Soviet Union, are on the threshold of a new relationship that can serve not only the interests of our two countries, but the cause of world peace. We are prepared to continue to build this relationship. The responsibility is yours if we fail to do so.

And finally, may I say to the American people, I ask you for the same strong support you have always given your President in difficult moments. It is you most of all that the world will be watching.

I know how much you want to end this war. I know how much you want to bring our men home. And I think you know from all that I have said and done these past 3½ years how much I, too, want to end the war to bring our men home.

You want peace. I want peace. But, you also want honor and not defeat. You want a genuine peace, not a peace that is merely a prelude to another war.

At this moment, we must stand together in purpose and resolve. As so often in the past, we Americans did not choose to resort to war. It has been forced upon us by an enemy that has shown utter contempt toward every overture we have made for peace. And that is why, my fellow Americans, tonight I ask for your support of this decision, a decision which has only one purpose, not to expand the war, not to escalate the war, but to end this war and to win the kind of peace that will last.

With God's help, with your support, we will accomplish that great goal.

Thank you and good night.

C. Vietnam in Election-Year Politics.

[Although the actions announced in President Nixon's speech of May 8, 1972 (Document 47) did not suffice to halt the enemy military campaign in the South, the threatened capture of major South Vietnamese cities was averted and Quang Tri itself was later recaptured by South Vietnamese forces. The U.S.-Soviet summit conference likewise took place without impediment, following what amounted to no more than a routine Soviet denunciation of the new American moves.[59] While the U.S. and Soviet governments continued to reaffirm their separate viewpoints on the Indochina problem (Document 10), there are indications that the Russians found sufficient flexibility in the American position to warrant a new attempt to persuade Hanoi to come to terms. The Chinese leaders, too, are said to have listened attentively to Dr. Kissinger's subsequent account of the Moscow meetings, and to have independently advised the North Vietnamese to moderate their ambitions.[60]

The United States, meanwhile, maintained its aerial campaign against North Vietnam even while continuing the gradual withdrawal of its forces in the South, whose number was to be down to slightly over 24,000 by the year's end. In a continuation of the retaliatory attacks against the North initiated in April, North Vietnamese communications, oil supplies, and industrial targets were now being subjected to the heaviest bombing of the entire war. Both Hanoi and Haiphong were attacked repeatedly, and there were recurrent allegations—peremptorily denied in Washington—that American aircraft were also attacking the network of dams and dikes in the Red River delta despite the risk of causing massive civilian casualties. Domestic and international opinion were further incensed when an American bomb demolished the headquarters of the French mission in Hanoi on October 11 and caused fatal injury to the French Delegate-General, Pierre Susini.

These activities inevitably tended to revive the antiwar agitation within the United States, after the period of relative calm that had accompanied the gradual reduction in the scale of combat and the continuing withdrawal of American forces. Senator McGovern, accepting the Democratic presidential nomination at Miami Beach on July 13, 1972, had left no doubt that Vietnam would be a central issue in his campaign, and that he proposed to "halt the senseless bombing of Indochina on Inauguration Day" (Document 4). In Washington, other Senators of both parties were moved to renew the effort to expedite the conclusion of the war by some form of legislative enactment along the lines of the Mansfield amendment of 1971, which had called for the setting of a definite date for the withdrawal of all U.S. forces from Indochina.[61]

The principal effort of this kind in 1972 was the so-called Brooke

[59] Soviet statement, May 11, 1972, in Keesing's, p. 25399.
[60] On the Kissinger visit, cf. Document 58; for discussions at the June meetings of the SEATO and ANZUS Councils, cf. Documents 64-65.
[61] *A.F.R., 1971*, nos. 79 and 81a.

amendment, named for Republican Senator Edward W. Brooke of Massachusetts, which called for the withdrawal of all U.S. ground, naval, and air forces from Vietnam, Laos and Cambodia within four months of enactment, provided all American prisoners of war held by the North Vietnamese and their allies were released within that period. Attached successively to the foreign aid authorization bill, the military procurement authorization bill, and the military assistance authorization bill, the amendment was approved by a vote of 50 to 45 on July 24 and again by 49 to 47 on August 2, but was rejected by 42 to 45 in a third and decisive vote on September 26. In the House, congenitally less sympathetic to "end-the-war" legislation, a parallel amendment calling for military withdrawal from Indochina by October 1, 1972 was defeated on August 10 by a vote of 178 to 228.[62]

Likewise defeated by a Senate vote of 26 to 55 on October 2 was an amendment to the Department of Defense appropriation bill, submitted by Democratic Senator William Proxmire of Wisconsin, prohibiting the use of appropriated funds for U.S. bombing over Vietnam, Laos, or Cambodia. Although the Senate did accept an amendment by Republican Senator Charles McC. Mathias of Maryland reiterating the 1971 demand that the President set a deadline for the withdrawal of U.S. military forces from Indochina, even this comparatively mild assertion of Senate views was eliminated in Senate-House conference on October 10, 1972.[63] This was the final attempt of the kind so far as the 92nd Congress was concerned, although a more successful effort in the next Congress was to result on July 1, 1973 in presidential acceptance of legislation barring any combat activities in Indochina by U.S. forces as from August 15, 1973.[64]

With the collapse of congressional "end-the-war" efforts, the presidential campaign came into its own as the primary focus of the continuing national debate on Indochina policy. Whereas the point of view of President Nixon had been repeatedly set forth in an official context and required no special elaboration in terms of campaign rhetoric, it was only on October 10 that the Democratic nominee came forward with an indictment of administration policy sufficiently comprehensive to be weighed against the official position (Document 48). The extreme reserve with which the McGovern formula was viewed in administration quarters is well reflected in a comment by Secretary of State Rogers (Document 49).]

[62] Senate Foreign Relations Committee History, pp. 57-66.
[63] *New York Times*, Oct. 3 and 11, 1972.
[64] Public Laws 93-50 and 93-52, July 1, 1973.

(48) Views of the Democratic Candidate: Television Address by Senator McGovern, October 10, 1972.[65]

(Complete Text)

Tonight, I ask you to think carefully about an issue that has troubled me more than any other for the last nine years—the war in Vietnam.

On Sept. 23, 1963, I warned that our deepening involvement in the affairs of the Vietnamese people was "a policy of moral debacle and political defeat."

Under three separate Presidents—two of them Democrats and one of them a Republican—I have opposed this war. During these same long years, Mr. Nixon has supported the war. This, I think, is the sharpest and most important difference between Mr. Nixon and me in the 1972 Presidential campaign.[66]

Mr. Nixon has described the Vietnam war as our finest hour. I regard it as the saddest chapter in our national history. Our problem with this terrible war does not stem from the lack of bravery or skill on the part of our fighting men. Indeed, no better American army has ever been sent abroad.

Our problem is that we have asked our armed forces to do the impossible—to save a political regime in Saigon that doesn't even have the respect of its own people. I've been to Vietnam more than once talking to our G.I.'s. They've told me in countless conversations of the frustrating and impossible nature of this assignment.

Before the 1968 election, the Republican candidate, Mr. Nixon, told you that he had a secret plan to end the war. He refused to discuss the details, but he asked your support in the election, and he offered peace in return.[67]

That promise has been broken, and the destruction in Southeast Asia has increased.

The war goes on for our sons who are still ordered into battle. It's true that men have been withdrawn from Vietnam, but half a million American fighting men ranged in the Pacific, Thailand and Guam are still carrying this war to Vietnam.

Tonight, as I speak to you, some of these men may die. Forty per cent of all the Americans lost in Vietnam have died in the last four years; died under the present Administration.

Since January of 1969, 20,000 young Americans have come home—

---

65 *New York Times,* Oct. 11, 1972.

66 For other campaign statements, see Documents 6-8.

67 For reports of Mr. Nixon's statements in Mar. 1968, cf. especially *New York Times,* Mar. 6 and 11, 1968. The assertion that he claimed to have a "secret plan" to end the war was critically examined by William Safire and Theodore C. Sorensen in same, Sept. 12, 1972.

not in glory, to the cheers of a grateful country—but in death, to the bitter tears of their families. The secret plan, the secret plan for peace will forever remain a secret to them.

The war goes on also for our prisoners in North Vietnam. Tonight, on the other side of the world, they sit and think of us—of their homes, their families, of children who are growing up without fathers, of a country they may never see again.

And in the last four years, 550 more Americans have been taken captive or listed as missing in action. More than 100 of them in the last six months. And if anyone says that the promise to end the war has been kept, let him tell that to the families of the brave men who waste away in the cells of Hanoi.

Now Mr. Nixon says we must bomb and fight to free our prisoners. But just the reverse is true. We must end the bombing—end the fighting—if we're ever to see these prisoners again. Prisoners of war come home when the war ends—not while the war continues.

The war also goes on for the millions of Americans like you who bear its cost. Every single week this war claims $250-million of your taxes. Every week it inflates the cost of everything you buy.

Each week it costs $250-million that we need to employ men to rebuild our cities, to fight crime and drugs, to strengthen our schools, and to assist our sick and elderly.

Since he came to the Presidency, Mr. Nixon has spent $60-billion of your money on this war, $60-billion of your taxes to kill human beings in Asia instead of protecting and improving human life in America; $60-billion in the last four years—not for a cause, but for a mistake—not to serve our ideals, but to save the face of our policy-makers.

And the war goes on also for the people of Indochina. Indeed, they are literally being crushed under the weight of the heaviest aerial bombardment the world has ever known.

The bombing of Indochina has doubled under the present administration, and while General Thieu is secure in his palace, six million of his fellow Vietnamese are victims—people dead, maimed or driven from their homes.

Most of these people are not enemies, but innocents. Our bombs bring them not freedom, but terror. Bombing does not save their land. It destroys it.

The reality of this war is seen in the newsphoto of the little South Vietnamese girl, Kim, fleeing in terror from her bombed-out school.[68] She has torn off her flaming clothes and she is running naked into the lens of that camera.

That picture ought to break the heart of every American. How can we rest with the grim knowledge that the burning napalm that splashed

68 Untitled photo by Nick Ut (Associated Press, 1972).

over little Kim and countless thousands of other children was dropped in the name of America?

Now, there are those who say that you will accept this because the toll of suffering now includes more Asians and fewer Americans. But, surely, conscience says to each of us that a wrong war is not made right because the color of the bodies has changed. We are all created in the image of God.

As a bomber pilot in World War II, like millions of you, I did what had to be done. Our nation took up arms and laid down lives because tyranny threatened all that we held precious.

I loved America enough to offer my life in war 30 years ago. And for nine years I have loved this country enough to risk my political life to call us home from a war in Asia that does not serve the interests and the ideals of the American nation.

What, after all, is our purpose in Southeast Asia?

Now, we used to say that we fought in Vietnam to stop Communist China or to stop Communist Russia. But these nations are now quarreling among themselves, and Mr. Nixon's public opinion ratings have gone up after he was wined and dined in the Communist capitals of Peking and Moscow.

How can we really argue that it is good to accommodate ourselves to a billion Russian and Chinese Communists—but that we must somehow fight to the bitter end against a tiny band of peasant guerrillas in the jungles of little Vietnam?

Incredible as it seems, when all is said and done, our purpose in Vietnam now comes down to this—our policy-makers want to save face and they want to save the Saigon regime of General Thieu.

Now, that is a fundamental difference between President Nixon and me on the issue of Vietnam. It is a choice, after all, between saving face or saving lives. It is a choice between four more years of war, or four years of peace.

The Nixon position is that the Thieu regime represents self-determination for the people of South Vietnam. Let me tell you what I think his regime represents.

I think our support for General Thieu actually denies the people of South Vietnam the right to choose their own government. The Saigon lawyer, a former president of Rotary International, who had the courage to run against General Thieu four years ago [Truong Dinh Dzu], was sent to jail for five years.

Last year, General Thieu issued a decree to force all the other candidates out of the race.[69] This year, he abolished all the local elections so he could extend his dictatorship to every village in South Vietnam.

69 Cf. A.F.R., 1971, p. 311.

General Thieu has closed newspapers simply for printing the truth. He has presided over the execution of 40,000 people without trial on the mere suspicion that they did not support his policies.

The Thieu regime stands for the theft of billions of dollars of our aid, stolen by powerful officials to enrich themselves while their country-men are in the grip of starvation and disease. And every G.I. who has served in Vietnam knows that that's the truth.

Corrupt Vietnamese officials have enriched themselves putting heroin into the veins of a hundred thousand of our G.I.'s. That same poisonous heroin from Southeast Asia is now being shipped into our cities, our suburbs, our streets and even into the schools of America. And every Vietnam G.I. knows that it is true.

This corrupt dictatorship that our precious young men and our tax dollars are supporting cannot be talked clean by American blood. Instead, our own most precious values are corrupted by the very Gov-ernment we fight to defend.

Now, Mr. Nixon would continue the war to preserve General Thieu's power. On that, he and I disagree. I say—General Thieu is not worth one more American dollar, one more American prisoner, one more drop of American blood. Mr. Nixon and I also disagree on how to find peace—and this is the second fundamental difference between us.

He has chosen what he calls "decisive military action" to end the fighting. Despite all the highly publicized "secret" meetings with the other side, he has persisted in the belief that we can find peace only in a wider war. But the escalations of 1965 and 1967 were also "decisive military actions" and they did not end the war. They only increased the killing and increased the costs.

Mr. Nixon's invasion of Cambodia,[70] made without the approval of Congress as required by our Constitution, that was a "decisive military action," but it did not end the war. It only brought the war to more people who had been living in peace and it brought Communist rule to two-thirds of that previously neutral country.

The mining of North Vietnamese harbor[s][71] was a decisive military action, but it did not end the war. The supplies still flow into the south, and our adversary is reported by our own observers to be as strong as ever.

For nearly 30 years, the people of Vietnam have been at war. For nearly 30 years, the Japanese, the French, the Americans have tried "decisive military action" to win a satisfactory peace. And for 30 years, each, in turn has failed.

Now, the answer to failure is not more of the same. And yet I fear continued war is what the Nixon Administration has in store if they

---

70 Cf. *Documents, 1970*, pp. 156-79.
71 Cf. Document 47.

stay in power.

Secretary of Defense [Melvin R.] Laird recently admitted to a Congressional committee that the fighting could continue far into the future under present policy.

Four years ago last night, on Oct. 9, 1968, Mr. Nixon, as a candidate for President, said to a crowd in California, and I quote:

"Those who have had a chance for four years and could not produce peace should not be given another chance."[72] Now, Mr. Nixon has had his chance. He could not produce peace in four years. And we have every indication that he cannot produce peace in eight years.

So, I ask the American people—shall we break free at last from General Thieu? Shall we forget about saving face and begin saving the soul of our nation? Shall we demonstrate that we are determined to stop the killing and to stand for peace? My answer is—yes.

Let me now set forth the specific steps that I would take as President to carry out that determination.

Immediately after taking my oath as President, if the war has not ended by then, I would issue a national security directive to the Secretary of Defense, to the Joint Chiefs of Staff, and to our commands in the field, with the following orders:

¶Immediately stop all bombing and acts of force in all parts of Indochina.

¶Immediately terminate any shipments of military supplies that continue the war.

¶Immediately begin the orderly withdrawal of all American forces from Vietnam, from Laos and Cambodia, along with all salvageable American military equipment. And we will assign whatever transportation is required to complete that process and to complete it within 90 days—a time period that I've been told by competent military authority is well within our capability.

Secondly, I would issue the following instructions to our negotiators in Paris:

¶Notify the representatives of the other side that we have taken these steps to end the hostilities, and that we now expect that they will accept their obligation under their own seven-point proposal of 1971[73]—to return all prisoners of war and to account for all missing in action. We will expect that process to be completed within 90 days to coincide with our complete withdrawal from the war.

¶We would further notify all parties that the United States will no longer interfere in the internal politics of Vietnam, and that we will allow the Vietnamese people to work out their own settlement. The United States is prepared to cooperate to see that any settlement,

---

[72] *New York Times*, Oct. 10, 1968.
[73] *A.F.R., 1971*, no. 74a.

including a coalition government, gains international recognition.

Thirdly, I would send the Vice President to Hanoi to speed the arrangements for the return of our prisoners and an accounting of the missing.

I would also instruct our diplomats to contact the opposing parties in Laos and Cambodia in order to secure release of prisoners held in those countries, and an accounting of missing in action, including American civilian newsmen now missing in Cambodia. There are six known prisoners in Laos, and nearly 300 missing. No effort has been made to secure their release.

Fourth, after all of our prisoners have been returned, and we have received a satisfactory accounting for any missing men, I would order the Secretary of Defense and the Joint Chiefs to close our bases in Thailand, to bring home any troops and equipment still there, and to reassign elsewhere any ships still stationed in the water adjoining Indochina.

Fifth, as the political solution in Vietnam is worked out by the Vietnamese themselves, we should join with other countries in repairing the wreckage left by this war.

Sixth, I would ask the Congress to take immediate action on an expanded program for our veterans. I think it's simply a disgrace that our Government is able to find these young men to send them off to war, but somehow, we look the other way when they come back in need of an education or decent medical treatment, or a decent job.

Now, like many other veterans of World War II, I received a four-year eduction under a generous G.I. Bill of Rights. I think Vietnam veterans need that help more than those of us who fought a generation ago because we came back with the welcome of a nation that knew we had fought and won a necessary war.

The Vietnam veterans come back to a country that largely believes this war was a mistake. So, we ought to literally put the arms of this nation around these young men and guarantee them either a good job or a fully funded higher education. Months ago, I sponsored in the Senate a Vietnam veterans bill of rights that would do precisely that.

Finally, when the war has ended, when our troops and prisoners are home, and when we have provided for the veterans of Vietnam, we must then consider the young men who chose jail or exile because they could not in conscience fight in this war.

So, following the example of earlier Presidents, I would give these young men the opportunity to come home. Personally, if I were in their position, I would volunteer for two years of public service on subsistence pay simply to demonstrate that my objection was not to serving the nation, but to participating in a war I thought was morally wrong.

We are not a vindictive or mean-spirited people. And we must act as Lincoln told us—"With malice toward none and charity for all." We must bind up the wounds of this nation, and we must bring all of our sons back.

In that same spirit, we must oppose any so-called war crimes trials to fix the blame for the past on any citizen or any group of citizens. Vietnam has been a terrible experience for all of us, on every side of this issue. And this is not the time for recrimination. It is the time for reconciliation.

So, this is what I would do to bring America home from a hated war, and it is a program that will work. The people of France were once trapped in Vietnam, even as we are. But in 1954, they chose a new President [Premier], Pierre Mendès-France, whose highest commitment was to achieve peace in Indochina. His program was very similar to mine. And within just five weeks, the war was over.

Within three months, every last French prisoner had been returned.

Now, I ask you to remember that I speak to you as one who has publicly opposed this war for nine years. I ask you to remember that my opponent has supported American military intervention in Vietnam ever since 1954. I ask you to recognize that every detail of my position is fully out in the open. It is a public plan—not a secret plan.

Often during this last tortured decade, I've reflected on a question from the Scriptures: "Which of us, if his son asked him for bread, would give him a stone?"

Our sons have asked for jobs—and we've sent them to an Asian jungle. Our sons have asked for an education—and we've taught them how to kill. Our sons have asked for a full measure of time—and 50,000 of them have been lost before their time.

So, let us seize the chance to lift from our sons and our selves the terror of this war, and bestow the blessings of peace. And then we can restore our sense of purpose and our character as a great nation.

This is not just a question of material wealth—although the billions which would otherwise be lost in Southeast Asia could then be used to secure a better life for our own people. But more important for America, there will be a special healing in the wings of peace. It will be a healing of our doubts and a rekindling of our faith in this great and good land, and in our own capacity to make it so.

On the night when the last American soldier from Vietnam has landed in San Francisco, there will be a new birth of confidence and hope for all of us. On that night, we will know that, once free of the waste of this war, we can begin the rebuilding of our own land—a task that can provide a fulfilling job for every man and woman in America, who is able to work.

On that night, America can begin to be America again. It can be the

America that we learned to love in the days of our youth—a country that once again stands as a witness to the world for what is noble and just in human affairs.

This is the choice of a century. But it is also the same choice that human beings have faced from the very beginning. So, let us heed the ancient words: "I have set before you life and death, blessing and cursing. Therefore, choose life, that thou and thy seed may live."

Thank you. God bless you.

(49) An Administration Rejoinder: Comments by Secretary of State Rogers, October 15, 1972.[74]

(Excerpts)

* * *

Mr. Koppel:[75] *Mr. Secretary, you have been very forceful about your reluctance to discuss private negotiations. Perhaps for a moment we can examine the public record. This administration has indicated on numerous occasions that it will not withdraw its support or hand over the Saigon government to the North Vietnamese. It has also indicated its opposition to a coalition government. Do we still at this time refuse to consider the Presidency of Nguyen Van Thieu as negotiable, and would we not accept any kind of coalition government with the NLF [National Liberation Front]?*

Secretary Rogers: Mr. Koppel, I must say you are persistent. I am not going to comment on the latter part of your question, for reasons I have already stated.

On the first part of the question, we are going to make certain that there is not a Communist takeover of South Viet-Nam by force. That is what it is all about. And that is what the President has said constantly. As you know, there have been recent suggestions that we should just quit, get out of Viet-Nam completely, walk away from it. In fact, the suggestions have been that we should take all of our military equipment with us, which in effect would deny the people in South Viet-Nam the right to defend their own country.

Now, that type of policy is totally unacceptable, and it is really difficult for me to understand how it could be seriously proposed. That

---

[74] Interview on ABC "Issues and Answers" television and radio program, Oct. 15, 1972; text (from Department of State Press Release 265, Oct. 19, 1972) in *Bulletin*, Nov. 6, 1972, pp. 519-22.

[75] Ted Koppel, ABC News diplomatic correspondent.

is not only throwing in the towel ourselves, throwing in the towel by the United States, but insisting that the South Vietnamese throw in the towel—that we throw in the towel for them, that we say to them "You can't defend your country; we are not going to even let you have the military equipment that we have given to you to defend your country."

So the answer to your question is: Yes, President Nixon is going to make certain that we do not have a Communist takeover of the South Vietnamese by force.

* * *

Mr. Koppel: Mr. Secretary, I am afraid my British heritage makes it a little tough for me to give up on a subject altogether. Avoiding political polemics as much as possible, and this is slightly related to the Viet-Nam question, did you find anything of value in Senator McGovern's speech the other day on the Viet-Nam—his Viet-Nam peace plan?

Secretary Rogers: No, I didn't. I was really—parts of it were incredible. I couldn't believe it.

For example, he talked about a tiny band that—that we were fighting a tiny band of peasant guerrillas. Now, it is unbelievable that that could be said. I am sure no one who has fought in Viet-Nam thinks we are fighting a tiny band of peasant guerrillas. They have hundreds of related tanks; they have field artillery pieces with a range of 17 or 18 miles; they have the most sophisticated SAM missile [surface-to-air missile] sites probably in the world, and how he could say that it was a tiny band of peasant guerrillas beats me.

I couldn't understand why he said we should take all the military supplies we could salvage out of South Viet-Nam. We have been fighting alongside the South Vietnamese since 1965. We have told them that we would give them an opportunity to defend their country. They have had a lot more casualties than we have had. Now for us to say that we are not only going to get out ourselves but we are going to take all the equipment that we can take out with us "so that you have no chance to defend yourself," and acknowledge the fact that there would be a Communist takeover at this stage, I don't understand it.

I hear people say it is surrender. It is not only an offer to surrender; it is a demand that the South Vietnamese surrender, too.

So, when you ask me did I find anything about it that was good, no. It is incredible. I can't believe that a man who is as sophisticated in foreign affairs could possibly say that.

All the nations in the area can't believe it, that he would say these things.

Mr. Koppel: For example, the Thai Government—Senator McGovern suggested once the prisoners come back he would remove American bases from Thailand. Have you gotten any communications from the Thai Government expressing concern over this?

Secretary Rogers: Oh, sure. He has also said he wasn't sure about that. Sometimes he referred to maybe he would insist on withdrawal and at other times he wasn't sure, so I am not sure about the prediction on that. But the Thai Government said he wouldn't have to worry about that; they would insist on our leaving.

*   *   *

D. The Breakthrough Toward Peace.

[While the United States' domestic debate regained momentum, the diplomatic impasse that had blocked agreement to end the war had imperceptibly softened. An intimation that Communist attitudes were changing had come on September 11, 1972 with the broadcast of an "important statement" by the P.R.G. that reiterated the demand for a "provisional government of national concord with three equal segments," but also acknowledged that any solution to the internal problems of South Vietnam must start from the reality of the "two administrations, two armies and other political forces" that actually existed there.[76] Le Duc Tho, in a meeting with Dr. Kissinger on September 26, appeared to shelve the notion of a coalition government entirely in proposing the establishment of a "National Council of Reconciliation and Concord" which, though also formed on a tripartite basis, would presumably have no governmental responsibilities.[77] The really decisive breakthrough appears to have occurred on October 8, 1972 when Le Duc Tho presented a full-scale draft agreement, ostensibly attuned to the American preference for settling the military issues before attacking political questions.

In reality, the North Vietnamese plan of October 8[78] envisaged a first-stage settlement of basic political principles as well as military issues, although the details of South Vietnam's internal situation would ostensibly be left to a second stage in which they would be dealt with by "the two South Vietnamese parties," the Saigon government and the Communist-dominated P.R.G. In essence, the bargain proposed by Hanoi had three main elements: (1) tacit

[76] *New York Times,* Sept. 12, 1972.
[77] Kalb, *Kissinger,* p. 349.
[78] Cf. below at note 89.

acceptance by North Vietnam and the P.R.G. of the continued existence of the Saigon government; (2) tacit acceptance by the United States of the continued presence ´of North Vietnamese troops in the South; and (3) acceptance by all concerned of the "National Council of National Reconciliation and Concord" as a tripartite "administrative structure" to be formed by Saigon, the P.R.G., and neutral elements and to be responsible for organizing internationally supervised free elections as the basis of South Vietnam's future government. Especially notable in the North Vietnamese draft was the absence of any demand for the immediate resignation of President Thieu or the formation of a coalition government in advance of elections.

These changes in Hanoi's position cleared the ground for rapid agreement on the outlines of a peace settlement that would be applicable to the whole of Indochina and would provide, among other things, for a prompt cessation of U.S. bombing and mining in North Vietnam; an immediate cease-fire throughout South Vietnam; withdrawal within 60 days of U.S. and allied military personnel in South Vietnam; and concurrent return of all captured and detained personnel. Political and military questions within South Vietnam would be settled within three months under the aegis of the "National Council of National Reconciliation and Concord." Control functions would be exercised by various military and international supervisory commissions, and an "international guarantee conference" would be convened within 30 days. In addition, the terms as published called for noninterference and withdrawal of foreign forces from Cambodia and Laos, and offered U.S. reconstruction aid in North Vietnam "and throughout Indochina."

Agreement in principle on a text embodying these provisions was apparently reached by October 17, 1972, and the United States undertook to do its best to meet the North Vietnamese desire to have the agreement signed before the end of October and well in advance of the November 7 election. From Paris, Dr. Kissinger planned to proceed to Saigon to obtain the agreement of President Thieu's government, and to go on from there to Hanoi to initial the agreement on October 24. But serious difficulties arose as soon as the proposed arrangement was explained to the South Vietnamese President, who found it deeply objectionable from several points of view. South Vietnamese objections, then and later, centered particularly on three features of the proposed agreement: the National Council of National Reconciliation and Concord, which was viewed in Saigon as a thinly disguised coalition; the lack of provision for withdrawal of North Vietnamese troops in the South, who were estimated by the United States at 145,000 and by South Vietnam at 300,000 to 400,000; and the absence of provision for restoring the Demilitarized Zone between North and South Vietnam, as a military barrier and a symbol of South Vietnam's independent existence.

Over and above the South Vietnamese objections, American authorities were disconcerted by indications that the Communists might even now be engaged in preparation for new military offensives and, in addition, might still be thinking in terms of a coalition government in South Vietnam. Although the United States as a gesture of good faith suspended the bombing of North Vietnam above the 20th parallel as from October 23, it also advised Hanoi that there was need for further negotiation on a number of points and that it would be unable to meet the October 31 target date for signature of the agreement. Hanoi's response took the form of a vehement public statement, released October 26 (local time), in which it presented its version of the negotiations and insisted that the United States live up to its "commitments" (Document 50).

Confirming the general accuracy of Hanoi's account, Dr. Kissinger in a news conference later on October 26 voiced the administration's continued belief "that peace is at hand" and that the remaining issues could be settled in one more negotiating session lasting not more than three or four days (Document 51). President Nixon, in a preelection broadcast on November 2, emphasized that the United States would not be "stampeded" into signing an agreement prematurely in order to meet "an election deadline or any other kind of deadline."[79]

Prospects for an early settlement failed to improve in the wake of President Nixon's election victory, which left the United States still facing the problem of President Thieu's resistance as well as various unresolved "ambiguities" in the arrangement with Hanoi. To strengthen the military position of the Saigon government in the event that an agreement was reached, the United States had initiated and continued through most of November a massive air- and sealift of aircraft, tanks, and other military items for the South Vietnamese forces. At the same time, a vigorous attempt was made to overcome the hesitation of the South Vietnamese President by assuring him of the United States' continued support and warning him of its determination to proceed with or without his agreement. President Nixon, in a letter addressed to President Thieu on November 14, 1972 and made public at the time of the Saigon regime's definitive collapse on April 30, 1975, promised to lay Saigon's concerns before the North Vietnamese, but intimated that the resolute attitude of the United States itself would constitute a more effective guarantee of South Vietnamese interests. ". . . Far more im-

[79] *Public Papers, 1972*, p. 1086.

portant than what we say in the agreement on this issue," Mr.
Nixon wrote, referring specifically to the matter of North Vietnamese troop withdrawals, "is what we do in the event the enemy
renews its aggression. You have my absolute assurance that if Hanoi
fails to abide by the terms of this agreement it is my intention to
take swift and severe retaliatory action. . . . I repeat my personal
assurances to you that the United States will react very strongly and
rapidly to any violation of the agreement. . . ."[80]

But neither South Vietnam's demands nor those of the United
States itself appeared acceptable to the North Vietnamese negotiators when Dr. Kissinger and Le Duc Tho met on November 20-25
for their first round of talks since the election. At a second round
on December 6-13, matters went from bad to worse as Le Duc Tho
and his associates began to reopen questions that had long since
been settled. Describing the changing North Vietnamese attitude at
another news conference held December 16 (Document 52), Dr.
Kissinger noted that Hanoi's negotiators had been particularly
resistant to any reference "which would make clear that the two
parts of Vietnam would live in peace with each other and that
neither side would impose its solution on the other by force." The
United States, according to the presidential assistant, was unwilling
on its side to "make a settlement which is a disguised form of
continued warfare" or "a disguised form of victory for the other
side."

Failure of this second round of Paris talks was the signal for
stronger American action, aimed at bringing matters to a head both
with Hanoi and with Saigon. According to the most detailed
account available, the North Vietnamese were advised on December
14 that the United States could wait no more than 72 hours for a
resumption of "serious negotiations"; and renewed bombing of
North Vietnamese objectives began with the expiration of this deadline on December 17.[81] The decision to resume full-scale bombing
of military targets throughout North Vietnam "until such time as a
settlement is arrived at" was publicly announced on December 18.
In the following days, Hanoi and Haiphong were subjected to the
heaviest air attacks of the entire war, interrupted only by a 36-hour
pause at Christmas. Hanoi alone, it was claimed, suffered 1,318
killed and 1,261 wounded, while the United States acknowledged
the loss of 93 airmen as well as fifteen B-52 bombers and eleven
other aircraft.

The counterpart of these actions was a decision by the President

[80] *New York Times*, May 1, 1975. These assurances were not communicated to
the Congress and are considered to have been superseded by the antiwar
legislation referred to at note 64 above.
[81] Kalb, *Kissinger*, pp. 412-15.

to talk "sternly" with "our friends in South Vietnam" and let them understand that the United States was definitely determined to conclude the agreement, if the North Vietnamese "should once again prove reasonable in Paris."[82] In a letter dated December 17 and conveyed to President Thieu by Major General Alexander M. Haig, Jr., his Deputy Assistant for National Security Affairs, the President wrote: "I am convinced that your refusal to join us would be an invitation to disaster—to the loss of all that we together have fought for over the past decade. It would be inexcusable above all because we will have lost a just and honorable alternative."[83]

Although additional correspondence would be required before President Thieu could be induced to sign the peace agreement worked out by American and North Vietnamese negotiators, no further difficulties of importance were encountered from the North Vietnamese side. Private communication with the latter had been maintained despite the bombing, and on December 30 the White House was able to announce that Dr. Kissinger and Le Duc Tho would resume negotiations in Paris on January 8, 1973. In the meantime, the White House spokesman added, the President had ordered the discontinuance of all bombing north of the 20th parallel "as long as serious negotiations are under way."

With the resumption of the negotiations in Paris, the remaining difficulties were rapidly overcome and an "Agreement on Ending the War and Restoring Peace in Vietnam" was initialed by Dr. Kissinger and Le Duc Tho on January 23 and signed in Paris on behalf of the four parties—including South Vietnam—on January 27, 1973.[84] By its terms, a cease-fire nominally entered into effect throughout South Vietnam as of 2400 hours G.M.T. (7:00 P.M. Washington time) on that date. The restoration of peaceful conditions, however, was never fully accomplished, and neither the political nor the military clauses of the agreement were effectively implemented. The opening of still another major Communist offensive early in 1975 was rapidly followed by the collapse of the South Vietnamese military position, the resignation of President Thieu on April 21, and the unconditional surrender of the Saigon government to the Provisional Revolutionary Government of South Vietnam on April 30, 1975.

A parallel evolution took place in Cambodia and Laos. In Cambodia, the civil war continued until April 6, 1975, when the U.S.-supported Khmer Republic government surrendered to insurgent leftist forces nominally loyal to the exiled Royal Cambodian

[82] Nixon Report, 1973, p. 56.

[83] Quoted in Nixon letter to Thieu, Jan. 5, 1973, in *New York Times*, May 1, 1975.

[84] TIAS 7542 (24 UST 1); text and related material in *Bulletin* , Feb. 12, 1973, pp. 153-90.

Government of Prince Norodom Sihanouk. In Laos, where a cease-fire agreement was concluded February 21, 1973 and a coalition government set up April 5, 1974, a new political offensive launched by the leftist Pathet Lao in May 1975 led to the abolition of the monarchy and the establishment of a left-wing People's Democratic Republic on December 3, 1975.]

(50) Negotiations Relating to the Vietnam Problem: Statement by the Government of the Democratic Republic of Vietnam, October 26, 1972.[85]

(Complete Text)

Following years of a glorious resistance war of our armed forces and people in both zones, the United States had to stop in October 1968 the bombardments against the Democratic Republic of Viet Nam and accept the holding of a four-party conference on Viet Nam in Paris.[86] That situation opened up prospects for restoring peace in Viet Nam.

The Nixon administration chose, however, to embark on the path of "Vietnamization of the war" and negotiation from a position of strength. As a result, the U.S. war of aggression in Viet Nam dragged on, was intensified and expanded, and the Viet Nam peace negotiation could not make any progress.

Over the past four years, the valiant and undaunted Vietnamese people have stepped up their just struggle on the military, political and diplomatic fronts, and have recorded unprecedented victories, especially since spring 1972, thus inflicted a very important setback on the "Vietnamization" policy.

At the same time, the Government of the Democratic Republic of Viet Nam has constantly shown its serious attitude and goodwill in the search for a peaceful solution to the Viet Nam problem on a basis guaranteeing the Vietnamese people's fundamental national rights and the south Vietnamese people's right to self-determination.

In full agreement with the Provisional Revolutionary Government of the Republic of South Viet Nam, the Government of the Democratic Republic of Viet Nam has held private meetings with the U.S. Government with a view to a peaceful settlement of the Viet Nam problem.[87] But till September 1972, the negotiations on the Viet Nam problem had remained without result.

With a view to making the negotiations progress, at the private meeting on October 8, 1972, the D.R.V.N. side took a new, extremely

[85] Text from *Peking Review*, Nov. 3, 1972, pp. 6-10.
[86] Cf. *Documents, 1968-69*, pp. 243-8.
[87] Cf. Documents 43-45.

important initiative: It put forward a draft "agreement on ending the war and restoring peace in Viet Nam," and proposed that the Government of the Democratic Republic of Viet Nam, with the concurrence of the Provisional Revolutionary Government of the Republic of South Viet Nam, and the Government of the United States of America, with the concurrence of the Government of the Republic of Viet Nam, immediately agreed upon and signed this agreement to rapidly restore peace in Viet Nam. In that draft agreement, the D.R.V.N. side proposed a cessation of the war throughout Viet Nam, a ceasefire in south Viet Nam, an end to all U.S. military involvement in south Viet Nam, a total withdrawal from south Viet Nam of troops of the United States and those of the foreign countries allied with the United States and with the Republic of Viet Nam, and the return of all captured and detained personnel of the parties. From the enforcement of the ceasefire to the installation of the government formed after free and democratic general elections, the two present administrations in south Viet Nam will remain in existence with their respective domestic and external functions. These two administrations shall immediately hold consultations with a view to the exercise of the south Vietnamese people's right to self-determination, achieving national concord, ensuring the democratic liberties of the south Vietnamese people, and forming an administration of national concord which shall have the task of promoting the south Vietnamese parties' implementation of the signed agreements and organizing general elections in south Viet Nam. The two south Vietnamese parties shall settle together the internal matters of south Viet Nam within three months after the ceasefire comes into effect. Thus the Viet Nam problem will be settled in two stages in accordance with the oft-expressed desire of the American side: the first stage will include a cessation of the war in Viet Nam, a ceasefire in south Viet Nam, a cessation of the U.S. military involvement in south Viet Nam and an agreement on the principles for the exercise of the south Vietnamese people's right to self-determination; in the second stage, the two south Vietnamese parties will settle together the internal matters of south Viet Nam. The D.R.V.N. side proposed that the Democratic Republic of Viet Nam and the United States sign this agreement by mid-October, 1972.

The above initiative of the Government of the Democratic Republic of Viet Nam brought the negotiations on the Viet Nam problem, which had dragged on for four years now, on to the path to a settlement. The American side itself admitted that the draft "agreement on ending the war and restoring peace in Viet Nam" put forward by the D.R.V.N. side was indeed an important and very fundamental document which opened up the way to an early settlement.

After several days of negotiations, on October 17, 1972, the Democratic Republic of Viet Nam and the United States reached agreement on almost all problems on the basis of the draft agreement of the Democratic Republic of Viet Nam, except for only two unagreed issues. With its goodwill, the D.R.V.N. side did its utmost to remove the last obstacles in accepting the American side's proposals on the two remaining questions in the agreement. In his October 20, 1972 message to the Premier of the Democratic Republic of Viet Nam [Pham Van Dong], the President of the United States appreciated the goodwill of the Democratic Republic of Viet Nam, and confirmed that the formulation of the agreement could be considered complete. But in the same message, he raised a number of complex points. Desirous of rapidly ending the war and restoring peace in Viet Nam, the Government of the Democratic Republic of Viet Nam clearly explained its views on this subject. In his October 22, 1972 message, the President of the United States expressed satisfaction with the explanations given by the Government of the Democratic Republic of Viet Nam.[88] Thus by October 22, 1972, the formulation of the agreement was complete.

The main issues of the agreement which have been agreed upon may be summarized as follows:

1) The United States respects the independence, sovereignty, unity and territorial integrity of Viet Nam as recognized by the 1954 Geneva Agreements.[89]

2) Twenty-four hours after the signing of the agreement, a ceasefire shall be observed throughout south Viet Nam. The United States will stop all its military activities, and end the bombing and mining in north Viet Nam. Within 60 days, there will be a total withdrawal from south Viet Nam of troops and military personnel of the United States and those of the foreign countries allied with the United States and with the Republic of Viet Nam. The two south Vietnamese parties shall not accept the introduction of troops, military advisers and military personnel, armaments, munitions, and war material into south Viet Nam. The two south Vietnamese parties shall be permitted to make periodical replacements of armaments, munitions, and war material that have been worn out or damaged after the ceasefire, on the basis of piece for piece of similar characteristics and properties. The United States will not continue its military involvement or intervene in the internal affairs of south Viet Nam.

3) The return of all captured and detained personnel of the parties shall be carried out simultaneously with the U.S. troops withdrawal.

4) The principles for the exercise of the south Vietnamese people's right to self-determination are as follows: The south Vietnamese people shall decide themselves the political future of south Viet Nam through

---

88 The exchange of messages between President Nixon and Prime Minister Dong has not been made public.
89 *Documents, 1954*, pp. 283-302 and 311-14.

genuinely free and democratic general elections under international supervision; the United States is not committed to any political tendency or to any personality in south Viet Nam, and it does not seek to impose a pro-American regime in Saigon; national reconciliation and concord will be achieved, the democratic liberties of the people, ensured; an administrative structure called the national council of national reconciliation and concord of three equal segments will be set up to promote the implementation of the signed agreements by the Provisional Revolutionary Government of the Republic of South Viet Nam and the Government of the Republic of Viet Nam and to organize the general elections, the two south Vietnamese parties will consult about the formation of councils at lower levels; the question of Vietnamese armed forces in south Viet Nam shall be settled by the two south Vietnamese parties in a spirit of national reconciliation and concord, equality and mutual respect, without foreign interference, in accordance with the postwar situation; among the question [s] to be discussed by the two south Vietnamese parties are steps to reduce the military numbers on both sides and to demobilize the troops being reduced; the two south Vietnamese parties shall sign an agreement on the internal matters of south Viet Nam as soon as possible and will do their utmost to accomplish this within three months after the ceasefire comes into effect.

5) The reunification of Viet Nam shall be carried out step by step through peaceful means.

6) There will be formed a four-party joint military commission, and a joint military commission of the two south Vietnamese parties.

An international commission of control and supervision shall be established.

An international guarantee conference on Viet Nam will be convened within 30 days of the signing of this agreement.

7) The Government of the Democratic Republic of Viet Nam, the Provisional Revolutionary of the Republic of South Viet Nam, the Government of the United States of America, and the Government of the Republic of Viet Nam shall strictly respect the Cambodian and Lao peoples' fundamental national rights as recognized by the 1954 Geneva Agreements on Indochina and the 1962 Geneva Agreements on Laos,[90] i.e., the independence, sovereignty, unity and territorial integrity of these countries. They shall respect the neutrality of Cambodia and Laos. The Government of the Democratic Republic of Viet Nam, the Provisional Revolutionary Government of the Republic of South Viet Nam, the Government of the United States of America and the Government of the Republic of Viet Nam undertake to refrain from using the territory of Cambodia and the territory of Laos to encroach on the sovereignty and security of other countries. Foreign countries shall put

90 Cf. note 26 above.

an end to all military activities in Laos and Cambodia, totally withdraw from and refrain from reintroducing into these two countries troops, military advisers and military personnel, armaments, munitions and war material.

The internal affairs of Cambodia and Laos shall be settled by the people of each of these countries without foreign interference.

The problems existing between the three Indochinese countries shall be settled by the Indochinese parties on the basis of respect for each other's independence, sovereignty, and territorial integrity, and non-interference in each other's internal affairs.

8) The ending of the war, the restoration of peace in Viet Nam will create conditions for establishing a new, equal, and mutually beneficial relationship between the Democratic Republic of Viet Nam and the United States. The United States will contribute to healing the wounds of war and to postwar reconstruction in the Democratic Republic of Viet Nam and throughout Indochina.

9) This agreement shall come into force as of its signing. It will be strictly implemented by all the parties concerned.

The two parties have also agreed on a schedule for the signing of the agreement. On October 9, 1972, at the proposal of the U.S. side, it was agreed that on October 18, 1972, the United States would stop the bombing and mining in north Viet Nam, on October 19, 1972, the two parties would initial the text of the agreement in Hanoi; on October 26, 1972, the Foreign Ministers of the two countries would formally sign the agreement in Paris.

On October 11, 1972, the U.S. side proposed the following change to the schedule: on October 21, 1972, the United States would stop the bombing and mining in north Viet Nam, on October 22, 1972, the two parties would initial the text of the agreement in Hanoi; on October 30, 1972, the Foreign Ministers of the two countries would formally sign the agreement in Paris. The Democratic Republic of Viet Nam agreed to the new U.S. schedule.

On October 20, 1972, under the pretext that there still remained a number of unagreed points, the U.S. side again put forth another schedule: on October 23, 1972, the United States would stop the bombing and mining in north Viet Nam, on October 24, 1972, the two parties would initial the text of the agreement in Hanoi; on October 31, 1972, the Foreign Ministers of the two countries would formally sign the agreement in Paris. Despite the fact that the U.S. side had changed many times what had been agreed upon, the D.R.V.N. side with its goodwill again agreed to the U.S. proposal while stressing that the U.S. side should not under any pretext change the agreed schedule.

Thus, by October 22, 1972, the D.R.V.N. side and the U.S. side had agreed both on the full text of the "agreement on ending the war and restoring peace in Viet Nam" and on a schedule to be observed for the formal signing of the agreement on October 31, 1972. Obviously, the two sides had agreed upon an agreement of extremely important significance, which meets the wishes of the peoples in Viet Nam, the United States and the world.

But on October 23, 1972, contrary to its pledges, the U.S. side again referred to difficulties in Saigon, demanded that the negotiations be continued for resolving new problems, and did not say anything about the implementation of its commitments under the agreed schedule. This behaviour of the U.S. side has brought about a very serious situation which risks to jeopardize the signing of the "agreement on ending the war and restoring peace in Viet Nam."

The so-called difficulties in Saigon represent a mere pretext to delay the implementation of the U.S. commitments, because it is public knowledge that the Saigon administration has been rigged up and fostered by the United States. With a mercenary army equipped and paid by the United States, this administration is a tool for carrying out the "Vietnamization" policy and the neo-colonialist policy of the United States in violation of the south Vietnamese people's national rights. It is an instrument for the United States to sabotage all peaceful settlement of the Viet Nam problem.

The above shows that the Nixon administration is not negotiating with a serious attitude and goodwill in order to end the war and restore peace in Viet Nam, all it is doing in fact is to drag out the talks so as to deceive public opinion and to cover up its scheme of maintaining the Saigon puppet administration for the purposes of continued war of aggression in Viet Nam and Indochina. The Nixon administration must bear before the people of the United States and the world responsibility for delaying the signing of the agreement, and thus prolonging the war in Viet Nam.

The Government of the Democratic Republic of Viet Nam deems it its duty to bring the present situation with respect to the private meetings between the Democratic Republic of Viet Nam and the United States to the notice of our countrymen and fighters throughout the country, and the peoples in the world and the United States so that the truth may be known. This information is in the interest of peace and will in no way affect the negotiations, the two parties have agreed upon the text of the agreement and the schedule for its signing. While pointing to the above situation, the Government of the Democratic Republic of Viet Nam strictly holds to the undertakings between the Democratic Republic of Viet Nam and the United States to the effect that no change should be brought to the agreed text of the agreement, and that the date scheduled for its signing is October 31, 1972.

The Government of the Democratic Republic of Viet Nam strongly denounces the Nixon administration's lack of goodwill and seriousness.

It firmly demands that the U.S. Government respond to its goodwill, keep its commitments, and sign on October 31, 1972, the agreement whose text has been agreed upon with a view to ending the war, restoring peace in Viet Nam, contributing to the consolidation of peace in Asia and the world, thus meeting the desire of the Vietnamese people, the American people and the peoples around the world.

Countrymen and fighters throughout the country,

We want peace in independence and freedom. We are animated with goodwill. But the U.S. imperialists still nurture the design of conquering the southern part of our country, turning it into a new-type colony and a military base of the United States, and perpetuating the partition of our country. We had rather sacrifice everything than submit. **"Nothing is more precious than independence and freedom!"**

For the independence and freedom of our fatherland, for peace, national independence, democracy, and socialism in the world, we are fighting and defeating the U.S. imperialist aggressors. Ours is a position of victory, of initiative, which is unceasingly improving. The position of the U.S. imperialists and their lackeys is one of defeat, passivity and decline.

More than ever, our countrymen and fighters throughout the country are enhancing their resolve to unite as one man, to brave all hardships and sacrifices, to do their utmost to carry out President Ho Chi Minh's sacred testament, to persist in, and step up the fight on the three fronts—military, political, and diplomatic, until these lofty objectives have been achieved, to liberate the south, to defend and build the socialist north, and to proceed to the peaceful reunification of the country. Our people are determined to fight shoulder to shoulder with the fraternal peoples of Laos and Cambodia, and inflict a total defeat on the U.S. imperialist aggressors and their lackeys.

Our people's patriotic struggle against U.S. aggression is a just one. The strength of our unity is invincible. We have traditions of valiant and undaunted struggle against the aggressors. Moreover, our people enjoy the sympathy and great support of the fraternal socialist countries and the progressive people around the world.

We will win!

The Government of the Democratic Republic of Viet Nam calls on the Governments and peoples of the Soviet Union, China and the other fraternal socialist countries, of the peace- and justice-loving countries, the international organizations, the American people, and the peoples around the world, which have been wholeheartedly supporting the Vietnamese people's patriotic struggle against U.S. aggression, to wage a resolute struggle to urge the U.S. Government to carry out immediately what has been agreed upon between the United States and the Democratic Republic of Viet Nam so as to rapidly end the war and restore peace in Viet Nam. The Government of the Democratic Republic of

Viet Nam calls on all brothers and friends around the five continents to extend even stronger support and assistance to the Vietnamese people's just struggle until total victory.

The Vietnamese people will win!

The three peoples of Indochina will win!

Hanoi, October 26, 1972

(51) Vietnam Peace Negotiations: News Conference Statement by Dr. Henry A. Kissinger, Assistant to the President for National Security Affairs, October 26, 1972.[91]

(Excerpt)

DR. KISSINGER. *Ladies and gentlemen:*

We have now heard from both Vietnams[92] and it is obvious that, as a war that has been raging for 10 years is drawing to a conclusion, that this is a traumatic experience for all of the participants. The President thought that it might be helpful if I came out here and spoke to you about what we have been doing, where we stand, and to put the various allegations and charges into perspective.

First, let me talk about the situation in three parts: Where do we stand procedurally; what is the substance of the negotiations; and where do we go from here?

We believe that peace is at hand. We believe that an agreement is within sight, based on the May 8th proposals of the President[93] and some adaptations of our January 25th proposal[94] which is just to all parties. It is inevitable that in a war of such complexity that there should be occasional difficulties in reaching a final solution, but we believe that by far the longest part of the road has been traversed and what stands in the way of an agreement now are issues that are relatively less important than those that have already been settled.

Let me first go through the procedural points, the arguments with respect to particular dates for signing the agreement. As you know, we have been negotiating in these private sessions with the North Vietnamese for nearly 4 years. We resumed the discussions on July 19 of this year. Up to now, the negotiations had always foundered on the North Vietnamese insistence that a political settlement be arrived at

---

[91] *Presidential Documents*, Oct. 30, 1972, pp. 1565-8.
[92] For the North Vietnamese statement, see Document 50. In a statement issued on the morning of Oct. 27 (local time), the South Vietnamese Foreign Ministry stated that South Vietnam was ready to accept a cease-fire but would never accept a political settlement that went against the interests and aspirations of the South Vietnamese people (*New York Times*, Oct. 27, 1972).
[93] Document 47.
[94] Document 44.

Now, let me first go briefly over the main provisions of the agreement as we understand them, and then let me say what, in our view, still remains to be done. We believe, incidentally, what remains to be done can be settled in one more negotiating session with the North Vietnamese negotiators lasting, I would think, no more than 3 or 4 days, so we are not talking of a delay of a very long period of time.

Let me, however, before I go into the issues that still remain, cover those that are contained in the draft agreement, of which, on the whole, a very fair account has been given in the radio broadcast from Hanoi. I don't refer to the last two pages of rhetoric; I am referring to the description of the agreement.

The principal provisions were and are that a cease-fire would be observed in South Vietnam at a time to be mutually agreed upon—it would be a cease-fire in place; that U.S. forces would be withdrawn within 60 days of the signing of the agreement; that there would be a total prohibition on the reinforcement of troops—that is to say, that infiltration into South Vietnam from whatever area, and from whatever country, would be prohibited. Existing military equipment within South Vietnam could be replaced on a one-to-one basis by weapons of the same characteristics and of similar characteristics and properties, under international supervision.

The agreement provides that all captured military personnel and foreign civilians be repatriated within the same time period as the withdrawal; that is to say, there will be a return of all American prisoners, military or civilian, within 60 days after the agreement comes into force.

North Vietnam has made itself responsible for an accounting of our prisoners and missing in action throughout Indochina and for the repatriation of American prisoners throughout Indochina.

There is a separate provision that South Vietnamese civilians detained in South Vietnam, that their future should be determined through negotiation among the South Vietnamese parties, so that the return of our prisoners is not conditional on the disposition of Vietnamese prisoners in Vietnamese jails on both sides of the conflict. With respect to the political provisions, there is an affirmation of general principles guaranteeing the right of self-determination of the South Vietnamese people and that the South Vietnamese people should decide their political future through free and democratic elections under international supervision.

As was pointed out by Radio Hanoi, the existing authorities with respect to both internal and external policies would remain in office; the two parties in Vietnam would negotiate about the timing of elections, the nature of the elections, and the offices for which these elections were to be held.

There would be created an institution called the National Council of National Reconciliation and Concord whose general task would be to help promote the maintenance of the cease-fire and to supervise the elections on which the parties might agree.

That council would be formed by appointment, and it would operate on the basis of unanimity. We view it as an institutionalization of the election commission that we proposed on January 25 in our plan.

There are provisions that the disposition of Vietnamese armed forces in the South should also be settled through negotiation among the South Vietnamese parties.

There are provisions that the unification of Vietnam also be achieved by negotiation among the parties without military pressure and without foreign interference, without coercion, and without annexation.

There is a very long and complex section on international supervision which will no doubt occupy graduate students for many years to come and which, as far as I can tell, only my colleague Ambassador Sullivan[98] understands completely.

But briefly, it provides for joint commissions of the participants, either two-party or four-party, for those parts of the agreement that are applicable either to two parties or to four parties; it provides for an international supervisory commission to which disagreements of the commissions composed of the parties would be referred, but which also had a right to make independent investigations, and an international conference to meet within 30 days of the signing of the agreement to develop the guarantees and to establish the relationship of the various parties to each other in greater detail.

There is finally a section on Cambodia and Laos in which the parties to the agreement agree to respect and recognize the independence and sovereignty of Cambodia and Laos, in which they agree to refrain from using the territory of Cambodia and the territory of Laos to encroach on the sovereignty and security of other countries.

There is an agreement that foreign countries shall withdraw their forces from Laos and Cambodia and there is a general section about the future relationship between the United States and the Democratic Republic of Vietnam in which both sides express their conviction that this agreement will usher in a new period of reconciliation between the two countries, and in which the United States expresses its view that it will in the postwar period contribute to the reconstruction of Indochina and that both countries will develop their relationships on a basis of mutual respect and noninterference in each other's affairs, and that they will move from hostility to normalcy.

Now, ladies and gentlemen, in the light of where we are, it is obvious that most of the most difficult problems have been dealt with, that if you consider what many of you might have thought possible some months ago compared to where we are, we have to say that both sides

---

[98] William H. Sullivan, Deputy Assistant Secretary of State for East Asian and Pacific Affairs.

peace is within reach in a matter of weeks, or less, dependent on when the meeting takes place, and that once peace is achieved, we will move from hostility to normalcy, and from normalcy to cooperation with the same seriousness with which we have conducted our previous less fortunate relationships with them.

As far as Saigon is concerned, it is, of course, entitled to participate in the settlement of a war fought on its territory. Its people have suffered much, and they will remain there after we leave. Their views deserve great respect. In order to accelerate negotiations, we had presented them with conclusions which obviously could not be fully settled in a matter of 4 days that I spent in Saigon. But we are confident that our consultations with Saigon will produce agreement within the same time frame that I have indicated is required to complete the agreement with Hanoi, and that the negotiations can continue on the schedule that I have outlined.

With respect to the American people—we have talked to you ladies and gentlemen here very often about the negotiations with respect to the peace, and we have been very conscious of the division and the anguish that the war has caused in this country. One reason why the President has been so concerned with ending the war by negotiation, and ending it in a manner that is consistent with our principles, is because of the hope that the act of making peace could restore the unity that had sometimes been lost at certain periods during the war, and so that the agreement could be an act of healing rather than a source of new division. This remains our policy.

We will not be stampeded into an agreement until its provisions are right. We will not be deflected from an agreement when its provisions are right. And with this attitude, and with some cooperation from the other side, we believe that we can restore both peace and unity to America very soon.

Thank you. I will be glad to answer your questions.

*   *   *

(52) Obstacles to Agreement: News Conference Statement by Dr. Kissinger, December 16, 1972.[100]

(Excerpt)

DR. KISSINGER. Ladies and gentlemen, as you know, I have been reporting to the President and meeting with the Secretary of State, the Vice President, the Secretary of Defense, the Chairman of the Joint

[100] *Presidential Documents*, Dec. 18, 1972, pp. 1764-7.

Chiefs, and other senior officials. I am meeting with you today because we wanted to give you an account of the negotiations as they stand today.

I am sure you will appreciate that I cannot go into the details of particular issues, but I will give you as fair and honest a description of the general trend of the negotiations as I can.

First, let me do this in three parts: what led us to believe, at the end of October, that peace was imminent;[101] second, what has happened since; third, where do we go from here?

At the end of October we had just concluded 3 weeks of negotiations with the North Vietnamese. As you all know, on October 8 the North Vietnamese presented to us a proposal which, as it later became elaborated, appeared to us to reflect the main principles that the President has always enunciated as being part of the American position. These principles were that there had to be an unconditional release of American prisoners throughout Indochina; secondly, that there should be a cease-fire in Indochina brought into being by various means suitable to the conditions of the countries concerned; third, that we were prepared to withdraw our forces under these conditions in a time period to be mutually agreed upon; fourth, that we would not pre-judge the political outcome of the future of South Vietnam, we would not impose a particular solution, we would not insist on our particular solution.

The agreement, as it was developed during October, seemed to us to reflect these principles precisely. Then, toward the end of October, we encountered a number of difficulties. At the time, because we wanted to maintain the atmosphere leading to a rapid settlement, we mentioned them at our briefings, but we did not elaborate on them.

Now let me sum up what the problems were at the end of October.

It became apparent that there was in preparation a massive Communist effort to launch an attack throughout South Vietnam to begin several days before the cease-fire would have been declared, and to continue for some weeks after the cease-fire came into being.

Second, there was an interview by the North Vietnamese Prime Minister which implied that the political solution that we had always insisted was part of our principles, namely that we would not impose a coalition government, was not as clear-cut as our record of the negotiations indicated.

Thirdly, as no one could miss, we encountered some specific objections from Saigon.

Under these conditions, we proposed to Hanoi that there should be one other round of negotiations to clear up these difficulties. We were convinced that, with good will on both sides, these difficulties could be relatively easily surmounted and that, if we conducted ourselves on

---

101 Cf. Document 51.

both sides in the spirit of the October negotiations, a settlement would be very rapid.

It was our conviction that if we were going to bring to an end 10 years of warfare, we should not do so with an armistice, but with a peace that had a chance of lasting. Therefore, we proposed three categories of clarifications in the agreement. First, we wanted the so-called linguistic difficulties cleared up so that they would not provide the seed for unending disputes and another eruption of the war. I will speak about those in a minute.

Secondly, the agreement always had provided that international machinery be put in place immediately after the cease-fire was declared. We wanted to spell out the operational meaning of the word "immediately" by developing the protocols that were required to bring the international machinery into being simultaneously with a cease-fire agreement. This, to us, seemed a largely technical matter.

Thirdly, we wanted some reference in the agreement, however vague, however allusive, however indirect, which would make clear that the two parts of Vietnam would live in peace with each other and that neither side would impose its solution on the other by force. These seemed to us modest requirements, relatively easily achievable.

Let me now tell you the sequence of events since that time.

We all know of the disagreements that have existed between Saigon and Washington. These disagreements are, to some extent, understandable. It is inevitable that a people on whose territory the war has been fought and that for 25 years has been exposed to devastation and suffering and assassination, would look at the prospects of a settlement in a more detailed way, in a more anguished way, than we who are 10,000 miles away. Many of the provisions of the agreement inevitably were seen in a different context in Vietnam than in Washington.

I think it is safe to say that we face, with respect to both Vietnamese parties, this problem. The people of Vietnam, North and South, have fought for so long that the risks and perils of war, however difficult, seem sometimes more bearable to them than the uncertainties and the risks and perils of peace.

Now, it is no secret, either, that the United States has not agreed with all the objections that were raised by Saigon. In particular, the United States' position with respect to the cease-fire had been made clear in October 1970.[102] It had been reiterated in the President's proposal of January 25, 1972.[103] It was repeated again in the President's proposal of May 8, 1972.[104] None of these proposals had asked for a withdrawal of North Vietnamese forces. Therefore, we could not agree with our allies in South Vietnam when they added conditions to the established

[102] *Documents, 1970,* pp. 196-201; cf. above at note 6.
[103] Document 44.
[104] Document 47.

positions after an agreement had been reached that reflected these established positions.

As was made clear in the press conference here on October 26, as the President has reiterated in his speeches,[105] the United States will not continue the war one day longer than it believes is necessary to reach an agreement we consider just and fair.

So, we want to leave no doubt about the fact that if an agreement is reached that meets the stated conditions of the President, if an agreement is reached that we consider just, that no other party will have a veto over our actions.

But I am also bound to tell you that today this question is moot because we have not yet reached an agreement that the President considers just and fair. Therefore, I want to explain to you the process of the negotiations since they resumed on November 20 and where we are.

The three objectives that we were seeking in these negotiations were stated in the press conference of October 26, in many speeches by the President afterwards, and in every communication to Hanoi since. They could not have been a surprise.

Now, let me say a word first about what were called "linguistic difficulties," which were called these in order not to inflame the situation. How did they arise? They arose because the North Vietnamese presented us a document in English which we then discussed with them, and in many places throughout this document, the original wording was changed as the negotiations proceeded and the phrases were frequently weakened compared to the original formulation. It was not until we received the Vietnamese text, after those negotiations were concluded, that we found that while the English terms had been changed, the Vietnamese terms had been left unchanged.

So, we suddenly found ourselves engaged in two negotiations, one about the English text, the other about the Vietnamese text. Having conducted many negotiations, I must say this was a novel procedure. It led to the view that perhaps these were not simply linguistic difficulties, but substantive difficulties.

Now I must say that all of these, except one, have now been eliminated. The second category of problems concerned bringing into being the international machinery so that it could operate simultaneously with the cease-fire and so as to avoid a situation where the cease-fire, rather than bring peace, would unleash another frenzy of warfare.

To that end we submitted on November 20, the first day that the negotiations resumed, a list of what are called protocols, technical instruments to bring this machinery into being. These protocols—and I will not go into the details of these protocols—they were normally technical documents and ours were certainly intended to conform to normal practices, despite the fact that this occurred 4 weeks after we had made clear that this was our intention and 3 weeks after Hanoi had pressed us to sign a cease-fire agreement. The North Vietnamese refused to discuss our protocols and refused to give us their protocols, so that the question of bringing the international machinery into being could not be addressed.

The first time we saw the North Vietnamese protocols was on the evening of December 12, the night before I was supposed to leave Paris, 6 weeks after we had stated what our aim was, 5 weeks after the cease-fire was supposed to be signed, a cease-fire which called for this machinery to be set up immediately.

These protocols were not technical instruments, but reopened a whole list of issues that had been settled, or we thought had been settled, in the agreement. They contained provisions that were not in the original agreement, and they excluded provisions that were in the original agreement. They are now in the process of being discussed by the technical experts in Paris, but some effort will be needed to remove the political provisions from them and to return them to a technical status.

Secondly, I think it is safe to say that the North Vietnamese perception of international machinery and our perception of international machinery is at drastic variance, and that, ladies and gentlemen, is an understatement.

We had thought that an effective machinery required, in effect, some freedom of movement, and our estimate was that several thousand people were needed to monitor the many provisions of the agreement. The North Vietnamese perception is that the total force should be no more than 250, of which nearly half should be located at headquarters; that it would be dependent for its communications, logistics, and even physical necessities entirely on the party in whose area it was located.

So it would have no jeeps, no telephones, no radios of its own; that it could not move without being accompanied by liaison officers of the party that was to be investigated, if that party decided to give it the jeeps to get to where the violation was taking place and if that party would then let it communicate what it found.

It is our impression that the members of this commission will not exhaust themselves in frenzies of activity if this procedure were adopted.

Now, thirdly, the substance of the agreement. The negotiations since November 20 really have taken place in two phases. The first phase, which lasted for 3 days, continued the spirit and the attitude of the meetings in October. We presented our proposals. Some were accepted; others were rejected.

But by the end of third day, we had made very substantial progress, and all of us thought that we were within a day or two of completing the arrangements. We do not know what decisions were made in Hanoi at that point, but from that point on, the negotiations have had the character where a settlement was always just within our reach, and was always pulled just beyond our reach when we attempted to grasp it.

I do not think it is proper for me to go into the details of the specific issues, but I think I should give you a general atmosphere and a general sense of the procedures that were followed.

When we returned on December 4, we of the American team, we thought that the meetings could not last more than 2 or 3 days because there were only two or three issues left to be resolved. You all know that the meetings lasted 9 days. They began with Hanoi withdrawing every change that had been agreed to 2 weeks previously.

We then spent the rest of the week getting back to where we had already been 2 weeks before. By Saturday [December 9], we thought we had narrowed the issues sufficiently where, if the other side had accepted again one section that they had already agreed to 2 weeks previously, the agreement could have been completed.

At that point, the President ordered General Haig to return to Washington so that he would be available for the mission that would then follow, of presenting the agreement to our allies. At that point, we thought we were sufficiently close so that experts could meet to conform the texts so that we would not again encounter the linguistic difficulties which we had experienced previously, and so that we could make sure that the changes that had been negotiated in English would also be reflected in Vietnamese.

When the experts met, they were presented with 17 new changes in the guise of linguistic changes. When I met again with the Special Adviser [Le Duc Tho], the one problem which we thought remained on Saturday had grown to two, and a new demand was presented. When we accepted that, it was withdrawn the next day and sharpened up. So we spent our time going through the 17 linguistic changes and reduced them again to two.

Then, on the last day of the meeting, we asked our experts to meet to compare whether the 15 changes that had been settled, of the 17 that had been proposed, now conformed in the two texts. At that point we were presented with 16 new changes, including four substantive ones, some of which now still remain unsettled.

Now, I will not go into the details or into the merits of these changes. The major difficulty that we now face is that provisions that were settled in the agreement appear again in a different form in the protocols; that matters of technical implementation which were implicit in the agreement from the beginning have not been addressed and were not presented to us until the very last day of a series of sessions that had been specifically designed to discuss them; and that as soon as one issue was settled, a new issue was raised.

It was very tempting for us to continue the process which is so close to everybody's heart, implicit in the many meetings, of indicating great progress, but the President decided that we could not engage in a charade with the American people.

We are now in this curious position: Great progress has been made, even in the talks. The only thing that is lacking is one decision in Hanoi, to settle the remaining issues in terms that 2 weeks previously they had already agreed to.

So, we are not talking of an issue of principle that is totally unacceptable.

Secondly, to complete the work that is required to bring the international machinery into being in the spirit that both sides have an interest of not ending the war in such a way that it is just the beginning of another round of conflict.

So, we are in a position where peace can be near, but peace requires a decision. This is why we wanted to restate once more what our basic attitude is.

With respect to Saigon, we have sympathy and compassion for the anguish of their people and for the concerns of their government. But if we can get an agreement that the President considers just, we will proceed with it.

With respect to Hanoi, our basic objective was stated in the press conference of October 26. We want an end to the war that is something more than an armistice. We want to move from hostility to normalization and from normalization to cooperation. But we will not make a settlement which is a disguised form of continued warfare and which brings about, by indirection, what we have always said we would not tolerate.

We have always stated that a fair solution cannot possibly give either side everything that it wants. We are not continuing a war in order to give total victory to our allies. We want to give them a reasonable opportunity to participate in a political structure, but we also will not make a settlement which is a disguised form of victory for the other side.

Therefore, we are at a point where we are again perhaps closer to an agreement than we were at the end of October, if the other side is willing to deal with us in good faith and with good will. But it cannot do that [if] every day an issue is settled a new one is raised, that when an issue is settled in an agreement, it is raised again as an understanding, and if it is settled in an understanding, it is raised again as a protocol. We will not be blackmailed into an agreement. We will not be stampeded into an agreement. And, if I may say so, we will not be charmed into an agreement until its conditions are right.

For the President and for all of us who have been engaged in these negotiations, nothing that we have done has meant more than attempting to bring an end to the war in Vietnam. Nothing that I have done since I have been in this position has made me feel more the trustee of so many hopes as the negotiations in which I have recently participated. It was painful at times to think of the hopes of millions and, indeed of the hopes of many of you ladies and gentlemen who were standing outs: these various meeting places expecting momentous events to be oc~urring, while inside one frivolous issue after another was surfaced in the last 3 days.

So, what we are saying to Hanoi is, we are prepared to continue in the spirit of the negotiations that were started in October. We are prepared to maintain an agreement that provides for the unconditional release of all American and allied prisoners, that imposes no political solution on either side, that brings about an internationally supervised cease-fire and the withdrawal of all American forces within 60 days. It is a settlement that is just to both sides and that requires only a decision to maintain provisions that had already been accepted and an end to procedures that can only mock the hopes of humanity.

On that basis, we can have a peace that justifies the hopes of mankind and the sense of justice of all participants.

Now, I will be glad to answer some of your questions.

*   *   *

VI.
AMERICAN POLICY IN ASIA:
EAST ASIA
AND THE PACIFIC

[The repercussions of President Nixon's visit to mainland China dominated the Far Eastern scene in 1972 in much the same way that its preparation had dominated the scene during a part of 1971. In opening a long-delayed dialogue with the principal power of the East Asian mainland, the United States eliminated an anomaly in its diplomatic stance and helped assuage anxieties that had long preoccupied allied and friendly governments in the Far East and Pacific. At the same time, the rapid thawing of relations between the United States and the People's Republic of China awakened new uncertainties about America's long-range intentions on the part of such old-established associates as Japan, Australia, and New Zealand, not to mention the allied Republic of China on Taiwan.

Contributing to these uncertainties was the new emphasis on a so-called "pentagonal world" that had begun to characterize some Washington foreign policy pronouncements, among them an interview with President Nixon made public by *Time* magazine in the last days of 1971. "We must remember," the President had said, in words that would later be quoted with misgivings by his Democratic rival for the presidency, "the only time in the history of the world that we have had any extended periods of peace is when there has been balance of power. It is when one nation becomes infinitely more powerful in relation to its potential competitor that the danger of war arises. So I believe in a world in which the United States is powerful. I think it will be a safer world and a better world if we have a strong, healthy United States, Europe, Soviet Union, China, Japan, each balancing the other, not playing one against the other, an even balance."[1]

---

[1] *Time*, Jan. 3, 1972, p. 15; cf. Document 6 at notes 73-74. (For an earlier expression of the same thought in an economic context, cf. *A.F.R., 1971*, no. 91.) More detailed discussion of the subject matter of this chapter will be found in Rogers Report, 1972, pp. 329-65, and in Nixon Reports, 1972 and 1973, as cited in notes 2, 49, and 85 below.

Both the achievements and the uncertainties of Far Eastern diplomacy are reflected in the following documents, which record the highlights of U.S. relations with mainland China, Japan, and the allied countries participating with the United States in the South-East Asia Treaty Organization (SEATO) and the ANZUS Pact.]

A. The People's Republic of China (P.R.C.).[2]

1. President Nixon's Visit to Mainland China, February 21-28, 1972.

[Originally announced July 15, 1971,[3] President Nixon's precedent-shattering visit to the Communist-ruled Chinese mainland occurred at a moment of extraordinary significance to each of two governments whose vehement hostility, extending back to the foundation of the People's Republic of China (P.R.C.) in 1949, had been generally regarded as a well-nigh immutable feature of the international scene. For the United States, the visit coincided with an expected crisis in Vietnam, as well as the planning for Mr. Nixon's visit to the Soviet Union in May and his expected bid for reelection in November 1972. For the Peking government, it occurred at a period which, though marked by continuing tension with the U.S.S.R., was also a time of internal consolidation after the upheavals of the "Great Proletarian Cultural Revolution" and the crisis that had surrounded the disappearance and death in September 1971 of Lin Piao, the "close comrade-in-arms" and former successor-designate of the 78-year-old Chairman Mao Tse-tung. The direction of China's day-to-day affairs, for the moment at least, appeared firmly in the hands of 73-year-old Premier Chou En-lai, one of the few Chinese statesmen to have emerged with undimmed prestige from the turmoil that had convulsed the mainland in recent years.

The outlines of the visit, as seen from an American viewpoint, emerge distinctly from President Nixon's predeparture account of his objectives (Document 53); the formal statement issued by the two governments at Shanghai as the visit neared its end (Document 54); the interpretive comments offered by Dr. Kissinger and others of the presidential party (Document 55); and the observations of the President himself immediately following his return to the United States (Document 56).]

---

[2] For more detailed discussion cf. Nixon Report, 1972, pp. 26-37; same, 1973, pp. 16-25.
[3] *A.F.R., 1971*, no. 91.

(53) Expectations for the Visit: News Conference Statement by President Nixon, February 10, 1972.[4]

(Excerpt)

THE PRESIDENT. Ladies and gentlemen, before going to your other questions, I would like to make an announcement with regard to the details of the trip to Mainland China. This will not cover all the details, but it will at least cover those that we can announce at this time.

The official party will be announced from Florida, Key Biscayne, on Saturday the 12th.[5] Of course, as you know, we have already announced that Dr. Kissinger, the Secretary of State, Mrs. Nixon, and I will be going, and the other members of the official party at that time will be announced from Washington.

On Monday, I have an event that I think has already been announced, a meeting with André Malraux, and I am giving a dinner that night for him to which several Congressional leaders will be invited, as well as members of the official party, the Secretary of State, Dr. Kissinger.

In mentioning André Malraux, I do not want to reflect on many of the other experts—and there are many experts in this field of China—whose books have been brought to my attention. I do not want to indicate I have read them all but I have been exposed to a great number. I asked him to come because there was an interesting coincidence.

In 1969, when I met with President de Gaulle in Paris, Mr. Malraux at that time was the Minister of Culture in the de Gaulle Cabinet. We had a discussion prior to the dinner on the subject of China generally, and I was particularly impressed with his analysis of the leaders. His book, at least the one I have read—he's written many—but his book, the one I particularly refer to was his Anti-Memoirs.[6] I would commend it to you not only for what it tells about China and its leaders, but also about France, its problems, and the whole World War II and post-World War II era.

I give you this only to indicate the breadth of the kind of briefings that all of us who are going to participate in the talks are trying to undertake. It is very different from the other meetings that we have had at the highest level with other governments. I have visited virtually all of the other countries, just as I, of course, have visited the Soviet Union.

But here it is essential to do an enormous amount of homework just to come up to the starting line. I don't want to say that after having read as much as I have, and as much as I will be reading between now and the time we arrive, that I will be an expert, but at least I will be

---

[4] *Presidential Documents*, Feb. 14, 1972, pp. 413-14.

[5] Same, Feb. 21, 1972, p. 444.

[6] André Malraux, *Anti-Memoirs* (New York: Holt, Rinehart and Winston, 1968).

familiar with the men that we will be meeting and the problems that may be discussed.

Tuesday and Wednesday [February 15 and 16] will be used primarily to finish up on many of the domestic matters that are, of course, the subject of matters that I will be discussing with Secretary [of the Treasury John B.] Connally and Mr. [John D.] Ehrlichman over this weekend, and also for further briefings from members of the NSC [National Security Council] staff and the State Department on the China trip.

The time of departure has now been set. It will be 10 o'clock, Thursday morning, the 17th, from Andrews.[7] We will fly directly to Hawaii. We will spend Thursday night and all day Friday in Hawaii.

The following morning, Saturday morning, on the 19th, the press plane will go directly to Mainland China, stopping at Shanghai first, and arriving in Peking. The Chinese Government is arranging this so that the members of the press can be on the ground prior to the time that I will be arriving.

On that same day, Saturday, the 19th, the Presidential plane, the Spirit of '76, will fly to Guam, and we will overnight in Guam and take off the next day, Monday, for Shanghai and Peking, arriving in Peking Monday morning at approximately 11:30 a.m.[8] The date, of course, is the 21st there and the 20th here. As you know, we cross the International Date Line on the way.

A couple of other points that I know have been raised in briefings and that I can only cover generally:

With regard to agenda, both governments have decided that we will not make any announcements on agenda items prior to the meetings. The agenda will be covered by a joint communiqué that will be issued at the conclusion of our talks[9] and consequently, questions on agenda, what will be discussed and so forth, on the part of both sides, will not be answered either before we get there or during the course of the meetings, unless the two sides decide, while we are meeting, that an agenda item can properly be discussed or disclosed.

With regard to this itinerary itself, the itinerary, generally as you know, has been announced for three cities. With regard to what we do in each city, it is being kept flexible and no final decisions have been made and none will be announced at this time.[10]

Mrs. Nixon's itinerary will be much more public than mine. And she will have an opportunity, which I hope many of you also will have, those of you who are going, to visit a number of institutions, places of

---

[7] For the President's departure remarks see *Public Papers, 1972*, p. 367.

[8] 10:30 P.M. Sunday E.S.T.

[9] Document 54.

[10] A chronology of the President's activities in China appears in *Public Papers, 1972*, pp. 365-7 and in *Bulletin*, Mar. 20, 1972, pp. 438-40. A detailed account of the visit will be found in Kalb, *Kissinger*, pp. 266-83.

interest in Peking, Hangchow, and Shanghai. She, having as you know, traveled to perhaps more countries than any First Lady, is looking forward to this with a great deal of interest and, I think, as she demonstrated on her trip to Africa,[11] her events, I think, will be worth covering.

One side note is that, and I am sure all of you who have been studying, as I have, will have noted this, is that one development in 20th century China that is very significant, is the enormous elevation in the status of women. Total equality is now recognized and looking back over Chinese history, that is, of course, a very significant change.

Consequently, I think Mrs. Nixon's activities will be significant for them. It will be, of course, very significant for us in the United States to see their schools and the other institutions and how they compare with ours and the other countries that we will visit.

As far as my agenda is concerned, there will not be a great deal of what I would call public—well, to put it perhaps rather plainly— sightseeing. There will be some. I mean actually I would hope to see some of the points of interest and the Chinese Government is arranging for some. But we have both agreed that this visit is one, taking place as it does at this time, in which first priority must be given to our talks and sightseeing and protocol must come second. And consequently, we have agreed that we will not get frozen in to any extended travel within the cities which we will be visiting, in the event that that might interfere with an extended conversation that might be taking place.

I do not want to suggest here what the length of the talks will be but, necessarily, because we are in truth at a beginning, they will be much longer, both with Mr. Chou En-lai and with Mr. Mao Tse-tung[12] than with the leaders of other governments that we have visited, because there we are not starting at the beginning. We had the opportunity to come immediately to matters of substance.

Finally, in order to perhaps put the trip in context, you have heard me discuss it in various speeches that I have made generally. I haven't really much to add, because as I pointed out, the agenda items will be decided at the beginning of the meetings, but they will be published at the end of our meetings and by communiqué.

But I think we could say this: This trip should not be one which would create very great optimism or very great pessimism. It is one in which we must recognize that 20 years of hostility and virtually no communication will not be swept away by one week of discussion.

However, it will mark a watershed in the relations between the two governments; the postwar era with respect to the People's Republic of China and the United States, that chapter now comes to an end from

11 Mrs. Nixon visited Liberia, Ghana, and the Ivory Coast on Jan. 1-9, 1972.
12 Respectively Chairman of the State Council (Premier) and Chairman of the Central Committee of the Chinese Communist Party.

the time that I set foot on the soil of Mainland China, and a new chapter begins.

Now, how the new chapter is written will be influenced, perhaps influenced substantially, by the talks that will take place. On our side and we believe also on their side we hope that the new chapter will be one of more communication and that it will be a chapter that will be marked by negotiation rather than confrontation and one that will be marked by the absence of armed conflict. These are our hopes.

We, of course, will now see to what extent those hopes can be realized in this first meeting.

I will go to any other questions.

QUESTIONS

MEETINGS WITH CHINESE LEADERS

Q. Mr. President, Mr. Malraux has been quoted as having said that he is sure that the first question that Mao will ask you is, "Will you provide aid for China?" and that the rest of the trip, the success of the talks, will be determined by your answer. Can you give us any indication that if that is true what you will say?

THE PRESIDENT. That gets into the area that I will decline to comment upon, because it involves the agenda items. I cannot really predict with as much confidence as Mr. Malraux perhaps can, as to what Mr. Mao Tse-tung's questions will be.

So, consequently, I don't believe it would be proper to comment now on a question that has not yet been asked by him. If it is asked, I will have an answer.

Q. Mr. President, do you look upon these talks—do you look upon your meeting with Chou En-lai and Mao Tse-tung as dialogue or negotiation?

THE PRESIDENT. They will be primarily dialogue. Here a very subtle but definite distinction is made between the talks that will take place in Peking and the talks that will take place in Moscow.

In the talks in Moscow there are certain subjects that we have been negotiating about and those subjects, therefore, will be negotiated, although, of course, there will be dialogue as well.[13] Dialogue is an essential part of negotiation.

In the case of Peking, there will necessarily have to be a substantial amount of dialogue before we can come to the point of negotiating on substantive matters. I should emphasize, too, that it has already been pointed out by Dr. Kissinger when he returned,[14] that when we speak

13 Cf. Documents 10-14.
14 Cf. A.F.R., 1971, no. 93

of these matters that they will be primarily bilateral matters. Beyond that, however, I will not go.

* * *

(54) The Shanghai Communiqué: Joint Statement Issued at the Conclusion of President Nixon's Visit, Shanghai, February 27, 1972. [15]

(Complete Text)

President Richard Nixon of the United States of America visited the People's Republic of China at the invitation of Premier Chou En-lai of the People's Republic of China from February 21 to February 28, 1972. Accompanying the President were Mrs. Nixon, U.S. Secretary of State William Rogers, Assistant to the President Dr. Henry Kissinger, and other American officials.

President Nixon met with Chairman Mao Tse-tung of the Communist Party of China on February 21. The two leaders had a serious and frank exchange of views on Sino-U.S. relations and world affairs.

During the visit, extensive, earnest and frank discussions were held between President Nixon and Premier Chou En-lai on the normalization of relations between the United States of America and the People's Republic of China, as well as on other matters of interest to both sides. In addition, Secretary of State William Rogers and Foreign Minister Chi Peng-fei held talks in the same spirit.

President Nixon and his party visited Peking and viewed cultural, industrial and agricultural sites, and they also toured Hangchow and Shanghai where, continuing discussions with Chinese leaders, they viewed similar places of interest.

The leaders of the People's Republic of China and the United States of America found it beneficial to have this opportunity, after so many years without contact, to present candidly to one another their views on a variety of issues. They reviewed the international situation in which important changes and great upheavals are taking place and expounded their respective positions and attitudes.

The U.S. side stated: Peace in Asia and peace in the world requires efforts both to reduce immediate tensions and to eliminate the basic causes of conflict. The United States will work for a just and secure peace: just, because it fulfills the aspirations of peoples and nations for freedom and progress; secure, because it removes the danger of foreign aggression. The United States supports individual freedom and social progress for all the peoples of the world, free of outside pressure or

[15] *Presidential Documents*, Feb. 28, 1972, pp. 473-6.

intervention. The United States believes that the effort to reduce tensions is served by improving communication between countries that have different ideologies so as to lessen the risks of confrontation through accident, miscalculation or misunderstanding. Countries should treat each other with mutual respect and be willing to compete peacefully, letting performance be the ultimate judge. No country should claim infallibility and each country should be prepared to re-examine its own attitudes for the common good. The United States stressed that the peoples of Indochina should be allowed to determine their destiny without outside intervention; its constant primary objective has been a negotiated solution; the eight-point proposal put forward by the Republic of Vietnam and the United States on January 27, 1972[16] represents a basis for the attainment of that objective; in the absence of a negotiated settlement the United States envisages the ultimate withdrawal of all U.S. forces from the region consistent with the aim of self-determination for each country of Indochina. The United States will maintain its close ties with and support for the Republic of Korea; the United States will support efforts of the Republic of Korea to seek a relaxation of tension and increased communication in the Korean peninsula. The United States places the highest value on its friendly relations with Japan; it will continue to develop the existing close bonds. Consistent with the United Nations Security Council Resolution of December 21, 1971,[17] the United States favors the continuation of the ceasefire between India and Pakistan and the withdrawal of all military forces to within their own territories and to their own sides of the ceasefire line in Jammu and Kashmir; the United States supports the right of the peoples of South Asia to shape their own future in peace, free of military threat, and without having the area become the subject of great power rivalry.

The Chinese side stated: Wherever there is oppression, there is resistance. Countries want independence, nations want liberation and the people want revolution—this has become the irresistible trend of history. All nations, big or small, should be equal; big nations should not bully the small and strong nations should not bully the weak. China will never be a superpower and it opposes hegemony and power politics of any kind. The Chinese side stated that it firmly supports the struggles of all the oppressed people and nations for freedom and liberation and that the people of all countries have the right to choose their social systems according to their own wishes and the right to safeguard the independence, sovereignty and territorial integrity of their own countries and oppose foreign aggression, interference, control and subversion. All foreign troops should be withdrawn to their own countries.

The Chinese side expressed its firm support to the peoples of

---

[16] Document 44, presented at the Paris talks on Vietnam on Jan. 27, 1972.
[17] A.F.R., 1971, no. 63.

Vietnam, Laos and Cambodia in their efforts for the attainment of their goal and its firm support to the seven-point proposal of the Provisional Revolutionary Government of the Republic of South Vietnam[18] and the elaboration of February this year on the two key problems in the proposal,[19] and to the Joint Declaration of the Summit conference of the Indochinese Peoples.[20] It firmly supports the eight-point program for the peaceful unification of Korea put forward by the Government of the Democratic People's Republic of Korea on April 12, 1971, and the stand for the abolition of the "U.N. Commission for the Unification and Rehabilitation of Korea."[21] It firmly opposes the revival and outward expansion of Japanese militarism and firmly supports the Japanese people's desire to build an independent, democratic, peaceful and neutral Japan. It firmly maintains that India and Pakistan should, in accordance with the United Nations resolutions on the India-Pakistan question, immediately withdraw all their forces to their respective territories and to their own sides of the ceasefire line in Jammu and Kashmir and firmly supports the Pakistan Government and people in their struggle to preserve their independence and sovereignty and the people of Jammu and Kashmir in their struggle for the right of self-determination.

There are essential differences between China and the United States in their social systems and foreign policies. However, the two sides agreed that countries, regardless of their social systems, should conduct their relations on the principles of respect for the sovereignty and territorial integrity of all states, non-aggression against other states, non-interference in the internal affairs of other states, equality and mutual benefit, and peaceful coexistence. International disputes should be settled on this basis, without resorting to the use or threat of force. The United States and the People's Republic of China are prepared to apply these principles to their mutual relations.

With these principles of international relations in mind the two sides stated that:

—progress toward the normalization of relations between China and the United States is in the interests of all countries;
—both wish to reduce the danger of international military conflict;
—neither should seek hegemony in the Asia-Pacific region and each is opposed to efforts by any other country or group of countries to establish such hegemony; and
—neither is prepared to negotiate on behalf of any third party or to enter into agreements or understandings with the other directed at other states.

[18] Same, no. 74a.
[19] Cf. Chapter V at note 9.
[20] Cf. *The United States in World Affairs, 1970*, pp. 134 and 309.
[21] Cf. note 85 below.

Both sides are of the view that it would be against the interests of the peoples of the world for any major country to collude with another against other countries, or for major countries to divide up the world into spheres of interest.

The two sides reviewed the long-standing serious disputes between China and the United States. The Chinese side reaffirmed its position: The Taiwan question is the crucial question obstructing the normalization of relations between China and the United States; the Government of the People's Republic of China is the sole legal government of China; Taiwan is a province of China which has long been returned to the motherland; the liberation of Taiwan is China's internal affair in which no other country has the right to interfere; and all U.S. forces and military installations must be withdrawn from Taiwan. The Chinese Government firmly opposes any activities which aim at the creation of "one China, one Taiwan," "one China, two governments," "two Chinas," and "independent Taiwan" or advocate that "the status of Taiwan remains to be determined."

The U.S. side declared: The United States acknowledges that all Chinese on either side of the Taiwan Strait maintain there is but one China and that Taiwan is a part of China. The United States Government does not challenge that position. It reaffirms its interest in a peaceful settlement of the Taiwan question by the Chinese themselves. With this prospect in mind, it affirms the ultimate objective of the withdrawal of all U.S. forces and military installations from Taiwan. In the meantime, it will progressively reduce its forces and military installations on Taiwan as the tension in the area diminishes.

The two sides agreed that it is desirable to broaden the understanding between the two peoples. To this end, they discussed specific areas in such fields as science, technology, culture, sports and journalism, in which people-to-people contacts and exchanges would be mutually beneficial. Each side undertakes to facilitate the further development of such contacts and exchanges.

Both sides view bilateral trade as another area from which mutual benefit can be derived, and agreed that economic relations based on equality and mutual benefit are in the interest of the peoples of the two countries. They agree to facilitate the progressive development of trade between their two countries.

The two sides agreed that they will stay in contact through various channels, including the sending of a senior U.S. representative to Peking from time to time for concrete consultations to further the normalization of relations between the two countries and continue to exchange views on issues of common interest.

The two sides expressed the hope that the gains achieved during this visit would open up new prospects for the relations between the two countries. They believe that the normalization of relations between the two countries is not only in the interest of the Chinese and American peoples but also contributes to the relaxation of tension in Asia and the world.

President Nixon, Mrs. Nixon and the American party expressed their appreciation for the gracious hospitality shown them by the Government and people of the People's Republic of China.

(55) Statements by Members of the Presidential Party, Shanghai, February 27, 1972.

(a) News Conference Statements by Dr. Kissinger and Marshall Green, Assistant Secretary of State for East Asian and Pacific Affairs. [22]

(Excerpt)

MR. ZIEGLER.[23] You have had a chance to read over the communiqué.[24] Dr. Kissinger is here to discuss it with you and take your questions. What Dr. Kissinger says is on the record. Together with Dr. Kissinger is Assistant Secretary of State Marshall Green who, as you know, participated in all the meetings with Secretary of State Rogers when he met with the Foreign Minister, and he is here also to discuss the communiqué with you and to take your questions, together with Dr. Kissinger.

We will begin with Dr. Kissinger.

DR. KISSINGER. Let me make a few preliminary observations before we go to your questions. Let me do it in two parts: the process, and there is obviously the communiqué produced, and secondly, what does it mean in general terms. Then I believe that I will be prepared to answer questions.

First, how was the communiqué produced? From the beginning of our contacts with the People's Republic of China, there were some obvious general considerations of what the outcome of a meeting between the President and the leaders of the People's Republic might be.

During the interim visit[25] there was some exploratory conversation of an outcome in the conventional sense in which both sides tend to state general positions which they afterwards choose to interpret, each in their own way.

It was, therefore, decided early in the meetings on this occasion be-

22 *Presidential Documents*, Feb. 28, 1972, pp. 476-7.
23 Ronald L. Ziegler, Press Secretary to the President.
24 Document 54.
25 *A.F.R., 1971*, no. 93a.

tween the President and Prime Minister [Chou En-lai] that such an approach would make no sense. It would not be worthy of the purposes that were attempted to be served.

It was therefore decided that each side would state its position on issues in a section which it would produce more or less independent of the other. It would not pretend to an agreement which did not exist and which would have to be interpreted away in subsequent implementations. Therefore, the beginning part of the communiqué represents, in effect, a statement by each side of some of its general principles.

On our side, they were deliberately not phrased in a contentious way. While in discussions some of the arguments made by the Chinese side were, of course, rebutted, we did not feel that this was the appropriate vehicle to do so, but rather to state what our positive view was.

For that matter, the Chinese side did not rebut arguments which we made in our section that they did not particularly agree with.

In order to present these two views on an equal basis, it had been decided that in the text issued by the American Government, the U.S. position would be stated first, and in the text to be issued by the Chinese Government, the Chinese version would be stated first.

I mention this only so that you will not be surprised if the Chinese version follows a different sequence from the American version. This is by agreement. Both versions are official and are being put out on the basis of this agreement.

The procedure that was followed here was that issues of general principle were first discussed in the meetings between the President and the Prime Minister. They were then, after they had been explored for some time, transferred to the meetings chaired by the Secretary of State and the Foreign Minister of the People's Republic of China [Chi Peng-fei]. Then, if any additional issues arose, they might be referred back to the meeting of the President and the Prime Minister.

In drafting the communiqué, various sections were produced by various elements of the American side. I played the role of go-between on our side and the Vice Foreign Minister, whose name I despair of ever learning to pronounce, on the Chinese side. [See next page.]

In this manner, as we put together the various paragraphs that were supplied to us on our side by various individuals, if we reached a point at which agreement seemed near or possible, we would then go back to our principals and to the Secretary of State. Through this process, the communiqué was finally achieved.

For example, some of the sessions were quite prolonged. The last few nights the sessions went on until the early hours of the morning with the President. In Peking, the Chinese delegation had a house in the guest complex, and most of the sessions took place in that house. As a paragraph was finished, it would typically go back then to the President who was in the next house, and this went on Friday night [February 25] until about 5 in the morning.

So much for the process. Let me say something about the content. Obviously neither side would have written this communiqué this way if it had been able to draft it entirely by itself. Therefore, it represented an attempt by two countries that had been out of contact for a long time to find a basis to convey first some immediate understandings, but beyond that, to start a process by which they could bring about a closer relationship over a period of time and by which they could, where interests converged, act in a more nearly parallel fashion and where interests differed, to mitigate the consequences of those disagreements.

So the communiqué ought to be seen in two aspects: first, in terms of the specific principles and conclusions it states, and secondly, in terms of the direction to which it seeks to point. It is on that basis that we are presenting it to the American people and on which the People's Republic is presenting it as well.

Now, this is all that I want to say by way of introduction. I wonder whether Marshall Green would like to add a few words, and then we will be glad to answer questions.

MR. GREEN. I have just a few words. First of all with regard to the P.R.C. authority with whom Dr. Kissinger was maintaining the discussions, it was Chiao Kuan-hua—just to clarify that point.

I don't think I really have much to add. Our talks under Secretary Rogers on our side, and Foreign Minister Chi Peng-fei for the People's Republic of China, extended over, I believe, 10 hours all together.

But it was not just the talks themselves. We had frequent occasion, as you could imagine with all the fine food you have eaten—occasionally waiting to have that fine food to have extensive talks also, and a number of matters could be discussed in that context.

Also, it was not just that, but the Secretary did have a chance to meet on a number of occasions with the Prime Minister. Most recently, coming down on the plane, he had an hour and a half from Peking to Hangchow. And then today the Prime Minister called on him in his hotel room for about 40 minutes.

I would say that the talks and the counterpart meetings were characterized by candor, friendliness, and courtesy and hospitality, as I am sure you have all seen, on the part of our Chinese hosts. There was no pulling of punches, not physically, of course. They were outspoken, no effort to cover up or paper over differences, but to have it out. It is good for the system. I think in so doing one has a much better appreciation of the other person's point of view.

As far as the specifics are concerned, in the talks, I really can't say much more than what already appears in the communiqué itself, although some of the points there may raise questions.

*   *   *

(b) Statement by Ronald L. Ziegler, Press Secretary to the President.[26]

(Complete Text)

President Nixon and Premier Chou En-lai have reached agreement on a joint communiqué.[27] This communiqué reflects the position of the United States and the People's Republic of China on various bilateral and international issues which were discussed during President Nixon's visit to the People's Republic of China.

The day President Nixon arrived in Peking [February 21] he met with Chairman Mao Tse-tung. The two leaders had a serious and frank exchange of views on Sino-U.S. relations and world affairs. During the President's 7-day visit to the People's Republic of China extensive, frank, and honest discussions were held between President Nixon and Premier Chou En-lai. The discussions were held on the normalization of relations between the United States and the People's Republic of China, as well as on other matters of interest to both sides.

The two leaders participated in over 15 hours of formal talks. In addition, Secretary of State Rogers and Foreign Minister Chi Peng-fei held discussions in the same spirit and participated in about 15 hours of formal discussions.

So the communiqué reflects over 30 hours of formal discussions between the United States and the People's Republic of China. The very fact of the joint communiqué between the two governments is symbolic of the greater understanding produced through the face-to-face discussions that have been held.

It is President Nixon's hope that this historic beginning to improve communications between the United States and the People's Republic of China will significantly contribute to a more stable structure of peace in the world.

The communiqué honestly reflects the differences that both sides recognize exist and states those areas where both sides found common views and have agreed to take specific steps to further improve their relationship. The communiqué, in stating its general attitude, says, "The leaders of the People's Republic of China and the United States of America found it beneficial to have this opportunity, after so many years without contact, to present candidly to one another their views on a variety of issues."

The communiqué goes on to say: "There are essential differences between China and the United States in their social systems and foreign policies. However, the two sides agreed that countries, regardless of their social systems, should conduct their relations on the principles of

---

[26] *Presidential Documents*, Feb. 28, 1972, p. 480.
[27] Document 54.

respect for the sovereignty and territorial integrity of all states, non-aggression against other states, non-interference in the internal affairs of other states, equality and mutual benefit, and peaceful coexistence. International disputes should be settled on this basis, without resorting to the use or threat of force. The United States and the People's Republic of China are prepared to apply these principles to their mutual relations."

(56) Return to the United States: Statement by President Nixon, Andrews Air Force Base, Maryland, February 28, 1972.[28]

(Complete Text)

THE PRESIDENT. *Mr. Vice President, Members of the Congress, Members of the Cabinet, Members of the Diplomatic Corps, and ladies and gentlemen:*

I want to express my very deep appreciation, and the appreciation of all of us, for this wonderfully warm welcome that you have given us and for the support that we have had on the trip that we have just completed from Americans of both political parties and all walks of life across this land.

Because of the superb efforts of the hardworking members of the press who accompanied us—they got even less sleep than I did—millions of Americans in this past week have seen more of China than I did. Consequently, tonight I would like to talk to you not about what we saw but about what we did, to sum up the results of the trip and to put it in perspective.

When I announced this trip last July,[29] I described it as a journey for peace. In the last 30 years, Americans have in three different wars gone off by the hundreds of thousands to fight, and some to die, in Asia and in the Pacific. One of the central motives behind my journey to China was to prevent that from happening a fourth time to another generation of Americans.

As I have often said, peace means more than the mere absence of war. In a technical sense, we were at peace with the People's Republic of China before this trip, but a gulf of almost 12,000 miles and 22 years of noncommunication and hostility separated the United States of America from the 750 million people who live in the People's Republic of China, and that is one-fourth of all the people in the world.

As a result of this trip, we have started the long process of building a bridge across that gulf, and even now we have something better than the mere absence of war. Not only have we completed a week of

[28] *Presidential Documents*, Feb. 28, 1972, pp. 483-5.
[29] *A.F.R., 1971*, no. 91.

intensive talks at the highest levels, we have set up a procedure whereby we can continue to have discussions in the future. We have demonstrated that nations with very deep and fundamental differences can learn to discuss those differences calmly, rationally, and frankly, without compromising their principles. This is the basis of a structure for peace, where we can talk about differences rather than fight about them.

The primary goal of this trip was to reestablish communication with the People's Republic of China after a generation of hostility. We achieved that goal. Let me turn now to our joint communiqué.[30]

We did not bring back any written or unwritten agreements that will guarantee peace in our time. We did not bring home any magic formula which will make unnecessary the efforts of the American people to continue to maintain the strength so that we can continue to be free.

We made some necessary and important beginnings, however, in several areas. We entered into agreements to expand cultural, educational, and journalistic contacts between the Chinese and the American people. We agreed to work to begin and broaden trade between our two countries. We have agreed that the communications that have now been established between our governments will be strengthened and expanded.

Most important, we have agreed on some rules of international conduct which will reduce the risk of confrontation and war in Asia and in the Pacific.

We agreed that we are opposed to domination of the Pacific area by any one power. We agreed that international disputes should be settled without the use of [or] the threat of force and we agreed that we are prepared to apply this principle to our mutual relations.

With respect to Taiwan, we stated our established policy that our forces overseas will be reduced gradually as tensions ease, and that our ultimate objective is to withdraw our forces as a peaceful settlement is achieved.

We have agreed that we will not negotiate the fate of other nations behind their backs, and we did not do so at Peking. There were no secret deals of any kind. We have done all this without giving up any United States commitment to any other country.

In our talks, the talks that I had with the leaders of the People's Republic and that the Secretary of State had with the office of the Government of the People's Republic in the foreign affairs area, we both realized that a bridge of understanding that spans almost 12,000 miles and 22 years of hostility can't be built in one week of discussions. But we have agreed to begin to build that bridge, recognizing that our work will require years of patient effort. We made no attempt to pre-

30 Document 54.

tend that major differences did not exist between our two governments, because they do exist.

This communiqué was unique in honestly setting forth differences rather than trying to cover them up with diplomatic doubletalk.

One of the gifts that we left behind in Hangchow was a planted sapling of the American redwood tree. As all Californians know, and as most Americans know, redwoods grow from saplings into the giants of the forest. But the process is not one of days or even years; it is a process of centuries.

Just as we hope that those saplings, those tiny saplings that we left in China, will grow one day into mighty redwoods, so we hope, too, that the seeds planted on this journey for peace will grow and prosper into a more enduring structure for peace and security in the Western Pacific.

But peace is too urgent to wait for centuries. We must seize the moment to move toward that goal now, and this is what we have done on this journey.

As I am sure you realize, it was a great experience for us to see the timeless wonders of ancient China, the changes that are being made in modern China. And one fact stands out, among many others, from my talks with the Chinese leaders. It is their total belief, their total dedication, to their system of government. That is their right, just as it is the right of any country to choose the kind of government it wants.

But as I return from this trip, just as has been the case on my return from other trips abroad which have taken me to over 80 countries, I come back to America with an even stronger faith in our system of government.

As I flew across America today, all the way from Alaska, over the Rockies, the Plains, and then on to Washington, I thought of the greatness of our country and, most of all, I thought of the freedom, the opportunity, the progress that 200 million Americans are privileged to enjoy. I realized again this is a beautiful country. And tonight my prayer and my hope is that as a result of this trip, our children will have a better chance to grow up in a peaceful world.

Thank you.

2. Developments Subsequent to the Visit.

[Some slowdown in the tempo of American-Chinese *rapprochement* was only to be expected in the months that followed the Nixon visit, a time when American attention was focused on developments in Vietnam and Moscow and when the Chinese leaders appeared to be concentrating heavily on the growth of China's economy and military potential. Although a channel for regular diplomatic communication was established soon after the presidential visit (Document 57) and Dr. Kissinger made a special trip to Peking to brief the Chinese leaders in the wake of the U.S.-Soviet summit (Document 58), by August Secretary of State Rogers was finding little that was new to report (Document 59).

China's subsequent veto of Bangladesh's application for U.N. membership on August 25, 1972 would be a fresh reminder that U.S. and Chinese Communist objectives did not invariably coincide. Although the United States had accepted the mainland government as the lawful representative of China in the United Nations, in accordance with the General Assembly's decision in 1971,[31] it continued to recognize its special commitments to the Republic of China government on Taiwan and showed no intention of according bilateral recognition to the People's Republic as the "sole legal government of China,"as numerous governments had done or were doing.

Trade between the United States and mainland China was meanwhile growing rapidly, from a one-sided $4.9 million imported from China by the United States in 1971 to a more nearly balanced $92.5 million in bilateral trade in 1972. Prospects for a further increase were authoritatively appraised in October in an address by Assistant Secretary of State Marshall Green (Document 60).]

(57) Establishment of a Channel of Communication: White House Announcement, March 10, 1972.[32]

(Complete Text)

The White House announced that the primary channel for further communication between the United States and the People's Republic of China will be the Ambassadors of the two countries in Paris. The United States Ambassador to France is Arthur K. Watson and the People's Republic's Ambassador to France is Huang Chen. Ambassador Watson met with the President today for consultation.[33]

---

[31] A.F.R., 1971, no. 125.
[32] Presidential Documents, Mar. 13, 1972, p. 556.
[33] An agreement by the two governments to establish liaison offices in each other's capitals was announced Feb. 19, 1973, and Ambassador David K.E. Bruce was designated Mar. 15, 1973 to head the U.S. liaison office in Peking.

(58) Visit by Dr. Kissinger to the People's Republic, June 19-23, 1972: Joint Statement Issued in Washington and Peking June 24, 1972.[34]

(Complete Text)

Premier Chou En-lai of the People's Republic of China and other Chinese officials held discussions with Dr. Henry A. Kissinger, Assistant to the U.S. President for National Security Affairs, and his party from June 19 to 23, 1972. The talks were extensive, earnest, and frank. They consisted of concrete consultations to promote the normalization of relations between the two countries and an exchange of views on issues of common interest.

Both sides agreed on the usefulness of these consultations which were foreseen in the Sino-U.S. joint communiqué of February 1972[35] and on the desirability of continuing them.

(59) Developments in U.S.-China Relations: Interview with Secretary of State Rogers, August 16, 1972.[36]

(Excerpt)

* * *

Mr. McCartney: The trip to China, as you know, has fascinated the world. Discussion about it has died down now some months later. What is developing, what has developed since the trip to further improve, if anything, the relationship with China, and what are we headed for there?

Secretary Rogers: Well, I think that the developments since the visit have been the developments that we expected—somewhat gradual, because it takes some effort to move quickly when you haven't had any contact with a nation for 22 years.

We have had meetings with the Chinese on a periodic basis. The things that we agreed to in terms of conversations, about admission of Americans to China and so forth, have gone on schedule. As you know,

---

34 *Presidential Documents*, June 26, 1972, p. 1086. For further reference to talks in Peking cf. Chapter V at note 60; also Kalb, *Kissinger*, pp. 337-8.
35 Document 54.
36 Department of State Press Release 202, Aug. 22, 1972; text from *Bulletin*, Sept. 11, 1972, p. 270. The interview was conducted Aug. 16 by James McCartney, Knight Newspapers, and first published Aug. 20, 1972.

Senators Mansfield and Scott[37] visited in China, and the majority leader and minority leader in the House[38] visited China. We have had Americans who went to the Chinese Trade Fair and received orders there. They were treated courteously and with respect by the Chinese. And we would expect that our relations would continue to improve and gradually we will develop more trade, we will have more exchanges.

As you know, Dr. Kissinger had a return trip after the Moscow visit.[39]

So that the relations are developing just about as we expected they would.

The Chinese have been very friendly. They have been restrained in their comments about the United States, and we on our part have, I think, been restrained in our comments. As far as we can tell, we are going to continue to improve our relations with the People's Republic of China. And we are particularly pleased that our allies in that part of the world have understood the President's purposes and have reported the success of his mission.[40]

* * *

(60) Trade in the Context of United States Relations with the People's Republic of China: Address by Assistant Secretary of State Green, Los Angeles, October 9, 1972.[41]

(Complete Text)

For more years than I care to count, I have looked to the day when China trade would be not just a subject of academic interest but a practical concern of practical men. This symposium, with its emphasis on the practical aspects of U.S.-China trade, is one more sign that that day has arrived. It is therefore with great personal satisfaction that I join your discussions.

In the panel meetings you will be attending today you will hear and talk with experts in this field, all of them men of wide experience and

---

[37] Senators Mike Mansfield (Democrat, Montana) and Hugh Scott (Republican, Pennsylvania), respectively majority and minority leaders of the Senate.
[38] Representatives Hale Boggs (Democrat, Louisiana) and Gerald R. Ford (Republican, Michigan).
[39] Cf. Document 58.
[40] Cf. Documents 64-65.
[41] Department of State Press Release 254; text from Bulletin, Oct. 30, 1972, pp. 489-94. The address was delivered before a China trade symposium sponsored by the Graduate School of Business Administration of the University of Southern California.

deserved international reputations. I could not add to the knowledge they will present to you.

What I would like to do instead is to place trade in the framework of our overall relationship with the People's Republic of China and to suggest why trade figures so importantly in the momentous changes we are witnessing.

To find a reference point in tackling a subject like this, I could go back a decade or more to a time when a number of us in the American Foreign Service, together with some of our colleagues in business and academe, were recommending that tight U.S. restrictions on trade and travel to mainland China be modified and that we enter into a real dialogue with Peking.[42] Or I could discuss the number of steps that were taken between 1962 and 1971 in modifying those restrictions, especially the rapid succession of measures undertaken by this administration from 1969 to 1971, to enable Americans to visit mainland China and to engage in trade.[43] These were unilateral administrative measures that required no U.S. legislative action or reciprocity from the Chinese side, and until recently they did not seem to produce much in the way of results. What changed the whole scene, of course, was the President's trip to China.

But rather than go over these events that are so well known to you, I would prefer to start with the joint communique issued at Shanghai on February 27 of this year.[44]

Those of you who have studied or had some experience in foreign affairs are well aware that communiques are often the least interesting or important result of diplomatic meetings. If that is the rule, then the joint communique is the exception. It is a remarkable document for several reasons. First of all, it is comprehensive, reflecting as it does all the understandings reached and all the discussions held. It is realistic, making no effort, either through omission or obscure language, to gloss over or minimize the differences that remain between us. On the contrary, it hits them head on. Indeed, the first area of common ground we found with the Chinese was that this is the style in which we both like to do business. The Chinese, no less than we, do not like to pretend that there are no differences when differences clearly exist.

Having stated our differences, however, we were able to outline possible areas of common interest and to specify ways in which we might proceed to work together toward the normalization of relations. Clearly implied in this document was the real breakthrough: that we could move forward without first resolving all those differences. Also clearly implied was the realization on both sides that whatever the broad ideological concerns that divide us, there should be few funda-

---

[42] Cf. *Documents, 1963*, pp. 301-11.
[43] Cf. *A.F.R., 1971*, nos. 86-87 and 90.
[44] Document 54.

mental differences in practical national-interest terms that time and mutual trust on both sides could not resolve. And most important of all, we agreed that improving relations was in the interest of both sides.

You will also note that the communique sets forth the specifics of how we will work to strengthen our relationships. We agreed to maintain contact through various channels, including the sending of a senior U.S. official to Peking from time to time. Later we announced that another channel or contact point had been established in Paris,[45] where discussions are continuing in the same constructive atmosphere that marked the summit meetings in Peking. We also agreed that increasing contact between our peoples was at least as important as official contact in developing and deepening this new relationship.

Neither of us meant by this that if we just get to know each other better, all our problems will disappear. There was a more practical consideration. For differing reasons, both the PRC and the United States evidently want to provide tangible evidence of a warming trend in our relations. Since, as the communique made clear, obstacles to improved relations remain, areas of common interest for the time being must be sought in less politically charged fields; hence, trade and exchanges.

On the specific subject of trade, the joint communique said:

> Both sides view bilateral trade as another area from which mutual benefit can be derived, and agreed that economic relations based on equality and mutual benefit are in the interest of the peoples of the two countries. They agree to facilitate the progressive development of trade between their two countries.

Note especially in that paragraph the repeated appearance of the phrase "mutual benefit" and its description of trade between our two countries as developing progressively. In other contexts the Chinese have talked about our relations, including trade, developing step by step. Implicit in this document is the thought that trade between our two countries has more than just economic significance. Or even if the volume of trade remained statistically microscopic—which is not likely—there are advantages to be derived from focusing attention on it.

ABSTRACT AND TANGIBLE GOALS

If the public eye is drawn to a succession of businessmen, trade groups, and technicians going back and forth between the United States

---

[45] Document 57.

and the PRC—sometimes concluding sales, sometimes not—the political point need not be stated. This very motion will testify to the existence of an improved relationship and will help create a climate in which cooperation in other areas may become possible.

There are other political advantages accruing to both sides which one should not lightly dismiss. Trade negotiations by private American firms may prove to be an especially significant arena for building mutual trust and confidence. Since major political issues are not likely to enter into these discussions, it should be possible to set a positive tone for future discussion of more troublesome matters. By the same token, the acquisition of negotiating skills and techniques can add to one nation's store of information about the other and thereby ease the way for later negotiations on improvement of political relations.

Moving from these relatively abstract goals to more tangible ones, Peking has beyond a doubt calculated the effect of improved trade relations with the United States on its chances for achieving its major policy goals. By trading with the PRC, the United States overtly demonstrates its acceptance of the Peking Government even if it does not involve formal recognition. In the speech of a top PRC leader, Marshal Yeh Chien-ying, delivered on the occasion of October 1 National Day celebrations a week ago, this theme comes across loud and clear. Even granting some of Peking's outdated perceptions of the nature of the present-day capitalist mind, it is not unreasonable for Chinese leaders to believe that U.S. businessmen who benefit from U.S.-PRC trade might influence American political opinion in ways that may be mutually beneficial.

By facilitating trade with the United States, Peking also moves toward its goal of diversifying its markets and sources of supply. Peking undoubtedly calculates that if it can develop new sources of supply for its import requirements, it will never again be so dependent on any single trading partner as to become vulnerable to efforts to exert political pressure on China through trade. Those of you who have read Chinese history, as well as the newspaper accounts of China's more recent national experience, will appreciate that the need to be economically independent holds a high priority in China.

To say that political considerations are important is not to suggest, however, that expanding PRC trade relations with the United States will not be of mutual economic benefit as well. While the U.S. economy as a whole may not be affected significantly by any foreseeable U.S.-PRC trade which may develop, specific U.S. industries will benefit. We have already seen this in the recent deals for Boeing aircraft, RCA communications equipment, and wheat, and we may see it again in other industries which can derive important benefit—machine tools, for example, or other sales of aircraft and parts.

CONSTRAINTS ON RAPID EXPANSION OF TRADE

Having mentioned these advantages related to expansion of Sino-U.S. trade, I want to inject a note of caution. There are definite constraints placed on rapid expansion of U.S.-PRC trade by both political and economic considerations. China's reputation as the most revolutionary of the revolutionaries is somewhat offset by its equal renown as one of the most conservative states in international financial dealings. Unlike many of the developing countries which have consciously borrowed heavily in order to finance economic development, the PRC has financed its imports either by immediate payment or on ordinary 18-month commercial terms. Even during the most revolutionary phases of its recent history, the PRC preserved its reputation for scrupulous financial dealings. Credits were and are paid off on schedule or even in advance. What this means, of course, is not that the PRC has unlimited cash reserves but that it has preferred to limit its imports to the extent of its ability to generate funds through export earnings.

This does not suggest that Peking insists on balanced trade with each and every partner; because of its large net export earnings from Hong Kong, it has a certain leeway to accept an unfavorable balance of trade on a bilateral basis with such nations as Japan. Moreover, there have recently been some indications that in special cases the PRC may be willing to incur a short-term debt in order to acquire a high-priority item. In general, though, China maintains the principle that it will stand on its own feet. We do not anticipate, therefore, that the PRC will choose to incur long-term debt or allow a significant or prolonged deficit in its balance of trade with another nation.

As long as Peking remains wedded to its policy of "self-sufficiency," it is difficult to envision a dramatic increase in the level of foreign trade. The "self-sufficiency" doctrine has a number of implications for the growth of foreign trade, none of them positive. This philosophy by definition places foreign trade almost in the category of a necessary evil; foreign trade can only be an adjunct of domestic economic development whereby China acquires abroad whatever technology and essential goods it cannot produce at home. Because Peking perceives trade in this light, there has been a disinclination to foster the development of export-oriented industries, even if these would afford the PRC competitive advantages in the world market. In fact, the PRC has at times in the past turned aside requests to modify its products to make them more marketable in the West. Finally, because the PRC remains basically a subsistence agricultural economy and because all imports are handled through state trading corporations, it is highly unlikely that consumer goods will appear for some time to come among the priority items in the annual state plan.

American businessmen must also consider that the PRC has developed well-established trading relationships over the years with low-cost suppliers of its major import needs. Most of the PRC's grain comes from Canada or Australia, while capital goods, metals, and fertilizers have been imported from Japanese and western European suppliers. While it will not be impossible for American firms to break into this market—in fact, given the PRC's desire to diversify its sources of supply, it is likely that some penetration will be accomplished—it would be unrealistic to anticipate major sales at the expense of the Japanese and western Europeans except in certain high-technology areas, particularly so long as the political impediments remain.

CHINESE PRAGMATISM AND FLEXIBILITY

As long as I am smashing misconceptions about the China market, I might as well throw some cold water on another popular myth. I want to emphasize that the PRC has established quite a record for pragmatism and flexibility in its business dealings, legends about the strong ideological orientation of the Chinese notwithstanding. Many of you have probably read reports of Chinese favoritism toward "ideologically correct" firms and refusal to deal with those firms considered to be "reactionary." This has occurred in isolated instances; the Chinese, as they themselves point out, do not separate politics and economics. But within that principle there is room for a considerable degree of flexibility and pragmatism. In most cases, then, I think you will find that PRC negotiators are more interested in the quality of your product and the size of your market than in your political opinions. What I am suggesting is that there is no advantage for an American businessman to suggest that he supports policies popular in Peking or that he has been a consistent opponent of some of his own government's policies. Indeed, such a bearing may only serve to place you at a negotiating disadvantage with the Chinese, who do not respect cheap devices for currying favor.

Little research is necessary to unearth confirmation that the Chinese are indeed pragmatic when it comes to business. Up to 1970, only three of the PRC's 10 largest trading partners had extended diplomatic recognition to Peking. The PRC recently concluded a major wheat deal with the Australians, in spite of the fact that the PRC leadership continued to differ with the foreign policy of the Australian Government. When Prime Minister Tanaka arrived in Peking at the end of last month to negotiate the normalization of relations between his country and the PRC, it was evidently made clear to him and other members of his party that continued trade ties with Taiwan would not constitute a barrier in PRC eyes to a Japan-PRC rapprochement.[46] Price and quality, not politics, generally determine the decision for the PRC negoti-

---

[46] Cf. below at note 53.

ators. None of this means, however, that you need not concern your-
selves with Chinese sensitivities or that you could engage in political
argument without affecting your business prospects. The Chinese are
perceptive people who appreciate normal courtesy; they are also quick
to detect insincerity.

DIALOGUE BETWEEN NATIONS

It seems to me that the great changes that have taken place in our
relations with the PRC could not have been achieved without certain
changes in the attitudes prevailing in both Peking and Washington. For
example, it is hardly conceivable that this evolution in our relationship
could have occurred at the time of the Great Leap Forward or its
aftermath or during the period of the subsequent Cultural Revolution
in China. In other words, it would have been very difficult indeed for
these changes to have come about before 1969. Similarly, I am convinced that this breakthrough would not have been possible without the
leadership and the commitment that President Nixon has given to the
task of ending the period of U.S.-PRC confrontation.

After 23 years of mutual antagonism and drearily sustained deadlock,
the task of persuading the PRC to join with us in greatly improving our
relations seemed herculean. Something more than small steps was called
for. A dramatic gesture was needed to dispel any suspicions in Peking
that our intentions might be directed at short-term domestic political
gains or at giving merely the appearance of progress. Despite the risks so
often associated with personal diplomacy, the President recognized that
the summitry approach would best convey to the Chinese his determination to stake the prestige and authority of his Presidency on the new
policy. Moreover, personal contact at the highest level was necessary to
overcome the misunderstandings and myths which had grown up during
decades of nondialogue. A new relationship had to be inaugurated on
the basis of candor, not evasiveness; on friendly discussion, not glacial
silence or steaming rhetoric; and above all, on growing mutual perceptions that perhaps there was more common ground in our national
interests than was apparent from our wide ideological differences. To
seize the moment, which could in fact be a fleeting moment, required
personal rapport between leaders. The result was the Peking summit
meetings.

Developing relations between the United States and the PRC during
the past seven months attest to the success of the Peking summit. Most
significantly, the leaders of China seem to have a clearer understanding
of U.S. policy and objectives in East Asia. Implementation of the Nixon
doctrine,[47] for example, supplied persuasive evidence that the United

---

[47] Cf. *A.F.R., 1971*, no. 82.

States did not in fact have designs on China and that it was not seeking to isolate or contain China. On the contrary, it was manifestly our view that the PRC should be involved in the international mainstream and that the great problems of our planet could not be resolved without the participation of China in finding solutions and implementing them.

It is not only in terms of U.S.-PRC relations that the summit was a success, however. As I suggested earlier, the approach to Peking was only a part of a coherent new world view. Perhaps even more significant than the opening of a PRC-U.S. dialogue was the impression made on other nations by this successful summitry. The U.S.-PRC precedent seemed to make all things possible. Longtime antagonists could approach each other on the basis of shared interests rather than abiding differences. We have recently seen a series of summit-type meetings between nations, some of which had just barely been on speaking terms, if indeed they had communicated at all. On July 4 of this year, South and North Korea jointly announced that they would meet to discuss ways and means of attaining the mutually desired objective of national reunification.[48] As a direct consequence of the Peking summit, there thus seems to have emerged a new pattern of international relations, a new mode of international behavior.

Encouraging as it may be that nations are now competing in image building and that countries which used to appear intransigent now worry less about appearing tough and more about appearing at least as flexible and conciliatory as their rivals, the millennium is not yet upon us. Serious problems and dangers remain. Yet for the first time in this generation there is at least the hope that there can eventuate a pattern of international relationships which can serve the legitimate interests of all nations and a climate in which each nation will see that it is in its interest to pursue its goals by means which do not undermine this new trend.

We proceed on the assumption that no nation is abandoning its goals or what it perceives as its major interests. But there now seems to be a trend among at least the greater powers to pursue their goals through means less likely to involve themselves in war. In other words, sharp competition will continue to mark relations between nations, and ideologies may not change; but it is to be hoped that in a world of expanded dialogue, trade, and exchanges between nations—even between nations of opposing ideologies—there can be the real beginnings of a lasting peace. The President's trip to Peking made a major contribution to that goal.

[48] Cf. note 85 below.

B. The United States and Japan.[49]

[In seeking *rapprochement* with mainland China, the Nixon administration entertained no thought of downgrading U.S. relations with Japan, America's second largest trading partner (after Canada) and a crucial element in the new "pentagonal" style of foreign policy thinking.[50] If anything, American leaders seemed specially anxious to reassure the Japanese and to enlist their continued cooperation following the "Nixon shocks" attendant on U.S. action regarding China policy and international economic matters in the summer of 1971.[51]

The many-sided American concern with Japanese affairs, analyzed in depth in another speech by Assistant Secretary of State Green (Document 61), gave rise to two successive bilateral meetings "at the summit" in what proved to be an important year of readjustment for Japan as well as the United States. In January 1972, President Nixon conferred at San Clemente, California, with Prime Minister Eisaku Sato (Document 62), a veteran statesman whose six-year tenure was to be crowned on May 15 by the reversion to Japanese authority of the formerly U.S.-occupied Ryukyu Islands in line with the agreement signed in 1971.[52] In August, the President met in Hawaii with Sato's successor, Kakuei Tanaka (Document 63), whose accession had been felt by many to mark the conclusion of Japan's "postwar" era and the opening of a new period marked by different problems and opportunities.

Beginning his administration with a burst of activity, Tanaka was to follow his meeting with the President by paying a visit to Peking, where he succeeded in "normalizing" Japan's relations with the People's Republic of China by accepting the latter's claim to be the "sole legal government" of China and agreeing to a severance of diplomatic (but not economic) relations with the Taiwan regime.[53] The new Prime Minister would be less successful, however, in his attempts to negotiate a peace treaty with the U.S.S.R., avoid a further revaluation of the yen against the dollar,[54] or improve the position of his Liberal Democratic Party in the elections to the Lower House of the Diet on December 10, 1972.]

[49] For more detailed discussion cf. Nixon Report, 1972, pp. 52-9; same, 1973, pp. 94-105.
[50] Cf. above at note 1.
[51] Cf. *A.F.R., 1971*, no. 97.
[52] Same, no. 95.
[53] Joint statement, Sept. 30, 1972; excerpts in Keesing's, pp. 25517-8.
[54] Under the Smithsonian agreement of Dec. 18, 1971, the yen was revalued upward against the dollar by 16.88 per cent, from 360 to the dollar to 308 to the dollar. The second devaluation of the dollar on Feb. 12, 1973 and the simultaneous floating of the yen resulted in a further upward revaluation of the yen, which stood at 263.1577 to the dollar as of Mar. 30, 1973.

(61) "Mutual Trust and Security in U.S.-Japan Relations": Address by Assistant Secretary of State Green Before the Japan-America Society, Washington, September 21, 1972.[55]

(Complete Text)

Speaking before the Japan-America Society for the first time inevitably calls to mind my first association with this society. It was back in 1939 when, fresh from Yale, I was signed on as Ambassador [Joseph Clark] Grew's private secretary and accompanied him back to Japan on the *Tatsuta Maru*. Almost immediately after our arrival in Japan, he delivered his famous October 19 address before the Japan-America Society.[56] This straight-from-the-horse's-mouth speech—as Grew was wont to call it because of its directness and frankness—was an attempt to bring home to the Japanese the realities of American public opinion and of American policy in the Far East.

The history of the relations of our two countries has undergone tumultuous changes since then, and great strides have been taken in recent years toward establishing our relations with Japan on a stable and durable base. Both America and Japan today recognize their interdependence. They both recognize that their relations with each other are more significant and important than their relations with any other countries.

Yet we are not without our problems. For example, there has been the series of so-called "Nixon shocks" of 1971:

—The sudden announcement on July 15 of the President's intention to visit Peking.[57]

—The August 15 announcement of our new economic policy and the imposition of an import surcharge that led to the Smithsonian agreement and the revaluation of the yen.[58]

—The decisions taken in October on Japanese synthetic textile exports to the United States.[59]

There was also the defeat we suffered a year ago on the resolution sponsored by both Japan and the United States that would have retained a seat in the U.N. General Assembly for the Republic of China.[60]

All of these events caused some observers to feel that we were mishandling this vital relationship with Japan, that somehow we had

[55] *Bulletin*, Dec. 18, 1972, pp. 703-7.
[56] *Documents, 1939-1940*, pp. 249-60.
[57] *A.F.R., 1971*, no. 91.
[58] Same, nos. 142 and 150; cf. note 54 above.
[59] *A.F.R., 1971*, p. 367.
[60] Same, no. 123c.

lost contact with each other, lost the ability to communicate, or that our policies were beginning to diverge seriously. While the President's initiative on China was widely applauded—including in Japan—there were those who felt that we were in danger of sacrificing the obvious benefits of close ties with a proven friend of immense economic power and enormous potential influence, namely, Japan, for uncertain gains through a new relationship with an adversary power, namely, the PRC [People's Republic of China].

Some have even attempted to draw direct parallels between the course of events in our relations with Japan during the early 1970's with those of the early 1930's. For example, last year at a staff meeting I read a confidential report received from the Embassy in Tokyo which commented as follows on Japan's burgeoning exports to an increasingly alarmed international community:

Japan now finds herself like nothing so much as a high-powered steam engine with a particularly stout gang of stokers shovelling fuel under the boilers; and a number of onlookers busy securing every orifice against the escape of steam. It requires no prophet to foresee the result.

Japanese goods of increasingly wider range and higher quality are finding their way into industrialized countries. The charges of "dumping" freely levelled against Japan are, in every case that it has been possible to investigate, found to be without foundation. Japanese wages are low. Japanese currency is undervalued. And these two great advantages are given a deadly effectiveness by the enterprise and industry of the Japanese. Many countries are considering measures to curtail Japanese exports by raising import duties or establishing import quotas or exchange compensation surtaxes. And as Japanese exports increase, Japanese competition has to be faced in practically every country of the world. Yet economic nationalism is a growing force to be reckoned with—and the days are numbered of unlimited exports of Japanese goods to countries from which Japan is unwilling to import anything in return.

After reading this excerpt, I asked whether the staff thought the Embassy's report was overdrawn. Some thought it was somewhat overdrawn, some didn't; but no one recalled seeing that particular Embassy report. I replied perhaps they were too young to remember it because it was a British Embassy, Tokyo, report dated March 1933. *Plus ça change—*

But tonight I would like to present to you a view that is a great deal more optimistic than the one I have just been discussing. The experiences that lead me to this more optimistic outlook are fairly recent in time and involve a relatively new and sometimes controversial element in international diplomacy—summitry, the meeting of heads of government for direct discussions of matters of moment. First, a word or two about summitry in general:

—Summitry is a fairly recent phenomenon. There have been many summits before, but thanks largely to the speed of jet aircraft, meetings by chiefs of government involve only a few days' absence from country or capital.

—Summitry is controversial. It builds expectations, and the glare of publicity tends either to magnify failures or overinflate successes. It also arouses suspicions of secret deals. Incidentally, there have been none of these in any of the President's summit meetings.

—Summitry has also proven very useful. It forces governments to focus hard on mutual problems. Summit meetings impose deadlines for the solution of pressing problems.

—Successful summitry involves careful preparation—mountains of memoranda and position papers and advance negotiations.

—Summitry also gives leaders the opportunity for personal talks and establishes rapport between leaders. Summitry is, in short, a difficult, intricate art which is potentially highly useful.

President Nixon has made it his personal style to meet world leaders, and he has been successful in dealing directly and systematically with the most important foreign policy issues. This has been particularly true with Japan. I have in mind three major summit meetings during President Nixon's administration:

President Nixon and Prime Minister [Eisaku] Sato met in Washington during November 1969;[61] they met again at San Clemente in January 1972;[62] and the President met Prime Minister [Kakuei] Tanaka at Kuilima, Hawaii, August 31-September 1, 1972.[63]

Each of these represented a step forward in the evolution of the U.S.-Japan relationship. Parenthetically, each seems to have brought President Nixon and the rest of his delegation further westward, closer to Japan itself.

As I have just said, summitry forces governments to face up to basic issues and reach decisions based on a realistic assessment of national interests. Certainly each of these three meetings had a substantive result that might not have been possible without participation at the highest levels. Let me illustrate this with a brief look at each of these occasions.

At the first meeting in November 1969, Prime Minister Sato was nearing the end of a long term in office in which he had set his sights on obtaining the reversion of Okinawa. President Nixon, new in office, was

61 *Documents, 1968-69,* pp. 336-41.
62 Document 62.
63 Document 63.

well aware that Japanese and Okinawan sentiment could no longer brook continued U.S. administration over the 1 million Japanese citizens on Okinawa. He was mindful that future U.S.-Japan relations depended on the United States now fulfilling its pledge to return Okinawa to Japan. And both governments wanted to prevent the Security Treaty[64] from becoming a serious issue when on June 26, 1970, after its initial 10 years, it entered a new phase under which either side could abrogate it upon one year's notice.

Details on terms of the Okinawa reversion had long been discussed by Embassy Tokyo, the State Department, and the Defense Department with our various Japanese opposites. On this and other issues raised at the Sato-Nixon summit in Washington, the ground had been carefully prepared.

I firmly believe that the Sato-Nixon communique[65] was the most significant single document in East Asian affairs these past three years. This is not to minimize the great importance of the Shanghai communique last February.[66] The effect of the Washington summit meeting in 1969 was to put our relations with Japan on a new footing based on interdependence. The two leaders agreed that:

—First, the Mutual Security Treaty of 1960 was of continuing importance;

—Second, the United States should continue to be in a position to carry out its security obligations in the Far East;

—Third, Okinawa should revert to Japan in 1972, with the United States retaining its bases there under the basic terms of the Mutual Security Treaty;

—Fourth, Japan would rapidly reduce its restrictions on the import of U.S. goods and capital to Japan; and

—Fifth, Japan in effect pledged itself to give far more concessional aid to developing countries. Incidentally, in the communique the President and Prime Minister recognized that there would be major requirements for the postwar rehabilitation in Viet-Nam and elsewhere in Southeast Asia. The Prime Minister stated the intention of the Japanese Government to make a substantial contribution to this end.

These agreements had the desired effect. The antitreaty movement in Japan subsided; June 26, 1970, became just another day.[67] Prime

[64] Treaty of Mutual Cooperation and Security between the United States and Japan, signed at Washington Jan. 19, 1960 and entered into force June 23, 1960 (TIAS 4509; 11 UST 1632); text and related documents in *Documents, 1960*, pp. 425-31.
[65] Same as note 61.
[66] Document 54.
[67] Cf. U.S. and Japanese statements of June 22, 1970 in *Documents, 1970*, pp. 217-19.

Minister Sato and the Liberal Democratic Party (LDP) won the national election the following month in impressive fashion, and Japan's relationship with the United States was not an issue in that election.

The second meeting, at San Clemente in January 1972, took place under very different circumstances.[68] It occurred six months after the July 15, 1971, announcement of the President's planned trip to Peking and at a time when Prime Minister Sato was in his last months in office. In fact, a political struggle was shaping up within the LDP between Foreign Minister [Takeo] Fukuda and MITI [Ministry of International Trade and Industry] Minister Tanaka, both of whom were present at San Clemente, as to who was going to succeed Prime Minister Sato. The Japanese were still recovering from the so-called "Nixon shocks," showing some signs of resentment. President Nixon was about to leave for Peking, with the Japanese uncertain of the outcome and frustrated over Peking's refusal to deal with them.

The task for us, however, was twofold:

—First, to restore Japanese confidence in our ability and intention to handle our relationship with the PRC without harming U.S.-Japanese relations;

—Second, to convince the Japanese of the need for action to correct our growing trade imbalance.

While the results of San Clemente were not immediately apparent, it proved to be helpful in preparing the way for the President's trip to Peking and in restoring confidence and understanding on both sides. I might add that although it was a less important meeting than either Washington or Kuilima, it was in some ways the most pleasant. This was because the Japanese and American delegations shared the same hotel at Newport Beach, and there were many informal meetings between old friends from the *Gaimusho* and the State Department.

This brings us to the third meeting, at Kuilima, Hawaii, August 31, 1972. Between the time of the San Clemente summit and the Kuilima summit, considerable change had occurred. President Nixon's trip to China had occurred, culminating in the Shanghai communique. The President had subsequently visited Moscow. The Ryukyus did revert to Japan on schedule—May 15—in an impressive Tokyo ceremony. The United States no longer held any Japanese territory. It was now up to the Russians to return to Japan what was rightfully Japanese.

In early July 1972, Mr. Tanaka became Prime Minister and was being wooed by Peking, which now seemed more conciliatory toward Japan and at least as eager as Japan to normalize relations. There were signs that Mr. Tanaka would shortly be going to Peking.

The joint statement issued at the conclusion of the Kuilima meet-

68 Cf. Document 62.

ing[69] reflected agreement and understanding on a wide range of issues. But the real message of Kuilima was that both Japan and the United States would pursue essentially the same goals but each would recognize the different circumstances in which the other must operate and accept the fact that the other may have to take somewhat different paths at times toward the same goals. In any case, it was clearly understood that Japan's normalization of relations with the PRC should in no way impair the Mutual Security Treaty or our ability to deliver on our commitments in the Far East.

Kuilima was preceded by a lot of hard diplomatic spadework, including agreement on specific short-term measures to reduce the imbalance in our bilateral trade account. This agreement was also announced at Kuilima.[70]

Prime Minister Tanaka described Kuilima as a family gathering. The President was obviously reassured that while Japan had a new pitcher on its ball team—with perhaps a different assortment of pitches—the team remained essentially the same and Prime Minister Tanaka would not move the franchise to another league.

For his part, Prime Minister Tanaka had every right to feel reassured that our policies toward Japan and toward China and toward other major issues remain steadfast, that we place the highest value on our relationship with Prime Minister Tanaka's government, and that we shared Prime Minister Tanaka's hope that his visit to the PRC would serve to further the trend toward relaxation of tension in Asia.

Japan, it would seem, had gained new awareness of its negotiating power and leverage; and despite its firm determination not to develop a military force for operations beyond Japan, it could play the diplomatic power game like any other nation in Japan's position.

By now, the so-called "Nixon shocks" had receded into the background. Japan had come to see that the President's initiative toward China, far from being a blow to Japan, was a boon to Japan.

And I might add, parenthetically, that for over two decades now American policies in East Asia have been almost uniformly of great benefit to Japan. These include our enlightened occupation policies, the stand we took in Korea in 1950, the stand we took in Viet-Nam and in Southeast Asia generally, and now the moves the President has taken to improve our relations with the PRC while maintaining our ties with the Republic of China on Taiwan.

I am told that in Hawaiian, *kuilima* means "arm in arm." That's a

---

[69] Document 63.

[70] Following a series of meetings between U.S. Ambassador to Japan Robert Ingersoll and Deputy Vice Minister for Foreign Affairs Kiyohiko Tsurumi, it was announced Sept. 1, 1972 that the two governments had agreed on a number of short-term measures that included Japanese purchase of U.S. goods and services exceeding $1 billion (*Presidential Documents*, Sept. 1, 1972, p. 1335).

good omen. It means that at least we are facing and moving in the same direction.

But I expect we will continue to face difficulties. There have always been some in Japan who would dispense with our security relationship. We will also continue to be competitors in our own markets and in third countries. So I wouldn't be so naive as to suggest that at Kuilima we settled all of our problems; for we clearly did not.

What the President, Prime Minister Tanaka, Secretary Rogers, and Foreign Minister [Masayoshi] Ohira did do at Kuilima was to help build a basis for resolving these and other problems and to achieve a greater degree of mutual trust and confidence than has marked our relations for years.

That, I submit, is achieving a great deal; and I doubt whether it could have been accomplished in any other way than through the atmosphere and evolving decisions reached at the major summits of Washington, San Clemente, and Kuilima.

(62) Meeting at San Clemente: Joint Statement by President Nixon and Prime Minister Eisaku Sato Following Their Meetings at the Western White House, San Clemente, January 7, 1972.[71]

(Complete Text)

Prime Minister Sato and President Nixon, meeting in San Clemente on January 6 and 7, 1972 had wide-ranging and productive discussions that reflected the close, friendly relations between Japan and the United States. They covered the general international situation with particular emphasis on Asia including China, as well as bilateral relations between Japan and the United States.

The Prime Minister and the President recognized that in the changing world situation today, there are hopeful trends pointing toward a relaxation of tension, and they emphasized the need for further efforts to encourage such trends so as to promote lasting peace and stability. These efforts would involve close cooperation between the two governments and other governments. They also recognized that the maintenance of cooperative relations between Japan and the United States is an indispensable factor for peace and stability in Asia, and accordingly they confirmed that the two Governments would continue to consult closely on their respective Asian policies.

The Prime Minister and the President, recalling the more than one hundred years of association between the two countries, emphasized the importance of U.S.-Japanese relations being founded on mutual

[71] *Presidential Documents*, Jan. 10, 1972, pp. 34-6.

trust and interdependence. In this connection, they highly valued the important role played by the Treaty of Mutual Cooperation and Security between Japan and the United States.[72]

The Prime Minister and the President discussed the problems relating to the return of Okinawa as contemplated in the Joint Communiqué of November 21, 1969.[73] They were gratified that the Reversion Agreement signed on June 17, 1971[74] had received the support of the respective legislatures, and decided to effect the return of Okinawa to Japan on May 15, 1972. The President indicated the intention of the United States Government to confirm upon reversion that the assurances of the United States Government concerning nuclear weapons on Okinawa have been fully carried out. To this the Prime Minister expressed his deep appreciation. The Prime Minister explained to the President why he felt it necessary that, after reversion, the facilities and areas of the United States armed forces located in Okinawa be realigned or reduced to the extent possible, particularly those in areas densely populated or closely related to industrial development. The President replied that these factors would be taken fully into consideration in working out after reversion mutually acceptable adjustments in the facilities and areas consistent with the purpose of the Treaty of Mutual Cooperation and Security.

Recognizing that the further strengthening of the already close economic ties between Japan and the United States was of vital importance to the overall relations between the two countries as well as to the expansion of the world economy as a whole, the Prime Minister and the President expressed their satisfaction that significant progress was being made, particularly since the meeting of the Japan-United States Committee on Trade and Economic Affairs last September,[75] towards improvement of trade conditions and economic relations between the two countries.

They shared the expectation that the international currency realignment of last December[76] would provide a firm basis on which to chart future development of the world economy, and stated their determination to exert renewed efforts, in combination with other countries, towards improved monetary arrangements, expanded world trade and assisting developing countries. In this connection they affirmed the importance of conditions that facilitate the flow of both public assistance and private capital.

The Prime Minister and the President reaffirmed the basic view that Japan and the United States, jointly ascribing [*sic*] to the principles of

---

[72] Cf. note 64 above.
[73] *Documents, 1968-69*, pp. 336-41.
[74] *A.F.R., 1971*, no. 95.
[75] Sept. 9-10, 1971; for communiqué see *Bulletin*, Oct. 4, 1971, pp. 346-54.
[76] *A.F.R., 1971*, no. 150; cf. note 54 above.

freedom and democracy, would cooperate closely with each other in all areas such as the political, cultural, economic, scientific and technological fields to achieve the common goals of maintaining and promoting peace and prosperity of the world and the well-being of their countrymen.

They agreed that the two Governments would expand cooperation in the fields of environment, of the peaceful uses of atomic energy and the peaceful exploration and use of outer space. They further agreed that experts of the two countries would examine concrete steps in this regard. They also agreed that steps be taken to increase cultural exchanges and in this regard the President welcomed the explanation given on the contemplated establishment of a Japanese cultural exchange program.

(63) Meeting at Kuilima: Joint Statement by President Nixon and Prime Minister Kakuei Tanaka Following Their Meetings at Kuilima Hotel, Oahu, Hawaii, September 1, 1972.[77]

(Complete Text)

1. Prime Minister Tanaka and President Nixon met in Hawaii August 31-September 1 for wide ranging discussions on a number of topics of mutual interest. The talks were held in an atmosphere of warmth and mutual trust reflecting the long history of friendship between Japan and the United States. Both leaders expressed the hope that their meeting would mark the beginning of a new chapter in the course of developing ever closer bonds between the two countries.

2. The Prime Minister and the President reviewed the current international situation and the prospects for the relaxation of tension and peaceful solutions to current problems in the world, with particular reference to Asia. It was stressed that the maintenance and strengthening of the close ties of friendship and cooperation between the two countries would continue to be an important factor for peace and stability in the evolving world situation. Both leaders reaffirmed the intention of the two governments to maintain the Treaty of Mutual Cooperation and Security between the two countries[78] and agreed that the two governments would continue to cooperate through close consultations with a view to ensuring smooth and effective implementation of the Treaty.

3. In discussing the increasing indications for peace and stability in Asia, the Prime Minister and the President welcomed the recent opening

---

[77] *Presidential Documents*, Sept. 11, 1972, pp. 1332-4.
[78] Cf. note 64 above.

of dialogue in the Korean Peninsula,[79] and the increasingly active efforts of Asian countries for self-reliance and regional cooperation, and shared the hope for an early realization of peace in Indochina. The Prime Minister and the President recognized that the President's recent visits to the People's Republic of China and the USSR were a significant step forward. In this context, they shared the hope that the forthcoming visit of the Prime Minister to the People's Republic of China[80] would also serve to further the trend for the relaxation of tension in Asia.

4. The Prime Minister and the President discussed the recent agreements reached by the United States and the USSR on the limitation of ballistic missile defenses and the interim arrangement on the limitation of strategic offensive missiles,[81] and they agreed that such measures represented an important step forward in limiting strategic arms and contributing to world peace. They agreed to consult on the need for further steps to control strategic arms.

5. The Prime Minister and the President exchanged views in a broad perspective on issues related to economic, trade and financial matters. The Prime Minister and the President emphasized the great importance of economic relations between Japan and the United States. Both leaders expressed their conviction that their talks would contribute to closer cooperation between the two countries in dealing with economic issues of a bilateral and global nature.

6. The Prime Minister and the President shared the view that fundamental reform of the international monetary system is essential. They committed their governments to work rapidly to achieve such reform. In trade, they reaffirmed the February 1972 commitments of both countries to initiate and actively support multilateral trade negotiations covering both industry and agriculture in 1973.[82] In this connection they noted the need in the forthcoming trade negotiations to lay the basis for further trade expansion through reduction of tariff and nontariff barriers as well as formulations of a multilateral non-discriminatory safeguard mechanism.

7. The Prime Minister and the President agreed that both countries would endeavor to move towards a better equilibrium in their balance of payments and trade positions. In this regard, the President explained the measures undertaken by the United States to improve its trade and payments position and stated that the Government of the United States was urging U.S. firms to expand the volume of exports through increased productivity and improved market research, particularly to Japan. The Prime Minister indicated that the Government of Japan

[79] Cf. note 85 below.
[80] Cf. above at note 53.
[81] Documents 13-14.
[82] Cf. Chapter X at note 28.

would also try to promote imports from the United States[83] and that it was the intention of the Government of Japan to reduce the imbalance to a more manageable size within a reasonable period of time. The Prime Minister and the President agreed that it would be most valuable to hold future meetings at a high level to review evolving economic relationships, and that they intend to hold a meeting of the Joint United States-Japan Committee on Trade and Economic Affairs as early in 1973 as feasible.[84]

8. The Prime Minister and the President noted the endeavors of the two countries, in cooperation with other developed countries, to help bring stability and prosperity to the developing countries in Asia and other regions of the world. They acknowledged the need for adequate levels of official development assistance on appropriate terms. They also reaffirmed that the two governments intend to continue to help strengthen the international financial institutions for the purpose of economic development of the developing countries.

9. The Prime Minister and the President reaffirmed the need to promote efforts to improve the mutual understanding of the cultural, social and other backgrounds between the peoples of the two countries. They agreed further that new and improved programs of cultural and educational exchange are an important means to this end. In this connection the President underlined his high hopes for the successful activities of the Japan Foundation to be inaugurated in October this year.

10. The Prime Minister and the President noted with satisfaction the growing momentum of cooperation between the two countries in increasingly diverse fields under the common aims of maintaining and promoting peace and prosperity of the world and the well-being of their countrymen. They agreed to strengthen and expand the already close cooperation between the two countries in controlling the illegal traffic in narcotics and other dangerous drugs, and they also agreed on the need for further bilateral and multilateral cooperation concerning the development and better utilization of energy and mineral resources and on the pressing problems of environmental protection and pollution control. They pledged to continue appropriate assistance through the UN and its specialized agencies for the solution of problems caused by too rapid population growth.

11. The Prime Minister and the President discussed cooperation in space exploration including Japan's goal of launching geo-stationary communications and other applications satellites. The President welcomed Japan's active interest in and study on the launching of a meteorological satellite in support of the global atmospheric research program.

[83] Cf. note 70 above.
[84] The ninth meeting of the Joint Committee was held in Tokyo July 16-17, 1973; text of final communiqué in *Bulletin*, Aug. 13, 1973, pp. 246-8.

12. The Prime Minister and the President expressed satisfaction with their talks and agreed to continue to maintain close personal contact.

C. SEATO and ANZUS.

[The problems of Pacific security that had loomed so large through much of the postwar period could be viewed with somewhat lessened concern in the early 1970s, thanks to the growing détente between the United States and its principal "cold war" adversaries, the gradual movement toward settlement of the Indo-china conflict, the opening of a cautious dialogue between North and South Korea,[85] and the consequent growth of emphasis on the economic and social aspects of international affairs in Asia and elsewhere. Despite these changes in the international climate, the regional security alliances negotiated during the 1950s remained in being and continued to provide a forum for the exchange of views on current trends in Asia and the Pacific.

As in earlier years, this intergovernmental dialogue was centered in the Council of the South-East Asia Treaty Organization (SEATO), whose seventeenth meeting took place in Canberra, Australia, on June 27-28 (Document 64), and in the three-nation ANZUS Council, whose annual meeting was held in the same city on June 29 (Document 65). Although participants in both meetings

---

[85] Some moderation of the long-standing hostility between the anti-Communist Republic of Korea (R.O.K.) in the South and the Communist-ruled Democratic People's Republic of Korea (D.P.R.K.) in the North had become evident during 1971 as both governments began to adapt their respective diplomatic postures to changing relations among the great powers. Although a North Korean plan for national reunification advanced Apr. 12, 1971 was scornfully rejected by South Korea, the latter subsequently agreed to the initiation on Aug. 20, 1971 of discussions between representatives of the North and South Korean Red Cross Societies with a view to possible reunion of families separated by the North-South division. In 1972, contact was also established at a governmental level. In a joint communiqué issued July 4, 1972, the two governments declared that unification must be achieved by peaceful means and not by force; promised not to slander, defame, or undertake armed provocations against one another; and announced their intention to conduct exchanges in various fields, establish an emergency telephone link, and set up a North-South Coordinating Committee to implement these agreements and "settle the unification problem on the basis of the agreed principles." In light of these developments, the U.N. General Assembly decided in 1971 and again in 1972 to postpone consideration of the Korean question. The need "to fully support the North-South dialogue" was also cited by South Korean President Park Chung Hee when he proclaimed martial law throughout South Korea on Oct. 17, 1972 in what proved to be a first step in the establishment of authoritarian rule.

For fuller discussion of the subject matter of this section, cf. Nixon Report, 1972, pp. 82-9; same, 1973, pp. 106-14.

stressed the continued relevance of their alliances to developing conditions in the Pacific, longstanding uncertainties about the future of SEATO were heightened at the 1972 Council session by the absence not only of France but also of Pakistan, whose recent loss of its former eastern province (now the independent Republic of Bangladesh) had excluded it geographically from the Southeast Asian region. In consequence of this development, Pakistan was to give formal notice on November 8, 1972 that its membership in SEATO would terminate on expiration of the prescribed one-year waiting period.

Additional uncertainties developed late in the year when both New Zealand and Australia inducted Labor Party governments of antimilitarist tendency whose respective leaders—Norman E. Kirk and E. Gough Whitlam—expressed strong reservations about existing arrangements for defense cooperation, particularly with respect to SEATO and to the recently inaugurated five-power defense arrangement for Malaysia and Singapore.]

(64) Seventeenth Meeting of the Council of the South-East Asia Treaty Organization (SEATO), Canberra, June 27-28, 1972.

(a) Statement by Secretary of State Rogers, June 27, 1972.[86]

(Complete Text)

In the past four months the United States has participated with others in critical developments which will leave their stamp on the history of this century. The success of the President's visits to Peking and Moscow, the signing of the U.S.-Soviet agreements to limit strategic arms,[87] the entering into force of an agreement to eliminate Berlin as a source of international tension[88]—singly and together, these events should make a profound contribution to the peaceful world which all of us in SEATO want.

In the steps we have taken with our major adversaries, American goals have been straightforward and undeviating: a world free of the risks of nuclear war and the dangers of great-power confrontation; a Europe in which reconciliation progressively replaces division; an Asia whose peoples, large and small, can guide their own destinies in peace without outside interference.

These goals will be approached more rapidly if the principles of inter-

[86] Department of State Press Release 154, June 27, 1972; text from Bulletin, Aug. 7, 1972, pp. 159-61.
[87] Documents 13-14.
[88] Document 25.

national relations which emerged from the Peking and Moscow visits are scrupulously observed. Only time can tell how fully those principles will be given practical effect. With each country we will remain, in varying degrees and for some time to come, competitors and vigorous ideological rivals with a diametrically different view of relations among human beings and among states. We believe, however, that a process has begun which could keep that competition peaceful and these rivalries restrained and realistic.

The paths to the summit meetings were not easy. For both China and the Soviet Union the ideological and practical barriers were formidable. We therefore assume that they have undertaken to improve relations with the United States with a seriousness of purpose. The changes of attitude on their part are no doubt of the head, not of the heart, as President Nixon has described it. But those changes offer the possibility of a more peaceful world for us all, and the United States will do its part, in that spirit, to see that possibility realized.

It is our hope, and it is our intention, that the bilateral progress made at the summit meetings can also aid the transition to more normal relations among other countries divided or estranged by the cold war. Such a process is already underway both in Europe and in Asia.

—In Europe, three weeks ago, Sir Alec Douglas-Home and I participated in signing an agreement which will ease travel restrictions and other conditions of life for the people of West Berlin,[89] innocent victims of the division of their city and their country. That agreement has opened up further prospects for improvements in Europe through increased bilateral contacts and the forthcoming European conference.

—In Asia, talks have been in progress for nearly a year between Red Cross representatives of the Republic of Korea and the Democratic People's Republic of Korea, initially directed toward reuniting families separated for decades. We share the hope President Park [Chung Hee] expressed at the recent meeting of the Asian and Pacific Council that such conversations and communications will be continued and developed.[90]

The Berlin achievement and the new openings in Korea demonstrate the progress that negotiations can bring to intractable problems. Unfortunately, in Viet-Nam—and areas of more direct concern to SEATO—such progress is still blocked by the refusal of North Viet-Nam to negotiate seriously. The Communist side even refuses to enter into talks with the Government of the Republic of Viet-Nam regarding a political

[89] Document 25b.
[90] The Seventh Ministerial Conference of the Asian and Pacific Council was held in Seoul, South Korea, on June 14-16, 1972. On the relations between South and North Korea, see note 85 above.

settlement. The President's proposals of May 8[91] have so far failed to move Hanoi from its insistence on terms which would prevent the people of South Viet-Nam from determining their own future. To this we cannot and will not agree. But our generous proposal for an equitable settlement is the basis for negotiation, whenever Hanoi is prepared to start. We have some reason to hope that the increased diplomatic pressure on Hanoi throughout the world will lead it to undertake serious negotiation.

American foreign policy in Asia and in the world is based on fidelity to our commitments and firmness in our principles. It is also based on the conviction that a willingness to alter traditional patterns, to search for solutions through negotiations and dialogue, and to seek mutually beneficial compromises will serve the interest of peace. Just as we are improving our relations with traditional adversaries, we understand and welcome the similar approaches of our allies and friends. A willingness on all sides to move away from the rigidities of the last two decades can only have positive results.

These changes can only develop within a matrix of stability. For our part the United States will continue to act in East Asia and the Pacific on these convictions:

—First, our new relationships will not be achieved by sacrificing the interests of our friends. We obtained explicit recognition of this fact in the principles to which we subscribed with China and the Soviet Union.

—Second, we are well aware that these new relationships will improve our security and that of our allies only if, in pursuing them, we remain convincingly strong. That is why President Nixon insists on an adequate national defense budget even in an election year. That awareness is at the heart of our policies, in the Pacific as in Europe. And we are aware as well that continued military and economic assistance will be necessary as others take on responsibility for their own security. We are determined to provide that assistance.

—Third, a peaceful Asia will not be sought, and could not be achieved, through U.S. abandonment of our obligations or our interests in this area. Our interests in Asia and the Pacific are fundamental. In our own self-interest and in the interest of our friends and allies, our involvement will not end with the end of our military involvement in Viet-Nam.

It is the necessity for stability in a time of change which makes an organization like SEATO of continuing importance. That is why the United States continues to support this Organization and its purposes. Indeed, our initiatives in East Asia are directed toward the primary

[91]Document 47.

objective set forth by the signers of the SEATO Treaty[92] 18 years ago: "to strengthen the fabric of peace and freedom." On behalf of President Nixon I can give you our solemn assurance that in Asia the United States will remain engaged in that endeavor.

I will now turn to Admiral [John S.] McCain, [Jr.] so that he can give you his analysis of the military threat to the treaty area. As you know, this is Jack's last Council meeting. I should like to express in this forum my personal gratitude to him for a job well done. During his years as Commander in Chief, Pacific, he has been an unfailing source of advice and strength to me as Secretary of State. Certainly, SEATO has no more loyal friend than Jack McCain.[93]

(b) Final Communiqué, June 28, 1972.[94]

(Complete Text)

The Council of the South-East Asia Treaty Organization held its Seventeenth Meeting in Canberra from 27 to 28 June 1972, under the Chairmanship of the Honorable Mr. Nigel Bowen, QC, the Minister of State for Foreign Affairs of the Commonwealth of Australia. The Governments of Australia, New Zealand, the Philippines, Thailand, the United Kingdom and the United States participated; France and Pakistan did not participate. The Republic of Vietnam, a protocol state, was represented by an observer.

General Observations

The Council discussed developments in South-East Asia during the fourteen months since it last met in London.[95] The Council noted that two principal changes had been, on the one hand, the full-scale attack against the Republic of Vietnam by virtually the entire North Vietnamese army, supported by new sophisticated weapons and, on the other, the further reduction of American forces in the Republic of Vietnam to 49,000.[96] It condemned the blatant violation of the Geneva Agreements by North Vietnam and regarded the aerial and naval response to it[97] as an appropriate and understandable measure against the flow of

---

[92] Southeast Asia Collective Defense Treaty, signed at Manila Sept. 8, 1954 (TIAS 3170; 6 UST 81); text in *Documents, 1954*, pp. 319-23.

[93] Adm. Noel Gayler succeeded Adm. McCain as Commander in Chief of the Pacific on Sept. 1, 1972.

[94] Department of State Press Release 157, June 28, 1972; text from *Bulletin*, Aug. 7, 1972, pp. 161-4.

[95] *A.F.R., 1971*, no. 83.

[96] Cf. Document 46.

[97] Cf. Document 47.

war material to North Vietnam which had made the attack feasible. The Council expressed the hope that this response would be helpful in bringing the invasion to an end and leading to meaningful negotiations.

The Council noted that, despite setbacks suffered in the invasion, the armed forces and people of the Republic of Vietnam have demonstrated their growing capacity to defend themselves effectively, notably in their determined defence of An Loc and Kontum. The Council also noted that the Khmer and Lao peoples and Governments have continued to resist North Vietnamese attacks.

The Council recognized the continuing needs of the Republic of Vietnam, the Khmer Republic and Laos for assistance to support their relief and rehabilitation efforts and to meet other problems stemming from the North Vietnamese military invasion. A considerable amount of assistance has already been provided to these countries in the form of direct grants, imports of essential items, commodity import assistance, exchange support and other programmes. The Council expressed the hope that all nations concerned with problems arising from the assault on the sovereignty and territorial integrity of independent states in Indo-China would increase their efforts to assist in these fields.

The Council noted with gratification that the President of the United States, while continuing to honour defence commitments in the treaty area, had visited the People's Republic of China and the Union of Soviet Socialist Republics with a view to improving both bilateral relations and the prospects for a world at peace. It welcomed these visits and expressed the hope that their success would open up opportunities for a lessening of the threat in the treaty area and for an equitable negotiated settlement of the war in Indo-China.

The Council was pleased to note the conclusion of agreements between the United States and the Union of Soviet Socialist Republics including those limiting defensive and offensive strategic weapons and setting the basis for further negotiations on strategic arms.[98]

In keeping with the spirit of the Pacific Charter,[99] the Council was pleased to note the progress made in regional co-operation in building up resilience amongst countries of South-East Asia. It noted the growing importance of various regional groupings and the initiatives they are taking towards progress and stability in the area. It observed that the growth of national self-reliance and increasingly close co-operation would promote the well-being and security of the countries of the region.

The Council noted with satisfaction the significant contribution to security in the area provided by ANZUS[100] and the Five Power defence

[98] Documents 13-14; other agreements listed in Document 10.

[99] Signed at Manila Sept. 8, 1954; text in *Documents. 1954*, pp. 318-19.

[100] Tripartite Security Treaty Between the Governments of Australia, New Zealand, and the United States (ANZUS Pact), signed in San Francisco Sept. 1, 1951

Philippines

The Council was given a comprehensive account of the security situation in the Philippines and, in particular, of increased subversive and insurgent activities by communist elements.

The Council expressed its support for the continuing political, economic and social measures taken by the Philippine Government to raise living standards and to initiate social reforms in the country.

Thailand

The Council noted the increased level of communist subversive and insurgent activity which had developed in Thailand over the past year, more seriously in the northern and north-eastern provinces of the country bordering Laos. It observed that insurgents in Thailand have stepped up the frequency and boldness of terrorist incidents against the local populace and authorities. It noted that the insurgents continued to receive political support and substantial material aid, including high-powered weapons, from sources outside the country.

The Council also noted the importance of the intensified efforts of the Royal Thai Government and Thai people to counter insurgency and to further economic and social development in the country, particularly at the grass roots level.

The Council was pleased that member countries, both individually and collectively, were lending assistance to the Royal Thai Government in these efforts.

Counter-subversion and other Activities of SEATO

The Council emphasized the importance of continued efforts to assist regional members to cope with the problems raised by externally-promoted subversion and insurgency. Solutions depended on increased understanding of problems and vigorous action to resolve them on the part of individual members as well as by SEATO.

The Council decided that SEATO programmes in the areas of information and research as well as its economic, social and cultural activities should be increasingly complementary to and closely co-ordinated with its counter-subversion and counter-insurgency activity. The Organization will assist wherever possible in training officials dealing with these problems.

The Council noted with satisfaction that member countries continued to provide aid to other member countries bilaterally in support of SEATO objectives.

Co-operation in the Military Field

The Council noted the report of the military advisers and commended the Military Planning Office for its continuing work in keeping plans up to date and in organizing military exercises. These exercises provide useful experience in co-operation between members as well as in the other aspects of military training. It commended the Civic Action Projects which were undertaken in the Philippines and Thailand in connection with SEATO exercises "Sea Hawk" and "Mittraparb".

Eighteenth Meeting of the Council

The Council accepted with pleasure the invitation of the Government of the United States of America to host the Eighteenth Council Meeting in 1973.[106]

Expression of Gratitude

The Council expressed its gratitude to the Government and people of Australia for their generous hospitality and warm welcome and its appreciation for the excellent arrangements made for the meeting.

The Secretary-General

The Council noted reports of the Secretary-General and expressed its appreciation for the work of the Civil Secretariat.

In taking note of the forthcoming retirement of the Secretary-General, the Council paid tribute to the active and devoted manner in which General [Jesus] Vargas has served SEATO over the past seven years.

The Council appointed His Excellency Mr. Sunthorn Hongladarom of Thailand as Secretary-General and extended a warm welcome to him.[107]

Leaders of Delegations

The Leaders of the Delegations to the Seventeenth Council Meeting were:

Australia

The Honorable Nigel Bowen, QC, MP, Minister for Foreign Affairs

New Zealand

The Right Honorable Sir Keith Holyoake, GCMG, CH, MP, Minister of Foreign Affairs

Philippines

His Excellency General Carlos P. Romulo, Secretary of Foreign Affairs

---

[106] The Eighteenth Meeting of the SEATO Council was held in New York Sept. 28, 1973 (*Bulletin*, Oct. 22, 1973, p. 512).
[107] Mr. Sunthorn began a three-year term as Secretary-General on Sept. 4, 1972.

Thailand

His Excellency Mr. Pote Sarasin, Assistant Chairman, National Executive Council

United Kingdom

The Right Honorable Sir Alec Douglas-Home, KT, MP, Secretary of State for Foreign and Commonwealth Affairs

United States

The Honorable William P. Rogers, Secretary of State

Republic of Vietnam (Observer)

His Excellency Mr. Tran Van Lam, Minister of Foreign Affairs

(65) 22nd Meeting of the ANZUS Council, Canberra, June 29, 1972: Final Communiqué.[108]

(Complete Text)

Continuing their series of meetings that began with the signature of the Security Treaty of 1 September 1951, between Australia, New Zealand, and the United States,[109] the ANZUS partners met as the ANZUS Council in Canberra on 29 June 1972. Attending were the Honorable Nigel H. Bowen, Minister for Foreign Affairs of Australia and the Honorable David Fairbairn, Minister for Defence; the Right Honorable Sir Keith Holyoake, Minister of Foreign Affairs of New Zealand; and the Honorable William P. Rogers, Secretary of State of the United States.

As in the case of previous meetings of the ANZUS partners, the Council conducted a full and frank review of major issues in the Pacific area which could affect the security of the three nations.

The Council reviewed the visits by President Nixon to the People's Republic of China in February 1972, and to the Soviet Union in May 1972, and underlined the role these visits played in the search for a reduction in international tension and the prevention of conflicts between nations. The ANZUS partners discussed the steps they have taken to normalize their respective relations with the People's Republic of China and reiterated that the search for new relationships should not be at the expense of old friendships.

The Council noted the continuing and indeed, increasing importance of Japan, both politically and economically, to the stability and welfare

108 Department of State Press Release 159, June 29, 1972; text from *Bulletin*, Aug. 7, 1972, pp. 164-5.
109 Cf. note 100 above.

of the Pacific area and reaffirmed the importance of a continuing close partnership and confidence between Japan and each of the three ANZUS partners.

The Council noted the growing solidarity among countries within the South East Asian region and steps being taken to strengthen Australia's and New Zealand's bilateral relations with them, including the recent visit by Prime Minister [William] McMahon [of Australia] to Indonesia, Singapore and Malaysia. The Council welcomed the entry into effect as from 1 November 1971 of the Five Power defence arrangements.[110]

The Council deeply regretted the decision by the North Vietnamese leaders to escalate their aggression against the Republic of Viet-Nam, rather than to negotiate seriously a political settlement of the long and destructive war in Indo-China. The Council noted the valiant and successful efforts by the people and Government of the Republic of Viet-Nam to defend themselves and the additional measures taken by the United States in response to the massive North Vietnamese invasion. It expressed the hope that North Viet-Nam and those who have facilitated its acts of aggression would at last realize that it is time to bring the war to a close and that North Viet-Nam would begin to negotiate seriously in Paris. In this connection it commended the generous proposals for a settlement made in January by Presidents Nixon and Thieu[111] and the practical basis for ending the military conflict contained in President Nixon's proposal of 8 May.[112]

The Council deplored the fact that Laos and the Khmer Republic also continued to be the victims of North Vietnamese aggression. Not only have North Vietnamese troops continued their unjustified attacks, but they occupy areas farther west than ever before while maintaining a high level of hostilities. The ANZUS partners observed that numbers of North Vietnamese troops were withdrawn recently from areas of Laos and the Khmer Republic in order to attack the people of the Republic of Viet-Nam. Where this happened, hostilities significantly declined, thus underlining the true nature of the conflict in both countries. A final and definitive withdrawal of North Vietnamese forces from Laos and the Khmer Republic would contribute greatly to the restoration of peace and security in Indo-China.

The ANZUS partners reviewed their security interests in the Pacific Ocean. They also had an exchange of views on their strategic interests in the Indian Ocean. The Council reaffirmed its hope that military competition in the Indian Ocean could be avoided and its belief that the area should remain under continuing surveillance.[113]

The Council welcomed the continuing growth of regional cooperation

110 Cf. note 101 above.
111 Document 44.
112 Document 47.
113 Cf. *A.F.R., 1971*, nos. 65-66.

among the independent and self-governing states in the South Pacific. It noted that the second meeting of the South Pacific Forum was held in Canberra in February 1972, and that a third would be held before the end of the year.[114]

The Council observed that, notwithstanding the mounting opposition amongst countries of the Pacific, nuclear tests were still being conducted in the atmosphere.[115] The ANZUS partners, being parties to the Nuclear Test Ban Treaty of 1963,[116] affirmed their hope that there should be universal adherence to this treaty. It was noted that, in response to the deep and widespread concern felt throughout their communities at the further series of tests in the South Pacific, the Prime Ministers of Australia and New Zealand had issued a joint call to the Conference of the Committee on Disarmament. It was agreed that progress in this area would respond to the deeply-held feelings and aspirations of the peoples of the Pacific area.

The ANZUS partners reaffirmed the deep importance that each of them continued to attach to the alliance. They emphasized that it is as vital to them in the changing circumstances of the 70's as it was during the Cold War of former years. The significant developments which had taken place in international relations since the Council last met, in October 1971,[117] and which would be long in the working out, underlined the need to continue to cooperate closely within the ANZUS Alliance in furtherance of the political and security interests of its members.

---

[114] Cf. *The World This Year, 1973*, p. 166.
[115] France conducted a series of atmospheric nuclear tests at Mururoa Atoll, French Polynesia, during June and July 1972.
[116] Treaty Banning Nuclear Weapon Tests in the Atmosphere, in Outer Space and Under Water, done at Moscow Aug. 5, 1963 and entered into force Oct. 10, 1973 (TIAS 5433; 14 UST 1313); text in *Documents, 1963*, pp. 130-32.
[117] *A.F.R., 1971*, no. 84.

VII.
THE UNITED STATES
AND AFRICA

[Africa continued during 1972 to occupy the comparatively subordinate position in American foreign policy it had held throughout the postwar years and more especially since the advent of the Nixon administration, with its characteristic absorption in great-power diplomacy. "For historical and geographical reasons," President Nixon wrote in his "State of the World" report for 1972, "Africa is resistant to involvement in alien conflicts and controversies. This accords with our purposes as well as Africa's. . . . Africans have demonstrated, in their drive for autonomy and self-reliance, their ability to solve their problems without outside interference."[1]

"Political restraint in our policy toward Africa," Mr. Nixon implied, was particularly to be cultivated in dealing with the issues created by the quest for racial justice in Southern Africa—one of the two "awesome problems" that most preoccupied contemporary Africans. Concerning the other problem—the "hope for modernization," which, he said, was "spreading across Africa more rapidly than the means to assure its realization"—the President saw greater opportunities for a fruitful American role. "African leaders look to the United States for help primarily in meeting their development objectives," he wrote. ". . . On our part, we consider this an area particularly appropriate for an active U.S. role in African affairs. As Africans diversify their economic relationships, our own economic interests and opportunities expand. Our interest in African trade and investment opportunities matches the African interest in American goods and their desire for American technology."[2]

This shared concern with economic matters was to inspire two of the more informative of Washington's infrequent pronouncements on African affairs during 1972. Both were speeches by David D.

---

[1] Nixon Report, 1972, p. 103. For further discussion see same, pp. 101-7; same, 1973, pp. 153-60; Rogers Report, 1972, pp. 447-72.
[2] Nixon Report, 1972, pp. 101-3.

Newsom, the Assistant Secretary of State for African Affairs and principal U.S. Government spokesman in this area (Documents 66 and 67). A third Newsom speech provides an unusually comprehensive review of U.S. relations with the countries of North Africa (Document 68); a fourth examines U.S. policy regarding the controversial issues of racial and political relations in Southern Africa (Document 70). Documents on the internal upheaval in Burundi (Document 69) and on the status of the Rhodesian problem (Documents 71-72) round out the necessarily somewhat fragmentary record of American policy toward Africa in 1972.]

A. The American Interest: Economic Aspects.

["Our interest in supporting Africa's development rests on many bases," President Nixon would point out in the last of his "State of the World" reports, made public in the spring of 1973. "A central motive is our humanitarian concern. We also believe that as the quality of life improves on the continent, so will the prospects for regional peace. In addition a developing African economy will mean expanding potential markets for American goods. Moreover, Africa is becoming a major source of energy for the United States and Western Europe. Libya is one of the world's most important producers of oil; Nigeria's oil production is increasing; Algerian natural gas is a rapidly growing source of world energy. One-fourth of the world's known uranium ore reserves are in Africa. As the West seeks new and alternative sources of energy, African development becomes increasingly important."[3]

Four distinct varieties of American aid to African development were singled out by the President as he surveyed the achievements of the early 1970s. First came development assistance under the foreign aid program, which, he reported, had increased from $450 million in 1970 to $600 million in 1972. Second was direct private investment, almost doubled since the late 1960s to a figure of approximately $4 billion. Third came two-way trade, which had also increased by 30 percent to a 1972 level of $3.1 billion. Last, the President specially stressed humanitarian assistance in combating illiteracy, starvation, disease, and the effects of natural disasters. As examples of this last type of effort, Mr. Nixon cited the United States' support of a seven-year campaign to control smallpox throughout Central and West Africa; emergency grain shipments to semiarid states south of the Sahara, where years of insufficient rainfall had posed a threat of large-scale starvation; and assistance to

3 Nixon Report, 1973, p. 154.

those made homeless by internal events in the Sudan, Burundi, and Uganda.[4]

A more detailed picture of the American economic role in Africa emerges from the following addresses by Assistant Secretary Newsom, the first of which is focused on the continent's needs for development aid (Document 66) while the second reviews a wider range of American business interests (Document 67).]

(66) "Aid to Africa—A Moral and Economic Necessity": Address by David D. Newsom, Assistant Secretary of State for African Affairs, Before the Santa Clara County Council for Social Studies, Palo Alto, January 22, 1972.[5]

(Complete Text)

On October 29, [1971] in a surprise vote, the Senate of the United States killed the bill authorizing a U.S. foreign aid program for the current fiscal year.[6] The program now is operating under a continuing resolution which permits spending only until February 22. Members of Congress this week returned to Washington after a monthlong recess, and the next few weeks will be decisive for the aid program.

In a parallel move before the recess, the Congress failed to complete action on Peace Corps appropriations. The continuing resolution reduces Peace Corps operations to a point where it may have to close down 15 of its 55 programs around the world.

The actions on foreign aid by your representatives and mine have great significance for our foreign relations. Often they are described as reflecting the criticism of foreign aid by the American people. But every American who wishes this country to play a meaningful role in today's world must give attention to this situation.

I can speak most knowingly of only one part of this world: Africa. In doing so, I speak of a continent where the needs are great but where much is being done and can be done.

I returned last month from my sixth trip to Africa in 2 years. I have now visited all but five of Africa's independent countries. On each trip, the overriding preoccupation of Africa's leaders is with one subject: the need for assistance in economic development. Their words to me reflect gratitude for what we as a nation have done, coupled with deep disappointment that we, as the world's wealthiest nation, cannot do more. On this last trip, they reflected puzzlement and deep concern over the doubtful future of U.S. aid.

---

[4] Same, pp. 155-7; cf. Section C below.
[5] Department of State Press Release 20; text from *Bulletin*, Feb. 14, 1972, pp. 199-205.
[6] Cf. *A.F.R., 1971*, no. 154.

Their preoccupation stems from their own frequently desperate awareness of their own needs and of the fact that both their own political futures and the future of their nations depend upon satisfying those needs. They face directly the pressures of poverty, unemployment, underemployment, problems of motivation, rising expectations, and the growing gap between the haves and the have-nots. These pressures exist in all the developing countries. In Africa they have a particular poignancy.

On this last trip, the President of one African country took me to a map of his country hanging on the wall of his office. In quiet tones he spelled out his problems.

In the north, the Sahara was creeping slowly southward, inundating farmland. Two years of drought were accelerating the process. Rains had failed this year, just at the critical time, and grain had failed to ripen.

One of the country's major cities faced a severe water shortage in the coming years. Substantial capital was needed to solve the problem.

In the south, one of the country's most fertile river valleys was made uninhabitable by onchocerciasis, or river blindness.

Cattle, the country's principal export, were forced to walk to markets in neighboring countries because of the lack of roads and railroads. They arrived with both their weight and their price sharply reduced.

I know the response of the skeptics to appeals of this kind:

—Africa is distant; our national interests are minimal. Why should we get involved?

—We have grave problems at home, problems of drought and disease. Let's solve our own problems first.

—Others, Britain and France, are helping in Africa. They have been there longer than we. Let them assume the burden. Why should we get involved?

—Experience to date with aid has been disappointing. We have spent billions of dollars and have little to show for it. Africa, in particular, gives little basis for hope.

REASONS FOR U.S. INVOLVEMENT

You can hear all these arguments and more. There are grains of truth in each. But they do not tell the whole story.

Africa is closer geographically to you here in Palo Alto than most of Asia. Eleven percent of our population traces its ancestry to Africa; few identifiable ethnic groups in our culture are larger. We will depend increasingly on mineral and energy resources from Africa. The question is not, "Why should we get involved?" We are involved.

We do have major problems at home requiring our resources. This does not mean that we turn our back on the rest of the world. All of the resources we put into foreign economic assistance probably represents less than 1½ percent of our Federal budget. It is far less than the 1 percent of gross national product established by the United Nations as a goal for the developed countries. We today rank 12th in the world in per capita participation in economic assistance to the developing countries. Is this the proper share for a country with more than one-third of the world's total gross national product?

It is true that the European countries carry a major share of help to Africa. They have much older direct ties with the continent than we. They have fewer commitments on other continents. The French-speaking European countries have the advantage of a common language with almost half the African countries. Many Europeans in Africa have been, and still are, reluctant to see the United States play a larger role.

We welcome the increased aid programs of the European countries, given the major burden we assumed in the early years of independence.

Yet all of these arguments ignore others.

The Africans want us involved. They need the resources. They also seek the greater independence that goes with a diversification of sources of support.

We have some very practical reasons for seeking involvement. Our economic assistance serves to introduce U.S. products and techniques at a time when the competition for exports is becoming more and more important to our own national economy. Africa, in particular, is an area where we face a particular problem of promoting our own exports. Most doors were closed to our traders in colonial times.

U.S. assistance to Africa, as does U.S. assistance to other areas of the world, results directly in benefits to our own industries at home. Ninety-nine percent of our aid commodity purchases are made in the United States. These purchases amounted to nearly a billion dollars in fiscal year 1971.

We have contributions to make to foreign economic development which are particularly sought by Africans. We have developed expertise in several areas, particularly in agriculture, unmatched by any other nation. The American spirit of willingness to work in remote areas and under difficult conditions, especially as exemplified in the Peace Corps, is rare and envied. In those major projects which require substantial capital, United States participation in financing is often essential to the success of the project.

Finally, we face the fact of African expectations of the United States. Both because of our size and wealth, and because of words with which we greeted African independence, Africans expected much of us. They feared us. They envied us. They looked to us for major support. They have been disappointed, both because their expectations were un-realistic and, perhaps, so were ours. They were disappointed that our programs, at the outset, were not larger. Many were bitter when, as the result of congressional action, we were required to limit the number of countries to which we can extend bilateral development loans. By frank discussions and experience, the African leaders now have a more realistic appraisal of what we can do and are becoming reconciled to our emphasis on projects which are regional and done in cooperation with other donors. The fact remains, however, that if we are to have a meaningful relationship with African nations and their leaders, we cannot ignore their expectations of us.

Both the givers and the receivers of aid have over the past 15 years learned of the limitations of political influence obtained through aid. Few donor countries have, except in very precise and limited circumstances, been able to impose their political will on the developing countries through either promises to grant aid or threats to withdraw it. Recipient countries have, at the same time, demonstrated a stout resistance to influences which will affect either their internal policies or their external policies related to African issues. The expectations of countries, both western and eastern, that aid would bring political benefits have proven false. Aid must be and can be justified largely on the basis of the needs of the developing nation and the direct economic and moral interests of the developed nations involved.

The Soviets and the Chinese are showing a renewed interest in economic assistance to Africa. In the last 6 months, the Soviet Union has announced its willingness to undertake major projects valued at nearly $100 million in one country, Somalia. The Chinese have extended $84 million in credits to Ethiopia and an estimated $190 million to the Sudan. These are credits which may be drawn down over a period of years, if at all. Exact comparisons with our own programs are therefore difficult. Nevertheless, it is worthy of note that, in African eyes, the two Communist powers have extended more credits to three countries in 6 months than we have provided through AID [Agency for International Development] to Africa in 2 years.

We have announced as a policy that we do not wish to continue the cold war in Africa. We welcome the constructive provision of economic resources by the Communist powers. We are no longer lured to respond to appeals from African countries by the fact or threat of Communist aid. We are more convinced than we were earlier of the African nations' ability to preserve their independence. There is less evidence than we expected some years ago to suggest that Communist political infiltration necessarily accompanies economic aid. The Communist countries, too, have their legitimate motivations for giving aid: promotion of exports and technology, securing of foreign exchange, prestige.

Nonetheless, the figure of $2 billion offered by the Soviets, eastern Europe, and the Chinese People's Republic in economic assistance to Africa over the past 10 years is impressive by comparison with our own.

It is impressive to the African nation which, for ideological reasons, has turned to us, with apparently lesser results. In assessing what we should do in a continent where we have ties and interests, we cannot ignore the effect of the efforts being made by the Soviet Union and China.

UNIQUE CONTRIBUTIONS OF U.S. AID

And now to a question frequently asked of me: Why can't we leave Africa to the European powers and to international organizations such as the World Bank and the United Nations Development Program?

British aid to Africa in the 1960's averaged $150 million per year; French aid, at an annual rate of almost $500 million, was even larger. World Bank loans and credits to Africa in fiscal 1971 amounted to $470 million. The U.N. programs for the continent were $70 million. Another important donor to Africa is the European Economic Community, which, through the Fund for Economic Development, funnels about $125 million a year into Africa.

These various sources give Africa the largest per capita share of the world's economic assistance dollar. Why, then, is U.S. aid needed?

First, the needs are great. Black Africa has one of the world's lowest per capita incomes. Coming late into the world's development, it has less basic infrastructure than other areas. Its skilled manpower base is minimal. In fact, by U.N. measurement, 16 of the 25 "least" developed countries in the world are in Africa, or 40 percent of the nations of the continent.

Secondly, we have a moral obligation as a wealthy nation to assist the poorest group of nations in the world.

Thirdly, with a black population second only to Nigeria, we have a special interest in Africa. We can demonstrate that interest most effectively by responding to the preoccupation of the Africans with their own economic development.

Fourthly, only we can project the advantages of our products and techniques into this continent of 340 million people. We are latecomers into one of the world's growing market areas. European assistance, also in part motivated by the desire for trade, is not intended to help us.

Fifthly, our aid is needed because the Africans want it. They want it for the diversification necessary to their genuine independence. They want it because the United States can provide, better than others, certain techniques and experience. They want it because major development requires ultimately assistance from the world's largest source of capital, the United States.

Finally, there are some nations in Africa with which the United States has had traditional ties and which do not have a special relationship with a European power. In other cases, difficulties with the former mother country at the time of independence left significant African countries to seek other sources of aid. Thus neither Ethiopia nor Liberia benefits from traditional European ties. In the early years of their independence Morocco and Tunisia faced difficulties because of problems with France; the United States assumed and continues a significant role in these key North African nations.

Another question often asked is, "Why cannot our private resources provide aid? Why does it have to be governmental aid?" Private resources, through foundations and educational institutions do provide considerable assistance, but this is very limited in terms of the needs. Private investment flows on the basis of profitable opportunities. This is a significant boost to development where such opportunities exist, but unfortunately the investment opportunities of Africa are not evenly spread.

The need for assistance is greatest in those nations without the resources which attract private capital. Substantial governmental help, in the form of grants and loans on exceptional terms, is often necessary before the basis for satisfactory private investment can be laid. Both we and many Africans believe that ultimately development is more sound if it can be based on profitable private enterprises. Aid is necessary, however, to create the conditions which make such enterprises possible.

What is the United States providing now? In comparative terms to assistance from other sources, it is supplemental, but it is not insubstantial.

In the fiscal year 1970-71, we provided through the Agency for International Development in loans and grants for capital projects and technical assistance $164 million.

In the same year, Peace Corps programs in Africa were valued at $20 million.

We provided $65 million through long-term Export-Import Bank credits for U.S. exports to Africa. Finally, we provided $99.5 million in surplus agricultural commodities to support various forms of humanitarian and development projects.

The total direct U.S. assistance thus amounted to about $350 million, slightly less than $2 per American, of which 40 percent was loaned to Africa. Added to this was another estimated $200 million contributed to Africa through international agencies, including the World Bank and the U.N. Development Program.

DRAMATIC SUCCESSES

It is this substantial but supplemental flow of resources to Africa which is now, with the remainder of our worldwide assistance program, at stake in the current congressional deliberations. It is this program which requires the support and interest of those Americans who wish to see us relate to Africa in a way responsive to the preoccupations of the Africans themselves.

But, someone will say, where is this money really going? Is it being efficiently used? Is it merely going into the pockets of rich elites or propping up unpopular regimes? Does it really reach the African people?

Our assistance to Africa has had its share of failures: projects that were overly ambitious, completed without the local resources or the manpower to operate them; projects extensively delayed by bureaucracy in Africa and in the United States; problems with contractors; the wrong man for the job. Those seeking to discredit any aid program can find examples if they seek them. The transfer of resources to the developing world is complex, often experimental, often agonizingly slow. This is the nature of the task.

The dramatic successes far outshine the failures:

Ten years ago the former Belgian Congo [Zaïre] was in the chaos of its immediate postindependence period. It was the substantial input of American resources which helped maintain the unity of this country and provide today a significant political and economic stability in the heart of Africa.

In country after country in Africa, the participant training program of AID has created groups of technicians and administrators who are today the backbone of many African governments. In one country which, at independence, had only eight university graduates, AID trained some 600 at the technical college and university level in 10 years.

In West Africa, the vital need for roads is being partly met by a highly successful road machinery maintenance center where Africans from 11 nations are being trained to build roads and maintain them.

Africa is filled today with the impact of small projects directly relating to the people at the village level, most of them created through cooperation between the Peace Corps and the "self-help" fund of AID.

On my latest trip, I visited several of these. In one place, a Peace Corps volunteer conceived of a small dam project and constructed it with the help of $806 from AID. Villagers who once walked 12 miles for water now have it available in their backyard. In another, self-help funds were used to aid villagers in constructing a school. One of them remarked to me, "You have no idea how this has changed the village life. Previously, the school was something imposed from outside. Now it is ours and the center of our village activity." Small bridges thrown across streams at minimum cost have opened areas to markets which were previously distant and impossible to reach in rainy seasons.

REGIONAL AND MULTILATERAL APPROACH

And what of the future?

Our economic assistance policies in Africa are, in many ways, shaped to meet the new circumstances of the future, as well as some of the particular concerns of critics of former aid programs.

More and more of our assistance is being worked out through African regional organizations and in cooperation with other donors.

There has been much misunderstanding of the fact that the United States has, because of congressional limitations, had to channel the bulk of its development aid into 10 selected countries. This should be seen not as an effort to choose among African leaders or political systems but as a means of encouraging the regional and multilateral approach. It was also intended to stimulate the reduction of the large missions, staffed by Americans, which were a much criticized feature, both in Africa and in America, of earlier aid programs.

Today about 30 percent of our economic assistance is provided to 15 African countries on a regional and multidonor basis. In one group of countries, the five nations of the Entente in West Africa,[7] we are providing more total resources on a regional basis than we provided to them on a bilateral basis 5 years ago.

The number of direct-hire Americans working in aid programs in Africa has dropped from 1,500 to 900, a much larger percentage drop than the reduction in the aid figures themselves.

To make our aid more effective we are concentrating on aspects of life where we believe our own experience will lead us to make the greatest contribution: in agriculture, transportation, health, and education.

A look at even the 10 countries to which we are providing bilateral development aid will belie the idea that we choose among types of regimes or political orientation.

They include the monarchies of Morocco and Ethiopia; countries with Socialist-oriented economies such as Tunisia and Tanzania; non-Socialist countries such as Kenya and Liberia; military-led regimes in Ghana, Uganda, Zaïre, and Nigeria, Africa's most staunchly independent and largest nation.

U.S. assistance on a regional basis and in cooperation with other donors touches 21 other countries, equally diverse in their styles of government and orientation.

Such assistance enables us to respond to the plea that I mentioned earlier was made to me by the African President beset by problems of a drought that threatened to ruin a portion of his country, by a disease that made another part uninhabitable, and by a lack of roads that diminishes the value of the principal export, cattle. What are we doing for his country?

Through a regional grain stabilization program we are providing surplus grains from the United States to meet the food needs and to stabilize prices. In the coming years, this immediate help will be sup-

[7] Dahomey, Ivory Coast, Niger, Togo, and Upper Volta.

plemented by research and development of new grain strains, storage facilities, and marketing systems which will give to this country the means of doing what now must be done with outside help.

Secondly, through a regional livestock project, we are, in cooperation with other donor countries, helping to improve the feeding and watering facilities of the livestock and the slaughtering and marketing facilities in neighboring countries.

Thirdly, we have committed ourselves through the African Development Bank to do the preliminary studies for a significant road to a neighboring country.

Fourthly, in cooperation with the World Health Organization, we are examining the techniques and possibilities of eradicating the larvae of the fly that causes river blindness.

Here in West Africa, in an area from which many of our own Afro-Americans came, we have the possibility to make a dramatic contribution in the years to come to the life of a proud and needy people.

In another significant area of Africa, southern Africa, our regional programs are becoming increasingly important. This administration consciously chose to funnel more assistance into the majority-ruled states which lie next to and are surrounded by South Africa, as a concrete indication of our belief in and support for majority regimes. I have seen the results of even our modest beginnings. They have provided hope to peoples in an area of the world particularly beset by questions of race and human dignity. Thus we are assisting in the development of agriculture in Swaziland and Lesotho. We are providing help to a major mineral complex in Botswana. We are completing the engineering studies for a road which will link Botswana with Zambia to the north.

I have tried this morning to give you some indication of what is at stake in one area of the world, Africa, as your representatives and mine contemplate the future of the foreign assistance program.[8]

I have given arguments, valid arguments, which have traditionally supported the foreign aid program. Naturally, at a time of a total reexamination of our national priorities, these, like other arguments, are being questioned.

In the last analysis, therefore, what we do depends not so much on these traditional justifications but on whether, as a nation, we continue to be interested in the fate of peoples on other continents in this shrinking world. It depends on whether we continue to recognize our special bounty—whatever our problems—and a responsibility to share that with those less endowed. It depends on whether disappointments and unrealized expectations will lead us to turn our backs on the world or to continue forward on a more realistic and sounder basis.

[8] Cf. Chapter X at notes 60-63.

The needs are there, in Africa and in the developing world. More and more the peoples of the developing world are showing their awareness of the realities of development. They are helping to make what we and others do more effective. The moment when both we and they realize, from experience, what can be done and what needs to be done is not the moment to turn away.

If we as Americans wish to have a meaningful relationship to Africa, in terms that match African preoccupations, if we desire a positive image in African nations, it is essential that we continue to respond to their development needs. I am sure that, with the support and help of groups such as yours, we will.

(67) "U.S. Government and Business—Partners in African Development": Address by Assistant Secretary Newsom Before the African-American Chamber of Commerce, New York, February 16, 1972. [9]

(Complete Text)

The American Government and American business are on the spot in Africa. Each has an interest in Africa's economic and political development.

Economics used to be considered the special domain of business, and politics the private preserve of government. It is no longer possible, if it ever was, to separate the two.

American business, as all of you know better than I, cannot afford to ignore the political climate in which it is to operate. Neither can government representatives ignore the concerns of business.

As a government our goals in Africa are simple. We desire friendly relations with all African governments. We desire equal access for our citizens to commercial and investment opportunities. We desire to contribute to economic development and to peaceful change. We seek to avoid major-power confrontation.

These are goals compatible with what business wishes. They are compatible with the interests of African countries seeking both the conditions and the resources for progress.

Africans want to do business with the United States. They value our expertise, our reputation for quality in many lines. They recognize that the United States is a major source of capital. Sensitive to unfair arrangements made in preindependence times, they want to do business on their terms. They do not necessarily look at contractual obligations the same way we do. But the fact is that American business is finding

9 Department of State Press Release 42; text from *Bulletin*, Mar. 20, 1972, pp. 441-5.

increasing opportunities and building increasing confidence in Africa.

U.S. investment in Africa has increased rapidly and steadily during the past decade. At the end of 1970 the book value of U.S. investments in Africa reached $3.5 billion. This was 17 percent more than the previous year and four times the value of U.S. investments in 1960.

The rise in American investments in developing areas of Africa has been particularly dramatic. The increase in the value just since 1967 has been $1 billion. This compares with an increase in the value of U.S. investment in the Republic of South Africa of $200 million in the same period. Today, the American investment in Africa is 75 percent in the developing countries and only 25 percent in South Africa.

Much of the dramatic rise has come from the increased investment in petroleum, particularly in Libya and in Nigeria. Today, petroleum accounts for 73 percent of the American investment in the developing countries of Africa. Mining accounts for 13 percent and manufacturing for only 3 percent.

On the other hand, the rise in trade has been much less satisfactory. Even though exports to Africa and, to a much lesser degree, imports from that continent have been increasing, Africa still occupies a relatively small place in American foreign trade, and our proportion of African trade is still small. In 1971 African markets took only 3.6 percent of our exports and supplied only 2.6 percent of imports into this country.

In terms of the proportion we hold of the African market, the United States supplies a little more than 12 percent of Africa's purchases from the industrialized nations—this, in a continent of 330 million people with growing demands and a slowly but definitely rising level of consumption. Annual imports by African countries have run from $9.5 billion to $14 billion during the last 5 years.

The markets are there waiting to be expanded. The resources are there waiting to be developed, and the interest is there waiting to be acted upon.

STIMULATION OF U.S. INVESTMENT

A word now about our approach and responsibilities as a government. Our frequently declared interest in the promotion of American investment in Africa has not slackened. Since I last spoke to this chamber 2 years ago, not only has U.S. investment risen, but so has the government's commitment to facilitate that investment.

OPIC, the Overseas Private Investment Corporation, was established in 1971 and is already involved in a number of projects on the continent. OPIC is concerned with stimulating investment in the developing countries of Africa. Its largest activity at present is in insurance for investors overseas. OPIC also guarantees commercial loans and has guaranteed loans amounting to approximately $160 million in Africa to date. Pre-investment assistance is another function of this organization, as is lending U.S.-owned currencies where they are [sic].

Through OPIC and through the Departments of State and Commerce, we are involved in pointing out opportunities to investors and in conveying back to potential investors the declared interest of the African countries.

While beginnings have been made in this, there is, in my view, much more that can be done to fit the interests and opportunities demonstrated by the Africans with the potential investor in this country. To the average African Embassy seeking to promote investment in its country, the United States is a huge supermarket with too many confusing signs. The need is constantly brought to my attention for some better machinery by which the African countries can make known to the American business community the possibilities for investment that exist.

As the statistics which I mentioned earlier demonstrate, investment in Africa today is largely in mining and petroleum. Manufacturing, which in many ways provides more jobs and is potentially of longer range benefit to a country, represents only a small percentage. Investment in agricultural production is even smaller. Yet today one can see in Africa dramatic indications of how small manufacturing can be profitably established on the continent. The agricultural opportunities are potentially boundless. With proper irrigation and improved farming techniques—and here American "know-how" is particularly applicable—Africa can become a significant producer of most of the world's crops.

The potential investor in Africa is naturally concerned about the question of longer range stability and the risk of expropriation or nationalization. These concerns are genuine. They were very much in the mind of the President when he issued the statement last month on the government's policy toward expropriations.[10] This statement set forth clearly our deep concern over expropriations of significant investments without compensation and made known the seriousness with which such actions are regarded in this country. It was not intended to trigger reactions automatically but was intended to suggest that where there is no forward movement toward prompt, adequate, and effective compensation the United States had actions which it could take, consistent with international law.

Opportunities exist for an even greater increase in commerce between the United States and Africa. We have shown our interest in the exports of Africa to this country by our participation in the International Coffee Agreement and by our positive stance during a recent conference in Geneva on a proposed cocoa agreement. The President has spoken of his plan to send to the Congress of the United States pro-

10 Document 97.

posed legislation to set up generalized tariff preferences for manufactured goods from the developing countries.[11]

Conscious of the particular problems facing the promotion of American exports to Africa, we are seeking to place a special emphasis on commercial promotion in even the smallest of our missions abroad. This was one subject in a conference of our economic and commercial officers which I attended in Abidjan [Ivory Coast] in December.

U.S. MISSION–PRIVATE SECTOR COOPERATION

Selling in the markets of the developing countries is a task that requires the closest cooperation between our missions and representatives of the private sector. This is especially true in the developing countries of Africa, where government is the primary purchaser. Some businessmen still cling to the belief that it is healthier to keep government at arm's distance. In Africa, however, commerce and politics are intertwined.

The government is frequently the largest purchaser of the very things which we export—heavy machinery and capital goods for development purposes. It is the most important purchaser of those items which account for the largest dollar flow. In many, if not most, of the developing African countries, the influence of government and of individuals associated with the government is highly important in determining purchases.

The Export-Import Bank makes an important contribution to American exports to Africa. By means of direct lending guarantees and some recent improvements in its procedures, the Eximbank has expanded its role in Africa in the past 2 or 3 years. President Henry Kearns and one of his directors have visited about a dozen African countries.

Today the Eximbank has almost $600 million of involvement in Africa, 91 percent of which is in the developing nations. Of that amount, 87 percent is in long-term credits and guarantees. This is a measure of the confidence of the U.S. Government in developing Africa.

The working out of Eximbank support inevitably involves our Embassies in negotiations with African governments.

For all these reasons, a very close relationship between U.S. Government representatives in an African country and the American exporter is highly desirable.

If we in the Embassies are to be truly effective, we need your help. There still seems to be some reluctance on the part of businessmen to

[11] Cf. Chapter X at notes 64-66.

check with us. The Embassy often can provide useful tips and background on the local situation that can save the businessman valuable time and trouble.

We need your help in following up on promises and correspondence with Africans. American business has too often been remiss in this practice.

We need your help in establishing a presence in the key market areas in Africa. It is not enough for a salesman to spend 3 or 4 days on the scene. Company representatives must make frequent visits and remain for longer periods if they hope to create the climate of familiarity and trust necessary to "do business." This investment in time pays off, especially with the African, who sets great store by personal contacts. Unfortunately many companies are not yet ready to make this investment, an investment which looks to the long term in a market of great potential.

We need your help in maintaining a high standard of quality. I am sure that other exporting countries face the problem of businessmen who think that Africa will take anything and who dump inferior goods on the African Continent; Africans will not take anything, and in the highly competitive situation in Africa, American goods must be goods of quality. I have been shocked in travels in Africa to see abandoned American products and to find that they were unloaded in Africa in a way that hurts our entire commercial presence.

We must not forget that we are not in on the ground floor with our exports in Africa. We face the competition of European firms long entrenched and, in the case of French speakers, familiar with both the language and the country. We face, as everywhere, the vigorous competition of the Japanese.

EXTRA RESPONSIBILITY OF AMERICAN BUSINESS

I have mentioned that we are on the spot in Africa. We are on the spot to invest. We are on the spot to trade in the face of major competition. We, both business and government, are increasingly on the spot to show a responsibility toward the environment in which we may be operating.

This is a delicate area as far as the United States is concerned. American business traditionally has felt that its responsibility does not extend except in exceptional circumstances beyond the purely business motives that take it to a country. There is frequently the feeling that extra effort should not be made lest that extra effort, which often means extra cost, be the opening wedge to other demands.

Yet, increasingly, American business abroad carries an American imprint and creates expectations that go along with the name "American." There is, therefore, created a certain assumption of responsibility which we cannot ignore.

First, the African government, conscious of European firms in a "European mold," expects American firms to be visibly American. Now, naturally, in this day of multinational business firms, the American enterprise is going to do business with Africa in the manner that is most profitable. Frequently this means dealing through European subsidiaries.

On many occasions in Africa, however, I have run into the very strong desire of Africans to deal directly with the American company and to talk with an American rather than the foreign representative of an American company. I have had Africans say to me, "But how is it that the representative of an American company is of another nationality?" Even if the dealings are through European firms it is important, often for political reasons, for the firm to send someone from its American office occasionally to the African countries.

In countries where the needs of development are great, and particularly the need for trained manpower, the willingness of business to contribute to these needs is becoming more and more important. In recognition of this, the Advisory Council on Africa, which works with us in the Department of State and which includes individuals who are members of this chamber, is looking into the adaptation for Africa of some of the excellent programs of education and training that American companies have created in other parts of the world and particularly in Latin America. This is an area where American firms may have an opportunity both to demonstrate their interest in the countries' development and to provide an extra dimension that can be helpful commercially.

In the southern sixth of the African Continent, one of the great problem areas in human relations exists.[12] In South Africa and Rhodesia white minority regimes rule, effectively excluding the majority from the political process. In the Portuguese territories colonial administrations are still in power.

As many of you know, the policies of firms which invest in these areas toward their employees is becoming more and more of an issue in this country.

Even among groups that feel very strongly on the situation in southern Africa, contact with the problem has changed attitudes.

There is less emphasis now on a withdrawal by American business from southern Africa. The Polaroid Company is demonstrating what a private company can do to equalize employment practices and improve labor relations. Other American companies are showing an interest in following Polaroid's example.

12 Cf. pp. 381 ff.

This, again, is a matter essentially between the American business and its employees in the countries of southern Africa. We as a Department, however, recognizing the growing importance of this problem, stand ready to counsel with American business firms on things that can be done consistent with the laws of the foreign land in which they operate, that can still put American business in the forefront of peaceful change. We have found, as I think many of the companies have found, that there is much that can be done, consistent with the local regulations, that can contribute to an improved relationship with the firms' environment.

As I travel about this country discussing African issues with various audiences, I find that the greatest emphasis among these people is on what the United States is doing to ameliorate the situation in southern Africa.

This interest and concern are understandable, but Africans themselves have one overriding concern when they speak to the U.S. Government, and that is, what role the United States can play in their economic development.

The help they seek is not just from us as a government. They know that aid may be a declining resource. They know, also, that true development will come only with a sound economy based as much as possible on trade and profitable investment. They are, therefore, seeking your help as well as ours.

American business has already made a valuable contribution to the development of Africa. The road lies open for an even greater contribution, mutually beneficial not only in economic progress but in strengthened ties between this country and Africa.

B. The United States and Northern Africa.

[Closely identified with the Arab world both ethnically and culturally, the countries of North Africa often seemed to share more interests with their fellow members of the Arab League than with the nations situated in the sub-Saharan sections of the African continent. Preoccupation with Middle Eastern affairs did not, however, prevent Algeria, Libya, Morocco, Sudan, and Tunisia from playing their full part as African states and members of the Organization of African Unity (O.A.U.). The following statement by Assistant Secretary Newsom provides an informative survey of American relations with these five countries toward the end of President Nixon's first term.]

(68) United States Policy Toward North Africa: Statement by Assistant Secretary Newsom Before the Subcommittees on Africa and the Near East of the House Committee on Foreign Affairs, July 19, 1972. [13]

(Complete Text)

Mr. Chairmen: I welcome this opportunity to meet with you and the members of your subcommittees today to discuss our policy toward North Africa. Your joining together for this review is symbolic of the significant way in which the problems and the currents of the Middle East and Africa meet in this area.

I have been associated with our relations with the Arab world for the better part of my career, going back to service in Iraq in 1951. My North African experience began with my assignment as Deputy Director of the Office of Northern African Affairs in the Department of State in 1962 and continued with my appointment as Ambassador to Libya in 1965. I continue to follow events in the area closely against the wider backdrop of my present African responsibilities. I have visited each of the countries we are discussing today several times. I have met all but one of the heads of state.

As you know, responsibility for our relations with the Arab states of North Africa, except for Egypt, falls within the Bureau of African Affairs. While there is no perfect way to divide the world for such purposes, this has proved a thoroughly feasible organization and has recognized the special links of these countries with the rest of the continent. At the same time we coordinate closely with the Bureau of Near Eastern and South Asian Affairs to insure that our policies take fully into account the fact that these countries are also Arab and inextricably linked as well in culture and interests with the Near East.

While there are common threads that run through these countries, they are distinct in character, culture, and background. In our policies, we recognize and encourage wider area links, but basically we treat them as individual countries. The actual relationships we have with each vary accordingly.

Each of these states is sovereign and jealously independent. No matter how close our relations may be, we recognize this as a fundamental basis for our relations. Their internal affairs are their own. While we may have some marginal influence on the implementation of economic and developmental policies through our aid programs, this does not extend to internal political policies or organizations. The latter is an area in which, in this day and age, our involvement is neither feasible nor consistent with our respect for the national political institutions.

With two of the states of the area, Algeria and the Sudan, we do not have diplomatic relations, a circumstance existing since the six-day Middle East war of 1967.[14] We take the position with each that we are prepared to resume relations whenever they are. Nevertheless, as I will show, our relations with each have steadily grown on the basis of developing mutual interests.

In the case of Mauritania, a state which has identified itself increasingly with North Africa because of its Arab and Islamic heritage, the diplomatic relations that had been broken in June 1967 were restored in 1970 with the reopening of a small American diplomatic mission in Nouakchott and of a small Mauritanian mission in Washington. Our relations with Mauritania are cordial but not extensive. In September 1971, President [Moktar] Ould Daddah visited Washington in his capacity as President of the Organization of African Unity (OAU) and held useful conversations with President Nixon[15] regarding the status of Namibia.

The leaders of the area have shown in the past several years a remarkable ability to resolve problems existing among them. While actual economic or political unity may still be a distant dream, their practical relationships and understanding has steadily grown closer. What seemed like intractable problems 10 years ago are now behind them.

Morocco's recognition of Mauritania in 1969 set aside centuries-old claims. Algeria and Tunisia found a common understanding on their frontier and on economic cooperation in 1969. The agreement concluded between Morocco and Algeria in June of this year resolved problems which resulted in actual conflict between the two states in 1963. Sudan, with the help of others, has resolved its 16-year-old internal southern problem. Each one of these, in a world of unresolved disputes, is a remarkable achievement that has received all too little attention in this country.

One regional problem that remains is the status of Spanish Sahara, which both Mauritania and Morocco claim and in whose eventual disposition Algeria is also interested. Discussions regarding the future of this territory have been held from time to time by the interested governments and in the United Nations. Spain has promised to hold a referendum of the inhabitants of the area to ascertain the wishes of the population regarding their political future, but a date for the referendum has not yet been fixed. One of the principal reasons for the interest of Morocco, Mauritania, and Algeria in Spanish Sahara is the territory's economic potential, represented chiefly by its substantial phosphate deposits. The territory might also provide a relatively nearby

---

[14] The resumption of diplomatic relations with the Sudan was announced July 25, 1972; relations with Algeria were resumed Nov. 12, 1974.
[15] *Presidential Documents*, Oct. 4, 1971, p. 1365.

exit point for Algerian exports of iron ore from mines in southwestern Algeria should they be developed in the future.

Now to take up the countries on an individual basis.

CLOSE RELATIONS WITH MOROCCO AND TUNISIA

Our relations have traditionally been closest with Morocco and Tunisia. Each has been going through a period of some political uncertainty.

In Morocco, since the abortive coup attempt on July 10 of last year, the King [Hassan II] has been seeking new constitutional arrangements which would widen the sharing of governmental responsibility. He has so far been unable to reach agreement on a more broadly based government with the leaders of the traditional political parties. An additional factor may be elements in the youth of the country who find identity neither with the traditional political parties nor the monarchy. The King, a shrewd political leader in his own right, is still very much in control.

Morocco remains one of the largest recipients of U.S. assistance in Africa. In fiscal year 1972, we provided $50 million in loans and grants, the largest part of this being in P.L. 480 commodities.[16] At the same time, U.S. investment in Morocco, already at the $47 million mark by December 1971, increased still further.

In the military field, Morocco permits us to utilize frequencies and facilities for U.S. naval communications, although the size of our contingent is being reduced as part of a worldwide reduction of U.S. personnel at similar installations elsewhere. The Moroccan facilities, however, remain an important and integral link in our worldwide communications system. We provide a limited amount of grant aid training for the Moroccan armed forces, as well as credit assistance for the purchase of U.S. military equipment that last year totaled $15 million.

Morocco is also the site of one of the two principal Voice of America relay points in Africa. The transmitters at Tangier are shared with the Moroccans under arrangements made in 1963.

In Tunisia, we have had a strong friend over many years in President [Habib] Bourguiba. He recalls early American help to him as a person and to his nation. His moderate views on many issues have been close to ours. After a period of inactivity because of illness, he has returned to active leadership in Tunisia, manifested by a vigorous appearance at the Organization of African Unity meeting in Rabat[17] and by a recent state

---

[16] Cf. Chapter III, note 17.

[17] The Ninth Regular Session of the O.A.U. Assembly of Heads of State and Government was held in Rabat (Morocco) on June 12-15, 1972.

visit to France. During this period, the Destourian Socialist Party organization has been considering the question of succession, and constitutional changes have been proposed. Under the current provisions of the Constitution the Prime Minister [Hedi Nouira] would fill out the remainder of the Presidential term; that is, until 1974.

We have for many years made a substantial input into Tunisia's economic development, recognizing the potential of this energetic nation with relatively few natural resources. In fiscal year 1972, our assistance will total about $43 million, a large part of this representing continuing help to the agricultural sector.

RELATIONS WITH ALGERIA AND LIBYA

Three major political differences have affected us in our relations with Algeria since before Algerian independence: their view of our relations with France during the Algerian war of independence; different views on Viet-Nam, Cuba, and the Middle East; their activist role in Third World movements. Relations reached their lowest point when Algeria broke diplomatic relations with us in 1967. The break was further aggravated by the Algerian nationalization of the assets of nine U.S. companies.

Since that time, we have worked slowly and realistically to find a common basis for improved relations. This has been found in the growing U.S. need for natural gas from external sources and the Algerian need for capital and markets for that country's extensive hydrocarbon resources.

Within the last few years we have, as a result, seen the settlement, with compensation, of the nine U.S. nationalization cases, a growing involvement in Algeria of U.S. technology and technicians, and an increasing exposure of the Export-Import Bank in Algerian projects. The largest project is one in which the El Paso Natural Gas Company proposes to purchase a very substantial quantity of gas for U.S. customers from Sonatrach, the Algerian national hydrocarbon company. The U.S. customers have obtained preliminary approval from the Federal Power Commission for the deal, but serious problems of future pricing remain to be worked out. Two other U.S. companies have contracted to purchase Algerian LNG [liquefied natural gas]. Conceivably, Algeria, by 1985, could be selling half of its natural gas output to the United States.

Meanwhile, diplomatic contact has been developing through the establishment and augmentation of interest sections in each country. Algeria is under the flag of Guinea in this country, and we are under the Swiss flag in Algeria.

The Libyan revolution of September 1969 changed the character of

Libyan-U.S. relations. The new regime, under the leadership of Colonel [Mu'ammar al-] Qadhaafi and a group of young military officers, sees its policies in exclusively Arab terms. It seeks closer cooperation among Arab states and sees that cooperation focused primarily on the cause of the Palestinians and the struggle with Israel. Although strongly anti-Communist, the regime is at the same time cool to the United States and Britain because of the stand of these governments on Arab issues.

The present Libyan Government has, at the same time, sought greater control, greater revenue, and greater participaton in the production of its basic resource, petroleum. U.S. companies which produce 90 percent of Libya's petroleum are under severe pressure as a result.

The Libyan revolution also ended the previous military relationship with the United States and Britain. We withdrew at the request of the Libyans from Wheelus Air Base, as the British withdrew from their base at El Adem. In keeping with the 1954 agreement, permanent construction reverted to the Libyan Government. Movable property was removed except for a small amount which was sold to the Libyans after screening our worldwide requirements. By a recent exchange of notes outstanding agreements were ended and conflicting claims canceled. The Libyans now use the former base as their principal military base in the Tripoli area.

SLOW IMPROVEMENT IN U.S.-SUDAN RELATIONS

President [Ja'far Muhammad] Nimeri of the Sudan has, since he came to power in a military coup in 1969, been charting a delicate course among the various political tendencies of that country, the largest geographically in Africa. Coming to power originally with support from the Sudanese Communists, he broke with them after the abortive coup of July 1971. Relations with the Soviet Union became particularly strained, although those with Communist China did not.

Today he is seeking to build improved relations with all his neighbors, to the south and to the north. He desires to insure the success of the recent agreement on the southern Sudan,[18] while at the same time keeping firm ties with Egypt and the Arab world. Because of the complex political and ethnic makeup of the Sudan, he has avoided any commitment to join the Confederation of Arab Republics.[19]

The slow improvement in our own relations with the Sudan began after Nimeri came to power, but predating his break with the Soviets.

---

[18] A longstanding insurgent movement in the southern Sudan was ended by an agreement on regional autonomy negotiated in Addis Ababa and ratified Mar. 27, 1972.

[19] A tripartite structure established by Egypt, Libya, and Syria pursuant to national referendums held Sept. 1, 1971.

We see our improved relationship as stemming from a desire on President Nimeri's part to resume effective relations with the United States and not only as a counterweight to the Soviet Union.[20]

Most recently we have demonstrated our admiration for the southern settlement and our hope for the future of the Sudan by giving emergency assistance to the Sudan Government for returning refugees in the south. We are making available more than $4 million in P.L. 480 title II food supplies and are also contributing some $18 million for food relief through the World Food Program. Much of our bilateral assistance will be funneled through U.S. voluntary agencies.

FOUR DIMENSIONS OF NORTH AFRICA'S POLICIES

North Africa is the hub of a wheel with spokes to the Near East, to Africa, to Europe, and to us. Its policies need to be seen in all these dimensions.

The countries are drawn to the Near East by their Arab language and culture and by their political concern over Near East issues. At the same time, other interests and priorities are present and none is as completely absorbed in these issues as are the states directly contiguous to Israel.

Each of these states points, also, toward Africa. Morocco and Mauritania are pressing the question of the Spanish Sahara. King Hassan of Morocco has just succeeded President Ould Daddah of Mauritania as President of the Organization of African Unity. As such he will, for the coming year, be deeply involved in African issues.

Algeria borders on Mauritania, Mali, and Niger. It has always taken an interest, and continues to do so, in the liberation movement in Africa. President [Houari] Boumediene recently visited Guinea, before his attendance at the OAU meeting in Rabat.

Tunisia has always taken a great interest in African issues and a significant role in the OAU. Libya has increasingly interested itself in sub-Saharan Africa through expressions in the past of support for Moslem populations in other states and opposition to what it regards as Israeli influence detrimental to the Arab cause in Africa. President Nimeri is striving to unite the Sudan, as the recent agreement with the southerners has shown. In this endeavor he has been aided by other African states, the good offices of the Imperial Ethiopian Government, and the personal efforts of Emperor Haile Selassie.

Relations with Europe have always been of great importance, particularly to the three states of the Maghreb: Morocco, Algeria, and Tunisia. They remain so today. Europe is the principal market and the principal source of supplies. Relationships of these nations with the European Common Market become increasingly important to them.

[20] Cf. note 14 above.

Common Market relations with Mediterranean countries are in a state of flux. Existing trade arrangements are to be modified as a result of the enlargement of the Community and the proposed changes in relations between the Community and the European Free Trade Area countries remaining outside.[21] For the longer run, the Community has under active consideration a coherent "Mediterranean policy" embracing the countries from Spain to Israel and including the Arab states.

Algeria, particularly, is also manifesting more and more interest in questions of European and Mediterranean security and is expressing a desire for Maghreb participation in any European Security Conference.

I have already outlined how the relationship of each of these states with us is also important, whether for reasons of investment, trade, or aid. I believe they will remain so. Though our direct relationship to the political events of this area may continue to diminish, though these countries may become increasingly allied to Europe economically, strong bases of common interest with the United States will remain. Our policies for the future will be designed to develop those common interests into strong and realistic links across the Atlantic.

C. The Upheaval in Burundi.

[Two African developments that produced widespread distress in 1972 took place in the equatorial region of East Central Africa that includes Uganda and Burundi. In August 1972, President Idi Amin Dada of Uganda abruptly decreed the expulsion of over 50,000 residents of Indian and other Asian origin, some 1,000 of whom were eventually admitted to the United States on an emergency basis while approximately 28,000 went to the United Kingdom. In Burundi, an alleged coup attempt against a government dominated by the minority Tutsi people resulted in the unleashing of a veritable wave of terror against members of the more numerous but less powerful Hutu group. This development was later described by Secretary of State Rogers in the following terms:

"A political upheaval in Burundi from April to October unfortunately contributed to a resurgence of the chronic instability that has plagued the central African region for a number of years. A report released by the United Nations in July said 'the proportions of the human tragedy which the people of Burundi are experiencing are staggering. The Burundi Government itself has reported that 80,000 persons had died since April 29 and that 500,000 persons are experiencing great suffering.' The tragedy in Burundi also sent thousands of refugees into neighboring Rwanda, Zaïre, and

[21] Cf. Document 20 at note 4.

Tanzania, where the local governments have responded generously with humanitarian assistance aided by U.N. and voluntary agencies. We have been concerned with the dimensions of the tragedy as well as the questions of human rights involved in the events since April 29. We therefore continue to support U.N. efforts to assure that relief assistance for victims of the tragedy is distributed equitably to all who need it, both inside Burundi and among refugees outside. . . .

"African governments regarded the tribal conflict which sparked the tragedy as an internal matter but, privately, several African leaders sought to encourage reconciliation among the deeply divided people."[22]

In line with the position adopted by African governments, the United States refrained from dramatizing the political or moral issues involved in the Burundi tragedy and limited itself for the most part to trying to mitigate the resultant human suffering. The record of American action is set forth in the following letter from the Assistant Secretary of State for Congressional Relations, David M. Abshire, to Chairman Fulbright of the Senate Foreign Relations Committee.]

(69) The Position of the United States: Letter from David M. Abshire, Assistant Secretary of State for Congressional Relations, to Senator J. William Fulbright, Chairman of the Senate Committee on Foreign Relations, August 18, 1972.[23]

(Complete Text)

AUGUST 18, 1972.

Honorable J. W. FULBRIGHT
Chairman, Committee on Foreign Relations
United States Senate
Washington, D.C.

DEAR MR. CHAIRMAN: The Secretary has asked me to respond to your letter of June 15 requesting comments on Senate Resolutions 315, 316, and 317 on civil strife in Burundi.

The Administration has been closely following the recent events in Burundi. As we understand the situation, a rebellion by elements of the Hutu people during the week of May 1 triggered a reaction by the ruling Tutsi who feared losing their dominant position and their lives as

22 Rogers Report, 1972, pp. 465-6.
23 *Bulletin*, Sept. 11, 1972, pp. 283-4.

the Tutsi had in Rwanda in the early sixties. The subsequent arrests and executions, which the Burundi Government claimed only involved those guilty of revolution against the state, are alleged to have included large numbers of Hutu government leaders, intellectuals, secondary school children, common workers and peasants.

The United States was the first government to extend relief to the victims of this crisis by allocating $100,000 to our Embassy for the purchase of ambulances, food, blankets, medicines and cooking utensils. In addition, our Embassy associated with the Embassies of Belgium, Great Britain, Rwanda, Switzerland, West Germany, and Zaire in supporting the demarche presented to the Government of Burundi by the dean of the diplomatic corps, the Papal Nuncio, calling for a return to peace and an end to reprisals.

Anticipating that the Burundi question would be considered at the June summit of the OAU,[24] prior to that meeting, we discussed the crisis with the governments of Ethiopia, Rwanda, and Zaire and with the President and Secretary-General of the OAU.[25] The members of the OAU, however, chose not to intervene in what they considered to be the internal affairs of another African state.

We then consulted with UN officials to ascertain what that organization could usefully do. On June 22, a three-man mission sent by Secretary-General [Kurt] Waldheim reached Burundi to investigate the requirements of humanitarian assistance and also, privately to assess the general situation and convey a message of concern to President [Michel] Micombero. The mission included a representative of the UN High Commissioner for Refugees [UNHCR].

We have not seen the report submitted to the Secretary-General, but we know that the Government of Burundi reported 80,000 dead and estimated that $8 million would be needed for immediate relief requirements. The Secretary-General subsequently issued a statement which noted that "the proportions of the human tragedy which the people of Burundi are experiencing are staggering." With respect to Burundi's request for relief assistance, Waldheim announced that "the United Nations system must be in a position to assure the international community, and donors in particular, that assistance will reach the entire population and benefit the country as a whole."

Partly to satisfy this requirement, the UN sent a second mission in late July. We hope that the mission made it clear to the Government of Burundi that relief aid will have to be equitably distributed. International organizations have previously had difficulty in securing appropriate cooperation with humanitarian efforts in Burundi. Early in the current crisis, UNICEF and UNDP [United Nations Children's Fund; United Nations Development Program] vehicles were comman-

24 Cf. note 17 above.
25 Respectively Moktar Ould Daddah (Mauritania) and Diallo Telli (Guinea).

deered by the Government for internal security use. The International Red Cross found itself unable to gain freedom of access to all parts of the country and all elements of the population and has withdrawn its staff and supplies. Catholic Relief Services (CRS) is continuing its operations within Burundi.

The United States is prepared to contribute further to emergency relief in Burundi but there must be adequate guarantees that the relief will benefit directly those requiring it.

In the states neighboring Burundi, the refugee problem has become more acute. The United States has expressed its concern about the refugee problem and about the situation within Burundi to the Governments of Rwanda, Tanzania and Zaire. The Presidents of Zaire and Tanzania[26] subsequently met with President Micombero and the President of Rwanda[27] received Foreign Minister [Artémon] Simbananiye. We hope that these contacts will produce initiatives which will involve Burundi's neighbors and other African states in cooperative efforts to provide assistance and assure peace.

In the meantime, public and private organizations are caring for the refugees along Burundi's borders. The United States has given an emergency allocation of $50,000 to the Catholic Relief Services to help the Burundi refugees in East Zaire and will further supplement the efforts of the asylum countries, UNHCR and other relief agencies as additional needs are identified.

It is clear from the above that the objectives of Senate Resolutions 315 and 317 have been realized. With regard to Senate Resolution 316, as already noted above, the OAU decided not to intervene in what they considered to be an internal Burundi problem. Furthermore, the United States is not a member of the Organization of African Unity and, therefore, would be in a difficult position to request an investigation by or a report from that body. Since the beginning of the crisis, we have discussed our concerns about Burundi with key leaders of the OAU. These discussions have revealed a concern on their part, but we are not aware of any specific steps being taken by the OAU.[28]

The Office of Management and Budget advises that from the standpoint of the Administration, there is no objection to the submission of this report.

Sincerely yours,

DAVID M. ABSHIRE

Assistant Secretary
for Congressional Relations

---

[26] Respectively Mobutu Sese Seko and Julius K. Nyerere.
[27] Grégoire Kayibanda.
[28] None of the proposed resolutions was adopted.

D. The United States and Southern Africa.

[More controversial than its policies in Northern, Central, and East Africa was the Nixon administration's attitude regarding conditions in Africa's southern region, particularly in the Republic of South Africa, Namibia (South West Africa), Southern Rhodesia (Zimbabwe), and the Portuguese-ruled "provinces" of Portuguese Guinea (Guinea-Bissau), Angola, and Mozambique. This was an area where, as President Nixon recognized, the aspirations of the black majorities for full participation in political and economic life were frustrated by "minority intransigence and repression" that were creating one of the continent's most explosive problems.[29] It was also an area in which American policy was being harshly criticized, both by black African governments and by a vocal segment of U.S. opinion, on the ground that it was in effect aligned with the white majority regimes in opposition to majority aspirations as well as to underlying principles of justice.[30]

The extent, if any, to which the policy of the Nixon administration may have been deliberately "tilted" in favor of Southern Africa's white regimes is obviously not susceptible of precise measurement. Official disclaimers of any lack of sympathy for African aspirations may be juxtaposed with secret documents, made public by the columnist Jack Anderson and others, that do not fully resolve this issue but afford some insight into the manner in which the administration's policies toward Southern Africa were originally formulated.

A range of options for dealing with the black-white confrontation in Southern Africa was apparently set forth initially in a National Security Study Memorandum (N.S.S.M. 39) that was completed under the auspices of the National Security Council in August 1969 as basis for a formal policy decision by the President. President Nixon, in turn, is said to have approved in January or February 1970 a recommendation by Dr. Kissinger envisaging, in effect, an attempt to promote conciliation between the two hostile groups through a combination of "selective relaxation of our stance toward the white regimes" and "more substantial assistance to the black states." This recommendation is said to have reflected a conviction that the whites were in Africa "to stay"; that constructive change could come about only through them; and that violence, far from enabling the blacks to gain the political rights they sought, would "only lead to chaos and increased opportunities for the Communists."[31]

[29] Nixon Report, 1972, pp. 101-2.
[30] Cf. *A.F.R., 1971*, pp. 429-31.
[31] Jack Anderson in *Washington Post*, Oct. 11, 1974; Murrey Marder in same, Oct. 13, 1974.

This line of reasoning is consistent with what is known of President Nixon's attitude from his public statements. "For more than a decade," the President pointed out in his "State of the World" report for 1972, "leading Americans in all fields have expressed this nations's profound concern over racial injustice in southern Africa, and decried the serious potential of the issue for bringing large scale conflict to this region.... I share the conviction that the United States cannot be indifferent to racial policies which violate our national ideals and constitute a direct affront to American citizens.... Americans alone, however, cannot solve the racial problems of southern Africa.... For our part, we look toward black and white *in Africa* to play the primary role in working toward progress consistent with human dignity. We support their efforts by:

—Encouraging communication between the races in Africa, and between African peoples and our own.
—Making known directly to the parties involved our views on their actions. My Administration will not condone recourse to violence, either as a means of enforcing submission of a majority to a minority or as a formula for effecting needed social change....

"Some call for the United States to take the prime responsibility for the racial problems of southern Africa. Some want the United States to force upon the minority governments of southern Africa immediate and, if need be, violent change. I have indicated why I reject that position. Southern Africa contains within itself the seeds of change. We can and will work with others to encourage that process."[32]]

1. An Overview.

[The principles enunciated by President Nixon found frequent application in dealing with those Southern African situations that figured regularly in international controversy and were a standing subject of United Nations debate. An unusually concentrated discussion of many of these issues took place early in 1972 when the Security Council held a special series of meetings in Addis Ababa, Ethiopia, for the express purpose of focusing world attention on African problems. Meeting in the Ethiopian capital from January 28 to February 4, 1972, the Security Council eventually adopted four resolutions that dealt respectively with (1) the launching of a U.N.

[32] Nixon Report, 1972, pp. 105-6.

diplomatic effort regarding Namibia;[33] (2) a renewed demand for South African withdrawal from Namibia;[34] (3) a condemnation of *apartheid* (racial segregation) in South Africa itself;[35] and (4) support for liberation movements in Portuguese Africa.[36] Three of these resolutions were adopted with the support of the United States—which, however, abstained on the resolution regarding Portuguese Africa, and also on a resolution concerning Southern Rhodesia that was vetoed by the United Kingdom.[37]

The significance of these actions was well brought out in Assistant Secretary Newsom's midyear review of U.S. policy on Southern African issues (Document 70), which is particularly helpful in clarifying the year's developments with respect to Namibia, Portuguese Africa, and Southern Rhodesia.]

(70) "Southern Africa—Constant Themes in U.S. Policy": Address by Assistant Secretary of State Newsom Before the Mid-America Committee, Chicago, June 28, 1972.[38]

(Complete Text)

Interest here at home in a meaningful U.S. policy toward Africa has clearly been growing in recent years. We welcome this interest. We feel it should be accompanied by an accurate knowledge and an increased understanding of what our policy is.

I regret to say that our policy and actions have been misunderstood on occasion and misinterpreted. It is not my purpose here today to make a partisan speech. As the steward of our African policy over the past three years, however, I should like to take this occasion to set the record straight.

The growing interest in Africa in this country was manifested most dramatically during the last weekend in May when a conference of 400 black Americans at Howard University was followed by an impressive demonstration by over 10,000 persons in Washington on behalf of African liberation. As is natural to an occasion totally directed to one area of policy, there were many critical of official policies—not always, however, with a full knowledge of what the policies are and of the

---

[33] Cf. below at note 46.
[34] Resolution 310 (1972), Feb. 4, 1972, adopted by a vote of 13-0-2 (France, U.K.).
[35] Resolution 311 (1972), Feb. 4, 1972, adopted by a vote of 14-0-1 (France).
[36] Resolution 312 (1972), Feb. 4, 1972, adopted by a vote of 9-0-6 (U.S.); cf. below at notes 49-51.
[37] Cf. below at note 54.
[38] Department of State Press Release 156; text from *Bulletin*, July 24, 1972, pp. 119-25.

complexities of making those policies. Charges ranged from "neglect" of Africa to assertions that present policies represented a shift from the past purposely in favor of the white-dominated regimes of southern Africa. Quite understandably, because of the identity with racial problems, the focus of attention of this surging interest in Africa is on the southern portion of the continent.

There have been other manifestations of both rising interest and serious misconception. The New York Times of April 2 highlighted what it called the deliberate increase of contacts and communication with the white-dominated regimes of southern Africa. A statement issued through the office of Congressman [Charles J.] Diggs [Jr.] of the House Subcommittee on Africa spoke of "collaboration" with the white regimes.

There has also been criticism from those who dislike our policies on the ground that these policies do not sufficiently recognize certain of our interests in southern Africa. Motivated by concern over strategic or economic considerations, by basic sympathies with the white populations of the area, or by reluctance to see us become involved in problems of distant regions, many express their disapproval of traditional U.S. restraint toward the regimes of southern Africa.

Individual American attitudes toward this area vary widely. Those making policy are in the middle.

To set the record straight on what our policies can be and what they are, let us examine first those elements that have been constant in U.S. policy toward southern Africa since the late fifties:

—First, the United States Government has consistently supported the principle of self-determination for all peoples in Africa.

—Second, we have strongly and actively indicated our abhorrence of the institution of apartheid.

—Third, we have consistently favored peaceful change in southern Africa through supporting constructive alternatives to the use of force.

Our implementation of these principles has been governed, for more than a decade and through several administrations, by our recognition of four realities:

1. As a nation, we have complex worldwide relationships. Our response to the needs of one area frequently is limited by our interests in another. For example, the difference between interests in Europe and in Africa has affected our position in both.

2. We are dealing in southern Africa with governments which react strongly to outside pressures and are not easily susceptible to persuasion.

3. We are dealing with complex societies, not with the interest of one

race, but of many. Justice requires a consideration of the future of all.

4. There are many real limitations on the extent to which we can influence the situation, both in terms of what might be supported domestically and of what we might be able to do in Africa.

The actions of the U.S. Government in this area over the past three years have been consistent with these general policy lines and limitations laid down in the years just after the emergence of independent Africa.

By the strict maintenance of arms embargoes toward both South Africa and the Portuguese territories, we have tangibly demonstrated our support for self-determination and our desire to avoid any support either for the imposition of apartheid or for the continuation of colonial rule.

The maintenance of an arms embargo may sound like a passive act. It is not. It requires constant vigilance over shipments to the area. It means considerable sacrifice on the part of U.S. exporters who have seen substantial sales in southern Africa go to countries less conscientious about the embargo and less criticized by the Africans. It means a continuing effort on our part to explain to those in this country opposed to the embargoes the absolute necessity of maintaining them in terms of our wider interests in Africa. We believe this policy has been effective. No proof has ever been presented that any weapons have gone from the United States to southern Africa since the embargoes were established in 1963.

The maintenance of the arms embargo has been accompanied, particularly in the case of South Africa, by a strict limitation on contact with that country's military. Because we have not wished to risk subjecting our men to apartheid, we have since 1967 avoided U.S. naval visits to South African ports despite the frequent need for U.S. Navy transit of this area. This has added to logistical problems for the Navy.

The U.S. Embassy and the U.S. consulates general in South Africa continue to constitute significant bridges between the races in that country. Multiracial entertaining, contact with South Africans of all races, and the facilitation of such contacts for American visitors in the country leave little doubt as to where the United States stands with respect to apartheid. The record of the U.S. mission in this regard is in important respects a unique one.

We have, further, during the past three years sought to add new dimensions to these efforts.

We have expanded our contacts with all elements of the South African population. We have offered significant members of the South African majority the opportunity to visit this country. During the past three years, we have had 45 official visitors from South Africa, of whom 30 have been from the black, colored, and Indian communities.

Many of the white as well as the black and colored South Africans whom we have invited here have been persons deeply involved in seeking alternatives to apartheid.

It is, perhaps, pertinent that the Foreign Minister of South Africa [Hilgard Muller] felt obliged to point out to his Parliament on May 5 that present U.S. policy did not accept the South African approach to evolution within that country but sought, through persuasion, to bring about peaceful change.

We have begun to break down racial barriers regarding the assignment of American official personnel to South Africa. Black diplomatic couriers have now been placed on the runs to South Africa. Three black Foreign Service officers have, during the past year, been on temporary duty assignments in the Republic. Black Americans have been sent to South Africa under our official cultural exchange program.

In the case of Namibia, or South West Africa, we strongly supported the proposal at the United Nations to have the International Court of Justice take up the question of South Africa's continued administration of the territory.[39] We accepted the Court's conclusions that South Africa's mandate over the territory was terminated and that South Africa's continued presence there is illegal.[40]

We alone among major countries have taken the position of discouraging any new investment in the territory. We encourage U.S. firms already in Namibia to set the pace in improved employee relations. We consistently have supported the U.N.'s responsibility in the territory.

In our support for alternatives in southern Africa, we have increased our assistance dramatically to the smaller majority-ruled states of southern Africa: Botswana, Lesotho, and Swaziland. We will in July be signing a $12 million loan agreement for the construction of a road linking Botswana to Zambia and providing an economic outlet to the north for that nation. In 1971 for the first time we appointed an Ambassador[41]—a black American—to represent us in these three countries.

In the continuing interplay of U.S. interests, decisions must be made in which one set of interests may prevail, in any specific case, over another. In the region of southern Africa there are five areas in particular where conflicting interests have affected policies—in every administration. For southern Africa has in the past 15 years presented particularly difficult policy problems: The Portuguese territories, relations with the liberation movements, pressures at the United Nations, Rhodesia, and investment in South Africa are some of these.

Critics of U.S. policies seek to take isolated decisions in these problem areas and read into them a basic change in the course of U.S.

[39] Security Council Resolution 284 (1970), July 29, 1970; *Documents, 1970*, pp. 259-60.
[40] Cf. below at note 45.
[41] Charles J. Nelson.

African policy. In doing so they tend to neglect decisions which with equal logic point in the opposite direction.

In the more extreme form, a few critics have claimed that there is a conscious effort on the part of the U.S. Government at this time to favor the white-ruled governments of southern Africa. I have had to deny both in Africa and in this country that we have chosen sides in the southern conflict and that the United States would intervene on the side of the white regimes in the event of trouble.

There is no basis for such assumptions. They ignore the large and growing U.S. interest in black Africa and, particularly, our interest in the majority-ruled states in southern Africa. They ignore the fact that our one major intervention in Africa, in close collaboration with the U.N., was to preserve the unity of the Congo—against efforts to dismember it supported by the white-dominated regimes. This intervention was ordered by President Eisenhower and fully supported and carried on by President Kennedy.

RELATIONS WITH PORTUGAL

The most difficult area relates to our relations with Portugal. Portugal is an ally, a charter member of the North Atlantic Treaty Organization. For more than two decades we have enjoyed the use of base facilities in the Azores, Portuguese islands in the mid-Atlantic. These base facilities are of great importance to our antisubmarine defenses in the face of a growing Soviet submarine presence in the area.

Although our last formal agreement to continue stationing forces in the Azores lapsed in 1962, the Portuguese permitted us to stay on. When a new Portuguese Government took office in 1968, it insisted that we formalize our presence in the Azores by renewing the lapsed agreement. We concurred and also agreed to a related request that we examine areas in which the United States could assist Portugal in economic and social development. The final agreement did not follow the usual pattern of granting military assistance for military bases but was instead solely related to economic and educational development in metropolitan Portugal.

Now, this base agreement[42] has drawn a great deal of attention and has attracted substantial comment both in the United States and in Africa. I am afraid that despite our best efforts at explaining the terms it has been greatly misunderstood, and even misrepresented. Much of the confusion has concerned Export-Import Bank credits for American exporters competing for contracts in Portugal. In a letter to the Portuguese on this subject, the Secretary of State said that we had reviewed a number of development projects that they had in mind and that the

42 Cf. above at Document 21.

Export-Import Bank would consider financing exports for those projects in accordance with the usual loan criteria and practices of the Bank. Export-Import Bank facilities have always been available for U.S. firms seeking business in Portugal, and this agreement represented absolutely no change in that policy. No commitment was made to extend credits in any amount, only to consider applications as before.

The principal objection voiced against the agreement holds that it releases Portuguese resources for use in the African wars. But in fact, Portugal has large exchange reserves as the result of conservative fiscal policies. Our refusal to grant credit would not lead others to do the same. There is no evidence to suggest that our withholding credit would in any sense deter the Portuguese from pursuing their present policies in Africa.

LIBERATION MOVEMENTS IN AFRICA

We recognize that the question of our relations with Portugal and with Portuguese Africa is becoming increasingly an emotional issue in this country. Closely related to this is the question of our relations with all liberation movements in Africa. Many in Africa and America judge one's attitude toward the southern African issues as a whole by the attitude taken toward the liberation movements and their leaders.

The African movements targeted against the several parts of white-ruled southern Africa vary widely in size, effectiveness, cohesion, and activity. Those targeted against the Portuguese territories appear to be militarily the most active. They are receiving help from the Soviets and Chinese. The leaders of the movements seek contacts with and help from the West.

The question of U.S. official relations with leaders of opposition movements in colonial territories has always posed a dilemma for American policymakers. It was true in the fifties with respect particularly to North Africa. It has been no less true throughout the sixties and today in that part of Africa still under colonial or white domination.

These movements are a political fact. On the one hand, the absence of contact or support from us leaves the leaders subject to certain other outside influences. On the other hand, the United States has traditionally been unwilling to recognize opposition elements in colonial territories until an internationally recognized transfer of power has taken place. That situation still prevails today. Nevertheless, in such areas, as in the past, both U.S. Government and private organizations seek opportunities to help with appropriate humanitarian and educational assistance to refugees affected by the conflicts.

AFRICAN ISSUES IN THE UNITED NATIONS

The problem in the United Nations is particularly difficult.

We have a basic sympathy with the aspirations of the Africans to see an end to apartheid and colonial government and to see a greater recognition of the need for racial justice and equality. Most African leaders understand and appreciate this. At the same time, because of our own traditions and historical experience, they expect more of the United States—more than they expect of others. We cannot always meet these expectations.

During 1971, if we take together General Assembly and Security Council votes on African issues, we voted for 15 specific African proposals, against 11, and abstained on 12.

Many Africans believe this record is inadequate. Yet, underlying the careful consideration given each vote was a deep dedication to many of the same principles motivating African representatives and our desire, whenever possible, to vote with the Africans. Ironically, we could have voted for most of these proposals if only one or two extreme or unrealistic features had been eliminated. We were able to negotiate, however, in many cases, agreements on language changes so we could vote with the Africans. Many of the problems we had did not relate to Africa per se, but involved broader questions. They related to:

—Our desire to avoid establishing worldwide legal precedents which could affect broader U.S. and U.N. interests.
—The need to verify facts before condemning another state.
—Our deep concern over increases in the budget of the United Nations.

ECONOMIC SANCTIONS AGAINST RHODESIA

With regard to Rhodesia, the U.S. Government has sought to support United Nations economic sanctions as an alternative to a violent solution and as a form of pressure on the Smith regime to negotiate a new basis for independence. We closed our consulate in Rhodesia. We closed off all contact with the Smith regime. We enforced sanctions against Rhodesia as conscientiously as any nation, and more so than most.

This has not been a universally popular policy in this country. There are those who dislike the idea of sanctions against anyone, those who are aware of extensive violations by other countries, those whose own interests have in some way been affected, and still others who are disillusioned with the United Nations and opposed to the concept of United Nations mandatory action infringing on the United States.

There are those who deplore the fact that while other countries have been ignoring sanctions with impunity, the United States was forced to pay higher prices to the Soviet Union for strategic materials. These attitudes resulted in the action of the Congress last year to exempt strategic materials from Rhodesian sanctions and allow their importation into the United States unless there is a similar embargo on such materials from Communist countries. Efforts this year to obtain the repeal of the resultant legislation[43] have not been successful.

This move has caused adverse reactions in Africa. It created a contradiction between our domestic and international obligations. It came at a time when Britain was seeking a settlement with Rhodesia and undoubtedly led the Rhodesians for a time to believe that sanctions as a whole were visibly crumbling. While there have been far more extensive sanctions violations by others, this open and official U.S. act has made us appear the principal culprit, in New York and in Africa, condemned by resolutions both in the U.N. and in the Organization of African Unity. I dislike deeply seeing ourselves in this position.

U.S. INVESTMENTS IN SOUTH AFRICA

Finally, there is the question of U.S. investments in South Africa. There are those who see the failure of the U.S. Government to seek to restrict such investments as an indication of sympathy for the policies of South Africa. There are those who assume that the presence of these investments automatically means that we will intervene in the event of trouble in that area. Neither assumption is correct. Here, again, the record needs to be set straight:

—First, U.S. investment in South Africa represents only 16 percent of total foreign investment in that country. It represents only a fourth of total U.S. investment in Africa, a ratio that is decreasing all the time. It is not likely that U.S. withdrawal of this investment, assuming this were feasible, would force change in South Africa. There is no valid basis for speculating that the United States would take extraordinary measures to protect this investment in the event of civil or other disturbance when, among other factors, more substantial investment in the rest of the continent would need to be weighed in the balance.

—Second, much of this investment is linked with South African business interests; withdrawal would not be easy even if the United States had authority to force withdrawal by American companies. New U.S. investment in South Africa comes to a large extent from current profits of U.S. firms operating there.

—Third, the United States does not encourage investment in South Africa nor extend guarantees covering such investment. It is the economic situation in that country that attracts investment.

[43] Cf. below at note 58.

—Fourth, while there is debate in the United States and in South Africa on this point, our soundings indicate that the black and colored populations of South Africa do not want to see U.S. investment withdrawn. The majority see U.S. investment as a constructive force; they wish to see it remain and make an impact on that society.

The United States Government, therefore, neither encourages nor discourages investment in South Africa. It does encourage U.S. firms that are there to lead the way in upgrading the status of non-white workers and in contributions to social and educational improvement. It is a misleading oversimplification to suggest that the presence of that investment either draws us into the conflict of races in that area or commits us to a policy favorable to apartheid.

The southern African aspect, however, is not the only element in U.S. policy toward Africa. There are 41 independent African states other than South Africa. In many of them we have major interests and investments. We desire satisfactory relations with all.

Cliches exist about this aspect of our policy as well. People speak of "neglect," and "low priority." The facts do not bear this out.

With patient effort, we have established reasonably satisfactory relations with all but one of these states. We have, in the past three years, resumed diplomatic relations with Mauritania; we have strengthened our relations with Algeria and the Sudan despite the continued absence of formal diplomatic ties.[44] Of all the states in Africa, only in Congo (Brazzaville) do we not have reasonable access to the leadership and a reasonably respected relationship.

African nations welcome the attention we have given to them and to their citizens as significant members of the world community. We have, from its inception, recognized the Organization of African Unity as a forward-looking institution representing the common interests and identities of Africans.

Through visits, correspondence, and the work of our diplomatic missions, we have established bonds of friendship and common interest which belie any suggestion of neglect. The Ambassador of one of the most militant African countries recently told one of our officers that he was preparing a memorandum for his government emphasizing the degree of attention given both personally to him and to the needs and interests of Africa by those in the U.S. Government. We are in continuing correspondence with several African heads of state, including one from another militant government who, while not agreeing with all that we are doing, emphasizes his appreciation for the attention we give to him and to the needs of his country.

In the last analysis, each African leader places the greatest emphasis on the needs of his own country, particularly in the desperate search

44 Cf. note 14 above.

for the means of development. Here, there is neither neglect nor low priority on the part of the United States.

During a period of increasing disillusionment with foreign aid and of declining overall appropriations, we have been able to maintain assistance to the African countries at a constant level. In 1972, in fact, the overall sum was the highest since 1968. Our role was part of an international effort which gives the African Continent the highest per capita development aid in the world.

The United States follows policies in Africa today which are consistent with the main themes of that policy since the late fifties. It follows policies which give us a meaningful relationship with a continent increasingly important in terms both of trade and investment and its role on the international stage.

2. Search for Political Settlements: Namibia and the Portuguese Territories.

[Though 1972 brought no *de facto* easing of South African *apartheid* and no real modification in the status of Namibia, Rhodesia, or the Portuguese territories, developments with respect to some of these areas appeared to open up at least a possibility of peaceful change of the kind the United States professed to favor. Particularly auspicious, in the American view, was the apparent tendency in U.N. quarters to switch from "confrontation to negotiation" in seeking a solution of the problems of Namibia and the Portuguese African provinces.]

a. Namibia (South West Africa).

[The most recent phase of the Namibian problem had been shaped by South Africa's uncompromising rejection of the advisory opinion of the International Court of Justice, delivered June 21, 1971, to the effect that the continued presence of South Africa in that territory was illegal and should be terminated forthwith.[45] In the absence of practical means of giving effect to this stand, the Security Council at its Addis Ababa meeting early in 1972 had sanctioned a new and more conciliatory approach whereby the U.N. Secretary-General was invited to establish direct contact with South Africa with a view to furthering Namibian self-determination and independence.[46] Contacts subsequently maintained by Secretary-

---

[45] *A.F.R., 1971*, no. 104; cf. above at note 40.
[46] Resolution 309 (1972), Feb. 4, 1972, adopted by a vote of 14(U.S.)-0 with China not participating; cf. above at notes 33-34.

General Waldheim and his special representative for Namibia, Alfred Martin Escher of Switzerland, resulted in November 1972 in an announcement by the United Nations that South Africa was in fact prepared to make certain political concessions within the territory, even though it remained unwilling to agree to Namibian independence in accordance with the U.N. concept. Regretting the absence of a "complete and unequivocal clarification" of South Africa's policy, the Security Council in a resolution adopted with U.S. support on December 6, 1972 invited the Secretary-General to continue his efforts and again called on South Africa to cooperate with the latter in bringing about a peaceful transfer of power.[47] The United States abstained, however, on a later resolution adopted by the General Assembly which urged the use of stronger measures to effect South Africa's ouster.[48]]

b. The Portuguese Territories.

[The principle of negotiations leading toward self-determination and independence was also invoked in 1972 on behalf of Portugal's African territories, where insurrectionary movements had been active since the early 1960s and in at least one instance—in Portuguese Guinea or "Guinea-Bissau"—had achieved an unmistakable measure of success. Repeated demands from within the United Nations for independence for Guinea-Bissau (with Cape Verde), Angola, and Mozambique were in no way satisfied by Portugal's action in May 1972 in granting a measure of local autonomy to its overseas provinces and giving Angola and Mozambique the title of "states." In a resolution adopted (over U.S. opposition) on November 14, 1972, the General Assembly again condemned the actions of Portugal in territories under its administration; appealed for all necessary moral and material assistance to the national liberation movements in Portuguese African territories; and asked the Secretary-General to provide assistance in getting Portugal to negotiate with the national liberation movements with a view to the "full and speedy" implementation of independence.[49] The United States did support, though with misgivings, a resolution unanimously adopted by the Security Council on November 22, 1972 which likewise reaffirmed the "inalienable right" of the peoples of the Portuguese territories to "self-determination and indepen-

---

[47] Resolution 323 (1972), Dec. 6, 1972, adopted by a vote of 13 (U.S.)-0-1 (U.S.S.R.) with China not participating.
[48] Resolution 3031 (XXVII), Dec. 18, 1972, adopted by a vote of 112-2-15 (U.S.).
[49] Resolution 2918 (XXVII), Nov. 14, 1972, adopted by a vote of 98-6 (U.S.)-8; cf. above at notes 36-37.

I

dence"; called on Portugal to cease forthwith its military operations and "all acts of repression" against the peoples of the territories; and called on Portugal "to enter into negotiations with the parties concerned" with a view to achieving a solution of the existing "armed confrontation" and permitting the peoples of the territories "to exercise their right to self-determination and independence."[50] Although both resolutions were rejected by Portuguese Premier Marcello Caetano on the ground that they amounted to interference in Portuguese internal affairs, Portugal did reaffirm earlier offers to permit the verification of insurgent claims by U.N. observers and offered to discuss the situation with interested African governments.[51]]

3. The Problem of Southern Rhodesia (Zimbabwe).

[Particularly embarrassing to the United States in the early 1970s were certain aspects of the situation regarding Southern Rhodesia (Zimbabwe), the white-ruled, self-governing British colony which had unilaterally declared itself independent in 1965 and had since maintained that status, in fact though not in law, in the face of the trade and financial sanctions imposed initially by the British Government and subsequently multilateralized on order of the U.N. Security Council. World concern with the Rhodesian problem at the beginning of the 1970s was dominated by two immediate issues: (1) the possibility that the United Kingdom might succeed in negotiating a political settlement with the *de facto* Rhodesian government headed by Premier Ian D. Smith; and (2) the increasingly obvious ineffectiveness of the U.N. sanctions, which were openly disregarded by a number of governments and no longer commanded full compliance even on the part of the United States.

Past attempts by the United Kingdom to arrive at a negotiated settlement of the Rhodesian problem had invariably foundered on the incompatibility between Britain's insistence that any settlement must be acceptable to the Rhodesian people "as a whole"— including the nonwhites who made up over 95 percent of the population—and the determination of the Rhodesian authorities to keep political control in the hands of the white minority and exclude any arrangement that could lead to African "majority rule." The advent of a Conservative government in Britain in 1970 had signaled a fresh attempt to resolve this impasse, and in November 1971 the two governments made public new proposals that purported to provide a basis for settlement through a very gradual

[50] Resolution 322 (1972), Nov. 22, 1972, adopted unanimously.
[51] *The World This Year, 1973*, p. 95.

increase in African parliamentary representation. Final approval by the U.K. was withheld, however, pending an examination of Rhodesian opinion by a fifteen-member British commission headed by Lord Pearce, and the proposals in fact were shelved in May 1972 when the commission reported that they were acceptable to the great majority of Rhodesia's European population of some 225,000 but had been unmistakably rejected by the majority of the country's 5,310,000 Africans.

International rejection did not await the report of the Pearce Commission. From the moment of their issuance, the proposals had been denounced as a "sell-out" by African governments, by the Organization of African Unity, by the U.N. General Assembly[52] and by a majority of the Security Council, where the adoption of a formal resolution had been blocked only by a British veto on December 30, 1971.[53] At Addis Ababa, on February 4, 1972, the United Kingdom vetoed another draft Security Council resolution in which it was urged to desist from implementing the proposals and to convene instead a contitutional conference in which the African people could participate through "genuine representatives."[54] As on previous occasions, the United States abstained in sympathy with Britain's contention that it could not accept a directive to change a policy that was still to be worked out.

The United States itself had meanwhile incurred an equal measure of opprobrium by reason of its admitted violation of a portion of the sanctions ordered by the Security Council. A hitherto flawless record of compliance with the sanctions program had been marred in 1971 by the congressional passage and presidential acceptance of the so-called Byrd amendment to the Strategic and Critical Materials Stock Piling Act, a provision that in effect directed the American President to disregard Security Council orders barring the import of chrome ore and other strategic and critical materials from Rhodesia.[55] This action, too, had elicited an immediate expression of "grave concern" by the U.N. General Assembly[56] and was later taken up by the Security Council, which adopted on February 28, 1972 (with the United States and Britain abstaining) a resolution reaffirming the sanctions program and deprecating any relaxation with respect to "any commodity . . . including chrome ore."[57]]

[52] Resolution 2877 (XXVI), Dec. 20, 1971, adopted by a vote of 94-8-22 (U.S.).
[53] U.N. document S/10489, Dec. 30, 1971; failed of adoption by a vote of 9-1 (U.K.)-5 (U.S.).
[54] U.N. document S/10606, Feb. 2, 1972; failed of adoption by a vote of 9-1 (U.K.)-5 (U.S.); cf. above at note 37.
[55] Sec. 503, Public Law 92-156, Nov. 17, 1971, in *A.F.R., 1971*, no. 108b.
[56] Resolution 2765 (XXVI), Nov. 16, 1971, adopted by a vote of 106-2-13 with the U.S. not participating; text in *A.F.R., 1971*, no. 109b.
[57] Resolution 314 (1972), Feb. 28, 1972, adopted by a vote of 13-0-2 (U.S.).

a. Retention of the "Byrd Amendment."

[To find the United States in direct violation of an order issued by the Security Council in the exercise of its authority under the U.N. Charter had been a painful experience for many Americans. An attempt to regularize the situation was instituted early in 1972 by Democratic Senator Gale W. McGee of Wyoming with the support of other members of the Senate Foreign Relations Committee. A provision calling for outright repeal of the Byrd amendment (so named for Independent Democratic Senator Harry F. Byrd of Virginia) was included in the pending State Department authorization measure that was favorably reported by the Foreign Relations Committee on April 20, 1972. Not only had the existing amendment adversely affected U.S. relations with Africa and the United Nations, the committee's report asserted; it was also unnecesary, since the United States had more than enough chrome ore to meet strategic needs for several years to come. "It is too late to undo all the damage by Congress' unwise action last year," the committee stated, "but reversal of the current U.S. posture will again pledge our support for the U.N. Security Council's decision and help improve our general relations with nations on the African Continent."[58]

This judgment was supported in a communication supplied to Senator McGee by Acting Secretary of State John N. Irwin II (Document 71). The administration cannot, however, be said to have thrown its full weight behind the drive for repeal of the Byrd amendment. That movement collapsed on May 31, 1972 when a motion by Senator Byrd to delete the McGee provision from the pending legislation was upheld on the Senate floor by a vote of 40 to 36.]

(71) United States Legislation on Rhodesian Chrome Imports: Letter from Acting Secretary of State John N. Irwin II to Senator Gale W. McGee, May 20, 1972.[59]

(Complete Text)

MAY 20, 1972.

DEAR SENATOR McGEE: In response to your request, I am writing to confirm the Administration's support for Section 503 of the

---

[58] S. Rept. 92-754, Apr. 20, 1972, quoted in Senate Foreign Relations Committee History, p. 74.
[59] *Bulletin*, June 12, 1972, pp. 815-16.

State Department Authorization Bill, S. 3526, which would repeal existing legislation permitting the importation of chrome and other strategic materials from Southern Rhodesia.

The Administration opposed that legislation last year and considers that there are several compelling reasons for its repeal now. As we pointed out prior to passage, the measure adopted last year has put the United States in violation of its international legal obligations: a most serious step which the Administration then maintained and still believes was not warranted by circumstances. The legislation now under consideration by the Senate would allow the United States once again to comply fully with its international treaty obligations.

Repeal now would serve to make us less vulnerable to unfavorable international reaction. As a result of the legislation now in force, our international interests have suffered in other respects. In Africa, where our position on Rhodesia has heretofore been seen as a test of our commitment to self-determination and racial equality, our credibility has suffered. The depth of African concern has been particularly strong in some nations where our interests far outweigh those in Rhodesia. In the United Nations, we will face, with each shipment of chrome or other commodity, an increasing erosion of our position. While we have sought and continue to seek means of making the existing sanctions against Rhodesia more effective, and less liable to circumvention by others, our ability to do so is seriously limited by the legislation now in effect.

Finally, the Administration continues to hold the view that neither economic nor national security considerations affecting chrome are sufficiently compelling to compensate for the adverse foreign policy consequences of the legislation now in effect. There are 2.2 million tons of excess chrome ore in the stockpile; legislation authorizing release of 1.3 million tons has already been approved this year by the Senate. This amount alone would meet our total chrome needs for about 18 months, and defense requirements amount to only about 10% of total needs. Industry stocks are high, and we continue to have access to chrome ore from a variety of other foreign sources. In short, there was no chrome shortage last year and there is none now. Moreover, the legislation now in effect permits the importation from Rhodesia of other strategic list items in addition to chrome, and under it we may expect a variety of materials including asbestos, nickel, and other minerals to be imported. The adverse international reactions to such transactions in our judgment would outweigh any possible economic advantage, and there is on strategic grounds no need to import any of these materials from Rhodesia.

As will be clear from the foregoing, we have been increasingly concerned about the serious effects of the existing legislation upon United States foreign policy interests. For all of the reasons mentioned, the

Administration believes that the passage of Section 503 would further those interests.

With kindest regards,
Sincerely,

JOHN N. IRWIN II,

Acting Secretary.

b. Action in the Security Council.

[With the failure of the British-Rhodesian settlement plan and of the attempt to repeal the Byrd amendment, the Security Council met again in late September 1972 to consider new proposals drawn up by Guinea, Somalia, and the Sudan, the leading protagonists of African interests in the Security Council membership. Of the two draft resolutions now proposed for Security Council consideration, the first referred to the United States' reported importation of Rhodesian chrome ore and other minerals as a source of deep concern and urged the United States to cooperate fully in the effective implementation of sanctions.[60] The second, directed primarily at the United Kingdom, insisted once again that there should be no independence in Southern Rhodesia before majority rule, and that any consultation of the people regarding their political future should be governed by the principle of one man, one vote.[61]

U.S. Representative Christopher H. Phillips deprecated both of these initiatives in a statement to the Security Council on September 29, 1972 (Document 72a). The United Kingdom, the Ambassador suggested, had acted in "a wholly responsible manner" in trying to bring the Rhodesian situation under control, and no purpose would be served by calling for "measures that could only become effective with the use of force." As for the sanctions issue, the U.S. representative endeavored to put the recent American action in perspective by calling attention to its limited scope and contrasting the United States' record of overall compliance with sanctions with the much less satisfactory performance of some other countries.

Apparently unmoved by these considerations, the Security Council proceeded to adopt the sanctions resolution by a vote of 13 to 0, with the United Kingdom and the United States abstaining.[62] The resolution on political procedures, like earlier resolutions of similar import, won ten positive votes but was vetoed by the United Kingdom, while the United States abstained together with Belgium,

---

[60] U.N. document S/10804, Sept. 29, 1972.
[61] U.N. document S/10805 and Rev.1, Sept. 29, 1972.
[62] Resolution 320 (1972), Sept. 29, 1972, adopted by a vote of 13-0-2 (U.S.).

France, and Italy. In a statement in explanation of the American votes (Document 72b), Ambassador Phillips stated that while U.S. law precluded a vote for sanctions "across the board" and the United States considered that it was being unfairly singled out for criticism, it was nevertheless the American intention "to continue to cooperate with the sanctions program to the fullest extent of our ability." As for the situation inside Southern Rhodesia, the Ambassador stressed the U.S. view that "all elements . . . should remain in contact and jointly demonstrate their will to work out a solution to the present impasse."]

(72) Consideration by the Security Council of the United Nations: Statements by Ambassador Christopher H. Phillips, United States Representative, to the Security Council, September 29, 1972.

(a) Statement on Pending Resolutions. [63]

(Complete Text)

My delegation has listened with great interest to the statements of the distinguished Foreign Ministers who have spoken here thus far.[64]

The United States remains concerned about the situation in Southern Rhodesia. We believe, however, that the Council should look at the problem from a practical point of view and in terms of measures that the members of the United Nations will actually carry out.

The United States continues to believe that racial equality and self-determination must become the inheritance of all of the people of Southern Rhodesia, and we share the abhorrence already expressed by previous speakers before this Council for an illegal regime that has tried to perpetuate control by a racist minority over an area of Africa which it has no right to govern. The United States will continue to support practical means toward achieving the realization of full political rights for all of the people of Rhodesia, but we recognize, perhaps more clearly now than in 1968, that the way will not be an easy one.

We believe that the Council should not turn a deaf ear to any practical efforts to seek a solution and that it should not hasten to condemn the attempt made recently by the British to seek a settlement. The United Kingdom has acted in a wholly responsible manner in seeking to bring the situation in Southern Rhodesia under control, and

---

[63] USUN Press Release 109, Sept. 29, 1972; text from *Bulletin*, Nov. 6, 1972, pp. 543-6.

[64] Participants in the debate, which coincided with the 27th Regular Session of the General Assembly, included (in order of participation) the Foreign Ministers of Zambia, Guyana, Senegal, Kenya, Guinea, Argentina, Nigeria, and Mali.

we see no purpose in attempting to push the British Government into taking measures that would not contribute to the best interests of the majority of the people of Rhodesia. Thus, we do not believe that it is appropriate for this Council to call upon the United Kingdom to take measures that could only become effective with the use of force.

In listening to the statements so far, we note that there has been great emphasis placed on imports by the United States of strategic materials from Southern Rhodesia, although several speakers have also called attention to widespread violations by others. Mr. President,[65] I wish briefly to set the subject in its proper perspective.

The sanctions program is, first of all, a matter which affects various states differently. For some, sanctions have been easy to comply with since they had no economic relations with Southern Rhodesia at all. For others, there were difficulties and in some cases hardships as well-established commercial ties were broken. Still others, however, have found ways of keeping such links more or less intact, and it is because of them that economic sanctions against Southern Rhodesia have thus far not had the success we originally hoped for.

The second point I wish to make is that the cooperation of all states is needed to make sanctions more effective. As you are well aware, the Congress of the United States has passed legislation which exempts certain strategic materials from its observance of Rhodesian sanctions. Though the executive branch opposed this legislation, it was nevertheless adopted and became effective as law on January 1, 1972.

My government has been forthright in making full and rigorous disclosures of our imports of these materials to the Security Council's Committee on Sanctions, and we would wish that the many other importers of Rhodesian commodities would be as candid about their transactions so as to enable the Sanctions Committee to gain a full and accurate picture of how Southern Rhodesia has for six years been able to surmount the mandatory economic sanctions established by the Security Council.

It has been pointed out in this session of the Council that sanctions have had some limited effect on Southern Rhodesia. The Smith regime has had difficulty in finding investment capital. Procedures adopted by the Southern Rhodesians to evade sanctions are complex and expensive. There is no doubt, however, that the program is far from achieving the goal set out in Security Council Resolution 253.[66]

In considering why the program has not been more effective, my delegation strongly hopes that other delegations will not succumb to the temptation to concentrate on one country, the United States,

[65] Huang Hua (China).
[66] Resolution 253 (1968), May 29, 1968, summarized in *Documents, 1968-69*, pp. 370-71.

simply because it is easy to do so since its imports of Southern Rhodesian products have been made a matter of public record.

Our last report on our imports to the Sanctions Committee covered the period April 1 to June 30. Projecting our estimated annual imports against Rhodesia's estimated annual exports, it appears that our share of Rhodesia's exports will be around 2 to 3 percent of the total. Despite the fact that most of Southern Rhodesia's exports are going to other countries, the discussion on sanctions in this Council has centered to an unwarranted degree on the comparatively small amount of imports by the United States.

Now, let us look at the record of importations from Rhodesia during the first half of 1972. A good estimate of Rhodesia's total exports for the first half of 1972 would be $200 to $220 million. Now, what was the total value of U.S. imports, all of which were reported to the Sanctions Committee during the same period? The answer, Mr. President, is $3 million, a very small fraction indeed of this total.

This is a troubling situation to us, not because so much time has been spent in examining U.S. imports but because so little time and effort has been expended to determine to whom Rhodesia sold the other 98.5 percent of its exports during the first half of this year.

I believe members of the Council are also aware of the lengths to which my government has gone to maintain and support the sanctions program. Our laws and regulations, with the excepted area of strategic imports, continue to reflect our determination to do so, and so does the actual record of the United States in not only enacting the appropriate laws and regulations—although some governments, I would note, have not even done that—but also in enforcing them. Of the nations represented in this chamber today, only two have actually taken appropriate enforcement measures. One of these two, I might add, is the United States.

It may be argued that the nationals of other countries have not been prosecuted because they have studiously avoided dealing with Rhodesia. But I believe, and I think most impartial observers would agree, that the Sanctions Committee's own reports and statistics suggest an alternative explanation. So, I might add, does the evidence that has been developed as a result of recent U.S. court actions. We continue to regard with concern the very large number of cases of reported transactions in violation of sanctions, some 130 in all, compared to the handful of cases in which violations have been confirmed or admitted.

In examining the volume of reported violations, which we must assume is only the tip of the iceberg of total Rhodesian trade, and Rhodesia's obvious ability to market its goods abroad, it is clear that some countries simply have not taken their responsibilities seriously. This is not a problem that began with a statute adopted by the United States in 1972. The problem began as soon as it became clear that the

United Nations Security Council Resolution 232[67] was being system-atically evaded.

Now, I appreciate the concern, Mr. President, of those who argue that our action, because of its open, official character, will lead others to similar actions and will undermine the sanctions effort. But the logic of that position needs close examination.

Those who attack us for this move are saying in effect, "By your actions you will encourage others to do likewise." Now, that puts it backward. No encouragement by us has been needed. The United States would not have acted as it did if it were not well known, widely and universally known, that the United States until this year was one of a handful of nations, along with the United Kingdom and a few others, who had taken the totality of the sanctions program seriously and had made it work.

The United States did not act to create a new situation regarding sanctions. It is one thing, Mr. President, to be the first to pierce a hole in the dike, but in this case the dike has been leaking, and leaking badly, for a long time.

With respect to chrome, for example, this Council is aware that U.S. firms have recently imported two lots of chrome ore totaling about 56,000 tons. But again, according to the estimates of the Sanctions Committee, Rhodesian chrome ore production since 1966, most of which has been sold abroad, has been about 400,000 tons a year, or more than 2 million tons since Resolution 232 was adopted by this Council. Obviously, singling out the United States will not deal respon-sibly or adequately with this situation.

In this connection it is also interesting to note that in the fourth report of the Sanctions Committee, the single largest number of re-ported cases of sanctions violations involved chrome ore and ferro-chrome, 34 such cases in all. Nationals of 23 nations reportedly were involved in this apparently widespread trafficking in chrome and ferro-chrome. The United States was not mentioned in any one of these cases.

Another important mineral export of Rhodesia is copper. The United States may now under the recent legislation import copper from Rhodesia, although none has in fact been imported into the United States from that territory since 1965. Nonetheless, copper since UDI [unilateral declaration of independence] has risen from third to first place among Rhodesia's mineral exports, and there are an estimated 30 to 40 copper mines now operating. The report of the Sanctions Com-mittee documents a sharp curtailment of Rhodesian copper exports since 1966. At the same time, the evidence is that Rhodesian copper production has continued and even increased during the same period. It

67 Resolution 232 (1966), Dec. 16, 1966, in *Documents, 1966*, pp. 320-22.

is, as the fourth report stated, "very difficult to determine the true situation." But there can be no serious doubt that Rhodesian copper is going somewhere, and in very substantial quantities. We have imported none, either this year or in years past.

My delegation believes that sanctions can be made more effective only if this matter is given the further study and analysis it deserves.

Mr. President, we should not confine our attention only to the area of strategic materials. Turning for a moment to the agricultural sector, the evidence again points to widespread violations on a truly massive scale.

The United States does not, and under law cannot, import any of Rhodesia's tobacco, corn, beef, or sugar. Yet these commodities continue to figure prominently in Rhodesia's exports.

Tobacco was Rhodesia's main export before sanctions. Although sanctions caused Rhodesia to lose its traditional tobacco market, much of the tobacco is being sold abroad. It is not going to the United States, but where is it going?

Analysis of this question would properly begin with the excellent information compiled by the Sanctions Committee's fourth report. Unfortunately, as far as we can determine, no further analysis has ever been attempted despite the 10 cases of suspected violations that have been brought to the committee for action and despite the information developed by the committee which demonstrates that Rhodesia's neighbors by their own figures exported 87,000 metric tons of tobacco in the period of 1968 to 1970, yet somehow trading nations elsewhere managed to import 142,000 tons of tobacco from the same countries during the same period.

Similarly, maize has grown substantially in its importance to the Rhodesian economy since UDI. No less than 11 cases of reported violations have been brought to the Sanctions Committee, and it is clear that Rhodesian exports of this commodity have increased. But no one seems to know where any of it is going, although the fourth report of the committee documents the remarkable fact that while Mozambique reported exports of 172,000 tons of maize in the period 1967 to 1969, various countries for the same period reported maize imports from Mozambique of upward of 1 million tons.

This kind of 600 percent discrepancy, one would think, would cause some serious questions to be asked. On the contrary, however, it seems to have escaped notice entirely.

Mr. President, we are also concerned that those who share our desire to see a fair and just outcome of the Rhodesian issue have not always focused on broader aspects of the problem. We can understand concerns about our legislation, but we would have hoped that the Council would pursue all sanctions violations more systematically.

We would expect to see more interest displayed in the vital question of total Rhodesian trade. If we have imported 56,000 tons of chrome in the first half of 1972, we naturally expect to hear expressions of concern. But we would also hope to see others ask, To whom has Rhodesia sold over 2 million tons of chrome ore since sanctions went into effect? If the United States during 1972 will buy 2 or 3 percent of Rhodesia's exports, who will buy the rest?

Finally, Mr. President, if this Council is serious about making sanctions work, it will avoid this one-sided approach and recognize that the real problem is far broader in nature and cannot usefully be addressed by singling out the U.S. Government or any other individual government without reference to the total problem.

(b) Statement in Explanation of Vote.[68]

(Complete Text)

In explanation of vote on the two draft resolutions upon which the Council has just voted, the United States abstained in the vote on draft resolution S/10804,[69] and I should like to explain very briefly why.

Given U.S. law, the United States could not vote for the call by the Security Council with regard to sanctions across the board. Moreover, I am compelled to say that we consider that this resolution focuses attention unfairly on the United States, but I want to make clear that the United States intends to continue to cooperate with the sanctions program to the fullest extent of our ability.

Mr. President, my delegation abstained on draft resolution S/10805.[70] We share the sentiments expressed by others that what is now needed and what has been needed since the Pearce Commission announced its findings is that all elements within Southern Rhodesia should remain in contact and jointly demonstrate their will to work out a solution to the present impasse.

We are therefore particularly concerned about the trend of events in Southern Rhodesia in recent months and the growing evidence there of polarization. As we have made clear, we do not believe force is an appropriate or effective means of resolving the Rhodesian problem or the other fundamental difficulties in southern Africa. But neither do we believe that steps taken by the Rhodesian regime to suppress those committed to peaceful and constructive change[71] can have any effect but to exacerbate an already difficult situation.

We would also hope that circumstances could be brought about in

[68] USUN Press Release 110, Sept. 29, 1972; text from *Bulletin*, Nov. 6, 1972, pp. 546-7.
[69] Adopted as Resolution 320 (1972); cf. above at notes 60 and 62.
[70] Cf. above at note 61.
[71] A reference to administrative measures affecting the African National Council led by Bishop Abel T. Muzorewa.

which a constitutional conference, including those representing all Rhodesians, African and European, could be called. We recognize that this would be impractical under present conditions, but we call upon those who seek an orderly and just outcome to the present impasse to continue to seek common ground of discussion and possible compromise.

C. Action in the General Assembly.

[One further round of U.N. voting on Rhodesian issues took place December 7, 1972 in the closing weeks of the General Assembly session. Both Britain and the United States (together with Portugal and South Africa) opposed a General Assembly resolution that reiterated the principle of no independence without majority rule and urged the United Kingdom to convene a "national constitutional conference" of "genuine political representatives" to work out a settlement for subsequent endorsement "through free and democratic processes."[72] In a second resolution that was likewise opposed by Britain, the United States, and other allied governments, the General Assembly declared among other things that it "*Condemns* the continued importation by the Government of the United States of America of chrome and nickel from Zimbabwe in open contravention of the provisions of Security Council resolutions ... and contrary to the specific obligations assumed by that Government under Article 25 of the Charter,[73] and calls upon the United States Government to desist forthwith from further violations of the sanctions and to observe faithfully and without exception the provisions of the above-mentioned resolutions."[74]

"The United States takes seriously its obligations under the United Nations Charter," President Nixon commented in his "State of the World" report for 1973. "Except for imports of small quantities of certain strategic materials exempted by U.S. public law—accounting for no more than a minute percentage of Rhodesia's exports—the United States, unlike many others, adheres strictly to the UN program of sanctions against Rhodesia. Many in the United Nations challenged our observance of sanctions. But there should not be a double standard which ignores the widespread, substantial—but unavowed—non-observance of sanctions by others."[75]]

---

[72] Resolution 2945 (XXVII), Dec. 27, 1972, adopted by a vote of 111-4 (U.S.)-9.
[73] Article 25 of the U.N. Charter reads: "The Members of the United Nations agree to accept and carry out the decisions of the Security Council in accordance with the present Charter."
[74] Resolution 2946 (XXVII), Dec. 7, 1972, adopted by a vote of 93-8 (U.S.)-23.
[75] Nixon Report, 1973, p. 214.

VIII.
WESTERN HEMISPHERE
RELATIONS

[Tensions between the United States and its Western Hemisphere neighbors continued during 1972 to strain the bonds of friendship traditional in U.S. relations both with Canada and with the Latin American countries. Increasing interaction at both governmental and private levels served not only to keep alive a certain sense of mutual good will, but also to accentuate the irritation prevailing elsewhere in the Americas at the disparities of power and wealth between the United States and its hemispheric neighbors. In Canada no less than in the Latin American countries, these trends had tended to undercut the "more balanced and reinvigorated partnership of the Americas" that Secretary of State Rogers had invoked in addressing the General Assembly of the Organization of American States (O.A.S.) at its First Regular Session in San José, Costa Rica, on April 15, 1971.[1] Existing dissatisfaction over U.S. attitudes and actions had been still further accentuated with the adoption of the United States' "New Economic Policy" on August 15, 1971.[2]

"Over the past few years, the New World community has undergone severe testing," Secretary Rogers later conceded in making public his report on the foreign policy developments of 1972. "The forces of nationalism—both positive and negative—have exerted an increasing pull on the policies of its members from Canada and ourselves in the north, to the Caribbean states, Mexico, Central and South America. Stress and tension have been undeniable facets of our community. But so, too, have common interests, cooperation and interdependence. For we are all concerned with achieving improved quality of life for all people of the hemisphere and with effective cooperation among ourselves toward this end. We are all

---

[1] *A.F.R., 1971*, no. 113.
[2] Same, no. 142. For fuller discussion of Western Hemisphere affairs, see Nixon Report, 1972, pp. 90-100; same, 1973, pp. 115-30; Rogers Report, 1972, pp. 403-40.

dedicated to a community of free nations, in which the sovereignty, dignity, and fundamental rights of each are respected."[3]]

A. Some Inter-American Problems.

[Notwithstanding his rather cautious assessment of overall trends in the hemisphere, Secretary Rogers insisted that U.S.-Latin American relations had continued their gradual evolution "from the uneasy predominance of earlier relations with Latin America toward the more mature partnership called for by President Nixon in October 1969."[4] "We are leaving behind the paternalistic attitudes of the past," Mr. Rogers emphasized; "we have relinquished a directive role while maintaining commitments and responsibilities that are ours as the most advantaged member of the inter-American community; and we have turned more to the support of Latin American initiatives reflecting their perception of needs and priorities."[5]

The Secretary of State conceded that some conflict was inevitable in the "pervasive relationship" created by "a broad and growing network of transnational links through which officials, businessmen, people from every walk of life, together with the communications media, bring our societies into contact." This was particularly true, he pointed out, in an era when the Latin American states were "increasingly intent upon asserting their own sense of national identity and independence," and in an area where the assertion of nationhood was "manifested most often in economic terms." United States interests were bound to be affected, sometimes adversely, as Latin American nations struggled to reconcile "the imperatives of development, the drive for national control, and the need for foreign economic cooperation." But while warning that the United States would insist on "fair and equitable treatment" where its legitimate interests were involved, Secretary Rogers also stressed that the United States itself "must approach each conflict in a spirit of compromise, not confrontation, and with a keen sense of the totality of American interests in play. It is reasonable to ask and expect," Mr. Rogers added, "that Latin American governments, looking closely at their own interests, adopt a reciprocal attitude."[6]

[3] Rogers Report, 1972, p. 403.
[4] Cf. Nixon remarks to the Inter American Press Association, Oct. 31, 1969, in *Documents, 1968-69*, pp. 429-38.
[5] Rogers Report, 1972, pp. 403-4.
[6] Same, p. 404.

Several of the more familiar problems of U.S.-Latin American relations were to persist through 1972 without fundamental change. The United States' relations with the Fidel Castro regime in Cuba, for example, remained immovably frozen despite the fact that a number of other governments in the hemisphere preferred to follow Chile's example in restoring or establishing relations with the Havana government.[7] With the "Popular Unity" government of Chilean President Salvador Allende, the United States maintained correct official relations even while it provided an undetermined amount of clandestine assistance to opposition forces and made plain its disapproval of Chile's failure to pay compensation for expropriated U.S. properties.[8] The attitude of the Allende government in this regard was largely responsible for the policy statement of January 19, 1972 in which President Nixon warned that the United States would not in future extend new bilateral economic benefits nor support loans by international development banks to countries that expropriated U.S. property without compensation (Document 97).

In Panama, the United States continued under heavy pressure from the regime of Brigadier General Omar Torrijos Herrera, which was demanding a fundamental revision in the status of the Panama Canal and the U.S.-administered Canal Zone; but bilateral negotiations to this end remained in abeyance through most of 1972 while both parties awaited the outcome of the U.S. presidential election.[9] Relations between the United States and Mexico maintained a smoother course but were also not free from friction, as was noted by leaders of both countries on the occasion of a state visit to the United States by President Luis Echeverría Alvarez (Document 79).

A broader problem that had adversely affected U.S. relations with a number of Latin American countries arose from differing interpretations of the legal principles governing oceanic fishing in waters adjacent to coastal states. A comprehensive review of the U.S. position on this controversial matter was provided by Charles A. Meyer, Assistant Secretary of State for Inter-American Affairs, in an appearance before the Subcommittee on Inter-American Affairs of the House Foreign Affairs Committee.]

---

[7] Cf. below at notes 76-77.
[8] Document 97. For background cf. *A.F.R., 1971*, no. 118.
[9] For background, cf. *A.F.R., 1971*, no. 119; further discussion appears in *Bulletin*, June 12, 1972, pp. 812-22.

(73) Fisheries Disputes and Their Effect on Inter-American Relations: Statement by Charles A. Meyer, Assistant Secretary of State for Inter-American Affairs, Before the Subcommittee on Inter-American Affairs of the House Committee on Foreign Affairs, February 3, 1972. [10]

(Complete Text)

Fisheries disputes between the United States and certain countries of Latin America have been a disturbing element in our relations with the hemisphere for almost 20 years. They have tended to cause periodic problems in the normal conduct of our affairs, which, when the boats went home, often were set aside until the next fishing season. Solutions have been either elusive or, when reached, temporary. The dimensions of these disputes changed significantly in 1971, so significantly that a problem which once could be dealt with primarily as a fisheries problem now forces itself on us as one which involves a range of important interests of the United States.

For this reason and because, in spite of the combined efforts of the Departments concerned, there is still no ready answer, I especially welcome this opportunity to review with you the nature of the disputes, the harm they cause, and the prospects for realizing our continuing hope that they can be resolved. With me today are, representing the Special Assistant to the Secretary for Fisheries and Wildlife and Coordinator for Ocean Affairs, Mr. Wilvan Van Campen, and Mr. Charles J. Pitman, representing the Department's Legal Adviser.

Fisheries disputes arise from differences we have with certain Latin American countries regarding the breadth of the territorial sea and coastal state rights over resources of the waters adjacent to their coasts. The United States recognizes a 3-mile territorial sea and, in addition, claims a 9-mile contiguous zone of exclusive jurisdiction over fisheries. Ecuador, Peru, and Brazil, the countries whose names are most closely associated with the fisheries problem, claim 200 miles of sovereignty or exclusive jurisdiction over the waters off their coasts. Thus, in some ways, fisheries disputes can be seen as the result of a contest between those who believe that the waters beyond 12 miles are high seas and those who claim 200 miles.

This is more than a numbers game, however, as basic to our dispute are differing concepts of how we approach rulemaking with respect to the world's oceans. The United States believes that the question of sovereignty and rights is one which must be settled within the international community in order to avoid the chaos of extensive and conflicting unilateral claims. Certain countries of Latin America, 10 in all,

[10] *Bulletin*, Feb. 28, 1972, pp. 284-7.

believe that it is the right of each coastal state to determine for itself, on the basis of its own requirements and needs, the extent and nature of its claims over the waters off its coast.

The elements of the fisheries disputes date from the middle and late 1940's. In 1945, when the world was populated by countries claiming less than 12 miles of territorial seas, President Truman issued two proclamations dealing with ocean resources off our own coasts.[11] One of these proclamations stated U.S. policy with respect to the resources of the continental shelf. In reserving for the coastal state the resources of the continental shelf, President Truman carefully reaffirmed the United States view that existing international law provided for a 3-mile territorial sea. We also clearly stated that it was not our intention to affect the high-seas character of the waters above the continental shelf and the right thereon to free and unimpeded navigation.

In spite of our intentions, in 1947, Peru and Chile, noting that the United States had acted unilaterally to protect resource interests in an area off its own coast, laid claim to sovereignty and national jurisdiction over the seas adjacent to their coasts extending to a distance of 200 nautical miles. They were joined in 1952 by Ecuador when all three countries signed the Santiago Declaration on the Maritime Zone.[12] It was the thesis of the three nations that the region delineated by this zone constitutes a distinct ecological unit within which a dynamic balance of nature is maintained.

The Declaration of Santiago suggests that the claim of Chile, Ecuador, and Peru is essentially a claim to resources, although in the years since 1952, it has been treated both as a resource claim and as a territorial sea claim. With it, conflict over fisheries resources became inevitable. I say "inevitable" because differences with countries that make claims with which we disagree, and which we protest, cannot always wait on the slow process of writing new international law. Where the American distant-water fishing fleet must continue to operate pending agreement, the differences manifest themselves not only in the exchange of notes protesting juridical positions but, most seriously, in fisheries disputes.

There are, as I said, now 10 Latin American countries with similar claims. In addition to Chile, Ecuador, and Peru, these are El Salvador, Nicaragua, Argentina, Panama, Uruguay, and Brazil. Costa Rica has had a 200-mile conservation zone. Of all of these states, the disputes which

---

[11] Proclamation on the Continental Shelf and Proclamation on Fisheries, Sept. 28, 1945; texts in *Bulletin*, Sept. 30, 1945, pp. 485 and 486 (10 Federal Register 12303 and 12304).

[12] Conferencia de Explotación y Conservación de las Riquezas marítimas del Pacífico Sur: Declaración sobre Zona Marítima (Annex 19; República del Perú, Memoria del Ministro de Relaciones Exteriores ... 4 de Agosto de 1952-27 de Julio de 1953 [Lima, 1954], pp. 70-72). For earlier discussion, cf. address by Herman Phleger, Department of State Legal Adviser, May 13, 1955, in *American Foreign Policy, 1950-55: Basic Documents*, vol. 1, pp. 1346-56.

concern us today involve only Ecuador, Peru, Chile (because of the tie of the Santiago Declaration), and Brazil.

Two international law-of-the-sea conferences, one in 1958 and one in 1960, have failed to resolve the basic issues on territorial seas and resource jurisdiction. We are now looking to a new conference in 1973 to do so.[13] Our experience with fisheries disputes and the proliferation of 200-mile claims in the hemisphere in the decade of the sixties compel us to conclude that this conference must be successful if we are to insure the navigational rights on the world's oceans which are essential to our security and if we are to resolve existing conflicts or, more, to prevent new conflicts over rights to the oceans' resources. Unfortunately, the necessity for international agreement and the difficulty of waiting for it are being most clearly demonstrated in the hemisphere.

Over the years the elements for a full-scale demonstration of the implications for the United States of disagreements over issues of law of the sea have been gathering, with little obvious relation to each other. The American distant-water fishing fleet, particularly our tuna fleet, has been modernizing and improving its technology. It has sailed to more distant seas in search of tuna for a growing American market. Flying the American flag, vessel owners are not obligated, in our view, to buy licenses to fish waters beyond 12 miles, although we do not object when they decide for themselves that they want to. As a consequence of the seizures which began in 1953, when Ecuador and Peru began enforcing their 200-mile claims against unlicensed American fishing vessels, the Congress acted in 1954 to begin assisting the tunaboat owners to meet the costs to them as individuals of an unresolved dispute between governments. Amended in 1968,[14] the Fishermen's Protective Act now permits reimbursement for fines paid and licenses purchased to obtain release after seizure. Other pieces of legislation have been passed by Congress as the vessel seizures have drawn increasing attention to the problem. This body of legislation calls upon the executive branch to act or consider acting against countries that seize American fishing vessels with respect to military sales, economic assistance, military assistance, and ship loan programs. Other drafts of legislation are periodically put forward which are either more stringent or are intended to add to the list of retaliations available for use against seizing countries. We have opposed punitive legislation consistently. Without exception, it does not address the problem of how we end seizures. Instead, it increases the scope of the problem, either by placing new obstacles in the way of returning to negotiations or by complicating the issue by adding others to it, or both.

Throughout 1967 and 1968, in a new effort to find a solution, we urged Chile, Ecuador, and Peru to join us at a conference table. Seizures

13 Cf. Document 86.
14 Public Law 90-482, Aug. 12, 1968.

in 1969, to which we responded by applying the laws then in force, threatened to lead us to bitter confrontation. At that time, however, perhaps because for a brief moment we all had a glimpse of what could happen in a spiral of escalating action and reaction, the United States, Chile, Ecuador; and Peru agreed at last to convene a Quadripartite Fisheries Conference. Taking note of the fact that by that time we were all engaged in the steps leading to the United Nations resolution of 1970 calling for a new law-of-the-sea conference, the Quadripartite Fisheries Conference was to consider practical solutions that set aside our differences on the broader issues of international law.

The Quadripartite Fisheries Conference met in its first session in Buenos Aires in 1969 and met again in that same city in 1970. It was to have reconvened in a third session no later than July 31, 1971.

As I indicated in the beginning of my statement, 1971 was the year for demonstrating the dimensions of the confrontation that can flow from unresolved fisheries disputes.[15] Between January 11 and March 27 and again in November and December, the Ecuadorean Navy made 51 seizures of American fishing vessels. The vessel owners paid a total of $2.4 million for the forced purchase of licenses and fines to obtain their release. This amount will be reimbursed to them under the terms of the Fishermen's Protective Act. The executive branch, because of the legislation passed throughout the years of the dispute, announced on January 18, 1971, the suspension of military sales and credits to Ecuador under the terms of the Foreign Military Sales Act.[16] All other programs which were the subject of discretionary legislation were placed under review. Given your own experience with the countries of the hemisphere, you will not be surprised when you recall that this step of January 18 was quickly followed by an Ecuadorean appeal to the OAS to consider charges of economic aggression and to the expulsion of the United States Military Group from Ecuador.

Mr. Chairman, we have not yet found a solution to this problem. We have not been able to return to negotiations such as a resumption of the Quadripartite Fisheries Conference, because Ecuador insists that measures first applied in January 1971 must be lifted. We have engaged in private conversations with the Ecuadoreans because they believe as firmly as we that the entire range of our relations must not be allowed to deteriorate. These private conversations were initiated in November by Presidential Counsellor Robert Finch. They were continued when I returned to Quito in December 1971 and again in early January of this year. Ambassador McKernan [Donald L. McKernan, Special Assistant to the Secretary of State for Fisheries and Wildlife] and the Legal Adviser of the Department of State, John R. Stevenson, were with me on both

15 For details, see *A.F.R., 1971*, pp. 441-3.
16 Public Law 90-629, Oct. 22, 1968, as amended by Public Law 91-672, Jan. 12, 1971 (excerpt in *A.F.R., 1971*, p. 442n).

of those trips. On our last visit we were accompanied by representatives of the Department of Defense.

The members of the delegation taken together represented the important U.S. interests which must be respected and reconciled in the course of our search for a temporary solution to our problems with Ecuador,[17] which we would hope also would be acceptable to the signatories of the Santiago Declaration. This west coast fishing problem is not necessarily related to the search for an agreement with Brazil on the issues arising from its new fisheries regulations, which, in effect, could exclude a distant-water American shrimp fleet from operating off Brazil's coast.[18]

We have sought a solution that takes into account all the interests of the United States—our security interests, our distant-water fishing interests, our bilateral political and economic interests, our broader interests in good relations in the hemisphere generally, and our interest in the achievement of United States objectives at the 1973 law-of-the-sea conference.

I would be less than frank if I held out to you and to this subcommittee a falsely optimistic prospect for an interim solution to these disputes. Although the law of the sea, with respect to resources, is evolving in a way which we hope eventually will make it possible to have an end to fisheries disputes in the hemisphere, this is a longer term hope only to be realized in the context of the conference that will begin in 1973. We look to other countries in Latin America that do not have extensive claims to help us identify the elements of an accommodation.

We hope that as our private conversations with Ecuador and our formal negotiations with Brazil continue, we will be able to show convincingly that we appreciate the resource concerns of the developing countries of the hemisphere and have no desire to deprive them of access to the wealth of the oceans in which they, as well as we, have a legitimate interest. In return, we hope they will recognize that for the United States as a major power, the question of how the world's oceans

[17] On Mar. 9, 1972 Secretary Rogers officially waived the application to Ecuador of an amendment to the Foreign Assistance and Related Programs Appropriation Act, 1972 (Public Law 92-242, Mar. 8, 1972) which would have barred assistance to that country in the absence of a determination that such assistance was important to the national interest of the United States. Text of determination in *Bulletin*, Apr. 10, 1972, p. 546; further comment in Rogers Report, 1972, pp. 417-18.
[18] An Agreement with Brazil Concerning Shrimp, signed at Brasilia May 9, 1972 (TIAS 7603; 24 UST 923), established agreed limits for U.S. shrimp fishing operations in disputed waters for an interim period ending Jan. 1, 1974. Approved by an 89-0 vote of the U.S. Senate on Oct. 3, 1972, the agreement was ratified Nov. 29, 1972 and entered into force Feb. 14, 1973. The agreement was extended by notes exchanged at Brasilia Dec. 31, 1973, and the conclusion of a new agreement for the period ending Dec. 31, 1976 was announced Mar. 24, 1975.

are governed in the years ahead must be answered in terms equally responsive to our national security interests.

B. The Organization of American States (O.A.S.).

[The 150th year of diplomatic contact between the United States and Latin America, which was later observed at a ceremonial meeting in Philadelphia on November 14, 1972 (Document 77), found the 24 contemporary members of the inter-American organization still somewhat at a loss to define the objectives and the ultimate significance of their common bond. "The inter-American system is searching for new meaning and purpose in old forms of association," Secretary of State Rogers wrote in the last of his annual reports on U.S. foreign policy. "It had yet to resolve fundamental questions about the future roles of the United States and the Latin American countries. But we are committed to the search."[19]

For the Organization of American States (O.A.S.) and its allied institutions, Secretary Rogers conceded, 1972 was "a year of only limited tangible achievements, coupled with some frictions and anxiety." Nevertheless, the Secretary contended, "the year's difficult passage was a necessary and useful stage in the Organization's progress toward better self-definition and clearer sense of purpose—essential ingredients in the more modern relationship which this Administration seeks with Latin America. Moreover, despite the broader political uncertainties among its members, the OAS as a multilateral entity continued to serve as an effective channel for the transfer of technical and developmental assistance to Latin American countries, and as a forum for airing and examining economic and political problems among its members."[20]]

1. Review of United States Economic Policy.

[One of the essential features of this reciprocal process was the annual review of U.S. economic policy by the Inter-American Committee on the Alliance for Progress (CIAP), established as an instrument of economic policy coordination in 1963 and endowed with permanent status in subsequent reorganization of the O.A.S. machinery. A first review of the U.S. economy had been caried out by

[19] Rogers Report, 1972, p. 405.
[20] Same, pp. 405-6.

CIAP in October 1970; the second, in March 1972, began with an illuminating survey of U.S. economic policies and their meaning for Latin America by Under Secretary of State John N. Irwin II.]

(74) United States Economic Policy and Inter-American Cooperation: Statement by Under Secretary of State John N. Irwin II Before the Inter-American Committee on the Alliance for Progress (CIAP), March 20, 1972.[21]

(Complete Text)

It is a pleasure to welcome CIAP once again to its annual country review of the United States. The first CIAP review, a year ago last October, was a tribute to the more mature relationship among the countries of the Americas which President Nixon first announced in 1969 as the goal of U.S. policy[22]—a goal which the other countries of the hemisphere have universally welcomed. The discussions in that first review session, under your able chairmanship, Dr. [Carlos] Sanz de Santamaría, were thorough, frank, and constructive. Above all, they were discussions among friends. They produced a most helpful report.

We will do our part, and I am confident the other CIAP members will do theirs, to see that this second annual review meets the high standard set by the first. The past year has been a difficult one, difficult for the United States economy and difficult for our economic relations with the Americas. The agenda prepared by the CIAP Secretariat for this review refers to 1971 as "a year of tension in inter-American relations." To the extent that this is true, I hope that our discussions here can help to defuse this tension. We are prepared to examine as fully as time allows the many issues raised in the several papers which the CIAP Secretariat staff, with their usual thoroughness and professionalism, have prepared for this review.

The other members of the United States delegation, most of whom are here, who will participate in the review are:

Mr. Charles A. Meyer, Assistant Secretary of State for Inter-American Affairs; Mr. Ezra Solomon, member of the President's Council of Economic Advisers, who will speak on the United States domestic economy; Mr. Maurice J. Williams, Deputy Administrator of the Agency for International Development, who will cover United States bilateral aid; Mr. Willis Armstrong, Assistant Secretary of State for Economic Affairs, who will cover United States trade policy; and Mr. John M. Hennessy, Acting Assistant Secretary of Treasury for Inter-

[21] Department of State Press Release 68; text from *Bulletin*, Apr. 10, 1972, pp. 539-44.
[22] Cf. note 4 above.

national Affairs, who will discuss the United States balance of payments, the international monetary system, and multilateral financing.

As background for later remarks about U.S. economic policy, let me sketch some basic concepts which underlie U.S. policy toward the countries of Latin America. The Latin American chapter of President Nixon's latest foreign policy report[23] stated that Latin America is not simply another region of the developing world but is unique for United States interests. We believe not only that Latin America is uniquely important for our own interests but also that our interests and those of the countries of Latin America are consonant. In fact, they are mutually supportive, rather than—as some would maintain—conflicting.

—We all desire economic and social progress for all nations of the hemisphere.

—We all want expanded trade.

—We all want an improved quality of life for our peoples and better understanding of how that improvement may best be achieved.

—We all believe in self-determination and in respect for all nations, large or small.

—We all believe in the enhancement of political and civil liberties.

—We all want to negotiate and settle disputes among ourselves peacefully and reasonably, rather than letting them escalate into confrontation or harden into hostility.

It is in our mutual interest to work together toward these common ends through a sharing of ideas and responsibilities. We have the institutions for doing so. CIAP is one. This review process, therefore, is a signal expression of a commitment on the part of all CIAP members to continue a common effort to achieve a better life for all of our peoples.

U.S. DOMESTIC ECONOMY AND BALANCE OF PAYMENTS

What the United States can do toward this common effort is strongly influenced by the condition of our domestic economy and by our international balance of payments. Adverse trends in unemployment, in the rate of inflation, and in our balance of payments came to a head in 1971. Although the economy was expanding and the increase in prices had slowed, it became increasingly clear as the summer of 1971 went on that output expansion and inflation restraint were not proceeding as rapidly as was desirable. The second quarter of the year brought our deteriorating balance of payments to a position where prompt action was imperative.

On August 15 President Nixon announced a new economic policy

[23] Nixon Report, 1972, pp. 90-100.

designed to deal with both the international and the domestic aspects of our economic problems.[24] At home a wage-price freeze was instituted to check inflation. Fiscal measures were adopted to speed up economic activity and cut unemployment. To restore equilibrium in our balance of payments, the President decided to seek a realignment of currency rates, to impose a temporary 10-percent surcharge on dutiable imports,[25] and to press for negotiations in two areas: (1) to correct what in our view were inequitable trade practices of some of our major trading partners and (2) to modernize the international monetary system. Convertibility of the dollar was suspended.

By the end of 1971 substantial progress had been made. The President's revenue bill was passed, with some modifications. On December 18 the United States and nine other industrial nations agreed to a major realignment of their currencies and to undertake urgent negotiations looking toward short-term measures of trade liberalization; they also agreed to longer term discussions on international trade and on the international monetary system.[26] The 10-percent surcharge was lifted.[27]

First results of the August 15 package were already visible at the end of the year. The rate of increase in domestic prices was sharply slowed. The total output of goods and services increased in the fourth quarter at an annual rate double that of the third quarter. The U.S. balance of payments, however, was still heavily in deficit. Improvement in this area will come only over time as the new monetary relationships and trade measures take effect.

As 1972 began, therefore, there were prospects for rising output, diminishing unemployment, greater price stability, and—eventually—a stronger U.S. balance of payments position.

INTERNATIONAL MONETARY REFORM

Two issues relating to the reform of the international monetary system are of obvious concern to Latin America and to this CIAP review: first, the effect on Latin America of the currency realignment already achieved and, second, the reform of the monetary system which we hope to negotiate in the future. The currency realignment should help Latin American exports. Sales in the markets of the revaluing countries should increase as Latin American goods become relatively cheaper. In the United States market, Latin American exports will become more competitive with the suppliers whose countries have appreciated their

[24] *A.F.R., 1971*, no. 142.
[25] Same, no. 143.
[26] Same, no. 150.
[27] Same, no. 151.

currency. In addition, as the United States economy expands, our ability to absorb more imports from the hemisphere will increase.

Looking to the future, we recognize that the countries of Latin America will wish to participate in the discussions leading to reform of the international monetary system. The question of [a] negotiating forum for these discussions is very much on our minds. The Smithsonian agreement[28] pointed to the International Monetary Fund as an appropriate forum; certainly any forum we might devise should be linked in some way to such relevant institutions as the IMF. At the same time, effective negotiations will require a forum in which the participants can reach agreement as well as exchange ideas and views. This suggests some limitation on the number of actual participants so that discussion remains manageable and decision is possible.

The Group of Ten[29] has proved to be a useful forum in the past. We recognize, however, that the Group of Ten is limited to the more industrialized and wealthier nations; it is not ideally suited to giving a representative voice to other nations whose interests must be taken into account. A forum modeled on the IMF Executive Board might provide suitably wider representation. Other models are possible. Under Secretary of the Treasury Paul Volcker has now been asked to explore this question with interested governments to see whether a mutually satisfactory solution can be found.[30]

UNITED STATES TRADE POLICY

Another focus of the CIAP annual review will be the impact of U.S. trade policies on Latin America. For three decades the United States has played a leadership role in removing trade barriers and liberalizing the international movement of goods, services, and capital. In such institutions as GATT, the OECD, and UNCTAD [General Agreement on Tariffs and Trade; Organization for Economic Cooperation and Development; U.N. Conference on Trade and Development], we have consistently supported freer access of goods from the developing countries into industrialized markets. With respect to agricultural products, such as sugar and meat—on which the United States has felt it necessary to retain import quotas—Latin America has received favorable conditions of access. The Sugar Act extension last year[31] continued generally the benefits to Latin America which it has enjoyed in recent years. United States participation in the International Coffee Agreement, which imposes worldwide quotas on coffee exports, has

---

[28] Cf. above at note 26.
[29] Cf. *A.F.R., 1971*, p. 592n.
[30] Cf. Chapter X at note 15.
[31] Sugar Act Amendments of 1971 (Public Law 92-138, Oct. 14, 1971).

materially benefited Latin American producers by insuring them equitable prices for their exports. Congress has now approved and sent to the President legislation extending our participation in the International Coffee Agreement until October 1973.[32]

There are undeniably strong and growing protectionist sentiments in the United States. They are manifested in the Congress, in the labor movement, and in several industrial sectors of our society. The administration's objective in the field of international economic policy, however, has not changed. We seek an open world economy in which trade and investment flows are not disturbed by national barriers. President Nixon has strongly endorsed the cautions raised in the report by Mr. Peter Peterson, then Chairman of the Council on International Economic Policy and now Secretary of Commerce, against erecting new barriers to imports.[33] The United States has, as you know, joined with the European Community and Japan in calling for multilateral trade negotiations in 1973.[34] The developing countries should play an important role in these negotiations.

The imposition of the 10-percent surcharge was probably the trade measure which elicited the most debate and criticism from Latin America in 1971.[35] While we recognized that the Latin Americans had not contributed to our trade deficit, we felt compelled to impose the surcharge on a worldwide basis in order to comply with our GATT obligations and to achieve the objectives of the new economic policy designed over the long run to benefit all of us in the hemisphere. The impact of the surcharge was somewhat lessened by the exemption of two categories of goods particularly important to Latin America— nondutiable items and items under quantitative restraints. As had been promised, the surcharge was a temporary measure and has now been eliminated.

Another issue of great interest to Latin America is a system of generalized tariff preferences.[36] Generalized preferences would help the countries of Latin America meet their needs to increase foreign exchange earnings and diversify exports. The United States has strongly supported efforts in recent years to establish generalized preferences for the developing countries. We took the lead in the OECD to develop a generally acceptable system. As a result of our efforts, the European Community, Japan, and the U.K. have already adopted some form of generalized preferences. As all of you know only too well, the United States has not yet been able to put its own plan into effect. The improvement in our balance of payments and trading position which we

[32] Public Law 92-262, Mar. 24, 1972.
[33] Cf. Nixon Report, 1972, pp. 70-71.
[34] Cf. Chapter X at notes 27-28.
[35] Cf. A.F.R., 1971, no. 115.
[36] Cf. below at note 56.

expect as a result of the Smithsonian agreement should create a more favorable climate for preference legislation. We intend to submit such legislation to Congress the moment we feel it would have a real chance of passage without crippling amendments.

The United States recognizes the importance of export development to the economies of Latin America. A recent meeting of experts in Bogotá brought out that substantial possibilities for assistance exist in this field and should be used. Discussions recently concluded between the United States and Latin American governments brought out that Latin American exports to the United States could be increased if producing countries would give greater attention to quarantine, sanitary, and health regulations designed to protect the consumer and the environment.

UNITED STATES ECONOMIC ASSISTANCE

Those participating in the CIAP review will be particularly interested in the assistance which the United States provides through multilateral and bilateral channels. The foreign assistance program had rough going in our Congress during the latter part of 1971. But with continued administration support, foreign aid authorization and appropriations bills were finally enacted this year.[37] In signing the authorizing legislation, the President expressed his serious concern over the large cut made by Congress in his foreign aid requests. In his foreign policy report he reemphasized that the vital role of foreign assistance deserves the continued support of the U.S. Congress and public.

In my remarks to the first annual CIAP review a year ago last October,[38] I outlined the proposals which the President had just transmitted to Congress for reorganizing U.S. bilateral assistance efforts.[39] Legislation embodying these proposals was submitted to the Congress last spring,[40] but to date Congress has been unwilling to act on them.

In the interim, a number of significant changes are being made in the existing Agency for International Development. The changes are designed to give our bilateral assistance programs sharper focus in those areas where the United States continues to have a distinctive bilateral contribution to make. The most significant changes involve separating the administration of security and developmental aid, trying to concentrate on sectors such as education and agriculture judged to have the highest priority, strengthening population and humanitarian efforts, and encouraging private United States organizations to use their techni-

---

[37] Cf. Chapter X at notes 59-60.
[38] *Bulletin*, Nov. 9, 1970, pp. 561-5.
[39] *Documents, 1970*, pp. 429-44.
[40] *A.F.R., 1971*, no. 153.

cal and scientific capabilities more effectively to help the developing world.

The administration continues to emphasize providing assistance through multilateral organizations. Broader cooperation and wider sharing of responsibility for assistance to the developing areas are essential if the common goals I spoke of earlier are ever to be reached. We expect the international organizations to take an effective lead in this common effort. The bill authorizing the United States share of replenishment for the Inter-American Development Bank has now been signed into law,[41] and most of the appropriations we sought for the Bank have been obtained. The administration will continue to seek adequate appropriations in this area. We also plan to continue financial and technical support for multilateral consultative institutions such as IA–ECOSOC [Inter-American Economic and Social Council] and CIAP.

The United States believes strongly that private foreign investment can make a significant contribution to the economic development of Latin America. Such investment not only transfers capital, which domestic savings cannot provide in sufficient quantities, but also contributes technology and creates trade and employment opportunities. Private investment usually concentrates on productive facilities and thereby complements public assistance, which of necessity usually concentrates on infrastructure.

I know that some of you participating in this review have philosophical differences with us on this issue. A frank exchange of views, however, may help us to find a common middle ground. President Nixon's January 19 statement on economic assistance and investment security[42] is a comprehensive and authoritative statement of the attitude of this government toward private foreign investment. As evidenced by the President's statement, the United States is deeply concerned that different philosophical attitudes toward the role of private foreign investment—attitudes which we recognize are entirely legitimate even though we may disagree with them—seem to be leading to actions in the area of governmental expropriations which in our view are not legitimate. I cannot overemphasize how important it is for all of us who are interested in the common development goals for the hemisphere which I outlined at the beginning of these remarks to come to an understanding on this issue. If the U.S. commitment to developmental assistance is to be maintained, we must work together to preserve an investment climate in which investors, whether private or public, can count on investment protection and the fulfillment of contractual obligations in accordance with recognized international legal standards.

As the CIAP review discusses the role of private foreign investment in

[41] Public Law 92-246, Mar. 10, 1972; cf. Chapter X at note 63.
[42] Document 97.

the overall U.S. economic assistance strategy, I urge you to consider the possible use of multilateral mechanisms for dealing with investment disputes. There are a range of available mechanisms, from consultation with or mediation by the international financial institutions and disinterested governments to formal arbitration in a forum such as the International Center for the Settlement of Investment Disputes. My government hopes that the International Investment Insurance Agency of the World Bank will soon be in a position to provide additional security for foreign investment in a multilateral framework acceptable to both investor and recipient nations.

Mr. Chairman, this has been but a brief sketch of the topics which the members of CIAP will review in much greater depth with my colleagues over the next few days. Let us hope that the review of the difficult year 1971 will lead all of our governments to the kind of common understanding we need to make 1972 a year of increased cooperation among us and progress toward the concrete goal of a better life for our peoples which remains the underlying purpose of the alliance.

2. Second Regular Session of the O.A.S. General Assembly, Washington, April 11-21, 1972.

[Of even broader interest was the Second Regular Session of the O.A.S. General Assembly, supreme organ of the recently reorganized inter-American system, whose memorable First Regular Session had been held in San José, Costa Rica, in April 1971.[43] The Second Regular Session, held in Washington on April 11-21, 1972, again provided a forum for a full-dress policy review by the Secretary of State (Document 75) as well as an informal greeting by the President (Document 76). The substantive achievements of the session, however, were admittedly somewhat limited, and Secretary Rogers took sympathetic note of the complaints of some of the sixteen attending Foreign Ministers that too much time had been spent on "mundane housekeeping and protocolary matters." While sharing the view that future meetings should be restructured in the interests of "freer and more penetrating examination of major hemispheric problems," Mr. Rogers observed that the 1972 Assembly had none the less served a useful purpose in helping to moderate a dispute between Guatemala and the United Kingdom about the British military presence in British Honduras. Another accomplishment noted in the Secretary of State's report was the adoption of a resolution defining and denouncing foreign subversive activities aimed at fomenting violence and terrorism.[44]]

43 Cf. *A.F.R., 1971*, no. 113.
44 Rogers Report, 1972, p. 406.

(75) "The Inter-American Community in a Larger World": Statement by Secretary of State Rogers to the General Assembly, April 12, 1972.[45]

(Complete Text)

This year marks the 150th anniversary of the establishment of diplomatic relations between the United States and a Latin American nation. On June 19, 1822, President Monroe accepted the credentials of Manuel Torres as Chargé d'Affaires of Gran Colombia, the first Latin American diplomatic representative to the United States. The United States made a wise decision—I suppose it was labeled a bold decision at the time—and thus became the first country outside Latin America to recognize the independence of a Latin American government.

For my country it is a privilege and an honor to celebrate 150 years of this association by meeting in Washington at the headquarters of an organization which embodies the successful evolution of relationships which were begun in 1822. Next year the Assembly may wish to meet elsewhere in the hemisphere as it did last year. However, it is my opinion that the time has come for the United States to be the official host of the Assembly, not just the site of its meeting. I therefore extend an invitation for the Assembly to meet in the United States in 1974, in a city other than Washington if that meets with your wishes.[46]

The 150 years of our ties testify to the durability of a fundamental relationship which has survived many changes. Today the nature of that relationship is advancing to a stage in which strong new elements of partnership exist. The process has not been easy; it is not over. But it was necessary and derives from the desires and policies both of Latin America and of the United States.

In the process we have discarded a number of myths which had become part of the standard rhetoric.

First is the concept that our historical experiences are very much the same. It is true that we share many things in common: in the achievement of our independence, in our acceptance of the validity of democratic principles, and in our hopes for peace and stability. But at the same time there are important differences: in language and culture, in our political systems and economic development. These differences, quite naturally, often provide different perspectives on current issues.

Second is the view that basic interests which are in the long run consonant must lead at any given time or on all subjects to harmonious

---

[45] Department of State Press Release 86; text from *Bulletin*, May 1, 1972, pp. 619-25.
[46] The Third Regular Session of the O.A.S. General Assembly was held in Washington on Apr. 4-15, 1973; the Fourth Regular Session was held in Atlanta, Georgia on Apr. 19-May 1, 1974.

relations. Over time they take us in that direction. But it is not un-natural nor unexpected that we should have specific and recurring differences—over such matters as fisheries, the law of the sea, and various economic problems. But these differences themselves prove the independence and sovereignty of each member state, which are so essential to the kind of relationship we desire and so essential to the strength of this Organization and its future.

Third is the belief held by some that this hemisphere is, or should be, a self-contained community. At the time Minister Torres was received by President Monroe the separateness of the hemisphere—apart from the rest of the world—was a progressive idea. The political, economic, and security ties we have forged remain unique, durable, and essential. But all of us also have separate and important contributions to make and interests to pursue throughout the world. In more recent times, not only the United States but also many other countries of the hemisphere have contributed importantly to global developments, not least in the creation of multilateral institutions like the United Nations. These contributions will be even more pronounced as the hemisphere grows in economic and political strength.

The United States is keeping such realities in mind in pursuing the concrete policy toward Latin America defined by President Nixon in 1969[47] and which I reiterated in San José last year.[48] First let me refer to the policy and then to its implementation.

—Our policy is one of involvement in the hemisphere and of firm adherence to the inter-American system.

—It is a policy of continuing commitment to Latin America's economic and social progress, through trade, through investment, through aid, and through our political attitudes.

—It is a policy of respect for the diversity of our national states and of determination not to permit any trace of hegemony in our relations in the hemisphere.

—It is a policy which recognizes that the United States does not have—and should not have—a monopoly on initiative or responsibility.

—It is, finally, a policy which encourages the growing participation of Latin American countries in global affairs and the growing interest of others in productive cooperation in Latin America.

This last point, Latin America's growing impact on world events, is one of particular relevance to this Assembly. For this Assembly reflects that broadening trend. We all welcome to the status of Permanent Observers to the OAS two states in this hemisphere, Canada and Guyana, and we look forward to even closer ties between them and this

[47] Cf. note 4 above.
[48] A.F.R., 1971, no. 113.

Organization. We all welcome also to Permanent Observer status three countries from outside the hemisphere, Spain, Israel, and the Netherlands, all of which participate generously in programs of this Organization.

TIME OF CHANGE IN GLOBAL POLITICS

We meet, as well, at a time when substantial changes are taking place in global politics. My own government is, of course, directly engaged in some of these efforts, notably in the effort to improve relations with the Soviet Union and the People's Republic of China. We are well aware that President Nixon's initiatives affect all of us, and I would like, therefore, to refer to them. You have already received reports from your Ambassadors about my consultation with them immediately after my return from China, so I shall be brief.

Most notable was the simple but profound fact that the visit[49] constituted a new beginning in relations which had been interrupted for 22 years. But it also produced several specific results which are important:

—It established a set of principles to govern bilateral relations under which both countries have placed themselves on record as forgoing the use of force. They were not new principles, but they are new in the bilateral context in which they were stated. They must of course be tested in practice, but we have every expectation that they are principles on which we can build.

—It produced a public proclamation by both sides that they share a number of parallel interests. This recognition may not have changed any of Peking's basic policies, or indeed of ours, but it has made a sharp break with the more than two decade period of unbroken contention.

—It has created opportunities for travel and exchanges among our peoples and for a resumption of trade. These bilateral improvements have been and will be pursued through our contacts in Paris.

—And, in bringing adjustments on both sides toward greater realism in our policies, it has opened the door to a more reasonable and stable set of relationships within Asia.

I am aware that the very boldness of President Nixon's initiatives toward China has raised questions whether we might not be on the verge of a shift, with similar surprise, in our attitude toward Cuba. Let me take this opportunity to say that we do not believe that circumstances justify altering the 1964 OAS decision.[50]

Cuba's continuing interventionist behavior and its support for revolu-

---

[49] Cf. Documents 53-56.
[50] Cf. note 76 below.

tion, even though on a different scale than in the past, still constitute a threat to the peace and security of the hemisphere within the meaning of the 1964 OAS decision which established diplomatic and economic sanctions. Moreover, Cuba continues its close and active military ties with the Soviet Union, a matter of obvious concern to this hemisphere.

If changes in Cuba's policies and actions should justify a reconsideration of the 1964 OAS resolutions, the United States of course would act in concert with our fellow members in the OAS. It is essential for us all to adhere to the process of consultation and decision within the OAS framework.

Unlike our relationship with the People's Republic of China, our relationship with the Soviet Union is a developed and complex one. Many issues are currently under discussion between us. None is of higher priority than achieving an agreement to limit our strategic arms. Such an agreement would have profound consequences not only for our two countries but for all countries. Intensive negotiations remain, but we are hopeful that agreement can be reached by the time of the Moscow summit.

The realistic prospect we now have to curb strategic arms is the product of many years of progress in reaching auxiliary arms agreements. The task of such limitation has not been and must not be restricted to the world's strongest powers, nor should it be restricted to nuclear arms. This Assembly, and particularly the Latin American delegations, will be considering arms limitation on a regional basis. The United States has, as you know, ratified protocol II of the treaty making Latin America a nuclear-free zone.[51] We hope that efforts will be insistently pursued to achieve agreements within the hemisphere limiting other armaments. Such agreements could help divert resources from military expenditure to the economic development and social progress which are still so vital.[52]

The President's visit to Moscow in late May will also enable us to discuss not only SALT [Strategic Arms Limitation Talks] but a range of subjects on which greater bilateral cooperation is possible; e.g., trade, the environment, health, maritime matters, and joint endeavors in space. It will also give us an opportunity to exchange views on major world problems where greater understanding between us could help the cause of peace. As I did following the visit to China, I will report to your Ambassadors in Washington early in June on the outcome of these talks.

---

[51] Done at Mexico City Feb. 14, 1967 and entered into force for the U.S. May 12, 1971 (TIAS 7137; 22 UST 754); text in *Documents, 1968-69*, pp. 392-4; see further *A.F.R., 1971*, no. 114.

[52] A General Assembly resolution in this sense (Resolution 95 [II-0/72] of Apr. 21, 1972) is reprinted in *Documents on Disarmament, 1972*, pp. 169-76.

DEVELOPMENTS IN MONETARY AND TRADE FIELDS

The hemisphere will be affected more immediately, however, by a number of other issues of a global nature. The international economic situation is the most important of these. In both the monetary and trade fields new developments are underway in which Latin America can make a major contribution and receive major benefits.[53]

Over the next few years a new international monetary and trade system affecting all the world's peoples will emerge. The basis for negotiating that system was laid in the actions taken during 1971, a year of landmark economic decisions. The new system must serve fully the needs of developing as well as industrialized countries. The developing world, and Latin America in particular, should participate fully in its creation and its operation.

In the monetary area, one suggestion under active consideration in the International Monetary Fund is for a Governor's Committee modeled on the Executive Board of the Fund, which has 20 representatives. If such a forum were chosen, it would include three representatives from Latin America. There may, however, be some merit in having a group smaller than 20. Whatever the forum, we believe it is important for Latin America to be equitably represented in these discussions.

We also believe the American states should take an active part in advancing their interests in the forthcoming negotiations on international trade, particularly those contemplated for next year within the GATT [General Agreement on Tariffs and Trade]. The communiques which we signed following our bilateral trade negotiations this year with Japan and the European Community[54] contained a pledge to give special attention to the problems of developing countries in the coming multilateral negotiations.

We take that pledge seriously and will consult with you as multilateral discussions proceed, taking full advantage of established regional mechanisms. The United States and Latin America have many trade interests in common. Our efforts to assure a liberal and global trading system should be mutually supportive. For example, as agricultural suppliers we will both want to insure that the expansion of the European Community and the increase in special trade preferences do not discriminate against our legitimate export interests.

The United States also remains intent on improving our own trading relationships with Latin America. In my foreign policy report earlier this year I said frankly that we were "unable to achieve as much as we would have liked" in 1971.[55] I had particularly in mind generalized

---

[53] For further discussion, cf. Document 74.
[54] Cf. Chapter X at notes 27-28.
[55] Rogers Report, 1971, p. ix.

tariff preferences. At the meeting in San José I told you that upon my return I would consult with Congress with a view toward early introduction of legislation to establish a generalized preference system for developing countries.[56] We had hoped to submit such legislation and press for its adoption last year, and we had certainly expected to introduce it before this Assembly met again. However, our consultations convinced us that submission of the legislation under prevailing economic circumstances would have intensified protectionist pressures and might have opened up the possibility of a less rather than more liberal import system. At present there are clear and encouraging signs of considerable progress in our domestic economy, and we will submit preference legislation as soon as we believe prospects for passage have improved.

Meanwhile, we are continuing in other ways to encourage the growth of Latin American exports—which we recognize as essential to your economic development. The recent extensions of sugar and coffee legislation[57] continue import arrangements which benefit Latin American exporters. In addition, meat imports under new agreements with suppliers will be about 7 percent above the 1971 level.

FOREIGN PRIVATE CAPITAL FOR DEVELOPMENT

I am convinced that the international economic arrangements which are emerging as a result of President Nixon's actions of last year will also bring longrun trade benefits to all countries, developing as well as developed. We will do our best to see that they do. Indeed, the realignment of world currencies already achieved should help Latin America's trading position. Latin American exports are now more competitive in the markets of revaluing countries and more competitive in the United States with the exports of revaluing countries.

A steady and significant increase in international trade is a primary requisite for sustained economic growth in developing countries. But also of great importance is the potential developmental value of foreign private investment. At San José last year I stressed the contribution it can make, not only in terms of capital but also in technical and scientific knowledge and in the expansion of export trade. Since then I have been struck by forecasts of a sizable gap in Latin America between external resource needs and anticipated receipts. CIAP [Inter-American Committee on the Alliance for Progress], for example, recently anticipated that by 1973 there will be a gap of $800 million between loan needs and actual or expected disbursements. It is unlikely that such a gap can be closed by further increases in public funds. Foreign private capital, as well as trade, is therefore essential.

[56] *A.F.R., 1971*, no. 113; cf. Chapter X at notes 64-66.
[57] Cf. notes 31-32 above.

By foreign capital, I do not mean U.S. capital alone, but capital from a variety of sources. The advantages of diversified sources of investment are obvious, and this is another area in which Latin America's worldwide involvement is increasing. Nor do I imply any external right to invest in a foreign country. Every country must determine whether it wants foreign investment, the kind of investment it wants, and the purposes for which it wants it. We for our part are convinced that mutual benefits will ensue from equitably regulated and equitably treated foreign investment. We also believe that once a country has determined that it would be beneficial to receive foreign capital, foreign investors should be able to rely on that determination.

Earlier this year we established a presumption that new public economic benefits would not be extended in cases of expropriation without reasonable provision for compensation.[58] We did this because of our responsibility to the legitimate interests of our citizens. But we also had in mind the importance of preserving a climate of confidence that will insure the continued flow of capital that will be needed for development for many years to come. It is in our mutual self-interest to work together to preserve a climate which attracts investment and insures the fulfillment of contractual obligations in accord with recognized international legal standards. When intractable investment disputes do arise, we believe more use should be made of a range of impartial settlement procedures, from consultation to international adjudication or arbitration.

DEVELOPMENT THROUGH PUBLIC ASSISTANCE

The most direct tool of development is of course public assistance. The record of development progress in this hemisphere is a solid one. Despite the highest rate of population increase in the world, and although income distribution in many cases remains inequitable, Latin America's gross national product per capita has risen by at least 3.4 percent each year since 1967. We are glad to have contributed to this progress.

We are encouraging the shift toward larger shares of assistance to Latin America through multilateral channels. Our aim in this is not to avoid our obligations in Latin America but to help fulfill them. Indeed the total of U.S. bilateral assistance and of the U.S. share of multilateral aid funds going to Latin America is at as high a level now as it was in the peak period of the mid-1960's.

We will continue to emphasize the multilateral framework for assistance. Congress has fully authorized the full amount necessary for replenishment of the Inter-American Development Bank's ordinary

[58] Document 97.

capital account and has approved our appropriation requests for $437 million. We are pressing for appropriation of the remaining $387 million due during the coming fiscal year. The $1 billion we have requested for the Bank's Fund for Special Operations has also been fully authorized by Congress,[59] although only half of the first $100 million due this fiscal year has so far been appropriated. The President has urged prompt appropriation of the full amount remaining. We are seeking $450 million in fiscal 1973, and we intend to seek the balance in fiscal 1974.

In our bilateral assistance, we are changing program emphasis. With the international lenders now concentrating on such aspects of the physical infrastructure as transportation, power, and water resources, our bilateral effort will be focused on the more direct needs of the people: on the economic area in which most of Latin America's people work, agriculture; on education; and on health, nutrition, and population. This new focus depends critically on your initiative and effort, because it involves improvements across major sectors rather than a concentration on specific projects. We believe that in this process we can help especially through the transfer and adaptation of U.S. technological and management skills and through encouraging better use of science and technology in development.

Further, we shall continue to give attention to the development of capital markets, to tourism, and to the stimulation of Latin American exports.

COOPERATION WITHOUT INTERFERENCE

Though we currently view our economic relations as central to closer cooperation in the Americas, we are also seeking to keep our political relationships under constant review and to improve them. In political no less than in economic policy, we seek to emphasize a policy of cooperation without interference, to recognize and encourage Latin American initiative and responsibility in the world as well as in the hemisphere, and to respect the interests of all nations large and small.

We are in particular endeavoring to clear away residual territorial problems between us and other countries in the hemisphere. Last year we eliminated the last remaining territorial issue with Mexico in a settlement which recognized Mexican sovereignty over certain territory long under our jurisdiction.[60] We terminated our exclusive right to build an interoceanic canal across Nicaragua.[61] And we signed a treaty recog-

[59] Same as note 41 above.
[60] Boundary treaty with Mexico, signed in Mexico City Nov. 23, 1970 and entered into force Apr. 18, 1972 (TIAS 7313; 23 UST 371).
[61] Convention signed at Managua July 14, 1970 and entered into force Apr. 25, 1971 (TIAS 7120; 22 UST 663).

nizing Honduran sovereignty over the Swan Islands,[62] which is now before the Senate for advice and consent to ratification.

As I noted earlier, shortrun political differences in the Americas are to be expected, and none of us pretend that solutions will always come easily. This is true, for example, on the issue of fisheries,[63] which is complicated by implications for general law-of-the-sea policy. The fisheries issue tests our ability to find solutions respecting the interests of all parties. We are convinced that it should be possible to negotiate pragmatic interim solutions which would meet those interests while setting aside—pending the 1973 U.N. Law of the Sea Conference—differing positions on law of the sea. We are heartened by the recently signed *ad referendum* agreement with Brazil which, without compromising the juridical position of either country, would provide an interim arrangement on fishing.[64] We will similarly continue to seek opportunities to resolve the west coast fisheries problems.

On one high-priority political issue for my government, narcotics, greater interaction between this hemisphere and the rest of the world has created a new problem with which we all must deal. Latin America is neither a major producer nor a major consumer of heroin; yet some areas are being used as transit points for heroin produced outside this hemisphere and destined for the United States. We appreciate the assistance and active cooperation you are giving us on this issue, because we recognize that drug addiction is not yet a serious problem in most of Latin America. We are particularly grateful for the close cooperation of Mexico and Canada on measures to suppress the illicit traffic across our common borders. During this year we plan to open negotiations with 15 countries of this hemisphere on detailed bilateral action programs to curb drug traffic. We welcome your initiatives, your suggestions, and your help in trying to shut off the illicit supply of drugs which are causing us severe domestic problems.

Nearly everything I have said today reinforces the fact that we in this hemisphere are not only a community with mutuality of interests but also an important part of a larger world. The prospects for peace implicit in the President's visits to Peking and Moscow, the reform of the international economic system, the trend toward putting assistance to developing countries on a multilateral basis, the arrangements on fisheries, the problem of narcotics—all these are not just issues which affect the interests of the countries represented here; they are global issues.[65]

The challenge for us all is to engage ourselves fully in such global

[62] Signed at San Pedro Sula Nov. 22, 1971 and entered into force Sept. 1, 1972 (TIAS 7453; 23 UST 2630).
[63] For fuller discussion, cf. Document 73.
[64] Cf. note 18 above.
[65] Cf. *A.F.R., 1971*, no. 136.

issues while maintaining our community of interest within the hemisphere. In a relationship which has developed and prospered for a century and a half, this is surely possible.

Consider for a moment the multiplicity of our ties today. Every Foreign Minister or chief of delegation around this table is involved in bilateral and multilateral programs for trade, for development, for social and political cooperation. My government, too, is involved, in a sense, in all these and in many other such programs around the world. Recognizing this, we have sought in our objectives to take fully into account an inter-American structure that was built over many years and has been strengthened in the recent past by the creation of the Inter-American Development Bank, the development of the Alliance [for Progress], the continuance of development programs through AID, the emergence of subregional development institutions such as the Central American Bank for Economic Integration and the Caribbean Development Bank, the International Coffee Agreement, the Sugar Act, a variety of new programs in the broad fields of science and education, and the expansion of the activities and modernization of the charter of this institution described by the Secretary General[66] yesterday.

Indeed, the scope of our mutual involvement is such that no one of us has even a partial inventory of all that is going on among us—not only officially but also in the multitude of unofficial contacts between businessmen, labor leaders, agriculturalists, scientists, students, and ordinary citizens. A truly inter-American policy, one which centers in this Organization of American States, has built this unique relationship.

Mr. President,[67] I have spoken today realistically and candidly. I have done so because we are convinced that such an approach serves and strengthens the common purposes which have guided our hemispheric community throughout its long and rich history. The United States is, and will remain, dedicated to those purposes.

(76) Remarks by President Nixon at a State Dinner for O.A.S. Representatives, the White House, April 15, 1972.[68]

(Complete Text)

President [José A.] Mora, Your Excellencies, and ladies and gentlemen:
I understand that during the past week that all of you have been exposed to a great number of speeches and tonight therefore, at this

---

[66] Galo Plaza Lasso of Ecuador. On the revision of the O.A.S. Charter cf. *Documents, 1968-69*, pp. 399-401 and *A.F.R., 1971*, p. 434n.
[67] José A. Mora, Minister of Foreign Affairs of Uruguay.
[68] *Presidential Documents*, Apr. 24, 1972, pp. 770-74.

very, shall we say, friendly occasion, I hesitate to impose upon you another speech. But I will speak briefly and then I would like to add a few words directly in a very personal sense to those who are members of what I call and what I think most of you call the American family, our family.

First, we want to welcome you here, as I have welcomed you previously. Yesterday in the Canadian Parliament, as Senator [George D.] Aiken [of Vermont], who is Canada's Senator in the United States Senate, they told me at least, in any event, knows, I was told that unless I spoke some French I would have no success in my speech. So I went back 37 years and picked out a few words and one way or another managed some French that some probably misunderstood.[69]

But whatever the case might be, let me say that as far as my Spanish is concerned, it is limited, but is from the heart when I say, *"Están ustedes en su casa,"*[70] and we are very honored to welcome you here again.

As you know, we come from southern California and we have a strong Spanish heritage—not only where we lived, but also our honeymoon was in Mexico and we have memories that we will always carry with us of those times. So our home in San Clemente, California, is one that we named Casa Pacifica. Casa Pacifica has two meanings. If you have seen this home, it is one that has a magnificent view of the Pacific so it is "The House on the Pacific" or "of the Pacific." But also it has another sense. It also, we believe and trust, will be recorded in history as a "House of Peace." And therefore we think that that Spanish word Casa Pacifica and that sentiment is one that should particularly characterize our thoughts tonight.

When we think of Pan American Week, it is hard to realize that 82 years ago the First International Conference[71] established the International Union of American Republics, which of course was the forerunner of this organization.

And we have to realize and I have noted that during the course of your discussions that we have had some differences, differences this week and differences over those 82 years, but considering what happened in those 82 years, in the Americas and in the world, it would be considered remarkable that an organization like this, which is comprised, as it is, of many diverse viewpoints, could endure at all over these eight decades of change.

So we stand tonight, not only in existence in the OAS, but we stand poised for even more progress as partners. But let me put the term partners in a different sense: Partners in principles, but not necessarily

---

[69] Cf. Document 78.
[70] "You are in your house."
[71] The International Conference of American States, held in Washington in 1890.

partners in every policy. And, of course, partners in principle, is what really matters.

This week has been Pan American Week,[72] in creative deeds as well as in the generalized words of the customary proclamations and resolutions. Yesterday, on Pan American Day, I addressed the Parliament of Canada,[73] as I referred to a moment ago, the American nation of the North. And tonight, here in Washington, we gather with the representatives of the American nations of the South, after a week of conferences that you have had.

We are, in the year 1972, in a year that world attention is focused on East-West relations, the relations for example of the great powers, great in terms of their military strength, their potential military strength. The Soviet Union and the United States, the Soviet Union and China, China and the United States, and in this year of East-West activities, it is good for the United States and for all our fellow American nations to devote this week to the vitality of the North-South relationship. Because, as I said in Canada, at a time that we, in the United States, we believe in the interest of world peace, are attempting to develop a new relationship with our adversary, it is enormously important to develop better relationships with our friends and particularly our friends in the American community.

Our Western Hemisphere ties provide the basic strengths which sustain us as we move toward that goal.

And now if I could turn to my good friend [Secretary-General] Galo Plaza [Lasso]. He spoke of the "fresh winds of change" that are blowing through the OAS and through the Americas in general and he is right. And we have felt those winds of change. That is good, that we have felt them and, frankly, that they are blowing, because we live in a world in which there must be change, change for the better, progress for all people.

Our basic policy position is a new practical acknowledgment that the general term "Latin America" now means something that it didn't used to mean. It means not a uniform voice, Latin America, all those countries down there speaking with one voice, one language, in a sense, but rather a plurality of views.

If I could interpolate here, I am the first President of the United States who has visited every country in Central America and every country in South America, and I know that what the State Department tells every visitor to these parts of the world before he goes, and what they told me is true. That the greatest mistake a traveler in Central America and South America and, for that matter, the Caribbean can make, is to assume that it is just one great part of the world that is very

[72] Text of Proclamation, Apr. 10, 1972, in *Presidential Documents*, Apr. 17, 1972, p. 746.
[73] Document 78.

much alike. It is alike in many ways, but very different in other ways. They are proud peoples, they are different peoples. Many speak the same language, many have the same ideals, but, on the other hand, the important thing for us in the United States to do is to recognize and respect each country in Latin America for what it is and what it stands for and to know them for what they are and what they stand for. This I know from having traveled to all of these countries.

We recognize that diversity has resulted in different kinds of government within Latin America, with varying national goals and methods and we realize that all of this presents problems.

The United States is no stranger to policy differences and to the efforts needed to forge strengths from the fires of discord.

Consequently, we stand prepared to work as a mature and equal partner on the inevitable differences that have arisen and have continued to arise because of the developing new realities in the American Hemisphere.

Let us all recognize that when we talk about differences there are some things that will not change as far as U.S. policy is concerned. We will continue to give a special priority to our unique relationships with Latin America.

I say that here; I could say it also with regard to all of the American Hemisphere, to the Americas generally, to Canada, and to the American family in its largest sense. We have special relationships with many countries in the world, but priority must necessarily go to our closest friends and our closest neighbors in the American Hemisphere.

We will deal realistically with governments as they are, not seeking to impose our political structure on other nations. We recognize that each nation must seek its own way and we respect the right of all people in the various countries with whom we deal in the American family to seek their own way, and we shall continue to demonstrate our deep humanitarian concern for the people of the Hemisphere.

I could interject here just a sense of the feeling that Mrs. Nixon and I have for the countries that you the Foreign Ministers, the Ambassadors, and the others represent here today.

We think of you as representatives of government and we respect you as representatives of government. But also, we think of you as representatives of people. When I think of Latin America I remember, for example, the friends I have met there. I remember a very handsome, vigorous, young man from the Foreign Office—he was young then, in 1955. He had gone to the University of California, had played football, had been a great star and was back in his country of El Salvador, his name means nothing to you. It was Quinones. But he was such a good man and strong man and spoke so fervently about his small country that I realized and sensed from him the sentiment that the people in the countries to the South have for their countries, the patriotism they feel for their countries, large or small.

I remember a ride one night, as we were going to a State dinner in Bolivia. We were riding down a mountain road. It was rather dark and we saw along the road a group of students gathered. They were young students and their teachers were there with them. I asked the driver, "Who are they?" They were waving. He said, "That is the school for the blind." We stopped the car. We got out. We shook their hands, a few of them. We talked to the Sister who was in charge of the school.

I have seen and my wife has, schools for the blind all over the world. But only as you see and feel the hand of a blind person can you realize the universality of the feelings each of us has in his heart for all the people of this world. And I shall always remember that school for the blind in La Paz, Bolivia.

And then my wife had an experience that she says was the mountain top experience of her travels in the world. She went to Peru after the 1970 earthquake, and she flew with Señora Velasco,[74] for whom we gave a dinner, a luncheon here, into the earthquake zone. She saw the great tragedy, all of the destruction, but what impressed her was the courage, the strength, the dignity of the people, young and old, those beautiful faces—in the face of adversity they are going to build a new country, and she brought back with her therefore a feeling for the people of Peru which she communicated to me, and I think also communicated to the American people.

What I am saying to my friends here in the American family, we do not think of you simply as representatives of government, but we think of you very truly as members of our family. There are blind people in our family. There are people who have suffered adversity, and Peru, of course, has had another earthquake. There are people who are old friends and dear friends, and it is that special relationship that we hope that all Americans can understand, because as we understand that we are a family, then we can develop a more understandable policy for the Americas.

What I am suggesting here is that an intangible force forms the basis of the solidarity among the Americas. This force was well defined over 50 years ago by another President standing in this room. Listen to his words—Woodrow Wilson: "We must prove ourselves their friends and champions upon terms of equality and honor. You cannot be friends upon any other terms than upon the terms of equality. You cannot be friends at all except upon the terms of honor. We must show ourselves friends by comprehending their interest whether it squares with our own interest or not."

I say to you tonight, we, the United States, do comprehend. The

[74] Wife of President Juan Velasco Alvarado. For background, cf. *The United States in World Affairs, 1970*, pp. 193-4.

United States is and will remain your friend, your champion, no matter what difficulties present themselves, in your countries, in ours, or any place on earth.

Now comes the time for the traditional toast at this dinner. There are so many people of high rank that we would have to go around the table Chinese style, tipping every glass in order to do it adequately, but I am afraid most of us probably couldn't survive the evening in the event we did that, so we have selected one of your members, the President of this Organization, as the one who will receive the toast on behalf of all of you.

Before toasting this very distinguished statesman, President Mora, let me say a word about the profession he represents. He is one who has been in diplomacy most of his life, as most of you have been in diplomacy. Now diplomats have very difficult times in every country, including the United States, but let me tell you how very important they are. I had it brought home to me today.

I signed a very thick treaty today with the Prime Minister of Canada.[75] They brought the treaty over, they turned the page, they said, "Sign here." And I signed. Now as a lawyer, or a former lawyer, I know better than to sign something without reading it. Why did I sign it? I will tell you why.

While the Prime Minister of Canada and I were being seen on television, while we were meeting, a meeting at the summit of our two countries, discussing these important things, the work was being done that made possible our agreements, by scores of able, dedicated people. Some were Foreign Ministers, some were Secretaries of State, others were at other levels in their Foreign Service, but all were enormously important.

I simply want to say that in this year of summitry, here is one who goes to the summit, who knows that without the help of those who make it possible for him to go, who dig out the little places on those mountains where you step before you get to the top, there could be no summitry whatever.

And for that reason, as I raise my glass with yours, to the President of this Organization, let me say, it is raised to all of those in this room who have given your lives to the service of diplomacy, to the service of peace and therefore, to the service of your own country and to the American family. So I ask that you rise, raise your glasses to *La Familia Americana* and to President Mora.

3. Other O.A.S. Matters.

[A most noticeable challenge to inter-American unity at the

[75] Cf. note 84 below.

O.A.S. level arose from a growing tendency on the part of some member states to disregard the organization's 1964 decision calling for suspension of diplomatic, trade, and maritime transport relations with Cuba until such time as the O.A.S. Council determined, by an affirmative two-thirds vote, that the Cuban Government had ceased to endanger the peace and security of the hemisphere.[76] Mexico had disregarded this recommendation from the beginning, and Chile had resumed relations with Cuba soon after the Allende government took office in 1970. But Secretary Rogers, in his address to the O.A.S. General Assembly (Document 75), expressed the definite view that "Cuba's continuing interventionist behavior and its support for revolution, even though on a different scale than in the past, still constitute a threat to the peace and security of the hemisphere." This negative judgment was later upheld by the O.A.S. Permanent Council when a Peruvian motion to lift the 1964 restrictions was rejected on June 8, 1972 by a vote of 7 in favor and 14 against (including the United States), with 3 abstentions. Peru nevertheless proceeded independently to establish relations with the Castro government in July 1972, and the prime ministers of Jamaica, Barbados, Trinidad and Tobago, and Guyana (a permanent observer but not a member state of the O.A.S.) later announced that their governments would take similar action. The United States, in contrast, continued to maintain that "any change in the O.A.S. sanctions should result from collective action by the O.A.S. member states and only after a finding by the Organization that Cuba no longer is a threat to the peace and security of the hemisphere."[77]

On a more harmonious theme, the inter-American organization commemorated in November 1972 the establishment, 150 years earlier, of diplomatic relations between the United States and the independent Latin American government of Gran Colombia, the predecessor of present-day Colombia, Venezuela, and Ecuador. This mainly ceremonial occasion permitted the Secretary of State to reiterate a number of the fundamental ideas that continued to shape the hemispheric relations of the U.S. Government.]

---

[76] *Documents, 1964*, pp. 294-5.
[77] Rogers Report, 1972, p. 427. For background on U.S.-Cuban relations, see also *A.F.R., 1971*, no. 117.

(77) "The Inter-American Community: Our Heritage and Our Future":
Statement by Secretary of State Rogers at a Protocolary Session of
the O.A.S. Permanent Council, Independence Hall, Philadelphia,
November 14, 1972. [78]

(Complete Text)

I am pleased to join you today to celebrate a century and a half of
diplomatic relations between the United States and the nations of Latin
America. It is especially fitting that we hold this commemorative session of the OAS Permanent Council in Philadelphia. This city was long
the home and is the resting place of Manuel Torres, the first accredited
Latin American diplomatic representative to the United States and a
man who helped construct the solid foundations on which our historic
association is built.

The idea of this hemisphere as a unique community had begun to
take root in 1796 when Manuel Torres arrived in this city a political
refugee. It flowered in June of 1822 when President Monroe accepted
Torres' credentials as Chargé d'Affaires of Gran Colombia. By this act
the United States became the first nation outside Latin America to
recognize the independence of a Latin American government.

This initial recognition, the first official bond between us, was not
fortuitous. Rather, it reflected the conviction of our early leaders that
the future of the hemisphere lay in cooperative association. From that
beginning there developed a common faith in the benefits of freedom,
in the importance of the individual, and in the possibility of human
reason to deal with the age-old afflictions of society. This bond was
sealed when many Latin American countries modeled their constitu-
tions after the one that was drafted in these halls. And our pursuit of a
common political destiny was reinforced by rapidly expanding trade, a
commerce which appropriately enough found this city at its forefront.

With their breadth of vision, the men who first sketched the outlines
of the inter-American community were as alive to its diversities as they
were to similarities that existed within the hemisphere. Diversity of
historical experience, diversity of economic condition, diversity of culture, were all manifestly present. And as was to be expected, over the
years there have indeed been differences in perception of national
interest.

Nevertheless, what is impressive to me in the record of our 150-year-
old association is the continued vitality of the idea that by circumstance and by choice we are a community—a community which has
brought great benefits to its members. We have forged significant

[78] Department of State Press Release 283; text from *Bulletin*, Dec. 4, 1972, pp.
655-6.

intellectual, economic, political, and security ties. Particularly, we have created together the inter-American system, which despite its imperfections has served our community in so many ways so well.

We must recognize, however, that the world in which our association began has been dramatically altered. Modern communications have collapsed time and space. The isolation of the hemisphere has disappeared. While all nations have developed significantly, material disparities still exist and in some instances have grown. Our intellectual community has been challenged by new ideas and changing values.

For our association to continue to draw spirit from the ideas that created it, we have to adjust our purposes to vastly different times and conditions from those in which Manuel Torres walked the streets of Philadelphia. We should welcome the challenge of adjustment, since no institution or idea can usefully survive if it is not constantly tested. As we examine our purposes and possibilities, we will need what Elihu Root, a distinguished predecessor of mine, called the "imagination which enlarges the historian's understanding of the past into the statesman's comprehension of the future."

One new development of great promise is the acceleration of Latin America's constructive involvement in an interdependent world. The United States has sought to encourage these trends. For example, Mexico, Brazil, and Argentina are, with our support, among the 20 nations which will be primarily concerned with developing a new international monetary policy.[79] We hope to work closely with them during those negotiations.

We will work on a similar basis with Latin American countries which will be involved in next year's trade negotiations,[80] for our economic interests in a world of freer trade should be mutually supporting. More broadly, we expect to expand our process of consultation with individual Latin American countries on specific international and bilateral issues. The enlargement of our individual roles in international affairs gives us the opportunity to deepen our community of interest on global as well as hemispheric issues.

It is equally important to maintain broad support for the regional organizations of the hemisphere, and in particular for the OAS—the linchpin of the inter-American system. We must continue to work together to find ways to make our system more effective. I hope, for example, we can enhance both the cooperative and consultative role of the OAS by finding ways for the Foreign Ministers to exchange views more frankly and freely when we meet together at its next General Assembly.[81]

Because economic relations are so vital to our community of interest,

[79] Cf. Chapter X at note 15.
[80] Cf. Chapter X at note 29.
[81] Cf. note 46 above.

I also welcome the initiative of our distinguished Secretary General, Mr. Galo Plaza, to place on the agenda of the next OAS General Assembly a review of inter-American cooperation in economic development with a view toward possible reform. We in the U.S. Government understand the priority you give to development in all its aspects. We give it the same priority, and we regret that it has not been possible so far to do as much as we both would have liked.

The changes we have undertaken in recent years in our policy toward Latin America are based on a genuine desire to modernize our relationships. President Nixon has asked me to tell you that during his second term we will remain committed to the interests of the hemisphere and determined to make a substantial contribution to its social and economic progress:

—We will pursue a policy of cooperation with Latin America in a relationship of greater equality, shared initiatives, and mutual responsibilities;

—We will work to insure that the legitimate interests of all the nations of Latin America are represented in the new international monetary and trade systems to be negotiated;

—We will cooperate with you directly in this hemisphere to strengthen and diversify our trade, investment, and assistance ties; and

—We will seek to resolve the issues between us, over fisheries, over territorial seas, over investment, and all others, in the spirit of friendship and mutual respect which is the essence of our inter-American system.

This ceremony today reminds us that our community is endowed with a rich heritage. We have an obligation to our forebears and a duty to our heirs to enrich what we have received. I am certain that, working together, we can be faithful to the past and worthy of the future. It remains the desire and the intention of the U.S. Government to help fulfill that trust.

C. Canada and Mexico.

[With the nations that shared its land frontiers, the United States quite naturally maintained a more intensive relationship than with countries situated at a greater distance. Geographical contiguity, though conducive in many ways to friendship and mutual understanding, was also apt to give rise to complex problems and even, on occasion, to a high degree of mutual irritation. Such ambiguities and contradictions were particularly apparent in the United States' relations with its northern and southern neighbors in a year when tension among friends and allies was not unknown in remoter parts of the world as well.]

1. Canada.

[President Nixon's state visit to Canada on April 13-15, 1972, highlighted by an address to the Canadian Parliament and the signature of an important agreement aimed at combating pollution in the Great Lakes Basin, occurred at a time when negative trends within the Canadian-American relationship had appeared to be rapidly gaining ground upon the traditional amity between the two countries. The reassertion of Canadian individuality under Prime Minister Pierre Elliott Trudeau was inevitably expressed to a considerable degree in resistance to what was seen by many Canadians as a threat of U.S. dominance, particularly in economic and cultural matters. The United States, on its side, was deeply concerned over Canadian economic policies directed, among other things, toward limiting the growth of foreign ownership of Canadian enterprises and reducing the susceptibility of the Canadian economy to external influences.

Some elements of this complex picture were touched upon in President Nixon's April 14 address to the Canadian Parliament (Document 78), which characteristically sought to place the irritations of the moment within a larger framework of shared beliefs and values. Although bilateral trade and economic problems between the United States and Canada were to persist through 1972 and beyond, Secretary Rogers later pointed out that "in many other areas, such as defense, preparations for the Conference on Security and Cooperation in Europe (CSCE) and mutual and balanced force reductions (MBFR) meetings, environmental protection, conservation and fisheries, narcotics control, and action against air piracy and terrorism, the year produced a number of bilateral and multilateral achievements reflecting a marked congruence of interests and close cooperation."[82]]

---

[82] Rogers Report, 1972, p. 419; for details, cf. same, pp. 420-23.

(78) Review of United States-Canadian Relations: Remarks by President Nixon to a Joint Meeting of the Canadian Parliament, Ottawa, April 14, 1972. [83]

(Complete Text)

Monsieur l'Orateur de la Chambre des Communes, Monsieur le Président du Sénat, Monsieur le Premier Ministre, Messieurs les Membres des Chambres du Parlement Canadien, éminents hôtes et amis: J'apprécie vivement votre aimable invitation ainsi que votre accueil chaleureux.

To all of you who have welcomed Mrs. Nixon and me so warmly on this occasion, I trust you will give me allowances for trying to speak in the language that I studied 37 years ago. When I tried it the day before I came on the top linguist of the American Government, [Major] General [Vernon A.] Walters, he said, "Go ahead. You speak French with a Canadian accent."

I will have to admit I am not very much at home in the French language, but as a former parliamentarian in my own country, I feel very much at home in this chamber. I am grateful for the high privilege which your invitation represents.

I am grateful, too, for this chance to return to Canada and for the opportunity of signing here an historic agreement to restore and protect forever the quality of the Great Lakes we share together. [84] That agreement testifies to the continuing vitality of our unique relationship, which has been described so eloquently by the Prime Minister. In discussing that relationship today, I wish to do so in a way that has not always been customary when leaders of our countries meet.

Through the years, our speeches on such occasions have often centered on the decades of unbroken friendship we have enjoyed, and our 4,000 miles of unfortified frontier. In focusing on our peaceful borders and our peaceful history, they have tended to gloss over the fact that there are real problems between us. They have tended to create the false impression that our countries are essentially alike.

It is time for Canadians and Americans to move beyond the sentimental rhetoric of the past. It is time for us to recognize:

—That we have very separate identities;
—That we have significant differences;
—And that nobody's interests are furthered when these realities are obscured.

---

[83] *Presidential Documents*, Apr. 17, 1972, pp. 757-61; additional documentation in same, pp. 752-7 and 761-2.
[84] Great Lakes Water Quality Agreement, signed in Ottawa Apr. 15, 1972 (TIAS 7312; 23 UST 301); summary in *Bulletin*, May 8, 1972, pp. 654-7.

Our peaceful borders and our peaceful history are important symbols, to be sure. What they symbolize, however, is the spirit of respect and restraint which allows us to cooperate despite our differences, in ways which help us both.

American policy toward Canada is rooted in that spirit. Our policy toward Canada reflects the new approach we are taking in all of our foreign relations—an approach which has been called the Nixon Doctrine. That doctrine rests on the premise that mature partners must have autonomous, independent policies:

—Each nation must define the nature of its own interests;
—Each nation must decide the requirements of its own security;
—Each nation must determine the path of its own progress.

What we seek is a policy which enables us to share international responsibilities in a spirit of international partnership. We believe that the spirit of partnership is strongest when partners are self-reliant, for among nations—as within' nations—the soundest unity is that which respects diversity, and the strongest cohesion is that which rejects coercion.

Over the years, the people of Canada have come to understand these concepts particularly well. Within your own borders, you have been working to bring a wide variety of peoples and provinces and points of view into a great national union—a union which honors the integrity of its constituent elements.

It was Prime Minister [Sir Wilfrid] Laurier who said of Canada's differing components: "I want the marble to remain the marble; I want the granite to remain the granite; I want the oak to remain the oak." This has been the Canadian way. As a result, Canadians have helped to teach the world, as Governor-General [Vincent] Massey once said, that the "toleration of differences is the measure of civilization."

Today, more than ever before, we need to apply that understanding to the whole range of world affairs. To begin with, we must apply it in our dealings with one another.

We must realize that we are friends not because there have been no problems between us, but because we have trusted one another enough to be candid about our problems—and because our candor has nourished our cooperation.

Last December, your Prime Minister and I met in Washington,[85] and he asked me if I thought the United States would always want a surplus trade balance with Canada so that we could always export capital here. My answer then, and my answer now, is "no."

As I said to him at that time, we in the United States saw this same

[85] Dec. 6, 1971; cf. *A.F.R., 1971*, pp. 180-81.

problem from the other side before World War I. We then depended on European capital for our development, and we wanted to free ourselves from that dependence. And so we fully understand that Canada is in that same position today.

Canada is the largest trading partner of the United States. It is very important that that be noted in Japan, too.[85a] Our economies have become highly interdependent. But the fact of our mutual interdependence and our mutual desire for independence need not be inconsistent traits. No self-respecting nation can or should accept the proposition that it should always be economically dependent upon any other nation. And so, let us recognize once and for all that the only basis for a sound and healthy relationship between our two proud peoples is to find a pattern of economic interaction which is beneficial to both our countries—and which respects Canada's right to chart its own economic course.

We must also build a new spirit of partnership within the Western Hemisphere that we share together.

It has been said that Canada is bounded "on the north by gold, on the west by the East, on the east by history—and on the south by friends." We hope that will always be the case, and we hope it will be the case not only with respect to the United States, your immediate neighbor on the south, but with respect to all your southern neighbors—and ours—who are bound by the great forces of geography and history which are distinctive to the New World.

But geography and history alone do not make a community. A true community must be a living entity in which the individuality of each member is a source of pride to all members, in which the unity of all is a source of strength to each, and the great community of the Americas cannot be complete without the participation of Canada.

That is why we have been encouraged by the recent decisions of Canada to upgrade its participation as an observer in the Organization of American States to ambassadorial status, and to apply for membership in the Inter-American Development Bank,[86] for both of these institutions made the abstract concept of community within the Americas a living reality.

A sound concept of community is also important in another international arena that we share, the Atlantic Alliance. Just one month after my inauguration as President of the United States, I observed that a new spirit of cooperation within that Alliance was essential as we

---

[85a] At a news conference on Sept. 16, 1971, President Nixon had incorrectly stated "that Japan is our biggest customer in the world and we are their biggest customer in the world" (*A.F.R., 1971*, pp. 590-91).

[86] Canada became a Permanent Observer to the O.A.S. in 1972 and joined the I.D.B. on May 3, 1972.

began a new search for cooperation between East and West.[87] The recent agreements concerning Berlin[88]—the fact, for example, that thousands of families were reunited this Easter for the first time in many years—these are among the first fruits of a new era of East-West negotiation.

But as we seek better relations with our adversaries, it becomes all the more important to strengthen the alliances with our friends. We must never forget that the strength and the unity of the West has been an indispensable element in helping to bring about the new era of negotiation with the East, and that is why we began our round of summit talks last December by meeting with the Prime Minister of Canada, and then with the leaders of other close allies.[89] That is why our East-West conversations will always be accompanied by a full and genuine consultation within the Atlantic Alliance.

That Alliance began as a way of pooling military resources. Today it is a way of pooling our intellectual and our diplomatic resources as well. Like our Federal approaches to nationhood, like our Canadian-American brotherhood, like our inter-American neighborhood, the Atlantic Alliance has achieved a creative unity in which the individuality of its members is respected and advanced.

Let us turn now to the world as a whole—for this is where the challenge of building a true community will be most difficult—and most important.

We in Canada and the United States have always been proud to live in what is called "the New World." Today there is a new world coming for everyone who lives on this globe. It is our responsibility to make this new world a better world than the world we have known.

We Canadians and Americans have fought and died together in two World Wars in this century. We live now in what has been called the post-war era. But mankind has known a long succession of post-war eras. And each one of them has turned out to be a pre-war era as well.

The challenge we face today is to build a permanent post-war era—an era of lasting peace.

My visit to Ottawa comes midway between my visits to Peking and Moscow.

In many respects, these journeys are very different. In the People's Republic of China we opened a new dialogue after 22 years of virtually no communication. In the Soviet Union there is an opportunity to bring a continuing dialogue to productive conclusions.[90]

But in their central aim, these journeys to Peking and Moscow are

87 Remarks to the North Atlantic Council, Brussels, Feb. 24, 1969, in *Documents, 1968-69*, pp. 144-8.
88 Cf. Document 25.
89 Cf. note 85 above.
90 Cf. Documents 53-56 and 9-12.

alike. Neither visit is directed against anyone—adversary or ally. Both are for the betterment of everyone—for the peace of all mankind.

However, we must not allow the fact of summit meetings to create any unrealistic euphoria.

The responsibility for building peace rests with special weight upon the great powers. Whether the great powers fulfill that responsibility depends not on the atmospherics of their diplomacy, but on the reality of their behavior.

Great powers must not treat a period of détente as an interlude between periods of tension. Better relations among all nations require restraint by great nations—both in dealing with each other and in dealing with the rest of the world.

We can agree to limit arms. We can declare our peaceful purposes. But neither the limitation of arms nor the declaration of peaceful purposes will bring peace if directly or indirectly the aggressive use of existing weapons is encouraged.

And great powers cannot avoid responsibility for the aggressive actions of those to whom they give the means for embarking on such actions.

The great powers must use their influence to halt aggression—and not to encourage it.

The structure of world peace cannot be built unless the great powers join together to build it, and its strength will grow only as all nations of all political and social systems, come to accept its validity and sustain its vitality. This does not mean that the great powers must always agree.

We expect to continue to have profound philosophical and significant diplomatic differences with the Soviet Union and with the People's Republic of China in a number of areas. But, through opening new lines of communication, we hope to increase the chance that in the future we can talk about our differences and not fight about them.

As we have prepared for both of these journeys, the experience of Canada has been most helpful. I am grateful to both the Prime Minister and to the Opposition Leader, Mr. [Robert L.] Stanfield, for sharing their insights with us as we embark on these endeavors.

As we continue toward our common quest for a better world order, let us apply the lessons we have learned so well on this continent:

—that we can walk our own road in our own way without moving farther apart; that we can grow closer together without growing more alike;

—that peaceful competition can produce winners without producing losers; that success for some need not mean setbacks for others;

—that a rising tide will lift all our boats; that to go forward at all is to go forward together;

—that the enemy of peace is not independence but isolation; and that the way to peace is an open world.

And let us remember, too, these truths that we have found together:

—that variety can mean vitality;
—that diversity can be a force for progress;
—and that our ultimate destiny is indivisible.

When I spoke at the St. Lawrence Seaway ceremonies in 1969,[91] I borrowed some words from the monument there which I had joined Queen Elizabeth [II] in dedicating just 10 years before. That monument, as its inscription puts it, "bears witness to the common purpose of two nations whose frontiers are the frontiers of friendship, whose ways are the ways of freedom, [and] whose works are the works of peace."[92]

The truth to which that inscription testifies is of profound importance to people everywhere in this world.

For the ability of our two nations, Canada and the United States, to preserve the frontiers of friendship, to walk in the ways of freedom, and to pursue the works of peace provides example and encouragement to all who seek those same objectives, wherever they may live.

There is nothing more exciting than a time of new beginnings. A member of this body caught that spirit when he spoke to Parliament about the beginnings of Canadian nationhood 100 years ago. Listen to him. "Blood pulsed in our veins, new hopes fired our hearts, new horizons lifted and widened, new visions came to us in the night watches."

May that same sense of excitement inspire our two nations as we help lead the world to new beginnings today.

2. Mexico.

[As with Canada, so with Mexico, affection and exasperation with regard to the United States were blended in a mixture that, in Mexico's case, may have been even more volatile because it reflected even wider economic and cultural disparities. President Luis Echeverría Álvarez, beginning a state visit to the United States with an address to a joint session of Congress on June 15, 1972, seemed to go out of his way in stressing the negative side of Mexico's evaluation of U.S. performance. "Mexico," said the neighboring

[91] June 27, 1969; text of President Nixon's remarks in *Public Papers, 1969*, pp. 483-5.
[92] Same, p. 484.

chief executive, "does not expect special treatment from the United States, but only asks that our contacts and exchanges be regulated by the standards of fairness and respect that should govern all international relations. . . . In any case, it is impossible to understand why the United States does not use the same boldness and imagination that it applies to solving complex problems with its enemies to the solution of simple problems with its friends." Rehearsing a familiar complaint of "third world" nations, the Mexican leader also declared: "We cannot be in agreement with those who try to reduce world politics to dealings among powerful nations. We agree even less with those who confuse power with the capacity to produce nuclear weapons. . . . It is more sensible to lay the foundations of security on a better distribution of wealth than on the progressive stockpiling of arms and technological resources."[93]

President Echeverría's conversations with President Nixon on June 15 and 16 provided the opportunity for a general review of current Mexican-American problems (Document 79) which focused especially on the high salinity of Colorado River water entering Mexico, described by Mr. Nixon as "the single most important irritant in relations with our nearest Latin neighbor."[94] As a result of the meeting, the United States arranged for prompt improvement, on an interim basis, of the quality of Colorado River water delivered to Mexico;[95] and an agreement on a permanent solution was embodied in diplomatic notes exchanged at Mexico City on August 30, 1973.[96]]

(79) State Visit of President Luis Echeverría Álvarez: Joint Communiqué Issued Following Meetings with President Nixon on June 15-16, 1972.[97]

(Complete Text)

President Richard Nixon and President Luis Echeverria Alvarez welcomed this opportunity to renew their personal friendship and the cordial dialogue which began at their first meeting here in 1970.[98] They regarded this visit as particularly appropriate at a time when the

[93] Bulletin, July 10, 1972, pp. 61-3.
[94] Nixon Report, 1973, p. 127; fuller discussion in Rogers Report, 1972, pp. 423-5.
[95] Bulletin, Aug. 14, 1972, pp. 197-9.
[96] Same, Sept. 24, 1973, pp. 388-96 and 416.
[97] Presidential Documents, June 19, 1972, pp. 1057-9; additional documentation in same, pp. 1052-6 and in Bulletin, July 10, 1972, pp. 57-67. The communiqué was issued at Key Biscayne, Florida on June 17, 1972.
[98] Nov. 13, 1970 (Presidential Documents, Nov. 16, 1970, p. 1559).

eyes of the world have been focused on President Nixon's recent visits to Peking and Moscow. The visit of the Mexican President to the United States serves to direct broad attention to the equally important tasks of advancing new approaches to Latin America and the less developed nations of the world.

They also agreed that their meetings had contributed to the establishment of a new era, an opening characterized by a spirit of frankness, with Mexico and which they hoped would characterize intra-Hemispheric relations.

The two Presidents exchanged impressions on world and Western Hemisphere affairs in considerable detail. President Nixon described his talks with the Chinese and Soviet leaders. President Echeverria recounted his experiences on recent visits to Japan, Chile and Peru. They found this review informative, useful as well as stimulating. They were firmly united in the view that world peace with social justice is essential to the well-being of all mankind.

The Presidents discussed overall relations between their two countries—political and economic affairs, and cooperation in the scientific, technical, cultural and other fields.

The President of the United States recognized the important role developing countries could and should play in erecting a new international monetary system and in progressing toward a free and fair trading system. In endorsing trade policies more responsive to the problems of both developed and developing countries, he reaffirmed his intention to seek congressional authorization at the appropriate time for the United States to participate with other industrialized countries in a system of Generalized Tariff Preferences for imports from developing countries.[99]

Regarding the problem of the salinity of the Colorado River, President Echeverria told President Nixon that Mexico reiterates its position as regards receiving its assignment of original waters from the Colorado River, to which the Treaty of February 3, 1944[100] refers, and therefore, with the same quality as those derived from the Imperial Dam.

To this, President Nixon replied that this was a highly complex problem that needed careful examination of all aspects. He was impressed by the presentation made by President Echeverria and would study it closely. It was his sincere desire to find a definitive, equitable and just solution to this problem at the earliest possible time because of the importance both nations attach to this matter.

As a demonstration of this intent and of the goodwill of the United States in this connection, he was prepared to:

[99] Cf. above at note 56.

[100] Treaty Relating to the Utilization of Waters of the Colorado and Tijuana Rivers and of the Rio Grande, signed at Washington Feb. 3, 1944 (Department of State *Treaty Series* 994); text in *Documents, 1943-44*, pp. 547-72.

(a) undertake certain actions immediately to improve the quality of water going to Mexico;

(b) designate a special representative to begin work immediately to find a permanent, definitive and just solution of this problem;

(c) instruct the special representative to submit a report to him by the end of this year;

(d) submit this proposal, once it has the approval of this Government to President Echeverria for his consideration and approval.[101]

President Echeverria said that he recognized the goodwill of President Nixon and his interest in finding a definitive solution to this problem at the earliest possible time. He added that based on two recent trips to the Mexicali Valley and his talks with farmers there, his Government, while reserving its legal rights, had decided to stop using waters from the Wellton-Mohawk project for irrigation purposes while waiting for receipt of the US proposal for a definitive solution.

Both Presidents agreed to instruct their Water and Border Commissioners to prepare and sign a Minute containing the above program and commitments as soon as possible.

The Presidents discussed the many areas of ongoing cooperation between Mexico and the United States, and their conviction that such cooperation serves to bind our people even closer together in mutual effort and understanding. They took note of the agreements concluded during the visit by their respective Secretaries for Foreign Relations: a bilateral agreement with regard to the exchange of information, training and research in the fields of science and technology; a subsidiary agreement which contemplates the exchange of young technicians and scientists (including the training of some 100 young Mexican technicians and scientists through US Government agencies); renewal of the agreement on Cultural Relations.[102]

President Nixon and President Echeverria discussed the serious nature of the illicit international traffic in narcotic drugs. They reviewed the joint enforcement measures which their countries have successfully undertaken over the past two years. President Nixon informed President Echeverria of recent measures taken to combat the drug problem in the United States. They agreed to acquire and employ additional equipment in the antinarcotics campaign and to make available increased training of personnel for this purpose.

With regard to the question of migratory Mexican workers, the two Presidents discussed the economic, social and political factors that produce this problem and agreed it was desirable for each government to undertake immediately a study of this question with a view to

---

101 Cf. above at notes 95-96.

102 For details, cf. joint announcement, June 17, 1972, in *Public Papers, 1972*, pp. 685-6.

finding a mutually satisfactory solution.

Recognizing the communality of many environmental problems and the need to seek cooperative solutions through the exchange of research and experience, the two Presidents have agreed that appropriate policy level officials from Mexico and the US will meet on a regular basis for discussion and consultation concerning current and future environmental problems of mutual concern and the methods for dealing with them in a more systematic way.

The conversations between Presidents Nixon and Echeverria were at all times cordial and marked by the spirit of good neighborliness which exists between Mexico and the US. At the same time problems were discussed frankly and openly as between true friends in an atmosphere of mutual respect and trust. President Echeverria particularly wished to convey on behalf of Mrs. Echeverria, his party and himself, his deep appreciation for the warm hospitality which was extended to them by President and Mrs. Nixon.

President Nixon expressed his great pleasure that President and Mrs. Echeverria will now have an opportunity to visit other areas and cities of the United States[103] and assured them they will receive a warm and friendly welcome from the American people.

[103] The advance program for the visit (Department of State Press Release 138, June 12, 1972) included stops in New York, Chicago, San Antonio, and Los Angeles prior to the return to Mexico June 21, 1972.

IX.
UNITED NATIONS
AND
INTERNATIONAL COOPERATION

[Awareness of the global character of many contemporary problems increased in 1972 as questions relating to space, the environment, the oceans, narcotics control, terrorism, and other matters transcending national boundaries became the object of heightened international attention. At the same time, effective action in many of these areas was inhibited by a growing disparity of outlook between the principal industrialized countries, particularly the United States, and numerous "third world" nations backed in most instances by the People's Republic of China. To an increasing extent, the familiar East-West polarity in international affairs was being superseded by a new "North-South" alignment that raised considerable doubt about the capacity of the international system to cope with the enlarged responsibilities born of technological and social change. Evidence of these parallel if somewhat contradictory trends is found not only within the United Nations organization as such[1] but also in the wider field of policy concern that President Nixon had dubbed the "New Dimensions of Diplomacy" or "The Global Challenges of Peace."[2]]

A. Review of United Nations Affairs.

[The limitations of the existing world organization "in solving or even abating many political disputes" were frankly recognized in the review of 1972 developments that accompanied President Nixon's annual report to Congress on United States participation in the United Nations (Document 80). Noting that "for the present

---

[1] For fuller discussion, cf. Nixon Report, 1972, pp. 184-94; same, 1973, pp. 210-15; Rogers Report, 1972, pp. 101-26.
[2] For fuller discussion, cf. Nixon Report, 1972, pp. 195-205 (A.F.R., 1971, no. 136); same, 1973, pp. 216-29; Rogers Report, 1972, pp. 91-5 and 127-85.

the most productive possibilities for United Nations action are on global problems of an economic, social, and technological nature," the President had relatively little to say of the frustrations engendered by the U.N.'s handling of political problems like the Arab-Israeli conflict[3] and the situation in Southern Africa.[4] Nor did the President dwell upon the increasingly tenacious resistance to U.S. views on the part of the General Assembly, which had ignored American counsels regarding the representation of China in 1971[5] and frustrated a major American initiative with reference to international terrorism in 1972. In spite of its tendency to minimize these frictions, President Nixon's statement provides a convenient summary of the world organization's activities in a characteristically busy year.]

(80) United States Participation in the United Nations, 1972: Message from President Nixon to the Congress Transmitting the 27th Annual Report on United States Participation, September 6, 1973.[6]

(Complete Text)

To the Congress of the United States:

I am pleased to transmit to the Congress the 27th annual report on United States participation in the work of the United Nations during calendar year 1972.[7]

This report reflects the increasing range of global concerns with which United Nations agencies are dealing. It highlights not only the opportunities but also the limits of operating through the United Nations system during an era of growing international interdependence.

In recent years, United Nations agencies have come to deal increasingly with the economic and technical agenda of the world in addition to the long-standing agenda of peace and security questions. Indeed, as this account makes clear, these agencies are now engaged in some manner in virtually every governmental activity that crosses national lines.

The United States participated actively in these cooperative efforts to help safeguard peace and lessen world tensions, to foster economic and social progress, and to cope with a wide array of legal and technological problems.

[3] Cf. above at Documents 37-38.
[4] Cf. above at Documents 70-72.
[5] *A.F.R., 1971*, no. 125.
[6] *Presidential Documents*, Sept. 10, 1973, pp. 1058-60.
[7] *U.S. Participation in the UN: Report by the President to the Congress for the Year 1972* (Department of State Publication 8731; Washington: G.P.O., 1973).

Three themes characterized our participation during 1972:

(1) Even though we recognized the limitations of the United Nations in solving or even abating many political disputes, we supported its participation where appropriate to reconcile such disputes, to curb international terrorism and outbreaks of violence, and to devise workable arrangements for peacekeeping operations. In order to serve the long-term interest of the international community, we worked in the General Assembly, the Security Council, and subsidiary bodies to have the United Nations deal evenhandedly and pragmatically with such politically-charged issues as the Middle East, decolonization, and human rights.

(2) We took the lead in seeking new arrangements and institutions to deal with worldwide social and technological concerns. Although we encountered some resistance, we pressed forward toward the goals of assuring the safety of civil aviation, protecting the environment, checking the illicit flow of narcotics, organizing relief for victims of disaster, strengthening the law of the sea, and slowing world population growth.

(3) We stressed the importance of having the United Nations act responsibly, equitably, and efficiently in ordering its financial and administrative affairs so that it could carry out its tasks more effectively. Progress was made in holding down the budgets of some agencies, budgeting procedures were improved, and the principle of a lower maximum ceiling for the United States assessment was endorsed. Nevertheless, the underlying financial problems were not solved and further administrative and procedural reforms are needed in the United Nations.

This report shows that, despite political and administrative shortcomings, multilateral agencies connected with the United Nations offered practical responses to worldwide problems of pressing concern to the American people. Given the fast pace of political, social, and technological change in recent years, it is not surprising that the record of accomplishments was uneven and there were setbacks as well as successes.

During 1972 developments at the United Nations were affected by certain long-term trends which both hold promise and pose problems for effective United Nations action.

—The loosening of old antagonisms, the entry of the People's Republic of China into the mainstream of United Nations work, and the growing importance of powers such as Japan could in the long run enable a near-universal United Nations to become a more effective instrument for dealing with serious world political and security problems.

—However, we also have to recognize that the continuing tendency to use the United Nations for propaganda advantage and to pursue political rivalries makes accommodation more difficult. For the near term, where the interests of its strongest members are engaged, the organization can deal only in a limited way with highly contentious political issues.

—The emergence in United Nations bodies and conferences of an active majority led by a number of the developing nations continued to make for some distortions in determining the areas of greatest United Nations attention. While we fully recognize the inherent right of all member nations to be heard, the voting weight of this majority, with its sometimes narrowly defined preoccupations, has tended to create imbalance and to place strains on the effective functioning of the organization.

This report reflects the growing cohesion which has taken place among the third world countries, notably with respect to colonial issues and to demands that rules of international trade and aid be altered in their favor. We were particularly concerned when, under the pressure of bloc voting, the organization adopted one-sided resolutions on certain political issues or failed to take concrete action on such important matters as international terrorism. To call this trend disturbing is not to depreciate the value to the United States of multilateral institutions in which all nations can be heard on matters that affect their security and welfare, conciliation can be pursued, and vital public services can be provided for the international community.

We attempted to adjust our policy during 1972 to take account of these changes. It became increasingly clear that for the present the most productive possibilities for United Nations action are on global problems of an economic, social, and technological nature. United Nations system expenditures reflected this concentration, with some 95 percent of the resources in 1972 going for programs designed to transfer techniques and skills to less developed nations, set standards for international behavior, and provide public services of benefit to all nations.

The following developments during the year were especially noteworthy:

We were gratified by the General Assembly's endorsement of the reduction of our United Nations budget assessment from 31.52 percent to 25 percent.[8] We believe this to be a healthy development for the organization, which should not be unduly dependent on the contributions of one member. The maximum assessment ceiling beginning next year is expected to fulfill the requirement enacted by the Congress that the United States should pay no more than 25 percent in the United

[8] Cf. below at notes 64-65.

Nations and in certain specialized agencies after January 1, 1974.[9] The vote of over two-thirds in favor of our position reflected a widespread recognition of the equities involved and of political reality, as well as concern for the maintenance of generous United States voluntary contributions to United Nations development programs.

Following the landmark conference in Stockholm in June, the institutional foundation was laid for international action to protect the environment and a work program was initiated for this purpose. Measures were taken to deal with environmental problems such as pollution from ocean dumping and the preservation of natural, cultural, and historic heritage areas, and a United Nations fund for the environment, which I had recommended earlier, brought pledges from a number of nations.[10]

On the other hand, a major setback was the United Nations failure to take strong and speedy international legal action to combat international terrorism and provide adequate protection for diplomats—measures advocated by the United States and other concerned nations. The Assembly did, however, set up a committee to study the comments of governments on the problem of international terrorism and submit a report to the next session.[11] While we regret the delay, we hope that the Assembly can make progress on this issue this fall. Progress was made in the International Civil Aviation Organization on the matter of aircraft safety.

The United Nations also advanced its programs for delivering technical assistance to developing nations and setting standards for international behavior in specific fields.

—Management reforms (notably adoption of a country programming system) were implemented which will enable the United Nations Development Program to handle an expanded program of technical assistance more efficiently.

—The organization's capacity to respond to disaster situations was strengthened by the establishment of a United Nations Disaster Relief Office in Geneva, largely as the result of a United States initiative in 1971.[12] The United Nations carried out an unprecedented number of

[9] Title I of the Departments of State, Justice, and Commerce, Judiciary, and Related Agencies Appropriation Act, 1973 (Public Law 92-544, Oct. 25, 1972) provides as follows: "That after December 31, 1973, no appropriation is authorized and no payment shall be made to the United Nations or any affiliated agency in excess of 25 per centum of the total annual assessment of such organization except that this proviso shall not apply to the International Atomic Energy Agency and to the joint financing program of the International Civil Aviation Organization."

[10] Cf. below at notes 37-39. On the U.N. Fund for the Environment, cf. the President's environmental message of Feb. 8, 1972 in *Public Papers, 1972*, pp. 186-7.

[11] Cf. below at notes 143-144.

[12] Cf. *A.F.R., 1971*, p. 498.

relief activities, notably in Bangladesh and the Sudan.

—There was growing cooperation in outer space. A United Nations working group cooperated in making available to other nations data from our first experimental satellite designed to survey earth resources, and the Convention on International Liability for Damage Caused by Space Objects, which had been negotiated by a United Nations committee, entered into force on September 1.[13]

—The momentum of international action against drug abuse was furthered in several ways: with the drafting of an amending protocol to the 1961 Single Convention on Narcotic Drugs, through increased activity by and contributions to the United Nations Fund for Drug Abuse Control, and through a more active role by the International Narcotics Control Board.[14]

—The population program was placed on a sounder administrative footing by linking the United Nations Fund for Population Activities to the United Nations Development Program. Preparations were continued for the World Population Conference in 1974,[15] which is expected to be as important as the 1972 environment conference.

—Perhaps of the greatest potential significance were the steps taken to accelerate preparations for the Law of the Sea Conference, which will come to grips with such matters as the nature of the international regime for the deep seabed, the breadth of the territorial sea, free transit through international straits, fisheries, marine pollution, and scientific research.[16] A successful resolution of these very difficult issues would help to prevent conflict and assure that the resources in and under the oceans will be equitably and rationally utilized.

The "quiet side" of the United Nations also produced important accomplishments which are covered in this report. Especially noteworthy were the International Atomic Energy Agency's expanded "safeguards" program to prevent the diversion to weapons use of nuclear materials intended for peaceful uses; the Inter-Governmental Maritime Consultative Organization's efforts at spurring agreement to control pollution from ocean dumping;[17] the International Civil Aviation Organization's efforts to devise effective measures for safe and efficient air travel;[18] the World Health Organization's continued cam-

---

[13] Opened for signature at Washington, London and Moscow Mar. 29, 1972 (TIAS 7762); text in *A.F.R., 1971*, no. 139. Although the convention entered into force for ratifying states on Sept. 1, 1972, it was not submitted to the U.S. Senate until June 15, 1972, and the United States did not become a party until Oct. 9, 1973.

[14] Cf. below at notes 21-26.

[15] Cf. note 109 below.

[16] Cf. below at notes 52-58.

[17] Cf. note 48 below.

[18] Cf. below at notes 70-74.

paign to suppress communicable diseases and raise the standards of health care; the Food and Agriculture Organization's work to expand agricultural production and improve nutrition; and the United Nations Educational, Scientific and Cultural Organization's activities to expand scientific communication and protect the world's cultural heritage.[19]

All these activities clearly demonstrate the stake we have in United Nations efforts to control new technologies for the common good, to bridge the gap between developed and developing countries on matters of trade and aid,[20] to facilitate the exchange of technical and scientific knowledge, and to set standards of behavior for international activity. To these concerns—and to the need to improve the functioning of all multilateral institutions—our nation must give increasing attention in the coming years.

RICHARD NIXON

The White House,
    September 6, 1973

B. Action on International Narcotics Problems.

[Described in a presidential message of mid-1971 as having already attained the proportions of a national emergency, the spreading problem of narcotics addiction continued during 1972 to engage the resources of American diplomacy in the leadership of "an intense international attack on the supply, demand, and illicit traffic in narcotics and other drugs."[21] The overall character and scope of this ongoing effort are suggested in the following statement by Secretary of State Rogers (Document 81).

A salient feature of this American-led campaign was the attempt to modernize and strengthen existing legal restrictions relating to harmful drugs through the negotiation and/or amendment of appropriate multilateral conventions. This enterprise involved a two-pronged strategy whose objects were, respectively, (1) a strengthening of existing controls over the traffic in narcotic drugs, especially heroin, whose principal destination was the United States; and (2) the establishment of similar controls over the so-called psychotropic drugs (LSD and other hallucinogens, together with amphetamines, barbiturates, and tranquilizers) which generally originated in the United States.

A first attempt to subject this second category of drugs to inter-

---

[19] Cf. note 49 below.
[20] Cf. below at note 52.
[21] Nixon Report, 1972, p. 199 (*A.F.R., 1971*, p. 536).

national control was the Convention on Psychotropic Substances which had been drawn up at a U.N. conference in Vienna and was opened for signature on February 21, 1971.[22] Immediately signed by 23 nations, including the United States, the convention was transmitted to the Senate by President Nixon on June 29, 1971 but failed to win the approval of the Foreign Relations Committee and had not yet been reported to the Senate as of early 1975.[23]

Narcotic drugs were already subject to a measure of international control under the provisions of the 1961 Single Convention on Narcotic Drugs,[24] which had superseded earlier conventions in this area and to which the United States had become a party in 1967. Proposals to strengthen the 1961 convention, primarily by increasing the authority of the International Narcotics Control Board, had been put forward by the United States in March 1971 in anticipation of a later U.N. conference. Meeting in Geneva on March 6-24, 1972, the 96-nation "United Nations Conference to Consider Amendments to the 1961 Single Convention on Narcotic Drugs" adopted a Protocol Amending the Single Convention on Narcotic Drugs[25] which was opened for signature and signed by 36 countries, including the United States, on March 25, 1972. Described in a laudatory statement by Secretary Rogers (Document 82), the protocol was transmitted to the U.S. Senate on May 4, 1972 and approved by a 69 to 0 vote of that body on September 18, 1972. The United States deposited its instrument of ratification on November 1, 1972, but entry into force was delayed until August 8, 1975.[26]]

[22] S. Ex. G, 92d Cong., 1st sess. (U.N. document E/CONF.58/6); cf. *A.F.R., 1971*, p. 538.

[23]Senate Foreign Relations Committee History, p. 39. Thailand on Nov. 21, 1975 became the 33rd party to the convention, which enters into force 90 days after 40 states have become parties.

[24] Done at New York Mar. 30, 1961 and entered into force for the U.S. June 24, 1967 (TIAS 6298; 18 UST 1407).

[25] S. Ex. J, 92d Cong., 2d sess. (U.N. document E/CONF.63/8); cf. *UN Monthly Chronicle*, Apr. 1972, pp. 52-3 and Senate Foreign Relations Committee History, pp. 28-9.

[26] The protocol entered into force Aug. 8, 1975 and bears TIAS no. 8118.

(81) "The United States International Campaign to Curb the Illicit Drug Supply": Address by Secretary of State Rogers Before the White House Conference on Drug Abuse, February 3, 1972.[27]

(Complete Text)

Drug addiction has become a major domestic problem in the United States. But we can never solve the problem at home unless we can succeed in winning comprehensive and effective cooperation abroad.

The basic reason why our campaign against drug abuse depends so greatly on our international diplomacy is a simple one. Much of the production and processing of illicit narcotics and other dangerous drugs takes place not in the United States but in other countries. To take a typical example, the heroin supplied to an addict in New York City or Washington, D.C., may well have originated—as opium—in Turkey and been converted to heroin in France. The chart behind me shows the principal areas where the opium poppy is grown: Turkey, Iran, the Soviet Union, the Afghanistan-Pakistan border area, India, and the so-called "golden triangle" area in the northern reaches of Burma, Thailand, and Laos.

There is another international link. While the United States—with more than 300,000 addicts is the country most plagued by heroin addiction, the problem is growing rapidly in other nations. The number of heroin addicts in western Europe may be as high as 100,000. In short, what has already become a major problem in the United States is fast becoming a major problem in other countries as well.

For these reasons the President last September established the Cabinet Committee on International Narcotics Control, with myself as its Chairman.[28] This Committee is responsible for formulating and coordinating all policies of the U.S. Government directed at stemming the flow of illegal narcotics and dangerous drugs into this country from abroad. To assist the President's all-out offensive against drug abuse I have directed that effective narcotics control be one of the major objectives of our diplomacy in contacts with other governments. And within the Department of State I have appointed in my own office a Senior Adviser and Coordinator for International Narcotics Matters, Mr. Nelson Gross.

We in the State Department are working in close collaboration with the Departments of Justice and Treasury in this large-scale international campaign. Our basic goal is to eliminate all opium production and the

[27] Department of State Press Release 29; text from *Bulletin*, Feb. 28, 1972, pp. 276-8. For additional details, cf. the statements by Ambassador Nelson Gross in same, Apr. 3, 1972, pp. 504-12 and Oct. 9, 1972, pp. 401-15.
[28] *Public Papers, 1971*, pp. 937-8.

growing of poppies, thus cutting off heroin at its source. But until substitutes for legitimate and medically useful opium derivatives like codeine can be developed, we must concentrate our efforts on illicit production of opium, on processing and trafficking, and on making national and international controls more effective. Meanwhile, we are pressing ahead with programs to develop synthetic substitutes for opium derivatives.

Now let me review for you the significant progress we have already made during the past year in our international campaign.

Most of the heroin entering the United States in recent years has originated in Turkey. Here, clearly, was where we had to start. Turkey is also a major source of opium grown for legitimate medical purposes; and for hundreds of years Turkish farmers have raised the opium poppy as a legitimate cash crop and for its edible oil and seed. Moreover, Turkey has no heroin addiction problem itself, and Turkish farmers had little awareness of the magnitude of the problem in the United States.

So you can see that the diplomatic task was not easy, either for us or for the Turkish Government. We were gratified, therefore, when our vigorous efforts resulted in Turkey's decision last June to ban the production of opium following the harvesting of the 1971–72 crop.[29] A strict licensing and control law has now been passed in Turkey to enforce the ban. Meanwhile, conscious of the effect on Turkey's economy, we assured the Turkish Government of financial assistance to offset foreign exchange losses from the export of legitimate opium products and to help establish alternative economic activities in the affected areas.

With the drying up of the Turkish opium supply, we expect illegal traffickers to turn increasingly to Southeast Asia, where there is substantial illegal or uncontrolled production of opium. We are therefore giving priority attention to engaging the cooperation of governments in this region.

Two major steps have already been taken to squeeze the producers in Southeast Asia. First, the United States and Thailand last September [28] signed a memorandum of understanding[30] by which the two countries pledged combined action against the supply and trafficking of illicit narcotics and dangerous drugs. Second, Laos has implemented a law prohibiting the growing, processing, trading, and use of opium and the opiates.

In other parts of the world the U.S. Government has been striving on

[29] Nixon Report, 1972, *loc. cit.* (note 21); cf. also *Public Papers, 1971*, pp. 788-90, and *Bulletin*, July 19, 1971, pp. 74-7. A partial lifting of the ban on opium poppy cultivation was announced by the Turkish Government on July 1, 1974.

[30] *Bulletin*, Oct. 18, 1971, pp. 411-13.

a day-to-day basis to limit production and supply. Cooperation has been very close with the Governments of Canada and Mexico to control traffic across our common borders. We have signed an agreement with France providing for French narcotics agents to operate in the United States and for U.S. narcotics agents to operate in France. The recent sizable heroin seizures are evidence of the close cooperation that now exists between the French and U.S. police. We were of course heartened by the discovery last week of a heroin laboratory in the Marseille area, complete with all the equipment and supplies to manufacture pure heroin.

In the multilateral area, a U.S. initiative led to the creation last spring of a U.N. Fund for Drug Abuse Control, to which we have made the major contribution of $2 million.[31] We have also led the effort to strengthen the enforcement provisions of the 1961 international convention on narcotics,[32] and we submitted to the Senate last June an international convention to control LSD and other manufactured substances.[33]

This, I believe, is a very creditable record. During 1972 we want to go even further:

—We are seeking to increase regional cooperation in Southeast Asia to prevent that area from becoming a major source of heroin for the U.S. market.

—In cooperation with governments in this hemisphere, we are stepping up efforts to intercept illicit narcotics from Latin America, which in recent months has become a major transfer route to the United States.

—Through the United Nations and other international organizations we are following through on the multilateral initiatives I have described.

—Finally, and perhaps most important, the Cabinet Committee is developing individual action plans for cooperation with each of the more than 50 countries considered to have a current or potential involvement in the production, processing, or transiting of illicit hard drugs. When these plans are completed, we will use them as the basis for opening discussions with foreign governments on the negotiation of bilateral action programs.

These, then, are the steps we have taken and will be taking in the international area to curb the supply of illicit drugs to the United States. Of course, this supply depends ultimately on the domestic demand for narcotics, and this is a problem which must be solved at

---

[31] Cf. *A.F.R., 1971*, p. 537.
[32] Cf. above at note 25.
[33] Cf. above at note 23.

home. Your efforts in educating Americans, particularly young Americans, to the dangers of drugs are making a major contribution toward solving it. Let me say in closing how much we appreciate those efforts. I hope you will continue and expand them, for the future welfare of our youth depends importantly on the steps we take today to eliminate the scourge of drug abuse.

(82) Protocol Amending the Single Convention on Narcotic Drugs, Opened for Signature at Geneva March 25, 1972: Statement by Secretary of State Rogers, March 27, 1972.[34]

(Complete Text)

The United States Government hails the decision by the U.N. conference in Geneva to add new muscle to the international narcotics control system by strengthening the 1961 Single Convention on Narcotic Drugs.[35]

For the United States, results of the Geneva session hold the promise of further curtailing the supply of heroin on the streets here at home.

For other countries where narcotic drugs are a present or potential menace, adoption of amendments to the convention will enable the U.N. International Narcotics Control Board to wage a more effective campaign against the plague of opium, heroin, and other narcotics.

President Nixon will submit the Geneva Protocol to the Senate for its advice and consent in the near future. As Chairman of his Cabinet Committee on International Narcotics Control, I urge the Senate to give it prompt and positive consideration.[36]

Implementation of the amendments will empower the International Narcotics Control Board to exercise new authority to curb illicit cultivation, production, manufacture, trafficking, and consumption of opium, heroin, and other narcotics. Now there will be important initial steps to limit opium production to legitimate medical and scientific requirements, beginning with cultivation of the opium poppy.

1. The International Narcotics Control Board will for the first time have authority to require reduction of opium poppy cultivation and opium production in countries shown to be sources of illicit traffic.

2. The international control system will henceforth intensify its efforts against the illicit narcotics traffic through access to better and

---

[34] Department of State Press Release 74, Mar. 27, 1972; text from *Bulletin*, Apr. 17, 1972, pp. 569-70. For the background, cf. above at notes 24-25.
[35] TIAS 6298; cf. note 24 above.
[36] Cf. above at note 26.

fuller information, on-the-spot examinations, and publicity of control violations or noncooperation at the highest levels of the United Nations.

3. The United States will have, along with other "victim countries," significantly greater ability to extradite and thus prosecute narcotics traffickers who have taken refuge in other nations.

4. For the first time under a narcotics control treaty, the control organ will have authority to recommend technical and financial assistance to help cooperating governments carry out their treaty obligations.

5. Also for the first time in international narcotics control, the nations undertake an obligation to drug abuse prevention and education and the treatment, rehabilitation, and social reintegration of drug abusers, as well as to more effective law enforcement.

I congratulate Nelson Gross, who is my Senior Adviser and Coordinator for International Narcotics Matters, and William I. Cargo, Director of Planning and Coordination Staff, for their productive leadership of the U.S. delegation in achieving the notable success at the Geneva conference to amend the 1961 Single Convention. Other administration agencies engaged in the President's antinarcotics program—Treasury; Justice; Health, Education, and Welfare; and the Special Action Office for Drug Abuse Prevention—were represented on the delegation.

The United States and 29 other countries cosponsored the amendments to strengthen the Single Convention on Narcotic Drugs. Ninety-seven countries joined in the U.N. conference at Geneva. Seventy-one countries voted for adoption of the amending protocol of Geneva on March 24, 1972. No country voted against. Thirty-six delegations signed the amending protocol, subject to ratification, on the first day it was opened for signature, March 25, 1972.

C. United Nations Conference on the Human Environment, Stockholm, June 5-16, 1972.

[The need for international action on environmental problems had been perceived at the United Nations as early as 1968, when the General Assembly had determined that a full-dress United Nations Conference on the Human Environment should be convened in 1972.[37] As a climax to years of preparatory effort, this conference met in Stockholm on June 5-16, 1972. Approximately 113 countries took part, although the Soviet Union and its East

[37] Resolution 2398 (XXIII), Dec. 3, 1968; *Documents, 1968-69*, pp. 460-62.

European allies (except Romania) declined to attend because the German Democratic Republic was not accorded full voting rights.

American expectations for the conference were set forth in an opening-day statement by Secretary of State Rogers (Document 83) as well as a lengthy declaration to the conference by Russell E. Train, Chairman of the Council on Environmental Quality and head of the U.S. delegation.[38] The most significant achievements of the conference were (1) the formulation of a 106-item "Action Plan" for governments and international organizations; (2) the adoption of a "Declaration on the Human Environment" (Document 84) that laid down various general principles, many of them reflecting the interests of "third world" and developing countries; and (3) determination of the form of the permanent environmental machinery to be set up by the U.N. General Assembly.

President Nixon, in a markedly optimistic review of conference highlights (Document 85), declared that "The United States achieved practically all of its objectives at Stockholm." American authorities evinced a more skeptical view of the institutional and financial arrangements approved at the autumn session of the General Assembly, involving the creation of a 58-member Governing Council for Environmental Programs, an Environmental Secretariat, a voluntary Environment Fund, and an Environmental Coordinating Board.[39] Maurice F. Strong of Canada, the Secretary-General of the Stockholm conference, was designated Executive Director of the new Environmental Secretariat. Especially questionable in American eyes was the decision to locate this body in Nairobi, Kenya, in response to the insistence of many U.N. members that it be situated in a developing country.]

(83) Significance of the Conference: Statement by Secretary of State Rogers, June 5, 1972.[40]

(Complete Text)

The United Nations Conference on the Human Environment, which opens today in Stockholm, marks the full emergence of an international concern which will increasingly occupy the world's peoples and governments in the years to come. The United States Government will be second to none in applying its energies to the task of preserving and

[38] *Bulletin*, July 24, 1972, pp. 106-12.
[39] Resolution 2997 (XXVII), Dec. 15, 1972, adopted by a nonrecorded vote of 116-0-10.
[40] Department of State Press Release 133; text from *Bulletin*, July 24, 1972, pp. 105-6.

enhancing the global environment.

We look for substantial progress at Stockholm in three areas:

First, the conference should spur efforts to acquire greater knowledge about what is happening to the world's environment. This requires a comprehensive monitoring system involving, for example, a global network of stations to measure the effect of air contaminants.

Second, the conference should encourage international conventions, agreements, and other arrangements to deal with problems where action, not research, is needed. We have particularly in mind conventions to control ocean dumping and to preserve heritage areas of special natural, cultural, or historic importance.

Third, because most environmental problems must be solved at the regional, national, or individual level, the conference should encourage and support regional and local efforts.

To help realize these and other important objectives, the President has proposed the creation of a United Nations Fund for the Environment, to be financed by voluntary contributions from governments.[41] We believe the initial funding goal, over a five-year period, should be $100 million. The United States is prepared to contribute up to $40 million to match the $60 million which we hope others will donate.

Firm centralized control and an agreed setting of priorities are essential to the effective administration of the United Nations environmental activities. Therefore, we will propose at Stockholm that a U.N. administrator be appointed. He should have authority, subject to policy guidance from an intergovernmental body within the ECOSOC [Economic and Social Council] framework, to administer the Fund to coordinate all U.N. programs on the environment.

The United States Government believes that the 1970's should be a decade in which the United Nations gives conscious priority to the coupling of scientific advance with the welfare of all peoples. As peacekeeping was its basic concern in the 1950's, as development was added as a second concern in the 1960's, we believe that in this decade the United Nations should adopt a third basic objective: to encourage, through cooperative international action, the application of science and technology to improving the quality of human life. In no area is this task more urgent than in the area of the human environment.

It is sometimes alleged that environment is a rich man's issue and that developing countries have little to gain from international activity in this field. This allegation is refuted by the presence in Stockholm of representatives of the vast majority of the people of the developing world.

41 Cf. note 10 above.

It is natural that developing countries should show particular concern that steps to preserve the environment must enhance rather than hinder the development process. We in the United States share this concern, and in our own policies regarding the environment we are taking it into full account:

—We pledge that environmental concerns will not be used as a pretext for trade discrimination against the products of developing, or other, countries or for their reduced access to U.S. markets. There should be no economic protectionism in the name of environmental protection.
   —We pledge that a commitment to environmental improvement will not diminish our commitment to development.

Environmental safeguards, far from being antithetical to development, are an integral part of it. This does not mean that they should be rigidly imposed by industrialized nations as a condition of their participation in development projects. The relative priority to be given such safeguards must be worked out between donor and recipient countries. In our own assistance policy we are emphasizing the primary responsibility of aid recipients for setting development priorities.
   We regret that the Soviet Union and a number of its allies have apparently decided, for political reasons, not to join the countries meeting in Stockholm. We hope, however, that the Soviet Union and the others will participate fully in the international initiatives and efforts which will be necessary following the conference.[42] The bilateral agreement we signed in Moscow May 23[43]—the most comprehensive environmental agreement yet reached between major countries—is an encouraging indication that the Soviet Union shares our belief in the importance of this issue.

(84) Declaration on the Human Environment, Adopted by the Conference June 16, 1972.[44]

(Complete Text)

The United Nations Conference on the Human Environment,
Having met at Stockholm from 5 to 16 June 1972,
Having considered the need for a common outlook and for common principles to inspire and guide the peoples of the world in the preservation and enhancement of the human environment,

---

[42] The U.S.S.R. and allied states are believed to have abstained on the General Assembly resolution listed in note 39.
[43] Cf. note 44 to Document 10.
[44] U.N. document A/CONF.48/14/Rev.1, pp. 3-5; text adapted from *UN Monthly Chronicle*, July 1972, pp. 86-90.

I

Proclaims that:

1. Man is both creature and moulder of his environment which gives him physical sustenance and affords him the opportunity for intellectual, moral, social and spiritual growth. In the long and tortuous evolution of the human race on this planet a stage has been reached when through the rapid acceleration of science and technology, man has acquired the power to transform his environment in countless ways and on an unprecedented scale. Both aspects of man's environment, the natural and the man-made, are essential to his well-being and to the enjoyment of basic human rights—even the right to life itself.

2. The protection and improvement of the human environment is a major issue which affects the well-being of peoples and economic development throughout the world; it is the urgent desire of the peoples of the whole world and the duty of all Governments.

3. Man has constantly to sum up experience and go on discovering, inventing, creating and advancing. In our time man's capability to transform his surroundings, if used wisely, can bring to all peoples the benefits of development and the opportunity to enhance the quality of life. Wrongly or heedlessly applied, the same power can do incalculable harm to human beings and the human environment. We see around us growing evidence of man-made harm in many regions of the earth: dangerous levels of pollution in water, air, earth and living beings; major and undesirable disturbances to the ecological balance of the biosphere; destruction and depletion of irreplaceable resources; and gross deficiencies harmful to the physical, mental and social health of man, in the man-made environment, particularly in the living and working environment

4. In the developing countries most of the environmental problems are caused by under-development. Millions continue to live far below the minimum levels required for a decent human existence, deprived of adequate food and clothing, shelter and education, health and sanitation. Therefore, the developing countries must direct their efforts to development, bearing in mind their priorities and the need to safeguard and improve the environment. For the same purpose, the industrialized countries should make efforts to reduce the gap between themselves and the developing countries. In the industrialized countries, environmental problems are generally related to industrialization and technological development.

5. The natural growth of population continuously presents problems on the preservation of the environment, and adequate policies and measures should be adopted as appropriate to face these problems. Of all things, in the world, people are the most precious. It is the people that propel social progress, create social wealth, develop science and technology, and through their hard work, continuously transform the human environment. Along with social progress and the advance of

production, science and technology, the capability of man to improve the environment increases with each passing day.

6. A point has been reached in history when we must shape our actions throughout the world with a more prudent care for their environmental consequences. Through ignorance or indifference we can do massive and irreversible harm to the earthly environment on which our life and well-being depend. Conversely, through fuller knowledge and wiser action, we can achieve for ourselves and our posterity a better life in an environment more in keeping with human needs and hopes. There are broad vistas for the enhancement of environmental quality and the creation of a good life. What is needed is an enthusiastic but calm state of mind and intense but orderly work. For the purpose of attaining freedom in the world of nature, man must use knowledge to build in collaboration with nature a better environment. To defend and improve the human environment for present and future generations has become an imperative goal for mankind—a goal to be pursued together with, and in harmony with, the established and fundamental goals of peace and of world-wide economic and social development.

7. To achieve this environmental goal will demand the acceptance of responsibility by citizens and communities and by enterprises and institutions at every level, all sharing equitably in common efforts. Individuals in all walks of life as well as organizations in many fields, by their values and the sum of their actions, will shape the world environment of the future. Local and national Governments will bear the greatest burden for large-scale environmental policy and action within their jurisdictions. International co-operation is also needed in order to raise resources to support the developing countries in carrying out their responsibilities in this field. A growing class of environmental problems, because they are regional or global in extent or because they affect the common international realm, will require extensive co-operation among nations and action by international organizations in the common interest. The Conference calls upon the Governments and peoples to exert common efforts for the preservation and improvement of the human environment, for the benefit of all the people and for their posterity.

II
Principles
States the common conviction that
1. Man has the fundamental right to freedom, equality and adequate conditions of life, in an environment of a quality which permits a life of dignity and well-being, and bears a solemn responsibility to protect and improve the environment for present and future generations. In this respect, policies promoting or perpetuating *apartheid*, racial segregation, discrimination, colonial and other forms of oppression and for-

eign domination stand condemned and must be eliminated.

2. The natural resources of the earth including the air, water, land, flora and fauna and especially representative samples of natural eco-systems must be safeguarded for the benefit of present and future generations through careful planning or management as appropriate.

3. The capacity of the earth to produce vital renewable resources must be maintained and wherever practicable restored or improved.

4. Man has a special responsibility to safeguard and wisely manage the heritage of wildlife and its habitat which are now gravely imperilled by a combination of adverse factors. Nature conservation including wildlife must therefore receive importance in planning for economic development.

5. The non-renewable resources of the earth must be employed in such a way as to guard against the danger of their future exhaustion and to ensure that benefits from such employment are shared by all mankind.

6. The discharge of toxic substances or of other substances and the release of heat, in such quantities or concentrations as to exceed the capacity of the environment to render them harmless, must be halted in order to ensure that serious or irreversible damage is not inflicted upon ecosystems. The just struggle of the peoples of all countries against pollution should be supported.

7. States shall take all possible steps to prevent pollution of the seas by substances that are liable to create hazards to human health, to harm living resources and marine life, to damage amenities or to interfere with other legitimate uses of the sea.

8. Economic and social development is essential for ensuring a favourable living and working environment for man and for creating conditions on earth that are necessary for the improvement of the quality of life.

9. Environmental deficiencies generated by the conditions of under-development and natural disasters pose grave problems and can best be remedied by accelerated development through the transfer of sub-stantial quantities of financial and technological assistance as a supple-ment to the domestic effort of the developing countries and such timely assistance as may be required.

10. For the developing countries, stability of prices and adequate earnings for primary commodities and raw material are essential to environmental management since economic factors as well as ecological processes must be taken into account.

11. The environmental policies of all States should enhance and not adversely affect the present or future development potential of devel-oping countries, nor should they hamper the attainment of better living conditions for all, and appropriate steps should be taken by States and international organizations with a view to reaching agree-

ment on meeting the possible national and international economic consequences resulting from the application of environmental measures.

12. Resources should be made available to preserve and improve the environment, taking into account the circumstances and particular requirements of developing countries and any costs which may emanate from their incorporating environmental safeguards into their development planning and the need for making available to them, upon their request, additional international technical and financial assistance for this purpose.

13. In order to achieve a more rational management of resources and thus to improve the environment, States should adopt an integrated and co-ordinated approach to their development planning so as to ensure that development is compatible with the need to protect and improve the human environment for the benefit of their population.

14. Rational planning constitutes an essential tool for reconciling any conflict between the needs of development and the need to protect and improve the environment.

15. Planning must be applied to human settlements and urbanization with a view to avoiding adverse effects on the environment and obtaining maximum social, economic and environmental benefits for all. In this respect projects which are designed for colonialist and racist domination must be abandoned.

16. Demographic policies, which are without prejudice to basic human rights and which are deemed appropriate by Governments concerned, should be applied in those regions where the rate of population growth or excessive population concentrations are likely to have adverse effects on the environment or development, or where low population density may prevent improvement of the human environment and impede development.

17. Appropriate national institutions must be entrusted with the task of planning, managing or controlling the environmental resources of States with the view to enhancing environmental quality.

18. Science and technology, as part of their contribution to economic and social development, must be applied to the identification, avoidance and control of environmental risks and the solution of environmental problems and for the common good of mankind.

19. Education in environmental matters, for the younger generation as well as adults, giving due consideration to the underprivileged, is essential in order to broaden the basis for an enlightened opinion and responsible conduct by individuals, enterprises and communities in protecting and improving the environment in its full human dimension. It is also essential that mass media of communications avoid contributing to the deterioration of the environment, but, on the contrary, dissemi-

nate information of an educational nature on the need to enable man to develop in every respect.

20. Scientific research and development in the context of environmental problems, both national and multinational, must be promoted in all countries, especially the developing countries. In this connexion, the free flow of up-to-date scientific information and transfer of experience must be supported and assisted, to facilitate the solution of environmental problems; environmental technologies should be made available to developing countries on terms which would encourage their wide dissemination without constituting an economic burden on the developing countries.

21. States have, in accordance with the Charter of the United Nations and the principles of international law, the sovereign right to exploit their own resources pursuant to their own environmental policies, and the responsibility to ensure that activities within their jurisdiction or control do not cause damage to the environment of other States or of areas beyond the limits of national jurisdiction.

22. States shall co-operate to develop further the international law regarding liability and compensation for the victims of pollution and other environmental damage caused by activities within the jurisdiction or control of such States to areas beyond their jurisdiction.

23. Without prejudice to such criteria as may be agreed upon by the international community, or to the standards which will have to be determined nationally, it will be essential in all cases to consider the systems of values prevailing in each country, and the extent of the applicability of standards which are valid for the most advanced countries but which may be inappropriate and of unwarranted social cost for the developing countries.

24. International matters concerning the protection and improvement of the environment should be handled in a co-operative spirit by all countries, big or small, on an equal footing. Co-operation through multilateral or bilateral arrangements or other appropriate means is essential to effectively control, prevent, reduce and eliminate adverse environmental effects resulting from activities conducted in all spheres, in such a way that due account is taken of the sovereignty and interests of all States.

25. States shall ensure that international organizations play a co-ordinated, efficient and dynamic role for the protection and improvement of the environment.

26. Man and his environment must be spared the effects of nuclear weapons and all other means of mass destruction. States must strive to reach prompt agreement, in the relevant international organs, on the elimination and complete destruction of such weapons.

(85) Results of the Conference: Statement by President Nixon, June 20, 1972.[45]

(Complete Text)

I have just received a report on the United Nations Conference on the Human Environment concluded last Friday at Stockholm from Chairman Train who headed the large and distinguished United States delegation.

The United States has worked long and hard over the past 18 months to help make the Conference a success. Representatives of 113 nations met together for 2 weeks to produce an impressive number of agreements on environmental principles and recommendations for further national and international action in this important field.

The United States achieved practically all of its objectives at Stockholm.

(1) The Conference approved establishment of a new United Nations unit to provide continued leadership and coordination of environmental action, an important step which had our full support.

(2) The Conference approved forming a $100 million United Nations environmental fund which I personally proposed last February.[46]

(3) The Conference overwhelmingly approved the U.S. proposal for a moratorium on commercial killing of whales.[47]

(4) The Conference endorsed our proposal for an international convention to regulate ocean dumping.[48]

---

[45] *Presidential Documents*, June 26, 1972, p. 1078. For a more detailed statement, cf. *Bulletin*, Sept. 18, 1972, pp. 313-14.

[46] Cf. note 10 above.

[47] A U.S. proposal for a ten-year moratorium on commercial whaling (*Bulletin*, July 24, 1972, pp. 112-14) was supported by the Stockholm conference but was subsequently rejected by the International Whaling Commission at its meeting in London on June 26-30, 1972. "Significant reductions in quotas," as well as improvements in the Commission, were nevertheless approved at the London meeting (*Bulletin*, Sept. 18, 1972, p. 314).

[48] Originally proposed by President Nixon in 1971, the completion of a convention to control ocean dumping of shore-generated wastes was endorsed by the Stockholm conference and effected by a special intergovernmental conference that met in London on Oct. 30-Nov. 13, 1972 and agreed on the text of a Convention on the Prevention of Marine Pollution by Dumping of Wastes and Other Matter (S. Ex. C, 93d Cong., 1st sess.; text and background in *Bulletin*, Dec. 18, 1972, pp. 710-17). Described as "the first positive action completed pursuant to recommendation by the Stockholm ... Conference," the convention was opened for signature at Washington, London, Mexico City, and Moscow and signed by the United States on Dec. 29, 1972 (same, Jan. 22, 1973, pp. 95-6). Following Senate approval by an 86-0 vote on Aug. 3, 1973, the United States on Apr. 29-May 6, 1974 became the sixth country to deposit its instrument of ratification (same, May 20, 1974, pp. 567-8). The convention entered into force Aug. 30, 1975.

(5) The Conference endorsed the U.S. proposal for the establishment of a World Heritage Trust to help preserve wilderness areas and other scenic natural landmarks.[49]

However, even more than in the specific agreements reached, I believe that the deepest significance of the Conference lies in the fact that for the first time in history, the nations of the world sat down together to seek better understanding of each other's environmental problems and to explore opportunities for positive action, individually and collectively.

The strong concern of the United States over the fate of our environment has also been demonstrated in our direct dealings with individual nations. The Great Lakes Water Quality Agreement which I signed in Ottawa this April with Prime Minister Trudeau[50] was evidence of the high priority this Administration places on protecting the environment. The Environmental Agreement which I signed in Moscow on May 23[51] is proof of the desire of our Nation to work together with the others on the common tasks of peace.

I am proud that the United States is taking a leading role in international environmental cooperation, and I congratulate our U.S. delegation on its success at Stockholm. The governments and people of the world must now work together to make the objectives of the Stockholm Conference a reality.

D. The Law of the Sea.

[Rivaling the U.N. Conference on the Environment as a focus of international attention during 1972 were two other U.N. conferences, one current and the other projected. The Third Ministerial Session of the U.N. Conference on Trade and Development (UNCTAD III), held in Santiago, Chile, on April 13 to May 21, 1972 with 141 countries participating, was notable primarily for

[49] Preparation of a World Heritage Trust Convention, likewise proposed by President Nixon in 1971, had been undertaken by the U.N. Educational, Scientific and Cultural Organization (UNESCO) and was completed, following endorsement by the Stockholm conference, at UNESCO's 17th General Conference in the fall of 1972. Done at Paris on Nov. 23, 1972, the Convention Concerning the Protection of the World Cultural and Natural Heritage (S. Ex. F, 93d Cong., 1st sess.) was transmitted to the Senate Mar. 28, 1973 (*Bulletin*, May 14, 1973, pp. 629-31) and, following Senate approval by a 95-0 vote on Oct. 30, 1973, was ratified by the President on Nov. 13, 1973. The U.S. instrument of ratification was deposited Dec. 7, 1973, and the convention was scheduled to enter into force on Dec. 17, 1975.
[50] Cf. note 84 to Chapter VIII.
[51] Cf. note 44 to Document 10.

the growing volume of third-world demands for favorable treatment in international trade and monetary discussions.[52] Of comparable import, though different in its subject matter, was the impending Third United Nations Conference on the Law of the Sea, which was due to convene in 1973 in conformity with a 1970 decision of the General Assembly.[53]

The First and Second U.N. Conferences on the Law of the Sea, held in 1958 and 1960 respectively, had settled a variety of outstanding problems but failed to resolve other critical issues, among them "the breadth of the territorial sea, the extent of fisheries jurisdiction, [and] the outer limits of the coastal states' exclusive rights over continental shelf resources." Since 1960, more novel problems had also begun to clamor for adjustment—e.g., "the growing need for protection of the marine environment and such uncertainties resulting from advances in technology as the mining of manganese nodules from the deep seabed."[54] The increasing urgency of an understanding on fisheries had likewise been underlined by a number of international incidents involving in particular the United States, Ecuador, and other Latin American countries.[55]

Preparations for an international conference that would, it was hoped, deal comprehensively with these issues had been entrusted by the General Assembly to its Committee on the Peaceful Uses of the Sea-Bed and the Ocean Floor Beyond the Limits of National Jurisdiction. Established on a permanent basis in 1968, this body currently had 90 members and was chaired by H.S. Amerasinghe of Sri Lanka (formerly Ceylon). It was to this committee that the United States had communicated its own proposals relating to the future regime of the oceans, which included a draft convention on the seabed, submitted in August 1970,[56] and a set of draft articles on the territorial sea, straits, and fisheries submitted a year later.[57] A restatement of the American position on these issues and a review of progress in the Seabed Committee were offered by John R. Stevenson, Legal Adviser of the Department of State and U.S. representative, in the course of the committee's session in Geneva on July 17-August 18, 1972 (Document 86).

Continuing disagreements in the Seabed Committee and in the General Assembly were to result in a decision late in 1972 that additional "preparatory work" would be required and that the sub-

[52] Cf. below at Document 98.
[53] Resolution 2750 C (XXV), Dec. 17, 1970.
[54] U.S. Department of State, U.N. Law of the Sea Conference 1975 (Department of State Publication 8764; Washington, Department of State, 1975), pp. 1-2. For more detailed background, cf. Bulletin, May 8, 1972, pp. 672-9.
[55] Cf. Document 73.
[56] Summary in Documents, 1970, pp. 334-41.
[57] A.F.R., 1971, no. 137.

stantive work of the projected conference should be postponed until 1974. In a resolution unanimously adopted by the General Assembly on December 18, 1972, that body determined that the first session of the Conference on the Law of the Sea should be convened in New York for approximately two weeks in November/ December 1973 for the purpose of dealing with organizational matters, while the second session, "for the purpose of dealing with substantive work," should be convened in Santiago, Chile, for an eight-week period in April/May 1974, any subsequent sessions that might prove necessary being decided upon by the conference itself and approved by the General Assembly.[58] Pursuant to these decisions as later modified, the organizational session of the conference was held in New York on December 3-15, 1973; the first substantive session took place in Caracas, Venezuela, on June 20-August 29, 1974; and a third session was held in Geneva on March 17-May 19, 1975, when plans were announced for a further session in New York in the spring of 1976.]

(86) Outlook for the Third United Nations Conference on the Law of the Sea: Statement by United States Representative John R. Stevenson to the United Nations Committee on the Peaceful Uses of the Sea-Bed and the Ocean Floor Beyond the Limits of National Jurisdiction, Geneva, August 10, 1972.[59]

(Complete Text)

Mr. Chairman [Hamilton Shirley Amerasinghe, of Sri Lanka] : In recent weeks, both you and your colleagues on the [Seabed Committee] Bureau have emphasized that this is a critical session for the United Nations Seabed Committee. We agree. Therefore we believe it is appropriate to consider the future of these negotiations and, in that context, the future of the law of the sea. It is over two years since President Nixon said:[60]

The stark fact is that the law of the sea is inadequate to meet the needs of modern technology and the concerns of the international community. If it is not modernized multilaterally, unilateral action and international conflict are inevitable.

Mr. Chairman, if we are to find negotiated international solutions to the law of the sea, we must do two things promptly.

[58] Resolution 3029 A (XXVII), Dec. 18, 1972; adopted unanimously.
[59] *Bulletin*, Oct. 2, 1972, pp. 382-6.
[60] Statement of May 23, 1970, in *Documents, 1970*, p. 332.

First, we must all be prepared to accommodate each other's interests and needs. We are preparing a comprehensive lawmaking treaty to govern not only the conduct of sovereign states and private persons in the ocean but also the natural resources of an area comprising two-thirds of the earth's surface. Its effectiveness will depend in large measure on the extent to which it represents a consensus of all, rather than a group of states. To achieve this, we must identify those national interests that are of fundamental importance to each of us and avoid time-consuming and potentially divisive debate on less important matters.

Second, we must achieve agreement before events overtake our ability to do so. I cannot stress too strongly that none of us can or should stop technology and its use. If we act wisely and in a timely manner, we can insure by agreement that the technology will be used in a manner that provides maximum benefit for all mankind.

Our efforts here, Mr. Chairman, are known to many people in my country and in many others represented here today. The people who use the seas, and the people whose livelihoods either now depend or will in the future depend on the sea, are watching us. In the United States there is a growing uneasiness about our work. Most Americans concerned with the sea are dedicated to multilateral solutions to problems which have international ramifications, but they are becoming increasingly skeptical about the chances for success. Other delegations here may perceive similar developments taking place in their own countries. We must not allow confidence to be shaken in our ability to negotiate timely solutions to the problems we face.

Against this background, I would like to comment on some aspects of the substance of these negotiations.

Ocean uses can be divided into two broad categories: resource uses and nonresource uses. The first group principally concerns fishing and seabed resources. The nonresource uses include such important interests as navigation and overflight, scientific research, and the preservation of the ocean environment.

The view of my delegation on nonresource uses has been clearly stated on a number of occasions. It is our candid assessment that there is no possibility for agreement on a breadth of the territorial sea other than 12 nautical miles. The United States and others have also made it clear that their vital interests require that agreement on a 12-mile territorial sea be coupled with agreement on free transit of straits used for international navigation, and these remain basic elements of our national policy which we will not sacrifice. We have, however, made clear that we are prepared to accommodate coastal state concerns regarding pollution and navigational safety in straits and have made proposals to that effect in Subcommittee II [on Law of Sea].[61]

[61] For details, cf. Rogers Report, 1972, pp. 133-4.

The views of my delegation on resource issues have also been stated on a number of occasions. Unfortunately, some delegations appear to have the impression that maritime countries in general, and the United States in particular, can be expected to sacrifice in these negotiations basic elements of their national policy on resources. This is not true. The reality is that every nation represented here has basic interests in both resource and nonresource uses that require accommodation. Accordingly, we believe it is important to dispel any possible misconceptions that my government would agree to a monopoly by an international operating agency over deep seabed exploitation or to any type of economic zone that does not accommodate basic United States interests with respect to resources as well as navigation. I would like to amplify this point with a few remarks on some of these basic elements.

COASTAL RESOURCES GENERALLY

Mr. Chairman, in order to achieve agreement, we are prepared to agree to broad coastal state economic jurisdiction in adjacent waters and seabed areas beyond the territorial sea as part of an overall law-of-the-sea settlement. However, the jurisdiction of the coastal state to manage the resources in these areas must be tempered by international standards which will offer reasonable prospects that the interests of other states and the international community will be protected. It is essential that coastal state jurisdiction over fisheries and over the mineral resources of the continental margins be subject to international standards and compulsory settlement of disputes.

SEABED RESOURCES–COASTAL AREAS

We can accept virtually complete coastal state resource-management jurisdiction over resources in adjacent seabed areas if this jurisdiction is subject to international treaty limitations in five respects:

1. *International treaty standards to prevent unreasonable interference with other uses of the ocean.* A settlement based on combining coastal state resource-management jurisdiction with protection of non-resource uses can only be effective if the different uses are accommodated. This requires internationally agreed standards pursuant to which the coastal state will insure, subject to compulsory dispute settlement, that there is no unreasonable interference with navigation, overflight, and other uses.

2. *International treaty standards to protect the ocean from pollution.* As a coastal state, we do not wish to suffer pollution of the ocean from seabed activities anywhere. We consider it basic that minimum interna-

tionally agreed pollution standards apply even to areas in which the coastal state enjoys resource jurisdiction.

3. *International treaty standards to protect the integrity of investment.* When a coastal state permits foreign nationals to make investments in areas under its resource-management jurisdiction, the integrity of such investments should be protected by the treaty. Security of tenure and a stable investment climate should attract foreign investment and technology to areas managed by developing coastal states. Without such protection in the treaty, investment may well go elsewhere.

4. *Sharing of revenues for international community purposes.* We continue to believe that the equitable distribution of benefits from the seabeds can best be assured if treaty standards provide for sharing some of the revenues from continental margin minerals with the international community, particularly for the benefit of developing countries. Coastal states in a particular region should not bear the entire burden of assuring equitable treatment for the landlocked and shelf-locked states in that region, nor should they bear the entire burden for states with narrow shelves and little petroleum potential off their coasts. The problem is international, and the best solution would be international. We repeat this offer as part of an overall settlement despite our conclusion from previous exploitation patterns that a significant portion of the total international revenues will come from the continental margin off the United States in early years. We are concerned about the opposition to this idea implicit in the position of those advocating an exclusive economic zone.

5. *Compulsory settlement of disputes.* International standards such as those I described are necessary to protect certain noncoastal and international interests and thus render agreement possible. Accordingly, effective assurance that the standards will be observed is a key element in achieving agreement. Adequate assurance can only be provided by an impartial procedure for the settlement of disputes. These disputes, in the view of my delegation, must be settled ultimately by the decision of a third party. For us, then, the principle of compulsory dispute settlement is essential.

SEABED RESOURCES–DEEP SEABEDS

In many respects, the deep seabeds present the newest and most exciting aspects of our work. Although we cannot agree that international law prohibits the exploitation of deep seabed resources in accordance with high seas principles, we fully share the desire to establish an equitable, internationally agreed regime for the area and its resources as the common heritage of mankind. The sooner we do so, the earlier we will terminate essentially divisive and counterproductive disputes over the present legal status of deep seabed exploitation as well as over the position taken by some delegations, with which we have consistently disagreed, that "common heritage" means the "common property" of mankind.

Our interest in the prompt establishment and effectiveness of an equitable international regime for the seabed is demonstrated both by the comprehensive draft treaty we presented two years ago and by President Nixon's statement that any prior exploitation of the deep seabed area must be "subject to the international regime to be agreed upon."[62]

The basic interests we seek to protect in an international seabed regime are reflected in the five points to which I referred earlier, coupled with our proposal for international machinery to authorize and regulate exploration and use of the resources of the area. An effective and equitable regime must protect not only the interests of the developing countries but also those of the developed countries by establishing reasonable and secure investment conditions for their nationals who will invest their capital and technology in the deep seabeds. In order to provide the necessary protections [sic] for all nations with important interests in the area, it is also necessary to establish a system of decisionmaking which takes this into account and provides for compulsory settlement of disputes. We do not regard these objectives as inconsistent with the desire of other countries for equitable participation in deep seabed exploitation and its benefits.

Finally, Mr. Chairman, it is our view that the benefits to be derived from the operation of this new treaty should only be made available to those nations who are prepared to ratify or accede to it. Those benefits, as all of us in this room know, are manifold. New technology for mining in the seabeds is rapidly opening up new prospects for important mineral supplies. As development proceeds, vast new knowledge will emerge as man begins the serious exploration of the ocean and its resources. Mining in the oceans will generate revenues as well. All these benefits, Mr. Chairman, should be shared. We are capable in this committee of making the decisions which will enable these benefits to be realized, but we must get about the business of making these decisions promptly or we will be precluded from doing so.

FISHERIES

With respect to fisheries, our basic interest is to assure rational use and conservation of all fish stocks. To achieve this, we believe coastal states should have substantial jurisdiction over all fisheries, including anadromous species, except where the migratory habits of certain fish

[62] *Documents, 1970*, pp. 333-41.

stocks dictate another system; for example, the highly migratory tuna should be managed pursuant to multilateral arrangements. In coastal areas, jurisdiction should be limited by such international standards as would assure conservation and full utilization of the living resources.

It is widely understood that the United States shares the interests of many other coastal states. However, the fact that over 80 percent of our fisheries are off our own coast does not mean that we are prepared to abandon the remaining 20 percent, the distant-water segment of our industry. There are reasonable ways to accommodate the interests of both coastal and distant-water fishing states and to assure the kind of special cooperation between states in a region that many delegations have urged. We believe that a solution of the fisheries problem should take into account the migratory habits of fish and the manner in which they are fished. Thus we can support broad coastal state jurisdiction over coastal and anadromous fisheries beyond the territorial sea subject to international standards designed to insure conservation, maximum utilization, and equitable allocation of fisheries, with compulsory dispute settlement, but with international regulation of highly migratory species such as tuna.

Our detailed proposals on this matter have been elaborated further in Subcommittee II. The proposals reflect our continuing belief that both sound conservation and rational utilization must take into account the biology and distribution of living marine resources. But they also respond to the expressed desire of coastal states for direct regulatory authority and preferential rights over coastal and anadromous fisheries. However, it is fundamental that fish stocks must be conserved and that there must be maximum utilization of stocks not fully utilized by local fishermen. Moreover, account should be taken of traditional fishing activities of other nations, as well as the desire of states to enter into special arrangements with their neighbors. We remain convinced that highly migratory oceanic species can only be properly regulated through international organizations. It is our hope that our new proposals will move the committee closer to a solution to the complex fisheries problems involved.

NEED FOR NEW POLITICAL WILL

Mr. Chairman, I would like to conclude my statement with some general comments. While my delegation must confess its disappointment in our progress to date, we must also point out those areas where we believe important progress has been made.

Looked at from a broad perspective, we see various signs that make us cautiously optimistic. It is clear that the negotiating positions of various states are now substantially closer together than their juridical positions. This is particularly the case with respect to the width of the territorial sea and coastal state jurisdiction over resources beyond the territorial sea.

Mr. Chairman, I welcomed the interesting reports of the distinguished Representatives of Venezuela and Kenya on the results of the Santo Domingo Conference of Caribbean States and the Yaoundé Seminar of African countries. While applauding their contribution to the continuing development of a generally acceptable agreement, I should point out they do not fully take into account a number of the factors I have discussed earlier in this statement. I note in particular the absence of any reference to international standards and dispute-settlement procedures applicable to coastal state resource jurisdiction and of any distinction in the treatment of living resources based on their migratory characteristics. However, these documents certainly provide a starting point for serious negotiations, and if harmonized with my own delegation's statement today, there might be a potential for merging together in a new treaty what are otherwise widely disparate positions. Perhaps then the very beginnings of an outline might emerge which could become the basis for a successful 1973 conference. I hope so, Mr. Chairman.

Another source of hope is the work of Subcommittee I [on International Régime]. We have given priority to the negotiation of the regime, and we are beginning to see not only concrete results but an open and constructive negotiating atmosphere. The distinguished Representative of the Cameroon [Paul Bamela Engo], chairman of the First Subcommittee, and your distinguished colleague from Sri Lanka, chairman of the working group, have through their tireless efforts helped break new ground in this committee, which makes us believe that where there is political will our negotiations will bear fruit.

This new political will, however, must infuse our work in the other subcommittees as well, and it must occur now. The "list" [of subjects and issues relating to the law of the sea] must be disposed of and work begun on the drafting of articles. We are confident, Mr. Chairman, that once such work begins it will move rapidly and a successful conference will be within our grasp. But if we wait longer, Mr. Chairman, we wonder if a successful conference will ever be possible. Let us all begin to work now to avoid such a tragedy.

Finally, in closing, Mr. Chairman, I want to express to you the sincere appreciation of my delegation for your wisdom, guidance, and firm leadership through what we hope will be one of the most important and successful negotiations to have taken place in our times. We wish you continued success at this endeavor and will give you all our support.

E. The 27th General Assembly and the Problem of International Terrorism.

[For many of the world's nations, the problem of international terrorism ranked in importance with the issues of narcotics control, the environment, the law of the sea, and the interests of the developing countries. It was indicative of the increasing gravity of the terrorist issue that it tended to dominate the proceedings of the 27th Regular Session of the U.N. General Assembly in 1972 in much the same way that the issue of Chinese representation had dominated the 26th Regular Session in 1971.[63] Like the 1971 debate on China representation, moreover, the 1972 debate on terrorism served to dramatize the minority position now occupied by the United States on many of the issues coming before the world organization.

The waning of U.S. influence in the General Assembly could be traced in various developments of the 27th Session, which took place at U.N. Headquarters in New York on September 19-December 19, 1972 under the presidency of Stanislaw Trepczynski, Poland's Deputy Foreign Minister. On the two issues of primary concern to the United States, its position was decisively defeated in one instance and only grudgingly upheld in the other. As will be seen below, a package of antiterrorist measures, proposed by the United States and inspired to a large extent by activities of Palestinian terrorist groups, was rejected in favor of a much weaker document reflecting the attitude of Arab and other "third world" governments and calling primarily for study of the underlying causes of terrorist acts (Documents 87-90). A second major U.S. proposal, calling for a reduction in the United States' assessed contribution from 31.52 percent to not over 25 percent of the United Nations' ordinary expenses, was approved only after long and bitter debate[64]—and with the understanding that its application would await an increase in operating funds following the admission of the two German states to U.N. membership in 1973.[65]

Among the numerous other matters on which the U.S. position diverged from that of the majority of U.N. members, the inability of the U.S. delegation to support a number of Assembly actions relating to the Middle East and Southern Africa has been noted in earlier chapters.[66] In addition, the United States placed itself in a

[63] Cf. *A.F.R., 1971*, nos. 122-126.
[64] Resolution 2961 B (XXVII), Dec. 13, 1972, adopted by a vote of 81 (U.S.)-27-22. For the U.S. position, cf. *Bulletin*, Jan. 8, 1973, pp. 43-51; for a congressional restriction on U.S. contributions, cf. note 9 above.
[65] The two German states were admitted to U.N. membership Sept. 18, 1973; cf. Chapter III at note 101.
[66] Cf. above at Documents 37-38 and 70-72.

minority of one by virtue of its inability to agree with two proposals originally advanced by the U.S.S.R. and widely accepted by
allied as well as neutral and Communist countries. As noted earlier,
unanimous approval of a resolution that looked toward the eventual
holding of a World Disarmament Conference was prevented by a
U.S. abstention.[67] Reacting to another Soviet proposal aimed at
curbing the use of space satellites for direct television broadcasting,
the United States cast the single negative vote against a resolution
that called for an elaboration of principles with a view to an eventual international agreement or agreements in this area.[68]]

1. International Terrorism: The Background.

[The growing resort to terrorist action for political ends had preoccupied the international community even before the shock ad-
ministered to world opinion by the massacre of the Israeli athletes
housed at the Olympic Village in Munich on September 5, 1972.
Two of the more prominent aspects of the problem—crimes against
civil aviation, and crimes against diplomats—had already been the
subject of international action extending over a period of years.[69]
   The attempt to deal on an international basis with crimes against
civil aviation went back to the conclusion in 1963 of the Convention on Offenses and Certain Other Acts Committed on Board Aircraft (Tokyo Convention),[70] drawn up at an international conference held under the auspices of the International Civil Aviation
Organization (I.C.A.O.), a specialized agency of the United Nations.
Directed against hijacking, among other things, the Tokyo Convention called upon contracting parties in whose territory a hijacked
aircraft landed to permit passengers and crew to continue their
journey as soon as practicable and to return the aircraft and its
cargo to the owners.
   Since the entry into force of the Tokyo Convention in 1969, the
I.C.A.O. had sponsored two further conventions which were primarily designed to ensure that aircraft hijackers and saboteurs
would not go unpunished. The Convention for the Suppression of

[67] Resolution 2930 (XXVII), Nov. 29, 1972, adoped by a vote of 105-0-1 (U.S.);
cf. Chapter II at note 155.
[68] Resolution 2916 (XXVII), Nov. 9, 1972, adopted by a vote of 102-1 (U.S.)-7.
For the U.S. position, cf. *Bulletin*, Dec. 11, 1972, pp. 686-8.
[69] For full discussion of the terrorist issue, see the address by Legal Adviser
Stevenson in *Bulletin*, Dec. 4, 1972, pp. 645-52.
[70] Done at Tokyo Sept. 14, 1963 and entered into force Dec. 4, 1969 (TIAS
6768; 20 UST 2941); on the U.S. ratification in 1969, cf. *Bulletin*, Sept. 22,
1969, p. 275.

Unlawful Seizure of Aircraft (Hijacking or Hague Convention),[71] which had been drawn up at an international conference in The Hague in 1970 and entered into force in 1971, required contracting states to take into custody and either extradite or prosecute hijackers found within their territory. The Convention for the Suppression of Unlawful Acts Against the Safety of Civil Aviation (Sabotage or Montreal Convention),[72] concluded at Montreal in September 1971 but not in force during 1972, imposed a similar obligation with regard to the extradition or prosecution of saboteurs and armed terrorists.

The system of deterrence embodied in the I.C.A.O. conventions would still be incomplete, in the American view, as long as potential hijackers and saboteurs could expect to find sanctuary in countries willing to flout the legal requirements these instruments imposed. In a statement issued September 11, 1970 on the heels of the hijacking of four New York-bound jet airliners by Palestinian terrorists, President Nixon had announced that the United States would favor an additional step amounting to the invocation of international sanctions against such countries. "I . . . call upon the international community," the President had said, "to take joint action to suspend airline services with those countries which refuse to punish or extradite hijackers involved in international blackmail."[73] Although the I.C.A.O. Assembly had since reacted negatively to a draft convention along these lines submitted by the United States and Canada, the issue was revived in 1972 under the stress of further hijacking and terrorist incidents which culminated on June 19 in an international shutdown of air services by striking pilots demanding more effective antihijacking measures. A fifteen-nation Special Subcommittee of the I.C.A.O., meeting in Washington on September 4-15, 1972, was presented with a reformulated U.S.-Canadian proposal that again involved collective suspension of international air navigation with an offending state. Its only definite action, however, was to pass the issue to the full I.C.A.O. Legal Committee, due to meet in January 1973.[74]

Crimes against diplomats had also figured on the international agenda since the beginning of 1971, when the United States had called attention to this increasingly serious problem at the Third Special Session of the General Assembly of the Organization of American States, held in Washington on January 25-February 2,

[71] Done at The Hague Dec. 16, 1970 and entered into force Oct. 14, 1971 (TIAS 7192; 22 UST 1641); text in *Documents, 1970*, pp. 350-55.
[72] Done at Montreal Sept. 23, 1971 and entered into force Jan. 26, 1973 (TIAS 7570; 24 UST 565); text in *A.F.R., 1971*, no. 138. On ratification and entry into force, cf. below at note 81.
[73] *Documents, 1970*, pp. 346-7.
[74] Details in *Bulletin*, Oct. 2, 1972, pp. 357-64; cf. below at note 157.

1971. By 13 votes out of a possible 23, that body had adopted a watered-down text officially entitled the Convention to Prevent and Punish the Acts of Terrorism Taking the Form of Crimes Against Persons and Related Extortion That Are of International Significance.[75] By its provisions, acts of violence against diplomats and others to whom governments owe special protection under international law were defined as common crimes and therefore as falling outside the category of political offenses for which territorial and diplomatic asylum have traditionally been granted. Transmitted to the U.S. Senate on May 11, 1971, the convention was approved by a 74 to 0 vote of that body on June 12, 1972, but ratification by the President was delayed while awaiting the enactment of implementing legislation.[76]

The United Nations was likewise involved with the question of crimes against diplomats by reason of a General Assembly resolution of 1971 in which the distinguished experts composing the International Law Commission had been asked to carry out a study with a view to the submission of draft articles for inclusion in an eventual international convention.[77] In response to this directive, the International Law Commission in the summer of 1972 gave tentative approval to a set of twelve articles inspired by the "extradite or prosecute" principle and designed, in the words of an official summary, "to ensure that safe havens will no longer be available to persons believed to have committed serious offenses against internationally protected persons."[78]

The Munich incident on September 5, 1972 prompted further action in the United States and the United Nations. In Washington, the Congress was already at work on a longstanding bill for the protection of foreign officials in the United States, originally proposed by the administration in an attempt to curb the harassment and occasional violence experienced by some foreign representatives at the hands of overeager political partisans.[79] Under the spur of the Munich incident, legislation making it a Federal offense to harass, assault, kidnap or murder a foreign official, a member of his family, or an official guest of the United States within the country

---

[75] Signed at Washington Feb. 2, 1971 and entered into force for ratifying states—but not for the U.S.—on Oct. 16, 1973; text (S. Ex. D, 92-1) in *A.F.R., 1971*, no. 111. Nicaragua, Costa Rica, Venezuela, and Mexico had become parties to the convention as of Mar. 17, 1975.

[76] Cf. *Bulletin*, July 5, 1971, p. 28; same, Dec. 4, 1972, p. 648; same, May 28, 1973, p. 678.

[77] Resolution 2780 (XXVI), Dec. 3, 1971, adopted by a vote of 107-0-0.

[78] *UN Monthly Chronicle*, Aug.-Sept., 1972, pp. 87-8. The text of the draft articles appears in the *Report of the International Law Commission on the Work of Its 24th Session, 2 May-7 July 1972* (U.N. General Assembly, *Official Records: 27th Session, Supplement No. 10* [A/8710/Rev.1]), pp. 91-101.

[79] Cf. *A.F.R., 1971*, no. 130.

was completed by the two houses of Congress and signed by the President on October 24.[80] In addition, on September 15 the President transmitted to the Senate the year-old text of the Montreal anti-sabotage convention, which was promptly approved by an 89 to 0 vote of that body on October 3, was ratified by the President on November 1, and entered into force January 26, 1973.[81]

Intensified action on still other fronts was forecast by President Nixon when he announced the establishment on September 25 of a Cabinet Committee to Combat Terrorism, chaired by the Secretary of State, to "consider the most effective means by which to combat terrorism here and abroad, and . . . take the lead in establishing procedures to ensure that our government can take appropriate action in response to acts of terrorism swiftly and effectively."[82] At virtually the same moment, Secretary of State Rogers in New York was calling upon the U.N. General Assembly to join a broadened anti-terrorist campaign directed not only against previously recognized offenses but also, in a significant broadening of the scope of international action, against the export of terrorism to otherwise uninvolved countries (Document 87).]

2. Proposals to the General Assembly.

[The inclusion of the terrorist issue on the agenda of the General Assembly's 27th Session was attributable in the first instance to the initiative of U.N. Secretary-General Kurt Waldheim. Dismayed by the long succession of terrorist incidents that culminated in the Munich massacre, the Secretary-General declared at a news conference on September 12, 1972 that the United Nations could not, in his opinion, remain a mute spectator of such developments but that the General Assembly had a duty to deal with the question and take adequate measures aimed at preventing acts of violence against innocent people. His decision to bring the matter before the Assembly, Mr. Waldheim emphasized, was not prompted by a specific act of violence but rather referred to all acts of violence against innocent people.[83]

Though warmly commended by the United States, the Secretary-General's initiative evoked a less than favorable reaction on the part of most Arab, African, and Communist countries. With few excep-

---

[80] Act for the Protection of Foreign Officials and Official Guests of the United States (Public Law 92-539, Oct. 24, 1972).
[81] Cf. *Bulletin*, Oct. 9, 1972, p. 418; same, Oct. 16, 1972, pp. 444-8; same, Nov. 20, 1972, pp. 607-8; same, Feb. 19, 1973, p. 215.
[82] Memorandum to the Secretary of State, Sept. 25, 1972, in *Public Papers, 1972*, pp. 912-13; further details in *Bulletin*, Oct. 23, 1972, pp. 476-80.
[83] *UN Monthly Chronicle*, Oct. 1972, p. 58.

tions, these governments seemed to fear that in denouncing terrorism, they would appear to be denouncing also the various causes in whose name the terrorists claimed to be acting. Unable to secure a year's postponement of the issue, these countries also reacted without enthusiasm to a proposed amendment to the agenda item, put forward by Saudi Arabia, that tended to dilute the emphasis on combating international terrorism by linking it with a study of the underlying causes of the phenomenon. As approved September 23 by a vote of 66 to 27 with 33 abstentions, the amended agenda item read: "Measures to prevent international terrorism which endangers or takes innocent human lives or jeopardizes fundamental freedoms, and study of the underlying causes of those forms of terrorism and acts of violence which lie in misery, frustration, grievance and despair which cause some people to sacrifice human lives, including their own, in an attempt to effect radical changes."[84]

Apparently undeterred by these unfavorable auguries, Secretary of State Rogers voiced an earnest plea for effective action against the terrorist menace in his September 25 address to the General Assembly (Document 87). Urging prompt adherence to the I.C.A.O. conventions, the American representative called also for (1) prompt completion of a treaty on crimes against diplomats; (2) prompt completion of a convention suspending air service to countries failing to punish or extradite hijackers or saboteurs of civil aircraft; and (3) conclusion of a new treaty requiring prosecution or extradition of persons "who kill, seriously injure, or kidnap innocent civilians in a foreign state for the purpose of harming or forcing concessions from a state or from an international organization." Recapitulated in a draft convention on terrorism against civilians (Document 88a) and an omnibus resolution submitted for consideration by the Assembly (Document 88b), this American action program was subsequently endorsed in a special statement by President Nixon (Document 89).]

(87) "A World Free of Violence": Statement by Secretary of State Rogers to the General Assembly, September 25, 1972.[85]

(Complete Text)

During the past few years the world has made remarkable advances toward the charter goal of practicing tolerance and living together in peace with one another as good neighbors. In 1972 alone:

84 Same, pp. 44-50.
85 Department of State Press Release 238, Sept. 26, 1972; text from *Bulletin*, Oct. 16, 1972, pp. 425-30.

—The United States and the Soviet Union have undertaken with each other to do "their utmost" to avoid military confrontations, to respect the sovereign equality of *all* countries, and to promote conditions in which no country would be subject to "outside interference in (its) internal affairs."[86]

—The Soviet Union and the United States have also placed precise limitations on our defensive and at least for the next five years on our offensive strategic missile systems.[87]

—The United States and the People's Republic of China have undertaken to broaden understanding between our peoples, to improve relations between us in the conviction that this would be "in the interests of all countries," and to oppose any efforts toward hegemony in Asia or toward divisions of the world "into spheres of interest."[88]

—The United Kingdom, France, the Soviet Union, and the United States have agreed on specific provisions to insure unimpeded movement to and from Berlin by road, rail, and waterways.[89]

—The Federal Republic of Germany and the German Democratic Republic have opened negotiations on a treaty to normalize their relations.[90]

—And North and South Korea have intensified their talks on the plight of divided families and have agreed to establish a joint committee to examine problems of unification.[91]

There were many other accomplishments toward the charter's objectives in 1972. I mention these merely to illustrate how old patterns of hostility are being eroded. If continued, this process in time will find positive reflection within the United Nations itself.

We are encouraged, too, by calls in both Eastern and Western capitals for a more secure and more open Europe.

A step toward realizing this goal would be creation of a more stable military balance in central Europe through negotiation of mutual and balanced force reductions. We are currently in consultation with our allies, and we believe exploratory talks on this subject could begin within several months. We trust they will be productive.[92]

It is equally important to move toward more normal relationships in Europe, relationships which have not existed since the end of the Second World War.

Toward this objective a Conference on Security and Cooperation in Europe, if it is carefully and constructively prepared, could play a

[86] Document 11.
[87] Documents 13-14.
[88] Document 54.
[89] Document 25.
[90] Cf. Chapter III at note 101.
[91] Cf. note 85 to Chapter VI.
[92] Cf. Chapter III at notes 102-103.

crucial role. A conference whose overall effect was to put a stamp of approval upon the rigid divisions of Europe would only prolong the problems of today into yet another generation. A conference which promoted a more normal relationship among all of Europe's states and peoples would reinforce the trend toward better relations on other levels. That is why we believe that the conference must take practical steps to promote the freer movement of people, ideas, and goods across the breadth of the continent.[93]

We are also now studying alternative approaches for the forthcoming SALT talks [Strategic Arms Limitation Talks].[94] The United States will pursue these general aims:

—First, our endeavor will be to negotiate on offensive weapons. In so doing we shall seek to expand the scope of strategic offensive weapons included in the limitations and to establish an equitable balance in the major delivery systems.

—Second, we will wish to examine carefully qualitative limitations which could enhance stability.

—Third, we will aim to reduce levels of strategic arms. As President Nixon said to this General Assembly in 1969, our objective is "not only to limit the buildup of strategic arms but to reverse it."[95]

Of course we also attach importance to the work of the Conference of the Committee on Disarmament, which has now turned its attention to preventing the accumulation of chemical weapons for use in warfare. Work in the Committee has come a long way toward resolving some of the important and complex issues related to possible significant restraints in this area. The United States is intensifying its study of all proposals, and we look forward to responding to them at an early date.[96]

It is clear from what I have said that the United States believes that a practical step-by-step approach is the best way to achieve genuine progress in disarmament.

Let me take note of other areas in the world in which progress needs to be accelerated.

In Africa, this Assembly must continue to champion the efforts of all people of all races for human dignity, self-determination, and social justice. The United States will continue to lend its full support to all practical efforts to these ends.[97]

In Latin America, while growth rates in recent years have far ex-

[93] Same.
[94] Cf. Document 17.
[95] *Documents, 1968-69*, p. 472.
[96] Cf. note 150 to Chapter II.
[97] Cf. Chapter VII at notes 47-50 and 73-76.

ceeded Alliance for Progress targets, economic development is still a primary concern and a primary need.[98] The U.S. Government remains committed to a substantial program of economic assistance, particularly through regional organizations. And in recognition of the importance of trade to development, we are actively supporting the participation of Latin American and other developing countries in the coming negotiations on a new international trading system.

In Viet-Nam the United States has reduced its armed forces from about 550,000 to 35,000. President Nixon has proposed a cease-fire in all of Indochina under international supervision, an exchange of prisoners of war, and a total withdrawal of all American forces.[99] Under this proposal the political future of Viet-Nam could be negotiated by the Vietnamese themselves. President Nixon has also pledged a major effort to assist both Vietnamese states in postwar reconstruction. In such circumstances it is hard to understand why the other side persists in believing the war should be continued.

CLIMATE FOR MIDDLE EAST PEACE SETTLEMENT

And in the Middle East, the momentum toward a peace settlement must be regained.

We should take note of two positive elements. The cease-fire is now in its 26th month. The climate for a settlement seemed to improve as 1972 progressed.[100]

We must, however, recognize that the Munich killings have set off deplorable patterns of action and counteraction and have seriously clouded prospects of early progress.[101] Nevertheless, neither side has permanently closed the door to future diplomatic efforts. We believe that forces favoring a peaceful settlement still have the upper hand. Our task is to do everything possible to see that they are supported.

The "no peace, no war" situation which prevails now in the Middle East does not and will not serve the interest of anyone in the area. Certainly a stable, just, and durable peace agreement based on Security Council Resolution 242[102] continues to be the objective of the United States.

But this cannot be achieved without the beginning of a genuine negotiating process between the parties concerned. No settlement imposed from the outside could long endure. Negotiation is not capitulation. Negotiating activity among longstanding antagonists across the world is presently occurring. Why should the Middle East be an exception?

[98] Cf. Document 74.
[99] Document 47.
[100] Cf. Document 35.
[101] Cf. Documents 36-37.
[102] Cf. Chapter IV at note 41.

When North Korea can talk with South Korea, when East Germans can talk with West Germans, when Indians and Pakistanis can meet in the immediate aftermath of war and prior to the withdrawal of troops[103] — then surely the Middle East should be no exception to the general rule that differences should be reconciled through an active dialogue between the parties concerned.

We do not hold that the process need necessarily begin with direct negotiations. Other diplomatic avenues exist. Ambassador Jarring [U.N. Special Representative Gunnar Jarring] remains available to help the parties negotiate the terms of a peace settlement in accordance with Security Council Resolution 242.

Another—in our view the most promising first step—would be proximity talks leading to an interim Suez Canal agreement. This would separate the combatants, restore to Egypt operation of and authority over the Suez Canal, involve some Israeli withdrawal, preserve the ceasefire, and provide momentum for further efforts toward an overall settlement.

It is encouraging that both sides agree that such an interim agreement would not be an end in itself but rather the first step toward an overall peace settlement. Such a practical test of peace on the ground would be in the interests of both sides, and the United States remains prepared to assist in achieving it. Moreover, an overall settlement in accordance with Resolution 242 must meet the legitimate aspirations and concerns of governments on both sides as well as of the Palestinian people.

U.N. WEAKNESSES AND STRENGTHS

In considering some of the great political developments of the past few years, one cannot help but observe that the United Nations has not been directly involved. This fact has often been cited in attacks against it.

We are all aware, of course, that the charter does not intend the United Nations to be the center of all diplomacy. Still, as the Secretary General puts it temperately in his annual report, "in the political sphere the Organization's place is . . . . uncertain."[104] With this thought most of us would agree.

Looking to the future, it is well to keep in mind that it is not so much in institutional reforms as in national wills that the solutions to the problem must be sought. Yet to the extent that better work methods

---

[103] On the Simla meeting between the leaders of India and Pakistan, cf. the discussion preceding Document 40.

[104] *Introduction to the Report of the Secretary-General on the Work of the Organization, August 1972* (U.N. General Assembly, *Official Records: 27th Session, Supplement No. 1A* [A/8701/Add.1]), p. 1.

and more realistic institutional arrangements will help, we also must bring them about. For example:

—We believe that for the Security Council to maintain its influence and authority, ways must be found to assure representation for states, other than the present permanent members, whose resources and influence are of major importance in world affairs. The absence of Japan, for example, is notable in a body designed to engage the responsibilities of the world's principal powers.

—We believe that greater recourse to fact-finding commissions, to good offices, and to quiet preventive diplomacy should be employed.

—We believe that the increase in bloc voting, often without independent regard for the merits of the issue, is leading increasingly to unrealistic results.

The discussion of United Nations weaknesses in dealing with political problems has reached its peak just at a time when its contribution to economic development and scientific and technological cooperation is making great strides.

Long before economic development became a major matter of international concern, the United Nations initiated efforts to reduce the economic gap between developed and developing countries. From the start the United States has supported that effort. It is an encouraging fact that during each of the last three years the per capita growth in production has finally achieved a higher rate in the less developed than in the developed world. Still, as the recent World Bank study showed, there are serious problems of income distribution, high rates of infant mortality, low rates of literacy, serious malnutrition, and widespread ill health. The United States intends to continue to devote serious efforts to solving such problems—through the improved United Nations Development Program and through other channels of economic assistance.

United Nations activities related to science and technology are also having an impact:

—The landmark United Nations Conference on the Human Environment has proposed a world monitoring of levels of pollution in water, air, earth, and living beings, measuring levels of specific chemicals, such as the hydrocarbons which poison the air of the world's cities. To launch this and other important programs without delay, we urge this Assembly to establish the Secretariat and the proposed $100 million Fund for the Environment.[105]

—The United Nations can also make a substantial contribution in the fight against drug traffic, particularly heroin traffic. A revised Single Convention on Narcotic Drugs will give the Narcotics Board authority

[105] Cf. above at notes 10 and 41.

to reduce poppy cultivation and opium production in countries shown to be sources of that traffic.[106] The U.N. Drug Abuse Fund is helping states to improve their drug administration, to train police and customs officials, to develop other means of livelihood for opium farmers, and to prevent and treat drug addiction.[107] As President Nixon said last week, "Every government which wants to move against narcotics should know that it can count on (the United States) for our whole-hearted support and assistance in doing so."[108]

—Just last week the Secretary General announced that 1974 will be the World Population Year and the time of a major U.N. population conference.[109] It is our hope that the conference will lead to the setting of concrete goals of reduced population growth.

—This General Assembly will review the progress of its Seabed Committee in preparing for a conference on the law of the sea.[110] It is important for us to use this opportunity to help make the oceans an example of international cooperation, rather than an area of future conflict.

Such activities as pollution, narcotics, the seabeds, and population control—most of them connected with new applications of science and technology—will increase in importance in the future. We believe they must acquire a greater focus and priority in the United Nations.

I have spoken today about some of the U.N.'s weaknesses as well as some of its strengths because I believe we must look at this organization realistically so that we may contribute to its future prospects. In that spirit, the United States will continue to support the United Nations. We remain committed to making it stronger and more effective.

DEALING WITH ACTS OF INTERNATIONAL TERRORISM

During this session the United Nations will have an opportunity and an obligation to take action of vital importance to the international community. The United Nations must deal effectively with criminal acts of international terrorism which are so tragically touching the lives of people everywhere, without warning, without discrimination, without regard for the sanctity of human life.

Twenty-four years ago the United Nations, in its Declaration of Human Rights,[111] affirmed that every human being has a right to life,

---

[106] Cf. above at notes 24-26.
[107] Cf. above at note 31.
[108] Statement of Sept. 18, 1972, in *Public Papers, 1972*, p. 875.
[109] The U.N. World Population Conference was held in Bucharest on August 19-30, 1974.
[110] Cf. above at note 58.
[111] Resolution 217 A (III), Dec. 10, 1948; *Documents, 1948*, pp. 430-35.

liberty, and "security of person." Yet what is happening in the world today to that security?

—In Sweden, 90 people boarding an international flight are made hostage and held for ransom by Croatian terrorists.

—In London, an Israeli diplomat is killed by a bomb sent through the mail. In New York, colleagues in the United Nations narrowly avert a similar fate.

—In Cyprus, 95 persons of many nationalities narrowly escape death on a Venezuelan plane when a bomb is discovered just in time.

—In New York, shots are fired into the apartment of a member of the Soviet Mission where children are playing.[112]

—In Munich, 11 Olympic athletes are kidnaped and murdered in a day of horror witnessed throughout the world.[113]

—In Czechoslovakia, a Czechoslovak pilot is killed and his plane hijacked and diverted to West Germany.

—In Israel, 26 tourists, 16 of them American citizens, are slaughtered in an insane attack at an international airport.[114]

In this year alone 25 airliners from 13 countries have been successfully hijacked, and 26 other attempts have been frustrated. In this year alone 140 airplane passengers and crew have been killed, and 97 wounded, in acts of terrorism. In five years 27 diplomats from 11 countries have been kidnaped and three assassinated. In New York, Arab and other missions have been threatened.

Is there any one of you here who has not had occasion, as you have journeyed by plane from around the globe, to be concerned about your own personal safety? Is there any one of you here who has not wondered what terrorist might strike next, or where?

The issue is not war—war between states, civil war, or revolutionary war. The issue is not the strivings of people to achieve self-determination and independence.

Rather, it is whether millions of air travelers can continue to fly in safety each year. It is whether a person who receives a letter can open it without the fear of being blown up. It is whether diplomats can safely carry out their duties. It is whether international meetings—like the Olympic games, like this Assembly—can proceed without the ever-present threat of violence.

In short, the issue is whether the vulnerable lines of international communication—the airways and the mails, diplomatic discourse and international meetings—can continue, without disruption, to bring

112 Same as note 79.
113 Cf. Document 36.
114 Cf. Chapter IV at note 51.

nations and peoples together. All who have a stake in this have a stake in decisive action to suppress these demented acts of terrorism.

We are all aware that, aside from the psychotic and the purely felonious, many criminal acts of terrorism derive from political origins. We all recognize that issues such as self-determination must continue to be addressed seriously by the international community. But political passion, however deeply held, cannot be a justification for criminal violence against innocent persons.

Certainly the terrorist acts I have cited are totally unacceptable attacks against the very fabric of international order. They must be universally condemned, whether we consider the cause the terrorists invoke noble or ignoble, legitimate or illegitimate.

We must take effective steps to prevent the hijacking of international civil aircraft.

We must take effective steps to prevent murderous attacks and kidnaping of diplomats.

We must take effective steps to prevent terrorists from sending bombs through the mails or murdering innocent civilians.

The United States welcomes the initiative the Secretary General has taken to place this matter on the agenda.[115]

Two years ago, before the problem had reached its present dimensions, the General Assembly took the first step, the step that must guide us now. In the Declaration on Friendly Relations Among States,[116] which so strongly reaffirmed the right of self-determination, the General Assembly also unanimously declared that each nation has a duty to refrain from assisting or in any way participating in "terrorist acts in another State or acquiescing in organized activities within its territory directed towards the commission of such acts."

The time has come to make that obligation, which this General Assembly solemnly undertook, more specific and meaningful.

In the past two years, the international community has taken certain steps in the field of hijacking. Conventions have been concluded prescribing severe penalties for the hijacking and sabotage of aircraft and requiring states to extradite or prosecute hijackers and saboteurs.[117] We urge all states which have not ratified these conventions to do so.

We are now faced with an urgent need to deter and punish international crimes of violence not only in the air but throughout our societies. The United States urges that this Assembly act, and act at once, to meet this challenge.

First, the draft treaty to prosecute or extradite those who attack or kidnap diplomats or officials of foreign governments or international organizations should be completed and opened for signature at this ses-

115 Cf. above at note 83.
116 Cf. below at note 133.
117 Cf. above at notes 71-72.

sion of the Assembly. The draft articles[118] are already before this Assembly in document A/8710.

Second, a treaty providing for suspension of all air service to countries which fail to punish or extradite hijackers or saboteurs of civil aircraft should be promptly completed and opened for signature. A nation which is a haven for hijackers should be outlawed by the international community. A draft of a treaty to do this has already been considered by a subcommittee of the International Civil Aviation Organization.[119] To achieve early action the process of deliberation should be accelerated, and a diplomatic conference to complete the treaty should be called without delay.

Third, a new treaty on the export of international terrorism should be concluded and opened for signature as soon as possible. It should include universal condemnation of and require the prosecution or extradition of persons who kill, seriously injure, or kidnap innocent civilians in a foreign state for the purpose of harming or forcing concessions from a state or from an international organization. To complete such a treaty a diplomatic conference should be convened as soon as possible. The U.S. Government is today circulating a first draft of a treaty.[120] We urge all governments to give it their earnest attention.

We have also embodied these various proposals in a draft resolution,[121] which we submitted to the Secretariat for distribution this morning.

These actions would mark a major advance in the struggle against international terrorism. Surely it is in the collective interest of every nation represented in this hall to arrest the growing assault on international order with which we are all faced.

Let this General Assembly be the driving force for the specific and vigorous steps that are required. Let it prove that the United Nations can meet this test. Let it show people everywhere that this organization—here, now—is capable of the concrete action necessary to bring us closer to a world free of violence, the kind of a world which is the great goal of the U.N. Charter.

---

[118] Cf. above at note 78.
[119] Cf. above at note 74.
[120] Document 88a.
[121] Document 88b.

(88) United States Draft Convention and Resolution, Circulated September 25, 1972.

(a) Draft Convention for the Prevention and Punishment of Certain Acts of International Terrorism. [122]

(Complete Text)

THE STATES PARTIES TO THIS CONVENTION—

RECALLING United Nations General Assembly Resolution 2625 (XXV) proclaiming principles of international law concerning friendly relations and co-operation among States in accordance with the Charter of the United Nations;[123]

CONSIDERING that this Resolution provides that every State has the duty to refrain from organizing, instigating, assisting or participating in terrorist acts in another State or acquiescing in organized activites within its territory directed towards the commission of such acts;

CONSIDERING the common danger posed by the spread of terrorist acts across national boundaries;

CONSIDERING that civilians must be protected from terrorist acts;

AFFIRMING that effective measures to control international terrorism are urgently needed and require international as well as national action;

HAVE AGREED AS FOLLOWS:

ARTICLE 1

1. Any person who unlawfully kills, causes serious bodily harm or kidnaps another person, attempts to commit any such act, or participates as an accomplice of a person who commits or attempts to commit any such act, commits an offense of international significance if the act:

(a) is committed or takes effect outside the territory of a State of which the alleged offender is a national; and
(b) is committed or takes effect:

(i) outside the territory of the State against which the act is directed, or

[122] U.N. document A/C.6/L.850, Sept. 25, 1972 (Department of State Press Release 238A, Sept. 26, 1972); text from *Bulletin*, Oct. 16, 1972, pp. 431-3.
[123] Cf. below at note 133.

(ii) within the territory of the State against which the act is directed and the alleged offender knows or has reason to know that a person against whom the act is directed is not a national of that State; and

(c) is committed neither by nor against a member of the Armed Forces of a State in the course of military hostilities; and

(d) is intended to damage the interests of or obtain concessions from a State or an international organization.

2. For the purposes of this Convention:

(a) An "international organization" means an international intergovernmental organization.

(b) An "alleged offender" means a person as to whom there are grounds to believe that he has committed one or more of the offenses of international significance set forth in this Article.

(c) The "territory" of a State includes all territory under the jurisdiction or administration of the State.

ARTICLE 2

Each State Party undertakes to make the offenses set forth in Article 1 punishable by severe penalties.

ARTICLE 3

A State Party in whose territory an alleged offender is found shall, if it does not extradite him, submit, without exception whatsoever and without undue delay, the case to its competent authorities for the purpose of prosecution, through proceedings in accordance with the laws of that State.

ARTICLE 4

1. Each State Party shall take such measures as may be necessary to establish its jurisdiction over the offenses set forth in Article 1:

(a) when the offense is committed in its territory, or
(b) when the offense is committed by its national.

2. Each State Party shall likewise take such measures as may be necessary to establish its jurisdiction over the offenses set forth in Article 1 in the case where an alleged offender is present in its territory

and the State does not extradite him to any of the States mentioned in Paragraph 1 of this Article.

3. This Convention does not exclude any criminal jurisdiction exercised in accordance with national law.

ARTICLE 5

A State Party in which one or more of the offenses set forth in Article 1 have been committed shall, if it has reason to believe an alleged offender has fled from its territory, communicate to all other States Parties all the pertinent facts regarding the offense committed and all available information regarding the identity of the alleged offender.

ARTICLE 6

1. The State Party in whose territory an alleged offender is found shall take appropriate measures under its internal law so as to ensure his presence for prosecution or extradition. Such measures shall be immediately notified to the States mentioned in Article 4, Paragraph 1, and all other interested States.

2. Any person regarding whom the measures referred to in Paragraph 1 of this Article are being taken shall be entitled to communicate immediately with the nearest appropriate representative of the State of which he is a national and to be visited by a representative of that State.

ARTICLE 7

1. To the extent that the offenses set forth in Article 1 are not listed as extraditable offenses in any extradition treaty existing between States Parties they shall be deemed to have been included as such therein. States Parties undertake to include those offenses in every future extradition treaty to be concluded between them.

2. If a State Party which makes extradition conditional on the existence of a treaty receives a request for extradition from another State Party with which it has no extradition treaty, it may, if it decides to extradite, consider the present articles as the legal basis for extradition in respect of the offenses. Extradition shall be subject to the provisions of the law of the requested State.

3. States Parties which do not make extradition conditional upon the existence of a treaty shall recognize the offenses as extraditable offenses between themselves subject to the provisions of the law of the requested State.

4. Each of the offenses shall be treated, for the purpose of extradition between States Parties as if it has been committed not only in the place in which it occurred but also in the territories of the States required to establish their jurisdiction in accordance with Article 4, Paragraph 1(b).

5. An extradition request from the State in which the offenses were committed shall have priority over other such requests if received by the State Party in whose territory the alleged offender has been found within thirty days after the communication required in Paragraph 1 of Article 6 has been made.

ARTICLE 8

Any person regarding whom proceedings are being carried out in connection with any of the offenses set forth in Article 1 shall be guaranteed fair treatment at all stages of the proceedings.

ARTICLE 9

The statutory limitation as to the time within which prosecution may be instituted for the offenses set forth in Article 1 shall be, in each State Party, that fixed for the most serious crimes under its internal law.

ARTICLE 10

1. States Parties shall, in accordance with international and national law, endeavor to take all practicable measures for the purpose of preventing the offenses set forth in Article 1.

2. Any State Party having reason to believe that one of the offenses set forth in Article 1 may be committed shall, in accordance with its national law, furnish any relevant information in its possession to those States which it believes would be the States mentioned in Article 4, Paragraph 1, if any such offense were committed.

ARTICLE 11

1. States Parties shall afford one another the greatest measure of assistance in connection with criminal proceedings brought in respect of the offenses set forth in Article 1, including the supply of all evidence at their disposal necessary for the proceedings.

2. The provisions of Paragraph 1 of this Article shall not affect obligations concerning mutual assistance embodied in any other treaty.

ARTICLE 12

States Parties shall consult together for the purpose of considering and implementing such other cooperative measures as may seem useful for carrying out the purposes of this Convention.

ARTICLE 13

In any case in which one or more of the Geneva Conventions of August 12, 1949,[124] or any other convention concerning the law of armed conflicts is applicable, such conventions shall, if in conflict with any provision of this Convention, take precedence. In particular:

(a) nothing in this Convention shall make an offense of any act which is permissible under the Geneva Convention Relative to the Protection of Civilian Persons in Time of War[125] or any other international law applicable in armed conflicts; and

(b) nothing in this Convention shall deprive any person of prisoner of war status if entitled to such status under the Geneva Convention Relative to the Treatment of Prisoners of War[126] or any other applicable convention concerning respect for human rights in armed conflicts.

ARTICLE 14

In any case in which the Convention on Offenses and Certain Other Acts Committed on Board Aircraft,[127] the Convention for the Suppression of Unlawful Seizure of Aircraft,[128] the Convention for the Suppression of Unlawful Acts Against the Safety of Civil Aviation,[129] the Convention to Prevent and Punish the Acts of Terrorism Taking the Form of Crimes Against Persons and Related Extortion that Are of International Significance,[130] or any other convention which has or may be concluded concerning the protection of civil aviation, diplomatic agents and other internationally protected persons, is applicable, such convention shall, if in conflict with any provision of this Convention, take precedence.

---

[124] TIAS 3362-5 (6 UST 3114, 3217, 3316, 3516).
[125] TIAS 3365 (6 UST 3516).
[126] TIAS 3364 (6 UST 3316).
[127] Cf. above at note 70.
[128] Cf. above at note 71.
[129] Cf. above at note 72.
[130] Cf. above at note 75.

ARTICLE 15

Nothing in this Convention shall derogate from any obligations of the Parties under the United Nations Charter.

ARTICLE 16

1. Any dispute between the Parties arising out of the application or interpretation of the present articles that is not settled through negotiation may be brought by any State party to the dispute before a Conciliation Commission to be constituted in accordance with the provisions of this Article by the giving of written notice to the other State or States party to the dispute and to the Secretary-General of the United Nations.

2. A Conciliation Commission will be composed of three members. One member shall be appointed by each party to the dispute. If there is more than one party on either side of the dispute they shall jointly appoint a member of the Conciliation Commission. These two appointments shall be made within two months of the written notice referred to in Paragraph 1. The third member, the Chairman, shall be chosen by the other two members.

3. If either side has failed to appoint its members within the time limit referred to in Paragraph 2, the Secretary-General of the United Nations shall appoint such member within a further period of two months. If no agreement is reached on the choice of the Chairman within five months of the written notice referred to in Paragraph 1, the Secretary-General shall within the further period of one month appoint as the Chairman a qualified jurist who is not a national of any State party to the dispute.

4. Any vacancy shall be filled in the same manner as the original appointment was made.

5. The Commission shall establish its own rules of procedure and shall reach its decisions and recommendations by a majority vote. It shall be competent to ask any organ that is authorized by or in accordance with the Charter of the United Nations to request an advisory opinion from the International Court of Justice to make such a request regarding the interpretation or application of the present articles.

6. If the Commission is unable to obtain an agreement among the parties on a settlement of the dispute within six months of its initial meeting, it shall prepare as soon as possible a report of its proceedings and transmit it to the parties and to the depositary. The report shall include the Commission's conclusions upon the facts and questions of law and the recommendations it has submitted to the parties in order to facilitate a settlement of the dispute. The six months time limit may be extended by decision of the Commission.

7. This Article is without prejudice to provisions concerning the settlement of disputes contained in international agreements in force between States.

(b) Draft Resolution Submitted for Consideration by the General Assembly. [131]

(Complete Text)

The General Assembly,

Gravely concerned by the increasing frequency of serious acts of international terrorism, inflicting injury and death to innocent persons and inflaming relations between peoples and states;

Deploring the tragic, unwarranted and unnecessary loss of innocent human lives from acts of international terrorism;

Recognizing that the continuation of international terrorism poses a grave threat to the safety and reliability of modern communications between states, including in particular international civil aviation and diplomatic intercourse;

Recognizing that governments have the responsibility to take appropriate steps to assure that all foreign diplomats engaging in normal pursuits and all foreign nationals travelling, visiting or residing abroad are afforded full legal protection against bodily harm or the threat thereof;

Noting the constructive initiative of the Secretary General to place an item on international terrorism before the General Assembly;[132]

Recalling the General Assembly's "Declaration on Principles of International Law concerning Friendly Relations and Cooperation among States in accordance with the Charter of the United Nations"[133] and in particular its statement that

Every State has the duty to refrain from organizing, instigating, assisting or participating in acts of civil strife or terrorist acts in another State or acquiescing in organized activities within its territory directed towards the commission of such acts, when the acts referred to in the present paragraph involve a threat or use of force.

1. *Calls upon* all states as a matter of urgency to become parties to and implement the following international conventions:

131 U.N. Document A/C.6/L.851, Sept. 25, 1972 (Department of State Press Release 238B, Sept. 26, 1972); text from *Bulletin*, Oct. 16, 1972, pp. 433-4.
132 Cf. above at note 83.
133 Resolution 2625 (XXV), Oct. 24, 1970, adopted without vote.

a. "Convention on Offenses and Certain Other Acts Committed on Board Aircraft," signed at Tokyo on September 14, 1963;[134]

b. "Convention for the Suppression of Unlawful Seizure of Aircraft," signed at The Hague on December 15, 1970;[135] and

c. "Convention for the Suppression of Unlawful Acts Against the Safety of Civil Aviation," signed at Montreal on September 23, 1971.[136]

2. *Requests* the International Civil Aviation Organization to pursue as a matter of urgency the drafting of a convention on arrangements for enforcement of principles and obligations embodied in the Tokyo, Hague and Montreal Conventions with a view to the calling of a plenipotentiary conference without delay.[137]

3. *Urges* all states to take immediate steps to prevent the use of their territory or resources to aid, encourage, or give sanctuary to those persons involved in directing, supporting, or participating in acts of international terrorism.

4. *Calls upon* all states urgently to take all necessary measures within their jurisdiction and in cooperation with other states to deter and prevent acts of international terrorism and to take effective measures to deal with those who perpetrate such acts.

5. *Strongly recommends* that member governments establish procedures for the exchange of information and data on the plans, activities and movements of terrorists, in order to strengthen the capability of governments to prevent and suppress acts of international terrorism and to prosecute and punish those perpetrating such acts.

6. *Calls upon* all states to become parties to a convention on the prevention and punishment of crimes against diplomatic agents and other internationally protected persons based on the draft articles prepared by the International Law Commission.[138]

7. *Decides* to convene a plenipotentiary conference in early 1973 to consider the adoption of a convention on the prevention and punishment of international terrorism and requests the Secretary General to transmit to member states for their consideration the texts of proposed draft articles on this subject submitted to the General Assembly.[139]

8. *Recommends* urgent efforts by all members to address the political problems which may, in some instances, provide a pretext for acts of international terrorism.

---

[134] Cf. above at note 70.
[135] Cf. above at note 71.
[136] Cf. above at note 72.
[137] Cf. below at note 158.
[138] Cf. above at note 78.
[139] Document 88a.

(89) Action to Combat Terrorism: Statement by President Nixon, New York, September 27, 1972. [140]

(Complete Text)

Monday [September 25], here in New York, Secretary of State Rogers urged prompt action by the United Nations on three measures to combat the inhuman wave of terrorism that has been loosed on the world.[141] I am gratified that the United Nations has agreed to take up the urgent matter of terrorism and—in the strongest possible terms—I endorse the plea which the Secretary made on behalf of the United States and of human decency.

Also Monday, in Washington, I directed the establishment of a Cabinet Committee to Combat Terrorism—to be chaired by Secretary Rogers—aimed at bringing the full resources of all appropriate United States agencies to bear effectively on the task of eliminating terrorism wherever it occurs.[142] I have charged it to move vigorously and immediately toward this end.

The use of terror is indefensible. It eliminates in one stroke those safeguards of civilization which mankind has painstakingly erected over the centuries.

But terror threatens more than the lives of the innocent. It threatens the very principles upon which nations are founded. In this sense, every nation in the United Nations, whatever its ideological assumptions, whoever its adversaries, wherever its sympathies, is united with every other nation by the common danger to the sovereignty of each. If the world cannot unite in opposition to terror, if we cannot establish some simple ground rules to hold back the perimeters of lawlessness; if, in short, we cannot act to defend the basic principles of national sovereignty in our own individual interests, then upon what foundations can we hope to establish international comity?

There are those who would tell us that terror is the last resort of the weak and the oppressed, a product of despair in an age of indifference, and that it seeks only political justice. This is nonsense. The way to seek justice is through negotiation. We have sought in our own relations to turn from confrontation to negotiation. We believe that this is the only way for grievances to be resolved in a way that will contribute to peace and stability.

In recent months we have seen nations moving to achieve accommodation and the resolution of differences, and we have seen terrorists acting to destroy those efforts. The time has come for civilized people to act in concert to remove the threat of terrorism from the world.

[140] *Presidential Documents*, Oct. 2, 1972, p. 1459.
[141] Document 87.
[142] Cf. above at note 82.

The world is reaching out for peace. The way may be hard and treacherous, but men of reason and decency are determined today, as perhaps never before, to make the effort. Let us not be disrupted or turned away by those who would loose anarchy upon the world; let us seek no accommodations with savagery, but rather act to eliminate it.

3. Action by the General Assembly.

[The proposals put forward by Secretary Rogers and the American delegation were favorably received by various Western and Latin American states but failed to dispel the reservations already expressed by most of the Arab, African, and Communist countries. While willing to authorize continued work on a convention for the protection of diplomats and other officials, these states appeared unwilling to sanction any broad intensification of antiterrorist efforts and effectively stalled the new U.S. initiative regarding the export of terrorism to third countries.

In its first action in this area, the General Assembly by a resolution adopted November 28, 1972 left the question of prevention and punishment of crimes against diplomatic agents and internationally protected persons in the hands of the International Law Commission. Noting with satisfaction the draft articles already prepared by that body, the resolution invited states and intergovernmental organizations to submit written comments and observations and decided that the question of elaborating a possible convention should be taken up at the Assembly's next annual session in 1973.[143]

As an alternative to the program of vigorous action laid down in the U.S. draft convention and resolution (Document 88), a majority of Assembly members preferred to take their cue from the amended agenda item and to shift the emphasis from a direct attack on terrorism to a search for "just and peaceful solutions" for its underlying causes. Led by Algeria, this group brought forward an alternative draft which emphasized study rather than concrete measures and, in the view of U.S. Delegate W. Tapley Bennett, Jr., appeared to signal an intention to take "minimal action rather than meaningful action."[144] Advised by Ambassador Bennett and later by Ambassador George Bush (Document 90a) that the United States would feel compelled to vote against a resolution that offered little beside a 35-nation study committee, the Assembly nonetheless

---

143 Resolution 2926 (XXVII), Nov. 28, 1972, adopted by a vote of 93-0-26 (U.S.); cf. below at notes 154-155.
144 Statement to the Sixth (Legal) Committee, Dec. 11, 1972, in *Bulletin*, Jan. 22, 1973, p. 90.

proceeded on December 18, 1972 to adopt the Algerian resolution in a slightly amended form by a vote of 76 in favor, 35 opposed (including the United States), and 17 abstentions. In what was generally considered the most serious defeat sustained by the United States at the 1972 Assembly session, no vote was taken on either the original U.S. resolution (Document 88b) or a subsequent draft submitted by Italy in an unsuccessful attempt to bridge the gap between the two positions.]

(90) Adoption of the Algerian Resolution, December 18, 1972.

(a) Statement by Ambassador Bush in Plenary Session. [145]

(Complete Text)

International terrorism poses a threat to all mankind—to individuals and to the developmental processes of nations. It poses a threat to the delicately interwoven network of modern transportation and communication facilities on which every country is dependent as it seeks to sustain or improve the life of its citizens. It poses a threat to the postal worker who sorts the mail and to the recipient of those letters. It poses a threat to the passenger who travels on an airplane and to the innocent passerby on the street.

Incidents of terrorist activity causing death and serious injury have taken place in every continent of the world and the islands in between. The dead and injured include the poor as well as the rich, men, women, and children of every race and religion. No one, no one of us, is immune from this scourge of violence.

It is understandable why the Secretary General took the exceptional step of bringing the item before this Assembly. It is understandable why public opinion, moved by a sense of personal involvement as in few other issues, takes a special interest in the problem of international terrorism.

The United Nations was given the opportunity to prove that it was capable of rising to the challenge of this world issue. It is an issue which should have united us in common purpose.

It is therefore with genuine regret that I announce that my delegation will vote against the resolution contained in the report of the Legal Committee.[146] We have only after lengthy and painful soul-searching determined our position. We would very much like to have been able to

145 USUN Press Release 166, Dec. 18, 1972; text from *Bulletin*, Jan. 22, 1973, pp. 92-3.
146 U.N. document A/8969; adopted in slightly amended form as Resolution 3034 (Document 90b).

vote at this 27th Assembly in favor of a resolution on international terrorism, but we could not in good conscience vote affirmatively on the resolution before us.

In order for us to have voted affirmatively, we would have needed a resolution which reflected an accurate and meaningful expression of the attitude of the international community toward random acts of violence which threaten the security of the individual enshrined in the Declaration of Human Rights,[147] which threaten the right to life itself. If acts are to be condemned then surely acts of the type which produced the atrocity of Munich, the killing and wounding of airline pilots and passengers on several continents in incidents which put the lives of hundreds of travelers in mortal danger, letters which explode in the hands of the recipient or maim postmen involved in their duty of serving the public, must be among those condemned. We would also have needed a resolution which established an objective process that could reasonably be expected to lead to concrete measures. We proposed a plenipotentiary conference.[148] Others suggested the International Law Commission as a first step in the process. Neither of these approaches could have deprived states members of the right to determine for themselves precisely what concrete measures they would be willing to take. Yet we find neither approach set forth in the resolution.

The resolution before us fails to meet either of these basic criteria of an adequate expression of community views and a program for future action.

The resolution, moreover, has other serious defects. But now is not the time for recrimination or for bickering over formulations which are so drafted as to be susceptible of being interpreted as aimed at raising rather than lowering the level of violence in our troubled world.

It is incumbent upon all of us to ask ourselves whether the General Assembly has risen to the challenge, whether it has given grounds for believing that it has the ability to respond to the needs of mankind. Does the resolution before us today represent the best we could have achieved? Does it represent the sum of the individual views of states members? Is it a true expression of the general will among us? Does it represent the views expressed by the assembled ministers during the general debate? Has there been an opportunity to negotiate toward the best possible goal? Has each state freely expressed its will on the matter? Can we say that the Assembly is functioning in a way such as to maximize international cooperation? Have we taken full advantage of the rich opportunities afforded by the United Nations system?

These are neither easy nor pleasant questions to have to ask ourselves. We believe the answers are profoundly disturbing.

This session has had some positive achievements, has taken forward

147 Same as note 111.
148 Document 88b.

steps in important fields, such as the human environment, the law of the sea, and earth resource surveying by satellite, that bring hope to us all. It is tragic that an adequate response to the deadly menace of international terrorism is not among the achievements of the 27th General Assembly.

We must not let our failure thus far to find common ground on this problem deter us from the continued search. Those who will continue to be directly associated with the work of this potentially great world body[149] must not lose heart. The time between now and when this Assembly next convenes should be used to demonstrate that this institution need not and must not be a captive of its present failures in this field. We should neither gloss over what has happened nor let our current despondency become a self-fulfilling prophecy of impotence.

The deeper currents of history are not always visible on the surface, but I am convinced that an international community of wider opportunity and greater security for the individual is forming. These currents will continue to flow.

My government will continue its positive efforts to find a solution to the problem of international terrorism through the machinery of the United Nations if at all possible.[150] We call on all other members to join in that effort. For the alternatives to working through the United Nations are bilateral efforts and efforts of groups of states and of individuals. There may be no alternative to such efforts, although we recognize that they can have neither the authority nor the overall effectiveness of measures taken through this great world body. They can only be a pale substitute born of the necessity to take partial steps at a time when broader ones prove impossible. When our inaction here forces states to look outside the United Nations, we weaken the only worldwide mechanism for international cooperation that exists. We deprive mankind of the hopes so eloquently set forth in our charter.

Let us make assets of our current failure. Let us use it as a spur to make the United Nations system function with greater effectiveness on the urgent problems of our day.

---

[149] Ambassador Bush's designation as Republican National Chairman was announced Dec. 11, 1972. He was succeeded as U.S. Permanent Representative to the U.N. by John A. Scali.
[150] Cf. below at notes 153-158.

(b) "Measures to prevent international terrorism which endangers or takes innocent human lives or jeopardizes fundamental freedoms, and study of the underlying causes of those forms of terrorism and acts of violence which lie in misery, frustration, grievance and despair and which cause some people to sacrifice human lives, including their own, in an attempt to effect radical changes": General Assembly Resolution 3034 (XXVII), Adopted December 18, 1972.[151]

(Complete Text)

The General Assembly,

Deeply perturbed over acts of international terrorism which are occurring with increasing frequency and which take a toll of innocent human lives,

Recognizing the importance of international co-operation in devising measures effectively to prevent their occurrence and of studying their underlying causes with a view to finding just and peaceful solutions as quickly as possible,

Recalling the Declaration on Principles of International Law concerning Friendly Relations and Co-operation among States in accordance with the Charter of the United Nations,[152]

1. *Expresses deep concern* over increasing acts of violence which endanger or take innocent human lives or jeopardize fundamental freedoms;

2. *Urges* States to devote their immediate attention to finding just and peaceful solutions to the underlying causes which give rise to such acts of violence;

3. *Reaffirms* the inalienable right to self-determination and independence of all peoples under colonial and racist régimes and other forms of alien domination and upholds the legitimacy of their struggle, in particular the struggle of national liberation movements, in accordance with the purposes and principles of the Charter and the relevant resolutions of the organs of the United Nations;

4. *Condemns* the continuation of repressive and terrorist acts by colonial, racist and alien régimes in denying peoples their legitimate right to self-determination and independence and other human rights and fundamental freedoms;

5. *Invites* States to become parties to the existing international conventions which relate to various aspects of the problem of international terrorism;

6. *Invites* States to take all appropriate measures at the national level

---

151 U.N. General Assembly, *Official Records: 27th Session, Supplement No. 30* (A/8730), p. 119; adopted by a vote of 76-35 (U.S.)-17.
152 Cf. above at note 133.

with a view to the speedy and final elimination of the problem, bearing in mind the provisions of paragraph 3 above;

7. *Invites* States to consider the subject-matter urgently and submit observations to the Secretary-General by 10 April 1973, including concrete proposals for finding an effective solution to the problem;

8. *Requests* the Secretary-General to transmit an analytical study of the observations of States submitted under paragraph 7 above to the *ad hoc* committee to be established under paragraph 9;

9. *Decides* to establish an *Ad Hoc* Committee on International Terrorism consisting of thirty-five members to be appointed by the President of the General Assembly bearing in mind the principle of equitable geographical representation;

10. *Requests* the *Ad Hoc* Committee to consider the observations of States under paragraph 7 above and submit its report with recommendations for possible co-operation for the speedy elimination of the problem, bearing in mind the provisions of paragraph 3, to the General Assembly at its twenty-eighth session;

11. *Requests* the Secretary-General to provide the *Ad Hoc* Committee with the necessary facilities and services;

12. *Decides* to include the item in the provisional agenda of its twenty-eighth session.

4. Summary of 1973-74 Developments.

[Although the United States did not abandon the search for solutions to the problems of international terrorism through the United Nations, the accomplishments of the next two years afforded it but limited satisfaction.

The 35-nation *Ad Hoc* Committee on International Terrorism, set up by the General Assembly resolution of December 18, 1972 (Document 90b), met in New York from July 16 to August 11, 1973 but was unable to agree on any recommendations to the General Assembly for dealing with the problem. The Assembly, acting on the advice of its Sixth (Legal) Committee, decided in December 1973 to postpone the matter to the following session, at which time it was once again postponed to the Assembly's 30th Session in the autumn of 1975.[153]

A more positive achievement was the adoption by the General Assembly in 1973 of the proposed Convention on the Prevention

---

153 *UN Monthly Chronicle*, Aug.-Sept., 1973, pp. 88-9; *Bulletin*, Sept. 3, 1973, pp. 337-9; General Assembly Resolution 3166 (XXVIII), Dec. 14, 1973, approved without objection; decision of December 14, 1974, approved without vote.

and Punishment of Crimes Against Internationally Protected Persons, Including Diplomatic Agents.[154] As drafted by the International Law Commission and accepted by the Assembly, the convention provides among other things for the extradition or prosecution of alleged offenders in cases of murder, kidnapping, or other attacks against heads of state or government, foreign ministers and other diplomatic representatives. Adopted without objection by the General Assembly on December 14, 1973, it was signed by the United States December 28, 1973 and approved by the Senate October 28, 1975.[155] Entry into force requires ratification or accession by 22 states, but only ten states had become parties as of November 1975.

The quest for more effective multilateral safeguards against aircraft hijacking and sabotage yielded few positive results except for the belated entry into force of the Montreal anti-sabotage convention on January 26, 1973.[156] The Legal Committee of the I.C.A.O., which held its previously scheduled meeting in Montreal on January 8-30, 1973, declined to approve the stringent measures recommended by the United States and Canada and recommended instead that further consideration be given either to a milder draft convention or to an appropriate amendment to the basic 1944 Convention on International Civil Aviation.[157] But a subsequent I.C.A.O. conference held in Rome on August 28-September 21, 1973— technically, a combined International Conference on Air Law and Extraordinary I.C.A.O. Assembly—proved "unable to agree upon any of the proposals . . . designed to enhance the security of civil aviation."[158] On a bilateral basis, however, the United States and Cuba by an agreement reached February 15, 1973 undertook a reciprocal obligation to prosecute or extradite persons involved in hijacking of aircraft or vessels.[159]]

154 Opened for signature at New York Dec. 14, 1973 (S. Ex. L, 93d Cong., 2d sess.); text, annexed to General Assembly Resolution 3166 (XXVIII), in *Bulletin*, Jan. 28, 1974, pp. 92-5.
155 General Assembly Resolution 3166 (XXVIII), Dec. 14, 1973, adopted without objection; *Presidential Documents*, Nov. 18, 1974, p. 1438.
156 Cf. above at note 81.
157 Done at Chicago Dec. 7, 1944 and entered into force Apr. 4, 1947 (TIAS 1591); text in *Documents, 1944-45*, pp. 585-607.
158 *Bulletin*, June 18, 1973, pp. 872-5; same, Oct. 29, 1973, pp. 550-51.
159 TIAS 7579 (24 UST 737); text in *Bulletin*, Mar. 5, 1973, pp. 260-62 (correction in same, Mar. 26, 1973, p. 372).

X

INTERNATIONAL ECONOMIC
AND
FINANCIAL AFFAIRS

[In international economic and monetary affairs, the year 1972 marks a period of uneasy transition between the turbulent developments surrounding the United States' "New Economic Policy" of 1971 and the more profound disturbances that accompanied and followed the Middle East war of 1973.[1]

Dominating the international economic landscape throughout this period were the varied obligations assumed in the Smithsonian Agreement of December 18, 1971, when the United States had accepted an 8.57 percent devaluation of the dollar, and other countries had made comparable adjustments, in preparation for negotiations on a general reform of trade and monetary relationships.[2] The creation of a suitable frame for such negotiations continued to occupy the leading industrial and financial powers through much of 1972. Their task was complicated by a variety of factors, among them the persistent instability of relationships among the major currencies; continued U.S.-European tensions, centering primarily around the policies of the European Economic Community (E.E.C.) and the expected entry of Denmark, Ireland, and the United Kingdom into that grouping on January 1, 1973;[3] the continuing demands of developing, "third world" countries for more generous attention to their economic and financial problems; and the still

---

[1] For more detailed discussion, cf. Nixon Report, 1972, pp. 60-79; same, 1973, pp. 162-75; Rogers Report, 1972, pp. 1-70.

[2] *A.F.R., 1971*, no. 150. The change in the par value of the dollar from one thirty-fifth to one thirty-eighth of a fine troy ounce of gold became effective May 8, 1972 pursuant to provisions of the Par Value Modification Act (Public Law 92-268, Mar. 31, 1972; for details, see *Bulletin*, Apr. 24, 1972, pp. 597-8; same, June 12, 1972, p. 808). A further, 10 percent reduction in the par value of the dollar was announced Feb. 12, 1973 (same, Mar. 12, 1973, pp. 298-305), and the new par value of "0.828948 Special Drawing Right or, the equivalent in terms of gold, of forty-two and two-ninths dollars per fine troy ounce of gold" was formally established by Public Law 93-110 of Sept. 21, 1973.

[3] For detailed discussion, cf. Document 20 and *Bulletin*, Mar. 27, 1972, pp. 484-8.

precarious state of the American economy as it struggled out of its 1970-71 recession.

Although the United States' gross national product (G.N.P.) increased from $1,055 million in 1971 to $1,158 million in 1972, with unemployment decreasing and inflation remaining within relatively manageable limits, the trade deficit which had first appeared in 1971 widened from $2 billion in that year to $6.3 billion in 1972, and the balance of payments again was heavily in deficit by all current measures. Hopes for a permanent, long-term improvement in America's international economic position thus remained bound up to a large extent with the trade and monetary negotiations on which the United States had insisted as the price of devaluing the dollar.

Contrary to U.S. hopes that a special negotiating forum could be established to deal concurrently with both trade and monetary issues, it was agreed in the course of the year that the projected negotiations on monetary reform would take place under the auspices of the International Monetary Fund (I.M.F.), while those on trade would go forward under the General Agreement on Tariffs and Trade (GATT). Serious discussions in both areas, it was anticipated, would get under way in 1973, although this expectation failed to take account of the new complications that were to arise in the course of that year.

The development of these questions through 1972 can be traced in the records of such key international bodies as the Organization for Economic Cooperation and Development (O.E.C.D.), the International Bank for Reconstruction and Development (I.B.R.D.) and International Monetary Fund (I.M.F.), and the General Agreement on Tariffs and Trade (GATT). Also documented in this chapter are the essentials of U.S. policy with respect to international development problems, a continuing concern of the international community that was in no way lessened by the current stress on trade and monetary matters.]

A. The Organization for Economic Cooperation and Development (O.E.C.D.): Meeting of the Council at Ministerial Level, Paris, May 24-26, 1972.

[As the first high-level encounter among developed nations since the Smithsonian Agreement of December 1971, the annual ministerial meeting of the O.E.C.D. Council in May 1972 was dominated by discussions of the contemplated reconstruction of the international monetary system, further liberalization of world trade, and the degree of linkage or separation to be maintained between these two endeavors. A sense of the essential interdependence of trade and monetary affairs inspired a proposal by the U.S. delegation, headed on this occasion by Under Secretary of State John N. Irwin II, that a special coordinating group be formed within O.E.C.D. to serve as an "umbrella" for the monetary negotiations to be carried on under the I.M.F. and the trade negotiations that were expected to take place under GATT. Although the American plan was not adopted, the Paris meeting marked a further stage in the O.E.C.D.'s developing emphasis on policy-level consultations regarding international trade, money and investment, and the relationship between internal economic policies and international transactions. Other notable aspects of the Paris meeting, as recorded in the official communiqué (Document 92), included a brief statement by Under Secretary Irwin about the emerging international energy problem (Document 91) and the approval of a formal Recommendation on Environmental Policies (Document 93) which testified to the growing international awareness of environmental problems on the eve of the U.N. environmental conference in Stockholm.[4]]

(91) The Coming Energy Crisis: Statement by Under Secretary of State Irwin, Head of the United States Delegation, May 26, 1972.[5]

(Complete Text)

Secretary General [Emile] van Lennep is to be commended for the initiative he has taken in bringing the Organization's attention to the developing world crisis in energy. We are in close agreement with his view of the implications of such a crisis for the world economic order.

This is a subject which we in the United States have recently been examining with increasing concern. We are now convinced that before the end of the present decade the United States and the other industrial countries of the world will face an energy shortage, possibly a serious one, in degree depending on the measures undertaken largely by the countries assembled here today.

During the 1950's, the United States was a net exporter of petroleum. Since 1967, however, we have become dependent on imports to the extent that today productive capacity in the United States would not be able to offset an interruption in our import supply. The figures indicate that U.S. domestic production has peaked out this year and that the trend of production will now be gradually downward, with the

---

[4] Cf. Documents 83-85.
[5] *Bulletin*, June 19, 1972, pp. 834-6. For a more detailed statement, cf. same, May 1, 1972, pp. 626-31.

result that by 1980 production of oil in the "lower" 48 States will be some 2 million barrels per day less than it is today.

The requirements for energy, moreover, and specifically for oil to supply that energy, are not standing still. By 1980, demand for oil in the United States is projected to rise from today's 16 million barrels per day to some 24 million barrels. Even with the Alaskan North Slope fields producing their expected 2 million barrels per day, production in the United States will probably be no more than what it is now—12 million barrels per day. Thus, an equal amount—50 percent of our entire consumption, or three times our present daily level of imports— will have to come from abroad.

The situation is little different in other major industrial areas. Western Europe, which today consumes some 12 million barrels per day, is expected to consume double that amount of oil by 1980. With luck, the North Sea fields may then be producing as much as 3 million barrels daily. The European members of the OECD will nevertheless have to import over 20 million barrels per day, roughly double their present import level. In the case of Japan, some figures we have seen indicate that the increase in consumption will be, if anything, even more startling. The present daily intake of just under 4 million barrels, virtually all of it imported, may rise by 1980 to as much as 10 million barrels.

Thus the OECD nations alone may well be confronted with a requirement for 26 million more barrels of oil per day by the end of this decade. This increase is almost equal to the combined present consumption of the United States and all European members of the OECD.

Most of this oil can come from only one source: the Middle East. Thus what is today regarded by many OECD members as an uncomfortable degree of dependence on the Middle East will by 1980 be far, far greater. In the case of the United States, imports from the Middle East today are negligible; by 1980 they could well entail 7 million or more barrels per day. They need not if we take effective measures now. Even so, we will still import substantial quantities by 1980.

Even if we make the most optimistic assumptions about political relations in and with the Middle East, governments there and elsewhere may be unwilling, for reasons of conservation or whatever, to supply the enormous new quantities of oil which will be needed. Libya has already cut production drastically. Kuwait and Venezuela have barred further increases in offtake. Other major producers give promise of following their lead. We are faced, therefore, with the real possibility of a major free-world shortfall of oil by 1980. Some estimates put this shortfall at close to 20 million barrels per day. An actual shortage, even of lesser proportions, would face us with a serious situation in which all of the countries represented at this table might well find themselves competing for the available supply. Such competition would inevitably be accompanied by further sharp increases in petroleum prices, by economic disruption in major consuming countries, and by particularly serious consequences for developing countries, except those fortunate few who have their own indigenous energy resources.

We are faced, therefore, with a challenge which is unprecedented. To meet the challenge, it is imperative for the world's major consumers of oil and other forms of energy to take joint and coordinated action—starting now—to increase the availability of all types of energy resources; to lessen, to the degree possible, an overdependence on oil from the Middle East; to coordinate the response of consuming countries to restrictions on the supply of Middle East petroleum; and to develop, jointly and cooperatively, a responsible program of action to meet the possibility of critical energy shortages by the end of this decade.

We believe that the OECD, which includes all the major energy consumers of the non-Communist world, is the logical forum for the development of such a program. The Secretary General, in his excellent memorandum, has suggested that the resources of the Organization be directed to a study of the world energy situation. We concur in this suggestion as an important step toward arriving at a common and widely accepted view of the problem.

We would hope and urge that the Organization's labors could be completed as soon as possible and that the study would produce concrete recommendations for action which would engage the attention of member governments at the highest political level. For this reason, we recommend that the Organization's world energy study be carried out under the direction of a prestigious body of senior, policy-level officials from capitals.

We believe that such a body already exists—the High Level Group of OECD's Oil Committee. The High Level Oil Group's record of dealing decisively with serious issues is unquestioned. It attracts senior, policy-level officials who are particularly well versed in oil, where the coming energy crisis will strike first, but whose responsibilities include the entire energy field. We would hope that the High Level Oil Group, in giving direction to the Organization's study and formulating recommendations in the light of its conclusions, would meet from time to time at or near the ministerial level and that it would not hesitate to recommend actions of substantial economic and political impact.

The urgency of the developing world energy crisis surely dictates that the time for our governments to take action is now. The place for such action, we believe, is a forum within the context of this institution which offers full scope for effective international cooperation among us.

(92) Communiqué of the Council Meeting.[6]

(Complete Text)

1. The Council of the O.E.C.D. met at Ministerial level in Paris on 24th, 25th and 26th May, 1972, under the Chairmanship of Mr. George Colley, Minister for Finance of Ireland.

The International Economic Situation

2. In considering the international economic situation, Ministers discussed Member countries' prospects and policies for the year ahead. They noted the expansionary policies already adopted and expressed the resolve of their Governments to restore, as soon as possible, high employment in the O.E.C.D. area. At the same time, Ministers reaffirmed the determination of their Governments to achieve further progress towards price stability. These prospects provide an appropriate setting for the adjustments to international balances of payments put in train by the realignment of currencies agreed upon in December 1971.[7]

International Monetary and Trade Issues

3. Ministers exchanged views on issues connected with forthcoming discussions and negotiations in the International Monetary Fund on monetary reform and in the framework of the GATT on international trade.

4. Ministers directed the Organisation to continue its work in the balance of payments field as a valuable contribution to international economic cooperation. Particular attention should be given to the balance of payments aims of Member countries, to the respective responsibilities for balance of payments adjustment of surplus and deficit countries, and to the problems of dealing with short-term capital flows.

5. Ministers noted with satisfaction the wide support given to the initiative taken by the European Economic Community, Japan and the United States to initiate in 1973 multilateral and comprehensive negotiations in the GATT, covering both industrial and agricultural trade.[8] The Organisation will continue to give consideration to the contribution which it could make, within its field of competence, to further progress in the liberalisation of trade.

6. Ministers heard an oral statement by Mr. Jean Rey, Chairman of the High Level Trade Group, formed by the Secretary-General fol-

---

[6] *Bulletin*, June 19, 1972, p. 836.
[7] Cf. *A.F.R., 1971*, no. 150.
[8] Cf. below at notes 27-28.

lowing the decision taken at the Meeting of the O.E.C.D. Council at Ministerial level in June 1971. They thanked Mr. Rey for the information given on the work of the Group and expressed appreciation for its efforts. They noted that the Group would submit its report at an early date.[9]

7. Ministers exchanged views on the issues arising in the areas of trade and international monetary reform and recognised that some important issues arise from their inter-relationship. They agreed that the O.E.C.D. has an important role to play in analysing and consulting on international monetary, trade, investment and related economic issues, including particularly their inter-relationships, and gave guidance on the way in which the Organisation can contribute to the progress of discussions on these issues.

8. Ministers stressed the importance of giving full attention to the views and interests of developing countries in the forthcoming discussions and negotiations. They also stressed the importance of the pursuit by O.E.C.D. countries of vigorous and forward-looking policies for development co-operation, including the provision of increased amounts of aid.

Environmental Policies

9. Ministers noted the progress of O.E.C.D. work on environmental problems and policies. They adopted a Council Recommendation[10] defining a set of guiding principles, the application of which by Member countries should reinforce the effectiveness of environmental policies, and should avoid distortions in international trade and other economic relations that might arise from pollution control measures.

Energy Policies

10. Bearing in mind the work on energy policies already carried out in the Organisation, Ministers approved a proposal by the Secretary-General to undertake an overall assessment of long-term energy problems, that might assist in the formulation of Member countries' energy policies in their domestic and international aspects. This analysis should take account of a variety of factors, such as energy demand, natural resource availability and accessibility, technological innovation and protection of the environment.

[9] For the communiqué of the June 1971 meeting, see *A.F.R., 1971*, no. 141b. The report of the High-level Group on Trade and Related Problems was published Sept. 5, 1972 under the title *Policy Perspectives for International Trade and Economic Relations* (Paris: O.E.C.D., 1972).
[10] Document 93b.

(93) Recommendation on the Environment.

(a) Department of State Announcement, June 1, 1972. [11]

(Complete Text)

Guiding principles designed to avoid distortions in international trade and other economic relations which might arise from differences in member countries pollution control measures were adopted at the May 24-26 Ministerial level meeting of the Organization for Economic Cooperation and Development.

The United States believes these principles represent an important first step in avoiding possible distortions and new barriers to international trade and investment among OECD members who account for about two-thirds of world trade. The principles also should help strengthen environmental protection since OECD countries will be less inhibited in taking necessary pollution control actions by concerns about placing their industries at a serious competitive disadvantage.

The guiding principles follow the general recommendations of the President's Commission on International Trade and Investment Policy. Among other things, they provide that OECD countries should observe the polluter-pays-principle in financing the costs of pollution control measures. In effect this means the costs of these measures should be reflected in the prices of the goods and services which cause pollution and the use of subsidies and similar devices to cover such costs should be avoided. The guidelines also call on governments to adopt more stringent standards to strengthen environmental protection and to seek the harmonization of environmental policies where valid reasons for differences do not exist. That is, governments facing essentially similar threats to their environment should adopt comparable controls and not seek to gain trade advantages at the expense of their environment. The principles further call on governments to frame their environmental policies so as to avoid the creation of new non-[tariff] barriers to trade.

To help ensure the effective implementation of the guidelines, a notification and consultation procedure is to be devised so that countries can confront each other regarding their environmental policies and practices.

Text of the guiding principles as adopted by the Ministerial Meeting of the OECD follows: [12]

11 Department of State Press Release 130, June 1, 1972.
12 Document 93b, Annex.

(b) Recommendation on Guiding Principles Concerning Environmental Policies. [13]

(Complete Text)

The Council

Having regard to Article 5(b) of the Convention on the Organisation for Economic Co-operation and Development of 14th December, 1960;[14]

Having regard to the Resolution of the Council of 22nd July, 1970 Establishing an Environment Committee [C(70)135] ;

Having regard to the Report by the Environment Committee on Guiding Principles Concerning the International Economic Aspects of Environmental Policies [C(72)69] ;

Having regard to the views expressed by interested committees;

Having regard to the Note by the Secretary-General [C(72)122 (Final)] ;

I. RECOMMENDS that the Governments of Member countries should, in determining environmental control policies and measures, observe the "Guiding Principles Concerning the International Economic Aspects of Environmental Policies" set forth in the Annex to this Recommendation.

II. INSTRUCTS the Environment Committee to review as it deems appropriate the implementation of this Recommendation.

III. INSTRUCTS the Environment Committee to recommend as soon as possible the adoption of appropriate mechanisms for notification and/or consultation or some other appropriate form of action.

ANNEX

GUIDING PRINCIPLES CONCERNING THE INTERNATIONAL
ECONOMIC ASPECTS OF ENVIRONMENTAL POLICIES

Introduction

1. The guiding principles described below concern mainly the international aspects of environmental policies with particular reference to their economic and trade implications. These principles do not cover for instance, the particular problems which may arise during the transitional periods following the implementation of the principles, instru-

---

[13] O.E.C.D. document C(72)122(Final); text from *Bulletin*, June 19, 1972, pp. 837-8.

[14] Signed at Paris Dec. 14, 1960 and entered into force Sept. 30, 1961 (TIAS 4891; 12 UST 1728); text in *Documents, 1960*, pp. 332-42.

ments for the implementation of the so-called "Polluter-Pays Principle", exceptions to this principle, trans-frontier pollution, or possible problems related to developing countries.

A. GUIDING PRINCIPLES

(a) Cost Allocation: the Polluter-Pays Principle

2. Environmental resources are in general limited and their use in production and consumption activities may lead to their deterioration. When the cost of this deterioration is not adequately taken into account in the price system, the market fails to reflect the scarcity of such resources both at the national and international levels. Public measures are thus necessary to reduce pollution and to reach a better allocation of resources by ensuring that prices of goods depending on the quality and/or quantity of environmental resources reflect more closely their relative scarcity and that economic agents concerned react accordingly.

3. In many circumstances, in order to ensure that the environment is in an acceptable state, the reduction of pollution beyond a certain level will not be practical or even necessary in view of the costs involved.

4. The principle to be used for allocating costs of pollution prevention and control measures to encourage rational use of scarce environmental resources and to avoid distortions in international trade and investment is the so-called "Polluter-Pays Principle". This Principle means that the polluter should bear the expenses of carrying out the above mentioned measures decided by public authorities to ensure that the environment is in an acceptable state. In other words, the cost of these measures should be reflected in the cost of goods and services which cause pollution in production and/or consumption. Such measures should not be accompanied by subsidies that would create significant distortions in international trade and investment.

5. This Principle should be an objective of Member countries; however, there may be exceptions or special arrangements, particularly for the transitional periods, provided that they do not lead to significant distortions in international trade and investment.

(b) Environmental Standards

6. Differing national environmental policies, for example with regard to the tolerable amount of pollution and to quality and emission standards, are justified by a variety of factors including among other things different pollution assimilative capacities of the environment in its present state, different social objectives and priorities attached to envi-

ronmental protection and different degrees of industrialisation and population density.

7. In view of this, a very high degree of harmonisation of environmental policies which would be otherwise desirable may be difficult to achieve in practice; however it is desirable to strive towards more stringent standards in order to strengthen environmental protection, particularly in cases where less stringent standards would not be fully justified by the above mentioned factors.

8. Where valid reasons for differences do not exist, Governments should seek harmonisation of environmental policies, for instance with respect to timing and the general scope of regulation for particular industries to avoid the unjustified disruption of international trade patterns and of the international allocation of resources which may arise from diversity of national environmental standards.

9. Measures taken to protect the environment should be framed as far as possible in such a manner as to avoid the creation of non-tariff barriers to trade.

10. Where products are traded internationally and where there could be significant obstacles to trade, Governments should seek common standards for polluting products and agree on the timing and general scope of regulations for particular products.

—National Treatment and Non-Discrimination

11. In conformity with the provisions of the GATT, measures taken within an environmental policy, regarding polluting products, should be applied in accordance with the principle of national treatment (i.e. identical treatment for imported products and similar domestic products) and with the principle of non-discrimination (identical treatment for imported products regardless of their national origin).

—Procedures of Control

12. It is highly desirable to define in common, as rapidly as possible, procedures for checking conformity to product standards established for the purpose of environmental control. Procedures for checking conformity to standards should be mutually agreed so as to be applied by an exporting country to the satisfaction of the importing country.

—Compensating Import Levies and Export Rebates

13. In accordance with the provisions of the GATT, differences in environmental policies should not lead to the introduction of compensating import levies or export rebates, or measures having an equivalent effect, designed to offset the consequences of these differences on

prices. Effective implementation of the guiding principles set forth herewith will make it unnecessary and undesirable to resort to such measures.

B. CONSULTATIONS

14. Consultations on the above mentioned principles should be pursued. In connection with the application of these guiding principles, a specific mechanism of consultation and/or notification or some other appropriate form of action should be determined as soon as possible taking into account the work done by other international organizations.

B. The International Bank and Monetary Fund: Annual Meeting of the Boards of Governors, Washington, September 25-29, 1972.

[Plans for the needed reconstruction of the international monetary system originally created in the closing months of World War II were the principal concern of the annual meeting of the Boards of Governors of the International Bank for Reconstruction and Development (I.B.R.D.) and the International Monetary Fund (I.M.F.), held in Washington in late September 1972 at a period when international monetary relationships, temporarily stabilized by the Smithsonian Agreement of December 1971, were exhibiting renewed volatility as evidenced by the floating of the pound sterling on June 23, 1972 and the readjustment of other exchange rates in agreement with international monetary authorities.

Although the selection of the I.M.F. as the sole forum for monetary reform negotiations had represented a setback to U.S. hopes of maintaining an organic link between the coming monetary and trade negotiations, American views were accorded great weight in the actual negotiating arrangements established within the Fund and publicly made known on July 28, 1972.[15] Ultimate responsibility was entrusted to a special, twenty-member *ad hoc* committee of the Board of Governors, the so-called Committee of Twenty, which would be so constituted as to give representation to both developed and developing countries and was to be chaired by Indonesian Finance Minister Ali Wardhana. The task of actually drafting the outlines of a monetary reform plan was assigned to the committee's deputies, also twenty in number, who were chaired by C. Jeremy Morse, an executive director of the Bank of England.

The relatively optimistic outlook prevailing at the Governor's

15 *IMF Survey*, Aug. 14, 1972, p. 3.

meeting was attributable not only to the successful completion of these arrangements but also to the relatively constructive posture adopted by the United States after what some had considered its egocentric behavior of the previous year. American views on the projected monetary reform, as outlined to delegates by President Nixon (Document 94) and Secretary of the Treasury George P. Shultz (Document 95), particularly stressed the obligation of surplus as well as deficit countries to take appropriate adjustment action when their payments were out of balance. But while this view continued to encounter resistance on the part of some other developed countries, it was widely anticipated that the differences could be sufficiently narrowed to permit the outlines of a reform plan to be presented at the ensuing annual meeting of the Board of Governors, to be held in Nairobi, Kenya, on September 24-28, 1973.

Inevitably, the completion of such plans was delayed by the deepening international financial crisis that accompanied the fourfold increase in world petroleum prices in 1973-74. Not until June 13, 1974 was the Committee of Twenty able to complete its work with the issuance of a series of recommendations that included, among other things, the establishment of an Interim Committee of the I.M.F. Board of Governors to continue the quest for basic reform of the international monetary system.[16]]

(94) Remarks by President Nixon at the Opening Session, September 25, 1972.[17]

(Complete Text)

Mr. Secretary [of the Treasury], distinguished guests, Governors, ladies and gentlemen:
I have had the privilege of visiting most of the 124 countries represented here in this distinguished audience, and on this occasion I would like to extend my welcome to you, my best wishes to the heads of government that I have also had the privilege to meet, and particularly the best wishes of the American people to all of the people of the many countries represented at this gathering.

It is customary in addressing such a significant international gathering to say that we are participating in a great moment of history. Great moments in history are easy to perceive. The headlines blaze and the world is riveted at television screens as world leaders meet. But great movements in history are much harder to perceive, and particularly while we are living through them. The action is slower, it is less dra-

16 Same, June 17, 1974, pp. 177-208.
17 *Presidential Documents*, Oct. 2, 1972, pp. 1446-50.

matic, it is infinitely more complex as changing circumstances and the new needs of people alter the behavior of nations.

I am convinced, on the basis of the evidence of the past year, that we are not only participating today in a great moment in history but that we are witnessing and helping to create a profound movement in history.

That movement is away from the resolution of potential conflict by war, and toward its resolution through peaceful means. The experienced people gathered in this room are not so naive as to expect the smoothing out of all differences between peoples and between nations. We anticipate that the potential for conflict will exist as long as men and nations have different interests, different approaches, different ideals.

Therefore, we must come to grips with the paradoxes of peace. As the danger of armed conflict between major powers is reduced, the potential for economic conflict increases. As the possibility of peace grows stronger, some of the original ties that first bound our postwar alliances together grow weaker. As nations around the world gain new economic strength, the points of commercial contact multiply along with the possibilities of disagreements.

There is another irony that we should recognize on this occasion. With one exception, the nations gathered here whose domestic economies are growing so strongly today can trace much of their postwar growth to the expansion of international trade. The one exception is the United States—the industrial nation with by far the smallest percentage of its gross national product in world trade.

Why, then, is the United States—seemingly with the least at stake—in the forefront of those working for prompt and thoroughgoing reform of the international monetary system, with all that will mean for the expansion of trade now and in the future?

One reason, of course, is our national self-interest. We want our working men and women, our business men and women, to have a fair chance to compete for their share of the expanding trade between nations. A generation ago, at the end of World War II, we deliberately set out to help our former enemies as well as our weakened allies, so that they would inevitably gain the economic strength which would enable them to compete with us in world markets. And now we expect our trading partners to help bring about equal and fair competition.

There is another reason, more far-reaching and fundamental, that motivates the United States in pressing for economic and monetary reform.

Working together, we must set in place an economic structure that will help and not hinder the world's historic movement toward peace.

We must make certain that international commerce becomes a source of stability and harmony, rather than a cause of friction and animosity.

Potential conflict must be channeled into cooperative competition. That is why the structure of the international monetary system and the future system of world trade are so central to our concerns today. The time has come for action across the entire front of international economic problems. Recurring monetary crises such as we have experienced all too often in the past decade, unfair currency alignments and trading agreements which put the workers of one nation at a disadvantage with workers of another nation, great disparities in development that breed resentment, a monetary system that makes no provision for the realities of the present and the needs of the future—all these not only injure our economies; they also create political tensions that subvert the cause of peace.

There must be a thoroughgoing reform of the world monetary system to clear the path for the healthy economic competition of the future.

We must see monetary reform as one part of a total reform of international economic affairs encompassing trade and investment opportunity for all.

We must create a realistic code of economic conduct to guide our mutual relations—a code which allows governments freedom to pursue legitimate domestic objectives, but which also gives them good reason to abide by agreed principles of international behavior.

Each nation must exercise the power of its example in the realistic and orderly conduct of internal economic affairs so that each nation exports its products and not its problems.

We can all agree that the health of the world economy and the stability of the international economic system rests largely on the successful management of domestic economies. The United States recognizes the importance of a strong, non-inflationary domestic economy, both in meeting the needs of our own citizens and in contributing to a healthy world economy. We are firmly committed to reaching our goals in this country of strong growth, full employment, price stability.

We are encouraged by the record of our current economic performance. We are now experiencing one of the lowest rates of inflation, one of the highest rates of real economic growth, of any industrial nation.

Recent gains in the productivity and the real income of American workers have been heartening. We intend to continue the policies that have produced those gains.

We also recognize that over the longer term, domestic policies alone cannot solve international problems. Even if all countries achieved a very large measure of success in managing their own economies, strains and tensions could arise at points of contact with other economies.

We cannot afford a system that almost every year presents a new invitation to a monetary crisis in the world. And that is why we face the need to develop procedures for prompt and orderly adjustment.

It is very easy for me to use the term "prompt and orderly adjustment." And many would say that that is a term that only concerns bankers and finance ministers and economists. But that phrase "prompt and orderly adjustment" in international monetary matters encompasses the real problems of working men and women, the fears and hopes of investors and managers of large and small businesses, and, consequently, it is the concern of the political leadership of every nation represented in this group today. No nation should be denied the opportunity to adjust, nor relieved of the obligation to adjust.

In the negotiations ahead, there will be differences of opinion and approaches. You saw some of those differences at the Smithsonian not a year ago, even. I had the opportunity to see them at another level in meetings with President Pompidou in the Azores, with Prime Minister Heath at Bermuda, with Chancellor Brandt in Florida,[18] with Prime Minister Sato in California,[19] and I know how intricate, how difficult the problems are that you will be considering at these meetings. Immediate interests inevitably will seem to be in conflict, and there will be times when impasses develop that may seem impossible to resolve.

But the world has had some experience recently with long, hard negotiations, and I refer in another field to a long, hard negotiation—the strategic arms limitation agreements signed by the Soviet Union and the United States early this summer.[20]

Now, that was bilateral negotiation. It involved just two nations, not 124. But its complexity, when those negotiations began 3 years or so ago, seemed almost infinite; the obstacles had been hardening for over 25 years; the issue of national security for each nation was as sensitive a matter as can exist in negotiations between two powers.

We came to an agreement in Moscow, nevertheless, because the issue that united us—seeking an end to the wasteful and dangerous arms race—was greater than the issues that divided us.

We reached agreement because we realized that it was impossible for either side to negotiate an advantage over the other that would prevail. The only agreement worth making was one in which each side had a stake in keeping.

Now, these two principles can guide us in building the monetary system of the future.

We recognize that the issues that divide us are many and they are very serious and infinitely complex and difficult. But the impetus that will make this negotiation successful is the force that unites us all, all the 124 nations represented here today: That is a common need to establish a sound and abiding foundation for commerce, leading to a better way of life for all the citizens of all the nations here and all the citizens of the world.

[18] *A.F.R., 1971*, nos. 43-45.
[19] Document 62.
[20] Documents 13-14.

The common need, let us call it the world interest, demands a new freedom of world trade, a new fairness in international economic conduct.

It is a mark of our maturity that we now see that an unfair advantage gained in an agreement today only sabotages that agreement tomorrow.

I well remember when I was a first-year law student, 32 years ago, what the professor of contracts said as he opened the course. He said, "A contract is only as good as the will of the parties to keep it."

The only system that can work is one that each nation has an active interest in making work. The need is self-evident. The will to reform the monetary system is here in this room and, in a proverb that has its counterpart in almost every language here, where there is a will there is a way.

We are gathered to create a responsible monetary system, responsive to the need for stability and openness, and responsive to the need of each country to reflect its unique character.

In this way we bring to bear one of the great lessons of federalism: that often the best way to enforce an agreed-upon discipline is to let each member take action to adhere to it in the way that is best suited to its local character, its stage of development, its economic structure.

For its part, I can assure you, the United States will continue to rise to its world responsibilities, joining with other nations to create and participate in a modern world economic order.

We are secure enough in our independence to freely assert our interdependence.

These are the principles that I profoundly believe should and will guide the United States in its international economic conduct now and in the years ahead.

We shall press for a more equitable and a more open world of trade. We shall meet competition rather than run away from it.

We shall be a stimulating trading partner, a straightforward bargainer.

We shall not turn inward and isolationist.

In turn we shall look to our friends for evidence of similar rejection of isolationism in economic and political affairs.

Let us all resolve to look at the ledgers of international commerce today with new eyes—to see that there is no heroism in a temporary surplus nor villainy in a temporary deficit, but to see that progress is possible only in the framework of long-term equilibrium. In this regard we must take bold action toward a more equitable and a more open world trading order.

Like every leader of the nations represented here, I want to see new jobs created all over the world, but I cannot condone the export of jobs out of the United States caused by any unfairness built into the world's trading system.

Let all nations in the more advanced stages of industrial development share the responsibility of helping those countries whose major development lies ahead, and let the great industrial nations, in offering that help, in providing it, forgo the temptation to use that help as an instrument of domination, discrimination, or rivalry.

Far more is at stake here than the mechanics of commerce and finance. At stake is the chance to add genuine opportunity to the lives of people, hundreds of millions of people in all nations, the chance to add stability and security to the savings and earnings of hundreds of millions of people in all of our nations, the chance to add economic muscle to the sinews of peace.

I have spoken this morning in general terms about how we can advance our economic interdependence. Later this week, Secretary Shultz will outline a number of proposals which represent the best thinking of my top economic advisers.[21] I commend those proposals to you for your careful consideration.

The word "economics," traced to its Greek root, means "the law of the house."

This house we live in—this community of nations—needs far better laws to guide our future economic conduct. Every nation can prosper and benefit working within a modern world economic order that it has a stake in preserving.

Now, very little of what is done in these negotiations will be widely understood in this country or in any of your countries as well. And very little of it will be generally appreciated.

But history will record the vital nature of the challenge before us. I am confident that the men and the nations gathered here will seize the opportunity to create a monetary and trading system that will work for the coming generation—and will help to shape the years ahead into a generation of peace for all nations in the world.

(95) American Views on International Monetary Reform: Statement by Secretary of the Treasury George P. Shultz, September 26, 1972.[22]

(Complete Text)

The nations gathered here have it in their power to strike a new balance in international economic affairs.

The new balance of which I speak does not confine itself to the concepts of a balance of trade or a balance of payments. The world needs a new balance between flexibility and stability in its basic ap-

---

[21] Cf. Document 95.
[22] Department of the Treasury Press Release, Sept. 26, 1972; text from *Bulletin*, Oct. 23, 1972, pp. 460-66.

proach to doing business. The world needs a new balance between a unity of purpose and a diversity of execution that will permit nations to cooperate closely without losing their individuality or sovereignty.

We lack that balance today. Success in the negotiations in which we are engaged will be measured in terms of how well we are able to achieve that balance in the future.

I anticipate working closely and intensively with you to that end, shaping and re-shaping the best of our thinking as we proceed in full recognition that the legitimate requirements of each nation must be meshed into a harmonious whole.

In that spirit, President Nixon has asked me to put certain ideas before you.

In so doing, I must necessarily concentrate my remarks today on monetary matters. However, I am deeply conscious that in approaching this great task of monetary reform we cannot neglect the needs of economic development. I am also conscious that the success of our development efforts will ultimately rest in large measure on our ability to achieve and maintain a monetary and trading environment in which all nations can prosper and profit from the flows of goods, services, and investment among us.

The formation of the Committee of Twenty, representing the entire membership of the Fund, properly reflects and symbolizes the fact that we are dealing with issues of deep interest to all members and in particular that the concerns of developing countries will be fully reflected in discussions of the reform of the monetary system.

As we enter into negotiations in that group, we have before us the useful report of the Executive Directors, identifying and clarifying some of the basic issues which need to be resolved.

We also look forward to participation by other international organizations, with each contributing where it is most qualified to help. The challenge before us calls for substantial modification of the institutions and practices over the entire range of international economic cooperation.

There have already been stimulating contributions to our thinking from a wide variety of other sources, public and private. I have examined with particular care the statements made over the past few months by other Governors individually and the eight points which emerged from the deliberations of the Finance Ministers of the European Community.

PRINCIPLES UNDERLYING MONETARY REFORM

Drawing from this interchange of views, and building upon the Smithsonian agreement,[23] we can now seek a firm consensus for new mone-

23 *A.F.R., 1971,* no. 150.

tary arrangements that will serve us all in the decades ahead. Indeed, I believe certain principles underlying monetary reform already command widespread support.

First is our mutual interest in encouraging freer trade in goods and services and the flow of capital to the places where it can contribute most to economic growth. We must avoid a breakup of the world into antagonistic blocs. We must not seek a refuge from our problems behind walls of protectionism.

The pursuit of the common welfare through more open trade is threatened by an ancient and recurring fallacy: Surpluses in payments are too often regarded as a symbol of success and of good management rather than as a measure of the goods and services provided from a nation's output without current return.

We must recognize, of course, that freer trade must be reconciled with the need for each country to avoid abrupt change involving serious disruptions of production and employment. We must aim to expand productive employment in all countries—and not at one another's expense.

A second fundamental is the need to develop a common code of conduct to protect and strengthen the fabric of a free and open international economic order.

Such basic rules as "no competitive devaluation" and "most-favored-nation treatment" have served us well, but they and others need to be reaffirmed, supplemented, and made applicable to today's conditions. Without such rules to guide us, close and fruitful cooperation on a day-to-day basis would not be possible.

Third, in shaping these rules we must recognize the need for clear disciplines and standards of behavior to guide the international adjustment process—a crucial gap in the Bretton Woods system. Amid the debate about the contributing causes of past imbalances and the responsibility for initiative toward correction, sight has too often been lost of the fact that adjustment is inherently a two-sided process—that for the world as a whole, every surplus is matched by a deficit.

Resistance of surplus countries to loss of their surpluses defeats the objective of monetary order as surely as failure of deficit countries to attack the source of their deficits. Any effort to develop a balanced and equitable monetary system must recognize that simple fact; effective and symmetrical incentives for adjustment are essential to a lasting system.

Fourth, while insisting on the need for adjustment, we can and should leave considerable flexibility to national governments in their choice among adjustment instruments. In a diverse world, equal responsibility and equal opportunity need not mean rigid uniformity in particular practices. But they do mean a common commitment to agreed international objectives. The belief is widespread—and we share it—that the exchange rate system must be more flexible. However, important as they are, exchange rates are not the only instrument of adjustment policy available; nor in specific instances will they necessarily be the most desirable.

Fifth, our monetary and trading systems are an interrelated complex. As we seek to reform monetary rules, we must at the same time seek to build in incentives for trade liberalization. Certainly, as we look ahead, ways must be found to integrate better the work of the GATT [General Agreement on Tariffs and Trade] and the IMF. Simultaneously we should insure that there are pressures which move us toward adequate development assistance and away from controls which stifle the free flow of investment.

Finally, and perhaps most fundamental, any stable and well-functioning international monetary system must rest upon sound policies to promote domestic growth and price stability in the major countries. These are imperative national goals for my government—and for yours. And no matter how well we design an international system, its prospects for survival will be doubtful without effective discharge of those responsibilities.

TOWARD A WORKABLE INTERNATIONAL AGREEMENT

Today is not the occasion for presenting a detailed blueprint for monetary reform. However, I do want to supplement these general principles with certain specific and interrelated ideas as to how to embody these principles in a workable international agreement.

These suggestions are designed to provide stability without rigidity. They take as a point of departure that most countries will want to operate within the framework of specified exchange rates. They would encourage these rates to be maintained within specified ranges so long as this is accomplished without distorting the fabric of trade and payments or domestic economic management. We aim to encourage freer flows of trade and capital while minimizing distortions from destabilizing flows of mobile capital. We would strengthen the voice of the international community operating through the IMF.

I shall organize these ideas under six headings, recognizing that much work remains to be done to determine the best techniques in each area: the exchange rate regime; the reserve mechanism; the balance of payments adjustment process; capital and other balance of payments controls; related negotiations; institutional implications.

1. The Exchange Rate Regime

We recognize that most countries want to maintain a fixed point of reference for their currencies; in other words, a "central" or "par" value. The corollary is a willingness to maintain and support these values by assuring convertibility of their currencies into other international assets.

A margin for fluctuation for market exchange rates around such central values will need to be provided sufficiently wide to dampen incentives for short-term capital movements and, when changes in central values are desirable, to ease the transition. The Smithsonian agreement took a major step in that direction. Building on that approach in the context of a symmetrical system, the permissible outer limits of these margins of fluctuation for all currencies—including the dollar— might be set in the same range as now permitted for nondollar currencies trading against each other.

We also visualize, for example, that countries in the process of forming a monetary union—with the higher degree of political and economic integration that that implies—may want to maintain narrower bands among themselves and should be allowed to do so. In addition, an individual nation, particularly in the developing world, may wish to seek the agreement of a principal trading partner to maintain a narrower range of exchange rate fluctuation between them.

Provision needs also to be made for countries which decide to float their currencies. However, a country that refrains from setting a central value, particularly beyond a brief transitional period, should be required to observe more stringent standards of behavior in other respects to assure the consistency of its actions with the basic requirements of a cooperative order.

2. The Reserve Mechanism

We contemplate that the SDR [special drawing rights] [24] would increase in importance and become the formal numéraire of the system. To facilitate its role, that instrument should be freed of those encumbrances of reconstitution obligations, designation procedures, and holding limits which would be unnecessary in a reformed system. Changes in the amount of SDR in the system as a whole will be required periodically to meet the aggregate need for reserves.

A "central value system" implies some fluctuation in official reserve holdings of individual countries to meet temporary disturbances in their balance of payments positions. In addition, countries should ordinarily remain free to borrow or lend, bilaterally or multilaterally, through the IMF or otherwise.

At the same time, official foreign currency holdings need be neither generally banned nor encouraged. Some countries may find holdings of foreign currencies provide a useful margin of flexibility in reserve management, and fluctuations in such holdings can provide some elas-

[24] Cf. *Documents, 1968-69*, pp. 509-15.

ticity for the system as a whole in meeting sudden flows of volatile capital. However, careful study should be given to proposals for exchanging part of existing reserve currency holdings into a special issue of SDR, at the option of the holder.

The suggested provisions for central values and convertibility do not imply restoration of a gold-based system. The rigidities of such a system, subject to the uncertainties of gold production, speculation, and demand for industrial uses, cannot meet the needs of today.

I do not expect governmental holdings of gold to disappear overnight. I do believe orderly procedures are available to facilitate a diminishing role of gold in international monetary affairs in the future.

3. The Balance of Payments Adjustment Process

In a system of convertibility and central values, an effective balance of payments adjustment process is inextricably linked to appropriate criteria for changes in central values and the appropriate level, trend, and distribution of reserves. Agreement on these matters, and on other elements of an effective and timely adjustment process, is essential to make a system both practical and durable.

There is, of course, usually a very close relationship between imbalances in payments and fluctuations in reserve positions. Countries experiencing large deterioration in their reserve positions generally have had to devalue their currencies or take other measures to strengthen their balance of payments. Surplus countries with disproportionate reserve gains have, however, been under much less pressure to revalue their currencies upward or to take other policy actions with a similar balance of payments effect. If the adjustment process is to be more effective and efficient in a reformed system, this asymmetry will need to be corrected.

I believe the most promising approach would be to insure that a surfeit of reserves indicates, and produces pressure for, adjustment on the surplus side, as losses of reserves already do for the deficit side. Supplementary guides and several technical approaches may be feasible and should be examined. Important transitional difficulties will need to be overcome. But, in essence, I believe disproportionate gains or losses in reserves may be the most equitable and effective single indicator we have to guide the adjustment process.

As I have already indicated, a variety of policy responses to affect the balance of payments can be contemplated. An individual country finding its reserves falling disproportionately would be expected to initiate corrective actions. For example, small devaluations would be freely permitted such a country. Under appropriate international surveillance, at some point a country would have a prima facie case for a larger devaluation.

While we must frankly face up to limitation on the use of domestic monetary, fiscal, or other internal policies in promoting international adjustments in some circumstances, we should also recognize that the country in deficit might well prefer—and be in a position to apply— stricter internal financial disciplines rather than devalue its currency. Only in exceptional circumstances, and for a limited period, should a country be permitted direct restraints; and these should be general and nondiscriminatory. Persistent refusal to take fundamental adjustment measures could result in withdrawal of borrowing, SDR allocation, or other privileges.

Conversely, a country permitting its reserves to rise disproportion- ately could lose its right to demand conversion, unless it undertook at least limited revaluation or other acceptable measures of adjustment. If reserves nonetheless continued to rise and were maintained at those higher levels over an extended period, then more forceful adjustment measures would be indicated.

For a surplus as for a deficit country, a change in the exchange rate need not be the only measure contemplated. Increasing the provision of concessionary aid on an untied basis, reduction of tariffs and other trade barriers, and elimination of obstacles to outward investment could, in specific circumstances at the option of the nation concerned, provide supplementary or alternative means. But in the absence of a truly effective combination of corrective measures, other countries should ultimately be free to protect their interests by a surcharge on the imports from the chronic surplus country.

For countries moving toward a monetary union, the guidelines might be applied on a collective basis, provided the countries were willing to speak with one voice and to be treated as a unit for purposes of ap- plying the basic rules of the international monetary and trading system.

4. Capital and Other Balance of Payments Controls

It is implicit in what I have said that I believe that the adjustment process should be directed toward encouraging freer trade and open capital markets. If trade controls are permitted temporarily in extreme cases on balance of payments grounds, they should be in the form of surcharges or across-the-board taxes. Controls on capital flows should not be allowed to become a means of maintaining a chronically under- valued currency. No country should be forced to use controls in lieu of other, more basic, adjustment measures.

5. Related Negotiations

We welcome the commitments which major nations have already made to start detailed trade negotiations under the GATT in the coming year.[25] These negotiations dealing with specific products and specific restraints need not wait on monetary reform, nor need monetary reform await the results of specific trade negotiations.

Those negotiations, and the development of rules of good behavior in the strictly monetary area, need to be supplemented by negotiations to achieve greater equity and uniformity with respect to the use of subsidies, and fiscal or administrative pressures on trade and investment transactions. Improper practices in these areas distort trade and investment relationships as surely as do trade barriers and currency disequilibrium. In some instances, such as the use of tariff surcharges or capital controls for balance of payments purposes, the linkage is so close that the Committee of Twenty must deal with the matter directly. As a supplement to its work, that group can help launch serious efforts in other bodies to harmonize countries' practices with respect to the taxation of international trade and investment, the granting of export credit, and the subsidization of international investment flows.

6. Institutional Implications

As I look to the future, it seems to me that there are several clear-cut institutional requirements of a sensible reform of the monetary and trading system.

Several times today I have stressed the need for a comprehensive new set of monetary rules. Those rules will need to be placed under guardianship of the IMF, which must be prepared to assume an even more critical role in the world economy.

Given the interrelationships between trade and payments, that role will not be effectively discharged without harmonizing the rules of the IMF and the GATT and achieving a close working relationship.

Finally, we need to recognize that we are inevitably dealing with matters of essential and sensitive national interest to specific countries. International decisionmaking will not be credible or effective unless it is carried out by representatives who clearly carry a high stature and influence in the councils of their own governments. Our international institutions will need to reflect that reality so that in the years ahead national governments will be intensively and continuously involved in their deliberations and processes. Without a commitment by national governments to make a new system work in this way, all our other labors may come to naught.

COOPERATION FOR EQUILIBRIUM

I am fully aware that the United States as well as other countries

25 Cf. below at notes 27-28.

cannot leap into new monetary and trading arrangements without a transitional period. I can state, however, that after such transitional period the United States would be prepared to undertake an obligation to convert official foreign dollar holdings into other reserve assets as a part of a satisfactory system such as I have suggested—a system assuring effective and equitable operation of the adjustment process. That decision will of course need to rest on our reaching a demonstrated capacity during the transitional period to meet the obligation in terms of our reserve and balance of payments position.

We fully recognize that we have not yet reached the strength we need in our external accounts. In the end, there can be no substitute for such strength in providing the underpinning for a stable dollar and a stable monetary system.

An acceptable monetary system requires a willingness on the part of all of us to contribute to the common goal of full international equilibrium. Lacking such equilibrium, no system will work. The equilibrium cannot be achieved by any one country acting alone.

We engage in discussions on trade and financial matters with a full realization of the necessity to continue our own efforts on a broad front to restore our balance of payments. I must add, in all candor, that our efforts to improve our position have in more than one instance been thwarted by the reluctance of others to give up an unjustified preferential and highly protected market position. Yet without success in our endeavor, we cannot maintain our desired share in the provision of aid and reduce our official debt to foreign monetary authorities.

We take considerable pride in our progress toward price stability, improved productivity, and more rapid growth during the past year. Sustained into the future, as it must be, that record will be the best possible medicine not only for our domestic prosperity but for the effective functioning of the international financial system.

My remarks today reflect the large agenda before us. I have raised difficult, complicated, and controversial issues. I did not shrink from so doing, for a simple reason: I know that you, as we, want to move ahead on the great task before us.

Let us see if, in Nairobi next year, we can say that a new balance is in prospect and that the main outlines of a new system are agreed. We owe ourselves and each other that effort.

C. The General Agreement on Tariffs and Trade (GATT): 28th Session of the Contracting Parties, Geneva, November 1-14, 1972.

[The interest of the United States in a resumption of the process of trade liberalization on a multilateral basis had been expressed on numerous occasions since the conclusion in 1967 of the Sixth or "Kennedy" Round of negotiations under the General Agreement on Tariffs and Trade (GATT), an exercise of unprecedented scope that had resulted among other things in cuts of one-third or more "across the board" in existing tariffs on industrial products. It was the well-established view of the United States that the next round of negotiations should be largely concerned with such matters as (1) the reduction or elimination of so-called nontariff barriers to trade, and (2) the establishment of a more satisfactory overall relationship between the United States and the expanding European Economic Community (E.E.C.). It was mainly through the implied promise of such negotiations that the American President, at his Azores meeting with French President Georges Pompidou in December 1971, had been induced to waive his long-standing objection to a devaluation of the dollar and thus make possible the general realignment of currencies embodied in the Smithsonian Agreement.[26]

The promise of trade negotiations through the GATT took on increased definition with the signature on February 11, 1972 of a joint declaration by the United States and the European Economic Community in which both parties stated that they "recognize the need for proceeding with a comprehensive review of international economic relations with a view to negotiating improvements in the light of structural changes which have taken place in recent years. The review shall cover inter alia all elements of trade, including measures which impede or distort agricultural, raw material and industrial trade. Special attention shall be given to the problems of developing countries." To this end, the two parties signified their intention "to initiate and actively support multilateral and comprehensive negotiations in the framework of GATT beginning in 1973 (subject to such internal authorization as may be required) with a view to the expansion and the ever greater liberalization of world trade and the improvement in the standard of living of the people of the world, aims which can be achieved inter alia through the progressive dismantling of obstacles to trade, and the improvement of the international framework for the conduct of world trade." The negotiations, it was further agreed, "shall be conducted on the basis of mutual advantage and mutual commitment with overall reciprocity," "shall cover agricultural as well as industrial trade," and "should involve active participation of as many countries as possible." During 1972, the two parties affirmed, they would "initiate and support . . . an analysis and evaluation in the GATT of alternative techniques and modalities for multilateral negotiations of long term problems affecting all elements of world

[26] *A.F.R., 1971*, nos. 43 and 149.

trade"; in addition, they would "seek to utilize every opportunity in the GATT for the settlement of particular trade problems" in the interests of lessening "current frictions" and smoothing the way toward "a new major initiative for dealing with longer term trade problems."[27] A similar joint statement was issued by the United States and Japan.[28]

The outlook for this "major new initiative" was still the principal concern when the 81 Contracting Parties to GATT held their 28th regular session in Geneva on November 1-14, 1972 and, among other actions, listened to a detailed exposé of U.S. views by Ambassador William D. Eberle, the President's Special Representative for Trade Negotiations (Document 96). By the time the Geneva meeting adjourned, it was generally anticipated that the new negotiations would be launched at a ministerial meeting of GATT in September, 1973, in the hope that they could be concluded in 1975.[29] But although the Seventh or "Tokyo" Round of multilateral trade negotiations was formally initiated on schedule at a meeting of contracting parties that took place in the Japanese capital on September 12-14, 1973,[30] substantive negotiations were postponed for a further seventeen months while Congress deliberated on President Nixon's request for the necessary negotiating mandate.

Since the expiration in 1967 of the Trade Expansion Act of 1962,[31] which had provided the legislative basis for U.S. participation in the Kennedy Round, the President had lacked authority to engage in new trade negotiations, and a renewal of this authority was the central feature of the proposed Trade Reform Act of 1973 which was submitted to the Congress by President Nixon on April 10, 1973.[32] Congressional action was delayed, however, primarily by objections to a separate feature of the proposed legislation which involved the granting of most-favored-nation tariff treatment to the U.S.S.R. at a time when that country was maintaining severe restrictions on Jewish emigration. Thus it was only with the passage of the long-delayed Trade Act of 1974 and its signature by President Ford on January 3, 1975[33] that the ground was cleared for the commencement of detailed negotiations in Geneva on February 11, 1975.[34]]

[27] Signed at Brussels Feb. 11, 1972; text in *Bulletin*, Apr. 3, 1972, pp. 515-16.
[28] Signed in Washington Feb. 9, 1972; text in same, p. 512.
[29] Office of the Special Representative for Trade Negotiations, Press Release 171, Nov. 22, 1972; text from *Bulletin*, Dec. 11, 1972, p. 679.
[30] Same, Oct. 8, 1973, pp. 445-52.
[31] Public Law 87-794, Oct. 11, 1962; summary in *Documents, 1962*, pp. 496-508.
[32] *Presidential Documents*, Apr. 16, 1973, pp. 343-55.
[33] Public Law 93-618, Jan. 3, 1975; cf. Chapter II at notes 207-209.
[34] *Bulletin*, Mar. 17, 1975, pp. 346-53.

(96) The Viewpoint of the United States: Statement by Ambassador William D. Eberle, Special Representative of the President for Trade Negotiations and Head of the United States Delegation, November 10, 1972.[35]

(Complete Text)

Since the last meeting of the Contracting Parties[36] there have been a number of significant developments which have changed the course of international economic relations. The scene has been set for negotiation of major improvements in the international trade and monetary systems.

The growing economic interdependence of the world has brought us all closer together, but at the same time it has intensified the difficulties resulting from the conflicts between our respective national economic policies. The international institutions, rules, and procedures have not adapted rapidly enough to keep pace. Faced with internal difficulties and with international mechanisms which did not provide adequate means of economic adjustment, nations have frequently been forced to take actions which created conflicts with the policies of other governments and which disturbed the economic interests of other countries. The consequent economic confrontations have put increasing stress on relations between nations generally.

The new circumstances which have evolved in the last year or so provide for us all the opportunity to move from a period of confrontation to an era of negotiation. It is imperative that governments develop the political will to seize this opportunity and to commit themselves to negotiations in a spirit of good will and cooperation.

The historic meeting of the Group of Ten at the Smithsonian Institution in December 1971[37] was but the first in a series of steps leading us to a new era of negotiation and reform. An essential catalyst was recognition of the need for a cooperative effort, by developed and developing countries alike, to steer the future of reform. The concept of a new Committee of Twenty was born. By the time of the September 1972 meeting of the IMF and the IBRD [International Monetary Fund; International Bank for Reconstruction and Development], it was possible to envisage not only broad terms of reference but a full program of work for the new Committee of Twenty. The Committee and its Deputies now have their work underway.[38]

But the countries most actively engaged in negotiation of a solution to the international monetary problems in late 1971 did not stop there.

[35] Office of the Special Representative for Trade Negotiations, Press Release 170, Nov. 10, 1972; text from *Bulletin*, Dec. 11, 1972, pp. 673-9.
[36] The 27th Session of the GATT Contracting Parties was held in Geneva Nov. 16-26, 1971.
[37] *A.F.R., 1971*, no. 150.
[38] Cf. above at note 15.

They also entered into mutual commitments to embark in 1973 on multilateral trade negotiations, involving as many countries as possible, aiming at further liberalization of trade.

Thus, as part of the broader effort to achieve basic reforms in the international economic system, it was recognized that the time had also come for fundamental improvements in international trade relations.

The commitments between the United States and Japan and the European Community[39] were discussed in the GATT Council in the spring of 1972. Since then, various countries have expressed their views on the need for trade negotiations and their own perspectives on what should be done. Many countries, both developed and developing, did so at the third UNCTAD conference [United Nations Conference on Trade and Development] at Santiago.[40] President Nixon and Prime Minister Tanaka jointly reaffirmed the intention to press ahead in 1973.[41] The most recent development was the statement on trade made by the leaders of the enlarged European Community (EC) in the communique of their October summit conference.[42] They stated that:

With regard to the industrial countries, the Community is determined, in order to ensure the harmonious development of world trade:

—To contribute, while respecting what has been achieved by the Community, to a progressive liberalisation of international trade by measures based on reciprocity and relating to both tariffs and non-tariff barriers;

—To maintain a constructive dialogue with the United States, Japan, Canada and its other industrialized trade partners in a forthcoming spirit, using the most appropriate methods.

In this context the Community attaches major importance to the multilateral negotiations in the context of G.A.T.T. in which it will participate in accordance with its earlier statement.

To this end, the Community institutions are invited to decide not later than 1st July, 1973 on a global approach covering all aspects affecting trade.

The Community hopes that an effort on the part of all partners will allow these negotiations to be completed in 1975.

With regard to the European summit communique, President Nixon issued the following statement on October 27:[43]

---

[39] Cf. above at notes 27-28.
[40] Cf. below at Document 98.
[41] Document 63.
[42] Held in Paris Oct. 19-20, 1972; text of communiqué in Keesing's, pp. 25540-42.
[43] Full text in *Public Papers, 1972*, p. 1047.

...I particularly welcome the Community's declared intent to maintain a constructive, forthcoming dialogue with us and its commitment to a progressive liberalization of tariff and nontariff barriers to trade on a comprehensive basis during the major multilateral negotiations to begin next year.

On behalf of the United States, I wish to reaffirm our commitment to work with the members of the European Community for reform of the international economic system in a way which will bring about a new freedom of world trade, new equity in international economic conduct, and effective solutions to the problems of the developing world.

These are the objectives with which the United States will approach forthcoming negotiations on monetary and trade reform. We will be prepared to take bold action with our European partners for a more equitable and open world economic order....

The new mood of cooperation and the common recognition of the need to negotiate improvements in our economic relationships are not, of course, shared everywhere. There are, I am afraid, in each of our nations those who wish to insulate their economies from outside forces or those who wish to return to the concepts of mercantilism in national policy. As governments, we cannot afford to accept such ideas. We have already become so economically interdependent that any turning back would necessarily result in reversal of the economic gains the world has achieved in recent years. Moreover, protectionist measures often cause serious damage to other countries and generate political conflict.

INTERNATIONAL ADJUSTMENTS BETWEEN ECONOMIES

The problem we must face is that the international economic system today does not prevent or adequately control politically divisive economic practices. Because the international balance of payments adjustment process does not function very well, pressures build up in particular sectors of industry or agriculture. The existing rules and procedural mechanisms for dealing with adjustment difficulties in specific sectors are not adequate, and governments are consequently encouraged to take unilateral actions to offset external forces.

This does not mean that we must give up our national objectives and our internal freedom to manage policy in relation to our own internal social and political considerations. We must, however, rule out predatory economic nationalism.

If we create a more effective, more liberalized international economic system which allows flexible, responsive adjustment by individual nations to changes between their internal and external circumstances, nations will be freer than they are now to pursue appropriate internal economic policies. If provisions for appropriate international balance of payments adjustments are built into the system, necessary domestic policies can be pursued with even greater vigor than in the past. There will then be less likelihood that actions needed for internal reasons will place heavy burdens of adjustment on other nations.

Secretary Shultz, in his statement to the IMF–IBRD annual meeting in September,[44] put the task in these words:

> The nations gathered here have it in their power to strike a new balance in international economic affairs.
>
> The new balance of which I speak does not confine itself to the concepts of a balance of trade or a balance of payments. The world needs a new balance between flexibility and stability in its basic approach to doing business. The world needs a new balance between a unity of purpose and a diversity of execution that will permit nations to cooperate closely without losing their individuality or sovereignty.

To strike this new balance, we must improve the whole international economic system, including the monetary, investment, trade, and other elements of it. It is not a matter of the processes of detailed monetary and trade negotiations being locked together procedurally at every step. What is crucial is that the system as a whole be seen and dealt with as a coherent whole and that all elements of it be adapted to the needs of the 1970's and 1980's.

International adjustments take place on a variety of levels between economies, sometimes affecting business conditions generally and at other times more specifically. They frequently occur in some sectors but not others. Adjustments can, in other words, take place in an overall manner, as when an exchange rate change shifts the position of a whole economy relative to the rest of the world. Sometimes governments prefer to limit adjustments to specific problems or areas. They may prefer to focus actions in the trade field for a time by imposing special measures to affect the trade account as a whole. Finally, governments frequently take special actions to assist or alter the circumstances of particular industries or regions. This is done through tax policies, regional development aids, trade restrictions, export subsidies, and other similar measures. These actions distort the conditions of trade.

The interrelationship between general and specific actions has frequently been unrecognized or ignored. In such cases, one type of action may thwart the purpose of other types of actions. This is an important aspect of what we mean by the interdependence of monetary and trading rules and the need for consistency in the two areas.

[44] Document 95.

GOALS OF MULTILATERAL TRADE NEGOTIATIONS

Turning to trade itself, my government is now preparing intensively for multilateral trade negotiations. We envisage such negotiations as covering all aspects of trade relations.

The GATT has made its most important contribution to trade liberalization in the area of tariffs. Clearly the importance of tariffs has greatly diminished over the last quarter century, relative to other impediments to trade and to trade-distorting policies. But we must not underestimate the importance of tariffs either, particularly in light of the effective levels of protection which they provide. Given the very significant progress in tariff reduction already made, the time may soon be at hand when we can seriously contemplate possible programs for their phased elimination.

In the field of nontariff barriers and other trade-distorting policies, we believe that every effort should be made to eliminate these sources of distortion and friction in trade relations. Where the problem is one of differing or conflicting national policies and practices but elimination of controls is not consistent with social objectives, we believe that there should be developed common commitments to common rules and procedures. This would at least reduce or eliminate the possibilities for using nontariff measures to favor one group over another or one nation over another. It would make us all subject to some harmonized concepts of what is right and what is wrong.

In this spirit, achievement of a more liberal world order for trade, together with common commitments to agreed rules and procedures, will lead us to what President Nixon has called a freer but fairer system.

We believe that it is essential to provide for a substantial expansion of world trade in agriculture and to bring under international discipline the various national instruments of agricultural policy which result in major forms of distortion and disruption. The need for reform in this field is great. Negotiations over the years have failed to bring about significant liberalization. The GATT rules are inadequate, and where they exist governments have often ignored them or found ways around them.

If I may give special emphasis to agriculture, it is because we believe that this area presents one of the clearest examples of the dangers of trade practices which are not governed by agreed rules. Developed and developing nations alike have a fundamental interest in building and preserving the strength of their farm sectors, but this should not be done in ways which burden farmers in other countries nor in ways which thwart pursuit of greater efficiency in world production in the long run.

We shall also need to find a means of bringing into some kind of harmony the various national safeguard actions which are taken to moderate trade flows for limited periods of time. We believe that a new multilateral safeguard system should be developed which would provide common procedures for all countries taking special actions to moderate the pace of domestic adjustment resulting from abrupt changes in the conditions of trade. This would, on the one hand, allow nations to implement special safeguard actions in particular cases where the external pressures cause significant domestic adjustment difficulties and, on the other hand, insure that nations adversely affected by such actions be treated equitably and that the special measures be subject to agreed rules and timetables. It would give opportunity and incentive to insure that such actions be aimed at longrun adjustment to changing world market circumstances. A multilateral safeguard system, if well constructed, should make the process of global trade liberalization easier to contemplate, while at the same time reducing the uncertainties of market access conditions which exporters may face in certain product areas.

Finally, we believe that those countries which have maintained internal discrimination against foreign products and old forms of protection appropriate to the circumstances of another era should now be willing to change substantially their policies and join in common commitments with us.

REVITALIZATION OF THE GATT

In contemplating liberalization and the development of new rules and procedures, we believe that the GATT, as an institution and as a set of rules and procedures,[45] remains valuable. Nonetheless, the time has come to reinforce the strengths of the GATT and repair its weaknesses. It must be recognized that major changes have taken place since the GATT was first drafted. Moreover, changes have occurred in the GATT as a result of day-to-day decisions and especially of failure to make decisions. Practice becomes the rule if repeated widely enough and if contracting parties are unwilling to take a stand on the issues involved.

We believe that the international trading system can no longer afford to have major provisions of the agreement honored largely in the breach. It is therefore urgent and essential to revitalize the day-to-day business of the GATT by using its procedures with a view to concrete decisions. Where, for example, the United States has had a long-standing import restriction inconsistent with the GATT applied against its trade, we are now moving to bring it forward for discussion with a view to reaching early agreement on a schedule of liberalization or

45 General Agreement on Tariffs and Trade, attached to the Final Act of the United Nations Conference on Trade and Employment, signed at Geneva Oct. 30, 1947 and entered into force for the U.S. Jan. 1, 1948 (TIAS 1700). For Part IV of the Agreement, cf. note 81.

compensation. We believe that effective action on these routine matters should be taken in the normal course of GATT business without hesitation and without political friction.

There is, as you all well know, growing concern in my country regarding the erosion of the applicability of the MFN [most-favored-nation] principle. The practice of negotiating special arrangements on a discriminatory basis tailored to the specific bilateral problems between two countries or groups of countries, in our view, runs counter to the spirit of the GATT as well as being contrary to the letter of the provisions of article XXIV. Indeed, we feel it is a clear threat to the philosophy of an equitable, "one world" economic system that has been so widely expressed by those directly involved in monetary reform. We share the growing concern that events will propel us into a division of the world into blocs or tight-knit spheres of influence.

Because of the differences of view among countries on the interpretation of the GATT, the GATT has avoided ruling on them. The practice of negotiating special arrangements is now widespread in relation to the European Community.[46] What, then, is the meaning of MFN? Does it only apply selectively to certain countries?

I could go on. The list would include the problems of inadequacy of and lack of adherence to the rules in agriculture, in use of trade measures for balance of payments purposes, in subsidies, and in restrictive safeguard actions. I could list areas where trade is affected by national policies but the rules for dealing with the problems raised are not adequate. Such areas include procurement policy, administrative actions, and internal industrial and regional policies. These problems in one way or another apply to all the contracting parties.

This is not to say that nothing is right any longer. In many respects the general agreement has served us well. GATT procedures and commitments have resulted in the substantial reduction of impediments to trade. They have also provided an important element of stability in commercial policy that has facilitated an enormous expansion of world trade during the postwar period.

But there have been sweeping changes in the world economy during the past 25 years—and the rules as well as their administration have not kept pace. We need to revitalize the GATT. In our forthcoming negotiations, we should seek further trade liberalization and develop new commitments. If this means improving the rules, as we believe it does, then let us admit that need and address ourselves to it without delay. As a beginning we could look at paragraph 328 of the OECD Rey group report[47] that suggests looking at some specific aspects of the general agreement "to strengthen its effectiveness while adapting it to present-day conditions." Obviously, those rules which involve interrelationships

46 Cf. note 3 above.
47 Cf. note 9 above.

between the monetary and trading systems, or which have a significant bearing on the international economic adjustment process, will be discussed in the monetary Committee of Twenty. The issues related to trade as such must, equally obviously, be dealt with here in the GATT.

PREPARATIONS FOR TRADE NEGOTIATIONS

In preparing for trade negotiations, we shall seek the advice of our trading partners, both developed countries and developing countries, in consultations over coming months. We hope they will do the same so that negotiations can be truly said to be a common initiative for the common welfare. In this connection, we will wish to study with care the thinking of the governments of developing countries regarding the role they envisage. Multilateral trade negotiations are crucial to their interests. Trade accounts for some three-fourths to four-fifths of their foreign exchange resources. Means for assisting the developing countries in their negotiating efforts, and procedures for the participation of countries not now members of the GATT, should be worked out carefully in the coming months. Indeed, we anticipate that the problems of developing countries will be an important element of the preparatory discussions which we believe ought to take place.

In the preparation for the negotiations, due account should be taken of differences between the economies of developed and developing countries. The overall framework for the negotiations should assure that the actual results in trade terms improve opportunities for access to developed countries' markets for the exports of developing countries.

My government is aware of the intense interest of developing countries in the generalized system of preferences. We intend to seek legislative authority to extend such preferences.[48] The fact should not be overlooked that even in the absence of preferences the United States accounted for one-half of the imports of manufactures of developed countries from developing countries in the period 1962 to 1969.

We strongly support the establishment of a preparatory committee to define the scope and goal of the 1973 negotiations and to provide policy guidance for the preparatory work of the various committees, CTIP [Committee on Trade in Industrial Products], Agricultural, Trade and Development. We agree with the Swedish suggestion that contracting parties should be represented in the preparatory committee by policy-level officials from capitals.

We must, at this session, give the strongest possible impetus to the work of the preparatory committee. Those in our various capitals who take whatever political, legislative, or procedural decisions may be re-

---

[48] Cf. below at notes 64-66.

quired also need a suitable international framework for the decision. To these ends, it is of the greatest importance that the Contracting Parties agree now to meet at ministerial level in September 1973 to establish a trade negotiations committee.[49]

We would also like to see the work of the CTIP and Agricultural Committee given new impetus. It should be possible in coming months to prepare as many issues as possible for agreement in broad outline, even though details might be subject later to final negotiations and political decision. It would be desirable in this context to give special attention to the broad outline of a multilateral safeguard system, on which I have already commented. Agreement on an acceptable multilateral system could facilitate progress on other matters.

In the immediate future, the Contracting Parties must deal promptly, fairly, and effectively with the consequences of the enlargement of the European Community. We believe the Contracting Parties should move expeditiously to complete the examination under article XXIV:5(a) of the relevant legal instruments. We are not happy that the working party charged with the matter has not been able to establish an agreed date and methodology for the examination. My delegation's views on the matter have been stated in the working party and in the discussion we had on the report of the Council. We have held the relevant item open in the hope that the EC and the acceding countries will give us a fuller statement of their views so that we may consider how best to expedite the examination. We welcome the announcement by the spokesman for the European Communities indicating that the article XXIV:6 negotiations can be opened soon. The working party on EC enlargement should follow closely the results of the negotiations, review their progress from time to time, and assist participating countries in eliminating difficulties that may arise. It would have been desirable for these negotiations to have been completed before February 1, 1973, when acceding countries begin to apply provisions of the accession treaty. Without forgoing any of our rights in concessions that may be breached, we realize that the renegotiations cannot be completed by February 1. We believe the negotiations should begin in February and be concluded by the August holidays. Hence, a firm February starting date must be fixed at this time in fairness to all contracting parties who must arrange for personnel to be in Geneva to conduct the negotiations. Concrete results must be achieved.[50]

---

[49] Cf. above at note 29.

[50] In his report on the Geneva session (note 29 above), the Special Representative cited an understanding to the effect that a renegotiation of GATT schedules of Denmark, Ireland, and the U.K. in consequence of their entry into the Common Market would begin Mar. 1, 1973 with a view to their completion in four or five months. The negotiations were actually completed May 31, 1974 (Keesing's, p. 26800).

I conclude by returning to my central theme—the need for early improvement in international trade relations and the importance we place on the forthcoming trade negotiations.

In summarizing the key elements of our position, allow me to remind you of the words of my President in his address to the IMF—IBRD meeting in September.[51] He said:

> We shall press for a more equitable and a more open world of trade. We shall meet competition rather than run away from it.
> We shall be a stimulating trading partner, a straightforward bargainer.
> We shall not turn inward and isolationist.

But the President also emphasized:

> There is another reason, more far-reaching and fundamental, that motivates the United States in pressing for economic and monetary reform.
> Working together, we must set in place an economic structure that will help and not hinder the world's historic movement toward peace.
> We must make certain that international commerce becomes a source of stability and harmony, rather than a cause of friction and animosity.
> Potential conflict must be channeled into cooperative competition. That is why the structure of the international monetary system and the future system of world trade are so central to our concerns today. The time has come for action across the entire front of international economic problems. Recurring monetary crises such as we have experienced all too often in the past decade, unfair currency alignments and trading arrangements which put the workers of one nation at a disadvantage with workers of another nation, great disparities in development that breed resentment, a monetary system that makes no provision for the realities of the present and the needs of the future—all these not only injure our economies; they also create political tensions that subvert the cause of peace.
> There must be a thoroughgoing reform of the world monetary system to clear the path for the healthy economic competition of the future.
> We must see monetary reform as one part of a total reform of international economic affairs encompassing trade and investment opportunity for all.
> We must create a realistic code of economic conduct to guide our

51 Document 94.

mutual relations, a code which allows governments freedom to pursue legitimate domestic objectives but which also gives them good reason to abide by agreed principles of international behavior.

Each nation must exercise the power of its example in the realistic and orderly conduct of internal economic affairs so that each nation exports its products and not its problems.

I hope all nations will join with us to meet these challenges expeditiously, for the benefit of all the countries of the world.

D. Economic Development Policy.

[Promotion of the economic and social progress of the world's developing countries no longer held the prominent place in American foreign policy it had assumed in the 1950s and early 1960s, when the United States had joined the Latin American nations in launching the Alliance for Progress[52] and had encouraged the U.N. General Assembly to designate the 1960s as the United Nations Development Decade.[53] Although the General Assembly had since proclaimed a Second United Nations Development Decade beginning January 1, 1971,[54] the United States by then had come to look upon such initiatives with visibly lessened enthusiasm. This change in the American outlook was mirrored in a steady decrease in the annual congressional allotments for foreign economic assistance, whether measured in absolute terms or as a proportion of national wealth. President Nixon took indirect note of the trend in submitting his report on the foreign aid program for the fiscal year 1971: "Whereas a decade or so ago the United States was the predominant source of development resources and guidance, other industrialized nations and international lending institutions have since expanded both their contributions and their administrative capabilities. Today the United States is the foremost of donor nations in absolute terms, but the other industrialized nations have increased their participation to the extent that in many cases they are contributing a greater percentage of their total resources to development assistance than is the United States."[55]

This gradual decline in the American contribution to development assistance had suddenly accelerated in October 1971 with the Senate's surprise rejection, by a vote of 41 to 27, of the basic foreign assistance legislation for the fiscal year 1972.[56] Although it

[52] *Documents, 1961*, pp. 395-437.
[53] Resolution 1710 (XVI), Dec. 19, 1961, in same, pp. 535-8.
[54] Resolution 2626 (XXV), Oct. 24, 1970; excerpts in same, *1970*, pp. 324-31.
[55] *Public Papers, 1972*, p. 877.
[56] *A.F.R., 1971*, pp. 615-16.

was correctly assumed at the time that Congress would eventually vote sufficient funds to keep the program from expiring, the Senate's action obviously reflected mounting impatience with a type of expenditure that was widely unpopular and had produced few unmistakable benefits from the standpoint of overall foreign policy. This disenchantment stemmed less from any specific short-comings in the economic performance of the developing countries than from a sense of dissatisfaction with their political and ideological attitudes, which had appeared increasingly at variance with those of the United States in recent years and, in Washington's view, were often directly harmful to the developing countries' own interests.

Particularly disturbing to governmental and business circles in the United States had been the determination shown by many developing countries to gain ownership and control of foreign-owned economic assets within their territory, often without making adequate provision for compensation of the previous owners. The recent expropriation of U.S.-owned copper companies by the left-wing government of President Salvador Allende Gossens of Chile,[57] which had been seen in Washington as an especially flagrant instance of such practices, was instrumental in evoking what was to become the most significant U.S. policy statement of 1972 in the whole field of international development endeavors. Concluding a lengthy discussion of the problems of investment security made public January 19, 1972 (Document 97), President Nixon warned that the United States not only would "not extend new bilateral economic benefits to the expropriating country" in cases of this kind, but would also "withhold its support from loans under consideration in multilateral development banks." The American answer to future uncompensated expropriations, in other words, would be a cutoff of direct aid (except humanitarian aid) together with an attempt to block or limit aid from international sources.

More positive elements of U.S. development policy were also touched upon in the Nixon statement, and were elaborated in greater detail in an address by Under Secretary of State Irwin at the Third Ministerial Session of the United Nations Conference on Trade and Development (UNCTAD III), held in Santiago, Chile, from April 13 to May 21, 1972. As noted earlier, this 141-nation meeting afforded the developing countries a unique occasion to voice their feelings of frustration and dissatisfaction with the attitude of the wealthy, industrialized powers, including the United States, and to demand full consideration of their interests in the forthcoming trade and monetary negotiations.

[57]Cf. A.F.R., 1971, no. 118.

The somewhat apologetic tone of Under Secretary Irwin's statement at Santiago (Document 98) was scarcely to be avoided under the circumstances, and recalls his earlier defense of U.S. development policies before the Inter-American Committee on the Alliance for Progress (Document 74). But while conceding that current U.S. policy left something to be desired from the standpoint of development needs, the U.S. delegation head could not himself foresee the extent to which the events of the next few months would undercut official protestations of concern regarding the fate of poorer countries. The largely negative record of American action in three key sectors—bilateral assistance, multilateral lending, and trade preferences—inevitably ranks 1972 as the least successful year thus far in terms of American support for global development objectives.

As had been foreseen at the time, the essentials of the United States' continuing program of military and economic aid to other nations were eventually salvaged, despite the Senate's rejection on October 29, 1971 of the annual foreign aid authorization bill for the fiscal year 1972.[58] A substitute Foreign Assistance Act of 1971, authorizing one year of military and two years of economic assistance, was signed by President Nixon on February 7, 1972, with a complaint, however, that the aid allotments had been reduced "below minimum acceptable levels" and that a proliferation of "restrictive and non-germane amendments" would further hamper efficient administration.[59] Actual appropriations for fiscal 1972 were further reduced in the subsequent Foreign Assistance and Related Programs Appropriation Act, 1972, which the President signed without comment on March 8, 1972.[60]

Although the President urged Congress in a special foreign aid message to improve upon this record in dealing with the aid program for the new fiscal year 1973,[61] no general foreign aid legislation was enacted at the 1972 congressional session. One version of the proposed Foreign Assistance Act of 1972 was rejected by a 48 to 42 vote of the Senate on July 24, 1972. A different version passed the House on August 10, 1972 but was subsequently amended in the Senate to a point where no agreement between the two houses could be achieved before Congress adjourned for the November election. Differing House and Senate versions of the companion measure, the Foreign Assistance and Related Agencies Appropriation Act, 1973, likewise remained unreconciled at ad-

---

[58] Cf. above at note 56.
[59] Public Law 92-226, Feb. 7, 1972; Nixon statement in *Public Papers, 1972*, p. 166.
[60] Public Law 92-242, Mar. 8, 1972.
[61] Message of Mar. 14, 1972, in *Public Papers, 1972*, pp. 412-13.

journment time. Continuation of the foreign aid program at current rates of expenditure was, however, authorized by separate legislation.[62]

American support for the principal multilateral development lending institutions—the Asian Development Bank (A.D.B.), the Inter-American Development Bank (I.D.B.), and the International Development Association (I.D.A.)—was also adversely affected by legislative delays, including nonenactment of the regular foreign aid legislation. As part of an effort to "multilateralize" developmental responsibilities, the United States had long favored an expansion of the lending capacity of these institutions, notably their ability to provide so-called concessional or "soft" loans on noncommercial terms. Mainly because of legislative delays, however, the United States by the early 1970s had fallen into arrears in fulfilling its commitments to contribute a share of the funds required for these purposes.

Prospects for overcoming this lag were nevertheless improved with the signature on March 10, 1972 of legislation authorizing U.S. contributions of $100 million to the Asian Development Bank, $900 million to the Inter-American Development Bank, and $960 million to the International Development Association, these payments to be made over periods of two or three years, subject to a variety of conditions and limitations.[63] Intended in each case to support concessional lending by the institutions in question, these allotments were separate from contributions to their ordinary capital, which normally presented fewer legislative problems. But actual payment of the funds—and, in some instances, of scheduled increases in ordinary capital as well—was to be further delayed by the lack of a foreign aid appropriation for the fiscal year 1973.

A third important measure for the benefit of developing countries had been announced by President Nixon on October 31, 1969, when he promised to recommend to Congress a system of generalized trade preferences designed to facilitate the access of developing countries' products to the markets of the United States and other industrialized countries.[64] Action along these lines had since been taken by the European Economic Community, the United Kingdom, and Japan; but the United States, alone among the major industrialized countries, had made no move to implement the Presi-

---

[62] Senate Foreign Relations Committee History, pp. 56-67.
[63] Public Law 92-245, 246, and 247, Mar. 20, 1972; cf. Nixon signature statement in *Public Papers, 1972*, pp. 410-11, and note 88 below.
[64] *Documents, 1968-69*, p. 433. For additional background, see *A.F.R., 1971*, pp. 616-17.

dent's plan—and, as Under Secretary Irwin explained at UNCTAD III, still saw no immediate prospect of doing so under existing conditions. Not until April 10, 1973, approximately a full year after the UNCTAD meeting, was a recommendation involving preferential treatment of certain products of developing countries over a temporary ten-year period laid before the Congress as part of the proposed Trade Reform Act.[65] Nearly two more years were to elapse before Congress approved and President Ford signed the Trade Act of 1974,[66] which authorized temporary ten-year duty-free treatment of various developing-country products but excluded members of the Organization of Petroleum Exporting Countries (OPEC) and certain other countries from the benefits of this provision.]

(97) Economic Assistance and Investment Security in Developing Nations: Statement by President Nixon, January 19, 1972.[67]

(Complete Text)

We live in an age that rightly attaches very high importance to economic development. The people of the developing societies in particular see in their own economic development the path to fulfillment of a whole range of national and human aspirations. The United States continues to support wholeheartedly, as we have done for decades, the efforts of those societies to grow economically—out of our deep conviction that, as I said in my inaugural address, "To go forward at all is to go forward together"; that the well-being of mankind is in the final analysis indivisible; and that a better fed, better clothed, healthier, and more literate world will be a more peaceful world as well.

As we enter 1972, therefore, I think it is appropriate to outline my views on some important aspects of overseas development policy. I shall discuss these matters in broader compass and greater detail in messages to be transmitted to the Congress in the coming weeks.[68] Nineteen seventy-one saw great changes in the international monetary and trade fields, especially among the developed nations. A new economic policy was charted for the United States, and a promising beginning was made on a broad reform of the international monetary system—starting with a realignment of international exchange rates.[69] Now, in 1972, the problem of how best to assist the development of the world's emerging nations will move more to the forefront of our concern.

[65] *Presidential Documents*, Apr. 16, 1973, p. 351.
[66] Public Law 93-618, Jan. 3, 1975.
[67] White House Press Release, Jan. 19, 1972; text from *Bulletin*, Feb. 7, 1972, pp. 152-4. For background, cf. above at note 57.
[68] Cf. above at note 61.
[69] Cf. *A.F.R., 1971*, no. 150.

Any policy for such assistance is prompted by a mutuality of interest. Through our development assistance programs, financing in the form of taxes paid by ordinary Americans at all income levels is made available to help people in other nations realize their aspirations. A variety of other mechanisms also serves to transfer economic resources from the United States to developing nations.

Three aspects of U.S. development assistance programs received concentrated attention during the past year. These were:

—Continuing a program of bilateral economic assistance.

—Meeting our international undertakings for the funding of multilateral development institutions.

—Clarifying the role of private foreign investment in overseas development and dealing with the problem of expropriations.

As to our bilateral economic program, it is my intention to seek a regular and adequate fiscal year 1972 appropriation to replace the present interim financing arrangement which expires February 22. I urge that this be one of the first items addressed and completed by the Congress after it reconvenes.[70] Looking beyond this immediate need, I hope the Congress will give early attention to the proposals which I submitted last year to reform our foreign assistance programs to meet the challenges of the seventies.[71]

In regard to our participation in multilateral institutions, I attach the highest importance to meeting in full the financial pledges we make. In 1970, the United States agreed with its hemispheric partners on replenishing the Inter-American Development Bank. Our contributions to this Bank represent our most concrete form of support for regional development in Latin America. While the Congress did approve partial financing for the Bank before the recess, it is urgent that the integrity of this international agreement be preserved through providing the needed payments in full.

These Inter-American Bank contributions—together with our vital contributions to the International Development Association, the World Bank, and the Asian Development Bank—are the heart of my announced policy of channeling substantial resources for development through these experienced and technically proficient multilateral institutions. These latter contributions also require prompt legislative action, and I look to the Congress to demonstrate to other nations that the United States will continue its longstanding cooperative approach to international development through multilateral financial mechanisms.[72]

---

70 Cf. above at note 60.
71 Cf. A.F.R., 1971, no. 153.
72 Cf. above at note 63.

I also wish to make clear the approach of this administration to the role of private investment in developing countries and, in particular, to one of the major problems affecting such private investment: upholding accepted principles of international law in the face of expropriations without adequate compensation.

A principal objective of foreign economic assistance programs is to assist developing countries in attracting private investment. A nation's ability to compete for this scarce and vital development ingredient is improved by programs which develop economic infrastructure, increase literacy, and raise health standards. Private investment, as a carrier of technology, of trade opportunities, and of capital itself, in turn becomes a major factor in promoting industrial and agricultural development. Further, a significant flow of private foreign capital stimulates the mobilization and formation of domestic capital within the recipient country.

A sort of symbiosis exists—with government aid efforts not only speeding the flow of, but actually depending for their success upon, private capital, both domestic and foreign. And of course, from the investor's point of view, foreign private investment must either yield financial benefits to him over time or cease to be available. Mutual benefit is thus the *sine qua non* of successful foreign private investment.

Unfortunately for all concerned, these virtually axiomatic views on the beneficial role of and necessary conditions for private capital have been challenged in recent and important instances. U.S. enterprises, and those of many other nations, operating abroad under valid contracts negotiated in good faith, and within the established legal codes of certain foreign countries, have found their contracts revoked and their assets seized with inadequate compensation or with no compensation.

Such actions by other governments are wasteful from a resource standpoint, shortsighted considering their adverse effects on the flow of private investment funds from all sources, and unfair to the legitimate interests of foreign private investors.

The wisdom of any expropriation is questionable, even when adequate compensation is paid. The resources diverted to compensate investments that are already producing employment and taxes often could be used more productively to finance new investment in the domestic economy, particularly in areas of high social priority to which foreign capital does not always flow. Consequently, countries that expropriate often postpone the attainment of their own development goals. Still more unfairly, expropriations in one developing country can and do impair the investment climate in other developing countries.

In light of all this, it seems to me imperative to state to our citizens and to other nations the policy of this government in future situations involving expropriatory acts.

1. Under international law, the United States has a right to expect:

—That any taking of American private property will be nondiscriminatory;

—That it will be for a public purpose; and

—That its citizens will receive prompt, adequate, and effective compensation from the expropriating country.

Thus, when a country expropriates a significant U.S. interest without making reasonable provision for such compensation to U.S. citizens, we will presume that the United States will not extend new bilateral economic benefits to the expropriating country unless and until it is determined that the country is taking reasonable steps to provide adequate compensation or that there are major factors affecting U.S. interests which require continuance of all or part of these benefits.

2. In the face of the expropriatory circumstances just described, we will presume that the United States Government will withhold its support from loans under consideration in multilateral development banks.

3. Humanitarian assistance will, of course, continue to receive special consideration under such circumstances.

4. In order to carry out this policy effectively, I have directed that each potential expropriation case be followed closely. A special interagency group will be established under the Council on International Economic Policy to review such cases and to recommend courses of action for the U.S. Government.

5. The Departments of State, Treasury, and Commerce are increasing their interchange of views with the business community on problems relating to private U.S. investment abroad in order to improve government and business awareness of each other's concerns, actions, and plans. The Department of State has set up a special office to follow expropriation cases in support of the Council on International Economic Policy.

6. Since these issues are of concern to a broad portion of the international community, the U.S. Government will consult with governments of developed and developing countries on expropriation matters to work out effective measures for dealing with these problems on a multilateral basis.

7. Along with other governments, we shall cooperate with the international financial institutions—in particular, the World Bank Group, the Inter-American Development Bank, and the Asian Development Bank— to achieve a mutually beneficial investment atmosphere. The international financial institutions have often assisted in the settlement of investment disputes, and we expect they will continue to do so.

8. One way to make reasonable provision for just compensation in an expropriation dispute is to refer the dispute to international adjudication or arbitration. Firm agreement in advance on dispute settlement procedures is a desirable means of anticipating possible disagreements between host governments and foreign investors. Accordingly, I support

the existing International Centre for the Settlement of Investment Disputes within the World Bank Group, as well as the establishment in the very near future of the International Investment Insurance Agency, now under discussion in the World Bank Group. The Overseas Private Investment Corporation will make every effort to incorporate independent dispute settlement procedures in its new insurance and guarantee agreements.

I announce these decisions because I believe there should be no uncertainty regarding U.S. policy. The adoption by the United States Government of this policy is consistent with international law. The policy will be implemented within the framework of existing domestic law until the Congress modifies present statutes along the lines already proposed by this administration. The United States fully respects the sovereign rights of others, but it will not ignore actions prejudicial to the rule of law and legitimate U.S. interest.

Finally, as we look beyond our proper national interests to the larger considerations of the world interest, let us not forget that only within a framework of international law will the developed nations be able to provide increasing support for the aspirations of our less developed neighbors around the world.

(98) "The Need for a Constructive Approach to Issues of Trade and Development": Statement by Under Secretary of State Irwin Before the Third Ministerial Session of the United Nations Conference on Trade and Development (UNCTAD III), Santiago, Chile, April 14, 1972. [73]

(Complete Text)

My delegation joins with our colleagues in congratulating the distinguished Foreign Minister of Chile [Clodomiro Almeyda] on his election as president of this historic conference. The conference agenda is long and complex. Your able leadership, Mr. President, will do much to help us deal with the issues before us and to guide us toward constructive results.

The Government and people of Chile richly deserve, and have, our warm thanks for hosting what I understand is the largest international economic conference ever to be held in Latin America and perhaps anywhere in the world. Their unstinting efforts and gracious hospitality have made it possible for us to meet today in the most impressive of international conference facilities.

[73] Department of State Press Release 89; text from *Bulletin*, May 8, 1972, pp. 661-6.

The years since the first United Nations Conference on Trade and Development[74] have seen an extraordinary cooperative effort to promote economic and social progress. The developing countries, as is normal, have assumed the primary responsibility for their own development. But the industrialized countries have helped significantly. They have provided large sums of official development capital, complemented by substantial private investment flows. Trade has been liberalized and expanded.

These cooperative efforts have brought concrete results. As one measure, during the First Development Decade, the gross national product of the developing countries grew at an average of 5.5 percent per year. Some developing countries grew at rates of almost 10 percent. Other countries have been less fortunate, growing at far less than the average. This is a situation we must work to correct.

The United States has supported and contributed substantially to the process of development. It has joined with others in establishing the concept that the wealthier countries have a responsibility to help the poorer nations accelerate their economic and social progress.

As convincingly stated by the Secretary General of the United Nations yesterday, UNCTAD, too, has made important contributions to this development process. As an institution, UNCTAD has advocated and supported trade and development objectives. It has provided a forum for surfacing new ideas, for frank discussions of trade and development problems between the developed and developing countries. It has acted as an important catalyst for action.

None of us, however, in either the developing or developed countries, can be satisfied with progress to date. Moreover, such progress as has been achieved has naturally tended to raise aspirations, to increase awareness of all that remains to be done, and to pose new or sharpened issues for the international community. Among those issues are the increasingly obvious ecological costs of economic growth when environmental considerations are not sufficiently taken into account, the high costs of rapid population growth, and the question of how best to achieve not just economic growth as measured in national income statistics but tangible improvements, equitably distributed, in the quality of life.

The Stockholm Conference later this year[75] will mark a milestone in international consideration of environmental issues. Unchecked population growth has been cited in the report of the Pearson Commission[76] and studies by United Nations experts as the single heaviest

---

74 Held in Geneva Mar. 23-June 16, 1964; cf. *Documents, 1964*, pp. 422-52.
75 Cf. Documents 83-5.
76 *Partners in Development: Report of the Commission on International Development* (Lester B. Pearson, Chairman), submitted Sept. 15, 1969; published by Praeger Publishers, New York, 1969.

burden on the efforts of many countries to attain their goals for economic development and social progress. Nor is population growth a
problem only for the developing countries. In the United States the
Commission on Population Growth and the American Future has recently submitted findings to President Nixon suggesting the need for
measures to slow our own population growth and to work toward a
stabilized population.[77]

Each nation rightfully will face the challenges and the unknowns of
the future in its own way according to its own philosophy and history.
Views and techniques will change over time in response to experience
and to changed situations. Yet one thing is clear. Never before has the
need for international cooperation and understanding been greater. We
live in one small, finite world. The challenges of the future can only be
met through working more closely together with a common will toward
shared objectives.

THE INTERNATIONAL ECONOMY

The international economy passed through a critical stage in 1971.
Serious strains had developed in the international trade and payments
system. By the summer of 1971, the situation of the United States
domestic economy and balance of payments had become particularly
critical. Five million workers, nearly 6 percent of the work force, were
unemployed. The rate of inflation continued to be unacceptably high.
We faced the possibility of an official settlements deficit at an annual
rate of $23 billion and the prospect of further deterioration. Reserves
had declined sharply. Our official liabilities had sharply increased. Before the President's program was announced, a $2.8 billion merchandise
trade deficit in 1971 and a much larger trade deficit in the following
years was forecast. The sluggishness of the domestic economy and the
alarming international monetary picture were contributing to the
growth of protectionist attitudes at home and eroding support for vital
government programs abroad, including those of particular importance
to the developing world.

Faced with this situation, the U.S. Government had to take difficult
decisions. Adjustments were required in our domestic economy and in
the international economic system. The new economic program announced by President Nixon last August 15 was a first step, followed
by the Smithsonian agreement in December.[78] The intent of both is
not just to improve the U.S. position but to make the system operate
more equitably for all countries.

[77] The report of the Commission, chaired by John D. Rockefeller 3d, was formally presented May 5, 1972; cf. *Public Papers, 1972*, pp. 576-7.
[78] *A.F.R., 1971*, nos. 142 and 150.

Improvements in our domestic economic situation are already visible. Improvements in our balance of payments situation will take more time but are expected to appear as the new monetary and trade measures take effect. Restored strength and stability of the United States economy will help us to continue our support for the growth and prosperity of the developing world.

Shaping the international monetary system for the next generation will require long and hard negotiations. Major differences, particularly relating to the optimum structure for international payments, need to be reconciled. Basic issues are involved which are matters of fundamental concern to both developing and developed countries and which have implications extending well beyond strictly monetary affairs.

An initial question to be faced is that of the appropriate forum for these negotiations. The International Monetary Fund (IMF) has been suggested as a possibly appropriate forum. Certainly any forum should be linked in some way to such relevant institutions as the Fund. At the same time, effective negotiations are possible only in a forum of limited size so that discussion remains manageable and decision is possible. The Group of Ten has been a useful negotiating forum in the past. Because it is limited to the more industrialized countries, however, it does not give a representative voice to other nations whose interests must be considered. A forum modeled on the IMF Executive Board might provide suitably wider representation, though other models are conceivable. In any event, the forum chosen should make it possible to take into account the implications of international monetary reform for other related issues, such as international trade. The decision as to specific forum must await the results of explorations among interested countries.[79] Whatever the forum, our firm view is that the developing countries must be effectively represented.

INTERNATIONAL TRADE

In the international trade sphere, multilateral negotiations are now scheduled for 1973 in the GATT [General Agreement on Tariffs and Trade].[80] These negotiations offer significant opportunities to both developing and developed countries to find ways to increase trade and improve standards of living. The negotiations will cover all trade barriers, tariff and nontariff, industrial and agricultural. Both in the preparatory phase and during the negotiations themselves, particular attention should be given to the problems of the developing countries. We hope these countries will participate actively. We encourage them to undertake careful preparatory work on the identification, description, and analysis of trade barriers which are of serious concern to them.

79 Cf. above at note 15.
80 Cf. above at notes 27-28.

The United States has accepted the special rules favoring the developing countries in part IV of the GATT.[81] We do not expect full reciprocity from these countries, nor do we expect them to make concessions inconsistent with their development needs. On the other hand, we urge that they be prepared to reduce their own tariff and nontariff barriers in the course of the new multilateral negotiations. We believe such action would be entirely consistent with their own interests. Strong evidence indicates that the reduction of their trade barriers can help expand their trade and promote development by producing increased competitiveness.

Satisfactory export performance is of course crucial to development. The exports of the developing countries have not increased as rapidly as would be desirable. For three decades the United States has taken a leading role in removing trade barriers and liberalizing the international movement of goods, services, and capital. In such institutions as the OECD [Organization for Economic Cooperation and Development], GATT, and UNCTAD we have consistently supported freer access of goods from the developing countries into industrialized markets. In particular, the United States has strongly supported efforts in recent years to establish generalized preferences for the developing countries.[82] We are happy that the European Community, Japan, the U.K., and other countries, have already adopted some form of generalized preferences.

As all of you know only too well, the United States has not yet been able to put its own plan into effect. We very much regret our inability to do so. In spite of the progress we have made since last August, concern remains in many quarters in the United States over our balance of payments situation and the general health of the economy. Strong forces exist favoring restrictive limitations on imports. In this atmosphere we have felt it would not be wise to submit generalized preferences legislation to the Congress. The administration remains committed to the adoption of such legislation. We will recommend action by Congress as soon as the chances for success improve.[83]

In examining the problem of how to expand LDC [less developed country] exports we recognize that external assistance can help support well-conceived national export development efforts. The United States has been providing direct technical assistance for projects in export development, and we have responded favorably to many specific requests in this area from individual developing countries. For fiscal year 1973 the administration has requested from Congress an additional

---

[81] Protocol Amending the General Agreement to Introduce a Part IV on Trade and Development, done at Geneva Feb. 8, 1965 and entered into force for the U.S. June 27, 1966 (TIAS 6139).
[82] Cf. above at note 64.
[83] Cf. above at note 65.

$3 million specifically to expand existing U.S. bilateral technical assistance programs for export development.

PRIMARY COMMODITIES

Although many developing countries are making progress toward industrialization, the bulk of their foreign exchange earnings will continue to come from the exports of primary commodities. We concur in the emphasis which the [UNCTAD] Secretary General's very thorough report[84] has placed on opening wider market opportunities for the primary-commodity exports of the developing countries. Expansion in the volume of these exports will remain the principal factor in the growth of their export earnings.

There is also an obvious need for healthy and stable commodity markets with prices that are remunerative to producers and fair to consumers. In some cases, these goals might be achieved through commodity agreements. The United States has supported the International Coffee Agreement.[85] We support the negotiation of a workable and effective cocoa agreement. Experience suggests, however, that there are relatively few cases where formal agreements will prove feasible and desirable. In general, our aim should be to open up markets rather than to proliferate controls.

We welcome an examination in depth by this conference of two additional approaches to commodity problems which have not yet received as much attention as they deserve. The first is research and development to help improve the competitive position of natural products subject to competition from synthetic substitutes. The second is diversification to help developing countries broaden their production base and reduce their dependence on particular commodity exports.

OFFICIAL ASSISTANCE AND PRIVATE INVESTMENT

The developing countries will continue to need high levels of capital flows to meet their development objectives. The United States is committed to maintaining and, where possible, increasing flows of official development assistance to the developing world. On March 8, 1972, President Nixon signed a bill providing for economic assistance appropriations for fiscal year 1972 of $1.7 billion, approximately the same level as the previous year.[86] To this should be added shipments of $1.4 billion in food and agricultural commodities under the P.L. 480[87] pro-

---

84 U.N. document TD/99. Manuel Perez Guerrero of Venezuela had become Secretary-General of UNCTAD in Mar. 1969.
85 Cf. Document 74 at note 32.
86 Cf. above at note 60.
87 Cf. note 17 to Document 21.

gram, as well as the United States commitment of $123 million of ordinary capital for the International Bank for Reconstruction and Development and $212 million for the ordinary capital of the Inter-American Development Bank, a total of over $3.4 billion. A request is now pending in Congress for a United States contribution of $320 million for the International Development Association capital replenishment.[88]

Thus, despite serious balance of payments difficulties, the United States in fiscal year 1972 continues to be the largest single contributor of official development assistance to developing countries. In 1970, the latest year for which comparable statistics are available, total United States official development assistance of nearly $3.1 billion comprised 45 percent of total assistance from all group B countries [developed country members of UNCTAD].

For fiscal year 1973 we plan to request from the Congress $2.3 billion for economic assistance,[89] while P.L. 480 shipments are expected to stay at the high 1972 level. We also plan to request from Congress next year a further $320 million for the International Development Association, $450 million for the Inter-American Development Bank's Fund for Special Operations, $387 million for its ordinary capital, $100 million for the Asian Development Bank's ordinary capital, and $100 million for its Special Funds. If Congress were to meet all these requests and if the projected level of P.L. 480 shipments is included, the total amounts of assistance available would be over $5 billion.

The contribution that foreign assistance can make to economic development, however, cannot be measured simply by the aggregate sums made available under developed country bilateral and multilateral aid programs. Increased attention must be given to particular human needs and social goals. The focus of United States bilateral assistance programs therefore will be concentrated on such human needs as education, nutrition, increased agricultural production and, for countries who wish it, help in family planning. Greater attention will also be given to employment and income distribution aspects of development so that the benefits of economic growth will be distributed widely and not confined just to the few.

There is also need for more detailed attention to the terms and conditions on which aid is offered. The United States has been actively supporting the current efforts in the Development Assistance Committee (DAC) of the OECD to upgrade the targets for "concessionality" of official development assistance. We expect to continue to play a

---

[88] Cf. above at note 63. Pursuant to formal notification on Sept. 22, 1972, of its accession to the third I.D.A. replenishment originally planned in 1970, the U.S. announced its intention to contribute $320 million during calendar year 1972 and make similar payments in 1973 and 1974 (*Bulletin*, Nov. 27, 1972, p. 637).

[89] Cf. above at note 61.

leading role in this effort. Our own terms have consistently been highly concessional.

Official development assistance by itself will not suffice to meet the urgent needs of the developing countries for higher volumes of capital and more technology. We believe that private foreign investment can help fill this gap by supplying and mobilizing capital, opening up new employment opportunities, providing management and marketing resources not available without foreign participation, and particularly by transferring technology.

I recognize that some countries represented here have philosophical attitudes differing from ours on this issue and do not share our beliefs in the benefits of private foreign investment. We do not contest the sovereign right of each country to decide for itself what role private investment, domestic or foreign, should play in its own economy. We are concerned, however, as President Nixon's statement of January 19, 1972, on this subject[90] made clear, that these different philosophical attitudes—whose legitimacy we recognize even though we may disagree with them—sometimes lead to actions in the area of governmental expropriations whose legitimacy we do not recognize because they are contrary to generally accepted principles of international law. We would like to work together with all developing countries to preserve a climate in which investors, whether private or public, can count on investment protection and the fulfillment of contractual obligations in accordance with recognized international legal standards, in which investment disputes are settled reasonably by normal processes of negotiation or arbitration, and in which present political commitments to development assistance will be sustained and strengthened.

THE LEAST DEVELOPED COUNTRIES

The United States is a firm supporter of the concept of special measures for the least developed countries. We have played an active role in consultations on this issue during the last year within the framework of the OECD and the UNDP [United Nations Development Program]. We have agreed in principle in the DAC to work toward easing the terms of financial assistance for the least developed. In cooperation with other bilateral and multilateral aid donors, we are prepared to engage in a concerted effort to improve the quantity and quality of our technical assistance.

As one example of our efforts in this area, we have been providing technical assistance to the African Development Bank; and at a meeting of potential contributing countries in Paris this week, we concurred in the provisions setting up the Bank's Special Fund. Although we can

90 Document 97.

make no financial commitment to the Special Fund at this time due to the need for prior congressional action, we are prepared to ask Congress for the necessary appropriations. We favor, too, a more active role for the UNDP in promoting the development of the least developed countries and will make recommendations to this effect at the next UNDP Governing Council meeting in June. At UNCTAD III, we look forward to working with other countries to develop specific, constructive action programs.

In closing, Mr. President, let me offer a few general thoughts. While there is no room for complacency, the results of the First Development Decade show substantial effort and measurable progress. To maintain and increase the political commitment in both the developed and the developing world to sound development efforts, we must give proper recognition to these positive accomplishments while candidly admitting where progress has been inadequate.

Looking to the future, the United States will continue its efforts to help meet the aspirations, shared by all peoples, for a better life with dignity and hope. We shall work toward this objective in partnership with other developed countries and in cooperation with an increasingly self-reliant developing world. This conference can play an important role in the ongoing examination of development issues for the Second Development Decade.[91] We look forward to participating actively and to contributing to the success of our joint endeavors.

[91] Cf. above at note 54.

APPENDIX:
PRINCIPAL SOURCES

"A.F.R.": *American Foreign Relations: A Documentary Record* (annual vols., 1971-   ). Continues the *"Documents"* series listed below. Volumes for 1971 and 1972 published for the Council on Foreign Relations by New York University Press (New York).

American Foreign Policy: Current Documents (Washington: G.P.O.;* 2 vols. for 1950-55, and annual vols. for 1956-67). The official documentary publication of the Department of State, now discontinued.

"Bulletin": *The Department of State Bulletin* (Washington: G.P.O., weekly). The official source for material of State Department origin appearing in this volume; contains also numerous documents originated by the White House and other governmental and international bodies.

"Documents": *Documents on American Foreign Relations* (annual vols., 1939-70). Volumes in this series were published prior to 1952 by Princeton University Press (Princeton, N.J.) for the World Peace Foundation; subsequent volumes published for the Council on Foreign Relations by Harper & Brothers/Harper & Row (New York and Evanston) for 1952-66; by Simon and Schuster (New York) for 1967-70. For subsequent volumes see *"A.F.R."* above.

Documents on Disarmament (Washington: G.P.O.; annual vols. for 1960-73). The most comprehensive collection of documents on disarmament and related topics, published annually by the U.S. Arms Control and Disarmament Agency.

Everyman's United Nations (New York: United Nations; eighth ed., 1968). A detailed account of the evolution of the U.N. system, brought up to date by occasional supplements.

IMF Survey (Washington: International Monetary Fund, semimonthly).

International Legal Materials: Current Documents (Washington: American Society of International Law, bimonthly). Includes numerous documents of non-U.S. origin.

Kalb, Marvin and Bernard, *Kissinger* (Boston: Little, Brown and Com-

---

*The abbreviation G.P.O. as used throughout this volume refers to the U.S. Government Printing Office.

573

pany, 1974). A detailed account of the diplomacy of the Nixon administration from 1969 until early 1974.

"Keesing's": *Keesing's Contemporary Archives* (Bristol: Keesing's Publications, Ltd., weekly). A detailed review of current developments throughout the world.

"Laird Posture Statement, FY 1973": U.S. Department of Defense, *National Security Strategy of Realistic Deterrence: Secretary of Defense Melvin R. Laird's Annual Defense Department Report FY 1973* [Statement . . . Before the House Armed Services Committee on the FY 1973 Defense Budget and FY 1973-1977 Program, February 17, 1972] (Washington: G.P.O., 1972). The annual review of U.S. defense policy as presented to Congress has superseded the *Annual Reports of the Department of Defense* issued through fiscal year 1968.

The New York Times (New York: The New York Times Co., daily). Contains unofficial texts of numerous documents of international interest.

"Nixon Report, 1970": *U.S. Foreign Policy for the 1970's: A New Strategy for Peace—A Report to the Congress by Richard Nixon, President of the United States, February 18, 1970* (Washington: G.P.O., 1970, 160 p.). Text appears also in *Presidential Documents*, Feb. 23, 1970, pp. 194-239; *Public Papers, 1970*, pp. 116-90; and *Bulletin*, Mar. 9, 1970, pp. 273-332. (Excerpts are printed in *Documents, 1970*, pp. 6-15.)

"Nixon Report, 1971": *U.S. Foreign Policy for the 1970's: Building for Peace—A Report to the Congress by Richard Nixon, President of the United States, February 25, 1971* (Washington: G.P.O., 1971, 235 p.). Text appears also in *Presidential Documents*, Mar. 1, 1971, pp. 305-77; *Public Papers, 1971*, pp. 219-345; and *Bulletin*, Mar. 22, 1971, pp. 341-432. (Excerpts are printed in *A.F.R., 1971*, nos. 3, 11, and 101.)

"Nixon Report, 1972": *U.S. Foreign Policy for the 1970's: The Emerging Structure of Peace—A Report to the Congress by Richard Nixon, President of the United States, February 9, 1972* (Washington: G.P.O., 1972, 215 p.). Text appears also in *Presidential Documents*, Feb. 14, 1972, pp. 235-411; *Public Papers, 1972*, pp. 194-346; and *Bulletin*, Mar. 13, 1972, pp. 311-418. (Excerpts are printed in *A.F.R., 1971*, nos. 121 and 136.)

"Nixon Report, 1973": *U.S. Foreign Policy for the 1970's: Shaping a Durable Peace—A Report to the Congress by Richard Nixon, President of the United States, May 3, 1973* (Washington: G.P.O., 1973, 234 p.). Text appears also in *Presidential Documents*, May 14, 1973, pp. 455-653; and *Bulletin*, June 4, 1973, pp. 717-834.

"OAS Chronicle": Chronicle of the OAS (Washington: Secretariat of the Organization of American States, quarterly).

OECD Observer (Paris: OECD Information Service, bimonthly). The official review of the Organization for Economic Cooperation and Development.

"Presidential Documents": *Weekly Compilation of Presidential Documents* (Washington: G.P.O., weekly). The official source for White House materials reproduced in this volume. Much of the contents is republished in *Public Papers*, and many texts relating to foreign affairs appear also in the Department of State *Bulletin* and/or *Documents on Disarmament*.

Public Laws of the United States, cited in this volume by serial number and date of approval (e.g., Public Law 92-156, Nov. 17, 1971), are issued by the G.P.O. in leaflet form and subsequently collected in the *United States Statutes at Large (Stat.)*.

"Public Papers": *Public Papers of the Presidents of the United States* (Washington: G.P.O., annual). Contains definitive texts of most presidential statements and some other material of White House origin, most of it previously published in *Presidential Documents*. Available volumes for the administration of Richard Nixon cover the years 1969, 1970, 1971, and 1972.

Rogers Report, 1969-70": *United States Foreign Policy 1969-1970: A Report of the Secretary of State* (Department of State Publication 8575; Washington: G.P.O., 1971, 617 p.).

"Rogers Report, 1971": *United States Foreign Policy 1971: A Report of the Secretary of State* (Department of State Publication 8634; Washington: G.P.O., 1972, 604 p.).

"Rogers Report, 1972": *United States Foreign Policy 1972: A Report of the Secretary of State* (Department of State Publication 8699; Washington: G.P.O., 1973, 743 p.).

"Senate Foreign Relations Committee History": U.S. Senate, 92nd Cong., *Legislative History of the Committee on Foreign Relations, . . . January 21, 1971-October 18, 1972* (Committee print; Washington: G.P.O., 1973, 160 p.). Records congressional action on treaties and legislation considered by the Foreign Relations Committee during the 92nd Congress in 1971-72.

Soviet News (London: Press Department of the Soviet Embassy, weekly). Includes unofficial texts or condensations of numerous documents of Soviet origin.

"TIAS": U.S. Department of State, *Treaties and Other International Acts Series* (Washington: G.P.O., published irregularly). This series presents the definitive texts of treaties and agreements to which the United States is a party, as authenticated by the Department of State. Issued in leaflet form under their individual serial numbers, items in this series are later republished with consecutive pagination in the official *United States Treaties and Other International Agreements* (UST) series, likewise published by the G.P.O. on behalf of the Department of State. Treaties and agreements that entered into force in 1971 (TIAS 7035-7264) are collected in 22 UST parts 1 and 2 (Washington: G.P.O., 1972); those that entered into force in 1972 (TIAS 7265ff.) are collected in 23 UST parts 1-4 (Washington: G.P.O., 1973) and 24 UST part 1 (Washington: G.P.O., 1974).

United Nations General Assembly, *Official Records* (New York: United Nations). The *Official Records* of each session of the General Assembly include official texts of all resolutions adopted during the session as well as much related material. Unofficial texts are frequently printed in the *UN Monthly Chronicle* and other publications.

United Nations Security Council, *Official Records* (New York: United Nations). Includes official texts of all resolutions adopted by the Security Council, with much related material. Unofficial texts are frequently printed in the *UN Monthly Chronicle* and other publications.

The United States in World Affairs (annual vols., 1931-40, 1945-67, and 1970). The annual survey of U.S. foreign policy developments, published for the Council on Foreign Relations by Harper & Brothers/Harper and Row (New York and Evanston) from 1931 through 1966 and by Simon and Schuster (New York) for 1967 and 1970.

UN Monthly Chronicle (New York: United Nations Office of Public Information, monthly), The official account of current U.N. activities, with texts of major resolutions and other documents.

"USUN Press Releases": Press releases of the U.S. Mission to the United Nations, as reprinted in the Department of State *Bulletin*.

The World This Year: Supplement to the Political Handbook and Atlas of the World (annual vols., 1971, 1972, and 1973). Condensed accounts of the organization and activities of governments and intergovernmental organizations, published for the Council on Foreign Relations by Simon and Schuster (New York).

Yearbook of the United Nations (New York: United Nations Office of Public Information). A comprehensive review of U.N. activities, issued annually.

INDEX

The following pages provide a detailed listing of the documents and editorial notes that make up the present volume. As in the *Documents on American Foreign Relations* series, each document is listed under (1) its official name, if any; (2) its main subject and principal subordinate subjects; (3) the name of the originating country, organization, or individual, and the addressee or recipient where appropriate; and (4) its place of origin when this is deemed historically significant. *Not* listed, in most cases, are names and subjects appearing in the body of the text but falling into none of the above categories. Acts and resolutions of the U.S. Congress will be found under the heading "Congress (U.S.)," where they are listed by subject and, where appropriate, by Public Law or Resolution number. Resolutions of the U.N. General Assembly and Security Council are also listed by subject and by resolution number.

B

C

D

G

H

I

M

N

O

P

T

V